THE JOHANNINE RENAISSANCE IN EARLY MODERN ENGLISH LITERATURE AND THEOLOGY

The Johannine Renaissance in Early Modern English Literature and Theology

PAUL CEFALU

OXFORD
UNIVERSITY PRESS

Great Clarendon Street, Oxford, OX2 6DP,
United Kingdom

Oxford University Press is a department of the University of Oxford.
It furthers the University's objective of excellence in research, scholarship,
and education by publishing worldwide. Oxford is a registered trade mark of
Oxford University Press in the UK and in certain other countries

First Edition published in 2017

Impression: 3

Published in the United States of America by Oxford University Press
198 Madison Avenue, New York, NY 10016, United States of America

British Library Cataloguing in Publication Data

Data available

Library of Congress Control Number: 2017942414

ISBN 978–0–19–880871–8

Printed and bound by
CPI Group (UK) Ltd, Croydon, CR0 4YY

For Chelsea

Acknowledgments

The idea for this book first presented itself while I was conducting research at the Folger Shakespeare Library on a related project on divine accommodation. I was fortunate to be able to present germinal material from this project to a number of astute scholars at the Folger, especially Pamela O. Long and Daniel Shore. At a certain point, Dan helped me in my decision to settle on a book-length study of John, and I have valued his insight ever since. I thank the Mellon Foundation and members of the Folger Institute, including Kathleen Lynch, Owen Williams, and Michael Witmore, for their scholarly engagement during my stay at the Folger. Carol Brobeck helped to make my stay there pleasant and productive. Other friends and scholarly interlocutors read large portions of the manuscript, offering sage advice, especially Gary Kuchar and Richard Strier. Gary applied his expertise in all things theological to every chapter of the manuscript. Richard, with his usual incisiveness, wit, and erudition, kept me returning to the poetry when I most needed to. Reid Barbour and Julia Reinhard Lupton, two of the most generous, leading scholars I know, have offered professional support over a many-year period. A special thanks goes to Maria Patricia Devlin for her painstaking and expert help in editing and proofreading an early version of the manuscript.

The editorial team at Oxford University has been a benchmark of professionalism and rigor. I thank especially Jacqueline Norton for her expertise, wisdom, and faith in this project during a two-year period. I thank as well the three anonymous readers for the press, two literary scholars, one biblical scholar, all of whom provided detailed and exacting suggestions for improvement.

At Lafayette College, the Academic Research Committee and the Frank Lee and Edna M. Smith endowment provided funds toward production of the book. I thank the hard-working staff of Skillman library, especially Karen Haduck and Kandyce Fisher. I am fortunate to have so many colleagues with interdisciplinary interests, including Joseph Shieber and Eric Ziolkowski. Eric has been an excellent mentor and conversationalist on the subject of religion and literature. Patricia Donahue, Head of the English Department at Lafayette College, has consistently supported this manuscript in small and large ways. For advice and supportive friendship, I also thank Steve Belletto, Tim Laquintano, and Owen McLeod.

I could not have written this book without the loving presence of my wife, Chelsea, and my daughter, Erica. Chelsea has provided patient and inspiring support over a long haul. I thank her for creating an ideal environment in which the rigors of scholarship in the office can be mingled with unfettered joy at home.

A version of chapter 6 was first published as "Johannine Poetics in George Herbert's Devotional Lyrics" in *ELH* 82.4 (2015), 1041–71. Copyright © 2015 The Johns Hopkins University Press. Reprinted with permission by Johns Hopkins University Press. I thank the editors of *ELH* and The Johns Hopkins University

Press for permission to reprint parts of the essay. I thank the staff at The National Gallery of London for permission to reprint an image of Titian's *Noli Me Tangere*, © The National Gallery, London. Bequeathed by Samuel Rogers, 1856. For permission to reprint an image of Hans Holbein's *Noli Me Tangere*, Royal Collection Trust/© Her Majesty Queen Elizabeth II 2016, I thank the staff of the Royal Collection Trust.

Contents

List of Illustrations

Introduction
The Johannine Renaissance

In an influential monograph entitled *The Pauline Renaissance in England*, John S. Coolidge some decades ago joined ranks with religious historians in declaring the singular influence of Saint Paul's theology on early modern English Calvinism and Puritanism.[1] For Coolidge and others, Paul's accounts of justification, the law–gospel relationship, and what now is typically described as Pauline universalism and political theology touched off the most fateful debates between sixteenth- and seventeenth-century Puritans and conformist Protestants regarding covenant theology, personal assurance, and church reform.[2] Heavily influenced by this so-called Pauline Renaissance in sixteenth- and seventeenth-century England, literary scholars for some time have argued that the devotional literature of the early modern period is in important respects Pauline in religious orientation.[3]

---

[1] Coolidge's emphasis is on the English Puritan use of Pauline theology, especially the deepening influence of Paul on English separatism and congregationalism: "The present study…argues that Puritanism originates as a response to elements of Pauline theology which are especially pertinent to a time of cultural dislocation, that English Separatism and Congregationalism are further developments of Paul's complex ecclesiology." *The Pauline Renaissance in England: Puritanism and the Bible* (Oxford: Oxford University Press, 1970), xiii. Several decades prior to the publication of Coolidge's book, William Haller had described the importance of Paul's conception of faith to the English Calvinist tradition, and Haller noted the English Calvinist attraction to the "spiritual egalitarianism" and "spiritual brotherhood" and "toleration" that one finds in Paul's epistles. See Haller, *The Rise of Puritanism* (New York: Harper & Row, 1957), 8, 86, 115, and 240. M. M. Knappen argued also for the influence of the Pauline epistles (as against the four Gospels) on sixteenth-century English Puritanism in *Tudor Puritanism: A Chapter in the History of Idealism* (Chicago: Phoenix Books, 1965), chapters 18–19, *passim*. In *Calvin and English Calvinism to 1649* (Eugene: Wipf & Stock, 1997), R. T. Kendall eventually offered a revisionist account of the Calvinist doctrines of perseverance, assurance, and universal atonement, and he maintained the influence of Paul on Theodore Beza and English experimental Bezan Reformers (chapters 1–2, *passim*).

[2] On the importance of Pauline theology to early modern political theology and literature, see Julia Reinhard Lupton, *Citizen-Saints: Shakespeare and Political Theology* (Chicago: University of Chicago Press, 2005), as well as Lupton's more recent essay, "Pauline Edifications: Staging the Sovereign Softscape in Renaissance England," in *Political Theology and Early Modernity*, eds. Graham Hammill and Julia Reinhard Lupton (Chicago: University of Chicago Press, 2012), 212–39. See also Nichole E. Miller, *Violence and Grace: Exceptional Life between Shakespeare and Modernity* (Evanston: Northwestern University Press, 2014), especially the Introduction and chapter 5, *passim*.

[3] That the Pauline *ordo salutis* is central to sixteenth- and seventeenth-century devotional poetry is the assumption of Barbara Lewalski's influential *Protestant Poetics and the Seventeenth-Century Religious Lyric* (Princeton: Princeton University Press, 1979): "The theological ideas that chiefly influenced the way in which these poets portrayed their own (and everyman's) spiritual condition were for the most part derived from the Pauline epistles.… From Paul's epistles, the Protestant extrapolated a paradigm against which to plot the spiritual drama of his own life" (14–15). For a more recent assessment of the

The title of this book, *The Johannine Renaissance in Early Modern English Literature and Theology*, announces at the outset the book's revisionist orientation. My fundamental claim is that the Fourth Gospel and First Epistle of Saint John the Evangelist were so influential during the period as to share with Pauline theology pride of place as leading apostolic texts on matters Christological, sacramental, pneumatological, and political. I argue further that, in several instances, Johannine theology is more central than Pauline theology and the theology of Matthew, Mark, and Luke, particularly with regard to early modern polemicizing on the Trinity, distinctions between *agape* and *eros*, and the ideologies of radical dissent, especially the antinomian challenge of free grace to traditional Puritan Pietism.

Johannine theology is influential during the period because it offers a distinctive depiction of Christ that is typically described as "high Christological." No other New Testament account of Christ's ministry underscores, as does the Johannine corpus, the divinity of the pre-existent Son of God. When the biblical scholar Ernst Käsemann influentially described the Johannine Christ as one who "strides across the face of the earth, avoiding touching it entirely," he was suggesting that, eschewing the Synoptic narrative of Jesus' humble origins and the way in which Jesus is abased during the Passion, John's Christ is more privileged than any other prophet, including Moses, because he has directly "seen God."[4] What Christ reveals to his believers is the immediate possibility of "eternal life" (John's realized eschatology) and, according to some interpretations of Johannine thought, a more intimate unity with God than is featured elsewhere in New Testament theology. Such high Christology lies behind John Donne's proclamation, for example, that the "Gospel of Saint *John* contains all *Divinity*."[5]

---

importance of St. Paul to early modern English literature, see Gregory Kneidel, *Rethinking the Turn to Religion in Early Modern English Literature: The Poetics of All Believers* (Basingstoke and New York: Palgrave Macmillan, 2008). The Pauline influence on George Herbert is frequently suggested. In *The Living Temple: George Herbert and Catechizing* (Berkeley: University of California Press, 1978), 62–3, Stanley Fish draws partly on Paul's epistles in his discussion of catechism in Herbert. On the importance of the Pauline intermingling of faith and love in Herbert's poetry, see Terry G. Sherwood's *Herbert's Prayerful Art* (Toronto: University of Toronto Press, 1989), chapter 2, *passim*. For a more recent expansion of Lewalski's notion of a Protestant-Pauline schema of salvation as it might have influenced Herbert, see Daniel W. Doerksen, *Picturing Religious Experience: George Herbert, Calvin, and the Scriptures* (Newark: University of Delaware Press, 2011), 61–2. On the influence of Paul on John Donne, see Gregory Kneidel, "John Donne's *Via Pauli*," *Journal of English and Germanic Philology*, vol. 100, no. 2 (Apr., 2001), 224–46. Due to the syncretistic nature of the poetry of Henry Vaughan and Thomas Traherne—in which neo-Platonism seems to prevail—scholars have not remarked as frequently on the Pauline orientation of those poets, although Lewalski averred that Vaughan's poems in particular trace the "familiar Protestant-Pauline paradigm of regeneration and the spiritual life." *Protestant Poetics*, 332.

  [4] Ernst Käsemann, *Testament of Jesus. Study of the Gospel of John in the Light of Chapter 17* (Minneapolis: Augsburg Fortress, 1978). The term "Synoptic," based on the Greek signification for "seeing alike," is typically used to designate the fact that the Gospels of Matthew, Mark, and Luke resemble one another more closely than they do the Gospel of John. For a recent collection of essays on the term and conception of Synoptic theology, see *Rethinking the Synoptic Problem*, eds. David Alan Black and David R. Beck (Grand Rapids: Baker Academic, 2001).

  [5] *The Sermons of John Donne*, eds. George R. Potter and Evelyn M. Simpson (Berkeley: University of California Press, 1957), vol. III, 351.

Fig. I.1 John the Evangelist, in William Tyndale, *The Newe Testament of Oure Saviour Jesus Christe* (London, 1553), RB 96524, The Huntington Library, San Marino, CA.

Early modern exegetes produced lengthy commentaries on the Johannine discourses that emphasize John's unique Christology, typically designating John as the Eagle among apostolic witnesses. Thus Anthony Wotton, in his *Sermons on John* (1609): "Who is not astonished with admiration of those wonderfull mysteries, concerning our Savior Christs eternal divinitie, which this sonne of thunder as it were ratleth out? Therefore did the antient writers compare him to an Eagle, as one that mounted up above the pitch of the other three Evangelists, even to the height of the Godhead, and that unsearchable mystery of the most glorious, and blessed Trinitie."[6] William Tyndale's *The Newe Testament of Oure Saviour Jesus Christe* (London, 1553) includes an image of a haloed Eagle situated atop a scribal John the Evangelist, emphasizing the Evangelist's soaring inspiration (Fig. I.1).

The moniker "Eagle" and other honorifics such as "Thunderer" and "Theologus" stem from the prevailing belief that the Johannine tradition departs from the Synoptics not only in celebrating Christ's intimate relationship with God but also in fulfilling or completing the work of the three earlier narratives of Matthew, Mark, and Luke.[7] Wotton continues that John adds a "great store of newe matter,

[6] Anthony Wotton, *Sermons Upon a Part of the First Chapter of the Gospell of S. John* (London, 1609), 17.

[7] The Eagle designation partly has its origins in Ezekiel 17:3–4: "Thus saith the Lord God, A great eagle with great wings, long wing'd, full of feathers, which had divers colours, came unto Lebanon, and tooke the highest branch of the Cedar. Hee cropt off the top of his yong twigs, and caried it into

not once touched by any of the other; the LORD having reserved, for him, the perfecting of that knowledge, which the rest did beginne and further."[8] Later in the century, John Arrowsmith will grant John a "preheminency" over the Synoptics in that the Fourth Gospel provides a "clearer truth" than the others and hence is "the Gospell of Gospells."[9] Part of this newness and preeminence derives from the unique content of the Fourth Gospel. Only in John's Gospel do we find Christ's dialogue with the Pharisee Nicodemus, Christ's turning water into wine in Cana, the raising of Lazarus, the frequently glossed bread of life discourse, and the well-known discourses of the vine and good shepherd.

John's "newness," however, consists less in the additional and redacted factual material found in his narratives and more in his distinctive Christological, pneu-matological, and soteriological approach to such material. If the Synoptics provide the historically grounded birth narrative and subsequent account of the ministry and Passion of Jesus of Nazareth, along the way sanctioning the use of miracles and parables to instruct belief, the Johannine discourses pass over many of the lineaments of the historical Jesus. John's birth narrative is simply the fateful proclamation in the Prologue to the Fourth Gospel: "In the beginning was the Word, & the Word was with God, and the Word was God" (1:1).[10] The basic (and distinctive) presuppos-ition of John's high Christology is that Jesus, as the "true light" having descended directly from God, is prepared to impart knowledge to a darkened world and then re-ascend. As Jesus informs Nicodemus in chapter 3, "And no man hath ascended up to heaven, but hee that came downe from heaven, even the Sonne of man which is in heaven....And as Moses lifted up the serpent in the wildernesse: even so must the Sonne of man be lifted up" (3:13–14). The "descent and return" motif, reprised in John 8:14—"I know whence I came, and whither I goe"—reflects the Johannine belief that Christ, as the only one who has ever seen God, is uniquely empowered to reveal God as his Word incarnate.

The singular nature and role of the Johannine Christ is best illustrated in the ways in which John's depiction of the baptism departs from the Synoptic account. According to Matthew's version of Jesus' baptism, after the Spirit descends like a dove a heavenly voice proclaims that Jesus is the "beloved son": "And Jesus, when hee was baptized, went up straightway out of the water: and loe, the heavens were opened unto him, and he saw the Spirit of God descending like a dove, and

---

a land of traffique; he set it in a city of merchants." Meister Eckhart prefaces his Johannine commen-tary with this citation as well as with Job 39:27–8, remarking: "John the Evangelist is the eagle who 'makes the nest' of his attention, contemplation and preaching 'among the steep crags and inaccessible rocks.'" *Meister Eckhart: The Essential Sermons, Commentaries, Treatises, and Defense*, trans. Edmund Colledge and Bernard McGinn (Mahwah: Paulist Press, 1981), 122.

    [8] Wotton, *Sermons Upon a Part of the First Chapter of the Gospell of S. John*, 17–18.
    [9] John Arrowsmith, *Theanthropos, or, God-Man* (London, 1660), 3.
    [10] For the sake of consistency, and since most of the texts discussed throughout this book date from the early to later seventeenth century, I will typically rely on the 1611 Authorized Version for passages from John's Gospel and First Epistle as well as for relevant verses from the Old and New Testaments. There are notable exceptions, however, since Zwingli relied on the Latin Vulgate, Cranmer on his own translations/Great Bible, and several other sixteenth- and early-seventeenth-century writers on the Geneva Bible. In such cases, I typically use the Bible translations provided in the primary text by the writer whose work is under scrutiny.

lighting upon him. And loe, a voice from heaven, saying, This is my beloved Sonne, in whom I am well pleased" (Matt. 3:16–17). In the Fourth Gospel, instead of the announcement by a heavenly voice, the Spirit reveals to John the Baptist that Jesus is the Son of God: "And John bare record saying, I saw the Spirit descending from heaven, like a Dove, and it abode upon him. And I knew him not: but he that sent me to baptize with water, the same said unto me, Upon whom thou shalt see the Spirit descending, & remaining on him, the same is he which baptizeth with the holy Ghost" (John 1:32–3).[11] In the Johannine narrative, the Baptist's anointing and prophetic powers are diminished relative to Christ's. The Baptist reveals Christ and proclaims that the latter will henceforth baptize via the Spirit.[12]

To suggest that the Spirit reveals to John the Baptist Christ's role as redeemer, the lamb who will expiate sin, is to provide the testimony and knowledge of Christ, here again establishing the incomparable and divine nature of the newly disclosed Son of God.[13] In the Synoptics, the Spirit descends in order to fill Christ with power, as if the infusion grants power to Christ or alters his human nature. In the Fourth Gospel, Christ is not impelled by the Spirit, which is reflected in the Markan account. For John, the Spirit affirms the power of God through the presence of the Son. And John is the only apostle who remarks that the Spirit will "remain" on Christ, suggesting further that Christ will anoint the brethren with the Spirit (which he will "breathe" on them) and, as we will discuss later, provide them with the Paraclete (Comforter) once he departs. The distinctiveness of Johannine pneumatology as against the Synoptics is just one example among several other differences that warrants John Downame's elevation of Johannine theology in the introduction to his mammoth *Annotations on the New Testament* (1657): "Having therefore read the other three Evangelists, recording principally those things which concerned the Humanity and Miracles of Christ; that which they omitted concerning his Deity and Doctrine, this high-flying Eagle discovereth."[14]

JOHANNINE QUESTIONS

Not only do the Johannine discourses extend the Synoptic writings in emphasizing a high Christology and in presenting a theology of "deity and doctrine," but those discourses are also the site of several controversies extending from the patristic

---

[11] On the revelation of the Spirit to the Baptist, see Marianne Meye Thompson, *The God of the Gospel of John* (Grand Rapids: Eerdmans Publishing Company, 2001), 161; and Craig R. Koester, *The Word of Life: A Theology of John's Gospel* (Grand Rapids: Eerdmans Publishing Company, 2008), 134–6.

[12] Thompson describes the power-affirming rather than power-granting role of the Johannine spirit in *The God of the Gospel of John*, 161–4.

[13] Ibid., 161.

[14] John Downame, *Annotations upon all the books of the Old and New Testament* (London, 1657), prefatory remarks to "Annotations on the Gospel According to S. John." The early modern appreciation of John's uniqueness is of a piece with the modern appraisal of John's departure from the Synoptics. If the Synoptic tradition provides the "basic facts" regarding baptism, Raymond E. Brown remarks, John provides "the rich background and meaning of baptism in references to the living water of rebirth." See Brown, *The Gospel and Epistles of John: A Concise Commentary* (Collegeville: Liturgical Press, 1988), 13.

through the early modern period.[15] Some of these controversies are narrowly editorial and philological in nature, particularly the perennially debated "Johannine question" as to who wrote and edited the several Johannine discourses.[16] While Justin Martyr had attributed all of the extant Johannine writings to John the Apostle—which includes the Fourth Gospel, three epistles, and the Book of Revelation—Eusebius of Caesarea (influenced by a surviving fragment from Papias, a second-century Anatolian Bishop) held that, while the Fourth Gospel and First Epistle were clearly authored toward the end of the first century by John the Apostle, Son of Zebedee, the remaining letters and Revelation were probably authored by another obscure author called John the Presbyter or Elder (who designates himself in Revelation as an exile on Patmos). Eusebius's position, developed further by Dionysius of Alexandria, was typically ranged against competing interpretations by Irenaeus and Clement of Alexandria that identify John the Apostle with the Elder or Presbyter.[17]

Since most of the early modern commentaries on John's Gospel and First Epistle are not especially interested in the later epistles or the Book of Revelation, the authorship question, unresolved in the early modern period and still currently debated, is not a primary concern of this book. Occasionally, radical appropriations of the Johannine corpus—as in writings by the illuminist John Everard, the

---

[15] A good discussion of the otherworldly sonority of the Johannine Jesus as against Synoptic Christology can be found in Robert Tompson Fortna, *The Fourth Gospel and its Predecessor* (Philadelphia: Fortress Press, 2007), 1–4.

[16] Another historically persistent crux is whether John is the "one whom Jesus loved" (13:23, 19:76, 20:2, 21:7, 21:20). I have found that most early modern English commentators follow Augustine and Calvin in assuming that John is indeed the "beloved disciple." Augustine remarks in a tractate on John 13:23: "What is meant by 'at the bosom' he states a little later where he says, 'against Jesus' chest.' This is John whose Gospel this is, as he makes clear later." Augustine, *Tractates on the Gospel of John, 55–111*, trans. John W. Rettig (Washington, D.C.: Catholic University Press, 2010), 34. The "later" clarification is 21:20, which for Augustine suggests a comparison of the ways in which Christ loves John relative to Peter. See Augustine, *Tractates on the Gospel of John, 112–24*, trans. John W. Rettig (Washington, D.C.: Catholic University Press, 1995), 86–7. Calvin, too, assumes that the beloved disciple is John. His gloss on 13:23 is an unapologetic explanation of the preference by Christ for John: "The special love which Christ had for John plainly testifies that it is not always inconsistent with Christian love (*caritas*) if we love some more than others." *The Gospel According to St. John*, in *Calvin's New Testament Commentaries*, vol. 5, eds. David W. Torrance and Thomas F. Torrance, trans. T. H. L. Parker (Grand Rapids: Eerdmans Publishing Company, 1959), 66. Post-Reformed English commentators also typically describe John as the beloved disciple. Thus Francis Bacon: "Apostle of our *Saviour*, and the *Beloved Disciple*, lived ninetie three yeares: He was rightly denoted…the *Eagle*, for his piercing [s]ight into the *Divinitie*." *Historie naturall and experimental* (London, 1638), 115–16. See also the biblical paraphrase, *Clavis Bibliorum* (London, 1648), by the Presbyterian Minister Francis Roberts, who refers to John as "that Disciple whom Jesus peculiarly loved above all the rest, Joh. 13.23. and 19.26. and 20.2, & 21.7.20…Who leaned on Jesus breast at supper" (164–5). Many other sixteenth-and seventeenth-century English examples of the attribution of the title "beloved disciple" to John could be adduced. One does find alternative identifications during the period—for example, the assumption in Thomas Gataker's *The decease of Lazarus Christ's friend* (London, 1640), 21–2, that the beloved disciple refers to Lazarus—but such ascriptions are relatively uncommon. Early Christian and patristic debates about the identity of the beloved disciple are described in Herman C. Waetjen, *The Gospel of the Beloved Disciple: A Work in Two Editions* (London: Bloomsbury T&T Clark, 2005), especially 15–53.

[17] For Eusebius's commentary on Johannine authorship, see *Fathers of the Church: Eusebius Pamphili, Ecclesiastical History, Books 1–5*, trans. Roy J. Defarrari (Washington, D.C.: Catholic University Press, 1957), Book III, chapter 39, 202–7.

Digger Gerrard Winstanley, or the American antinomian Anne Hutchinson—will polemically (and promiscuously) run together the Fourth Gospel and Apocalypse, assuming that John of Patmos was the primary author of all of the Johannine material. To the extent that the authorship question is raised in a sustained manner, we typically find it in commentaries on the Apocalypse, given the author's invocation in that text of his name as John and his role of testifier of Jesus Christ. Thus Timothy Brightman, in his *Revelation of S. John* (1619), in his zeal to legitimate and elevate the canonical status of the Book of Revelation, sets out to prove that John of Patmos was none other than John the Evangelist, dismissing the "vayne conjectures" of Dionysius of Alexandria, for only John the Apostle could have witnessed the "deeds and miracles of Christ."[18] Given that the Book of Revelation will only glancingly be referred to in the following pages, I will have little to say about the hand-wringing over the authorship question. Several important studies have been written on the influence of the Apocalyptic writings in the English Renaissance, but no study has been written on the more widely influential Fourth Gospel and First Epistle of John (two texts that comprise what I will often describe as the "Johannine tradition" or "Johannine writings").[19] In presenting material for this book at various venues, I have been surprised to learn that so many early modernists immediately associate "John" with the Book of Revelation and only secondarily with the author of the Fourth Gospel and First Epistle. One of my goals is to change that order of priority such that we appreciate the profound influence of John's evangelical writings on early modern culture and literature.

If I will not be concerned with the authorship controversy, I will be concerned with the most influential early modern exegetical controversies and polemics that issue from the unique Johannine embellishments in the Fourth Gospel and First Epistle on Christological and ontological themes that are partially covered in Paul and the Synoptics. The sixth chapter of John's Gospel, for example, the "bread of life" discourse in which Christ uniquely remarks that "the flesh profiteth nothing" (6:63), inspires the foundational debates on the Eucharist between Zwingli and Lutherans regarding the symbolic versus real presence of Christ's body during the Lord's Supper.[20] John 6 also shapes the sacramental theology of Thomas Cranmer, whose concern at the beginning of his influential *Defence of the True and Catholic Doctrine of the Sacrament* (1550) is not the otherwise pivotal Matthew 26 ("This is my Body") but John's bread of life narrative and the enfolded account of the Ascension that appear in John 16 and elsewhere. For Cranmer and so many sixteenth-century English divines, Christ's remark that he forsakes the world and will go to

---

[18] Timothy Brightman, *Revelation of S. John* (London, 1619), 9.

[19] See, for example, *The Apocalypse in English Renaissance Thought and Literature*, eds. C. A. Patrides and Joseph Anthony Wittreich (Ithaca: Cornell University Press, 1985).

[20] On the importance of John 6 to Augustine, Erasmus, and Zwingli, see W. P. Stephens, "Zwingli on John 6:63: *Spiritus est qui vivificat, caro nihil prodest*," in *Biblical Interpretation in the Era of the Reformation: Essays Presented to David C. Steinmetz*, eds. Richard A. Muller and John A. Thompson (Grand Rapids: Eerdmans Publishing Company, 1996). For Zwingli's careful exposition of John 6, see Ulrich Zwingli, *Commentary on True and False Religion*, eds. Samuel Macauley Jackson and Clarence Nevin Heller (Durham: Labyrinth Press, 1981), 198–210; and *Zwingli and Bullinger*, ed. and trans. G. W. Bromiley (Philadelphia: Westminster Press, 1963), 200–38.

his Father provides evidence that the Son could not have been present corporeally on earth during the Lord's Supper (an argument commonly marshaled against the Lutheran claim of Christ's ubiquity). Throughout the sixteenth and seventeenth centuries, liberal Reformers influenced by Zwingli and Cranmer consistently turned to John's Gospel in order to legitimate the claims, developed most clearly in Augustine's foundational *Homilies on John*, of the symbolic nature of the host and the provocative Johannine idea that "eating is believing."[21]

John's unique influence on Reformed polemics again surfaces in the Trinitarian and anti-Trinitarian debates of the middle to latter part of the seventeenth century. The two fateful announcements at the outset of his Gospel—"In the beginning was the Word" (1:1) and "The Word was made Flesh" (1:14)—provide Socinians such as Stephen Nye, John Biddle, and Johannes Crell polemical material for their arguments against the divinity of Christ, arguments that are controverted by the skillful lexical polemicizing of Trinitarians such as John Downame, Bartholomew Traheron, and John Trapp, who draw on Johannine theology and patristic authorities to claim, for example, that "the Word was God"(1:1) should not include an article ("a God"); hence the Trinitarians conclude that John 1:1 evinces Christ's co-eternal nature.[22] Not only John 1:1 and 1:14 but also 6:62 and 8:58, texts traditionally used to defend the eternal pre-existence of Christ, become the subject of intense scrutiny in the Racovian Catechism, the Socinian statement of faith. Surveying the polemical debates on the Trinity in the middle of the seventeenth century, Paul C. H. Lim remarks that the "Gospel of John played a formative role in the Christological controversies of both the patristic and the Reformation periods."[23] Lim goes on to show John's centrality to the Trinitarian/anti-Trinitarian debates of the seventeenth century, drawing on J. G. A. Pocock's work on the importance of the Johannine literature to emerging discourses of toleration. Lim concludes that the Fourth Gospel was "the single biblical book which became the key epicenter of the polemical exchange and the various ways in which the notion of orthodoxy and its seemingly ever-porous membrane was contested and re-negotiated during this period."[24]

In addition to the well-known debates regarding the Eucharist and Trinity, most early modern discoursing on the nature of *agape* or God's descending love focuses on John's ontological conception of love in his First Epistle: "God is love, and hee that dwelleth in love, dwelleth in God, and God in him" (1 John 4: 16). While the Synoptics as well as Paul allude to *agapic* or vertical love from God to man, only

---

[21] On the importance of John 6 to the debates on the Eucharistic among early English Reformers such as Cranmer, John Frith, Hugh Latimer, and Stephen Gardiner, see C. W. Dugmore, *The Mass and the English Reformers* (London: Macmillan, 1958), especially chapter viii, *passim*.

[22] For the most extensive recent discussion of the use of key Johannine texts by both mid-seventeenth-century Trinitarians and anti-Trinitarians, see Paul C. H. Lim, *Mystery Unveiled: The Crisis of the Trinity in Early Modern England* (Oxford: Oxford University Press, 2012), chapter 6, *passim*.

[23] Ibid., 271.

[24] Ibid., 273. Lim draws on J. G. A. Pocock's comments on the Fourth Gospel that can be found in Pocock's "Within the Margins: The Definitions of Orthodoxy," in *The Margins of Orthodoxy: Heterodox Writing and Cultural Response, 1660–1750*, ed. Roger D. Lund (Cambridge: Cambridge University Press, 1995), 50.

John directly identifies God with love as such. The importance of this single passage from John's First Epistle is sounded again and again by Augustine, who remarks: "If nothing else were said in praise of love, in all the pages of this Epistle, nothing else whatever in any other page of Scripture, and this were the one and only thing we heard from the voice of God's Spirit—'For God is love'—we should ask for nothing more."[25]

Distinctive, too, is John's presentation of Christ's prayer for believers in which Christ proclaims the unique and eternal nature of God's love for his Son—"Thou lovedst mee before the foundation of the world" (17:24)—one passage among several that convinced Anders Nygren that John, more complexly than the Synoptics and Paul, provocatively conflated the *agape* and *eros* motifs (John 17 presupposes, for Nygren, a measure of assumed merit on the Son's part that warrants God's eternal love for him).[26] John's unique conception of *agape* raises the question of how God's essence as love can be approached by humans whose creaturely love will always fall short of the essential love that is itself God, a topic featured not only in commentaries on Johannine theology by Heinrich Bullinger and Calvin but also in more particularized treatises of love by several English theologians and homilists.[27]

THE APOSTLE JOHN AND DEVOTIONAL POETRY

Given the unbridled early modern enthusiasm for John's writings, one expects to find the influence of John in the devotional lyrics of poets such as George Herbert, John Donne, Henry Vaughan, and Richard Crashaw, whose work is typically interested not only in the nature of Christ relative to God but also in those mysteries of devotion that were held to be located exceptionally in Johannine theology. While some critical work has drawn out Donne's use of the Johannine *Logos* theme in his sermons, Vaughan's treatment of the figure of Nicodemus in "The Night," and Herbert's use of the Johannine true vine image in several of his typological lyrics, early modernists have yet to offer a thoroughgoing interpretation of Johannine themes in seventeenth-century religious poetry.[28]

---

[25] Saint Augustine, *Ten Homilies on the First Epistle General of St. John,* in *Augustine: Later Works,* ed. John Burnaby (Philadelphia: Westminster Press, 1955), 314. For Augustine's fuller conception of Johannine *agape,* see his *On the Trinity,* same volume, 157–68.

[26] See Anders Nygren, *Agape and Eros,* trans. Philip S. Watson (London: S.P.C.K., 1953), 146–59.

[27] Bullinger's conception of Johannine *agape* can be found in *Fiftie Godlie and Learned Sermons* (London, 1577), 856–7; on Calvin and Johannine love, see *The comentaries of M. John Calvin upon the First Epistle of Sainct Jhon* (London, 1580), 91–3. See also commentaries and treatises on love by, for example, Thomas Collier, *The Marrow of Christianity* (London, 1647), 21–2, 34; Miles Coverdale, *Fruitful Lessons* (London, 1593), 10; and Richard Stock, *A Stock of Divine Knowledge* (London, 1641), chapter xv, *passim.*

[28] On Donne and *Logos,* see Helen Wilcox, "Devotional Writing," in *The Cambridge Companion to John Donne,* ed. Achsah Guibbory (New York: Cambridge University Press, 2006), 149. On Vaughan and Nicodemus, see Jonathan Post, "Vaughan's 'The Night' and His 'Late and Dusky' Age," *SEL* 19:1 (1979), 127–41, although Post downplays the centrality of Nicodemus to Vaughan's poem. On Herbert's typological use of the vine image, see Joseph H. Summers, *George Herbert: His Religion and*

This is a notable omission, given the frequent reference in devotional poetry to so many of the key Johannine texts on the sacrament of eating, the Trinity, and the *agape* motif mentioned above. Henry Vaughan's preparatory Eucharistic prayer in *The Mount of Olives*, for example, is directly inspired by the Johannine bread of life discourse; and John 6:50–5 as well as the good shepherd discourse of John 10 provide the scriptural material for "The Holy Communion," "The Sap," and "The Feast," three of Vaughan's well-regarded poems on the Eucharist.[29] Richard Crashaw's Divine Epigrams 19 and 20 are also both inspired by John's account of the feeding of the five thousand (described in 6:35–9); and across the ocean, the Puritan poet Edward Taylor not only provides a careful exposition of John 6:53–5 in his *Treatise Concerning the Lord's Supper* (polemically using the passage to justify restricting the Supper to only the most devout), but also devotes several lengthy poems, especially his first set of *Meditations* 8, 9, and 10, to the Johannine understanding of the ways in which the Ascension implies the purely signifying function of the Eucharist.[30]

With respect to Johannine conceptions of the Trinity, John Donne devotes two sermons explicitly to the Johannine Farewell Discourse (John 13–17), focusing on the role of the Paraclete or Holy Spirit in providing comfort to the disciples and testimony of Jesus' ways in a post-resurrectional context.[31] And John Milton, in *De Doctrina Christiana*, explicates controversial Johannine texts—especially 1 John 5:7–8 and John 10:30—in order to advance his seemingly anti-Trinitarian, specifically Arian conception of the Son's relationship to the Father.[32] Regarding the nature of *agape* or God's love, John's unique contributions inspire Vaughan's "The Law, and the Gospel," which is oriented around John 14:15—"If ye love me, keepe my commandements"—and Vaughan's fine meditation on the relationship between grief and divine love—"Jesus Weeping"—is inspired by John's unique account of

Art (London: Chatto & Windus, 1954), 126–8. A provocative discussion of Johannine theology in relation to Herbert's lyrics, especially on the subject of discontinuous dialogue, can be found in A. D. Nuttall, *Overheard by God: Fiction and Prayer in Herbert, Milton, Dante, and St. John* (London: Methuen, 1980), 128–43.

[29] See, for example, Henry Vaughan, *The Mount of Olives: or Solitary Devotions* (London, 1652), in *The Works of Henry Vaughan*, ed. L. C. Martin (Oxford: Clarendon Press, 1957), especially 162–4.

[30] In particular, see Edward Taylor, *Treatise Concerning the Lord's Supper*, ed. Norman S. Grabo (East Lansing: Michigan State University Press, 1966), 132–8.

[31] See John Donne, *Sermon 18*, in *The Sermons of John Donne*, vol. vii, 434–51; and John Donne, *Sermon 11*, in *The Sermons of John Donne*, vol. viii, 253–69.

[32] The importance of John's Gospel to Milton's conception of the Son and Holy Spirit is featured in John Milton, *De Doctrina Christiana*, in *The Works of John Milton*, vol. xiv, eds. James Holly Hanford and Waldo Hilary Dunn (New York: Columbia University Press, 1933), chapters v and vi. Toward the end of his discussion of the Holy Spirit in chapter vi, Milton acknowledges the importance of the famously disputed "Johannine Comma" at 1 John 5:7–8, reminding his readers of its alleged "spuriousness" (the passage had been redacted in early Greek translations, reappeared in early Latin versions, and then was fatefully included in Erasmus's 1522 Greek New Testament). Milton denies, in any case, that the Comma suggests a unity of essence. For a recent overview of the critical debates on Milton's seeming anti-Trinitarianism, see Russell Hillier, *Milton's Messiah: The Son of God in the Works of John Milton* (Oxford: Oxford University Press, 2011), 9–23. Miltonists have long noted the reference to the Paraclete and John 15:26 in Book XII of *Paradise Lost*—"But from Heav'n / Hee to his own a Comforter will send" (485–6)—but critical work still needs to be done on Milton's reliance on key Johannine source texts in *De Doctrina*.

the death of Lazarus, the topic of which motivates Donne's sermon on Christ's weeping at Lazarus's feet.[33] Notable devotional texts shaped by Johannine notions of *agape* include Thomas Traherne's *Christian Ethicks*, which uses John's epistolary remark, "God is love" (1 John 4:16), to direct its entire discussion of divine love; and, as we will see in Chapter 4, several poems of George Herbert rely on Johannine conceptions of love in order to poeticize the fraught relationship between human and divine love.

The relative neglect of the shaping influence of Johannine theology on devotional poetry is notable given that, by all accounts, John's Gospel stands apart from the Gospels of Matthew, Mark, and Luke as well as from the apostolic theology of Paul in that the Fourth Gospel offers the most *poetic* and *dramatic* depictions of Christ's ministry. John's rhetorical and literary devices are well known among religious historians. Stable and unstable irony, chiasmic structures, anaphoric comparisons, amplification, recurrent light and dark symbolism, a reliance on re-lexicalization, and the construction of a veritable "anti-language" all frame John's distinctive presentation of Christ.[34] Perhaps the most notable rhetorical device is the Johannine conception of discipleship misunderstanding. Presented through a Socratic method, Christ's messages are initially misunderstood, after which Christ accommodates his discourse to creaturely understanding. As so many commentators have pointed out, John's Gospel relies on irony and the heavy use of interrogatives to a much greater extent than do the Synoptic Gospels.[35] "A Johannine misunderstanding is a statement, normally involving ambiguity, metaphor, or double entendre, whose intended meaning is not properly identified by the person making the statement (most frequently Jesus) or the narrator."[36] Such misunderstandings analogize the discipleship failure that one finds in Matthew, Mark, and Luke, yet they are distinctively Johannine in their use of dramatic irony. Sent by God to illumine a darkened world, Christ's narratives work rhetorically to pique interest, which often leads to some confusion, after which Christ (or the narrator) clarifies his initial intent and the significance of the event or symbol under consideration. For example, Christ remarks to Nicodemus that only those who are reborn can see the kingdom of God, which Nicodemus obtusely takes to mean a literal rebirth until Christ gently rebukes him and provides clarification (3:4, 9). Other examples include the belief by the woman of Samaria that Christ's reference to "living water" refers to an actual spring or well (4:10–15); the disbelief among Jesus' hearers that he can build a literal "temple" in three days (Jesus refers to a spiritual temple) (2:20); and the disciples' erroneous belief that, when Jesus refers to Lazarus as having "fallen asleep," he means literally asleep rather than dead

[33] See John Donne, *Sermon* 13, in *The Sermons of John Donne*, vol. iv, 324–44.

[34] The most thorough account of the literary qualities of the Johannine writings is R. Alan Culpepper's *Anatomy of the Fourth Gospel: A Study in Literary Design* (Philadelphia: Fortress Press, 1983).

[35] Culpepper assesses Johannine style and the rhetoric of misunderstanding in *Anatomy of the Fourth Gospel*; see also Edwin E. Reynolds, "The Role of Misunderstanding in the Fourth Gospel," *Journal of the Adventist Theological Society* 9/1–2 (1998): 150–9.

[36] Andreas J. Köstenberger, *A Theology of John's Gospel and Letters* (Grand Rapids: Zondervan, 2009), 143–4.

(11:13).[37] To the extent that the Johannine Jesus asks more ironical questions than we find in the Synoptics, Johannine irony is more dialogic and Socratic in approach than is the irony of the other Gospels. Paul Duke aptly remarks: "The Johannine Jesus is a different sort of ironist than we meet in the other Gospels. He is more Socratic.... While the Synoptic Jesus is not without humor, his irony is spoken with fire in his eyes. The heavenly revealer of John's Gospel speaks irony too, but his eyebrows are raised, and there is the trace of a smile on his lips."[38] Another biblical scholar, emphasizing the fundamental irony of the *Logos* becoming flesh and dwelling among humankind, concludes that, in the Fourth Gospel, "theology *is* irony."[39]

As we will see throughout the following pages, early modern exegetes were keenly attuned to the pedagogical benefits of Johannine discipleship misunderstanding. William Perkins, for example, uses the Samaritan episode to caution that a reliance on our unaided reason will lead us astray: "When Christ tolde her he would give her *of the water of life*; she replied, *Sir, thou hast nothing to drawe with and the Well is deepe: whence then hast thou that water of life?* Thus we obiect and reason against God with carnall obiections, and waigh Gods Commaundements in the balance of reason.... But contrariwise...when we heare Gods word, we must with him captivate our reason, and subdue our affections to it."[40] While Perkins has in mind here the particular misunderstanding of the Samaritan woman, English divines frequently point to Nicodemus as an instructive example of spiritual obtuseness. Nicodemus fails to understand even the accommodated sense of Christ's remarks on rebirth by means of the Spirit. When Christ responds to Nicodemus, "If I have tolde you earthly things, and ye beleeve not: how shall ye beleeve if I tell you of heavenly things?" (3:12), he testifies to the ways in which he brings lofty or otherwise mysterious sayings down to the level of creaturely

---

[37] In an early-seventeenth-century sermon on the good shepherd discourse, William Ressold describes some of these Johannine misunderstandings: "The sheepe of Christ doe heare the voyce of Christ Intelligently, that is, with understanding and knowledge, not like those carnall Capernaites in *Johns* Gospell, who when our Saviour told them of that great mysterie, the eating of his flesh, and the drinking of his bloud, they dreampt of a carnall and corporeall eating thereof; therfore they cry out...this is a hard speech, who is able to abide it? Such also were those in the second of *John,* who required a signe of our Saviour: To whom he replied, *Destroy this Temple, and in three dayes I will raise it up againe:* but alas, they understood him not, he meant the corporeall Temple of his body, and they meant the matereall Temple of Ierusalem?...And such are many in these times, they doe not truly understand the word of God, but are apt to pervert it and abuse it, to the deep dishonour of God, and burthen of their owne soules." *Four Sermons* (London, 1627), 33–4.

[38] Paul D. Duke, *Irony in the Fourth Gospel* (Atlanta: John Knox Press, 1985), 53. John's dramatic irony stems from what has been described by Hans Windisch as the Fourth Gospel's tendency to offer "dramatically presented narratives" as against the brief pericope-system of the Synoptics. "John's Narrative Style," in *The Gospel of John as Literature: An Anthology of Twentieth-Century Perspectives*, ed. Mark W. G. Stibbe (Leiden: E. J. Brill, 1993), 27. Windisch adds: "The strange thing about John is...that he does not, like the synoptic, present a colourful mosaic of innumerable vignettes but a small number (in comparison to the synoptic) of mainly fully elaborated narratives, discussions and dispute scenes" (26).

[39] George W. MacRae, "Theology and Irony in the Fourth Gospel," in *The Word in the World: Essays in Honor of F. L. Moriarty*, eds. R. J. Clifford and G. W. MacRae (Cambridge: Weston College Press, 1973), 89.

[40] William Perkins, *A cloud of faithfull witnesses* (London, 1607), 193–4.

understanding. Calvin memorably describes such an accommodative mode of tutelage as "divine lisping" or baby talk: "For who, even of the meanest capacity, understands not, that God lisps, as it were, with us, just as nurses are accustomed to speak to infants? Wherefore, such forms of expression do not clearly explain the nature of God, but accommodate the knowledge of him to our narrow capacity."[41] Nicodemus's inability to understand an accommodated notion of rebirth prompts John Trapp, in *A brief commentary or exposition upon the Gospel according to St John* (1646), to liken Nicodemus's darkened understanding to that of a cowherd's: "He understands no more of the doctrine of Regeneration (though he could not but have often read of it in *Ezekiel* elsewhere) then a common cowherd doth the darkest precepts of Astronomy.... All this is gibbrish to him. Water ariseth no higher then the spring whence it came; so the naturall man can ascend no higher then nature."[42] Richard Baxter, along with so many other post-Reformed commentators, acknowledges Nicodemus's obtuseness but takes such a position a step further when reminding his auditors that misunderstanding in the manner of Nicodemus suggests the need for further pedagogical illumination by the Holy Ghost: "Some that do understand the *Words* that we speak, yet because they are carnal, understand not the *matter;* for the natural Man receiveth not the things of the Spirit of God.... They are earthly, and these things are heavenly.... The things of the Spirit are not well known by bare hearsay, but by a spiritual tast."[43]

To the extent that early modern commentaries on Johannine discipleship misunderstanding might be enlisted in arguments against scriptural perspicuity, such commentaries have important implications for the proper reading and construal of pivotal biblical passages. Peter Martyr references a range of Johannine examples of misconstrual in his claim that scriptural verses such as Matthew's "This is my Body" (26:26) cannot be understood uncritically in the plain or perspicuous sense:

> It is not méete therefore to pretend always a perspicuitie of words...Neither is it convenient foorthwith to take quicke holde of the first sense, neglecting and not considering other places. He said...*Lazarus our friend sleepeth.* There lykewise the Apostles misunderstood him: *If he sleepe he shall be safe,* when as he spake of death. Againe, the Lord said: *Destroy this Temple, and in three dayes I will raise it up againe:* Neither understood they, that he meant as touching his bodie....Grossely did *Nicodemus* understand the new byrth. No lesse did that woman of Samaria erre, as concerning that water which Christ promised her.... Wherefore, let them not always say unto us, that this scripture, *This is my bodie,* is plaine: for we will aunswere them: it is playne, as touching the signification of the wordes. But the sense of them is not plaine, as in the lyke sentences it dooth appeare.[44]

[41] John Calvin, *Institutes of the Christian Religion*, Book I, xiii, trans. Henry Beveridge (Peabody: Hendrickson Publishers, 2008), 64.

[42] John Trapp, *A brief commentary or exposition upon the Gospel according to St John* (London, 1646), 14–15.

[43] Richard Baxter, *Making light of Christ and salvation* (London, 1691), 5.

[44] Pietro Martire Vermigli, *The common places of the most famous and renowmed divine Doctor Peter Martyr* (London, 1583), 166.

For Martyr, both Christ's original hearers and post-Apostolic readers of scripture can only understand such gnomic statements when the seeming plain sense is weighed in the larger context of Christ's further instruction and related sayings, a process that requires thinking more incisively about Christological testimony: "It behooveth by other places and circumstances of the scripture to regard well what is héere meant. Wherefore wee will expound this proposition in scanning of it more déepely."[45] All of these uses of irony and misunderstanding, which typically focus on death and resurrection, serve not only to soften the spiritual obduracy of Jesus' hearers but also to engage and edify the reader through the presentation of riddles that will eventually be resolved.[46] Only from a post-resurrectional point of view (whether directly from Jesus or from the narrator) are the true meanings divulged; such misunderstandings serve as both efficacious vehicles and results of revelation.[47] Because Christ primarily clarifies and disseminates knowledge and only to a lesser extent preaches about faith, Johannine theology has at times been held to have been influenced by Hellenistic culture as well as Gnosticism.[48]

Given the importance of John's narratives to early modern theological controversy and the manifestly literary quality of those narratives and topical relevance to early modern devotional poetry, we might ask why there has been a neglect of John's shaping influence on early modern English literature. The answer lies partly in the critical perception that soteriological and forensic Pauline-Protestant notions of justification by faith are central to the work of Donne, Herbert, Vaughan, Traherne, Crashaw, and others. But as we will see, so many of the well-known poems of Herbert, Vaughan, Crashaw, Traherne, Edward Taylor, and, to a lesser extent, Donne, are concerned less with soteriology and the nuances of justification by faith—the nature of election, who deserves grace, how grace is transmitted, the relationship between justifying grace and regeneration, and the nature of heritable sin—than they are with ontological and epistemological, often Johannine-inspired themes, including the relationship between Christ and God, the nature of God's hiddenness relative to what he reveals, and the pedagogical process by which, through irony, misunderstanding, and illumination, Christ's hearers come to understand his message.[49] I suggest further that a good deal of seventeenth-century English devotional poetry marks something of a Johannine Renaissance in early modern England (if we take "Renaissance" in the etymological sense to describe an enthusiastic return to the Johannine discourses themselves and to the earliest scriptural commentaries thereon). Reformed exegetes appropriated the notion of a renaissance from classical humanists, reconceptualizing their return to scriptural purity as a *renovatio ecclesiae*, as in the title page of Theodore de Beze's *Histoire*

---

[45] Ibid., 166–7.   [46] Köstenberger, *A Theology of John's Gospel and Letters*, 143.
[47] Ibid., 142.
[48] Rudolf Bultmann provided a foundational assessment of John and Gnosticism in *Theology of the New Testament*, trans. Kendrick Grobel (New York: Charles Scribner's Sons, 1955), vol. II, part III, as well as in *The Gospel of John: A Commentary* (Westminster: John Knox Press, 1971). C. H. Dodd offers an influential Hellenistic interpretation of Johannine theology in *The Interpretation of the Fourth Gospel* (Cambridge: Cambridge University Press, 1968).
[49] On God's hiddenness and *apophatic* theology in Herbert's poetry, see Hillary Kelleher, "'Light thy Darkness is': George Herbert and Negative Theology," *George Herbert Journal* 28:1/2 (2004–5), 47–64.

ecclesiastique (1580), which describes its subject as "la renaissance et accroisment" of ancient scriptural texts.[50] While the devotional poets undoubtedly relied for their understanding of Johannine theology on some of the magisterial commentaries on John's Fourth Gospel and First Epistle by Aquinas, Meister Eckhart, Erasmus, Calvin, Luther, Martin Bucer, Wolfgang Musculus, and William Tyndale (commentaries on which I will at times rely in order to clarify nuanced exegetical points), much of the overall spirit of this literature looks beyond the contemporary (Reformed) reinterpretation of John's Gospel and back to the Augustinian and patristic reception of the text (especially commentaries by Chrysostom, Ambrose, Cyril of Alexandria, and Origen) as well as to the Fourth Gospel and First Epistle themselves.[51] My use of the term "Johannine Renaissance" does not suggest a break with earlier medieval appropriations of Johannine theology. One can trace, for example, a line of continuity from Augustine's Johannine commentaries through Ratramnus's ninth-century account of John 6 (*De Corpore et Sanguine Domini*), to Cranmer's and later seventeenth-century Johannine conceptions of "eating" as believing. The designation "Renaissance" simply emphasizes the persistent turn throughout the post-Reformation period to earlier, foundational scriptural commentaries on the Johannine confessions, despite typical Reformed and post-Reformed skepticism regarding the reliance on authoritative sources of exegesis relative to scriptural sufficiency.

This return to Johannine scriptural sources in the devotional literature of the period is itself part of a more diffusive turn to seminal Johannine scriptural passages in the pressured theological polemics of the Reformed and post-Reformed

---

[50] On Theodore de Beze and such appropriations among Reformation theologians of the term and concept of "renaissance," see *The Idea of the Renaissance*, eds. William Kerrigan and Gordon Braden (Baltimore: Johns Hopkins University Press, 1989), 9.

[51] Recent scholarship has maintained that, to a certain extent, Calvin and Luther read Pauline views of justification, atonement, and salvation into John's Gospel, thus breaking with the conventional patristic and medieval focus on the revelatory role of the Johannine Christ. Barbara Pitkin remarks that Luther enthusiastically embraced the fourth Evangelist because, along with Paul's epistles, especially Romans and Galatians, John's writings depicted for Luther "how faith in Christ overcomes sin, death, and hell, and gives life, righteousness, and salvation." "Calvin as Commentator on the Gospel of John," in *Calvin and the Bible*, ed. Donald K. McKim (Cambridge: Cambridge University Press, 2006), 180. For Pitkin, Calvin, like Luther, privileged John over Matthew, Mark, and Luke, but because Paul's account of salvation achieved priority in Calvin's mind, Calvin's interpretation of John is ultimately shaped by his interpretation of Paul. While earlier commentators focus on the *Logos* theme and Christ's divinity, Calvin is more interested in faith, the Incarnation, and, as Pitkin remarks, "what Christ does for humans rather than who he is" (192). In this context, Craig Farmer has recently demonstrated that, because Calvin's concerns were to explicate the importance of self-knowledge and what early modernists for some time have described as "affective individualism," Calvin reversed standard portraits of the symbolism of key Johannine figures like the Samaritan woman. For example, although the Samaritan woman is typically described as an amenable and earnest pupil of Christ, Calvin saw her as irreverent and brash. See Farmer, "Changing Images of the Samaritan Woman in Early Reformed Commentaries on John," *Church History* 65/3 (1996), 366, cited in Pitkin, "Calvin as Commentator on the Gospel of John," 195. Given the multifaceted nature of the Johannine writings, including their internal disunity in several places, I would caution against ascribing a univocal position to any Reformed and post-Reformed commentary on Johannine theology. I have found that Calvin's, Luther's, and Erasmus's commentaries on John are all useful (and in accordance mostly with Augustine's *Homilies on John*) on fine exegetical points, including the traditional perception of John's high Christology.

periods. To take just a few representative comments from religious historians regarding the profound influence of the Fourth Gospel and First Epistle on so many hot-topic issues: Jaroslav Pelikan describes John 6 as the "iron wall" of the Reformed position on the Eucharist.[52] Susan Schreiner points out that, on the subject of false spirits, 1 John 4:1 ("Beleeve not every spirit, but trie the spirits, whether they are of God: because many false prophets are gone out into the world") "took an urgency in Luther's thought that revealed the crisis of certainty and authority of his time."[53] D. Elton Trueblood, quoting directly the leading seventeenth-century Quaker Robert Barclay, remarks that John 1:9 ("That was the true light, which lighteth every man that commeth into the world") was "*the Quaker[s'] text*."[54] And I have already noted Paul C. H. Lim's belief that the Fourth Gospel was the "key epicenter" of seventeenth-century emergent discourses of toleration.[55] If we add to all of this an iconographical turn to John in the paintings of Renaissance and Reformed artists such as Titian, Correggio, and Hans Holbein, the appearance in early English books of woodcuts, engravings, emblems, and illustrations of key Johannine discourses and characters, the use of influential verses from the Fourth Gospel on the title pages and frontispieces of works as diverse as Cranmer's *Defence*, Hooker's *Of The Lawes of Ecclesiastical Politie* (1594–7), and the prophetic writings of the leading Familist Hendrik Niclaes, we can begin to appreciate the extent to which we find a Johannine Renaissance in sixteenth- and seventeenth-century English culture and theology.[56]

JOHANNINE DEVOTION

As an organizing framework, I will be describing throughout this book a distinct-ive Johannine devotionalism that can be found in some of the best-known English religious writings of the sixteenth and seventeenth centuries. The first feature, already described above, is a focus on the divine, pre-existent nature of Christ as *Logos*. This emphasis on John's high Christology should not be taken to mean that the Fourth Gospel correspondingly neglects attention to the cross or to the humanity of Jesus. That the Fourth Gospel is insistently incarnational is proclaimed

---

[52] Jaroslav Pelikan, *The Christian Tradition: A History of the Development of Doctrine, Volume 4: Reformation of Church and Dogma (1300–1700)* (Chicago: University of Chicago Press, 1984), 195.

[53] Susan Schreiner, *Are You Alone Wise? The Search for Certainty in the Early Modern Era* (Oxford: Oxford University Press, 2011), 300.

[54] Barclay's statement can be found in *An apology for the true Christian divinity* (London?, 1678), Fifth Proposition, 103. D. Elton Trueblood cites Barclay's estimation of John 1:9 in *Robert Barclay* (New York: Harper & Row, 1968), 155.

[55] Lim, *Mystery Unveiled*, 273.

[56] See, for example, Titian, *Noli Me Tangere* (1512–15), The National Gallery of London, and Antonio da Correggio, *Noli Me Tangere* (1525), Prado, Madrid. For a discussion of Holbein's depiction of Magdalene at the tomb, see Chapter 2. On the raising of Lazarus, see, for example, Jacopo Tintoretto, *The Raising of Lazarus* (1519–20), Minneapolis Museum of Art. An important iconographic use of Johannine verses can be found in Hubert and Jan Van Eyck's Ghent Altarpiece (1432), particularly the center panel (typically entitled the Adoration of the Mystic Lamb) that bears inscriptions of John 1:29 and 14:26; additionally, the foregrounded fountain of life is inspired by the Johannine theme of the waters of life found in John 3–4. References to Johannine images or verses in English bibles and treatises will be discussed in context later in this book, in accordance with the List of Illustrations.

famously in the Prologue: "And the Word was made flesh, and dwelt among us" (1:14). One of the great paradoxes of Johannine Christology is its integration of Christ's divinity (whose "I am" sayings testify to his Godly stature) with the passible aspects of Jesus who, for example, weeps after the death of his friend Lazarus (11:35). At times the high Christology of the privileged Christ is qualified by the seeming subordinationism of verses that suggest that the Son can do little through his own authority: "The sonne can doe nothing of himselfe, but what he seeth the Father doe" (5:19). Such dualities raise a larger question regarding the relationship between revelation and the cross in the Johannine writings. Tord Larsson, a contemporary biblical scholar, puts the question as follows: "Does the uplifted Revealer sail above the earth as a kind of radiant hovercraft or is he uplifted because he is being executed? And is he glorified *in spite of* or *because of* dying on the cross?"[57] Larsson maintains that, while Luther (and to a lesser extent Erasmus) are revisionists in assuming that the Johannine God paradoxically acquires glory through Jesus' distress, Calvin is more of a "traditionalist" in proclaiming a commonsensical notion of God's glory in John's writings: "The main purpose of the Gospel of John [for Calvin] is to proclaim the glory of God, a glory firmly connected with the miracles, resurrection, ascension, and heavenly power of Christ."[58] While we should be skeptical of such overriding ascriptions of revisionism or traditionalism to Luther's and Calvin's approaches to the multifaceted Johannine confessions, I will be arguing that, on balance, early modern English exegetes and literary authors do tend to follow a traditional, high Christological emphasis on the divine qualities of the Johannine Christ whose death is regarded as the definitive manifestation of God's glory. The high Christological stance, often embraced by both Calvin and Luther, is justified by the Johannine material itself. This is not to deny that, in Paul Anderson's terms, Johannine "disunity" is at times present in the Fourth Gospel (and that such disunity surfaces in the early modern reception of the Johannine writings), especially regarding more particularized topics such as the relationship between John's realized and futurist eschatology, the nature of the Trinity, or the question of the sacramentalism of John 6.[59] The open-endedness of Johannine Christology inspires some of the richest devotional poetry of the period and fuels some of the most bruising theological polemic during the Interregnum years.

The second feature of Johannine devotion is John's distinctive account of the Atonement and Passion. In John's writings the Atonement is not understood, as it

---

[57] Tord Larsson, "Glory or Persecution: the God of the Gospel of John in the History of Interpretation," in *The Gospel of John and Christian Theology*, eds. Richard Bauckham and Carl Mosser (Grand Rapids: Eerdmans Publishing Company, 2008), 84.

[58] Ibid., 86–7.

[59] Paul N. Anderson, *The Christology of the Fourth Gospel: Its Unity and Disunity in the Light of John 6*, third printing (Eugene: Cascade Books, 2010), 1–15. On the more general movement from anthropology to Christology in the Fourth Gospel (and on antinomies between theology and Christology in John's writings), see the important essay by C. K. Barrett, "Christocentric or Theocentric? Observations on the Theological Method of the Fourth Gospel," in Barrett, *Essays on John* (Philadelphia: Westminster Press, 1982), 1–18. On the "heavenliness" of the Johannine Christ, see Jerome H. Neyrey, *An Ideology of Revolt: John's Christology in Social-Science Perspective* (Philadelphia: Fortress Press, 1988), chapter 5, *passim*.

is in Paul's letters, in forensic terms as a penal or substitutionary sacrifice according to which God's wrath has been paid for by the ransom of Christ. The language of expiation and reconciliation is typical of the Pauline epistles, as in 2 Corinthians 5:20–2: "We pray you in Christs stead, that be ye reconciled to God. For he hath made him to be sinne for us, who knewe no sinne, that wee might bee made the righteousnesse of God in him"; and 1 Corinthians 6:20: "For yee are bought with a price." A Pauline theology of objective atonement and expiatory sin as the means to salvation is largely absent in John, whose theology is fundamentally revelatory in its emphasis on redemption through knowledge and the hearing of Christ's Word.[60] John will, of course, treat of sin and the Passion, even employing the language of sacrifice, as in John the Baptist's proclamation—"Behold the Lambe of God, which taketh away the sinne of the world" (1:29)—a proclamation that is included in Article 15 of the 1571 edition of the Thirty-nine Articles.[61] Yet for John the Incarnation serves not to satisfy divine justice through God's mercy but rather to foster belief and to evoke faith among the disciples. For most post-Reformed exegetes and poets, John's distinctive *kerygmatic* treatment of the Passion is of a piece with his high Christology. A Sonship of humiliation or abasement has little place in the Fourth Gospel. Christ's mission is not to substitute himself for creaturely sin so much as to reveal *agape* through his own intimate and eternal relationship with the Father.[62]

---

[60] Not only is the Pauline rhetoric of grace and mercy absent in the Fourth Gospel, but the Pauline "atmosphere and temperament," remarks W. F. Howard, cannot be found in the Fourth Gospel: "St. Paul pours out a torrent of superlatives as he looks back in wondering gratitude at the inconceivable mercy of God who, in the person of Jesus Christ, came to him and found him in the lowest depths of despair, only to turn the black and bitter shame of defeat into the most amazing victory. . . . These passionate outbursts of jubilation are not native to St. John." *Christianity According to St. John* (London: Duckworth, 1943), 102–3. Another formulation of the difference can be found in Colwell and Titus, for whom Paul's transactional account of the cross is not present in John: "The fourth evangelist, apparently, felt no attraction to this aspect of Paul's thought for it is absent from his Gospel. For him the death of Jesus far from being a transaction was the divine mechanism for the universalizing of the gospel: the crucifixion is the breaking of the crucible containing the precious ointment of the Spirit." Ernest Cadman Colwell and Eric Lane Titus, *The Gospel of the Spirit: A Study in the Fourth Gospel* (New York: Harper & Brothers, 1954), 48–9.

[61] For a recent discussion of the similarities and differences between Pauline and Johannine theology, see Colin G. Kruse, "Paul and John: Two Witnesses, One Gospel," in *Paul and the Gospels: Christologies, Conflicts and Convergences*, eds. Michael F. Bird and Joel Willitts (London: T&T Clark, 2011), 197–219; and Robin Scroggs, *Christology in Paul and John: The Reality and Revelation of God* (Eugene: Wipf & Stock, 1988).

[62] Seventeenth-century interpretations of John 1:29 emphasize this aspect of the Passion that evokes faith and belief rather than punishment or atonement, at times joining 1:29 to 3:16, as in Obadiah Howe's mid-century apology for orthodoxy and treatise on free grace, *The Universalist Examined and Convicted* (London, 1648): "He doth take away the sin of the world, that is of men living in the world: as he is said to be beleeved on in the world, that is, by men living in the world. He taketh away sins from the world *(quoad partem credentem)* in them that beleeve: as *John 3.16*" (C, 1). In the hands of a dissenting Quaker like William Smith, even the sacrificial implication of 1:29 is displaced by a focus on Christ's glory: "There is not another Saviour but he that is born of God, and comes into the world to redeem out of the world, and take away the sin of the world, in whom the Fathers bosom is opened, and his love tendered unto all people that none might perish. . . . [F]or this is the onely begotten of the Father, which is come in power and great glory, to put an end to sin." *The day-spring from on high visiting the world* (London, 1658), 10. We do find John 1:29 interpreted forensically during the period. Yet such interpretations tend to run together Johannine and Pauline

The third feature of Johannine devotion is a privileging of realized eschatology over more traditional versions of futurist and apocalyptic eschatology. One of the hallmarks of the Fourth Gospel is its emphasis on the "eternal life" that will be granted to Christ's faithful ministry. Whoever believes in the Son of God, Christ assures Nicodemus, "should not perish, but have eternall life" (3:15). This is a promise that resonates in the more overtly eschatological and dualistic overtones in John's summary of the testament of Jesus—"He that beleeveth on the Sonne, hath everlasting life: and he that beleeveth not the Sonne, shall not see life" (3:36)—and this promise is reprised elsewhere in the Gospel, especially in the good shepherd allegory: "My sheepe heare my voyce, and I know them, and they follow me. And I give unto them eternall life, and they shall never perish" (10:27–8). Eternal life, understood as a full and present "experience of blessedness," issues from the know-ledgeable relationship between the communicant and God, itself achieved through belief in Christ's testimony.[63]

Given that eternal life can be experienced in the presence of the descended Johannine Christ, it should not be conflated with the resurrection of the dead. The latter is referenced several times in the Fourth Gospel, most notably in Jesus' warning to his disbelievers: "The houre is comming, & now is, when the dead shall heare the voice of the Sonne of God: and they that heare, shall live" (5:25). The granting of present-day eternal life for the faithful does not obviate the post-resurrectional glory that awaits those faithful.[64] It suggests more of a seal or promise of the literal resurrection. Another way of thinking of the relationship between eternal life and resurrection is that, if the former provides the unassailable knowledge of God through Christ's words, including the adoption of the believer into the Trinitarian family, the latter involves the full beatific vision of God that remains on the horizon.[65] We will see that the possibility of inhabiting everlasting life while still a warfaring Christian offered proleptic comfort to a wide range of devotional poets and dissenting writers throughout the seventeenth century.

In his varied expressions of realized eschatology, John closely parallels Paul, both of whom transpose cosmic Jewish apocalyptic into historical eschatology. Paul's

passages and appear in polemical treatises defending justification by faith that are waged against, for example, Socinian denials of the atonement. Thus Anthony Burgess's treatise on Romans 3:24–5 closes by folding the Johannine into the Pauline conception of pardoning: "God is described by pardoning *iniquity, transgressions and sins.* Christ is said to take away the sin of the world." *The true doctrine of justification asserted and vindicated, from the errours of Papists, Arminians, Socinians, and more especially antinomians* (London, 1651), 23. For a modern assessment of the Johannine conception of sacrifice, see Craig R. Koester, *The Word of Life: A Theology of John's Gospel,* 112–16.

[63] R. Alan Culpepper, "Realized Eschatology in the Experience of the Johannine Community," in *Resurrection of Jesus in the Gospel of John*, eds. Craig R. Koester and Reimund Bieringer (Tübingen: Mohr Siebeck, 2008), 255. On John's realized eschatology, see also C. H. Dodd, "The Kingdom of God has Come," *Expository Times* 48 (1936), 138–42.

[64] Martin Luther addresses this question in his commentary on John 6:54, concluding that by faith the individual achieves eternal life "in an invisible and hidden manner," which will then be clarified and made visible after death. *Sermons on the Gospel of St. John, Chapters 6–8,* in *Luther's Works,* vol. 23, ed. Jaroslav Pelikan (Saint Louis: Concordia Publishing, 1959), 130–1.

[65] On this fundamental difference between realized eschatology and the resurrection of the dead, see Thompson, *The God of the Gospel of John,* 87.

later writings locate the death and resurrection of Jesus as eschatological moments, as in Colossians 3:1–3: "If yee then bee risen with Christ, seeke those things which are above, where Christ sitteth on the right hand of God: Set your affection on things above, not on things on the earth. For yee are dead, and your life is hid with Christ in God." While these passages and comparable verses in Ephesians 1 and 2 converge with the Christ-mysticism that one finds in Johannine eschatology, John, as has sometimes been noted, radicalizes the kind of eschatology associated with Paul. Both John and Paul assume that the arrival of Christ reflects the inbreaking of salvation history, a redemptive event that is consolidated by the death and resurrection of Christ (and the indwelling of the Spirit), which occurs before the *Parousia* (Christ's Second Coming). Yet to a greater degree than Paul, John focuses on the redemptive eschatology of Christ's ministry prior to his death and resurrection, which itself testifies to the Platonic cast of the Johannine writings. For the Johannine believer, the sensible world is in many respects just a phenomenal representation of the eternal order of being.[66] John "takes a step beyond Paul," C. H. Dodd remarks, because for John the "whole life of Jesus is in the fullest sense the revelation of His glory," whereas, on balance, Paul is more interested in Jesus' ministry insofar as it is a preparation for the savior's death and resurrection.[67]

Realized eschatology is closely related to the fourth feature of the Johannine devotionalism that I will be discussing in the following pages: an enthusiastic theology of assurance and perseverance. The bestowal of eternal life offered to the Johannine community the experience of "abiding" with Jesus, as implied throughout Jesus' prayer for believers: "And the glory which thou gavest me, I have given them: that they may be one, even as we are one: I in them, and thou in mee, that they may bee made perfect in one" (17:22–3). The soteriological, ethical, and sociopolitical implications of this passage are wide ranging in Reformed and post-Reformed discourse, so influential that Melanchthon remarked, "There was never a more excellent, more holy, more fruitfull, and more affectionate voice ever heard in Heaven or Earth, then this Prayer."[68] What the Prayer offered was the assured conviction among the faithful that they have achieved in the present life an eternal oneness with God and, according to the most enthusiastic interpreters of the verse, a habitual and unshakeable degree of spiritual perfection.

---

[66] On the Platonic phenomenal/eternal disposition of Johannine eschatology, see C. H. Dodd, *The Apostolic Preaching and its Developments: Three Lectures* (New York and London: Harper & Brothers, 1951), 66.

[67] Ibid., 68–9. On John's radicalization of Pauline eschatology, see also Rudolf Bultmann, *Theology of the New Testament*, vol. 2. Herman Ridderbos provides a comprehensive discussion of the tensions between Paul's realized and futurist eschatologies in *Paul: An Outline of His Theology*, trans. John Richard De Witt (Grand Rapids: Eerdmans Publishing Company, 1975), chapter xii, *passim*. An important foundational discussion of Paul's transformation of scribal apocalyptic can be found in Albert Schweitzer, *The Mysticism of Paul the Apostle*, trans. William Montgomery (New York: Henry Holt & Company, 1931), especially chapter v, *passim*. On Pauline apocalyptic generally, see J. Christiaan Beker, *Paul's Apocalyptic Gospel: The Coming Triumph of God* (Philadelphia: Fortress Press, 1982).

[68] Cited in Anthony Burgess, *CXLV expository sermons upon the whole 17th chapter of the Gospel according to St. John* (London, 1646), A3. For a good history of the reception of John beginning with the patristics and extending to the early modern period, see Pitkin, "Calvin as Commentator on the Gospel of John," 164–98.

The perfectionist language of the Prayer is often mentioned in tandem with the rhetoric of mutual abiding that one finds earlier in the vine allegory: "Abide in me, and in you: As the branch cannot beare fruit of itselfe, except it abide in the vine: no more can ye, except ye abide in me" (15:4). Such perfectionism reaches its apotheosis in Johannine pneumatology regarding Jesus' promise of the Paraclete or Comforter in his Farewell Speech: "And I will pray the Father, and hee shall give you another Comforter, that he may abide with you for ever. Even the Spirit of trueth, whom the world cannot receive, because it seeth him not, neither knoweth him: but ye know him, for hee dwelleth with you, and shall be in you" (14:16–17). No other Gospel or apostolic description of Christ's departure directly invokes the Paraclete, a manifestation of the Holy Spirit who will provide not simply testimony and advocacy of Jesus' ministry once he has departed but spiritual comfort and assurance to the brethren. I will discuss at length the missiological role of the Paraclete in Chapter 3. For many early modern writers, the Johannine depiction of eternal life, in which communicants mutually abide in Christ and God, enjoying the perseverance provided by the Paraclete, serves to offset in various contexts the well-known "fear and trembling" that runs throughout the writings of the English Calvinist and especially the experimental Puritan traditions.

A proper Johannine devotional poetics assumes that the principal literary texts that I assess in this book will include some combination of the following features: 1) a high Christology that emphasizes the divine rather than human nature of Christ; 2) the belief that salvation is achieved more through revelation than objective atonement and expiatory sin; 3) a realized eschatology according to which eternal life has been achieved and the end-time has already partially arrived; 4) a robust doctrine of assurance and comfort, usually tied to Johannine eschatology and pneumatology; and 5) a stylistic and rhetorical approach to representing these theological features that often emulates John's mode of discipleship misunderstanding and irony not found to a comparable degree in the Synoptic writings. The last feature knits together the preceding four. Rather than simply appropriating Johannine proof-texts in the context of varying rhetorical strategies, the poets and theologians discussed in this book often express Johannine theology through the very form of Johannine address.

JOHANNINE SECTARIANISM: A POLITICAL THEOLOGY OF THE *KOSMOS*

The Johannine writings also bespeak a unique and influential historical political tradition. In later sections of the book, I shift attention away from Johannine Christology and toward the sociopolitical influences of the Johannine writings on mid-seventeenth-century English radical dissent and sectarianism. Through the theoretical work of Carl Schmitt, Giorgio Agamben, Alain Badiou, and the important early modern scholarship of Julia Reinhard Lupton and others, we have come to associate early modern political theology largely with the Pauline tradition of ecumenical universalism.[69] Paul's vision of an inclusive, Great Church of all believers is well known among early modernists. Perhaps less well known is the fact that the emerging Johannine church in the first century fashioned itself much differently as a sectarian conventicle that was cut off from the synagogues.[70] This sectarian, Johannine "anti-community" responds with its own idiosyncratic vision of an enlightened and zealous community of brethren who rely on an appropriation of the more canonical language of the Synoptics in order to cultivate an identity distinct from the Jewish and Gentile dominant powers.

Johannine sectarianism is nowhere more evident than in the organizing dualisms that can be found throughout the Fourth Gospel and First Epistle. The term "world" or *kosmos* appears some fifteen times in John's Gospel and typically proclaims a horizontal dualism between believers and unbelievers rather than a cosmological dualism between the supramundane and mundane orders: "If the world hate you, yee know that it hated me before it hated you. If ye were of the world, the world would love his owne: But because yee are not of the world, but I have chosen you out of the world, therfore the world hateth you" (15:18–19). Those who remain under thrall to the world languish in darkness; those who follow Jesus and his brethren walk in the true light, as conveyed in Jesus' address to the unbelieving Pharisees at Mount Olivet: "And hee said unto them, Yee are from beneath, I am from above: Yee are of this world, I am not of this world" (8:23). Richard Crashaw provides a direct poetic paraphrase of the Johannine conception of the world in his Epigram on John 3: "The worlds light shines; shines as it will, / The world will love its Darknesse Still: / I doubt though when the World's in Hell, / It will not love its Darknesse halfe so well."[71]

Scholars have long debated the historical and sociological circumstances that eventuate in this frank dualism and its implied Johannine sectarianism. The earliest Johannine community, which has been described as an outlying maverick conventicle or "sociology of light," is believed to have splintered from the Jewish synagogues sometime around 50–80 CE.[72] This sect of Jewish Christians, having been influenced not only by the earlier Synoptic Gospels (especially Mark) but also by Greek Hellenism, Judean sources, Qumran philosophy, and emerging Gnosticism, was

[69] On Pauline universalism, see note 2 above.

[70] J. Louis Martyn, "A Gentile Mission That Replaced an Earlier Jewish Mission?" in *Exploring the Gospel of John: In Honor of D. Moody Smith*, eds. R. Alan Culpepper and C. Clifton Black (Louisville: Westminster John Knox Press, 1996), 124. Martyn's foundational work in this area is *History and Theology in the Fourth Gospel* (Louisville: Westminster John Knox Press, 2003). See also the influential essay on the dualism of the Johannine group by Wayne A. Meeks, "The Man from Heaven in Johannine Sectarianism," *Journal of Biblical Literature* 91:1 (1972), 44–72. Raymond E. Brown also provides important insights into the historical circumstances that shaped early Johannine ecclesiology in *The Community of the Beloved Disciple: The Life, Loves, and Hates of an Individual Church in New Testament Times* (New York: Paulist Press, 1979).

[71] See *The Complete Poetry of Richard Crashaw*, ed. George Walton Williams (New York: New York University Press, 1972), 13.

[72] I borrow the phrase "sociology of light" from Norman R. Petersen's *The Gospel of John and the Sociology of Light: Language and Characterization in the Fourth Gospel* (Valley Forge: Trinity Press International, 1993), especially chapter 4, *passim*. On the "maverick" quality of Johannine discourse, see Robert Kysar, *John, The Maverick Gospel* (Louisville: Westminster John Knox Press, 2007); and Neyrey, *An Ideology of Revolt*, chapter 6, *passim*.

expelled from Pharisaic culture for preaching high Christology and for refusing to honor cultic rituals, especially preaching or performing miracles on the Sabbath.[73] The result is the deeply sectarian rhetoric of the Fourth Gospel. According to many biblical scholars, the Christological in-group, typically relying on subcultural rephrasings of canonical terms and concepts—terms such as "light," "belief," "faith," etc., all acquire newly complex signification in Johannine discourse—is ranged against both first-century Roman and Jewish culture.[74] A later phase of sectarianism, the occasion of which leads to the composition of John's First Epistle, describes intra-Johannine tensions in which secessionists further radicalize Johannine theology and go on to form the dissenting traditions of Montanism, Cerinthianism, and other versions of Docetism and high Christology that threaten the formation of a catholic Church.[75]

It makes intuitive sense that the language and approach of Johannine sectarianism would appeal to those sixteenth- and seventeenth-century interest groups who typically refused to conform to official theological and ecclesiological dogma. The burden of Chapter 5 is to illustrate the ways in which the Johannine tradition is unqualifiedly embraced by early modern English nonconforming dissenters, including the Familists, Traskites, Eatonists, Ranters, Diggers, Quakers, and modes of English antinomianism that extend to seventeenth-century Boston during the Antinomian Controversy. John provides antinomians with the theological material and proof-texts for their doctrines of free grace, assurance, and, in more radical strains, an inherentist and adoptionist union with Christ and God as well as with the Holy Spirit. The Johannine temper of English antinomianism and radical dissent has gone largely unnoticed by religious historians; but again, that is partly because we have been looking too intently at Paul and not closely enough at John. If we can speak broadly of a Johannine renaissance in early modern culture, regarding the political theology of the dissenting English tradition, we can speak more particularly of a Johannine counter-renaissance against models of church citizenship

---

[73] For a systematic reconstruction of the early history of Johannine community life, see Brown, *The Community of the Beloved Disciple*, 22–4. On the Judaizing influence on the Fourth Gospel, see Howard, *Christianity According to St. John*, 30–2. A nuanced earlier comparison of the Fourth Gospel and the Synoptic Gospels, in which John is distanced from the other Gospel narratives, can be found in P. Gardner-Smith, *Saint John and the Synoptic Gospels* (Cambridge: Cambridge University Press, 1938). The "expulsion" theory and the two-level "Johannine community" hypothesis have been modified, at times questioned, in recent scholarship. For example, in "Building Skyscrapers on Toothpicks: The Literary-Critical Challenge to Historical Criticism," in *Anatomies of Narrative Criticism*, eds. T. Thatcher and S. D. Moore, 55–76, Adele Reinhartz argues that the expulsion passages in the Fourth Gospel were written to deter backsliding rather than to prepare a specific enclave of Johannine believers for persecution. In a more recent revision of the expulsion theory, Raimo Hakola argues that the secession of Johannine Christians resulted more from their differences of opinion regarding temple worship, Sabbath rituals, and the significance of the Sinai revelation than it did from the hostile rabbinic expulsion of the Johannine community from the synagogues. See Hakola, *Identity Matters: John, the Jews, and Jewishness* (Leiden: Brill, 2005), especially chapter 7, *passim*.

[74] In his comments on the Prologue to the Fourth Gospel, D. Moody Smith briefly compares Johannine dualism to the dualistic rhetoric of Palestinian Judaism in the Dead Sea Scrolls as well as to the philosophy of Philo. *John* (Nashville: Abingdon Press, 1999), 53–4.

[75] Ibid., 24.

founded on the principles of experimental Puritanism. As I describe in Chapter 5, one of the recurring politico-theological strategies in the writings of mid-century dissenters, especially in the writings of John Everard, Gerrard Winstanley, and George Fox, is recourse to a biblical-historical justification and analogue for English antinomianism. The ancient Johannine community of the Fourth Gospel, sequestered from the Jewish and Gentile dominant powers, is held up as a historical model for the antinomian separation from official soteriological and ecclesiological dogma.

In locating in the Johannine discourses a scriptural justification for sectarianism, the antinomians craft distinctive politico-theological views that have not been accounted for in recent scholarly work on early modern conceptions of political theology. In complementary but ultimately diverging studies of early modern political theology, Graham Hammill and Victoria Kahn argue that thinkers such as Machiavelli, Hobbes, and Spinoza offer a conception of political making and invention that is legitimated, in Hammill's case, by the Mosaic constitution itself, or in Kahn's case, by the nominalist inheritance in the seventeenth century of a *deus absconditus*.[76] For both Hammill and Kahn, Hans Blumenberg's "reoccupation" model of the transition to modernity offers a more subtle and capacious conception of political theology than does the standard secularization thesis according to which, as Carl Schmitt influentially remarked, "all significant concepts of the modern theory of the state are secularized modern concepts."[77] For Blumenberg, the path to secularization is forged by the complex ways in which pivotal early modern thinkers reoccupied or responded to a series of challenges that Gnostic heresies pose to Christian dogmatics. By locating the origin of degraded matter in the hands of a demiurge rather than in the transcendent God of salvation, early Christianity, despite Augustine's important inroads against Gnostic dualism, had trouble reconciling creation and redemption in the work of a single God.[78] Medieval nominalists, by separating God's *potentia absoluta* from

---

[76] For Hammill's introductory discussion of the use of Hebrew scripture in human making as well as the use of metaphor in the Mosaic constitution, see *The Mosaic Constitution: Political Theology and Imagination from Machiavelli and Hobbes* (Chicago: University of Chicago Press, 2012), 3–11. For Kahn's introductory discussion of the influence of medieval nominalism on *poiesis*, see *The Future of Illusion: Political Theology and Early Modern Texts* (Chicago: University of Chicago Press, 2014), 6–7. Although Kahn remarks that she agrees with Hammill's conception of political theology as a "vehicle of democratic transformation," she states clearly her divergence from Hammill on the question of transcendence: "Where I take issue with Hammill is in the interpretation he offers of the theological dimension of politics. Even as he argues that early modern theological fictions help produce and sustain allegiance to the state, he wants to hold onto, or argue that Machiavelli and Spinoza held onto, the theological dimension of this democratic 'imaginary' as irreducible to the human imagination." *The Future of Illusion*, 5.

[77] Carl Schmitt, *Political Theology: Four Chapters on the Concept of Sovereignty*, trans. George Schwab (Chicago: University of Chicago Press, 1985), 36. Hammill's discussion of Blumenberg's critique of Schmitt can be found in *The Mosaic Constitution*, 10–11. Kahn's discussion of Blumenberg's conception of secularization can be found in *The Future of Illusion*, 5–6. See also Graham Hammill, "Blumenberg and Schmitt on the Rhetoric of Political Theology," in *Political Theology and Early Modernity*, eds. Hammill and Lupton, 84–101.

[78] Hans Blumenberg, *The Legitimacy of the Modern Age*, trans. Robert M. Wallace (Cambridge, MA: M.I.T. Press, 1983), 128–9.

his *potentia ordinata*, attempt to curtail the historical persistence of Gnostic dualism, but in the process they erect a too-hidden predestinarian God. Nominalism thus voids the world of metaphysical certainties and encourages human pragmatism: "Deprived by God's hiddenness of metaphysical guarantees for the world, man constructs for himself a counterworld of elementary rationality and manipulability."[79] The resultant separation of God from nature opens up the space, in Kahn's view, for *poiesis* and "human self-assertion."[80]

In their own terms, Kahn and Hammill advance convincing arguments regarding the ways in which early modern writers rely on imagination and *poiesis* as responses to the challenge of theological legitimation. Yet as a broadly argued, history-of-ideas approach to secularization, Blumenberg's work as a frame for early modern English conceptions of political theology is limited by its cursory attention to relevant biblical and scriptural warrants for its arguments, and by its tendency to rely on mainstream early modern philosophers and political theorists— Hobbes, Leibniz, Descartes, etc.—in order to conceptualize a notion of modernity as a "second overcoming of Gnosticism."[81] The enthusiastic early modern appropriation of the Johannine confessions suggests that, for many literary writers, theologians, and political conventicles, Johannine theology questions the very assumption of an unpredictable and receded *deus absconditus*. Ancient and early modern enthusiasts for the Johannine discourses believe that they share intimate fellowship and union with God through the only-begotten Son, fellowship that might be achievable, given John's strongly realized eschatology, well before the *Parousia*. In its insistence that such indwelling is achievable primarily through the Incarnation, the Johannine confessions, especially the First Epistle, were conceived as a direct response to Gnostic skepticism about the presence of the divine in the historical figure of Jesus.[82] In a certain measure, the Johannine discourses themselves help early moderns overcome the very Gnostic worldview that Blumenberg sees as an otherwise intractable threat to post-Reformed theological legitimation. Drawing on Carl Schmitt's conception of divine voluntarism, Terry Eagleton, neither a theologian nor an early modernist, makes a shrewd but only partly true observation: a nominalist God is a "hidden God whose ways are not ours, inscrutable to reason.... He is the God of radical Protestantism, not the God of the New Testament who in the Johannine phrase pitches his tent amongst us."[83] Eagleton is correct in claiming that Johannine Christology imagines an

---

[79] Ibid., 173. Carl Schmitt assesses Blumenberg's conception of Gnostic recidivism in *Political Theology II: The Myth of the Closure of any Political Theology*, trans. Michael Hoelzl and Graham Ward (Cambridge: Polity Press, 2016), 123–5.

[80] Kahn, *The Future of Illusion*, 6.   [81] Blumenberg, *The Legitimacy of the Modern Age*, 126.

[82] According to Raymond Brown's influential schismatic theory of Johannine Gnosticism, the First Epistle in particular implies that a radicalized section of the Johannine community eventually splinters from the community and embraces forms of Gnosticism that are rejected by mainstream Johannine confessors. See Brown, *The Epistles of John* (Garden City: Doubleday, 1982), 55–68. On the influence of Brown's schismatic position, see the most recent survey of John's relationship to Gnosticism in Urban C. von Wahlde, *Gnosticism, Docetism, and the Judaisms of the First Century* (London: Bloomsbury T&T Clark, 2015), 28–9. On John and Gnosticism, see also Pheme Perkins, *Gnosticism and the New Testament* (Minneapolis: Augsburg Fortress, 1993), chapters 8–9.

[83] Terry Eagleton, *The Event of Literature* (New Haven: Yale University Press, 2012), 4.

accessible and indwelt God (via the teachings of the Son) rather than a *deus absconditus*. Yet this is precisely the sort of comfort that the Johannine confessions offer to "radical Protestants" such as mid-century antinomians and dissenters.[84]

What founds a uniquely Johannine early modern political theology is the emphasis in the Fourth Gospel and First Epistle on the ways in which the divinely-sent, historical Jesus fosters a separation of the world of unbelief from belief. As I describe in Chapter 5, although antinomian and dissenting writers are well known as proponents of a spirit-based rather than purely scriptural piety, much of their polemic against Puritan pastoralism in favor of free grace and liberty of conscience is based on their emulation of the perceived historical example of Johannine sect-arianism as outlined in John's writings.[85] When Everard, Winstanley, or Fox compare their separation from church dogma and oaths of uniformity to the segregation of the ancient Johannine community from the fallen world of unbelievers, these dissenters offer a political theology legitimated by what they deem to be an exemplary, scripturally recorded model of separatism. Although radical dissenters such as Hendrik Niclaes will at times distort Johannine scripture in order to legitimate anti-legalism and perfectionistic conceptions of grace, these writers do not typically find in Johannine scripture a legitimation for purely imaginative political theologies. Early modern Johannine-inspired dissent promotes a political theology that is based primarily on historical analogy, even as it might rely on exegetical imagination, metaphor, or *poiesis*.

Johannine sectarianism also manifests, as has often been recognized, in some of the most virulent anti-Judaism that can be found in the New Testament writings.[86] Much of the Fourth Gospel's hostility toward the Judean culture is expressed in passages that center on the excommunication of the Johannine Christ-confessors from the first-century synagogal culture. The expulsion motif is prominent, for example,

---

[84] Although he writes more generally about the continental Reformation, Brad S. Gregory's caution in *The Unintended Reformation: How a Religious Revolution Secularized Society* (Cambridge, MA: Harvard University Press, 2012), 203 that scholars should not "cordon off the radical Reformation from the magisterial Reformation" is advice that I would apply to an understanding of the Johannine temper in post-Reformed England, particularly regarding mid-seventeenth-century dissent and antinomianism.

[85] I write "perceived" historical example of sectarianism in order to emphasize, along with recent Johannine scholarship, that descriptions in the Fourth Gospel of the late-first-century separation of the Johannine community from Jewish culture might stem more from the Johannine community's quest for self-definition than from historical fact. As Adele Reinhartz remarks in "The Johannine Community and its Jewish Neighbors: A Reappraisal," in *"What is John?" Volume II: Literary and Social Readings of the Fourth Gospel*, ed. Fernando F. Segovia (Atlanta: Scholars Press, 1999), "The Gospel reflects the complex social situation of the Johannine community but not the specific historical circumstances which gave rise to that situation" (137). Additional scholarship that weighs Johannine identity construction against the history of the "expulsion" of the Johannine community includes Wayne O. McCready, "Johannine Self-Understanding and the Synagogue Episode of John 9," in *Self-Definition and Self-Discovery in Early Christianity: A Study in Changing Horizons*, eds. D. J. Hawkin and T. Robinson (Lewiston, N.Y.: Edwin Mellen Press, 1990); and Hakola, *Identity Matters*, 20–2.

[86] For recent accounts of Johannine theology and Judaism, see the essays in the section entitled "John and 'The Jews'" in *The Gospel of John and Christian Theology*, 143–208; Adele Reinhartz, *Befriending the Beloved Disciple: A Jewish Reading of the Gospel of John* (London: Bloomsbury Press, 2002); *Anti-Judaism and the Fourth Gospel*, eds. Reimund Bieringer, Didier Pollefeyt, and Frederique Vandecasteele-Vanneuville (Louisville: Westminster John Knox Press, 2002); and Hakola, *Identity Matters*.

in John 9, which records the refusal of the parents of the healed blind man to explain the miracle on their son's behalf lest they suffer removal from the synagogues: "These words spake his parents, because they feared the Jewes: for the Jewes had agreed already, that if any man did confesse that he was Christ, he should be put out of the Synagogues" (9:22). Comparable verses appear in 12:42 and 16:2, the latter, along with sentiments in John 8, perhaps the most unabashedly anti-Judean moments in the Fourth Gospel: "They shall put you out of the Synagogues: yea, the time commeth, that whosoever killeth you, will thinke that hee doeth God service" (16:2). Such passages are typically appropriated in the seventeenth century by those separatists who draw analogies between their own marginalization from conformist or Puritan culture and the sequestration of the original Johannine Christians. We will see later that such anti-Judaism runs throughout several of George Fox's Quaker treatises, including his well-known *Journal*, in which Fox compares Jewish and Pharisaical "professors" of the Word to those of his contemporaries who would question the Quaker belief in the personal experience of the inward light as a fount of spiritual illumination.[87] That the Fourth Gospel was often used in post-Reformed English culture to justify various forms of anti-Judaism is undeniable, and this reminds us of some of the more unseemly uses of Johannine dualism. And that the Fourth Gospel is often exclusionary is evidenced further by the fact that John's well-known love commandments, unlike what we find in the Synoptic Gospels, exhort the "friends" or brethren to love one another (15:12–17) but make no explicit mention of loving enemies or out-groups. As we track in the following pages some of these exclusionary manifestations and appropriations of Johannine theology, we would do well to keep in mind Wayne Meeks's remark that, as a countercultural sect of believers, the ancient Johannine Christians offer little in the way of explicit moral tutelage: "The kind of ethos that the narrative of the Fourth Gospel seems designed to reinforce, when taken at its face value in its historical rather than canonical context, is not one that many of us would happily call 'Christian' in a normative sense."[88] While the Johannine writings offered unrivaled spiritual consolation and illumination to so many facets of post-Reformed English society, at times offering uplift to the most marginalized sectors of English society, including women, this egalitarianism needs always to be weighed against the darker uses to which John's writings might be put.

JOHANNINE HERMENEUTICS

I offer here a few preliminary remarks on hermeneutics and the denominational labeling of the work of the early modern theologians and literary authors described throughout this study. When discussing a treatise such as Robert Southwell's *Marie*

[87] George Fox, *A journal or historical account of the life, travels, sufferings, Christian experiences and labour of love in the work of the ministry, of… George Fox* (London, 1694), 575.
[88] Wayne A. Meeks, "The Ethics of the Fourth Evangelist," in *Exploring the Gospel of John: In Honor of D. Moody Smith*, eds. R. Alan Culpepper and C. Clifton Black (Louisville: Westminster John Knox Press, 1996), 317–18.

Magdalens Funerall Teares (1591), or Herbert's sacramentalist poetry, or the divine
epigrams of Richard Crashaw, my interpretive starting point is not the Catholicism
of Southwell, conformism of Herbert, or Counter-Reformation or Baroque sensibility of Crashaw. My interpretive premise is that all such material is deeply
Johannine in conformity with several or all of the aspects of Johannine forms of
devotion as described above. The assumption here is that, while denominational
allegiances and religious ideologies will inevitably inflect the reception by an author
of the Johannine material (especially in the antinomian literature referenced
above), a proper understanding of the Johannine writings and worldview is not
simply a means to ideological ends but also, in many cases, an end unto itself. This
does not entail that the writers discussed in this book who appropriate the
Johannine writings serve merely as exegetes. The Johannine literature is itself so
richly literary—hymnic, densely troped and symbolic, structured, inspired—that
such writers will often find sustenance in emulating or simply puzzling over the
Johannine material rather than merely using the Johannine writings as proof-texts
for extra-literary goals.

Early modernists have at times assumed that seventeenth-century devotional
poems at their best transcend exegesis or theological interpretation and analysis.[89]
Yet distinctions between poetry and exegesis—and related distinctions between
doctrine and experience or theology and metaphor—emerge as false dichotomies
when discussing the most Johannine-inspired verse of the devotional poets of the
period. Frances Cruickshank has recently remarked of George Herbert's approach
to scriptural metaphor: "The metaphors by which God communicates His nature
and His activities are not mysterious but efficacious. They are not given as a code
to be deciphered, but as instructions to be followed."[90] But Christ's manner of
address in the Johannine writings indeed requires (among Christ's original hearers
and subsequent readers and authors) just such a critical decoding or, more properly
(and less infelicitously), a revelatory inquiry into and understanding of Christ's
teachings. Consider the metaphorical description that Christ offers of his death at
12:24 of the Fourth Gospel: "Verely, verely, I say unto you, Except a corne of
wheat fall into the ground, and die, it abideth alone: but if it die, it bringeth forth
much fruit." Only gradually does Christ explain in subsequent verses that he is
describing the glory that redounds when one's "hatred" of the world is apotheosized in death. And only gradually does Christ clarify the fundamental lesson of
the metaphor: that to follow him in this manner will foster indwelling and participation with God: "If any man serve me, let him follow me, and where I am, there
shall also my servant be: If any man serve me, him will my father honour" (12:26).
I argue later that George Herbert relies on 12:24 as a source text for "Peace," an
entirely original lyric meditation on where peace resides, but the poem's originality
partly lies in its tendency to reveal the elusive meaning of that establishing

---

[89] For a recent account of such distinctions, see Frances Cruickshank, *Verse and Poetics in George
Herbert and John Donne* (Aldershot and Burlington: Ashgate Publishing, 2010), especially chapter 2,
passim. See also Helen Vendler's reading of Herbert's "The Call" in *The Poetry of George Herbert*
(Cambridge, MA: Harvard University Press, 1975), 203–9.
[90] Cruickshank, *Verse and Poetics*, 46.

Johannine verse. In the Fourth Gospel, the interpretive key to 12:24 emerges at verse 12:26. The language of the latter, explanatory verse itself nowhere appears in Herbert's poem. Instead, Herbert poeticizes (through original diction and key syntactical and formal transitions) his own answer to 12:24—"Take of this grain, which in my garden grows, / And grows for you" (37–8)—which then brings us back to John's exegetical explanation at 12:26. In addition to Herbert's devotional verse, much of the Johannine-inspired verses of Vaughan, Crashaw, Traherne, and others discussed throughout this book are at once stunningly original poetic meditations *and* exegetical devices. These verses do not simply decode or interpret their sources but rather fashion responses to the questions that the Johannine sources raise; and such literary clarifications themselves emulate Christ's own explanations of the otherwise riddling statements that are typically established at the opening of a particular chapter or pericope of John's Gospel or First Epistle. In their imitation of the style and address of the Johannine narrator and of Christ himself, Herbert and other devotional poets of the period practice above all a revelatory poetics.

An understanding of the revelatory sense of seventeenth-century English verse prompts a reconsideration of the use and meaning of the term "devotion" in relation to the religious poetry of the period. Louis Martz, who believed that the "aim of meditation" is a "state of devotion," rested his understanding of devotion on comments such as the following by St François de Sales: "Devotion . . . is nothing els but a spirituall swiftnesse and nimblenesse of love, by which charitie worketh our actions in us . . . so it is the proper function of devotion, to fulfill the commandements with promptnesse, fervor, and nimble vigour of our minds."[91] Meditative poems are "molded," Martz concludes, to "express the unique being of an individual who is seeking to learn, through intense mental discipline, how to live his life in the presence of divinity."[92] To the extent that it carries a pastoral, ethical burden and is part of the duty of every man's life, meditation is essential for the "ordinary conduct of 'good life'."[93] The genre of meditative or devotional poetry thus represents an effort "to evoke and discipline the natural powers of the mind."[94]

Yet an appreciation of the ways in which the poems described in this book are devotional requires an understanding, among other hermeneutical and formal aspects, of the epistemological and exegetical inquiries that such devotional poetry undertakes. To make the intuitive argument, as Martz does, that devotional poetry is concerned with disciplining the self or with the conduct of life is to put the pastoral and ontological cart before the epistemological horse. Early modern treatises on devotion point out that an informed, clarifying knowledge of scripture is a formative step in the devotional process. In his tract on devotion, *A spiritual spicerie containing sundrie sweet tractates of devotion and piety* (1638), the poet and playwright Richard Brathwaite emphasizes that knowledge precedes prayer and devotion proper: "Holy Meditation may beget in thee knowledge, knowledge compunction,

---

[91] Louis L. Martz, *The Poetry of Meditation: A Study in English Religious Literature of the Seventeenth Century* (New Haven: Yale University Press, 1965), 15.
[92] Ibid., 324.   [93] Ibid., 16.   [94] Ibid., 330.

compunction devotion, devotion may produce prayer."[95] Daniel Featley, chaplain to Archbishop George Abbot in the early seventeenth century, demonstrates in *Ancilla pietatis: or, The hand-maid to private devotion* (1626) that a "descanting" upon relevant verses on Christ's feast is exemplary of devotional practice: "In the Devotion fitted to these dayes, first I lay the *ground* out of Scripture, and then *descant* upon it in the Admonition, Hymne, and Prayer."[96] Later in the century, in another treatise on devotion, John Norris, philosopher and clergyman, acknowledging that wisdom and knowledge of scripture do not always lead to devotion, concludes nonetheless that "Knowledge has a *natural* aptness to excite Devotion, and will infallibly do it if not hinder'd by some other cause. So that we may take this for a never-failing Rule, That all other things being equal, the more knowing and considering, still the more Devout."[97] We will have occasion later to meditate on the role of knowledge and understanding in devotion. Suffice it to say here that Johannine devotion requires a keen ability to sort through multiple levels of irony and theological accommodation in order to glean a proper application of Christ's messages. In his compendium of the varieties of devotional poetry during the early modern period, Anthony Low describes four types of devotion: vocal, meditative, affective, and contemplative.[98] While the meditative and contemplative modes naturally assume a level of scriptural attunement, none of the four modes sufficiently captures the exegetical labors required of Johannine devotion. To Low's four categories, I would add the exegetical/epistemological mode of devotion that I will be describing in this book.

Martz's conception of the religious lyric has, of course, been scrutinized and upgraded. Few early modernists now uphold the influence on such poetry of the Jesuit structure of meditation (most scholars are informed by some version of Barbara Lewalski's notion that the Pauline conception of the order of salvation strongly influences the devotional verse of the period).[99] Yet once shorn of its denominational biases, Martz's focus on the "process of mind" reflected in such

---

[95] Richard Brathwaite, *A spiritual spicerie containing sundrie sweet tractates of devotion and piety* (London, 1638), 79.

[96] Daniel Featley, *Ancilla pietatis: or, The hand-maid to private devotion presenting a manuell to furnish her with necessary principles of faith* (London, 1626), 113.

[97] John Norris, *Reason and religion, or, The grounds and measures of devotion* (London, 1689), xii, 11.

[98] Anthony Low, *Love's Architecture: Devotional Modes in Seventeenth-Century English Poetry* (New York: New York University Press, 1978), 6–7; 295–7.

[99] See Lewalski, *Protestant Poetics*, chapter 1, *passim*. Despite their divergences, both Jesuit-meditative and Pauline-Protestant modes of devotion assume a more or less formal, step-wise economy of salvation. The meditative structure of salvation urges penitents to undertake preparatory steps toward salvation (such as the composition of places), meditation proper (an application of the senses, for example), and then prayer and colloquies with Christ/God (see Martz, *The Poetry of Meditation*, 25–8). The Pauline-Protestant order of salvation asks penitents to measure their spiritual progress according to sequential but interfused stages of salvation, including election, calling, justification, adoption, sanctification, and glorification (see Lewalski, *Protestant Poetics*, 16). The Johannine confessions are not as concerned with such a structured soteriology or method of salvation through repentance—indeed, terms such as "repent" or "repentance," which appear over fifty times in the New Testament, are not used in the Fourth Gospel. The Johannine confessions offer salvation or eternal life through the very Incarnation and a coming to knowledge of God through Christ's testimony. On the question of repentance in the Johannine writings, see George Allen Turner, "Soteriology in the Gospel of John," *Journal of the Evangelical Theological Society*, vol. 19 (Fall 1976), 271–7.

verse—as against a primary focus on scriptural context, proof-texts, and exegesis—is consistent with Ryan Netzley's notion that early modern religious poems are "expressions of devotion," not simply "representations of belief," and with Kimberly Johnson's tendency to focus less on the "theological argument" or "thematic content" of such poetry and more on "poetic strategies" for responding to the hermeneutic challenges of sacramentalism.[100] In different ways, Netzley and Johnson provide salutary turns toward poetics and processes of reading that are enacted in devotional lyrics, and both make convincing arguments that devotional lyrics face the challenge of understanding immanence and presence rather than an aloof *deus absconditus*. Yet, like Cruickshank, their tendency is to set propositional content against method, strategy, and process. A Johannine devotional poetics, as I outline it in the pages that follow, does not draw distinctions between the scriptural content of a poem and a poem's method, mode of enactment, or performance as a speech act. A poem might strive simultaneously 1) to provide propositional knowledge and theological argument (the meaning of the bread of life, *agape*, the Comforter); 2) to serve as a performative (a re-enactment of Jesus' relationship to the disciples, Capernaites, or Pharisees); and 3) to offer a formal meditation on the poetic use of dramatic irony. Among the many irreducible aspects and effects of a Johannine-inspired poem is an adequate, even if unresolved, inquiry into the subtleties of the founding Johannine verses. Netzley asks a provocative question about some of the typical speakers of the early modern religious lyric: "Once we believe, or have faith, or receive grace, or are saved, what do devotees, or readers, do other than wait?"[101] Yet this question glosses too quickly past the very challenges of belief enacted in these poems. The insistent question is more fundamentally "What does it take to believe properly and adequately?" And this epistemological burden—what does the Word signify?—is indeed heightened when we locate God's presence immanently, as I think Netzley correctly does. The devotional poems discussed in the following pages typically do not struggle to reach a withdrawn deity; their authors and diegetic speakers labor to clarify common misunderstandings of the often elliptical messages that Christ vouchsafes to them (as readers) and to the prototypical disciples precisely as a means to apprehend the *visio dei*.

Such discipleship misunderstanding, central to John's dramatic irony and an important feature of the Johannine-inspired poems discussed throughout this book, provides a frame for understanding what Heather Dubrow has recently described as the labile shifting of voicing that occurs in early modern devotional writing.[102] Pushing against traditional conceptions of lyric voicing that assume that lyrics are conceived as overheard private meditations and, as Helen Vendler argues, are intended to be voiceable by readers regardless of social specification,

[100] Ryan Netzley, *Reading, Desire, and the Eucharist in Early Modern Religious Poetry* (Toronto: University of Toronto Press, 2011), 17; Kimberly Johnson, *Made Flesh: Sacrament and Poetics in Post-Reformation England* (Philadelphia: University of Pennsylvania Press, 2014), 27.
[101] Netzley, *Reading, Desire, and the Eucharist*, 196.
[102] On the labile quality of lyric voicing, see Heather Dubrow, *The Challenge of Orpheus: Lyric Poetry and Early Modern England* (Baltimore: Johns Hopkins University Press, 2008), 252, n. 6.

Dubrow emphasizes the multiple identifications and voicings of early modern poems.[103] Devotional lyrics might, like the Davidic Psalms, meditation, and prayer, "involve the suppliant shifting among the positions of principal speaker, animator, and audience."[104] Particularly relevant to our discussion of Johannine verse is Dubrow's recognition, drawing lightly on the work of Northrop Frye, that identificatory voicing (in which implied readers stably or univocally identify with speakers or authors) can give way to readerly skepticism; lyrics might "encourage some measure of ironizing distance, either throughout or at some junctures."[105] It is precisely this sense of skeptical distancing that I argue so many devotional lyrics share with the Johannine penchant for dramatic irony. As I have already remarked, the Fourth Gospel assumes a shared revelatory understanding between reader and the Evangelist that is typically lost on a gallery of recalcitrant speakers, characters, and unsuspecting victims of Johannine irony. Readers of Nicodemus's dialogue with Christ have a keen sense of Nicodemus's inability to get past a grossly literal understanding of rebirth, just as they realize, against the Samaritan woman's puzzlement, that Christ's reference to living waters needs to be understood symbolically, not literally. Because the Evangelist in the Prologue has already explained to readers that Christ is the incarnate Word, readers are elevated, in R. Alan Culpepper's terms, "to the implied author's Apollonian vantage point before the spectacle begins."[106] The Evangelist therefore approaches implied readers with a "wink" that reflects their shared wisdom as against the veil of ignorance worn by so many diegetic interlocutors: "Various textual features, principally the misunderstandings, irony, and symbolism, constantly lead the reader to view the story from a higher vantage point and share the judgments which the 'whispering wizard' conveys by various nods, winks, and gestures."[107]

One of my arguments is that the devotional writers discussed in this book provide just such a comforting wink to their implied or ideal readers.[108] And they wink because they and their readers do not typically share the conversion *pathos* of a poem's speakers. Of course, some readers might be naive to the directed irony, or, consistent with Dubrow's conception of shifting voicing, some readers might move from an identification with a dim speaker to an inspired author. More often than

---

[103] Vendler's discussion of identificatory voicing can be found in *The Art of Shakespeare's Sonnets* (Cambridge, MA: Harvard University Press, 1997), 2, 18, cited in Dubrow, *The Challenge of Orpheus*, 94. The conception of lyric as "overheard" harks back to John Stuart Mill's notion of the "poet's utter unconsciousness of a listener" as expressed in Mill's, "What is Poetry," in *Essays on Poetry by John Stuart Mill*, ed. F. Parvin Sharpless (Columbia: University of South Carolina Press, 1976), 12, cited in William Waters, *Poetry's Touch: On Lyric Address* (Ithaca: Cornell University Press, 2003), 2.

[104] Dubrow, *The Challenge of Orpheus*, 80.

[105] Ibid., 98. See also Northrop Frye, *The Anatomy of Criticism: Four Essays* (Princeton: Princeton University Press, 1957), 271.

[106] Culpepper, *Anatomy of the Fourth Gospel*, 169.   [107] Ibid., 151.

[108] By "implied reader" I mean the ideal narrative audience, following Peter Rabinowitz: "The ideal narrative audience agrees with the narrator that certain events are good or that a particular analysis is correct, while the narrative audience is called upon to judge him." "Truth in Fiction: A Reexamination of Audiences," *Critical Inquiry* 4 (1977), 135, cited in Culpepper, *Anatomy of the Fourth Gospel*, 208, where Culpepper goes on to remark: "In John the ideal narrative audience adopts the narrator's ideological point of view, penetrates the misunderstandings, appreciates the irony, and is moved to fresh appreciations of transcendent mystery" (208).

not, though, implied readers are encouraged to plume themselves on their skeptical distancing from the texts' many obtuse speakers and poetic characters.[109] Such literary works serve more as devotional allegories of their source texts than as private records of their authors' and readers' agony of conversion. Readers who encounter Southwell's narrator plying Mary with questions about her grief, or who mark the travails of the ignorant speaker of Herbert's "Love unknown," or who witness the biting irony of Crashaw's Johannine epigrams, are readers who ideally find common voice, in keeping with the dualism of the Johannine writings, with enlightened insiders. This helps to explain why the most Johannine-inspired verse of the period often emerges as the most theologically comforting. A poem that depicts backsliding or a self-persecutory *ethos* can often be read paradoxically as a poem of theological uplift if one identifies with authors, presumably enlightened by the Evangelist, rather than with forlorn speakers sunk in sin.

To argue that a Johannine devotional poetics is on one level exegetical and epistemological, and that it works toward understanding and clarifying dramatic irony, does not mean that early modern poets, theologians, and other writers strive to restore a scriptural perspicuity to the Johannine writings. Perhaps no early modernist has argued more convincingly than Brian Cummings that the early continental and English Reformation revealed a crisis in language, that, for example, the Lutheran contention that meaning resides in the purity of words emerges as something of a lexical chimera in the scurrilous sixteenth-century interpretive debates among Luther, Erasmus, and Thomas More.[110] But if the Bibliology of the early Reformers (which includes, in England, the scripturalist approaches of Wyclif, Tyndale, and Cranmer) and the kindred grammatico-historical method of interpretation (which emphasizes literalism and letterism) proved unsustainable during the period, we should not assume that interpretations of John were so open-ended as to invite a receptionist hermeneutics on the other extreme.[111] It is well known that early Reformers such as Luther and Calvin were suspicious of allegorical interpretations of scripture and the frequent recourse to a tradition of patristic exegesis by Catholic polemicists.[112] It is easy to assume

---

[109] In the context specifically of Herbert's "awareness of manipulative courtliness," Richard Strier remarks that Herbert is "fully aware" of the "strategic nature of courtly supplication and makes ironic, critical use of this awareness." For Strier, "Herbert knows…that the joke is always on him." *Resistant Structures: Particularity, Radicalism, and Renaissance Texts* (Berkeley: University of California Press, 1995), 112. I agree with the spirit of this formulation, particularly its appreciation of Herbert's ironic detachment, but I would add that, in the poems discussed throughout this book, the spiritual, if not courtly, joke is more typically on the implied speakers than on the real or implied authors.

[110] Cummings describes the textual and "grammatical" history of such sixteenth-century theological debates in *The Literary Culture of the Reformation: Grammar and Grace* (Oxford: Oxford University Press, 2002), especially chapter 1, *passim*.

[111] A recent account of the ideal of scriptural perspicuity as touted by the early English Reformers can be found in Richard M. Edwards, *Scriptural Perspicuity in the Early English Reformation in Historical Theology* (New York: Peter Lang, 2009), especially chapters 5–7.

[112] For an important reconsideration of the ways in which Reformed exegetes would integrate the allegorical or figurative approach to interpretation with an appreciation of the literal or plain sense of scripture, see Mary Morrissey, "Ornament and Repetition: Biblical Interpretation in Early Modern English Preaching," in Kevin Killeen, Helen Smith, and Rachel Willie, *The Oxford Handbook of the Bible in Early Modern England, c. 1530–1700* (Oxford: Oxford University Press, 2015), 303–16.

that the crisis in language and endless debating about words emerge from the ashes of anti-traditionalism. If one cannot rely on patristic exegeses, *catenae*, and Roman Catholic formularies for a univocal interpretation, one makes recourse to the words themselves, only to discover that debating over words reveals an ever-receding primary text and the need for the very authoritative translation or inter-pretation that *sola scriptura* questions in the first place.

Yet we would be wrong to argue that this hermeneutical spiral captures the early modern appropriations of the Johannine writings. While some passages and verses, particularly the notorious Johannine Comma, provoked debates about proper translation and grammatical *minutiae*, revealing that exegetes did not agree on any particular traditional or consensual interpretation, other pericopes such as the pier-cing of Christ's side at John 19 do not invite as much competitive textual glossing. Most early modern glossators accept Augustine's canonical sacramentalist view that the blood and water streaming from Christ's wound symbolize, respectively, justification and baptism. And the Augustinian and patristic interpretations of John's bread of life verses bring more Reformed and post-Reformed exegetes to agreement than disagreement on the meaning of the reference to true bread. In these cases and many others, to argue that the Reformed elevation of *sola scriptura* iconoclastically tears down the patrological edifice is to neglect the formative influence of the Augustinian tradition on the reception of Johannine theology in the early modern period.

When tradition is not embraced, exegetes, homilists, and poets will often resort to a contextualist approach to interpretation, often described in hermeneutical theory as "scripture interpreting scripture," according to which difficult Johannine passages are glossed in the context of other relevant passages elsewhere in the Fourth Gospel or First Epistle.[113] For example, when Nicholas Breton sets out to clarify his interpretation of Mary's weeping in John 20, he leans heavily on the Lazarus pericope at John 11. And when John Milton advances his skeptical cri-tique of the power and personhood of the Holy Ghost, he plays not one but several key Johannine verses against one another. Allowing scripture to interpret scripture also entails an appreciation of the intertextual unity of the Bible, evident in the syncretistic manner in which, for example, John Donne incorporates a Johannine poetics into a Pauline frame in several of his most theologically complex *Holy Sonnets*. For George Herbert, the interpretive unity of the Bible is expressed in the "constellations of the storie" (4), in the manner in which "This verse marks that, and both do make a motion / Unto a third, that ten leaves off doth lie" (5–6).[114]

It is true that several post-Reformed discourses rely on neither tradition nor contextualization in their appropriations of the Johannine writings. Yet I have

---

[113] On Calvin's harmonization of the Gospels through a method of "scripture interpreting scrip-ture," see Edward, *Scriptural Perspicuity*, citing Bernard Ramm, *Protestant Biblical Interpretation: A Textbook of Hermeneutics* (Ada: Baker Academic, 1980), 58.

[114] George Herbert, "The H. Scriptures (II)," in *The Works of George Herbert*, ed. F. E. Hutchinson (Oxford: Clarendon Press, 1941), 58. Chana Bloch discusses at length Herbert's approach to scrip-tural unity and collation in *Spelling the Word: George Herbert and the Bible* (Berkeley: University of California Press, 1985), especially chapter 2, *passim*.

found that most such approaches occur in the seventeenth-century polemical writings of antinomians and the Pietist opposition. As we will see, the far-reaching Johannine verse that seemed to legitimate dissenting arguments for free grace— "But if wee walke in the light, as he is in the light, wee have fellowship one with another, and the blood of Jesus Christ his Sonne clenseth us from all sinne" (1 John 1:7)—is typically removed from its immediate context in which the very succeeding verse in the First Epistle reminds the penitent that no one is free from sin entirely: "If we say that we have no sinne, we deceive our selves, and the trueth is not in us" (1 John 1:8). Opponents of antinomianism will frequently recontextualize such verses in their invectives against free grace. And for their part, Pietists will strategically decontextualize important Johannine passages on personal assurance in order to counter antinomian claims of spiritual perfection and eternal life.

Throughout this book, I will be tracking still another important early modern approach to exegeting properly the Johannine writings. Most of the writers treated in this book are as interested in the Johannine material as speech acts and in the illocutionary force of Christ's sayings, especially his use of a rhetoric of irony and misunderstanding, as they are in the content of that material. Rudolf Bultmann's influential notion that, in the Fourth Gospel, Christ reveals little more than that he is the revealer is almost clairvoyantly expressed in the early modern interest in John's writings.[115] Post-Reformed commentators, especially those tending toward separatism and dissent, will often imitate the manner in which Christ reveals himself as true light and direct witness of God to the brethren. And in recapitulating Christ's distinct manner of revelation, such writers will draw parallels between the marginalization of their own communities and the historical circumstances in which the prototypical ancient Johannine community emerged. This early modern historical-critical approach to John often anticipates the more recent hermeneutical attention to provenance and the social and historical circumstances that gave rise to John's unique Christology, eschatology, and soteriology.

The post-Reformed English approach to the Johannine material is thus context-sensitive. At times debate centers on the nuances of grammar and translation; at times tradition is wheeled in to justify an interpretation of an elusive passage; at times contextualization, intertextuality, and a comparative approach are used; at other times a historical-critical approach seems to be more fruitful, and the performative is elevated above the ideational. Despite this multiform hermeneutic, a radically subjective early modern account of Johannine theology does not emerge. Rather, what emerges (or what stubbornly refuses to be exegeted away) is a relatively stable and distinctive early modern English Johannine tradition. And I have found that a reconstruction of this Johannine tradition yields some surprising discoveries: that Southwell's treatment of Magdalene's grief is not radically different from the approach of a "Protestant" such as Breton, Markham, or even Vaughan; that Donne is as concerned with spiritual comfort and perseverance as he is fear and trembling; that Crashaw, the poet of the seemingly material and grotesque, is not especially concerned with Christ's body at the Supper; and that Vaughan, deeply

---

[115] See Rudolf Bultmann, *Theology of the New Testament*, vol. II, 66.

alienated from his own membership in High Church culture, finds the same solace in Johannine dualism that is experienced by antinomian enthusiasts. All of these writers were so insufflated with the Johannine Spirit that the comforts of Johannine theology at times helped to elevate them above the theological quibbles and ideological wrangling of the time.

Johannine comfort and assurance brings us finally to the important question of sacrality in post-Reformed English culture. Recent scholarship on the cultural historiography of Reformation England has questioned the widely held belief that Reformed theology systematically disenchanted or desacramentalized the preceding medieval-Catholic worldview.[116] Rather than draw boundaries between the sacred and profane or between the immaterial and material, revisionist historians, skeptical of metanarratives such as Weberian secularization, have argued for continuities rather than ruptures between the ritualized superstitions of medieval sacramentalism and Protestant theology. Certainly the anti-ritualist attacks on the local presence by Luther, Zwingli, and Calvin served to question in various and competing formulations the mysteries of transubstantiation. But anti-ritualism entailed for neither Luther nor Calvin the withdrawal of sacralization from the world. Luther, for example, whose work has been described as "apocalyptic and eschatological rather than desacralizing," premises his *theologia crucis* on a conception of Christ, the Word of God, as the sacramental link between the creaturely and divine and as the means through which the cosmic battle against Antichrist might be fought.[117] And Calvin's pneumatological account of the real presence, as I will discuss in more detail in Chapter 3, assumes that the sacramental body is the integral conduit between the creaturely and divine realms.[118]

I argue in this book that Johannine soteriology and theology likewise were sacralizing and enchanting to those early moderns who pledged a Johannine confession of Christ. This will become particularly evident in our discussion of the non-Eucharistic message of John 6. If Christ's exhortation to "eateth my flesh" needs to be understood symbolically, that is, as unconnected to any ordained or institutionalized rite, it also needs to be understood as thoroughly sacramental, at least according to a conception of sacramentalism that views the Incarnation itself

---

[116] See Alexandra Walsham, "Migrations of the Holy: Explaining Religious Change in Medieval and Early Modern Europe," *Journal of Medieval and Early Modern Studies*, 44:2 (2014), 246–8, as well as Walsham's earlier piece, "The Reformation and the 'Disenchantment of the World,' Reassessed," *Historical Journal* 51:2 (2008), especially 499–500. See also the earlier and foundational work by Robert W. Scribner, "The Reformation, Popular Magic, and the 'Disenchantment of the World,'" *Journal of Interdisciplinary History* 23:3 (1993), 475–94. Jennifer Waldron provides a useful account of this critique of the disenchantment narrative in *Reformations of the Body: Idolatry, Sacrifice, and Early Modern Theater* (Basingstoke and New York: Palgrave Macmillan, 2013), especially 1–5. For a fresh and provocative discussion of God's immanence (and a critique of the metanarrative of loss) in early modern devotional writing, see Netzley, *Reading, Desire, and the Eucharist*, especially 6–10.

[117] Scribner, "The Reformation, Popular Magic, and the 'Disenchantment of the World,'" 483. For a detailed discussion of Luther and the sacred presence of God in nature, see Richard Strier, "Martin Luther and the Real Presence in Nature," *Journal of Medieval and Early Modern Studies* 37:2 (2007), 271–303.

[118] On the sacramental elevation and efficacy of the body for Calvin, see Waldron, *Reformations of the Body*, chapter 2, especially 58–66.

as the "ultimate sacrament" and assumes that through the vehicle of the Son God is rendered present to the world.[119] When Robert W. Scribner remarks that, for theologians such as Luther, "the Word of God" is the "overwhelming sacramental experience, the sole means through which created humanity could come to knowledge of the divine," he might as well be summarizing the guiding sacramental principle of the Fourth Gospel.[120] We will reconstruct in the following pages the ways in which the distinctiveness of Johannine sacramentalism (what has been described as "symbolic sacramentalism") emphatically links the temporal orders to God not only through participation and fellowship with Christ (as described in the vine allegory, for example) but also through the promise of the Spirit-Paraclete once Christ has departed.[121] When one imagines a Christocentric conventicle of believers set apart from the hostilities of the reprobate world, enjoying eternal life through an indwelling with God, itself achieved through shared *agape*, then one begins to understand the ways in which the Johannine confession of Christ was one of the most sacralizing of such confessions in early modern English Reformed culture. Alec Ryrie asks us to imagine what the Reformation felt like to its lived inhabitants.[122] An early modern English Johannine enthusiast would respond that it felt assuring, uplifting, even magical in the access that it offered to the several manifestations of Christ's sacred presence.

CHAPTER SUMMARIES

I have organized the following chapters according to Johannine theme, typically connected to a historical-theological crux and polemic raised by a widely influential Johannine pericope. I have elected to organize chapters by theme rather than by single authors for several reasons. First, no single author treated here reveals a univocal or even reducible position on the varied Johannine topics treated throughout the book. Too often thematic studies that organize chapters according to single authors tend to project stable theologies or denominational worldviews onto the authors under consideration. Additionally, because John's discourses themselves are often internally fraught or seemingly contradictory, internal tensions relative to Johannine sacramentalism, pneumatology, *agape*, or free grace require discrete and extended treatment before they can be discussed in the context of the imaginative

---

[119] Paul N. Anderson describes the Johannine conception of the Incarnation as the "ultimate sacrament" in *The Christology of the Fourth Gospel*, 113.

[120] Scribner, "The Reformation, Popular Magic, and the 'Disenchantment of the World,'" 483.

[121] On the Johannine spiritualizing of the sacraments, see K. Matsunaga, "Is John's Gospel Anti-Sacramental?—A New Solution in Light of the Evangelist's Milieu," *NTS* 27 (1981), 516–25, cited in Anderson, *The Christology of the Fourth Gospel*, 116–17.

[122] See Alec Ryrie, *Being Protestant in Reformation Britain* (Oxford: Oxford University Press, 2013), 20. Ryrie's question regarding how it felt to be an early Protestant is inspired by C. S. Lewis's *English Literature in the Sixteenth Century Excluding Drama* (Oxford: Oxford University Press, 1973), 32, the latter of which is cited by John Stachniewski, *The Persecutory Imagination: English Puritanism and the Literature of Religious Despair* (Oxford: Oxford University Press, 1991), 1. I believe that the Johannine confessions of Christ serve as salves and religious antidotes to Stachniewski's notion of a persecutory poetics during the period.

literature of the period. Finally, and perhaps most importantly, because the imaginative literature often emulates Johannine language and approach and is revelatory in its attention to Johannine puzzles, the Johannine resonances of the literary texts emerge most clearly when the guiding themes of these texts are discussed as closely as possible in the context of the corresponding Johannine verses.

The first chapter reviews the interpretive fortunes of perhaps the most influential Johannine passages from the patristic through early modern periods: the bread of life discourses at John 6:26–59. Jesus has just arrived in Capernaum after miraculously producing food for five thousand. The Capernaites question why he has crossed over from Galilee, to which Jesus responds: "Ye seeke me, not because ye saw the miracles, but because yee did eate of the loaves, and were filled. Labour not for the meat which perisheth, but for that meat which endureth unto everlasting life" (6:26–7). What follows are several of Jesus' most influential but also most ambiguously worded sacramental comments, including the designation of himself as the "bread of life" and "living bread" and his remarks on eating his flesh: "For my flesh is meate indeed, and my blood is drinke indeed. He that eateth my flesh, and drinketh my blood, dwelleth in me, and I in him" (6:55–6). Such exhortations exert a profound influence on conceptions of the Eucharist from Augustine onward, prompting not only Zwingli but also Thomas Cranmer and several English theologians to equate "eating" with believing. And much exegetical labor is spent on proving that the bread of life allegory does not refer to the institution of the Supper but only serves as a preparative seal for the meal proper. The burden of this chapter is to reconstruct the neglected influence of the bread of life discourse on the sacramental poems of George Herbert, Henry Vaughan, Richard Crashaw, and Edward Taylor.

The second chapter reassesses the scholarship on the early modern reception of Christ's poignant words to Mary Magdalene at the tomb: *noli me tangere*, or "touch me not." Recent interpretations of the early modern approach to these words (as well as the related *hortulanus* sequence) have understood the lines to suggest a displacement of material touching with an Augustinian posture of spiritual seeing that accommodates itself to the Reformed emphasis on the signifying rather than the corporeal/sacramental function of Christ's body.[123] Much of this criticism, however, fails to put *noli me tangere* in its larger Johannine context. As the most revelatory of the Gospel accounts of Christ's evangelizing, the Fourth Gospel (the only Gospel in which *noli me tangere* appears) elevates the hearing of Christ's Word over spiritual seeing (or touching of Christ). We will see that Robert Southwell, Gervase Markham, Thomas Walkington, and Nicholas Breton all reconstruct the pedagogical lessons vouchsafed to Mary throughout John 20. Mary is petitioned to recall to herself the words of Christ that she has already heard and hence patiently await her post-resurrection reconciliation with Christ as Word of God. And we will see that several of the sixteenth- and seventeenth-century treatments of Mary at the tomb show a keen appreciation of the method of discipleship misunderstanding

---

[123] See, for example, Patricia Badir, *The Maudlin Impression: English Literary Images of Mary Magdalene, 1550–1700* (Notre Dame: University of Notre Dame Press, 2009), 65–8.

used by John, even emulating that rhetorical approach in their treatments of Magdalene's misplaced grief.

As I have already remarked, John's Gospel uniquely describes the Holy Spirit as the Paraclete who will provide testimony/advocacy as well as spiritual comfort and assurance to those disciples whom Jesus will leave behind. The Paraclete is also instrumental as the Spirit of truth in helping to establish and guide the mission of the future Johannine church. In the third chapter, I provide a more detailed account of the multivariate role of the Paraclete, especially as it is referenced in John Donne's and John Milton's poetry and prose. Donne devotes two sermons to the Paraclete, providing a comprehensive portrait of this influential figure in Johannine pneumatology. Donne's sermons describe the intimate relationship between sanctified individuals and the third person, and the sermons gesture at the perseverance provided to those individuals once such a bestowal has occurred. I then offer readings of selected *Holy Sonnets*, each of which provides an implicit legitimation of Trinitarianism but does so through an elevation of the Spirit, in particular. If Donne takes a traditional Johannine position on the nature and role of the Spirit, Milton shows less confidence in the ongoing (and historical) service of the Paraclete to establish truth within an infallible church. We find in Milton's writings that enthusiasm for the Paraclete is qualified both by Milton's tendency to elevate Christ over the third person and by his political experiences with false spirits who would claim the Paraclete's influence in establishing an authoritarian and rule-governed ecclesiology.

The fourth chapter is oriented around another foundational although more metaphysical proclamation of the Johannine discourses: the identification of God as love in 1 John 4:8–9: "Hee that loveth not, knoweth not God: for God is love. In this was manifested the love of God towards us, because that God sent his only begotten Sonne into the world, that we might live through him." Here again John departs significantly from the Synoptics and Paul, none of whom directly identifies God with love as such and all of whom privilege an ethics of horizontal or neighbor-love as the path through which communicants might unite with God. According to the Johannine metaphysic, responsive love of God is achieved fundamentally through an embrace of Christ's Word, particularly because God's love for Christ is expressed eternally for the Son prior to the Incarnation. Not only does Johannine *agape* raise the question of the proper role for the love of God's faithful outside of a circle of believers but, for critics such as Anders Nygren, it also creates a tension between *agape* and *eros*. If *agape* is expressed from Father to Son eternally, the implication is that Christ merits an unqualified form of abiding love not directly available to creatures; since the Father–Son bond serves as a prototype for the circuit of love among creatures, Christ, and God, any individual's loving relationship with Christ and God would seem to be bound up with meritorious *eros* rather than gratuitous *agape*.[124] This chapter addresses these and related questions as they are debated in early modern treatises on John's uniquely ontological and metaphysical conception of love. I then turn to four seventeenth-century poets, each of whom

---

[124] Nygren, *Agape and Eros*, 152.

borrows a distinctive feature of Johannine *agape* in his own approach to the divine love. For Herbert, responsive love of God is the surest means of knowing (seeing) God. Vaughan is less optimistic that he can sustain union with God's effulgent love, and so his poetics of *agape* is tempered by an almost Donnean preoccupation with both servile and filial fear. Thomas Traherne, too, makes liberal use of John's identification of God and love, although I argue that Traherne takes a Thomistic line in presenting an analogical relationship between God and creatures that is warranted by Johannine Christology. When we look across the ocean to Edward Taylor, we find in several exegetical poems an unashamed embrace of the idiosyncratic sectarianism seemingly justified by the Johannine material.

As I remarked above, the penultimate chapter of the book is the most politically and sociologically grounded. Here I track the manner in which Johannine sectarianism and dualism is appropriated first by Hendrik Niclaes, the leader of the sixteenth-century Familists, and then by a like-minded group of radical dissenters, antinomians, and enthusiasts, many of whom were influenced by the Familist belief in a radical union with God. These antinomians who believed, as Niclaes did, that they were "Godded with God" or "vined in the vine" make recurring use of dozens of Johannine tropes, pericopes, and images, all coalescing around the antinomian claims to free grace. Our focus on Johannine poetics of style will emerge as particularly apt in this context. The dissenting tradition will appropriate the spirit and letter of the Johannine discourses. Niclaes, John Everard, Gerrard Winstanley, and George Fox, in particular, draw parallels between the historical formation of their own maverick group of dissenters and the prototypical Johannine minority that historically separates from the synagogues. These writers will variously re-lexicalize Johannine tropes in ways analogous to the manner in which John's Gospel co-opts language from the Synoptics; and they will arrogate to themselves the roles of both John and Christ as true lights who are uniquely endowed to disseminate the good news to their nonconforming brethren. We will see that Johannine sectarianism and dualism provide the antinomian tradition with the scriptural material and rhetorical approach to counter some of the cherished pastoral assumptions of the practical divinity of experimental Puritanism. I can imagine that some readers will question the relevance of such a lengthy discussion of mid-century English antinomianism in a book that is largely devoted to the influence of Johannine theology on devotional poetry. I believe, however, that a detailed discussion of the Johannine aspects of antinomian enthusiasm can help us contextualize the Johannine poetry of two radically different mid-century devotional poets: Richard Crashaw and Henry Vaughan. If Crashaw, as Nicholas McDowell has already suggested in an important essay, does show antinomian leanings despite his embrace of Laudian fundamentals, Vaughan emerges as something of an anti-enthusiast in his more politically topical poems of *Silex Scintillans*.[125] Toward

---

[125] Nicholas McDowell, "The Beauty of Holiness and the Poetics of Antinomianism: Richard Crashaw, John Saltmarsh, and the Language of Religious Radicalism in the 1640's," in *Varieties of Seventeenth- and Early Eighteenth-Century English Radicalism in Context*, eds. Ariel Hessayon and David Finnegan (Abingdon and New York: Routledge, 2011), 31–50.

the end of Chapter 5, I develop these somewhat unexpected linkages between non-conformism/antinomianism and Crashaw's and Vaughan's devotionalism.

Although the material described above is organized according to Johannine themes rather than particular authors, the final chapter takes a closer look at two of the most Johannine poets of the early modern period: George Herbert and Henry Vaughan. In both poets' work the Johannine influence is present not merely in the range of source material—the Longinus wounding of Christ, the vine discourse, the figure of Nicodemus, the typological embrace of Isaiah—but also in the poems' overall form and mode of address. I will be especially interested in this chapter in the role of discipleship misunderstanding and in the use of irony in three beloved poems by Herbert—"The Bag," "The Bunch of Grapes," and "Love unknown"—as well as in Vaughan's highly regarded "The Night." We will see the ways in which Herbert's and Vaughan's speakers often find themselves productively confused by some of the Johannine riddles, tropes, and Christological sayings that are misconstrued by the faithful ministry of Jesus as well as by the Samaritans and Capernaites. I hope to show that in most cases, especially in Herbert's verse, such ironic misconstruals issue not in instability or paradox but in a clarification and heightened understanding of some of the deepest mysteries of Johannine Christology.

1

The Flesh Profiteth Nothing
John 6, the Bread of Life, and
Devotional Poetry of Belief

Early modernists have recognized for some time the profound ways in which sixteenth- and seventeenth-century debates regarding the sacrament of the Eucharist influenced not merely the theological content and approach of the period's devotional poetry but also, as one scholar recently has remarked, "new ways of understanding signification itself."[1] Much of this attention has centered on those fateful words of institution that can be found in Matthew, *Hoc est enim corpus meum* ("This is my body"). In the exegetical hands of a radical reformer such as Zwingli, these words might substitute "signifies" for "is," thereby calling into question centuries of more orthodox and literal translations that seem to warrant transubstantiation. Reformation polemicizing on the sacrament influences the manner in which imaginative writing treats figuration itself, what another scholar calls the "precarious relationship between materiality and signification."[2]

However, much of this recent scholarship has overlooked the foundational influence of key Johannine passages on the sixteenth-century continental and English debates regarding the real presence, as well as the influence of John on the matter and point of view of the sacramental poems of George Herbert, Henry Vaughan, Richard Crashaw, and Edward Taylor. I argue in this chapter that John 6, particularly the frequently cited bread of life discourse, exerts as profound an influence on devotional writing as Matthew's "This is my body." And with respect to debates on the role of the Ascension and the presence of Christ in the sacrament, John's theology is also as influential as the accounts of the Lord's Supper that are found in the Synoptic Gospels.[3] Perhaps the most frequently referenced text on the Eucharist is Augustine's *Homilies on John*, in which Augustine advances his notion that "eating is believing," a Johannine position that significantly influences various

---

[1] Sophie Read, *Eucharist and the Poetic Imagination in Early Modern England* (Cambridge: Cambridge University Press, 2013), 3.

[2] Kimberly Johnson, *Made Flesh: Sacrament and Poetics in Post-Reformation England* (Philadelphia: University of Pennsylvania Press, 2014), 6.

[3] A compendious summary of the early continental debates surrounding John 6 can be found in Jaroslav Pelikan, *The Christian Tradition: A History of the Development of Doctrine, Volume 4: Reformation of Church and Dogma (1300–1700)* (Chicago: University of Chicago Press, 1984), 195–7. Pelikan, drawing on the writings of Oecolampadius, describes John 6 as the "iron wall" of the Reformed position (195).

competing continental positions, including Zwingli's memorialism, Luther's notion of the ubiquity of Christ, and Calvin's pneumatological theory of the real presence. In England, Cranmer's *Defence of the True and Catholic Doctrine of the Sacrament* (1550) is steeped in John's theology both directly and by means of Augustine's scrupulous exegeses. What follows is an overview of the use of Johannine theology in the early Reformation debates on the sacrament, followed by a series of close readings of key seventeenth-century devotional poems that rely on John's theology in their representation of the Eucharist theme. We will see that the Johannine emphasis on the Ascension warrants in both the theology and the imaginative literature of the period the Reformed claim that Christ cannot be present bodily in the elements of the sacrament because he remains in heaven with God. This basic assumption influences further polemicizing on the role of belief, grace, and faith in the sacrament and on the related question of who is permitted to receive the Eucharist.

AUGUSTINE: EATING IS BELIEVING

Since all Reformed positions on the Eucharist were directly or indirectly influenced by Augustine's *Homilies on John*, we should provide a brief account of Augustine's treatment of John 6, particularly the bread of life pericope. At the outset of Homily 27, Augustine takes up the pivotal question of the role of the Ascension in the sacramental offering. In his gloss on John 6:62 ("What and if yee shall see the sonne of man ascend up where hee was before"), Augustine remarks that the Capernaites were scandalized because they could not reconcile eating Christ's flesh with his ascent to heaven: "For they were thinking he was going to give them helpings of his body; but he said that he was going to ascend into heaven—the whole of him, of course. *When you see the Son of Man ascending where he was before*, then at least you will see that he is not giving you helpings of his body in the way you are thinking; then at least you will understand that his grace is not something finished off in mouthfuls."[4] For Augustine, the grace that is set off against material food in the sacrament is directly associated with belief. The Capernaites were scandalized by the meaning of the bread of life because they failed to appreciate that eating is identified with believing: "The Lord, who was going to give the Holy Spirit, said that he was himself the bread who came down from heaven, urging us to believe in him. To believe in him, in fact, is to eat the living bread. The one who believes, eats; he is invisibly filled, because he is invisibly reborn."[5]

Augustine's interpretation of the bread of life verses, and his particular notion that eating Christ's flesh is equivalent to believing in his message, are premised on his greater understanding of John's depiction of Christ's relationship to the hidden Father. An important intertext for John 6 is the *noli me tangere* episode at John 20,

---

[4] Saint Augustine, *Homilies on the Gospel of John: 1–40*, ed. Allan D. Fitzgerald and trans. Edmund Hill (Hyde Park: New City Press, 2009), 467.
[5] Ibid., 450.

to which Augustine turns immediately after his interpretation of the bread of life narrative. Mary is not permitted to touch Christ until she truly believes that Christ is one with the Father: "What does 'touch' mean, if not 'believe?'"[6] That purer form of spiritual touching cannot be achieved until Christ has ascended and abides with the Father: "How was she to touch the one ascending to the Father? That, however, is the way he wished to be touched; that is the way he is touched by those who touch him rightly: as the one ascending to the Father, abiding with the Father, equal to the Father."[7] Mary and the Capernaites will be granted eternal life if they eat (believe) properly in the signification of Christ's flesh; that is, they need to believe without material, visual evidence. The problem with the Fathers who ate manna in the desert and died (John 6:48–9) is that "they believed in what they could see; they had no understanding of what they could not see."[8] Those who eat properly, those who eat nourished by belief, reveal a "spiritual understanding of that visible food" and receive the power or *virtus* of the sacrament.[9] Augustine's Johannine focus on the Ascension as a frame for understanding the spiritual rather than real (substantial) presence of Christ, as well as his externalist identification of belief with eating, casts a long influence not only on the sixteenth-century Reformed continental and English accounts of the Eucharist but also on an influential Carolingian interlude on the Eucharist, to which we now briefly turn.

The Johannine–Augustinian contribution to the early Christian understanding of sacramentalism and the Eucharist is fatefully reprised in the ninth century when, at Emperor Charles the Bald's request, a Carolingian Abbot, Paschasius Radbertus, publishes a short explanation and defense of the real presence entitled *De Corpore et Sanguine Domini* (831–3). Although the term "transubstantiation" does not come into typical parlance until the 1215 statement of faith of the Lateran Council, Radbertus anticipates the early medieval usage of the term in arguing that the substance of the bread and wine were effectively changed (*efficaciter interius commutatur*) into the body and blood of Christ, although our limited senses prevent us from discerning the transformation.[10] In a quest for further clarification on

---

[6] Ibid., 452.

[7] Ibid., 452. Augustine's intertextual mingling of John 6 and John 20 is reprised in Richard Sibbes's lengthy mid-seventeenth-century treatise on *noli me tangere*, *A heavenly conference between Christ and Mary after His resurrection* (London, 1654): "And therefore *touch me not*. She came with too much a carnall mind to touch him, when we said *Rabboni*, it was not satisfaction enough for her to answer *Rabboni;* but she runneth to him, and claspeth him, and clingeth about him, as the affection of love did dictate to her.... She was too much addicted to his bodily presence. 1. It is that, men will labour after, and have laboured for, even from the beginning of the world, to be too much addicted to present things, and to sense.... They will adore Christ; but they must bring his body down into a peece of bread, they must have a presence" (35–7).

[8] Ibid., 458.   [9] Ibid., 458.

[10] On Radbertus and the real presence, see Philip Schaff, *History of the Christian Church*, vol. VI (Grand Rapids: Eerdmans Publishing Company, 1963). Radbertus's position is summarized in Louis Ellies Du Pin's 1691 ecclesiastical history: "That no Man ought to doubt of its being the *Body of Jesus Christ*, and that his Flesh and Blood be really there; and shews, that none ought to be ignorant of so great a Mystery, daily Celebrated in the Church, and such as ought to be Received by the Faithful. Which they cannot do Worthily and Effectually, unless they can discern the Excellency of the Mystical Body and Blood of Jesus Christ from what they perceive by the Tast." *A new history of ecclesiastical*

the Eucharist theme, Charles later asks a Benedictine monk, Ratramnus, the Abbot of Corbie, to respond to Radbertus's earlier treatise.

The result is Ratramnus's *De Corpore et Sanguine Domini* (*c.*850). Ratramnus, turning immediately to John's Gospel, outlines the manner in which scripture relies on "figures," or "certaine vailes & covertures," in order to make "dark" declarations.[11] Two of his illustrative texts are John 6:53 and 15:15: "*I am the living bread which came downe from heaven.* Likewise, when hee calleth himselfe a *Vine,* and his Disciples *branches,* saying, *I am the true Vine, and yee are the branches.* For all these sayings, seeme to speake one thing, and yet meane another thing."[12] It follows that when Christ says "*Except yee eate the flesh of the Sonne of man and drinke his blood, yee shall not have life in you,*" "hee doth not say or meane, that his flesh, which afterwards hanged on the Crosse, should bee cut in peeces and parts, and so be eaten by his Disciples."[13] To those who would claim that John 6:53 should be understood in "verity and truth" rather than as a figure or mystery, Ratramnus defers to the authority of Augustine, specifically the third book of *De Doctrina Christiana* in which Augustine (consistent with his position in his commentary on John 6) remarks that John 6:53 provides a "*figurative speech commanding us to communicate in the Lords passion,*" about which Ratramnus concludes: "Here we perceive, that this Doctor saith and affirmeth, that the mysteries of the bodie & blood of Christ, are under a figure celebrated and received of the faithfull: for hee saith plainely, that it belongeth not to religion, but is rather a wicked thing, carnally to eate Christs body, or to drink his blood."[14]

Ratramnus likewise appreciates Augustine's important distinction between the material thing or matter of the sacrament (*res sacramenti*) and the sacrament as such (*sacramentum*): "We perceive that Saint *Augustine* saith, that the Sacrament is one thing, and the things whereof they are Sacraments, is another thing. Now the body, in which Christ suffered, and the blood that came out of his side, are the things of the Sacrament: but the mysteries by which these things are represented ... are the Sacraments of the body and blood of Christ, which are celebrated and administred, in remembrance of the Lords passion."[15] If the Eucharistic elements serve to memorialize the passion, they do so, Ratramnus reasons, because they are similitudes and likenesses of the "things which they represent and shew forth."[16]

Throughout the remaining parts of his treatise, and with further help from the Johannine commentaries by Ambrose and Jerome, Ratramnus continues to use

writers containing an account of the authors of the several books of the Old and New Testament (London, 1691), chapter 7, 69.

[11] Ratramnus, *A booke of Bertram the priest, concerning the body and blood of Christ written in Latin to Charles the Great* (London, 1623), 3. I have used this 1623 edition of Ratramnus's *De corpore et sanguine Domini.* Earlier translations had appeared in 1548 and 1582, the former apparently a partial translation. The preface to the 1623 edition, written by the Anglican theologian Humphrey Lynde, occasions the publication of John Floyd's *A plea for the reall-presence* (London, 1624), a Jesuit defense of Bellarmine's conception of the real presence. On the question of the dating of Ratramnus's Latin treatise, see Celia Chazelle, *The Crucified God in the Carolingian Era: Theology and the Art of Christ's Passion* (Cambridge: Cambridge University Press, 2007), 211–15.

[12] Ratramnus, *A booke of Bertram the priest,* 3.   [13] Ibid., 23.   [14] Ibid., 25–6.
[15] Ibid., 28.   [16] Ibid., 29.

John 6 as evidence for the spiritual rather than carnal presence. If Christ's body is indeed "chawed with the teeth," Ratramnus, after Ambrose, asks, how can it provide promised "incorrupted" eternal life to the faithful?[17] Ratramnus, however, does not go so far as offering a purely memorializing or symbolist conception of the Eucharist. The communicant does receive the body and blood of Christ, although in spiritual rather than carnal form: "I would have no man thinke, that because wee speake thus, that therefore the faithfull doe not in the mystery of the Sacrament, receive the Lords body and blood, because faith receiveth that thing, not which the eye seeth, but that which the hart beleeveth: for it is a spirituall meate, and a spirituall drinke, spiritually feeding the soule."[18] This is an argument for the ingestion of the real presence, although that presence mystically and spiritually feeds only the souls of the faithful, to whom it grants everlasting life.[19] Still, Ratramnus's *De Corpore et Sanguine Domini*, republished in 1531 and then translated into English in 1548, is a text that, in its defense of a Johannine–Augustinian conception of the Eucharist, comes to exert its influence on Thomas Cranmer as well as the Zwinglians and Swiss Reformers, to whose comparable engagement with John 6 we now turn.[20]

Motivated to expound his religious views to the faithful in France and Italy, Ulrich Zwingli positions sections of his *Commentary on the True and False Religion*

---

[17] Ibid., 39.   [18] Ibid., 79.

[19] In his ecclesiastical history, Du Pin notes that Ratramnus, who agrees in principle with Radbertus on the real presence, deviates from the spiritualist interpretations of the Eucharist that one finds in Augustine and Ambrose. Ratramnus and his followers "look'd upon *Paschasius* as one that receded from the express Words of S. *Austin* and S. *Jerom*, who said, our Saviour's Body might be taken in two or three manners, and they could by no means approve of such Expressions. Their Controversie was not about the real Presence, which they owned with *Paschasius,* but only about the Expression it self. *Paschasius* maintained, that not only the Body of our Saviour was really in the Eucharist, but also that Christians ought plainly to say, that there was no Difference betwixt the one and the other. His Adversaries on the other side, to whom this Expression appeared too harsh, as if there were no Figure in the Eucharist, and the outward Species were the very Body of our Saviour, were disgusted at it. So that the state of their Controversie was not, whether Christ's Body was truly and really in the Eucharist, but whether we ought to say that he was there in the same manner as he was born, crucified, and raised from the dead." *A new history of ecclesiastical writers*, chapter 7, 72.

[20] Cranmer shows his enthusiasm for Ratramnus (who is commonly referred to as Bertram in the sixteenth century) in his reply to Gardiner (and Richard Smith): "As the fathers had the same Christ and mediator that we have (as you here confesse) so did they spiritually eat his flesh and drinke his bloud (as we doe) and spiritually feed of him.... This besides saynt Augustine is plainely set out by Bertrame above ... whose judgement in this matter of the sacrament, although you allow not (because it utterly condemneth your doctrine therein) yet forasmuch as hytherto his teaching was never reproved by none, but by you alone, and that he is commended of other, as an excellent learned man in holy scripture." *An aunswere by the Reuerend Father in God Thomas Archbyshop of Canterbury, primate of all England and metropolitane, unto a craftie and sophisticall cavillation, devised by Stephen Gardiner Doctour of Law* (London, 1580), 77–8. Zwingli is more directly influenced by the work of Berengar of Tours, whose *De Sacra Cana* (1050) radicalizes Ratramnus in its defense of a more symbolist understanding of the Eucharist, a position that Berengar is forced to repudiate in 1059. Zwingli's reference to Berengar's repudiation in *On the Lord's Supper* can be found in *Zwingli and Bullinger*, trans. G. W. Bromiley (Philadelphia: Westminster Press, 1953), 197–9. On Zwingli's knowledge of Berengar, see Joar Haga, *Was there a Lutheran Metaphysics? The Interpretation of Communicatio Idiomatum in Early Modern Lutheranism* (Gottingen: Vandenhoeck & Ruprecht, 2012), 40, n. 80. Berengar, too, returns to John 6, arguing, as Philip Schaff points out, that John 6 refers to "the believing reception of Christ's death." See Schaff, *History of the Christian Church: Medieval Christianity* (New York: Scribner's, 1890), 565.

(*Commentarius de vera et falsa religion*, 1525) against the prevailing notion that the elements of the Holy Communion become the crucified or resurrected body of Christ.[21] As is perhaps well known, Zwingli also vehemently rejects what becomes known as Lutheran consubstantiality, the notion that the bodily presence of Christ coexists with the bread.[22] En route to advancing his own position according to which the words "This is my body" describe a figurative or symbolic presence of Christ in the sacrament, Zwingli provides lengthy exegeses of John 6. The *Commentary* systematically interprets relevant passages extending from the beginning of the bread of life pericope at 6:29 through Jesus' claim that the flesh profits nothing at 6:63. As I have noted, the narrative opens with Jesus' upbraiding of the Capernaites for seeking him out because he has already provided them with loaves of bread. The Capernaites ask what they can do to make satisfaction, how they can "worke the workes of God" (6:28), to which Jesus responds, "This is the worke of God, that ye beleeve on him whom he hath sent" (6:29). Zwingli's first claim, consistent with Augustine's gloss, is that 6:29 warrants the notion that feeding should be identified with belief rather than carnal eating: "The work of God is that wherewith we believe on the Son whom the Father hath sent.... The food He bids us seek is, therefore, belief on the Son. Faith, therefore, is the food of which He talks so impressively all through this chapter."[23] Once he has established that "by 'eating bread' He [Jesus] means believing the word of the Gospel," Zwingli turns to verses 6:49–50, which read in his translation of the Vulgate: "No one denies that your fathers did eat manna in the wilderness, and they died [Jn 6:49]; but he that eateth of this bread, me to wit, that is, that believeth on me, hath eternal life. This is that bread which cometh down from heaven, that a man may eat thereof, and not die [Jn. 6:50]."[24] These verses support Zwingli's contention, again consistent with Augustine's understanding of the Ascension (and manifestly against Lutheran theories of the ubiquity of Christ) that Christ's divine nature rather than his human nature descends from heaven: "Christ is our salvation by virtue of that part of His nature by which He came down from heaven, not of that by which He was born of an immaculate virgin, though He had to suffer and die by this part."[25] Zwingli pauses to emphasize that Christ is not speaking here of sacramental eating; rather, Christ is reminding the Capernaites that he is the means of salvation "not by being eaten, but by being slain."[26] Christ is indeed the food of the soul, but while he is slain according to the flesh, he is "salvation bringing only according to His Divinity."[27] From these interpretations of 6:48–51, Zwingli develops his controversial belief that sacramental eating serves simply to memorialize Christ's Passion.

---

[21] Zwingli dedicates his treatise to the King of France, to whom the preface is directly addressed. For a discussion of the circumstances leading up to the publication of the *Commentary*, see Jean Rilliet, *Zwingli: Third Man of the Reformation*, trans. Harold Knight (Philadelphia: Westminster Press, 1964), 97–100.

[22] For the pivotal use by Zwingli of John 6:63 in the controversy with Luther, see W. P. Stephens, *Zwingli: An Introduction to his Thought* (Oxford: Clarendon Press, 1992), chapter 10, *passim*.

[23] Ulrich Zwingli, *Commentary on True and False Religion*, eds. Samuel Macauley Jackson and Clarence Nevin Heller (Durham: Labyrinth Press, 1981), 201.

[24] Ibid., 204.   [25] Ibid., 204–5.   [26] Ibid., 205.   [27] Ibid., 205.

Zwingli's third important gloss on John 6 focuses on Jesus' statement that "He that eateth my flesh, and drinketh my blood, dwelleth in me, and I in him" (6:56). The verse serves to distinguish those hardened unbelievers from the pious righteous, suggesting that John 6 must refer to the "eating of faith," since so many who take the sacrament do not properly abide in Christ: "There are numberless persons, alas! who eat and drink the body and blood of Christ sacramentally, and yet are not in God nor God in them, except in the same way He is in the elephant and the flea."[28] Zwingli's interpretation here leads naturally into John 6:63, the textual linchpin of his argument: "The flesh profiteth absolutely nothing. The words that I speak unto you are spirit, and are life."[29] Not only does 6:63 reinforce Zwingli's belief that the Spirit "alone draws the heart to itself and refreshes it," but it substantiates his view that, although the flesh profits greatly, it does so again by being forsaken, not by being eaten. Zwingli will go so far as to imagine that in these words Christ is "providing by law, as it were, against our ever indulging in dreams about bodily flesh."[30]

I would note that, despite Zwingli's contentious debates with Luther on the issue of whether Christ's body is present during the bread of life and Eucharistic offerings, Luther's position on John 6 partly overlaps with Zwingli's (and Augustine's). In his commentary on John 6, Luther does distinguish himself from the "fanatics" who would contend that it is Christ's "divinity and not His humanity which imparts eternal life," but Luther agrees that John 6 does not refer distinctly to the Supper, going so far as to say that it is non-sacramental and refers to "spiritual nourishment and eating."[31] Indeed, Luther gathers his rhetoric of scriptural perspicuity, as against overly allegorical interpretations of John 6, to argue that the "true meaning" of eating and drinking in this context is "synonymous" with "to believe," and that the words of Christ "bear no supplement."[32]

THOMAS CRANMER'S JOHANNINE RENAISSANCE

Not simply Zwingli's figurative account of Christ's body in John 6, but specifically his identification of eating with believing, as well as his anti-Lutheran views on the restrictions of Christ's human nature, all influenced Thomas Cranmer's *Defence of*

---

[28] Ibid., 206.   [29] Ibid., 210.   [30] Ibid., 209.

[31] Martin Luther, *Sermons on the Gospel of St. John*, chapters 6–8, in *Luther's Works*, vol. 23, ed. Jaroslav Pelikan (Saint Louis: Concordia Publishing, 1959), 101, 119. Luther objects here and elsewhere to Zwingli's conception of "alloeosis," according to which Christ's divine nature is exchanged for his human nature during the sacrament. *Sermons on the Gospel of St. John*, n. 80, 101.

[32] Luther, *Sermons on the Gospel of St. John*, 135. Luther's more pointed critique of Zwingli's interpretation of John 6 can be found in his 1527 treatise *That These Words of Christ, "This is my Body," etc., Still Stand Firm Against the Fanatics*, trans. Robert H. Fischer, *Luther's Works*, vol. 37, ed. Robert H. Fischer (Philadelphia: Muhlenberg Press, 1961). In that treatise, Luther argues against Zwingli that the phrase the "flesh is of no avail" from John 6:63 does not refer to Christ's body, for the passage contrasts flesh with spirit and so refers to the old Adamic flesh rather than Christ's body: "Here you see manifestly that he distinguishes flesh from the Spirit and sets it in opposition to the Spirit. For he certainly teaches that life and spirit are in his words and not in the flesh; but in regard to the flesh he concedes that it is of no avail. How could it avail, if neither life nor spirit is in it?" (96).

the True and Catholic Doctrine of the Sacrament, first published in 1550. While the immediate occasion for the *Defence* was a response to an apologetic sermon on the real presence delivered by Bishop Stephen Gardiner in 1548, Cranmer had already begun to move from his earlier conciliar position on the Mass and Eucharistic sacrifice to one more in accordance with the views on spiritual presence and receptionism articulated by Martin Bucer, Heinrich Bullinger, and Peter Martyr.[33] Foxe remarks in his *Acts and Monuments* that Cranmer had passed through a Lutheran phase, yet the modern consensus agrees with Cranmer's own testimony in 1555 that he "taught but two contrary doctrines" on the Eucharist until his famous recantation and martyred death in 1556.[34] The *Defence* is notable, as we will see later in this section, not only for its turn to Johannine theology at the outset but also for Cranmer's twin reliance on scriptural literalism and patristic tradition. The title page (Fig. 1.1) establishes that his polemic will be "grounded and stablished upon God's holy word and approved by the consent of the most ancient doctors of the Church."[35] Directly underneath these lines appears the only epigraph used on the title page, John 6:63: "It is the spirit that giveth life, the flesh profiteth nothing."[36] When Cranmer turns to John in the *Defence*, he does so with the weighty support of the authority of the early Church, itself disseminated through the writings of the Church Fathers.[37]

---

[33] In *Thomas Cranmer: A Life* (New Haven: Yale University Press, 1996), Diarmaid MacCulloch marks 1548 as the year in which Cranmer's theology "had decisively crossed the Rubicon" (391); see also chapter 9, *passim*, in which MacCulloch describes in detail the influence of Bucer and kindred Reformers on Cranmer during this period. For a brief discussion of the formative debates between Gardiner and Cranmer, see A. F. Pollard, *Thomas Cranmer and the English Reformation, 1489–1556* (Hamden, CT: Archon Books, 1965), 237–41.

[34] *The Works of Thomas Cranmer* (Cambridge: Cambridge University Press, 1844–46), vol. ii, 218. Cited in Pollard, *Thomas Cranmer and the English Reformation,* 235.

[35] Cited in MacCulloch, *Thomas Cranmer,* 467. MacCulloch points out that Cranmer's use of the honorific "doctors" to describe the patristics strained against his increasing suspicion of Church authority; hence Cranmer more typically preferred the term "authors" to describe the Church Fathers (467).

[36] Anticipating Cranmer, the pseudonymous Lollard tract *Wycklyffes wycket* had used John 6:51–2 as its epigraph. That text extrapolates from the vine discourse in its conclusion that the bread of Christ needs to be understood figuratively: "Also Chryst sayeth John. xv. I am a very vyne/wherfore worshyppe ye not the vyne for god, as ye do the breade. wherein was Chryst a verye vyne or where in was the breade chrystes bodye, in fyguratyve speache, whiche is hyd in the understandyng of synners Then yf Chryste became not a materiall either an early vyne, neyther materiall vyne became the bodye of Chryste. So neyther the bread materiall breade was not chaunged from his substaunce to the flesshe and blode of Chryste." *Wycklyffes wycket* (London?, 1546), 12. For publication details of *Wycklyffes wycket*, see Alec Ryrie, *The Gospel and Henry VIII: Evangelicals in the Early English Reformation* (Cambridge: Cambridge University Press, 2003), 235–6. For Wyclif's own commentary on John 6 in *De Eucharistia*, where he relies directly on Augustine's gloss, see David Aers, *Sanctifying Signs: Making Christian Tradition in late Medieval England* (Notre Dame: University of Notre Dame Press, 2004), 55–6. On Wyclif's use of John 6 in support of his overarching contention that the real presence signifies not a substantial but rather a real, virtual, and sacramental presence, see Ian Christopher Levy, *John Wyclif: Scriptural Logic, Real Presence, and the Parameters of Orthodoxy* (Milwaukee: Marquette University Press, 2003), 249–50.

[37] Interesting to note is that Richard Bonner's *A treatyse of ye ryght honourynge a wourshyppyng of our saviour Jesus Christe in the sacrament of bread and wyne* (London, 1548), the authorship of which MacCulloch attributes to Cranmer, also uses John on its title page, in this case John 4:23: "But the houre commeth, and now is, when the true worshippers shall worship the Father in spirit, and in trueth: for the Father seeketh such to worship him." On the authorship of the tract, see MacCulloch, *Thomas Cranmer,* 399–403.

A DEFENCE
OF THE TRVE AND CA-
tholike doctrine of the sacrament of the body and bloud
of our sauiour CHRIST, with
a confutation of sundry errors
concernyng the same, grounded and stablished vpon God-
des holy woorde, & approued
by y consent of the moste auncient doctors of the Churche.
Made by the moste Reuerende
father in GOD
THOMAS ARCHEBYSHOP
of Canterbury, Primate of all
ENGLANDE
and Metropolitane.

Yt ys the spirite that giueth lyfe, the
fleshe profiteth nothinge .Ioannis.6.

Fig. 1.1 Title page, Thomas Cranmer, *Defence of the True and Catholic Doctrine of the Sacrament* (London, 1550), Photo Courtesy of the Newberry Library, Chicago, Call # Case C 823.197.

Rather than open his *Defence* with an evaluation of Matthew 26, Mark 14, or Luke 22—all important passages on the Eucharist—Cranmer opens with John 6:53: "Verily, verily, I say unto you, Except you eat the flesh of the Son of man, and drink his blood, you have no life in you."[38] At the outset Cranmer supposes that, given John's emphasis on eternal life as a consequence of eating, proper eating entails a mutual indwelling of the communicant and Christ. Reprobates might indeed eat the "sacrament" but not truly the body of Christ.[39] From these establishing premises, Cranmer undertakes his lengthy exegesis of the Ascension, emphasizing throughout that, given Christ's statement in John 16:28—"I forsake the world, and go to my Father"—Christ is not corporeally on Earth during the Eucharistic offering: "Our Saviour Christ...is gone unto heaven, and sitteth at the right hand of his Father, and there shall he tarry until the world's end, at what time he shall come again to judge both the quick and the dead."[40] Against objections of the Lutheran sort that would argue for Christ's ubiquity, Cranmer concludes, drawing on Origen's commentaries on Matthew and John, that Christ's two natures are such that, while his body resides in heaven, his divine nature is everywhere.[41] But Augustine's *Homilies on John* provides Cranmer with the surest justification for the location of Christ's heavenly body. As Augustine says of John 12—"You shall ever have poor men with you, but me you shall not ever have"—which prompts Cranmer to repeat Augustine's words: "*As concerning the flesh* which he took in his incarnation, as concerning that which was born of the Virgin, as concerning that which was apprehended by the Jews...he said, *You shall not ever have me with you*."[42] After further support from Cyril's Johannine commentary, Cranmer concludes that Christ's body cannot be in several places at one time, and hence he cannot be corporeally present in the elements of the sacrament.[43]

Once Cranmer has established that Christ is not present bodily in the Eucharist, he has to offer some explanation of the real presence, and so he makes recourse to John's bread of life narrative. After Christ describes himself as the "bread of life, the which whosoever did eat, should not die, but live forever," the disciples cavil, noting that "this is an hard saying: for how can he give us flesh to be eaten? (John 6:58–60)."[44] Adding to his earlier gloss on the Ascension, Cranmer reasons: "These words our Saviour Christ spake, to lift up their minds from earth to heaven, that

---

[38] Cited in Thomas Cranmer, *Defence of the True and Catholic Doctrine of the Sacrament* (1550), in *The Works of Thomas Cranmer*, ed. G. E. Duffield (Philadelphia: Fortress Press, 1965), 60. The modern translation of the verse approximates closely the version in the Cranmer or Coverdale Bible of 1540: "Then Jesus sayde unto them: Verely, verely, I saye unto you, except ye eate the flesshe of the sonne of man, and drinke his bloude: ye have no lyfe in you" (6:53). Throughout this section I rely, wherever possible, on Cranmer's own citation of the Fourth Gospel as slightly modernized in the Duffield edition.

[39] William Tyndale had already legitimated the Augustinian interpretation of John 6:53 in *A Brief Declaration of the Sacraments* (1536), in which he concludes that the bread there can only be a reference to faith and not a sacramental eating, since Abraham and the holy fathers had eaten the bread without "their holy mouths." *Doctrinal Treatises and Introductions to Different Portions of the Holy Scriptures*, ed. Henry Walter (Cambridge: Cambridge University Press, 1858), 369.

[40] Cranmer, *Defence*, 79.   [41] Ibid., 128–9.

[42] Ibid., 131. A modern translation of this passage from Augustine's Tractate 50 on John can be found in Saint Augustine, *Tractates on the Gospel of John, 28–54*, ed. John W. Rettig (Washington, D.C.: Catholic University Press, 2010), 269.

[43] Cranmer, *Defence*, 133.   [44] Ibid., 145.

they should not phantasy that they should with their teeth eat him present here on earth . . . for he would take his body from them, and ascend with it into heaven . . . and therefore . . . we shall spiritually and ghostly with our faith eat him."[45] When Cranmer elaborates his view of the relationship of faith to spiritual eating, he maintains that belief is sufficient for the sacramental eating: "The true eating and drinking of the said body and blood of Christ, is with a constant and lively faith to believe, that Christ gave his body and shed his blood for us. . . . And this faith God worketh inwardly in our hearts by his Holy Spirit, and confirmeth the same out-wardly to our ears by hearing of his word."[46] Cranmer's interpretation of John 6 leads him to conclude, as is consistent with so many Reformed commentaries of his time, that Johannine references to Christ's flesh, particularly the bread of life figuration, cannot, in any case, imply the consecration of the elements in the Lord's Supper. The bread of life discourse historically precedes by several years the Supper proper (the latter of which is not included in John's Gospel): "This place of St. John can in no wise be understand of the sacramental bread, which neither came from heaven, neither giveth life to all that eat it. Nor of such bread Christ could have then presently said, *This is my flesh*, except they will say that Christ did then conse-crate, so many years before the institution of his holy Supper."[47] It follows that John 6, so often used by Catholic apologists to argue for the real presence and transubstantiation, must refer to spiritual eating and the commemoration of the Passion. John 6 offers a typological clarification of the reasons why the Fathers ate manna in the desert but did not achieve eternal life in doing so.

That Cranmer opens his *Defence* with a lengthy and careful exposition of John 6 is not surprising, given his appreciation of the foundational patrological inter-pretations of the true bread that he found in Augustine's and Cyril's Johannine commentaries. But the use of John at the gate indeed provokes Bishop Gardiner who, in his 1551 response, *An explication and assertion of the true Catholique fayth*, accuses Cranmer of beginning too "low" in beginning his salvo with John: "In the rehersal of the wordes of Christ out of the gospel of saint John he begynneth a litle to lowe and passeth over that perteyneth to the matter and therfore should have begon a litle hygher at this clause."[48] Protesting too much, perhaps aware that Cranmer's decision to open with John was a carefully planned strategy, the Bishop of Winchester turns to nuances of grammar and translation. As he points out in his *Answer*, Cranmer had relied on commentaries by Origen and Augustine as well as, in Cranmer's own words, a "hundreth places" to justify his use of "very meat" (*verus cibus*) rather than "verily meat."[49] But the latter translation seems more appropriate to Gardiner:

Here is also a faulte in the translacion of the texte . . . whiche should be thus in one place. For my fleshe is verely meat and my bloud is verely drinke. In whiche speache

---

[45] Ibid., 146.   [46] Ibid., 74.   [47] Ibid., 107.

[48] Stephen Gardiner, *An explication and assertion of the true Catholique fayth, touchyng the moost blessed sacrament of the aulter* (Rouen, 1551), 7.

[49] Thomas Cranmer, *An aunswere by the Reuerend Father in God Thomas Archbyshop of Canterbury, primate of all England and metropolitane, unto a craftie and sophisticall cavillation, devised by Stephen Gardiner Doctour of Law* (London, 1580), 19.

the verbe that cuppleth the wordes (fleshe) and (meat) together: knitteth them together in their propre significacion....And in these words of Christ may appere plainly how Christ taught the mysterie of the fode of his humanitie...that he said he would geve for the life of the worlde and so expresseth the first sentence of this scripture....And the bread whiche I shall geve you is my fleshe whiche I shall geve for the life of the worlde. And so it is plaine that Christ spake of fleshe in the same sence that Sainct [John] speaketh in, saiyng: The worde was made fleshe, signifiyng by fleshe the hole humanitie.[50]

Cranmer dismisses the question of translation as a linguistic non-starter: "And what skilleth it for the diversitye of the wordes, where no diversity is in the sence? And whether we say, very meat, or verely meate, it is a figurative speache in this place, and the sence is all one."[51] He then proceeds to refute Gardiner's overall use of a Nestorian argument in defense of Christ's corporeity and implicitly Gardiner's use of John 1:14 as an intratextual source for John 6. Notable about the debate is, again, Cranmer's turn to tradition in his defense of Johannine fundamentals and a proper understanding of the real presence, a legacy of interpreting John grounded in Augustine, Origen, and Cyril (and legitimated in Greek translations by Cranmer's contemporary Robert Stevens) of which Gardiner, Cranmer quips, is deemed ignorant: "But your understanding of the sixt chapter of John is such as never was uttered of any man before your time, and as declareth you to be utterly ignoraunte of Gods misteries."[52] Cranmer begins with John not because he begins too "low," as Gardiner avers, but because he found a converging patristic tradition of Johannine explication the sheer weight of which impelled his shift from Eucharistic materialism to spiritualism.[53]

Cranmer's enthusiasm for John never wavered. Epigraphs from John 6 are used twice in the preface to his reply to Gardiner. Cranmer's early Johannine position in the *Defence* is sensibly summed up, as we have begun to see, in the marrow of his reply. Throughout his trial at Oxford in 1554, Cranmer returns to his use of Johannine texts in his explication to the university doctors. He reiterates that Christ is in the sacrament effectually rather than substantially, and he reaffirms his understanding of the true bread and wine as promissory signs and seals: "True bread and true wine remayn full in the Eucharist untill they be consumed of the

---

[50] Gardiner, *An explication and assertion of the true Catholique faith*, 7–8.
[51] Cranmer, *An aunswere by the Reuerend Father in God Thomas Archbyshop of Canterbury*, 19.
[52] Ibid., 20.
[53] Heiko Oberman's otherwise useful distinction between Tradition I and Tradition II in Reformed polemic does not exactly capture Cranmer's shuttling between direct exegesis of John 6 and a reliance on authoritative sources. If Tradition I signifies for Oberman canonical scriptural sufficiency (which is then passed on by means of the Fathers), Tradition II accords more priority to oral tradition and the authority of the Church. See Oberman, *The Harvest of Medieval Theology: Gabriel Biel and Late Medieval Nominalism* (Cambridge, MA: Harvard University Press, 1963). Cranmer's integration of *sola scriptura* and patristic exegesis agrees more with George Tavard's conception of a "classical synthesis," evident in medieval scholasticism and extending to the Reformation, that did not hierarchize canonical scripture relative to traditional exegesis. See Tavard, *Holy Writ or Holy Church: The Crisis of the Protestant Reformation* (London: Burns & Oates, 1959), 2. The merits of both Oberman's and Tavard's positions are evaluated at length in Nicholas Thompson, *Eucharistic Sacrifice and Tradition in the Theology of Martin Bucer, 1534–1546* (Leiden: Brill Academic Publishers, 2005), 21–5.

faythfull to be signes & as seales unto us annexed unto Gods promises making us certayne of Gods gifts towardes us."[54] Suffice it to say that John remains with Cranmer until he proudly gives up the ghost on March 21, 1556. During his confession of faith, minutes before his famous recantation and spectacular death at the stake, Cranmer invokes John twice in his four final exhortations to his hearers, begging them to refrain from the allurements of "this glozing world" according to his own example and to "learn to know what this lesson meaneth which St. John teacheth, that *the love of this world is hatred against God.*"[55]

We should note that, although Cranmer polemicizes convincingly against the conciliar notion of the real presence, we will find that, for many later English theologians and poets, the argument that John 6 is not directly about the Supper is an academic distinction, for such writers will use Johannine language and imagery precisely to argue against the real presence of the Eucharist. It should also be emphasized that Cranmer's theology of the sacrament is not reducible to any singular polemical position. To a certain extent, Cranmer appreciates the Zwinglian standpoint, itself based on a detailed reading of John 6, that the elements are signs that serve to memorialize the Passion.[56] But Cranmer's is also a pneumatological theory that shares much with Calvin's account of the sacrament: the communicant is prepared to believe/receive the sacrament through an infusion of the grace made available to the believer through the Holy Ghost. A brief look at Calvin's influential Eucharistic theology can help further contextualize Cranmer's Johannine contribution to the Eucharist controversy.

Calvin, too, builds his case against the Catholic real presence on Augustine's *Homilies on John*. Yet Calvin denies that Augustine argues that eating is equivalent to believing: "When Augustine...wrote, that we eat by believing, all he meant was to indicate that eating is of faith, and not of the mouth. This I deny not; but I at the same time add, that by faith we embrace Christ, not as appearing at a distance, but as uniting himself to us, he being our head, and we his members."[57] Calvin's goal is to reinstate the presence of Christ in the sacrament against those who would divest Christ of his flesh and transfigure him into a "phantom."[58] Calvin provides lengthy interpretations of key passages in John, including 5:26—"For as the Father hath life in himselfe: so hath he given to the Sonne to have life in himself"—that seem to elevate the importance of Christ's flesh in providing us "life-giving" power: "The flesh and blood of Christ feed our souls just as bread and wine maintain and

---

[54] John Foxe, *Actes and monuments of matters most speciall and memorable, happenyng in the Church with an vniuersall history of the same* (London, 1583), 1431.

[55] Cranmer's references to John during his final hour are taken from John Foxe's *Acts and Monuments*, ed. S. R. Cattley (London, 1837–9), vol. iii, 667, cited in Duffield, *The Work of Thomas Cranmer*, 335–6.

[56] The influence of Zwingli on Cranmer is argued in Dom Gregory Dix, *The Shape of the Liturgy* (London: Dacre Press, 1964), 64–6. See also Cyril C. Richardson, *Zwingli and Cranmer on the Eucharist: Cranmer dixit et contradixit* (Evanston: Seabury Western Theological Seminary, 1949).

[57] John Calvin, *Institutes of the Christian Religion*, trans. Henry Beveridge (Grand Rapids: Eerdmans Publishing Company, 1995), Book IV, 560.

[58] Ibid., 561.

support our corporeal life."[59] While Calvin clearly departs from the spiritual memorialism of the Zwinglians, the question remains how he is able to steer clear of both the traditional and Lutheran accounts of the real, corporeal presence of Christ in the elements, given statements such as the following: "There would be no aptitude in the sign, did not our souls find their nourishment in Christ. This could not be, did not Christ truly form one with us, and refresh us by the eating of his flesh, and the drinking of his blood."[60]

The crux of Calvin's unique account of the Eucharist theme can be found in his position on the Ascension. As do Augustine and the Edwardian and later English theologians cited earlier in this section, Calvin, too, denies the corporeal ubiquity of Christ. After acknowledging that Christ has "withdrawn" his flesh from us and has ascended "with his body" to heaven where he resides at the right hand of God, Calvin warns that we should not assume that Christ's powers are thereby circumscribed: "This kingdom is not limited by any intervals of space, nor circumscribed by any dimensions. Christ can exert his energy wherever he pleases, in earth and heaven, can manifest his presence by the exercise of his power, can always be present with his people, breathing into them his own life...just as if he were with them in the body."[61] The emphasis on the pneumatological "breathing into them his own life" and then the later mention of "transfusing" communion into the communicants make clear that, if Christ's physical body is not present in the elements, the Holy Spirit is the intermediary that indissolubly connects Christ in Heaven with the faithful on Earth.[62] Calvin concludes: "Though it seems an incredible thing that the flesh of Christ, while at such a distance from us in respect of place, should be food to us, let us remember how far the secret virtue of the Holy Spirit surpasses all our conceptions, and how foolish it is to wish to measure its immensity by our feeble capacity."[63] For our purposes, it is important to note that Calvin's justification of his pneumatological account of the real presence is his understanding of Johannine theology directly and indirectly inflected by Augustine's tractates.[64] Calvin makes reference several times to Christ's statements in John 12 and 14 to the effect that his disciples will not always "have" him; he then uses Augustine's gloss on the passages to justify his conclusion that Christ remains present to us in three ways: "in majesty, providence, and ineffable grace; under which I comprehend that wondrous communion of his body and blood, provided we understand that it is effected by the power of the Holy Spirit, and not by that fictitious enclosing of his body under the element."[65] Calvin reiterates the point in his 1561 polemical tract *The Clear Explanation of Sound Doctrine Concerning the True Partaking of the Flesh and Blood of Christ in the Holy Supper*, where he describes as his "axiom" the belief that "Christ, considered as the living bread and the victim immolated on the cross, cannot enter

---

[59] Ibid., 563.   [60] Ibid., 563.   [61] Ibid., 571.   [62] Ibid., 571.
[63] Ibid., 563.
[64] On the importance of Augustine's account of the Eucharist to Calvin's, see B. A. Gerrish, *Grace and Gratitude: The Eucharistic Theology of John Calvin* (Eugene: Wipf & Stock Publishers, 1993), 165–6.
[65] John Calvin, *Institutes*, Book IV, 580.

the human body devoid of his Spirit."[66] Later in the treatise, glossing John 6:63, Calvin reminds his readers that, for Augustine, "the flesh profiteth nothing" should include the words "alone" or "by itself," since the flesh is only useless when it is "separated from the Spirit": "How then," Calvin asks, "has flesh the power of vivifying, except by being spiritual?"[67] The Eucharistic efficacy of the Holy Spirit (the latter described, as will see in Chapter 3, slightly differently as the Paraclete or Comforter in the Fourth Gospel's Farewell Discourse) allows for Christ's continuing presence in a post-resurrectional context.

Cranmer, like Calvin, also elevates the role of the Spirit during the Communion, particularly in his response to Gardiner: "Doth not Gods word teach a true presence of Christ in spirit, where he is not present in his corporall substance?"[68] Such a spiritual as opposed to a real presence assumes that those who worthily receive the sacrament "be turned into divine substaunce, through the working of the holy Ghost, who maketh the godly receavers to be the partakers of the divine nature and substaunce."[69] As in Calvin's pneumatology, Cranmer's promotion of the Spirit during the Communion helps him to explain how Christ can be instrumentally present even while his body remains in heaven:

> Where S. Chrisostome and other Authors do speak of the wonderfull operation of God in his sacraments…they meane…the marvaylous working of God in the hartes of them that receave the sacramentes, secretly, inwardly, and spiritually transforming them, renuing, feding, comforting and nourishing them with his flesh and bloud, through his most holy spirite, the same flesh and bloud still remayning in heaven.[70]

---

[66] *Calvin: Theological Treatises*, trans. J. K. S. Reid (Philadelphia: Westminster Press, 1954), 285.

[67] Ibid., 316. See also the *Short Treatise on the Lord's Supper* (1541) in which Calvin concludes: "For the chief thing is that he cares for us internally by his Holy Spirit, so as to give efficacy to his ordinance, which he has destined for this purpose, as an instrument by which he will do his work in us" (*Theological Treatises*, 149).

[68] Cranmer, *An aunswere by the Reuerend Father in God Thomas Archbyshop of Canterbury* (London, 1580), 60. Cranmer's elevation of the instrumentality of the Spirit does recall Calvin, but Cranmer typically attempts to integrate Christology with pneumatology. Because he objected to Gardiner's dividing of the Spirit from Christ's body (the former present at Baptism, the latter present during the Supper), Cranmer at times remarks that both Christ and the Spirit are mystically or truly, although not substantially, present during the Supper: "Christ hath promised in both the sacramentes to be assistant with us wholl both in body and spirite (in the one to be our spirituall regeneration and apparell, and in the other to be our spirituall meate and drinke)" (42). While Cranmer claims that the Spirit might provide the nourishing conduit between Christ's ascended body and the communicant, he still maintains that Christ is present in terms of instrumental grace and effectual operation: "For our regeneration in Christ is spirituall…which kind of regeneration and feeding requireth no reall and corporall presence of Christ, but onely his presence in spirit, grace, and effectuall operation" (158). For Cyril C. Richardson, the crux of the matter that ultimately distinguishes Cranmer (and Zwingli) from Calvin (and Bucer) is that the former's nominalist position cannot admit of any substantial participation of the communicant in Christ's body. An important analogy that the Reformers used to differentiate their positions was that of the sun in relation to Christ's presence. If, for Calvin, the sun's rays share in the substance of the sun itself (and so, although Christ is located in heaven, we can share in his substance through the radiant Spirit), for Cranmer, the sun's rays (even when metaphorized as the Holy Ghost) do not carry the substantial presence of Christ's body. See Richardson, *Zwingli and Cranmer on the Eucharist*, 23–6. For a more recent account of Cranmer's view of the Spirit in relation to the true presence, see David J. Kennedy, *Eucharistic Sacramentality in an Ecumenical Context: The Anglican Epiclesis* (Aldershot and Burlington: Ashgate Publishing, 2008), 11–14.

[69] Cranmer, *An aunswere*, 316.   [70] Ibid., 190–1.

Again Cranmer turns to patristic authority, this time Chrysostom's Johannine commentary, in order to explain the manner in which the mystical or "true" presence of Christ inheres in the elements in the absence of any corporeal presence.[71]

JOHN 6 AND THE EUCHARIST IN ENGLAND: BEYOND CRANMER

Returning to the Reformed English contributions to the Eucharist debates, we can see that Cranmer's *Defence* marks the emergence of a veritable Johannine renaissance in sixteenth- and seventeenth-century England.[72] His account of the Eucharist,

---

[71] For more on the "true" as opposed to "real" presence, see Peter Newman Brooks, *Thomas Cranmer's Doctrine of the Eucharist: An Essay in Historical Development* (London: Macmillan, 1965), particularly chapter IV. For Brooks, Cranmer's mature conception of the Eucharist is influenced above all by the Archbishop's embrace of justification by faith. Since eating and drinking are acts of faith, the sacraments as such are not instruments of grace. Brooks, too, sees the importance of the Holy Spirit to Cranmer's conception of communion with Christ, although Brooks does not spell out the relationship between Cranmer's pneumatolology and the Eucharist: "Although Cranmer certainly held that grace is conferred in the Sacrament, this comes to pass for him solely by man's faith operated by the Holy Spirit" (95).

[72] Although Cranmer provides the earliest English Reformed systematic exposition of John 6, his reliance on the patristic reception of John 6 was anticipated about seventeen years earlier in a series of publications in which the Reformer John Frith contended with Thomas More on the proper meaning of John 6. The polemic ensued after Frith wrote a short letter on the Eucharist—*A christen sentence* (first published in London, 1545)—that had come into More's hands sometime in the early 1530s. The letter occasioned More's response—*A letter of syr Tho. More knyght impugnynge the erronyouse wrytyng of John Fryth* (London, 1533)—to which Frith responds in kind with a detailed explication of key scriptural passages on the Eucharist in *A Boke made by John Frith* (Antwerp?, 1533), drawing heavily on Augustine's spiritualist interpretation of John 6. Around this time a pseudonymous defense of the evangelical position on the Eucharist is published as *The souper of the Lorde* (Antwerp?, 1533), which is attributed to Tyndale, to which More also responds (folding into his response additional rebuttals of Frith's *Boke*) in *The answere to the fyrst parte of the poysened booke* (London, 1533). Frith, more overtly than Cranmer, had argued for an allegorical interpretation of John 6: "Some textes are only to be understond spiritually or in the waye of an allegory" (Frith, *A Boke*, 19). And Frith makes clear that his belief that John 6 speaks "not of the carnall eatynge or drynkynge of hys bodye or bloude / but of the spirituall eatynge / which is done by faythe" (*A Boke*, 15) is an interpretation grounded not simply in the works of Wyclif, Oecolampadius, Tyndale or Zwingli but rather according to "scripture / reason of nature / and doctors" (*A Boke*, 15), anticipating Cranmer's own irreducible commingling of literalism and a reliance on the patristic use of John 6 as against churchly inerrancy. Note also that, in *The answere to the fyrst parte of the poysened booke* (London, 1533), More takes issue with Frith's and Tyndale's seeming "spyrytuall exposicyon of allegoryes or parables" (20), arguing that John 6 needs to be understood to refer literally to the eating of Christ's (transformed) flesh: "Yet are these wordes here spoken so playne & so ful, that they must nedes make any man that were wyllyng to byleve hym, clerly perceyve and knowe that in one maner or other, he wolde gyve us hys awne very flesshe verely to be receyved and eaten" (92). The debate among More, Frith, and Tyndale suggests that the early English sixteenth-century exegeses of John 6 cannot be easily parsed between evangelical literalism and Catholic or controversialist traditionalism. Given the complexity and sometimes seemingly contradictory sense of the verses of John 6, context (and not always sedimented beliefs on scriptural hermeneutics) determines a particular exegetical approach. It makes sense that, despite More's general tendency to question the sufficiency of scripture, he would resort to literalism when glossing a passage such as John 6:55: "For my flesh is meate indeed, and my blood is drinke indeed." In *Burning to Read: English Fundamentalism and its Reformation Opponents* (Cambridge, MA: Harvard University Press, 2007), 248–9, James Simpson describes More's skepticism toward textual truths and scriptural sufficiency

which rests squarely on the fact of the Ascension and consequent denial of Christ's ubiquity, a denial that itself justifies the spiritualist or virtualist interpretation of the elements, is later picked up by legions of Reformed commentators on the Eucharist. The basic Zwinglian notion that to believe in Christ is to eat his flesh and blood is developed in one of the earliest sustained commentaries on John's Fourth Gospel by the French expatriate Reformer Augustin Marlorat. The proof-text for Marlorat is John 6:53–4: "Jesus therefore sayde unto them: verelye I saye unto you, except ye eate the flesh of the sonne of man, and drink his bloode ye have no lyfe in you. Who so eateth my fleshe and drinketh my bloude, hath eternall lyfe, and I will rayse him up at the last daye."[73] Because infants do receive baptism but not the Supper, thereby enjoying Christian fellowship, and because many others do receive the Supper but remain reprobate, Marlorat maintains that John refers here not to the Supper but to a "continual eating by fayth"; Marlorat concludes that to "eate the fleshe, and to drinke the bloude of Christe, is to beléeve that Christe suffered for oure synnes."[74]

In *The Badges of Christianity* (1606), William Attersoll, an English Puritan divine, reaches the same conclusion based on his interpretation of John 6:56. The verse reads: "He that eateth my flesh, and drinketh my blood, dwelleth in me, and I in him." Given the lack of correlation between eating Christ's flesh/drinking his blood and the shared indwelling described here, Attersoll reasons: "To eat him, is to beleeve in him: and therfore he useth these words, as being of one force, to beleeve in him and to eat him: to drinke him, and to come unto him.... Christ attributeth the same fruit and effect to them that beleeve in him, that hee doth to them which eat his body & drink his blood: therefore by eating and drinking hee meaneth nothing but beleeving."[75] Another Puritan divine, John Downame, who served as a member of the Westminster Assembly in the 1640s (and who is well remembered for his licensing of Milton's polemical treatises), agrees with Attersoll and Marlorat, again focusing on John 6:54 but buttressing his argument with John 5:24 and 10:28 (verses concerned with Christ's granting of eternal life to believers). In the *Christian Warfare* (1604) Downame remarks: "Now whosoever beleeve in Christ, they eate his flesh and drinke his blood; for faith is the mouth of the soule whereby we feede on this heavenly foode; and therefore all the faithfull shall have everlasting life; nay as he saith they have it alreadie and *shall not come into condemnation, but have passed from death to life*."[76] To partake of the flesh is to believe in

as pragmatic in that More located authority in the pre-textual faith and opinions of interpretive communities. Yet in his treatise on John 6, More's pragmatism manifests more simply as an attempt to seize on the literal meaning of a passage when the plain sense seems readily available and prior to a secondary, allegorical sense. When it comes to interpreting John 6, More's pragmatic hermeneutic is conditioned by interpretive expediency.

[73] Augustin Marlorat, *A catholike and ecclesiasticall exposition of the holy Gospell after S. John* (London, 1575), 226.

[74] Ibid., 225–6.

[75] William Attersoll, *The badges of Christianity. Or, A treatise of the sacraments fully declared out of the word of God* (London, 1606), 320–1.

[76] John Downame, *The Christian warfare wherein is first generally shewed the malice, power and politike stratagems of the spirituall ennemies of our saluation* (London, 1604), 668.

Christ. Consistent with the realized eschatology of the Fourth Gospel, faith is a manifestation of the eternal life of the communicant.[77]

Rather than multiply other examples of the importance of John's bread of life discourse to the English Reformed notion that faith and belief are identical with the eating and drinking recommended there, I would add that John's relevant verses are actually used to clarify misunderstandings or misappropriations of verses regarding the sacrament that can be found in the Synoptics, especially Matthew 26:26.[78] In *A most excellent sermon of the Lordes Supper* (1577), Heinrich Bullinger provides a knockdown critique of the Roman literalist interpretation of "This is my body," asking how Jesus can give of his corporeal body in the elements with his own hand. Bullinger points out that individuals eat "in suche sort, as he may be eaten: that is to say, spiritually by fayth: as the Lord hym selfe expoundeth this misterie unto us at large, in *S. John,* the sixt chapter."[79] Rather than distinguish John's words on eating in the sixth chapter from the Supper proper (a standard practice among other commentators), Bullinger boldly reads the Johannine figurative interpretation into the sacramentalist lines of Matthew 26:

> Yea, and this place [John 6] may wel be applyed to the woordes of the Supper of the Lord. For seeyng our Lord hath but one true bodye, the which he gave up to death for us, & that in these two places he speaketh of this selfe same body, it seemeth unto me, that this place of *Saint Matthewe* ought to be expounded by that of *S. John*.... [T]here cannot be found a better interpretour or expounder of the Lordes woord then the Lord himselfe, who for so much as he saith in the vi. Chapter of Saint *John,* that his flesh being eaten (to wit, corporally, as the Capernaites tooke it) profiteth nothing: It is most certayne, that hee would not geve in the xxvi. of Saint *Matthewe* that which profiteth nothing, and that he hath not ordayned here, that which he rejecteth and reprooveth there.[80]

John's profanation of the flesh at 6:63 is here used not simply intertextually to argue for a spiritualist interpretation of John's bread of life example but also to

---

[77] Compare Erasmus's deviation from the Augustinian identification of believing and eating. In his commentary on John 6, Erasmus concludes: "Beleve, eate it, and lyve. By thys sayyng our Lord Jesus did sumwhat (after an obscure sorte) open unto them the misterie of his godhed, whereby he was alwaye with God the father, and of his death also.... Finallye he did insinuate herein unto them, the privitie of hys mysticall bodye." *The first tome or volume of the Paraphrase of Erasmus upon the Newe Testamente* (London, 1548), 489. Rather than equate belief and manuduction, Erasmus turns the believing/eating identification into a three-fold process of believing, eating, and living, emphasizing the mystery of Christ's body.

[78] On the "spiritual" understanding of John 6:53, see, for example, Nicholas Byfield, *A commentary upon the three first chapters of the first Epistle generall of St. Peter* (London, 1637): "Thou must inwardly lay up Christ in thy heart, so as spiritually ever to eat his flesh, and drinke his bloud, by applying all he hath done or suffered for thee in particular, *John* 6.53. 1 *John* 5.12" (661), For an Augustinian interpretation of John 6:53, see Daniel Featley, *Transubstantiation exploded: or An encounter with Richard the titularie Bishop of Chalcedon concerning Christ his presence at his holy table* (London, 1638): "The words of our Saviour, *John* 6. 53. are to be taken in a figurative and improper sense, and consequently that the proper eating Christs flesh with the mouth, cannot be inferred from them" (79). For a similar interpretation of John 6:54, see William Sclater, *The worthy communicant rewarded Laid forth in a sermon* (London, 1639), 24–5; and regarding John 6:56, see Henry Ainsworth, *Annotations upon the five bookes of Moses* (London, 1627), 35.

[79] Heinrich Bullinger, *A most excellent sermon of the Lordes Supper* (London, 1577), 22.

[80] Ibid., 22.

delegitimate those readings of Matthew's depiction of the Supper that would associate eating with corporeal manuduction.

The use of John 6 as an alternative or counter-text to Matthew 26 is more clearly set out in Thomas Bilson's *The True Difference Between Christian Subjection and Unchristian Rebellion* (1585). An Anglican and Conformist Bishop of Winchester, Bilson draws on patristic theologians to point out that, as Chrysostom remarks, the disciples at the Supper, when confronted with Christ's words, "This is my Body," had already been prepared to understand the figurative and symbolic meaning of the words by Christ's earlier bread of life offering: "*How chanced*, saieth *Chrysostome, the (Disciples) were not troubled when they heard this: take, eate, this is my body? Because (their master) had debated the same matter largely and profoundly before.*"[81] Bilson concludes:

> You see by the constant opinion of these Fathers, that our Saviour in the sixt of *John* taught his Disciples what manner of eating his flesh and drinking his blood they should expect at his last Supper, and that they therefore started not at these words *this is my body*, because they learned of him before what to looke for, and well remembred his interpretation of himselfe, when the Capernites staggered at the like speech. Then perforce what sense the wordes of Christ in the sixt of *John* doe beare, the same must the wordes of the supper retaine: but there Christ teacheth the spirituall eating of his fleshe by faith, his wordes bee figuratiue: *ergo* the Lordes supper doeth not import any corporal eating of his flesh, nor literall exposition of his wordes.[82]

Bilson highlights to a greater degree than Bullinger the sense in which John's chronologically earlier discourse, although not directly referring to the Supper, serves as a promise or "seal" of the later Holy Communion discourse. Hence the meaning of the former discourse must shape the meaning of the latter: "For Seales doe not alter or infringe, but strengthen and confirme that which was promised."[83] The figurative construal of John 6 displaces and stands in for the literal meaning of Matthew 26. We find a more compendious version of the argument a few years later in Henry Smith's *Treatise on the Lord's Supper* (1591), although Smith uses John 6:63 in particular against the literal interpretation of Matthew 26: "As it is plainlie sayd, *This is my body;* so it is plainlie said, *these wordes are spirite:* that is, they must be understood spiritually, and not literally."[84]

The deployment of John against Matthew (or the simple displacement of the latter by the former) has the effect of reading John not simply as the basis on which to understand the Supper but as preparatory to the Supper. This Johannine–Augustinian position that the bread of life provides a seal and preparation runs throughout continental and English treatises and sermons of the period. We have already seen that Cranmer separates the bread of life from the sacramental bread, given that the institution of the Supper historically happens later. Attersoll reaches a similar conclusion: "These words are not understood of the Sacrament, they were uttered long before the

---

[81] Thomas Bilson, *The True Difference Between Christian Subjection and Unchristian Rebellion* (Oxford, 1585), 741.

[82] Ibid., 741.   [83] Ibid., 742.

[84] Henry Smith, *Treatise of the Lord's Supper* (London, 1591), 21.

institution of the Supper, and therefore coulde not be referred unto that which as yet was not: so that Christ speaketh of spirituall eating, not of carnall: by faith, not by the mouth, whereby wee abide in him and he in us."[85] Marlorat goes further in arguing that the spiritual eating and drinking described in John 6 serve as an initiatory seal for the entire Communion: "Notwithstanding wée must confesse that there is nothing spoken here which is not figured in the Supper and truelye given to the faythfull: and therfore Christ made his holy Supper to bée as it were a seale to this sermon. And this is the cause why our Evaungelist John maketh mention of thys Supper."[86] And Bilson points out that the pedagogical function of John 6 is to instruct the communicants on the significance of the later sacramental eating: "Our Saviour in the sixt of *John* taught his Disciples what manner of eating his flesh and drinking his blood they should expect at his last Supper."[87] In these treatises and others, detailed expositions of John 6 do not merely provide evidence for a figurative understanding of eating and drinking; they serve, in some cases, to downgrade the importance of the Supper proper for salvation.

Perhaps the most extensive discussion of John in relation to the Supper can be found in an early Lutheran-inspired treatise on the whole of John 6 by the German theologian, Johannes Brenz. Brenz is best known for his Lutheran-inspired *Syngramma Suevicum* (1525), a defense of the real presence against Oecolampadius and the Swiss Reformers. But in a later treatise on John, *A verye fruitful exposicion upon the syxte chapter of Saynte John* (London, 1550), Brenz uses John 6:54–5 in his polemic against those who would argue that, because John maintains that the sacrament provides eternal life, it should therefore be given to infants.[88] Having established that the eating and drinking of John 6 do not refer to sacramental ingestion, Brenz remarks that, while the Supper is essential to the remembrance of Christ's death, it does not in itself conduce to salvation:

> But Christe in thys place speaketh nothynge at all of the eatynge of that supper, whyche afterwardes he ordained for a remembraunce of hys death. For thys eatyng of Christes fleshe, & drinking of his bloud…we speake of nowe is plainly necessary to salvacion. Verely verely (sayeth he unto you) except ye shal eate the fleshe of the sonne of man and drynke hys blud, ye have not life in you. What can be spoken more playnely of the necessytye of thys eating and drinckyng? But the eatyng of the lordes supper is not simplye necessarye to salvacion. In dede great is the profit of that supper, and in dede when you maye, muste be taken, and that after the institucion of Christe, and in very dede great thankes must be gyven unto the Lorde for this gift, but the use of it is not simply necessary.[89]

Given that they cannot express faith, discretion, and Christological knowledge, infants should not receive the Communion, a position on the figurative sense of

[85] Attersoll, *Badges of Christianity*, 312.

[86] Marlorat, *A catholike and ecclesiasticall exposition of the holy Gospell after S. John*, 226.

[87] Bilson, *The True Difference*, 741.

[88] Jean Rilliet makes brief mention of Brenz's role in the Eucharist controversy in *Zwingli: Third Man of the Reformation*, trans. Harold Knight (Philadelphia: Westminster Press, 1964), 226.

[89] Johannes Brenz, *A verye fruitful exposicion upon the syxte chapter of Saynte John* (London?, 1550), 123–4.

John 6 that is reiterated in Thomas Tuke's *A fit guest for the Lords table* (1609): "Albeit our *Saviour* saith that none shall have life in them, unles they eat his flesh and drink his blood, yet it doth not follow that the sacrament of his body and blood should be given unto infants: for he speaketh not of sacramentall eating and drinking, but of that which is meerly spirituall or by faith. Neither doth he there meane infants at all, seeing they are utterly destitute of actuall faith."[90] Here again, while the Supper carries a memorializing and evidentiary function—we testify to our remembrance of the Passion upon receiving the elements—the Supper is not instrumental or necessary to salvation in the way that the continual eating through faith and believing is necessary according to the message of John 6.

We turn now to the Eucharist theme as understood through a Johannine lens in the poetry of several seventeenth-century devotional poets who show a keen interest in John 6: George Herbert, Henry Vaughan, Richard Crashaw, and the American Congregationalist poet Edward Taylor. Such poetic treatments of the sacrament are shaped not only by Calvin's pneumatology but also by several of the themes that I have collated from the most important Reformed treatises on John 6: the Augustinian contention that eating is believing; the role of the Ascension when it comes to polemicizing about the real presence of Christ's body; and the relative diminishing of the institution of the Supper proper in comparison to the import-ance of an ongoing "eating" by believing that is recommended throughout John's bread of life allegory.

THE SACRAMENT AND THE ASCENSION: GEORGE HERBERT

C. A. Patrides once asserted confidently that "The Eucharist is the marrow of [George] Herbert's sensibility."[91] From the starting assumption that Herbert's poetry is sacramentalist in some sense, Herbert's critics have acknowledged that Herbert's irenicism mostly follows Hooker, who proclaims a retreat from theo-logical wrangling on the real presence with the well-known comment in *Of the Lawes of Ecclesiasticall Politie* (1597): "Let it therefore be sufficient for me, present-ing my self at the Lords Table, to know what there I receive from him; without searching or enquiring of the manner, how Christ performeth his promise."[92] Despite Herbert's like-minded eschewal of theological quibbling on the real presence, Kimberly Johnson has suggestively remarked that Herbert does indeed "wrestle with 'the manner how' in a number of poems that consider the Eucharist

---

[90] Thomas Tuke, *A fit guest for the Lords table. Or, a treatise declaring the true use of the Lords Supper Profitable for all communicants* (London, 1609), 131.

[91] C. A. Patrides, *The English Poems of George Herbert* (London: J. M. Dent, 1974), 17. Cited in Johnson, *Made Flesh*, 35.

[92] Richard Hooker, *Of The Lawes of Ecclesiasticall Politie, Book V*, in *The works of Mr. Richard Hooker (that learned and judicious divine), in eight books of ecclesiasticall polity* (London, 1666), 263. The Hooker passage is quoted in Johnson, *Made Flesh*, 34–5, and Robert Whalen, *The Poetry of Immanence: Sacrament in Donne and Herbert* (Toronto: University of Toronto Press, 2002), 115.

directly."[93] I argue in this section that Herbert is less interested in the substance of Christ's presence during the Eucharist than he is in the fundamentally Johannine conceptions of the profitless nature of the flesh, Christ as bread of life, and the importance of the Ascension to an understanding of the Communion. While Herbert does descend into particulars regarding the Eucharist, he is especially concerned with the "manner *why*" Christ offers himself as true bread and the "manner *where*" Christ's body is during the sacramental offering.

Herbert's most Johannine meditation on the sacrament of eating is the version of "The H. Communion" included in the Williams manuscript that dates from between 1615 and 1625.[94] The speaker's indifferent attitude toward the nuanced question of the nature of Christ's presence in the bread is declared at the outset: "first I am sure, / whether bread stay / Or whether Bread doe fly away / Concerneth bread, not mee" (7–9).[95] What does preoccupy the speaker is his peculiar relationship to Christ: "But that both thou and all thy traine / Bee there, to thy truth, & my gaine, / Concerneth mee & Thee" (9–12). The designation of Christ's "truth" in the context of the preceding conundrum of the bread recalls Christ's description of himself in John 6:33 as "the true bread from heaven." The rest of the poem will refocus attention away from the question of the precise location of Christ's flesh regarding the sacramental offering and toward the symbolic significance of Christ's association with true bread. The speaker realizes that his thoughts on the true bread should not bring him to the super-subtleties of "impanation" (the view that Christ's corporeal presence manifests itself after the Incarnation) but rather toward the Incarnation itself, particularly the manner in which his own flesh or "fleshly villany" (29) is responsible for Christ's death on his behalf: "My flesh, & fleshly villany, / That allso made thee dead" (30). The speaker's awareness that his meditations on the bread should remind him of his own fleshly responsibility in killing Christ is a startlingly close approximation to Zwingli's conclusion regarding the message of John 6. As Zwingli remarks in his *Commentary*, Christ is the means of salvation "not by being eaten, but by being slain,"[96] an interpretation also offered in John Frith's *A boke made by John Frith*, in which Frith points out that the flesh "doth moche profit to be slayne that thorough yt and the shedinge of hys bloude."[97] For Herbert, Zwingli, and Frith (not to mention all of the commentators earlier discussed in relation to John 6), to focus narrowly on whether Christ is corporeally present in the bread is to divert one's attention from the real issue—namely, the very reason why Christ must offer himself as living bread in the first place, the signifying rather than the material cause of salvation.[98]

---

[93] Johnson, *Made Flesh*, 35.

[94] For a brief description of the uncertain publication history of the Williams manuscript, see *The English Poems of George Herbert*, ed. Helen Wilcox (Cambridge: Cambridge University Press, 2007), xxxvii.

[95] *The Works of George Herbert*, ed. F. E. Hutchinson (Oxford: Clarendon Press, 1941), 200. All quotes from Herbert's verse will be taken from this edition.

[96] Zwingli, *Commentary on True and False Religion*, 205.

[97] Frith, *A boke made by John Frith*, 23.

[98] That John 6 serves to remind the communicant of the death of Christ is explained, for example, in John Etherington's *The defence of John Etherington against Steven Denison* (London?, 1641): "But the

Herbert also relates the extent to which, in order to understand properly the significance of this salvific "gift of all gifts" (43) provided to the speaker by Christ, the speaker needs to accept that he will not discover the nature of the real presence, if it exists, through sight: "That flesh is there, mine eyes deny: / And what shold flesh but flesh discry, / The noblest sence of five? / If glorious bodies pass the sight / Shall they be food & strength & might / Even there, where they deceive" (30–6). Augustine's paraphrase of the manna reference at John 6:48 can help contextualize the speaker's musings on the need to relinquish an attempt to see the corporeal presence: "They ate manna, and they died. Why did they eat and die? Because they believed in what they could see; they had no understanding of what they could not see."[99] To understand what one cannot visualize signifies, for Augustine, a proper "spiritual understanding of that visible food"; while "a sacrament is one thing," Augustine points out, "quite another is the benefit of the sacrament."[100] Herbert's speaker makes just such a perspectival shift. He forsakes seeing with his eyes for a spiritual understanding of such "benefits" or "gifts" by and through the means of his soul and mind: "Into my soul this cannot pass... Bodyes & Minds are different Spheres" (37–40).

When Herbert's speaker accepts the villainy of his own flesh and reasons that the least thing he wants from Christ is his flesh—"Thy flesh the least that I request" (44)—the speaker might as well be recapitulating the fateful words of John 6:63: "It is the Spirit that quickeneth, the flesh profiteth nothing." The poem, which is preoccupied with the profitless nature of such flesh, reflects the speaker's appreciation that, once he forsakes his own body and desists from puzzling over the substantial presence, he can achieve a spiritual understanding of the significance of the true bread.[101] The result of that orientation or new "pledge" is that he will abide in Christ: "My God, give me all Thee" (48), faintly echoing the language of mutual indwelling at John 6:56: "He that eateth my flesh, and drinketh my blood, dwelleth in me, and I in him."

Although more typologically rich than "The H. Communion" (Williams), Herbert's "Peace" also offers a Johannine meditation on the bread of life. Consider the scriptural metaphor at lines 25–32: "But after death out of his grave / There

---

death and resurrection of Christ, the sacrifice of his body and blood, the value, vertue, price, and purchase thereof, he hath tyed himselfe unto, so as that without it... there is no salvation, as Christ pronounceth saying, *Except yee eate the flesh of the Son of man and drinke his blood, yee have no life in you, John 6. 53*" (58).

[99] Augustine, *Homilies on the Gospel of John*, 458.   [100] Ibid., 458.

[101] Failing to appreciate the important Johannine resonances of the poem, Helen Vendler too quickly dismisses the Williams manuscript's version of "The H. Communion" when remarking that, beyond the opening sallies, "the poem contains nothing of value. The logic by which Herbert decides what is present in the Communion is neither flesh nor a glorious body is sophistic, to say the least, and tastes of clever wit. Even Herbert's devoted editor Hutchinson does not attempt to gloss the last three stanzas, though he offers paraphrases elsewhere of passages far less complicated." *The Poetry of George Herbert* (Cambridge, MA: Harvard University Press, 1975), 141. For a more recent and appreciative interpretation of the poem, albeit one that only ambiguously describes its theology as deriving from a patristic "unitive" theology, see Esther Gilman Richey, "Unitive Theology: George Herbert's Revision of 'The H. Communion,'" *George Herbert Journal*, 35:1–2 (2011), 97–109. Ryan Netzley provides an engaging discussion of "The H. Communion" in terms of the Eucharist as gift in *Reading, Desire, and the Eucharist in Early Modern Religious Poetry* (Toronto: University of Toronto Press, 2011), 29–33.

sprang twelve stalks of wheat: / Which many wondring at, got some of those / To plant and set. / It prosper'd strangely, and did soon disperse / Through all the earth" (27–32). The lines recall Jesus' prediction of his death to the brethren: "Verely, verely, I say unto you, Except a corne of wheat fall into the ground, and die, it abideth alone: but if it die, it bringeth forth much fruit. He that loveth his life, shall lose it: and hee that hateth his life in this world, shall keepe it unto life eternall" (12:24–5). Calvin remarks that Jesus compares his death to the sowing of fructifying seeds that will lead, through his resurrection, to the dispersal of his glory and the continuing life of the members of his ministry as well as to the formation of the church.[102] Here, as in so many comparable passages of the Fourth Gospel, although Jesus will eventually depart from the disciples, the latter are offered the consolation of eternal life, as expressed in the subsequent verse: "He that loveth his life, shall lose it: and hee that hateth his life in this world, shall keepe it unto life eternall" (12:25).

In Herbert's poem, the lines borrowed from 12:24 lead into the grain and bread references in the final stanza: "Take of this grain, which in my garden grows, / And grows for you; / Make bread of it: and that repose / And peace, which ev'ry where / With so much earnestnesse you do pursue, / Is only there" (37–42). Following Rosemond Tuve, who maintains that the grain references are Eucharistic in keeping with medieval liturgical treatises and homilies (including the *Glossa ordinaria*), Helen Wilcox has argued that the instruction to "taste" the wheat "confirms the link between the wheat metaphor (line 28 onwards) and the bread eaten at the Eucharist" (115, n. 33); and that "take" at line 37 recalls the Matthean words of institution so crucial to the liturgy of the Holy Communion.[103]

Yet such Eucharistic interpretations neglect to explain any link between John 12:24 (lines which are not concerned with the Communion) and the subsequent grain and bread references. The last two stanzas should be read in the larger context of the typological and Johannine references in the poem. "Peace" is a good example of a Herbert poem that poeticizes Herbert's own notion, as described in "The H. Scriptures (II)," of marking the "constellations of the storie" (4) in order to extract the richest meaning possible from a range of scriptural sources.[104] The opening lines of "Peace"—"Sweet Peace, where dost thou dwell? I humbly crave, / Let

---

[102] John Calvin, *The Gospel According to St. John*, in *Calvin's New Testament Commentaries*, vol. 4, eds. David W. Torrance and Thomas F. Torrance, trans. T. H. L. Parker (Grand Rapids: Eerdmans Publishing Company, 1959), 36–7.

[103] See Wilcox, *The English Poems of George Herbert*, 441, nn. 33, 37. Tuve's Eucharistic interpretation can be found in *A Reading of George Herbert* (Chicago: University of Chicago Press, 1952), 162–4. In *Reformation Spirituality: The Religion of George Herbert* (Eugene: Wipf & Stock, 1985), 225–6, Gene Edward Veith, Jr. observes the Matthean echo in the reference to "seed," but Veith also links the bread references to John 6.

[104] I agree with Alison Knight, who remarks that Herbert does not simply showcase this aspect of the Bible's composition; rather, Herbert incorporates himself (and his verse) into that very scriptural unity. Biblical unity, for Herbert, is "something that the scriptural text is able to extend to, and effect in, his work. In 'The H. Scriptures. II,' it is no accident that scripture is the agent of the lines; scripture incorporates him into its own unity, as though he were a verse himself." "'This Verse Marks That': George Herbert's *The Temple* and Scripture in Context," in Kevin Killeen, Helen Smith, and Rachel Willie, eds., *The Oxford Handbook of the Bible in Early Modern England, c.1530–1700* (Oxford: Oxford University Press, 2015), 523.

me know" (1–2)—recall Isaiah 32:18: "And my people shall dwell in a peaceable habitation, and in sure dwellings, and in quiet resting places." Isaiah refers literally to a peaceful dwelling place for the Israelites. Yet in his commentary on Isaiah, Calvin rightly sees the Isaian verse as typologically linked to John 14:27: "This peace Christ left with his disciples, which the world could not give unto them."[105] The peace that Christ promises to the brethren in 14:27—"Peace I leave with you, my peace I give unto you, not as the world giveth, give I unto you"—is the pledge of the Comforter or Spirit-Paraclete who will "abide" (14:16) and "dwelleth" (14:17) with the followers once Christ has departed and who will further instruct the disciples as they establish the emergent church.[106]

The question of the proper dwelling place figures centrally in Herbert's poem. "Dwell" is reprised at line 16—"Peace at the root must dwell"—and mentioned in the other typological reference to the Fourth Gospel at line 23. Melchisedec, the "king of Salem" (linked to Christ as the "King of Peace" in Hebrews 7:2), typologizes the Johannine Christ of the good shepherd discourse of John 10: "There was a Prince of old / At Salem dwelt, who liv'd with good increase / Of flock and fold" (22–4).[107] The shepherd discourse is particularly apt in the context of the poem's preoccupation with dwelling. Christ's express mission is to bring all of the sheep into *union* with him: "them also I must bring, and they shall heare my voyce; and there shall be one fold, and one shepheard" (10:16).

Connecting the constellated points of the narrative that "Peace" provides, we can see that to dwell properly with Christ is to find everlasting life and peace, itself enabled through the tasting of Christ's grain or bread.[108] Not surprisingly, given the Johannine resonances of dwelling throughout the poem, the nearest and most compendious scriptural approximation to such a narrative of post-resurrectional comfort is provided not in Matthew 26 or in comparable lines on the Eucharist but in John 6:56 and the bread of life narrative: "He that eateth my flesh, and drinketh my blood, dwelleth in me, and I in him." In the context of "Peace," to eat or "taste" the bread is not to eat Christ bodily so much as to believe with "earnestnesse" (41) in Christ's example and to remember the "vertue" (34) of Christ's passion.[109]

---

[105] John Calvin, *A commentary upon the prophecie of Isaiah* (London, 1609), 326.

[106] The repeated references to "dwell" in "Peace" might also recall the Temple *topos* of 1 Corinthians 3:16–17 and 2 Corinthians 6:16, verses that, as Herbert's critics have noted, influence the "living temple" motif running throughout Herbert's poetry. In the context of the "bread of life" references in this particular poem, however (as well as in the context of Calvin's gloss on the typological verses), "dwell" more specifically recalls John 6 and the Farewell Discourse. On Herbert's use of the temple metaphor, see Chana Bloch, *Spelling the Word: George Herbert and the Bible* (Berkeley: University of California Press, 1985), 117–27, and Stanley Fish, *The Living Temple: George Herbert and Catechizing* (Berkeley: University of California Press, 1978), 68–89. On the many uses of the trope of dwelling in Herbert's poetry, see Terry G. Sherwood, *Herbert's Prayerful Art* (Toronto: University of Toronto Press, 1989), 90–4.

[107] Wilcox provides detailed glosses on the typology of the poem in *The English Poems of George Herbert*, 439–41.

[108] Without explicitly referencing John 6, Joseph H. Summers also sees the poem's typological references as issuing in the "bread of life" narrative: "The 'twelve stalks of wheat' involved the twelve tribes, the twelve apostles, and primarily that 'bread of life' which is Christ and His message." *George Herbert: His Religion and Art* (Cambridge, MA: Harvard University Press, 1968), 176.

[109] Compare John Cotton's later gloss on the love commandments in John's First Epistle. Cotton, personifying "Peace," brings together, as does Herbert's poem, the theme of dwelling, peace, and

Yet what renders "Peace" so much more than a proof-text for its Old and New Testament sources is a subtle transition from the allegorical and sermonic quality of stanzas 4–6, which place the speaker's personal quest to find peace in an instructive yet communal and figural narrative, to the intensely local and personal address of line 37: "Take of this grain, which in my garden grows, / And grows for you" (37). From the "many" wonderers at line 39, to the collective "they" that taste the wheat (33), the poem returns attentively to the speaker, the amplification and slight polysyndeton (relevant to the earlier verses) of "And grows for you" accenting the speaker's indwelt relationship with Christ. Christ's garden ("my" garden) grows or is grafted specifically, purposefully onto the speaker. It is a garden that is entitled "for" him as much as it is for anyone else. The speaker's humble craving to find out "where" peace dwells is not so much explained as experienced, a veritable growth of the speaker's awareness that peace is located in Christ with whom he participates. And as in so many Herbertian poeticizations of Johannine sources, "Peace" rings a beautiful and original note even as it is exegetical. The growing of Christ into the speaker, the repose and comfort offered in the speaker's awareness of that fellowship, recapitulate not the principal source text (John 12:24) but the concluding point of the Johannine allegory of the stalks which is explained two verses later: "Where I am, there shall also my servant be" (John 12:26). This verse provides the answer to Herbert's opening question in "Peace": "Sweet Peace, where dost thou dwell?" (1). There is good reason to agree with Joseph Summers's concluding remarks about "Peace": "With all its disparate elements the poem is a freshly created whole."[110] As I remarked in the Introduction, Herbert's Johannine poems do not set out to decode or merely to interpret their immediate sources. The poems offer rich poetic responses to the questions that the Johannine sources raise. And such versified responses themselves reflect Christ's own explanations to the otherwise cryptic statements that are laid out in relevant chapters or pericopes of the Johannine writings.

If "The H. Communion" (Williams) and "Peace" direct attention away from the substance of the real presence, even away from the Eucharist proper and toward the symbolism of the true bread, several other of Herbert's meditations on sacramental eating are notable for their consistent emphasis on the location of Christ in heaven despite the varying processes of eating and drinking that are described in a given poem. The sacramental poems typically place the speaker under thrall to earthly goods, longing to unite with Christ and to re-attain some trace of the beatific vision. The uplifting process often requires an administration of grace in the form of charity that impels the speaker heavenward. This *agapic* frame in turn shapes Herbert's representation of the sacrament such that Christ's body and blood are not typically located in the earthly elements. The speaker of "The Banquet," sunk

---

contrition, although Cotton adds more explicitly that the proper dwelling place is the spirit of love: "God being a God of peace, loves to dwell in a place of peace, or else he dwels not.... Where God dwels, he pardons sin, and purifies the conscience, or prospers the outward man, and there is a spirit of love in that mans heart." *A practicall commentary, or An exposition with observations, reasons, and uses upon the first Epistle generall of John* (London, 1658), 307.

[110] Summers, *George Herbert: His Religion and Art*, 176.

in earthly sin—"When I had forgot my birth, / And on earth / In delights of earth was drown'd" (31–3)—is reminded that, as a means of showing "how farre his love / Could improve" (28–9), God "took bloud" (33) and raises the speaker up through the Eucharistic meal: "Having rais'd me to look up, / In a cup / Sweetly he doth meet my taste. / But I still being low and short, / Farre from court, / Wine becomes a wing at last" (37–42). The one-sided emphasis here is on the force of the sacrament to enable the speaker to rise to the ascended Christ; the emphasis is not on Christ's descent in bodily form to the elements of the Eucharist. Herbert makes no fuss at all over what exactly is contained in the cup. The premise of the poem is that Christ remains in heaven and can only become visible to the speaker by means of the beatific vision, itself a result of the power of the meal. While the speaker drinks from "the cup" (38), he is already looking "up" (39), and he then realizes that, because he remains too earthbound and "farre from court" (41), the wine will bridge the geographical gap and send him up to Christ: "Wine becomes a wing at last. / For with it alone I flie / To the skie" (42–4). The wine provides efficacious power, already signified as God's "love" (28), to allow the speaker to repair from the corporeal to the incorporeal realm.[111]

Through God's grace, figured as love/charity, the speaker of "The Banquet" partakes of a sacramental offering and witnessing of God in heaven that, if it depicts Christ's presence at all, refuses to consign that presence to the earthly elements: "Where I wipe mine eyes, and see / What I seek, for what I sue; / Him I view, / Who hath done so much for me" (45–8). The process has an unmistakable Johannine aspect to it, or at least an Augustinian–Calvinist aspect itself linked to John 6. As we have seen, Augustine's gloss on John 6:56 underlines the point that sacramental eating allows the believer to dwell in Christ so that "he sticks to Christ so as not to be left behind."[112] Mutual participation (which the speaker of Herbert's poem has achieved) itself results from what Augustine describes as the "assistance of grace," nothing more than the "love of God," the very charity that advances the speaker's spiritual process in Herbert's "The Banquet" and that prompts his conclusion that we must "love the strife" (53), presumably his own embattlements but also Christ's passional strife on our behalf.[113] The mutual indwelling is further described by Augustine as an attaching of flesh to the spirit, a hybrid commingling that, through charity, provides spiritual knowledge: "*The flesh is no use at all*, but that means flesh by itself; let spirit be joined to flesh, in the way charity is attached to knowledge, and flesh is very useful."[114] The knowledge achieved by the speaker in "The Banquet" is none other than the spiritual "seeing" of Christ/God in the penultimate stanza. He has wiped his eyes and now sees/understands, with Christ in "view" (47), the signification of Christ's sacrifice on his behalf: "Who hath done so much for me" (48).

Herbert is able to represent a sacramental eating/drinking and maintain the utmost dignity of Christ's body because that body does not descend earthward.

---

[111] Compare Wilcox's suggestion that "meet my taste" carries also "the sensual aspect of the Eucharist": *The English Poems of George Herbert*, 630, n. 42.

[112] Augustine, *Homilies on the Gospel of John*, 466.   [113] Ibid., 450.   [114] Ibid., 469.

The speaker can achieve this seemingly miraculous flight because, as Calvin recommends, he has set his sights on Christ in heaven: "But if we are carried to heaven with our eyes and minds, that we may there behold Christ in the glory of his kingdom, as the symbols invite us to him in his integrity, so, under the symbol of bread, we must feed on his body, and, under the symbol of wine, drink separately of his blood, and thereby have the full enjoyment of him."[115] It is precisely the apprehending of Christ in heaven that serves as both impetus (in terms of the speaker's desire) and result (in terms of the beatific vision) that allows the speaker to partake of the "full" enjoyment of Christ by the close of "The Banquet." And he has done so in keeping with Calvin's supposition that "there be nothing derogatory to the heavenly glory of Christ" because Christ is not brought "under the corruptible elements of this world."[116]

There are moments in Herbert's devotional lyrics when the otherwise mysterious link between the heavenly or ascended Christ and the communicant, not to mention the consecrated elements themselves, becomes the focus of a particular poem. "The H. Communion" poem included in *The Temple* is quite like "The Banquet" in its firm heavenly placement of Christ throughout the process of Eucharistic eating. Here again the speaker bemoans his captivity to his "rebel-flesh" (17), setting his sights high on the "ease" (37) of heaven. He remarks that heaven would have been bequeathed to him—"a fervent sigh might well have blown / Our innocent earth to heaven" (31–2)—if not for Adamic sin: "He might to heav'n from Paradise go, / As from one room t'another" (35–6). Here, as in "The Banquet," Christ's blood is somehow connected to the sacramental elements even though it remains "heav'nly bloud" (38). But as Wilcox rightly notes, the idea of restoring through "blood" the union of heaven and earth echoes John 6:56: "The blood of the sacrament has restored earth and heaven to closeness and mutuality."[117] And here, too, sacramental eating can only achieve its spiritual effects through a complementary bestowal of grace: "Onely thy grace, which with these elements comes, / Knoweth the ready way" (19–20).

Yet *The Temple* version of "The H. Communion" meditates in more detail on precisely what the communicant receives when drinking Christ's "heav'nly bloud," which is to say that the poem attempts more readily to resolve the seeming paradox that Christ's body is both within the elements and within heaven. Just what the communicant receives is described at length in the second stanza: "But by the way of nourishment and strength / Thou creep'st into my breast; / Making thy way my rest, / And thy small quantities my length; / Which spread their forces into every part, / Meeting sinnes force and art" (7–12). This is certainly not a purely symbolic and extrinsic sort of eating in keeping with Zwingli's memorialism, for example. But we should not be too quick to assume that what has entered the speaker's body is Christ's corporeal body as such. The language of participation that Herbert uses—"nourishment," "creep'st," "forces," etc.—implies a pneumatological presence, in keeping both with Augustine's notion that the sacrament

---

[115] Calvin, *Institutes*, Book IV, 570.   [116] Ibid., 571.
[117] Wilcox, *The English Poems of George Herbert*, 185, n. 38.

provides efficacious power or *virtus*—"A sacrament is one thing, quite another is the 'benefit' [*virtus*] of the sacrament"—and with the Calvinist belief that the Holy Spirit serves as the intermediary between the heavenly Christ and earth-bound penitent.[118] The claim that the Spirit's role is to strengthen is frequently made during the period.[119] In *The Christians apparelling by Christ* (1625), Robert Jenison describes the "Christian mans strength by the spirit, in withstanding and resisting Satan."[120] Later in the century, Thomas Hall points out that "Christ draws in this yoke with us, and bears the heavier part of the yoke for us, and by his Spirit strengthens us to bear it."[121] The Puritan divine John Preston devotes an entire 1634 treatise, *The saints spirituall strength*, to a discussion of the way in which, according to Ephesians, the Spirit strengthens the "inner man" and sanctified holiness:

> The spirit strengthens grace in the soule, is this, by giving unto the soule, an effectuall operative and powerfull facultie, and that is done by rearing the inward man in the soule, and setting up the building of grace, and this Hee doth by shedding abroad in the heart the blessed effects of grace unto every facultie: as the blood is infused into every veine, or as the soule goes through every part of the body, and so gives life unto it; so doth the Spirit goe through all the parts of the soule, by infusing spirituall life and power into them.[122]

The Spirit spreads throughout the soul as the soul infuses itself throughout each part of the body, analogizing the infusion of blood into "every facultie"; the spirit strengthens the soul by erecting a building of grace, depositing power into each part of the soul. Compare Preston's description here to the second stanza of Herbert's "The H. Communion" (*Temple*). Christ, "by the way" (7) of strength, spreads his quantities into "every part" (11) in order to combat sin, providing the "outworks" (16) or battlements that would control the rebellious flesh. The means by which Christ courses throughout the speaker's body in order to provide spiritual strength and nourishment makes more sense if it refers to the manifestation of Christ's grace via the Spirit rather than the substantial body of Christ. This is how Christ's ascended body—the "heav'nly bloud"—participates with the speaker who has otherwise been dejected in sin (6).

Preston's elaboration of the building metaphor bears further comparison to stanza three of "The H. Communion" (*Temple*). The Spirit "strengthens grace in the soul," Preston continues, "by giving efficacy and power unto the meanes of growth.... [F]or as hee sets up the building, and furnisheth the roomes, and gives power unto the soule to use them, so that which makes all these effectuall, is this, when hee gives power and efficacy unto the meanes that are for the strengthning of the inward man."[123] Herbert, too, uses the vehicle of a building in order to suggest that,

---

[118] Augustine, *Homilies on the Gospel of John*, 458.
[119] Jean de Serres, *The three partes of commentaries containing the whole and perfect discourse of the ciuill warres of Fraunce* (London, 1574), 75.
[120] Robert Jenison, *The Christians apparelling by Christ* (London, 1625), 314.
[121] Thomas Hall, *The beauty of holiness* (London, 1655), 265.
[122] John Preston, *Remaines of that reverend and learned divine, John Preston* (London, 1634), 128.
[123] Ibid., 131.

through the means of strengthened grace, which must accompany the "elements," the soul's "subtile rooms" (22) will be opened and fortified. For Preston, the Spirit strengthens grace by providing the "rooms with new habits and qualities of grace," approximating the renewal described in the reprisal of the building metaphor found in the penultimate stanza of Herbert's poem. Once strengthened, once restored to Adamic ease, the speaker will be able to move from "one room t'another" (36) in the way that prelapsarian Adam might have traveled freely from Paradise to heaven.

The more particular ascription of the Spirit's role in "nourishing" the penitent is also frequently made throughout the period. Jean de Serres occupies the late-sixteenth-century Calvinist position: "Although he be now in heaven, and shall abide there untill he come to judge the worlde, yet notwithstanding we beleve that he doth by the secrete and incomprehensible power of his spirite nouryshe and quicken us."[124] Serres's treatise (and the English commentaries mentioned above on spiritual fortification) bring us back to Calvin's pneumatological précis on the real presence in the *Institutes*. Just prior to advancing his view that the Holy Spirit unites things separated by space, Calvin underlines his belief that the Eucharist, through the means of the Spirit, provides nourishment in Christ:

> There would be no aptitude in the sign, did not our souls find their nourishment in Christ. This could not be, did not Christ truly form one with us, and refresh us by the eating of his flesh, and the drinking of his blood. But though it seems an incredible thing that the flesh of Christ, while at such a distance from us in respect of place, should be food to us, let us remember how far the secret virtue of the Holy Spirit surpasses all our conceptions, and how foolish it is to wish to measure its immensity by our feeble capacity. Therefore, what our mind does not comprehend let faith conceive—viz. that the Spirit truly unites things separated by space.[125]

The nourishment in Christ, for Calvin, is indeed the very matter of the Eucharist. Yet this efficacy inheres not in the flesh of Christ but in the otherwise secret virtue of the Holy Spirit. Calvin reiterates the point in his partial agreement with Peter Lombard: "To his distinction between the flesh of Christ and the power of nourishing which it possesses, I assent."[126] Robert Whalen, after suggesting, against R. V. Young, that Herbert's position in the first two stanzas is one that is "bordering on a Roman Catholic sacramental position," concludes that, if the phrase "with these elements comes" might be accommodated to Calvin's notion that the sacraments announce the arrival of grace, the phrase "nourishment and strength" cannot be so accommodated to Calvin's sacramentalism.[127] Whalen remarks, "'Nourishment and strength'...would appear to invite Calvin's condemnation of the idea that

---

[124] Jean de Serres, *The three partes of commentaries containing the whole and perfect discourse of the ciuill warres of Fraunce* (London, 1574), 75.
[125] Calvin, *Institutes*, Book IV, 563.   [126] Ibid., Book IV, 589.
[127] Whalen, *The Poetry of Immanence*, 118–19. R. V. Young believes that, in the "H. Communion," Christ is "present in the eucharist species," and that the phrase "comes with" the elements is not typical of the Reformed belief that the sacrament provides only a seal or ratification of grace. *Doctrine and Devotion in Seventeenth-Century Poetry: Studies in Donne, Herbert, Crashaw, and Vaughan* (Cambridge: D. S. Brewer, 2000), 138.

heaven's king might go a progress through the guts of a beggarly sinner, suggesting that the elements are in fact changed at the moment of ingestion."[128] Yet we have just seen that Calvin explicitly associates "nourishment" with the power of the Holy Spirit and not with anything carnal, fleshly, or physiologically ingested.

I would further note that, here again, not only John 6 but also John's view of the Ascension provide Calvin with the scriptural warrant to endow the Spirit with the Eucharistic work of linking Christ at the right hand of God with the communicant on Earth: "Whenever Christ says that he will leave the world and go away (John xiv. 2, 28), they reply, that that departure was nothing more than a change in mortal state. Were this so, Christ would not substitute the Holy Spirit, to supply, as they express it, the defect of his absence....Certainly the advent of the Spirit and the ascension of Christ are set against each other, and hence it necessarily follows that Christ dwells with us according to the flesh, in the same way as that in which he sends his Spirit."[129] The exchange of Christ for the Spirit allows for Christ's "flesh" miraculously to be present in the Eucharist despite the fact that Christ's body is circumscribed in heaven.

Returning to Herbert's "The H. Communion" (*Temple*), we can see that Calvin's and the English Calvinist identification of the Spirit as Christ's agent or vehicle of the effectual sacrament helps to put in a more nuanced context Wilcox's correct assumption that lines 37–8—"Thou hast restor'd us to this ease / By this thy heav'nly bloud"—bring us to John 6:56: "He that eateth my flesh and drinketh my blood abideth in me, and I in him." For Wilcox, the sense of lines 37–8 of the poem is that "The blood of the sacrament has restored earth and heaven to closeness and mutuality," but the speaker's final claim that he can now "leave th' earth to their food" (40) signifies, as does the rhetoric of mystical abiding in John 6, that, because his soul has been spiritually strengthened, he will depart from earth and find Christ's presence in heaven.[130] That Christ's body has been in heaven from the outset of the speaker's meditation is reflected in the speaker's awareness that Christ has already been "sold" (4) and that Christ has (or should have) left him. The rising of the speaker to Christ's body, not the descent of Christ's body to the corruptible elements (a process that can only be achieved through the intermediate agency of the Spirit), is the whole point of the communion process as described in the poem. Calvin's cavil against those who would locate Christ's body in the elements is apt: "They thus leave nothing for the secret operation of the Spirit which unites Christ himself to us. Christ does not seem to them to be present unless he descends to us, as if we did not equally gain his presence when he raises us to himself."[131]

But this still leaves unaddressed perhaps the most puzzling aspect of *The Temple's* version of "The H. Communion," the sense in which some manifestation of Christ "creep'st" (8). In the context of stanza 2, the term "creep" is understandable. Christ's work is gradual, incremental. It must start in small but gathering "quantities" (10)

---

[128] Whalen, *The Poetry of Immanence*, 119. [129] Calvin, *Institutes*, Book IV, 579.
[130] Wilcox, *The English Poems of George Herbert*, 185, n. 38.
[131] Calvin, *Institutes*, Book IV, 586–7.

if it is to meet and overcome the "rebel-flesh" (17) operatively and lastingly. This is exactly what renovation, or more technically, sanctification, requires: step-wise spiritual progress, not a once-and-for-all improvement. Yet even assuming Herbert's innovatory poetics, the association of Christ's body with a creeping process would not seem to be a fitting ascription of the motions of Christ during the Communion. In the seventeenth century, "creep" is frequently associated with the insidious motions of Satan, especially the imbruted serpent. Likewise, sin, darkness, fear, falsehood, the world, agues, and papists all work "creepingly" to offset spiritual advancement.[132] In the more particular context of the Eucharist, the Protestant controversialist William Middleton directly associates the creeping of Christ's body with the metaphysical improprieties of transubstantiation: "These men makes us beleeve, that the body of Christ *creepes* in at the hole the bread went out, and so fils the vacuity of the roome, that the accidents or skinne of the bread remaines still as well stuffed, as it was before, without corrupting, or shrinking, or any alteration in the world" (italics mine).[133] Surely Herbert's Christ, in any imaginable form, is not the substantial stuffing for the accidental husk of the Eucharistic bread.

Yet there are positive connotations of creeping during the period that suggest an association with the renovating office of the Spirit. Later in the century Obadiah Sedgwick explains that renovation or sanctification is through the Spirit of grace, comparing the saving motion to a child's growth: "Like a Childe that is nourished by a dayly addition and reception of food, and so creeps up into more strength in time: Beloved, you must not expect (though you be united to Christ) such an immediate and compleat supply of the Spirit of grace from Christ as at once to make you strong Christians."[134] A similar analogy is used in a mid-century treatise, *Saints duty discoursed*: "As a child that hath life *in operari & esse*, goeth but by this support, and that assistance, for but weak now, new going.... So a poore soule at first creeps, cannot go; but his grace strengthened, renewed, he ventures *in nomine Domini*."[135] Putting such comments in the context of Herbert's Eucharistic use of "creep'st," alongside the Calvinist assumption that the Spirit provides the nourishment and strength during the Communion, we can see that it is not Christ's body as such that finds its way into the speaker's breast of "The H. Communion" (*Temple*) but rather the sanctified efficacy or power that Christ provides, the Spirit of grace that "knoweth the ready way" (20).

An appreciation of the Eucharistic pneumatology of "The H. Communion" (*Temple*) can help negotiate an ongoing critical controversy over whether the poem was originally written as two discrete poems, given the radical break in meter

---

[132] On the negative connotations of "creep," any number of extant texts and citations might be adduced. See, for example, Henry Smith, *Two sermons, of Jonahs punishment* (London, 1607): "Sinne creepes upon us, while doubt fulnesse remaineth in us" (12); and Sir William Cornwallis, *Essayes* (London, 1600–1): "Feare creepes in & over-valuing life, drawes preservation from wrong places" (149)

[133] William Middleton, *Papisto-mastix, or The protestants religion defended Shewing briefely when the great compound heresie of poperie first sprange* (London, 1606), 93.

[134] Obadiah Sedgwick, *The bowels of tender mercy sealed in the everlasting covenant* (London, 1661), 215.

[135] R. A., *Saints duty discoursed* (London, 1649), 23.

beginning with the fourth stanza.[136] For those Herbertians, including Hutchinson, who see the poem as a thematic, if not formal whole, the last four stanzas complement well the earlier stanzas. As Edmund Miller remarks, the focus in the opening stanzas on "public" exposition transitions well to a focus in the later stanzas on private emotion, a change that is marked by the simpler metric form of the final stanzas.[137] I agree that the poem works as a continuous whole. And I would add that the motion of creeping is pivotal both thematically and formally. As a compact meditation on the service of the Eucharist in the economy of salvation, the poem's first stanzas do creep along relative to the latter stanzas, reflecting the *process* by which the speaker has received the special grace through the operations of the Spirit. By the end of the poem, the speaker has made significant spiritual progress. He has been "restor'd" to Adamic "ease," having received the "heav'nly bloud," the latter reference retroactively clarifying that Christ has been in heaven throughout the process. The restorative ease has allowed him to put behind him mere earthbound food. Wilcox rightly notes the tenor of "comfort" in the reference to spiritual "ease" at line 37. It is precisely such spiritual "comfort" that, as I will discuss in Chapter 3, is the peculiar office of the Johannine Spirit-Paraclete or "Comforter."

Should we say with Patrides that the Eucharist is the "marrow" of Herbert's theology, or with Wilcox that poems such as "Peace" rely on Eucharistic motifs and passages culled from scripture? Some terminological clarification that distinguishes sacramentalism generally from the particular ordinance of the Eucharist is warranted. The standard medieval rule of faith regarding the sacrament as a visible form of an invisible grace, itself cobbled together from Augustine's several comments on the sacraments as sacred signs in Book X of the *City of God* and in his writings on the Donatist controversy, emphasized the instrumental power of the sacrament. This is a conception of the sacrament shared by Calvin, for whom a sacrament is an "external sign by which the Lord seals on our consciences his promises of good-will toward us," or more simply a "testimony of the divine favour toward us, confirmed by an external sign."[138] And for both Augustine and Calvin, sacraments consist of both the "word and the external sign."[139] Recall, for example, Augustine's influential view of baptism in his tractate on John 15: "Take away the word, and what is the water except water? The word is added to the elemental

[136] On the controversy regarding the composition and publication of "The H. Communion" (*Temple*), see Wilcox, *The English Poems of George Herbert*, 181–2.

[137] On the distinction between meaning and feeling in the poem, see Edmund Miller, *Drudgerie Divine: The Rhetoric of God and Man in George Herbert* (Salzburg: Institut für Anglistik und Amerikanistik, University of Salzburg, 1979), 164–6, as cited and discussed in Wilcox, *The English Poems of George Herbert*, 182. On the public–private distinctions in the poem, see Coburn Freer, *Music for a King: George Herbert's Style and Metrical Psalms* (Baltimore: Johns Hopkins University Press, 1972), 166–8, also cited and discussed in Wilcox, *The English Poems of George Herbert*, 182.

[138] Calvin, *Institutes*, Book IV, ch. XIV, 491–2. For a discussion of the medieval conception of sacramentalism that can be found in Hugh St. Victor, Peter Lombard, and Aquinas, see *The Book of Concord: The Confessions of the Evangelical Lutheran Church*, eds. Robert Kolb and Timothy J. Wengert, trans. Charles Arrand (Minneapolis: Augsburg Fortress, 2000), 219–20. On the influence of Augustine's definition of the sacrament on later medieval conceptions, see Donald K. McKim, *Theological Turning Points: Major Issues in Christian Thought* (Louisville: Westminster John Knox Press, 1988), 119–20.

[139] Calvin, *Institutes*, Book IV, 493.

substance, and it becomes a sacrament, also itself, as it were, a visible word."[140] While the number of sacraments proliferated during the Middle Ages, Peter Lombard's *Sentences* eventually distinguished seven, after which Reformed confessions (including Article XXV of the Thirty-nine Articles) further narrowed the list to the Eucharist and Baptism, both of which were understood to be institutional sacraments ordained by the Church and associated with particular ritualistic forms. With respect to John 6, we have seen that, while Christ's references to eating his flesh are sacramental affirmations in the broad sense, John 6 does not link this sacramentalism to the Eucharist proper, especially since the Lord's Supper is omitted from John's Farewell Discourse (John 13–17).[141]

Regarding the several poems of Herbert that in some sense borrow scriptural imagery associated with bread and wine (poems that rely on a Johannine semiotic), we can say that these lyrics are sacramental but not pointedly or doctrinally Eucharistic in orientation. That we should not too quickly assume that Herbert's sacramental language is narrowly Eucharistic is a view advanced compellingly by Richard Strier. After remarking that Herbert's sacramentalism follows Cranmer (and Calvin), Strier argues that Herbert's "Eucharistic-sounding language" is typically used metaphorically and that we should not collapse Herbert's "rhetoric with doctrine in Eucharistic contexts."[142] I would argue that, as in John 6, Herbert is less interested in the institutionalization of the sacrament or the question of this or that Eucharistic rite or confessional position than he is in what has been described as the "ultimate sacrament," namely, the Incarnation (through which the physical body of Christ becomes a vehicle for the spiritual), as well as in the death and resurrection of Christ.[143] This is not to say that poems such as "The H. Communion" from *The Temple* eschew all pondering over the subtleties of the real presence, only that at such moments Herbert is more interested in a post-Ascension communion with Christ than he is the ritual of the Eucharist. Christ's body is not locatable in the institution of the bread and wine because Christ remains in heaven. To the extent that there is an operative power conveyed from the host to the communicant, that agency resides more in the life-giving Spirit than it does in any corporeal

---

[140] Saint Augustine, *Tractates on the Gospel of John: 55–111*, vol. 4, trans. John W. Rettig (Washington, D.C.: Catholic University Press, 1994), 117.

[141] The most comprehensive recent discussion of the non-Eucharistic aspects of John 6 can be found in Paul N. Anderson, *The Christology of the Fourth Gospel: Its Unity and Disunity in the Light of John 6* (Eugene: Cascade Books, 2010), especially chapter 6, *passim*. C. K. Barrett discusses the sacramentalism of the Fourth Gospel in *The Gospel According to St. John* (London: S.P.C.K., 1965), 69–71. For a somewhat different discussion of the incarnational but non-sacramental semantics of John 6, see Herman N. Ridderbos, *The Gospel According to John: A Theological Commentary* (Grand Rapids: Eerdmans Publishing Company, 1997), 240–3. See also Meredith Warren, *My Flesh is Meat Indeed: A Nonsacramental Reading of John 6:51–58* (Philadelphia: Fortress Press, 2015).

[142] Richard Strier, *Love Known: Theology and Experience in George Herbert's Poetry* (Chicago: University of Chicago Press, 1983), xiv, 47, n. 41. Strier also cites Malcolm Mackenzie Ross, *Poetry and Dogma: The Transformation of Eucharistic Symbols in Seventeenth-Century Poetry* (New Brunswick: Rutgers University Press, 1954), 62 ff., 100, 180.

[143] Anderson, *The Christology of the Fourth Gospel*, 113. Remarking that John 6 nowhere describes the rite of the Eucharist, Anderson concludes: "Rather, the ultimate 'sacrament' for John is the *incarnation*, and to 'eat and drink' the 'flesh and blood' of Jesus is to assimilate the salvific reality of the incarnation by faith and communal faithfulness" (134).

presence in the elements. We find a similar Johannine poetics, inflected by the reception of Johannine material in the works of Augustine and Calvin, in Henry Vaughan's sacramental writings, although as we will see, Vaughan meditates more fundamentally than Herbert on the Eucharist proper.

HENRY VAUGHAN'S MOUNT OF OLIVES

Heavily influenced by Herbert, Henry Vaughan's approaches to the sacrament of eating are also informed by the importance of the Ascension to the question of the real presence. The preparatory prayers on the Lord's Supper in Vaughan's prose work *The Mount of Olives* (1652) are framed by the placement of Christ at the right hand of God: "When thou hast thus considered him in his acts of love and humility, consider him again in his glory, take thine Eyes off from Bethlehem and Golgotha, and look up to the mount of *Olives*, yea, to heaven where he sits now upon the right hand of his Father."[144] Vaughan uses John's good shepherd narrative and 7:37 in particular—"*If any man thirst, let him come unto me, and drink*" (162)—in order to situate Christ's vantage point in heaven during the Eucharist: "This is the voyce of the great Shepherd, and thy sheep hear thy voyce. Thus thou didst cry, and these were the words thou didst speak while thou wert here upon earth, and shall I turn away from thee, *that speakest now from heaven?*" (162). The difficulty Vaughan faces throughout his prosodic and poetic treatments of the sacrament is to keep Christ glorified firmly in heaven, away from the corporeal humilities of Golgotha, even while hinting at the "ful oblation" ("Dressing," 10) and sacrificial nature of the Eucharist. Again and again Vaughan elaborates the mysterious quality of the elements, describing them variously as "this divin mystery" (156), "mysterious solemnity" (156), "mysticall *Communion*" ("Dressing," 14), and "secret meals" ("The Sap," 14) that lie "under veyls here" ("The Feast," 40).

Vaughan does not so much reconcile his focus on Christ in heaven with the mysterious ontology of the sacrament as shift the focus away from what the sacrament is to a concern with both the means of preparation for the sacramental participation and the spiritual benefits of having eaten. In doing so he relies even more directly than Herbert on Johannine material. The preparatory prayer of *The Mount of Olives*—"A Prayer when thou art upon going to the Lords Table" (163)—is devised from a compilation of verses found in John 6:51–5: "*Jesus Christ*, the Lamb, the Branch, the bright and morning-Starre, the bread of life that came down from heaven, have mercy upon me! It is thy promise, that whosoever eateth thy flesh, and drinketh thy blood, he shall have eternal life in him....I am now coming to thee....[B]e unto me the bread of life to strengthen me in my pilgrimage towards heaven....O give me grace to receive both worthily" (163). This prayer is followed by both an admonition and then an additional prayer to be taken under

---

[144] *The Works of Henry Vaughan*, ed. L. C. Martin (Oxford: Clarendon Press, 1957), 158. Subsequent citations from *The Mount of Olives* will be included in the text according to page number; all references to Vaughan's poems will be taken from this edition and cited by line number.

advisement once the Supper has been received, which prompts Vaughan to instruct his auditors to read John 6:22 "to the end," along with relevant verses from Paul and Wisdom literature (165). These preparatory meditations serve to ready the communicant for an administration of grace and to remind him that the sacrament will provide spiritual passage to heaven and eternal life. Although Vaughan does not equate the act of eating with testimony and belief, he recommends an avowal of belief just before eating: "I believe all that thou hast said, and all that thou hast promised, helpe thou mine unbelief" (164).

The relationship between the preparation for and then consequence of eating becomes provocatively blurred in poems such as "Dressing": "Give to thy wretched one / Thy mysticall *Communion*, / That, absent, he may see, / Live, die, and rise with thee; / Let him so follow here, that in the end / He may take thee, as thou doest him intend" (13–17). On the one hand, the efficacious Communion once given will provide the spiritual illumination—"he may see" (15)—reminiscent of the beatific vision and eternal life gestured at in Herbert's verse. On the other hand, proper seeing seems to be the preparatory means that will allow the communicant to "follow" Christ and so "take" the Lord as he is intended to be taken. At times the speaker seems to be putting the sanctified cart before the initiatory horse, as in the opening of the final stanza: "Give me, my God! thy grace, / The beams, and brightnes of thy face, / That never like a beast / I take thy sacred feast" (31–4). To see God's face is typically a vision granted to those in the glorified afterlife; even then, according to the Augustinian tradition, it is a dimly seen face at best. Such an apprehension would more intuitively result from the shared indwelling afforded by the sacrament; it would not serve as a means to accepting the sacrament in its proper signification. The poem proffers its own resolution to such puzzling causality. The speaker makes clear in the final stanza that his principal concern is to avoid confusing material and spiritual eating, which would derogate the sanctity of the elements. To take the elements like a beast would be to use such "dread mysteries" (35) as rank "Kitchin food" (36), the speaker's worst fear: "Some sit to thee, and eat / Thy body as their Common meat, / O let not me do so! / Poor dust should ly still low" (37–40). This is a speaker who is so concerned about his own lack of preparation for the Supper and a subsequent debasing of Christ that he begs to be spiritually overprepared for the meal.

The speaker of "The Holy Communion" similarly blurs the preparation for and the effects of the Supper in the second stanza: "But that great darkness at thy death / When the veyl broke with thy last breath, / Did make us see / The way to thee" (21–3). The speaker relates that the proper witnessing of Christ's death has already been achieved; he then adds, "And now by these sure, sacred ties, / After thy blood / (Our sov'rain good,) / Had clear'd our eies, / And given us sight; / Thou dost unto thy self betroth / Our souls, and bodies both / In everlasting light" (25–32). The clearing of sight now seems to be a consequence of the Eucharistic sacred ties. Later in the poem, the speaker introduces a similar ambiguity with the notion of spiritual sealing: "Was't not enough to lose thy breath / And blood by an accursed death, / But thou must also leave / To us that did bereave / Thee of them both, these seals the means / That should both cleanse / And keep us so" (41–7). The Eucharistic "seals," which of course follow from the "accursed death," are clearly described as the means of cleansing, although earlier in the poem a significant amount of cleansing seemed to be required in order to prepare one to receive those very seals.

Vaughan's turn to John at the end of "The Holy Communion" helps to explain the ambiguous causal nexus described above. The final couplet pivots on John 10 and the good shepherd discourse: "How art thou now, thy flock to keep, / Become both *food*, and *Shepheard* to thy sheep" (50–1). Vaughan has superimposed onto a poem about the Lord's Supper a Johannine theme that not only has little to do with the Eucharist but, in its proper Johannine context (a context established, as we have seen, in discussions of the Eucharist in the shaping theology of Cranmer and beyond), would diminish the importance of the Supper itself to salvation. Toward the end of the shepherd example, Jesus remarks, "My sheepe heare my voyce, and I know them, and they follow me. And I give unto them eternall life, and they shall never perish, neither shall any man plucke them out of my hand. My father which gave them me, is greater then all: and no man is able to plucke them out of my fathers hand" (10:27–9). Although John will elsewhere remark that eternal life awaits the faithful who have died (5:29), the good shepherd allegory bespeaks a uniquely Johannine realized eschatology. Such passages from the Fourth Gospel help to explain why John does not include a depiction of the Last Supper proper. John primarily relates the manner in which, through instruction and faithful belief and worship, Jesus' disciples can enjoy salvation and the eternal life that is already made available to them. If we read into Vaughan's poem this emphasis on salvation through a proper belief in Christ as good shepherd, we can understand why salvation and spiritual "seeing" seem to precede the Supper, even though Vaughan's elevation of the importance of the Supper strains against that Johannine approach.

Consider the way in which the bread of life narrative is used in "The Feast." Having established the weakness of his "poor flesh" (9), the speaker recalls John 6: "Come then true bread, / Quickning the dead, / Whose eater shall not, cannot dye, / Come, antedate / On me that state / Which brings poor dust the victory" (13–19). So far the true bread has not been lifted out of its Johannine context. Yet the middle of the poem describes the bread in unmistakably sacramental terms: "The food of mans immortal being! / Under veyls here / Thou art my chear, / Present and sure without my seeing" (39–42). Recall that the whole point of Christ's bread of life self-designation is to clarify the meaning of the true bread for those Capernaites who confuse Christ with the manna of the Old Testament. The burden of that narrative is to unveil rather than obscure Christ's message (although the spiritually ignorant will still not understand the meaning of the eternal life that spiritual eating/believing will grant). Vaughan has yoked a Johannine theme originally unconnected to the Eucharist to his meditation on the real presence of the Supper. The last line of the poem especially reflects Vaughan's fondness for intermingling scriptural notions: "But let me heed, / Why thou didst bleed, / And what in the next world to eat" (76–8). As if to place the Johannine material back in its proper context, the final lines focus more on a deferral of sacramental eating and the speaker's attempt to understand properly the signification of the Passion.

Directly influenced by Herbert's "Peace" and "The H. Communion" (*Temple*), "The Sap" is perhaps Vaughan's most thoroughly Johannine meditation on the Eucharist. Unlike comparable lyrics, "The Sap" relies on John 6 less for its identification of eating and believing and more for the Christological coming–going motif that frames the poem. "Come sapless Blossom" (1), the narrator entreats, to a place beyond the stars, "an hil of myrrh / From which some drops fal here" (11–12), which immediately recalls the typological correction Jesus provides in John 6. If Moses promised manna from heaven, Christ provides the true bread "which commeth downe from heaven, and giveth life unto the world" (6:33). That is where Christ now dwells, providing the "way" (15) back (recalling John 14:6), but the speaker is reminded that this Prince of Salem had made a temporary sojourn on Earth—"Yet liv'd he here sometimes" (17)—before bearing a world of misery. To partake of the "sap" (27), his "sacred bloud" (26) and cordial, the speaker will "exalt and rise" (32) such that he will "Confess the Comfort such, as even / Brings to, and comes from Heaven" (49–50). The speaker's movement from earth to heaven parallels Christ's coming and returning from heaven. The implication is that the speaker had been sanctified through his baptismal "first birth" (then in a metaphorical heaven) but is now desperately in need of exaltation. In the final couplet's emphasis on the speaker's "Comfort" (49) that comes from but brings him to heaven (the use of "comes" recalling the opening invitation, "Come sapless Blossom"), the ending reinforces the idea that Christ, too, came from heaven, paused momentarily on Earth, and then returned to his Father, providing to his believers perseverance and spiritual ease: "assures that you / Shal find a Joy so true" (45–6).

The sending or commissioning of Christ by the Father is a distinctive Johannine theme, voiced throughout the Fourth Gospel, especially in chapters 6 and 8. That the divinely pre-existent Son makes a temporary stop on earth is also suggested in Christ's pithy claim, "I know whence I came, and whither I goe: but ye cannot tell whence I come, and whither I goe" (8:14). John 6, in particular, uses the terminology of "coming" and "sending" in several verses to describe Christ's unique commission by the Father: "The bread of God is hee which commeth downe from heaven" (6:33); "I am the bread of life: hee that commeth to me, shall never hunger" (6:35); "All that the Father giveth mee, shall come to mee; and him that commeth to me, I will in no wise cast out. For I came downe from heaven, not to doe mine owne will, but the will of him that sent me" (6:37–8). While the Son returns to the Father from whom he is sent, he provides special comfort in returning or coming again to the brethren through the agency of the Spirit-Paraclete: "I wil not leave you comfortlesse, I will come to you" (14:18).

Borrowing much of the language of the Johannine commissioning of Christ, Vaughan is able, as is Herbert, his master, to maintain a high Christological focus on Christ's presence mostly in heaven. To this end, the ambiguous syntax of the couplet—"That you'l Confess the Comfort such, as even / Brings to, and comes from Heaven" (49–50)—is explained in the context of John 14:18. The partaking of Christ's blood or sap will provide comfort to the speaker not merely because he (along with Christ) will have been brought to heaven, but also because Christ, in the manifestation of the Comforter, will "come" down from heaven again to help seal the sacrament. Vaughan's speaker has earlier anticipated this comforting office of Christ as Spirit when remarking: "But going hence, and knowing wel what woes / Might his friends discompose" (23–4), Christ gave his sacred blood. Again we hear the echo of Christ's farewell speech: "Let not your heart bee troubled, neither let it bee afraid. Ye have heard how I saide unto you, I goe away, and come againe unto you" (14:27–8).

The gesturing toward Christ and the Spirit as Comforter helps us to realize that Vaughan's "The Sap" is, like Herbert's "The H. Communion" (*Temple*), a pneumatological meditation on the Eucharist. What exactly is the restorative sap in Vaughan's poem? It is evidently Christ's sacred blood: "He gave his sacred bloud / By wil our sap" (26–7). Yet that sacramental gift works its restorative efficacy pneumatologically, the only way that Christ can enter into the communicant given that he has returned to the "hil of myrrh" (11). Calvin makes much the same point in a sermon on Ephesians: "We live of his owne substance, as a tree draweth his sap from his roote…so have wee a secret union…bycause that although Jesus Christ bee in heaven, yit he fayleth not too dwell in us."[145] The sap provides to Vaughan's communicant the "secret life" and "virtue" (31), echoing Calvin's conception of the "secret virtue of the Holy Spirit" that bequeaths Eucharistic strength and nourishment.[146] The identification of Christ as "spiritual sap," especially regarding his Eucharistic presence, is commonly found in seventeenth-century English commentaries. Thus George Downame: "For by faith we are rooted in Christ, & by it, we apprehending Christ and his righteousnes, draw from him spirituall sappe & nourishment, which in the scriptures is called the eating of his body and drinking of his blood."[147] A later treatise by Samuel Hudson on the corporate body of Christ more explicitly invokes the Spirit as sap: "By mystical body be meant the company of elect, faithful ones, that are knit to Christ by the Spirit on his part, and by faith on their part, and receive spiritual sap and vertue."[148] In Vaughan's poem, the "secret" meal that will exalt the speaker and "actuate such spirits as are shed / Or ready to be dead" (33–4)—the very meal that will provide spiritual "Comfort" (49) while Christ is in heaven—is not the meal of Christ's body and blood but the exalting and assuring Spirit that provides a balm to his aching soul.

Yet "The Sap," like all of Vaughan's Eucharistic meditations, is as concerned with protocols of spiritual preparation for the sacrament as it is with the actual taking of Christ's mystical body. From the outset, the personified sapless blossom is reminded of a prior benevolent infusion (9) that explains its stretching toward heaven and informs the communicant of the good news ahead. That infusion is later described as the speaker's residual but efficacious rare dew: "There is at all times (though shut up) in you / A powerful, rare dew, / Which only grief and love extract; with this / Be sure, and never miss, / To wash your vessel wel" (39–43). Much of the language

---

[145] John Calvin, *The sermons of M. John Caluin, upon the Epistle of S. Paule to the Ephesians*, trans. Arthur Golding (London, 1577), 140.

[146] Calvin, *Institutes*, Book IV, 563.

[147] George Downame, *The covenant of grace or An exposition upon Luke 1. 73.74.75* (London, 1631), 341.

[148] Samuel Hudson, *A vindication of the essence and unity of the church catholike visible* (London, 1650), 6.

here recalls Vaughan's preparative meditations in *The Mount of Olives*, where communicants are advised that they need to spend three days preparing their "vessel" before they can conscientiously receive the Eucharist.[149] Notable about the preparation in "The Sap" is the extent to which the verses on preparation, besides being more frequent and detailed than the verses on the ordinance proper, so praise the virtuous results of the cleansing exercises that the consequences of the preparatory exercises are rendered nearly as efficacious as the Communion itself. Prior to the Eucharist, the communicant can extract the always-present and "powerful, rare dew" through the purifying means of grief and love. The rare dew, itself recalling the earlier referenced shedding spirits, is not so much transformed or displaced by the sacramental sap as it is "actuated" by the sap, as if the sap, which might "add" some spirit, fundamentally restores the potency of the dew. Note the repetition of the word "sure" in the section on preparation. The enjambed "for sure / To all your pow'r most pure" (37–8) and the metrically clipped spondee of "Be sure" (42) help to conflate the preparatory exercise with the assured spiritual outcome. In addition to the enjambment of "sure," the word's repetition five lines later—"with this / Be sure, and never miss" (41–2)—accents the spiritual surety that the preparatory exercises sufficiently can achieve. Here, as in Vaughan's other Eucharistic meditations, the ordinance of the Eucharist serves primarily to seal or at most to rekindle the communicant's spirit-guided growth toward Christ.

Another way of saying this, in keeping with the final lines of "The Sap," is that the spiritual sap administered during the Eucharist provides assurance of salvation that is itself partially achievable through the preparatory exercises. Like Herbert's "Assurance," Vaughan's "The Sap" asserts that personal assurance is the endpoint of the sacramental process: "Then humbly take / This balm for souls that ake, / And one who drank it thus, assures that you / Shal find a Joy so true, / Such perfect Ease, and such a lively sense / Of grace against all sins" (43–8). The emphasis on the "true" and perfect joy recalls the lines on assurance in 1 John 3:19—"And hereby wee know that wee are of the trueth, and shall assure our hearts before him"—as well as (given the poem's final emphasis on the ease and comfort that the coming and going of the Son and Spirit provide) the assurance promised by Christ in the Farewell Discourse: "Peace I leave with you, my peace I give unto you . . . let not your heart bee troubled, neither let it bee afraid. Ye have heard how I saide unto you, I goe away, and come againe unto you" (14:27–8). In the context of Vaughan's poem, we would do well to recall that the Johannine promise of a peaceful, assured union with Christ through the comforting office of the Spirit-Paraclete, which depends on creaturely love and a reception of divine *agape*, is achievable in the absence of a specified Eucharistic rite. "The Sap" is an unmistakably Eucharistic poem. Yet as in all of his other Eucharist lyrics, Vaughan relies on the non-Eucharistic sense and language of key Johannine verses in order to underscore the importance of the Communion itself, in this case the partaking of the spiritual presence of Christ's body. And again, the preparatory exercises are so integral to the process that they tend to qualify the relative importance of the sacramental eating.

[149] See, for example, Vaughan, *The Mount of Olives*, 155.

Vaughan shares with Herbert an appreciation of the symbolic and preparatory function of the bread of life narrative. Yet he conflates this appreciation of Johannine belief, through which the communicant is ideally granted grace and eternal life, with a much different conception of the sacramental efficacy of the elements of the institution. In a certain sense, Vaughan wants his Johannine spiritual bread and wants his speaker to eat it too. Much has been written about Vaughan's tendency to rewrite Anglican rites and liturgical practices in the poems of *Silex Scintillans* and devotional manuals such as *The Mount of Olives*. The latter book serves, in some respects, as a surrogate or alternative Prayer Book for steadfast Anglicans during the Interregnum.[150] Jonathan Post has argued that sections of *The Mount of Olives* recreate the "structure and experience of the Holy Communion, as Vaughan plays both minister and communicant."[151] As Post notes, the sensitive political context dictated that Vaughan replace public aspects of the ceremony such as the Creed and Lord's Prayer with a more private desire to imitate Christ, a model "'life of Christ,' the archetypal sufferer, on whom the partaker is to meditate before, during, and after the ceremony."[152] I would suggest that Vaughan's desire to integrate such a personal Christology with more formal ceremonialism is itself reflected in his tendency to mold Johannine material to more purely Eucharistic ends. The bread of life discourse helps Vaughan meditate on the signification of the Incarnation and Passion and the extent to which his poetic personae are fit objects to receive the Communion. Vaughan does not set out simply to justify covertly or allegorically the liturgy and Prayer Book Communion. His fraught and uncertain reflections on the sacramental presence suggest that the very inaccessibility of the Prayer Book forced him to ponder more broadly the significance and personal experience of receiving the Eucharist. It is as if his recasting the bread of life in Eucharistic terms is Vaughan's way of cultivating, perhaps rationalizing, belief in the truth of the real presence in the absence of the practiced ritual. This positions Vaughan's lyrics closer to a Eucharistic poetics proper than even Richard Crashaw's treatment of the sacrament. Despite his counter-Reformation sensibilities, Crashaw adheres to a more faithful embrace of the Johannine tradition on which he, too, draws. We turn now to Crashaw's appropriation of an earlier passage in John 6, the well-known narrative of the "feeding of the five thousand" at John 6:1–11.

RICHARD CRASHAW AND JOHANNINE MISUNDERSTANDING

All of the Gospels provide commentary on Christ's feeding of the five thousand, the miracle that Christ performs, upon arriving in Galilee, whereby he feeds five thousand with five loaves of bread. John's reconstruction is as follows:

---

[150] See Jonathan F. S. Post, *Henry Vaughan: The Unfolding Vision* (Princeton: Princeton University Press, 1982), 123–7; and Philip West, *Henry Vaughan's Silex Scintillans: Scripture Uses* (Oxford: Oxford University Press, 2001), 72–5.
[151] Post, *Henry Vaughan: The Unfolding Vision*, 126. [152] Ibid., 126.

> After these things Jesus went ouer the sea of Galilee, which is the sea of Tiberias: And
> a great multitude followed him, because they saw his miracles which hee did on them
> that were diseased. And Jesus went up into a mountaine, and there hee sate with his
> disciples. And the Passeover, a feast of the Iewes, was nigh. When Jesus then lift up his
> eyes, and saw a great company come unto him, he saith unto Philip, Whence shall we
> buy bread, that these may eate? (And this he said to prove him: for he himselfe knew
> what he would doe). Philip answered him, Two hundred peny-worth of bread is not
> sufficient for them, that every one of them may take a litle. One of his disciples,
> Andrew, Simon Peters brother, saith unto him, There is a lad here, which hath five
> barley loaves, and two small fishes: but what are they among so many? And Jesus said,
> Make the men sit downe. Now there was much grasse in the place. So the men sate
> downe, in number about five thousand. And Jesus tooke the loaves, and when he had
> given thankes, hee distributed to the disciples, and the disciples to them that were set
> downe. (6:1–11)

John's recounting is notably distinguished from the other three Gospel depictions
in terms of its context. In Matthew, Mark, and Luke, the miracle of the multiplied
loaves is framed by the preceding beheading of John the Baptist and further miracles of Jesus, including his walking on water and the healing at Gennesaret.
However, John's narrative, which does include a brief account of Jesus' walking on
water, serves as a thematic preface to the bread of life pericope. Calvin reminds his
readers that the prefatory service of the miracle of the loaves is paramount for John,
who includes the miracle "expressly to go on to the discourse Christ delivered the
next day at Capernaum, since the two were connected. So this narrative, though
common to the other three Evangelists as well, is peculiar in being directed to
another object, as we shall see."[153] That other object, the bread of life narrative, is
tied to the feeding of the five thousand account by Jesus' important transitional
statement at 6:25–6. Once the disciples re-encounter Jesus across the sea at
Capernaum, they ask: "Rabbi, when camest thou hither?" to which Jesus responds:
"Verely, verely I say unto you, Ye seeke me, not because ye saw the miracles, but
because yee did eate of the loaves, and were filled." The meaning of this statement—
that the disciples seek Christ, as Calvin remarks, "for the sake of the belly and not
of the signs" and so do not recognize him as the Messiah—retroactively clarifies
the meaning of the feeding of the five thousand and anticipates the concluding
sentiment of the bread of life verses that, as we have seen, signify that the flesh
profits nothing.[154] We should not miss the irony of the Johannine narrative. John
proclaims at the outset, unlike the Synoptics, that the disciples have followed Jesus
in order to witness additional miracles: "And a great multitude followed him,
because they saw his miracles which hee did on them that were diseased" (6:2).
That appreciation of Jesus' power as pedagogically evidenced by his miracles is
sloughed off by the miracle of multiplied loaves, which whets a desire for further
carnal rather than spiritual eating.

---

[153] John Calvin, *The Gospel According to St. John*, in *Calvin's New Testament Commentaries*, vol. 4,
eds. David W. Torrance and Thomas F. Torrance, trans. T. H. L. Parker (Grand Rapids: Eerdmans
Publishing Company, 1959), 144.
[154] Ibid., 153.

It is precisely this Johannine irony that is expressed in Crashaw's well-known Divine Epigrams 19 and 20 on Christ's feeding of the five thousand. Both epigrams have erroneously been described as "types" of the institution of the Eucharist.[155] Epigram 19, "On the miracle of multiplied loaves," reads: "See here an easie Feast that knowes no wound, / That under Hungers Teeth will needs be sound: / A subtle Harvest of unbounded bread, / What would ye more? Here food it selfe is fed."[156] One editor of Crashaw's verse remarks that "notable in the epigrams are the ideas of abundance and effortlessness: 'food itself' (4) is the body of Christ."[157] Certainly Christ's body, particularly in the communitarian/corporate sense of the Church itself, is fed by the bountiful bread. But the point of Epigram 19 is that "abundance" has not been properly understood in its spiritual signification. "Hungers teeth" points to a carnal appetite that will not find satisfaction in Christ's message but only in additional corporeal eating. The crucial line is "What would ye more?" (4), which refers not only to the unsatisfied desire for more food but also to the desire for further miracles that would compare to the "subtlety" of the miracle of food feeding on itself.

The meaning behind Crashaw's question—"What would ye more?"—echoes the interrogative phrasing and significations of John 6:28–32:

> Then said they unto him, What shall we doe, that we might worke the workes of God? Jesus answered, and said unto them, This is the worke of God, that ye beleeve on him whom he hath sent. They said therefore unto him, What signe shewest thou then, that we may see, and beleeve thee? What doest thou worke? Our fathers did eate Manna in the desert, as it is written, He gave them bread from heaven to eate. Then Jesus said unto them, Verely, verely I say unto you, Moses gave you not that bread from heaven, but my Father giveth you the true bread from heaven.

Not content with the signs of Christ's power and feebly playing the Mosaic account of manna in the desert against Christ's miraculous provisions, the crowd asks for yet additional miracles, further evidence of his power. Crashaw's "What would ye more?" recalls the chastising of those Capernaites who need continual instruction regarding both the tenor and vehicles of Jesus' miracles.

Crashaw's subsequent Divine Epigram 20, "On the Miracle of Loaves," achieves its irony when read alongside the earlier Divine Epigram 19 and in the context of John 6:35–9. "On the Miracle of Loaves" reads economically: "Now Lord, or never, they'l beleeve on thee, / Thou to their Teeth hast prov'd thy Deity." Epigram 20 crucially adds two elements to the preceding Epigram 19. The proper witnessing of the miracle should foster "belief" not merely in Jesus' power to feed the hungry but also in Jesus' divine nature. If the irony of Epigram 19 is explained in the context of John 6:28–32, the irony of Epigram 20 is explained in the context

---

[155] George Walton Williams notes that Epigrams 19–21 "are two of the seven epigrams that Crashaw devoted to this miracle [of multiplied loaves], regarding it as a type of the institution of the Eucharist." *The Complete Poetry of Richard Crashaw*, ed. George Walton Williams (New York: New York University Press, 1972), 15.

[156] All references to Crashaw's poetry will be taken from Williams, ed., *The Complete Poetry of Richard Crashaw*.

[157] Ibid., 15.

of John 6:35–8: "And Jesus said unto them, I am the bread of life: hee that commeth to me, shall neuer hunger: and he that beleeveth on me, shall never thirst.
But I said unto you, that ye also have seene me, and beleeve not. All that the Father
giveth mee, shall come to mee; and him that commeth to me, I will in no wise
cast out. For I came downe from heaven, not to doe mine owne will, but the will
of him that sent me." The point of this passage, the very passage that informs
Augustine's identification of eating with believing, is that the disciples' focus on
carnal eating over the signification of Jesus' miracles itself reveals their refusal to
recognize Jesus' divinity. If we assume that Crashaw is vindicating the local, corporeal presence in the bread by baring the "teeth" of the partakers, we import the
entire Johannine context of the feeding of the five thousand into a sacramental
context that the performance of the miracle does not suggest. To appreciate that
eating with the teeth will not enable belief in Christ as God is to realize not so
much Crashaw's ingenuity as his subtle understanding of the Johannine passages
on which Epigrams 19 and 20 are based.

Of Crashaw's use of the epigrammatic form, which Crashaw clearly borrows
from the classical heritage, especially Martial and Catullus, Austin Warren has
remarked: "The 'point' of Crashaw's epigrams lies customarily in…paradox or
antithesis."[158] Sacred epigrammatists in the Jesuit tradition indeed favored these
and related rhetorical figures (including apostrophe, maxim, and pun) over elaborate metaphorical conceits. And sacred epigrammatists could find models of antithesis
throughout the New Testament, as in the fundamental paradox of "mors tibi vita
mea" (Christ's death is our salvation) or more pastorally in the Pauline maxim:
"The wisdom of this world is foolishness with God."[159] The Davidic Psalms rely on
so many epigrammatic tropes of antithesis that John Trapp describes them as
"Epigrammes of the Holy Ghost himself."[160] However, a distinguishing feature of
the Fourth Gospel is that it does not employ the epigrammatic style in the manner
of the Synoptic Gospels (a style borrowed from Wisdom texts). Rather than rely on
pithy, epigrammatic sayings, the Fourth Gospel, as we have begun to see, relies
on dramatic irony in order to underscore discipleship misunderstanding, and such
irony employs a technique of repetition and amplification rather than an emblematic or epigrammatic distillation of Christ's teachings.[161] Crashaw's Johannine-
inspired epigrams are remarkable in merging the distinctive epigrammatic use of
distichs with the less traditional use of epigrammatic irony (as opposed to paradox
and antithesis) in order to convey the fundamental ironies of disbelief particular to

---

[158] Austin Warren, *Richard Crashaw: A Study in Baroque Sensibility* (Ann Arbor: University of
Michigan Press, 1957), 83.

[159] On such scriptural uses of paradox and antithesis, see Warren, *Richard Crashaw*, 82–3.

[160] John Trapp, *A commentary or exposition upon the books of Ezra, Nehemiah, Esther, Job and Psalms*
(London, 1657), 892.

[161] On the use of repetition and amplification in the Fourth Gospel, see *Repetitions and Variations
in the Fourth Gospel: Style, Text, Interpretation*, eds. G. Van Belle, M. Labhan, and P. Maritz (Leuven:
Uitgeverij Peeters, 2009), especially Gilbert Van Belle, "Theory of Repetitions and Variations in the
Fourth Gospel: A Neglected Field of Research?" 25–6.

the Fourth Gospel.[162] It has been said that Crashaw's sacred verse should be described as sacred parody or satire, given that the epigrams and shorter poems transform the secular into the sacred.[163] Another manifestation of such sacred satire is vested in those divine epigrams that satirize the unbelief of the prototypical Pharisees of the Fourth Gospel.

Two of Crashaw's other well-known epigrams, Divine Epigram 44, "On our crucified Lord Naked, and bloody," and Divine Epigram 17, "Blessed be the paps which Thou hast sucked," find their principal source texts in the piercing of Christ's side during the crucifixion, a piercing that, among the four Gospels, appears only in John:

> But one of the souldiers with a speare pierced his side, and forthwith came there out blood and water. And he that saw it, bare record, and his record is true, and he knoweth that hee saith true, that yee might beleeve. For these things were done, that the Scripture should be fulfilled, A bone of him shall not be broken. And againe another Scripture saith, They shall looke on him whom they pierced. (19:34-7)

The centurion who pierces Christ (who comes to be known as Longinus, since the etymology of the name suggests "holy lance") sets out to discover whether Christ has really died.[164] Patristic through early modern commentators were particularly interested in the symbolism of the blood and water that pour from Jesus' open wound.[165] Augustine's commentary heavily influenced early modern exegetes. In his Homily on John 19, Augustine writes:

> The Evangelist used a wide awake word so that he did not say, 'pierced his side' or 'wounded' or anything else, but 'opened,' so that there, in a manner of speaking, the door of life was thrown open from which the mystical rites of the Church flowed, without which one does not enter into the life which is true life. That blood was shed for the remission of sins; that water provides the proper mix for the health-giving cup; it offers both bath and drink. There was a foretelling of this in that Noe was ordered to make a door in the side of the ark where the animals that were not going to perish in the flood might enter, and in these [animals] the Church was prefigured. For this reason the first woman was made from the side of a sleeping man.... For indeed it signified a great good, before the great evil of collusive transgression. Here the second Adam, his head bowed, slept on the cross in order that from there might be found for him a wife—that one who flowed from the side of the One sleeping. O death from which the dead live again! What is cleaner than this blood? What is more healthful than this wound?[166]

---

[162] English epigrammatists of course employed the figure of irony, although one finds its use typically in the secular, more satirical verse of poets such as Ben Jonson. On Jonson's epigrammatic irony, see R. V. Young, "Style and Structure in Jonson's Epigrams," *Criticism* 17:3 (1975), 201–22.

[163] See R. V. Young, *Richard Crashaw and the Spanish Golden Age* (New Haven: Yale University Press, 1982), chapter 2, *passim*.

[164] As in the early English anonymous poem "O, my heart is woe": "I looked on my sweet son on the cross that I stood under; / Then came Longeus with a spear and cleft his heart in sunder" (21–2). *The Faber Book of Religious Verse*, ed. Helen Gardner (London: Faber & Faber, 1972), 66–7.

[165] In *A Reading of George Herbert*, 32–3, Rosemond Tuve provides several images of the piercing that were popularized in the *Biblia Pauperum*.

[166] Saint Augustine, *Tractates on the Gospel of John, 111–24*, ed. John W. Rettig (Washington, D.C.: Catholic University Press, 1995), 50–1.

Augustine and early modern exegetes interpret the blood as a symbol of justification and the water as a symbol of baptism. The opening is read typologically as the door provided by Noah, itself a prefiguration of the invisible and visible church. Much interpretive labor focused on the exact nature and location of the wound, given the difficulty of explaining why the blood would be intermixed with water. Calvin, for example, denies that anything miraculous had transpired: "It is natural for congealed blood to lose its red colour and become like water. It is also well known that water is contained in the membranes next to the heart."[167] As I describe at length in Chapter 6, early modern commentators typically locate the wound at the site of the "pericardion," a sack-like bag or film variously described as a "cawl," "pannicle," or "casket" that surrounded and protected the heart and that would have emitted blood in addition to water.[168] For example, in *The Golden Chaine* (1600), William Perkins describes the pericardion as a casket or "coate": "For seeing that water and blood gushed forth together, it is very like, the casket or coate which inuesteth the heart called *Pericardion,* was pierced"; comparable descriptions of the pericardion appear in manuals on health and the humours, as in Levinus Lemnius's *Touchstone of Complexions* (1576), where the pericardion is described as a "pannicle or coffin."[169]

Crashaw's "On our crucified Lord Naked, and bloody" describes the outpouring blood from Jesus' pierced side as a garment or wardrobe: "Thee with thy selfe they have too richly clad, / Opening the purple wardrobe of thy side. / O never could bee found Garments too good / For thee to weare, but these, of thine owne blood" (3–6). Commentators have typically understood Mark 15 and Matthew 27 to be the source texts for the purple or scarlet robe first given to Christ by the centurions but then removed just before the crucifixion. According to the most sacramentalist interpretations of the poem, the literal robe, the governing vehicle of the poem (which is replaced by Jesus' robe of blood), motivates a typically odd and puzzling, even grotesque Crashavian conceit, one concerned to legitimate the real presence of transubstantiation. For Sophie Read, for example, the blood, congealing into another substance, evokes through metonymic sliding "the familiar but elusive paradoxes associated with the doctrine of transubstantiation, where wine and blood become, in substance, blood and body while remaining, in appearance, themselves."[170]

[167] John Calvin, *The Gospel According to St. John*, in *Calvin's New Testament Commentaries*, vol. 5, eds. David W. Torrance and Thomas F. Torrance, trans. T. H. L. Parker (Grand Rapids: Eerdmans Publishing Company, 1959), 185.

[168] Compare Origen's interpretation of the blood and water as presented in the 1660 English translation of his tract against Celsus. Despite his criticism of Celsus's incredible notion of the Homeric "immortal" blood from Christ's side, Origen still finds the effusion to be "preternatural": "In Dead Bodies, 'tis common for the Blood to stagnate, and we don't use, to see Water trickle down from the Veins; but when our *Saviour* was dead, Water, and Blood flow'd from his pierced Side, in a praeternatural Way. And if instead of putting an improper, and forc'd Sence, upon some Passages in the Gospels…one might easily perceive, that the Centurion, and they who were set to watch the dead Body of our *Saviour*…were struck with an unusual Terror, and said, *Truly this was the SON of GOD.*" *Origen against Celsus*, trans. James Bellamy (London, 1660), Book II, 95–6.

[169] William Perkins, *The Golden Chaine* (London, 1600), 31; Levinus Lemnius, *Touchstone of Complexions* (London, 1576), 113. The use of "cawl" to describe the pericardion itself derives from Hosea xiii 8, as noted in the *OED*: "I…will rent the kall of their hearts."

[170] Read, *Eucharist and the Poetic Imagination*, 142.

Without denying the inventiveness, even grotesquerie, of Crashaw's conceit of Christ wearing the garment of his own blood, we may reach a different interpretation if we put the poem in its guiding Johannine context. The paradox of the poem is that the horrific blood of Christ's wounds acquires a positive valence: "O ever could bee found Garments too good" (5). The benefit of the garments certainly stems from the sacramental benefits that the blood will come to signify. But the fact that Christ wears his own garment of blood is not necessarily suggestive of transubstantiation or the real presence. The metaphor is fitting, assuming the exegetical tradition that associated the wound with the piercing of the protective pericardion, that film or "garment" that shrouded the heart. To wear the blood that pours from the pierced wound is to transpose (not transubstantiate) that blood into another protective garment around Christ's body. It is as if the pericardion has been relocated from the interior to the exterior of Christ's body, no doubt an arresting image and process but not one necessarily linked to a poetics of real presence. This is Crashaw, like Vaughan, superimposing Johannine themes and source texts onto other scriptural texts through which he invents a novel conceit on the Passion.

A similar superimposition occurs in "Blessed be the paps." Here the Lukan source text is placed in the context of the Johannine piercing of Christ's side. Luke 11:27–8 reads: "And it came to passe as hee spake these things, a certaine woman of the company lift up her voice, and said unto him, Blessed is the wombe that bare thee, and the pappes which thou hast sucked. But hee said, Yea, rather blessed are they that heare the word of God, and keepe it." The meaning of the Lukan passage is clear. The woman's indirect praise of Mary is qualified by Christ's reminder that it is more of a blessing to embrace God's Word. While the opportunity to nurse Jesus is a gift, the more significant spiritual bestowal was to have been chosen by God to be Jesus' mother.

Crashaw's poem has been variously admired and vilified for its arresting image of the mother sucking on the bloody breast of Christ: "Hee'l have his Teat e're long (a bloody one) / The Mother then must suck the Son" (3–4). Empson famously found the poem perverse, attributing phallic qualities to the "long teat": "The second couplet is 'primitive' enough; a wide variety of sexual perversions can be included in the notion of sucking a long bloody teat which is also a deep wound."[171] Recent interpretations have shifted attention from the sexual to the sacramental. Sophie Read concludes of "Blessed be the paps" and "On the wounds of our crucified Lord" that both epigrams surprise the reader into an "absolutely visceral understanding of Christ's presence in the Host, and they do this by effacing the interim stages between crucifixion and communion: the blood-and-water that streams from the wounded Christ is shockingly figured as flowing directly into the mouths of the faithful. 'This is my blood indeed.'"[172] But again, the Johannine context assumes neither a sexual nor sacramental (corporeal) understanding of the

---

[171] See William Empson, *Seven Types of Ambiguity* (New York: New Directions, 1966), 221, cited in Williams, *The Complete Poetry of Richard Crashaw*, 14.
[172] Read, *Eucharist and the Poetic Imagination*, 137.

conceit. And since Crashaw's readers would have known that the blood issuing from Christ's piercing streamed from his side, and that the wound was most probably a heart wound, the association of the wound with the breast renders contrived any erotic connotation according to which the epigram figures a sexual perversion, as Empson would have it. Regarding the belief that the epigram depicts graphically the real presence of the communion: Crashaw's image of sucking Christ's bloody teat follows naturally from his chiasmic manipulation of the Lukan passage on the nursing of Christ by Mary. Crashaw doesn't invent the conceit whole cloth; he justifies the conceit from the source text. And the source text has little to do with sacramental eating. Sucking the blood of the Son can be associated during the period with spiritual nourishment and "divine milk" that do not imply the Lord's Supper.[173] Even when the image of sucking blood from Christ's breast does evoke the Supper, it does not necessarily signify the real presence. Vaughan, for example, incorporates the image (typically associated with Cyprian's *De Coena Domini*) into his Johannine prayer on the bread of life in *The Mount of Olives*: "Grant that I may suck salvation from thy heart, that spring of the blood of God, which flowes into all believers."[174] The blood flows from the heart, providing salvation to all, a metaphor of spiritual nourishment that can as easily suggest a spiritual eating as a corporeal one.

Where we might expect a poetics of the real presence, Crashaw's graphic reconstruction of the Passion in his several epigrams and shorter verse appropriates both the spirit and the letter of Johannine source texts. Not only do his best epigrams convey the importance of belief in Christ and the Spirit rather than corporeal eating or a partaking of the real presence, but, as is the case especially with Epigrams 19 and 20, they reveal Crashaw's appreciation and emulation of the use of irony in the Johannine material, particularly the subtle rhetorical ways in which Christ reprimands the unenlightened who cannot understand the symbolic nature of his perfective work. Does this mean that, as revisionist criticism has pointed out, Crashaw's counter-Reformation sensibilities have been exaggerated, especially given the fact that Crashaw most likely composed most of his poems while still firmly a member of the Anglican Church?[175] Perhaps so, although my goal here has been only to point out that our first approach to the Crashavian material glossed above should align with Crashaw's tendency above all to render faithfully

---

[173] See Williams, *The Complete Poetry of Richard Crashaw*, 14.

[174] See Vaughan, *The Mount of Olives*, 163. On the vexed authorship of *De Coena Domini*, which is typically attributed to Cyprian but which seems to have its source in Ernaldus Bonaevallis's *Liber de Cardinalibus*, see Nicholas Thompson, *Eucharistic Sacrifice and Patristic Tradition in the Theology of Martin Bucer*, 1534–46 (Leiden: Brill, 2005), 76. In its fuller signification, the image from Bonaevallis does suggest a carnal eating—"[We] fasten a tongue between the very wounds of our redeemer"—but neither Vaughan nor Crashaw follows the letter of the source text. On the manipulability of the image, see Jeremy Taylor's *The real presence and spirituall of Christ in the blessed sacrament* (London, 1653), 65.

[175] On the reductive tendency to canonize Crashaw as a one-sidedly Catholic poet, see Thomas F. Healy, *Richard Crashaw: A Biography* (Leiden: E. G. Brill, 1986), as well as Alison Shell, *Catholicism, Controversy, and the English Literary Imagination, 1558–1660* (Cambridge: Cambridge University Press, 1999), 97–104.

the content and signification of the Johannine material, even as Crashaw's imagery inevitably startles us with its extravagance, whether or not we deem that aestheticism to be Baroque in nature.

EDWARD TAYLOR'S PREPARATIONISM

I close this chapter with a turn to the work of the late-seventeenth-century American Puritan poet Edward Taylor. Taylor's provenance might seem to place him outside of the purview of this discussion of the Johannine influence on English devotional poeticizing on the nature of the Communion. Yet as Taylor's critics tend to agree, the influence of Herbert's poetry on Taylor's meditations is unmistakable, as are the larger concerns of a so-called Protestant poetics that seem to have influenced the devotional writings of his English "metaphysical" forebears. As the leader of the gathered Church in late-seventeenth-century Connecticut, Taylor displays a more stern Puritanism of the elect than do Herbert or Vaughan, particularly in his polemical work on the exclusionary and rigorist aspects of the *ordo salutis*. But I hope to show that he shares with his English devotional forebears a keen interest in the Johannine literature, particularly the bread of life figuration.

Taylor's *Treatise Concerning the Lord's Supper* was written in response to the polemical writings of Solomon Stoddard, leading pastor of the Congregationalist Church of Northampton, Massachusetts, and grandfather of Jonathan Edwards. Stoddard had rejected the so-called "Half-Way Covenant" developed at the Synod of 1662 in the Massachusetts Bay colony. The Covenant had dictated that all children of lapsed parents, those who might have received baptism but not the Lord's Supper, were to receive infant baptism. Although these children were halfway in the church, they eventually would be permitted to receive the Supper.[176] Stoddard believed that the Covenant remained too exclusionary. He argued, in a series of polemical writings, most notably *The Safety of Appearing at the Day of Judgment*, that the Supper should be made available to anyone who asked for it.[177] The premise of Stoddard's argument was that the Lord's Supper should serve as a converting ordinance, one that would serve as a "strengthening of faith," comparable to hearing and reading the Word.[178] Taylor's response, set forth in his *Treatise*, rejects Stoddard's notion of the Supper as a converting ordinance, claiming instead, through his recurring metaphor of wearing a proper "wedden garment" to the Supper, that preparation for the Supper requires a degree of evangelical righteousness approaching sanctified status. The crux of the debate centers on the causal nexus regarding grace and the Supper. For Stoddard the Supper is a means of begetting grace; for Taylor the Supper provides a seal and ratification of the grace that the communicant brings to the Table.

---

[176] I owe much of this summary to Norman S. Grabo's introduction to Taylor's *Treatise* in *Edward Taylor's Treatise Concerning the Lord's Supper*, ed. Norman S. Grabo (East Lansing: Michigan State University Press, 1966), xix–xx.

[177] Ibid., xix–xx. [178] Ibid., 22.

As we might expect, a proper understanding of John 6 frames much of the debate between Taylor and Stoddard. Stoddard had used key passages in John 6, especially the bread of life verses, to support his argument for opening the Supper to all desiring communicants. For Stoddard, God's gift of manna in the desert typologically mandates that spiritual nourishment should be bequeathed to all individuals regardless of whether they are spiritually dead. In his careful exposition of John 6:53–5, Taylor reminds his readers that Christ represents the true bread and means to eternal life for those who show genuine faith, concluding that the eating and drinking of John 6 should not be conflated with the sacramental inges- tion of the Supper: "He calls them therefore to eat His flesh and drink His blood, not in the sacrament of His Supper, for that was not as yet instituted; nor is it of such absolute necessity unto life as this is. But by true faith, which is the instru- ment of spiritual and eternal life."[179] Taylor's larger point is that, as a consecrated Church ordinance administered by ecclesiastical officials, the Supper demands a level of exclusionary solemnity that provides the "seals of the covenant of grace" only to worthy saints.[180] To treat the Supper as a fulfillment type of the distribu- tion of manna to the Israelites would be to divest it of its sanctified nature and reduce it to a "common matter to all, clean and unclean, baptized and unbaptized, to be used as our common food."[181]

Noteworthy about Taylor's remarks is that, although he clearly elevates the Supper in arguing that it should be granted only to the demonstrably faithful, he simultaneously diminishes its importance in the scheme of salvation, given his belief that the Supper alone will not lead to the eternal life promised by Christ in John's Gospel. So it is that Taylor follows those Reformed exegetes who, in the Augustinian tradition, tout the importance of proper belief in the economy of sal- vation, although he is more interested in arguing that the eating and drinking recommended in John is identifiable as a mode of belief than he is in promoting the idea that belief is fostered by the sacramental eating during the Supper. Preparation for the Supper is his primary debating point; and preparation requires a level of spiritual eating/believing that renders the communicant suitably garmented and ready to be called to the wedding feast of the Lord's Table: "Here is no offer of Christ to the unregenerate but only to the regenerate as appears in the duty called for: and this it to take, and eat, and drink, which are the duties of faith. To receive is in scripture to believe, and so is this eating and drinking, as John 6:53, 54."[182]

This elevation of the preparationist aspect of John's theology of eating and drink- ing Christ is fundamental to Taylor's poetic treatment of the theme in his *Meditations*. The sacramentalist poems consistently use John's verses to identify their relevance not to the Supper proper but to the required preparation thereof. In the First Series, "Meditation 40" reads the piercing of Christ's side at John 19 into the context of 1 John 2:2, the latter of which reveals the extent to which Christ's

---

[179] Ibid., 132.
[180] Ibid., 135. For a good although brief discussion of the sealing function of the Supper, see Johnson, *Made Flesh*, 63–5.
[181] Ibid., 135.   [182] Ibid., 137.

death satisfies our sins ("And he is the propitiation for our sinnes: and not for ours onely, but also for the sinnes of the whole world"). The blood and water that pour from Christ's side do not anticipate the Eucharist so much as they do the baptismal washing and purging that would precede it: "Thus quench thy burning flame / In that clear stream that from his side forth brake.... From all Defilement me cleanse, wash and rub... This reeching Vertue of Christs blood will quench / Thy Wrath, slay Sin and in thy Love mee bench" (51–2, 57, 65–6).[183] There is no question here of interpreting the receiving of Christ's blood as an ingestion of a real (substantial) presence. The blood is identified with the propitiatory "virtue" that will slay sin and provide the speaker's renewal in God.

When the poems more explicitly make reference to sacramental eating and drinking, as in the several meditations on John 6:51 and 6:55, they reflect, in proper Johannine context (and consistent with what we've seen in Herbert's verse), the nature of the Ascension, focusing on Christ's location in heaven and the eternal life that will redound to those faithful who spiritually eat/drink Christ. "Meditation 8" in the First Series imagines, against any Catholic or traditional view of the priest consecrating the host, that the consecration itself takes place in heaven: "And he to end all strife / The Purest Wheate in Heaven, his deare-dear Son / Grinds, and kneads up into this Bread of life. / Which Bread of life from Heaven down came and stands / Disht on thy Table up by Angells Hands" (20–4). The conduit that links the communicant's soul to God passes over any earthly intermediary: God does "mould" (25) the bread in heaven, and it arrives on the Table for the communicant. The result is the very "Grace" (31) kneaded in the loaf, the process of "eating" conducing to the eternal life promised in the source text: "Eate, Eate me, Soul, and thou shalt never dy" (35–6). Indeed, the speaker's sightline, established by the metaphor of "kening though Astronomy Divine" (1) wherein he espies a "Golden Path" (3) to the bright throne of heaven, never really resituates its vision toward anything but the celestial. "Heaven" and its cognates are invoked five times in the last three stanzas of a relatively short poem. To the extent that the speaker is convinced that he should eat "Heavens Sugar Cake" (30), he would only be eating the "grace" (31) kneaded into the loaf. If we take seriously Taylor's demonstrated polemical belief that the Johannine bread of life does not refer to the Eucharist, we can appreciate that the eating and feeding to which he refers here and elsewhere is a means of preparing the communicant for the consecrated eating of the Supper but it is no less important for serving as such, given that the Supper provides a seal of sanctified righteousness. As "Meditation 9" in the First Series suggests, the living bread is marvelous not only because it can "feed Dead Dust" (32) but because it can begin to renovate the most unregenerate of sinners: "Yet Wonder more by far may all, and some / That my Dull Heart's so dumpish when thus fed" (33–4). Like Vaughan's preparatory prayers that precede the Eucharist, Taylor's sentiments conclude beseechingly: "Lord Pardon this, and feed mee all my dayes, / With Living Bread to thy Eternall Prayse" (35–6).

---

[183] All references to Edward Taylor's poetry are taken from *The Poems of Edward Taylor*, ed. Donald E. Stanford (New Haven: Yale University Press, 1960).

This is not to say that Taylor's poems avoid puzzling over the mystery of the institution of the sacrament and the presence of Christ's body therein. Nor should we assume that Taylor's *Treatise on the Supper* serves as a proof-text for the theology of the poetry. "Meditation 10" in the First Series, on "My blood is drink indeed" from John 6:55, opens with an acknowledgement of the way in which the speaker's backsliding—"My Soule had Caught an Ague, and like Hell / Her thirst did burn" (7–8)—is reversed by Christ's well-sprung blood: "But this bright blazing Love did spring a Well / Of Aqua-Vitae in the Deity, / Which on the top of Heav'ns high Hill out burst / And down came running thence t'ally my thirst" (8–12). The blood spills down from heaven, again keeping the element away from Christ's corporeality. But then Taylor's speaker directly confronts the wondrous question of the Communion: "But how it came, amazeth all Communion. / Gods onely Son doth hug Humanity, / Into his very person. By which Union / His Humane Veans its golden gutters ly. / And rather than my Soule should dy by thirst, / These Golden Pipes, to give me drink, did burst" (13–18). In bringing the focus to the "very person" of Christ that hugs humanity in the offering of blood, Taylor comes close to locating the element of blood in the accessible body of Christ. Yet what he provides prosodically he qualifies poetically, for all of the metaphors lift that body back up to heaven. The veins and vessels of the blood are described as "golden gutters" and "Golden Pipes"; the sparkling liquor is crafted by "Art Divine" (19); and the blessed nectar is locked up with "Saph'rine Taps" (26). If this is "drink indeed," the refrain to the poetic meditation, the poem refuses to settle on any earthly source for that drink, the speaker content to be thankful for this "strange thing": "Nay, though I make no pay for this Red Wine, / And scarce do say I thank-ye-for't; strange thing! / Yet were thy silver skies my Beer bowle fine / I finde my Lord, would fil it to the brim" (37–40). Taylor provocatively leaves open the question of whether the speaker has received the Eucharist proper or whether he has simply been prepared for that participatory seal. The final couplet hints that he has been renewed to the extent that he will continue to praise the Lord for the gift of blood: "Then make my life, Lord, to thy praise proceed / For thy rich blood, which is my Drink-Indeed" (41–2).

We can see that Taylor follows Vaughan, despite their much different denominational allegiances, in refusing to conflate the bread of life and the Eucharistic meal. Both writers understand the bread of life source text in the manner of their English and continental forebears: not simply as a preparation for the Supper but as the means by which Christ's Johannine community, through the testimony of its belief, becomes properly incorporated into Christ and God. The Supper proper is more a manifestation and seal of eternal life than a ritualistic means to holiness. When Taylor does directly poeticize the Supper, he further follows Vaughan as well as Herbert in isolating the heavenly and hence incorporeal nature of Christ, which renders impossible the location of Christ's body in the elements of the Eucharistic meal. Of course, all of the devotional poets discussed above deviate from any singular or dogmatic theology, inventively playing on the store of terms, symbols, and emblems associated with eating Christ's body and drinking his blood. Despite such poeticization of the source material, however, all four poets draw either directly or

indirectly on the seminal, if often overlooked, Johannine approach to the relationship between the bread of life and the Eucharist. And we have begun to see, at least
in Crashaw's epigrams, the ways in which the rhetorical approach of Johannine
irony itself underlies the poetic treatment of the source material on the sacrament.
This Johannine use of irony becomes particularly evident in the sixteenth- and
seventeenth-century treatments of another frequently glossed set of verses that
appear only in John's Gospel, the *noli me tangere* and *hortulanus* narratives of John
20, to which we now turn.

2

Noli Me Tangere and the Reception of Mary Magdalene in Early Modern England

Recent criticism of the early modern understanding of the *noli me tangere* ("touch me not") pericope of John 20 has emphasized the extent to which devotional writers such as Robert Southwell, Gervase Markham, Thomas Walkington, and Nicholas Breton weigh the importance of Mary's spiritual seeing versus physical touching of the newly resurrected Christ. On the early modern reception of Christ's puzzling words to Mary regarding her excessive weeping and desire to touch Christ corporeally, Patricia Badir remarks that the early modern literary treatments of Magdalene at the sepulchre interpret *noli me tangere* and the preceding *hortulanus* sequence (in which Mary mistakes Christ for a gardener) as Christ's instruction to Mary to look for him within the recesses of her soul and memory. This fundamentally Augustinian, sublime, and purely figural way of seeing articulates a "sensual poetics of recollection that captures an idea of Christ's haunting, ever lively presence."[1] The Augustinian interpretation doubles with the transition from Catholic sacramentalism to Protestant iconophobia. Many of the homilists who memorialize Mary are forced simultaneously to negotiate the shift from a focus on the nourishment provided by Christ's body to an appreciation of the purely signifying effect of that body for the penitent.[2]

Such recent criticism has productively situated the early modern treatment of Mary Magdalene in the context of paradigmatic transitions from medieval-Catholic forms of devotional worship to Protestant spiritualism and affective individualism. Yet what gets left out of these treatments is the Johannine theology that informs Mary's colloquies with Christ in the Easter theology. Early modernists have made little of the fact that the *hortulanus* episode and the *noli me tangere* admonition appear only in the Fourth Gospel, a Gospel that, as we have begun to see, departs uniquely from the other New Testament accounts of Christology, soteriology, eschatology, and the very form and method of revelation that Christ employs in order to communicate with his brethren. I argue in this chapter that the early modern literary treatments of John 20 share with patristic, medieval, Reformed, and modern commentators a set of uniquely Johannine assumptions regarding Mary's encounter with Christ outside the tomb, assumptions that render the widely accepted "spiritual seeing" interpretation reductive and facile.

---

[1] Patricia Badir, *The Maudlin Impression: English Literary Images of Mary Magdalene, 1550–1700* (Notre Dame: University of Notre Dame Press, 2009), 65.
[2] Ibid., 70.

John relies in the Magdalene passages and throughout his Gospel on an ironic method of productive misunderstanding as a means of revelation. One crucial lesson entrusted to Christ's brethren is that, since Christ is identified at the outset with *Logos*, having descended from God, "hearing" Christ's words is superior to "seeing" Christ, whether seeing is understood literally or figuratively.[3] The early modern treatments of John 20, especially Southwell's *Marie Magdalens Funerall Teares* (1591), not only register the Johannine use of irony and misunderstanding to emphasize the importance of hearing over seeing but at times recapitulate the very form of Johannine tutelage. Southwell, for example, discourses with Mary in the manner in which Christ and the Johannine narrator engage with the disciples. When Southwell as narrator voices the obtuse or questioning disciple on Mary's behalf, he is, as Gary Kuchar has argued, enacting a mode of critical peripety in order to engage readers, but such an engagement is as much part of the Johannine source texts as it is Ignatian meditation or post-Reformed catechizing.[4] Additionally, most of the literary treatments of the *noli me tangere* and *hortulanus* episodes use John's Gospel as an intertext, referencing other Johannine passages, personages, and images in order to help illuminate the more circumscribed message of John 20.

I should state at the outset that, in reconstructing what I take to be the Johannine labors of Southwell and those poets influenced heavily by the "tears poetry" of which Southwell's work provides the finest example, I will not be recapitulating in detail the doctrinal disputes that critics have argued is poeticized in this tradition. Scholarly work on Southwell tends to be dominated by the assumption that his Jesuit recusancy and an early Baroque sensibility shape his portrait of Magdalene.[5] In her emotionalism and sensual eroticism rather than austere repentance, Southwell's Magdalene pines for Christ, according to recent criticism, as if she were crying for the loss of his body from the Roman Catholic Mass.[6] It might be true that the setting and atmosphere of Southwell's (and Crashaw's) graphic depiction of Magdalene's weeping, as opposed to what we find in the more restrained accounts of Markham or Breton, for example, rely on a counter-Reformation

---

   [3] The role of irony in Johannine revelation is described in detail in Gail R. O'Day, *Revelation in the Fourth Gospel: Narrative Mode and Theological Claim* (Philadelphia: Fortress Press, 1986): "Just as every irony statement requires an act of judgement on the reader's part to size up both levels of meaning and to make the correct move from the literal to the intended meaning, Jesus as revealer presupposes the same dynamic of understanding" (9).
   [4] Regarding Southwell's *St. Peters Complaint* in particular Gary Kuchar remarks in *The Poetry of Religious Sorrow in Early Modern England* (Cambridge: Cambridge University Press, 2008): "Through characterization by peripety, readers are being attuned to the gap between intention and meaning; they are being encouraged to recognize how the Spirit signifies in excess of Peter's knowledge as the saint tarries with the double motions of compunction, its oscillations between sin and grace" (34). I believe that the same pedagogy holds regarding Mary's errors but that we should trace this pedagogy to the Johannine writings before we do any particularized sixteenth-century denominational or confessional exercise.
   [5] That Southwell's portrait of Magdalene is informed by both a Jesuit and an early Baroque sensibility is the argument of Anne Sweeney's *Robert Southwell: Snow in Arcadia: Redrawing the English Lyric Landscape, 1586–1595* (Manchester: Manchester University Press, 2006), 140–57. See also F. W. Brownlow, *Robert Southwell* (New York: Twayne Publishers, 1996), especially chapter 1, *passim*.
   [6] Sweeney, *Robert Southwell*, 141.

aesthetic.[7] Yet my concern is to point out that Southwell's spiritual guide to understanding Magdalene is John's Gospel itself, which will help to explain why Southwell's account of John 20 converges with the early modern Protestant accounts of Magdalene at the tomb and with glosses that we find in Augustine's, Aquinas's, and Calvin's detailed commentaries on *noli me tangere*. The Southwell described in this chapter is more of an exegete and imitator of the Johannine presentation of Mary at Christ's tomb than he is a missionary Catholic.[8]

THE JOHANNINE ART OF HEARING

In the Fourth Gospel, Christ reveals himself primarily through words rather than signs. Christ establishes that, because he has directly heard from God the words that he preaches, to listen to him is to listen to God Himself: "I have many things to say, and to judge of you: But hee that sent mee is true, and I speake to the world, those things which I have heard of him" (8:26). To believe what Christ says is to evince discipleship, faith, and knowledge. And to hear productively is to hear Christ's words *directly*, as the Samaritans display after learning of the content and meaning of his miraculous provision of water: "Now we beleeve, not because of thy saying, for we have heard him our selves, and know that this is indeed the Christ, the Saviour of the world" (4:42). From faith through hearing comes the promise of eternal life, as Jesus avows in the Bethesda pericope: "Hee that heareth my word, & beleeveth on him that sent mee, hath everlasting life, and shall not come into condemnation: but is passed from death unto life" (5:24). To hear God's Word without creaturely mediation is rare and nearly as sacrosanct as seeing God directly, for only Jesus has had such a privilege: "And the Father himselfe which hath sent me, hath borne witnesse of me. Ye have neither heard his voyce at any time, nor seene his shape. And ye have not his word abiding in you: for whom he hath sent, him ye beleeve not" (5:37–8). Drawing on these passages and many others,

---

[7] One can find a Catholic or Jesuit position on repentance or co-operating grace in Southwell's *Funerall Teares*. In a compelling recent interpretation of the text, Brian Cummings remarks that Southwell's belief that Mary has "purchased" God's pardon relies on the language of contract or reciprocity: "The rub of the matter comes in the word 'purchased', which clearly implies a 'faculty' in Mary to procure Christ's forgiveness through repentance." *The Literary Culture of the Reformation: Grammar and Grace* (Oxford: Oxford University Press, 2002), 356. This indeed recalls some of the nuances of post-Tridentine doctrine. My point is only that Southwell's concern might also be to recover a tradition of exegeses on John 20, especially for pastoral purposes, that focuses on the importance of Christ's words in her conversion. This is an exercise in exegetical recovery that is not necessarily bent toward Catholic or Jesuit ends. Not everything Southwell says theologically about John 20 in *Funerall Teares* needs to be seen as Catholic or Tridentine; and not every Catholic or Tridentine moment of *Funerall Teares* is directly justified by a particular gloss on John 20.

[8] In *Catholicism, Controversy, and the English Literary Imagination, 1558–1660* (Cambridge: Cambridge University Press, 1999), Alison Shell, in her attention to Southwell's poetic vocationalism rather than doctrinal agenda, is much less willing to pin Southwell's depiction of Magdalene on a Catholic poetics. Shell rightly points out that the tears tradition appealed equally to Catholics and Protestants: "Accounts of the struggle of Peter or Mary Magdalen could also be used for exemplary purposes both by Protestant and Catholic: even more efficaciously than Christ's temptation in some ways, since they begin from a presumption that the protagonist is sinful" (80).

a number of modern commentators have remarked that, for John, revelatory words are superior to signs and miracles.[9] Rudolf Bultmann argues that the works of God that are mediated by the Son are primarily accessible through words/hearing.[10] One such passage in this context occurs in John 14:10, in Christ's response to Philip's request to show the Father to the disciples: "Beleevest thou not that I am in the father, and the father in mee? The words that I speake unto you, I speak not of my selfe: but the Father that dwelleth in me, he doth the works" (14:10). For Bultmann, Christ's works amount to nothing more nor less than the revelation of God to the disciples, and all such works and signs acquire their force and meaning through the medium of Christ's spoken testimony. In Johannine theology, signs and miracles are but "concessions" of faith. The genuine witness is through the words of Christ that are the direct means of God's revelation.[11] This is not to say that eyewitness testimony is derogated in the Fourth Gospel. The prospect of "seeing God," to the extent that it is the exclusive privilege of the Son, is in many respects the ideal goal toward which revelatory hearing should lead. But the Fourth Gospel will repeatedly emphasize the proximate, more accessible goal of acquiring creaturely faith and belief through auditory testimony.[12]

Scholars of early modern English religious culture have recently turned attention to a sizable body of early modern literature oriented toward instructing the English laity on the proper way to hear sermons. According to Arnold Hunt, art-of-hearing treatises such as Robert Wilkinson's *A Jewell for the Eare* (1593), Wilhelm Zepper's *The art or skil, well and fruitfullie to heare the holy sermons of the church* (1599), and Stephen Egerton's *The Boring of the Eare* (1623) not only elevate the status of listening to and appropriately hearing Christ's words through sermons; they provide guidelines as to how best to internalize and recall sermonic messages once away from the church.[13] Various techniques of self-application, including note-taking,

---

[9] Hearing Christ's words directly rather than relying on secondary testimony is featured elsewhere in the Fourth Gospel: "We have heard him our selves, and know that this is indeed the Christ, the Saviour of the world" (4:42). For a discussion of such passages in relation to the hearing/seeing dyad, see Marianne Meye Thompson, *The God of the Gospel of John* (Grand Rapids: Eerdmans Publishing Company, 2001), 107.

[10] Bultmann's discussion of the role of hearing in faith can be found in his *Theology of the New Testament*, vol. I (New York: Charles Scribner's Sons, 1955), 70–4. On Bultmann's privileging of hearing over seeing, see John Ashton, *Understanding the Fourth Gospel* (Oxford: Clarendon Press, 1991), 518–22.

[11] Cited in Thompson, *The God of the Gospel of John*, 107. In her revision of Bultmann's emphasis on the primacy of hearing, Thompson describes at length the importance of both hearing as revelation and seeing as eyewitnessing, the latter being particularly important to the Father–Son relationship (106–20).

[12] On hearing as a means to the end of faith and belief (and seeing as, in some cases, an end unto itself), see Thompson, *The God of the Gospel of John*, 108–14. See also her more recent revision of Bultmann's views in Thompson, "Jesus: 'The Man Who Sees God,'" in *Israel's God and Rebecca's Children: Christology and Community in Early Judaism and Christianity*, eds. Larry W. Hurtado and Alan F. Segal (Waco: Baylor University Press, 2007), 215–26. On Jesus' privilege to see God, see Catrin H. Williams, "(Not) Seeing God in the Prologue and Body of John's Gospel," in *The Prologue of the Gospel of John*, eds. Jan G. van der Watt, R. Alan Culpepper, and Udo Schnelle (Tübingen: Mohr Siebeck, 2016), 79–98.

[13] Arnold Hunt, *The Art of Hearing: English Preachers and Their Audiences, 1590–1640* (Cambridge: Cambridge University Press, 2010), especially chapter 2, *passim*.

ritualized practices of repetition in order to facilitate memory, and the cultivation of the emotions through an appreciation of the grand style of sermonizing, all contributed to a mode of household government designed to instruct churchgoers to "*heare well*," in Henry Smith's prescriptive phrase.[14]

Religious historians have often noted that Paul's expression in Romans 10:17—"Faith commeth by hearing"—helps to shape the Reformed, especially Lutheran elevation of *sola scriptura* and a word- rather than image-based piety.[15] Yet if we pause to look at some of the important early modern treatises on hearing, we find that the Fourth Gospel, too, is enlisted frequently as a guide or manual on practices of attentive hearing. In the first sermon of the *Art of Hearing*, Henry Smith remarks at the outset that John 1:14 justifies the importance of receiving Christ through hearing the Word: "Although our heartes are contrarie to the *Worde* more than to any thing beside, yet no man can thinke that this is the *Word* of GOD, but hee thinkes it necessarie to bee heard. Besides, if Christ bee the *Word* (as Saint John calleth him in the first chapter and fourteenth verse) and the *Worde* is received by no other meanes, but by *hearing* onely can anie man then receive Christ without *hearing?*"[16] Yet Smith will also remark, as several other writers in this tradition do, that one must hear attentively, properly, in order to receive profit. Christ's remark in the good shepherd discourse—"My sheepe heare my voyce, and I know them, and they follow me" (10:27)—is a recurring verse cited in the art-of-hearing literature. In that passage, Christ points out that the true disciples will be able to distinguish his voice from others and so hear his message efficaciously: "In the 10th of John he sends us to the sheep: as they know the voice of their shepheard, and will not heare a stranger, so we shuld know the voice of Christ from the voice of Popes, or Doctors, or Counsels, or Traditions.... [W]e should learne to sing the tune of the spirite: for they which heare the word aright, learne to speake even as the *Worde* speaketh."[17] Stephen Egerton more overtly aligns those who hear properly with the elect, suggesting that effective hearing is a gracious gift: "What other reasons may be gathered out of the words of Christ, to prove the profit, necessitie, and difficultie of hearing? Divers: as first, to be a good and fruitfull hearer is a speciall gift of God, and peculiar to the Elect, *My sheepe heare my voyce*. And againe, *hee that is of God, heareth Gods Word*."[18] In *Hearing and doing the ready way to blessednesse* (1635), Henry Mason draws on John 12:48 to make much the same point: "There are some, which received not profit by their hearing, no, not of the gratious words that proceeded out of our Saviours mouth: & thence I conclude, that therefore they heard amisse."[19]

---

[14] Henry Smith, *The Sermons of Mr. Henry Smith* (London, 1631), T6r–T8r. Cited in Hunt, *The Art of Hearing*, 65. On techniques of self-application, see Hunt, *The Art of Hearing*, 68–94.

[15] See, for example, James Kearney, *The Incarnate Text: Imagining the Book in Reformation England* (Philadelphia: University of Pennsylvania Press, 2009), 26–7.

[16] Henry Smith, *The sermons of Maister Henrie Smith gathered into one volume* (London, 1593), 635.

[17] Ibid., 653.

[18] Stephen Egerton, *The boring of the eare contayning a plaine and profitable discourse by way of dialogue* (London, 1623), 3.

[19] Henry Mason, *Hearing and doing the ready way to blessednesse* (London, 1635), 478.

That the good shepherd discourse of John 10 provides influential scriptural material on the necessity of hearing Christ's words properly is suggested in the iconographic use of a popular illustration of Christ as good shepherd that accompanies, for example, John Jewel's widely circulated *A Defence of the Apologie of the Churche of England* (1567). At Pope Pius IV's prompting, Jewel had earlier written an *An apologie, or aunswer in defence of the Church of England* (1562), a defense of the English Church in response to the third meeting of the Council of Trent in 1562. The text elicited a Catholic response in a lengthy treatise by Christopher Harding, *Confutation of a booke intituled "An apologie of the Church of England"* (1565), to which Jewel responds with his *Defence*. The *Defence* uses on its title page an image of Christ as good shepherd (in which Christ carries a sheep atop his shoulders), versions of which are reproduced in later sixteenth-century Protestant treatises and conversion narratives (Fig. 2.1).

As expected, given the imprint on the title page, the good shepherd narrative is a pivotal text in both Harding's *Confutation* and Jewel's *Defence*. Jewel declares forthrightly that one of the "principle Grounds" of Harding's whole book is the notion that "the Pope, although he maie erre by personal errour, in his owne Private Judgement, yet as he is Pope, as he is the Successour of Peter, and as he is the Shepheard of the Universal Churche, in Publique Judgement, in deliberation, and Definitive Sentence, he never erreth."[20] On papal inerrancy, Jewel accuses Harding of misreading John 10, 12, and 21 (as none of those verses in the Fourth Gospel decrees that the Pope as good shepherd is nominated as Peter's apostolic successor), and Jewel asserts that the words of the shepherd belong exclusively to Christ: "*The woordes, whiche M. Hardinge allegeth out of S. John, Christe him selfe expoundeth, not of the Pope, but of him selfe:* I am the good Shephearde.... Them muste I bringe, that they maye heare my Voice: and so shal there be one Shepheard, and one Flocke."[21] Jewel is especially concerned to accuse Harding of impiously failing to appreciate Christ's important advisement that only those who properly "hear [his] voice" (10:16) will enter the fold:

> Heare you the voice of God: leave your Fables: speake Goddes Holy Woord, and speake it truely: be ye faitheful Ministers of the Truthe. Then whosoever shal be founde to despise your Doctrine, be he kinge, or Emperour, wée will not doubte to calle him an Heathen.... But if he be an Heathen, that wil not beare your Churche, what is he then that wil not heare Christe? *Aeneas Syluius,* beinge afterwarde Pope him selfe, saithe thus... *If the Bishop of Rome wil not heare the Churche, he wil not heare Christe: and therefore muste be taken as an Heathen, and Publicane.* S. Augustine saith... *My Sheepe heare my voice, and folowe me. Awaie with Mannes Writtinges: Let the Voice of God sounde unto us.*[22]

Even heathens, Jewel avers, heed the call of attentive listening laid out in the good shepherd narrative. The unity of the Church depends upon hearing the shepherd properly: the Word of that "*one Shepehearde* is Christe the Sonne of God," and not the Pope.[23]

---

[20] John Jewel, *A Defence of the Apologie of the Churche of England* (London, 1567), ch. 1, 10.
[21] Ibid., ch. 3, 102.   [22] Ibid., ch. 8, 55.   [23] Ibid., ch. 18, 245.

A Defence of the Apologie of
the Churche of Englande,

Conteininge an Anfweare to a certaine
Booke lately fet foorthe by M.
Hardinge, and Entituled,
A Confutation of &c.

By Iohn Iewel *Biſhop*
of Sariſburie.

3. ESDRAE. 4.
Magna eſt Veritas & præualet.
Greate is the Truthe, and preuaileth.

Imprinted at London in Fleeteſtreate,
at the figne of the Elephante,
by Henry VVykes.
Anno 1567. 27. Octobris.

Cum Gratia & Priuilegio Regiæ
Maieſtatis.

Fig. 2.1 Title page, John Jewel, *A Defence of the Apologie of the Churche of England* (London, 1567), RB 61829, The Huntington Library, San Marino, CA.

Fig. 2.2 Christ as Good Shepherd, Richard Vennar, *The Right Way to Heaven* (London, 1602), RB 69720, The Huntington Library, San Marino, CA.

Jewel's debate with Harding over the proper interpretation of the shepherd discourse, as well as the image used on the title page to Jewel's *Defence*, seems to have influenced later English Protestant appropriations of John 10 in discussions of the art of hearing. Richard Vennar was a colorful, by most accounts prodigal mid-century pamphleteer and playwright best remembered for his inability successfully to launch his play *England's Joy* (1602). In and out of prison for several counts of fraud, Vennar penned an autobiography as well the apologetic *The Right Way to Heaven*, first published in 1601 and then revised in 1602. The revised edition of the confessional narrative includes a woodcut by Thomas East that is reminiscent of the good shepherd imprint used as the title page to Jewel's *Defence* (Fig. 2.2).[24]

The poem that accompanies the image brings together the motif of Christ as shepherd with a somewhat graphic depiction of the Passion, and it is preceded by Vennar's advice, in keeping with the approach to John 10 of the art-of-hearing

---

[24] The good shepherd image reappears in *The Map of Mortalitie* (London, 1604). For more information on Vennar and the shepherd image, see David J. Davis, *Seeing Faith, Printing Pictures: Religious Identity during the English Reformation* (Leiden: Brill, 2013), 134–6.

manuals, that, in contrast to his own prodigal example, the efficacious use of Christ's words involves more than simply a facile listening to them: "Blessed are they that heare the word of *God* and keepe it. Hee that heareth the word willingly, understandeth it rightly, beleeveth it faithfully, applieth it profitably, and keepeth it diligently, shall joy with *Christ* assuredly."[25] True reformation and spiritual comfort, Vennar realizes (prompted by further reflection on John 13), is to act on the correct understanding gleaned from attentive hearing: "If yee understand these things, saith our *Saviour*, happy are ye, if ye doe them."[26] Not surprisingly, the exemplar of such reformation and repentance is Mary Magdalene, who, upon witnessing Christ and hearing his words, "fell downe behinde *Jesus* and lamented pitefully."[27]

Vennar's emphasis on the importance of putting what one has heard into practice is echoed in several of the art-of-hearing treatises. Zepper, for example, reminds his readers of John's practical advice to Simon Peter. Convinced that he understands Christ's message, Simon Peter is instructed by Christ to practice conscientiously what he has heard: "If yee know these things, happy are ye if ye doe them" (13:17). "Wherefore the doctrine of Gods holy word, must not onely be put into our eares," Zepper remarks, "but into our head, and not into our brain or head only, but into our harts also, yea, and not into our heart only, but into our hands also, that the more sound fruit of it, may appeare in us."[28] Similarly, for Robert Wilkinson, not to use Christ's words pastorally and reformatively is to act in the manner of the Pharisees who are upbraided for mishearing Jesus' direct testimony: "He that is of God, heareth Gods words: ye therefore heare them not, because ye are not of God" (8:47), about which Wilkinson concludes, "Some come not to have their lives reformed, but to have their eares tickled as at a play: some come for novelty, some for fashion, some to sléepe, some to sée, and some to be seen, but few to practise: but let these things be farre from you, for our saviour Christ sayth. *He that is of God, beareth gods words...* nay he goeth further in the same place speaking to the unbeleeving Jewes, *ye therefore heare them not, beecause ye are not of God.*"[29] Zepper will more pointedly remark that realizing Christ's words practically should transform one's affections, as when, in John 7:46, the officers sent by the Pharisees to bind Christ decide against their charge: "Those officers that the Pharises sent out to take or to trippe Christ, were so transformed, and had put upon them such other affections and mindes, that they did not onely not bring Christ bound (a matter that was given them in charge to doe) but they did commend and imbrace both him and his doctrine."[30] The passage signifies for Zepper that Christ's words should be so transformative as to realign one's emotions in such a way that hearers and teachers can meet one another and find "the like will and mind."[31] Notable about all of these uses of John in the art-of-hearing treatises is that John is valued

---

[25] Richard Vennar, *The right way to heaven and a good presedent for lawyers and all other good Christians* (London, 1602), 12.

[26] Ibid., 12.   [27] Ibid., 11.

[28] Wilhelm Zepper, *The art or skil, well and fruitfullie to heare the holy sermons of the church*, trans. Thomas Wilcox (London, 1599), 90.

[29] Robert Wilkinson, *A Jewell for the Eare* (London, 1602), 20.

[30] Zepper, *The art or skil*, 92.   [31] Ibid., 92.

especially for the instructional guidelines laid down in the Fourth Gospel for internalizing Christ's words. In various ways, Smith, Egerton, Wilkinson, Zepper, and Mason treat the Fourth Gospel itself as an art-of-hearing manual from which they pull precepts for a regimen of hearing well.

MAGDALENE AND HEARING CHRIST'S WORD

If we turn to the most extensive early modern literary meditations on Mary's encounter with Christ at the tomb, we find that Mary's inability to recall accurately what she has heard from or about Christ helps to explain the prohibition against her touching him. In *Marie Magdalens Funerall Teares* (1591), Robert Southwell laments Mary's failure to regard the consolations of the angels who are sent to guide her after she has witnessed the empty tomb. The angels ask, "Woman, why weepest thou?" but Mary's response, "Because they have taken away my Lord, and I know not where they have laied him" (20:13), suggests that she erroneously concludes that the angels' knowledge is limited: "They know not where he is.... Whatsoever they could tell me, if they told me not of him, and whatsoever they should tell me of him, if they told me not where he were, both their telling and my hearing were but a wasting of time. I neither came to sée them, nor desire to heare them."[32] Mary proclaims that she desires not to hear/listen to the angels. Her refusal to see them, given the context, translates as her refusal to hear them, given that she is directly apprehending them. The angels play a role analogous to that of the Paraclete or Holy Spirit in John's theology. They provide instruction in Christ's stead through direct testimony. The reluctance to listen to the angels marks Mary's refusal to honor Christ's words to her regarding his disappearance, suggesting not simply that she has forgotten Christ's earlier messages but that she refuses to hear his *present* messages. Her problem is not merely that she forgets particulars about Christ; her problem is that she misunderstands the entire process through which Christ has revealed himself.

We find that the focus on a similar pedagogy of hearing well becomes especially pronounced during the *hortulanus* scene as well as the succeeding *noli me tangere* admonition. The account in the Fourth Gospel is as follows:

> Jesus saith unto her, Woman, why weepest thou? whom seekest thou? She supposing him to be the gardiner, saith unto him, Sir, if thou have borne him hence, tell me where thou hast laied him, and I will take him away. Jesus saith unto her, Mary. She turned herselfe, and saith unto him, Rabboni, which is to say, Master. Jesus saith unto her, Touch me not: for I am not yet ascended to my Father: but goe to my brethren, and say unto them, I ascend unto my Father, and your Father, and to my God, and your God. (20:15–17)

Initially mistaking Jesus for a gardener, Mary's epiphanic recognition occurs only upon Jesus' speaking her name. Mary's initial failure to understand Christ's and the

---

[32] Ibid., 15.

angels' words to her, which is interpreted repeatedly as a failure of hearing, is the principal reason for her epistemological limitations. In *Funerall Teares* (1591), Southwell remarks that Mary's plight stems from her inability to remember Christ's teachings: "Yea shée had forgotten all things. . . . And yet her love by reason of her losse, drowned both her mind and memory so déepe in sorrow, and so busied her wittes in the conceite of his absence, that al remembraunce of his former promises, was diverted with the throng of present discomforts."[33] Significantly, the failure to remember typically signifies an inability to recall what she has heard either directly or indirectly from Christ: "O *Mary* thou didst not marke what thy maister was woont to say, when he told thee, that the third day he shuld rise againe. For if thou hadst heard him, or at the least understoode him, thou wouldest not thinke, but that hée now useth both his heart and soule in the life of his owne body."[34] Even if Mary has forgotten what Christ has directly divulged to her, she should have recalled what she had heard Christ say to the thieves during the Passion: "And if sorrow at the crosse did not make thée as deafe, as at the tomb it maketh thée forgetfull, thou diddest in confirmation hereof heare him selfe say to one of the théeves, that the same day he shuld be with him in Paradise?"[35] To forget Christ's "promises" is to forget his words to her; and to forget his words is to forget the witness of Christ's ways, which ultimately marks a crisis of faith.

In *Mary Magdalens Lamentations* (1601), Gervase Markham's poetic reconstruction makes great weight of the invocation of Mary's name in her regeneration and veritable turning of her faith: "When I heard thee call in wonted sort, / And with thy usuall voice, my only Name, / Issuing from that thy heavenly mouths report; / So strange an alteration it did frame, / As if I had been wholly made anew, / Being only nam'd by thee (whose voice I knew)."[36] It is not merely that Mary recognizes Christ through hearing his voice. She recollects herself to herself, as if the simple address has impelled her conversion from weeping apostate to regenerated disciple. The restoration of her benumbed senses depends on her listening to rather than touching Christ: "But now this one word hath my sence restored, / Lightned my mind, and quicknd my heart, / And in my soule a living spirit poured."[37] That Mary is still not assured in her faith, however, is shown in the subsequent stanzas. She acknowledges that, despite her recognition (and recollecting) of Christ, she pines to touch him: "To hear more words I listed not to stay, / Being with the word it selfe now happie made / But deeme a greater blisse for to assay, To have at once my wishes full apaide / In honouring and kissing of his feet."[38] Christ's immediate explanation for disallowing her touch is that he has not yet ascended to his Father. Saint Gregory had seized on this plausible explanation for the admonition against touching, about which Lancelot Andrewes remarks that had Mary touched Christ, she would not have let go: "So, much time spent in impertinencies, which neither He nor she the better for. So, she to let her *touching* alone, and put it of till another

---

[33] Robert Southwell, *Marie Magdalens Funerall Teares* (London, 1591), 7.
[34] Ibid., 20–1.   [35] Ibid., 36.
[36] Gervase Markham, *Marie Magdalens lamentations for the losse of her master Jesus* (London, 1601), *Sixth Lamentation*, 21. Here and throughout, I have slightly modernized Markham's original text.
[37] Markham, *Sixth Lamentation*, 22.   [38] Markham, *Sixth Lamentation*, 24.

time, being to be imployed in a businesse of more hast, and importance."[39] But Christ's subsequent comments point out the lesson that she has failed to learn. She need not internally visualize and "feel" Christ since, as Markham reasons, his words should be sufficient: "If thou my former promises beleeve, My present words may be a constant proofe, / Doe not thy eies and eares true witnesse give, Must hands and face most feele for hearts behoofe: / If eies and eares deceived be by me, As well may hands and face deluded be."[40]

We can see here a subtle ranking of the proper means by which Christ's disciples can enjoy a faithful encounter with Christ. Mary only truly sees Christ when she hearkens to his speech, recalling his voice. Seeing provides "true witness" because it is preceded by hearing. The touching of hands and feet is at a further proprietary remove.[41] If Christ's privileged speech will not provide efficacious access, then a physical encounter with his body will certainly fail to provide comparable assurance. The causal primacy and efficacy of speaking/hearing is itself brought out in Markham's description of Mary's acknowledgement of her inability to understand what has been spoken to her by the angels and Christ: "Of understanding robd, I stand agaz'd, / Not able to conceit what I doe heare: / That in the end, finding I did not know, / And seeing, could not well discerne the show."[42] Mary can palpably see the show, but she cannot understand it because she has not functionally listened to the show's message. To touch Christ spiritually and not corporeally entails a strict identification of spirituality and hearing, a point made by Lancelot Andrewes who, explaining the admonition against touching, brings John 6 to bear on John 20: "CHRIST resolves the point, in that very place. The *flesh,* the *touching,* the eating it, *profits nothing. The words He spake, were spirit:* So, the *touching,* the eating, to be spirituall."[43] The spoken sentiments are not just a vehicle for a spiritual significa-tion: they "were spirit" themselves. The same year of Andrewes's 1629 sermon, the Independent minister Henry Burton, citing Saint Bernard, likewise identifies the touching not merely with faith but with the Word as such: "Touch me not, saith Christ; that is, dis-wont thy selfe with this seducible sense: rest on the Word, acquaint thy selfe with faith; faith that knowes not how to bee deceived."[44]

That this conversion process depends on Mary's internalizing Christ's words is the subject of another early modern recounting of *noli me tangere,* Thomas Walkington's contribution to the tears' tradition, *Rabboni: Mary Magdalen's Tears* (1620). Walkington also believes that the effective moment of conversion occurs before Mary addresses Christ as "Rabboni," when she hears Christ call her name: "Unto whom shee turning with an open and a nimble eare, for…having thus heard his sweet and gracious voyce, in terming her *Mary,* she out of a singular, dutifull, & strict obligation of her love to him, ecchoes backe this one and sole

---

[39] Lancelot Andrewes, *XCVI Sermons* (London, 1629), 551.

[40] Markham, *Seventh Lamentation,* 25.

[41] An important discussion on the seeing–hearing distinction in the Fourth Gospel can be found in Craig R. Koester, "Seeing, Hearing, and Believing in the Gospel of John," *Biblica* 70 (1989), 327–48.

[42] Markham, *Second Lamentation,* 10.   [43] Andrewes, *XCVI Sermons,* 551.

[44] Henry Burton, *Truth's Triumph Over Trent* (London, 1629), 321.

reciprocall word of her lowly love, and most humble respect unto him, *Rabboni*."[45]
Unable to recognize Christ by sight, given his rough garments of a gardener, Mary
comes to Christ through his voice: "*Non novit ex vultu, fides ex auditu.* She knew
him not at first by his outward lineaments: faith comes by hearing. Shee heard him,
and then beleeved in him."[46] Even more pronouncedly than Southwell or Markham,
Walkington identifies faith with belief (a basic Johannine presupposition) and
belief with the witness of what Christ has spoken. That conversion through the
Word is uppermost in Walkington's interpretation of the scene is reprised later
in the treatise. Walkington goes so far as to identify Mary's tears with the silent
word that stands in for Christ's words: "Her Teares are her best Advocates and
Proctours.... *O Taciturnitas clamosissima:* A silence that spoke much in the eares of
Almighty God, who though the everliving *Word* respects sad and sighing thoughts,
as well as words.... Never a word she spake, for shee knew it was unto the *Word*,
who knew her speech that was retired into her inner Cabinet."[47] Mary herself has
come to appreciate the singularity of her vocal exchanges (and inner dialogues)
with Christ. She has learned a lesson that even Christ's disciples have had trouble
understanding: the proper route to Christ is decidedly not through manna from
heaven: "Thou art the *Manna*, Angels food, the food I fed upon... the bread which
I most now hunger after, for man liveth not by other bread onely, but by thy word,
oh thou ever-blessed *Word*."[48]

An important distinction should be drawn between Southwell's, Markham's,
and Walkington's Johannine emphasis on faith through a belief in what is heard
rather than seen and the more typical Reformed, especially Calvinist assumption
that hearing Christ's words heightens the other senses, ultimately fostering an
inner seeing. In folding John 20 into the good shepherd discourse at John 10:3,
Calvin describes Mary's *volta* that is effected by her apprehension of Christ's voice
just prior to the *hortulanus* scene:

> That Christ let Mary err for a little while, was useful for confirming her faith. Now, by
> one word, He corrects her mistake.... He now assumes the character of the Master
> and addresses His disciple by name—as we read in chapter 10 that the Good Shepherd
> calls every sheep of His flock to Him by name. And so the voice of the Shepherd
> penetrates Mary's mind, opens her eyes, arouses all her senses and so affects her that
> she forthwith entrusts herself to Christ.[49]

On the one hand, Calvin prioritizes hearing over the other senses. Christ's words
serve as an efficient cause of whatever sensual arousal is needed for Mary to bind
herself to Christ. On the other hand, Christ's words are instrumental in "opening
Mary's eyes," as if an inner vision of Christ is the outcome of her epiphany and
conversion. Calvin's position here is consistent with his overall tendency in his
critique of worship by images to argue that faith is formed through an apprehension

---

[45] Thomas Walkington, *Rabboni: Mary Magdalens teares, of sorrow, solace* (London, 1620), 34–5.
[46] Ibid., 35.   [47] Ibid., 59–60.   [48] Ibid., 96.
[49] John Calvin, *The Gospel According to St. John*, in *Calvin's New Testament Commentaries*, vol. 5,
eds. David W. Torrance and Thomas F. Torrance, trans. T. H. L. Parker (Grand Rapids: Eerdmans
Publishing Company, 1959), 197–8.

of the preached word, although Calvin understands faith to be a "special kind of perception" that is often attached to metaphors of sight and inner vision.[50] To see properly through the eyes of faith presupposes for Calvin that the available and invisible words have penetrated the believer's heart.[51]

The Calvinist position, however, is not exactly a Johannine one. For John, the interplay between hearing and seeing typically works in two ways: either signs will confirm what Christ's disciples have already heard from or about Christ, or hearing will help to explain the meaning of visible signs already witnessed.[52] An example of the first instance occurs when John the Baptist remarks that he only recognizes Christ as the one on whom the Spirit has descended because God has told him as much (1:32–3). Similarly, the disciples understand the symbolism of Christ's turning water into wine because they have already heard of Christ's ministry. Instances in which hearing explains the meaning of signs already witnessed are more typical, including not only the manner in which, as we have been discussing, Mary understands the sight of the open tomb, two angels, and risen Christ once she is addressed aurally by Christ, but also the manner in which the blind man, Martha, and royal official described in other verses all understand Christ's actions on their behalf because they have come to trust in what they have heard directly and indirectly about Christ's mission.[53] In none of these examples does hearing primarily induce an inner seeing or vision of Christ. Hearing works properly to contextualize, explain, and ultimately substitute for what is simply seen or witnessed. An especially incisive declaration of the causal primacy of hearing relative to seeing can be found in Richard Sibbes's lengthy treatise on John 20, *A heavenly conference between Christ and Mary after His resurrection* (1654):

> That Christ when he teacheth, he doth it by words, not by Crucifixes, not by sights. We lost our salvation, and all our happiness by the ear, and we must come to it by the ear again. *Adam* by hearkening to *Eve,* and *Eve* to the Serpent, lost all, and we must recover salvation therefore by the ear. As we have heard, so we shall see. We must first hear, and then see. Life cometh in at the eare, as well as death.[54]

For Sibbes, the words of Christ, which have "a mighty efficacy" in "creating all things," clarify for Mary that which she has seen but not righteously understood.[55]

---

[50] William A. Dyrness, *Reformed Theology and Visual Culture: The Protestant Imagination from Calvin to Edwards* (Cambridge: Cambridge University Press, 2004), 69. In his discussion of Calvin's recourse to metaphors of sight, Dyrness draws on Barbara Pitkin's *What Pure Eyes Could See: Calvin's Doctrine of Faith in its Exegetical Context* (Oxford: Oxford University Press, 1999), 128–30.

[51] Dyrness, *Reformed Theology and Visual Culture,* 69. Debora Kuller Shuger, too, remarks on Calvin's tendency toward "inner iconoclasm," although she more compellingly stresses the importance of Calvin's verbal and "textualized" epistemology, which, I would argue, accords with the emphasis on aurality in John 20. See Shuger, *The Renaissance Bible: Scholarship, Sacrifice, and Subjectivity* (Berkeley: University of California Press, 1994), 174–5.

[52] On this interplay between hearing and sight, see Craig R. Koester, *Symbolism in the Fourth Gospel: Meaning, Mystery, Community* (Minneapolis: Augsburg Fortress, 2003), 138–40.

[53] Ibid., 139.

[54] Richard Sibbes, *A heavenly conference between Christ and Mary after His resurrection* (London, 1654), 16.

[55] Ibid., 17.

For John and the writers discussed above, to internalize faith is to internalize Christ's words as such, without necessarily transmuting those words into higher or more abstract and metaphorical sense-impressions. And all of the treatments of Magdalene so far discussed bear out the Johannine pedagogical process through which initial misunderstandings (typically based on a misinterpretation of signs) are clarified through aural testimony. If for John, "In the beginning was the Word," so too, throughout and following Christ's ministry, the record of Christ's mission is the continual manifestation of that *Logos.*[56]

What these thoroughly Johannine conceptions of *noli me tangere* suggest is that we should refocus the standard narrative according to which early modern Protestant writers worry about the loss of the immediacy of Christ's material body as implied in John 20, a loss registered more generally in the Reformed rejection of transubstantiation and in Protestant iconophobia. Regina Schwartz provides a recent summary of this disenchanting narrative of loss:

> When Reformers gave up the doctrine of transubstantiation (even as they held on to revised forms of the Eucharist), they lost a doctrine that infuses all materiality, spirituality, and signification with the presence of God. Their world was shaken by reformers' challenges to the medieval system of sacramentality, challenges to the sacred order as they had known it, an order that regulated both their actions and beliefs.[57]

Schwartz argues that, while the loss of sacramental presence was often mourned, this loss was innovatively displaced onto "other cultural forms," including modern domains of the "state and the arts."[58] Whether or not the loss of sacred presence is seen as productively sublimated into modern secular forms, such a metanarrative typically assumes that post-Reformed poetics struggles to compensate for the anxieties conditioned by a suspicion and decline of faith in sacramental metaphysics.[59]

---

[56] In their preoccupation with hearing over seeing, Southwell, Markham, and Walkington depart from the important medieval source text *De beata maria Magdalena*, which was typically attributed to the Pseudo-Origenist, translated as *An Homelie of Marye Magdalene* (London, 1555) and as *An Homilie of Marye Magdalene* (London, 1565). At the beginning of the 1565 edition, attention is given to Mary's inability to see or hear Christ properly: "Shee became as it were without life, without sense: having sence she used no sence: Seinge, she dyd not see: hearing, shee heard not" (6). For a good portion of the text, seeing and hearing are treated on equal planes, although as the text unfolds Mary is exhorted above all to contemplate seeing Christ in her heart: "But bicause she languished in her love, of this languishinge the eyes of her heart became so dym, that she coulde not se him whome she sawe. For she did see Jesus, but she knew not it was Jesus" (17). In the *Maudlin Impression*, 65–8, Patricia Badir offers a convincing reading of the homily's suggestion that Mary might "see absence," although I believe that Southwell, Markham, and Walkington, in their recovery of the Johannine understanding of Magdalene at the sepulchre, do not privilege seeing over hearing.

[57] Regina Mara Schwartz, *Sacramental Poetics at the Dawn of Secularism: When God Left the World* (Stanford: Stanford University Press, 2006), 12–13.

[58] Ibid., 13.

[59] Versions of such a desacralization thesis as a frame for understanding early modern devotional poetry can be found in, for example, Malcolm Mackenzie Ross, *Poetry and Dogma: The Transfiguration of Eucharistic Symbols in Seventeenth-Century English Poetry* (New York: Octagon Books, 1969), vii. R. V. Young agrees with Ross's conception of a post-Reformation sacramental crisis in post-Reformed England, but Young believes that the crisis is partly responsible for the irreducible tensions in the writing of the best devotional poets of the period: "It is precisely an awareness of the threatened loss of the sacraments' power to make grace present in the world that gives such tremendous tension and poignancy to their sacred poetry." *Doctrine and Devotion in Seventeenth-Century Poetry: Studies in*

But we have begun to see here (and in Chapter 1 on John 6) that the distance between Christ's materiality and the convert's desire for union is more than offset by John's high Christology. Through the pious expression of belief (often signifying the Johannine substitute for faith), one not only arrives at knowledge of God but also achieves eternal life and, as we will see in more detail in later chapters, enjoys a mutual indwelling or co-presence with God's holy family.[60]

Indeed, English Reformers followed those early Reformers such as Cornelius Hoen, Johannes Oecolampadius, and Heinrich Bullinger in using the Fourth Gospel to argue that the Ascension and inaccessibility of Christ's corporeity were advantageous or "expedient," given the redemptive promise of the Farewell Discourse, especially verse 16:7, in which Jesus remarks, "Neverthelesse; I tell you the trueth, it is expedient for you that I goe away: for if I goe not away, the Comforter will not come unto you: but if I depart, I will send him unto you. And when he is come, he will reprove the world of sinne, and of righteousnesse, and of judgement" (16:7–8).[61] The local, corporeal presence of Christ might deprive the Church of the Holy Ghost, opined Thomas Cartwright: "This opinion doth deprive us of all the spirituall graces and comforts, that God the father in his sonne Christ, by sending the holy Ghost the third person in the Deitie, hath bestowed upon the whole Church generally, and every particular member thereof."[62] In his commonplace book, John Merbecke (paraphrasing the English martyr John Cheke as well as the Lutheran Reformer Joachim Camerarius) remarks bluntly that the bodily presence is "hurtful" in diminishing the presence of the Spirit: "I tell you truth, it is expedient for you that I goe awaie. The corporall presence of Christ is hurtfull unto men, and that through their owne fault. For why? they are too much adicted unto it. Therefore his flesh must be taken awaie from us, that we maie waxe and increase in the spirite."[63] Furthermore, the "absence" of Christ in the flesh is "profitable" to the Church so "that we maie wholie depend upon the spirituall power."[64]

Donne, Herbert, Crashaw, and Vaughan (Cambridge: D. S. Brewer, 2000), 83. For more on Ross's and Young's viewpoints, see Robert Whalen, *The Poetry of Immanence: Sacrament in Donne and Herbert* (Toronto: University of Toronto Press, 2002), xvi–vii.

[60] The Johannine indwelling with God, itself anticipated by the Ignatian Hellenization of Paul's eschatological conception of union with Christ, distinguishes Johannine from Pauline mysticism. In *The Mysticism of Saint Paul the Apostle*, trans. William Montgomery (New York: Henry Holt & Company, 1931), Albert Schweitzer remarks, "Whereas Paul thinks of the believer, up to the beginning of the eternal blessedness, as only 'in-Christ,' not at the same time 'in-God,' in Ignatius the thought is beginning to come in that 'being-in-Christ' mediates 'being-in-God'.…Justin and the Gospel of John carry forward the work of Ignatius by inserting the Hellenistic union-with-Christ into the doctrine of Jesus Christ as the organ of the Logos" (347–8).

[61] Jaroslav Pelikan remarks that the century-long Christological controversy over the real presence had its genesis in debates over John 16:7: "What precipitated it was the contention, which seems to have been first advanced by Cornelius Hoen, that the ascension of Christ to the right hand of God precluded his bodily presence in the elements of the Eucharist, since it was to the 'advantage' of his disciples that they should no longer have direct physical access to him." *The Christian Tradition: A History of the Development of Doctrine, Volume 4: Reformation of Church and Dogma (1300–1700)* (Chicago: University of Chicago Press, 1984), 158.

[62] Thomas Cartwright, *Two Treatises* (London, 1610), 30–1. For a similar contention, see Heinrich Bullinger, *A most excellent sermon of the Lordes Supper* (London, 1577), 11–12.

[63] John Merbecke, *A booke of notes and common places* (London, 1581), 197.

[64] Ibid., 197. For the Puritan Divine Arthur Hildersam, the arrival of the Comforter in Christ's stead is expedient in that the Comforter prompts communicants to unburden themselves of sin: "The

Perhaps the most direct use of John 16 to justify the expediency of the loss of Christ's body can be found in Erasmus's *Enchiridion*. Excoriating those who would worship relics of the flesh over spiritual goods, Erasmus remarks that the Apostles' "crass understanding" of Christ's messages continued "as long as" they "enjoyed the physical company of Christ.... It was the flesh of Christ that stood in the way, and that is what prompted him to say: 'If I do not go away, the Paraclete will not come.'"[65] James Kearney is absolutely correct in concluding from this passage that "in a fallen world absence is the precondition of presence"; however, Kearney describes Erasmus's claims as "astonishing" and motivated by Erasmus's denunciation of the worship of fleshly goods.[66] We have begun to see that, given the widespread uses of such related Johannine passages on the exchange of Christ's body for the Paraclete, Erasmus's sentiment is not an astonishing exception but a typical reading of John 16.[67] A discussion of the spiritual comfort provided by the Paraclete to facilitate union with Christ/God (and to consolidate the Church) will await Chapter 3. Suffice it to say here that in the Johannine tradition, what one loses in Christ's body, one gains in the promise of an intimate dwelling or participation with God that would not be achievable through the rituals of a purely sacramentalist, particularly Eucharistic Christology.[68]

If hearing is privileged over seeing in the early modern treatments of *noli me tangere* and identified with a metaphorical "touching" for Mary, productive hearing serves as a means to the end of the proper touching of Christ that Mary might enjoy once Christ has been resurrected properly and once she has attained to the proper knowledge of his divinity. Markham describes Christ's promises: "Though to my Father I have not ascended, / I shortly shall, let thy demeanure then / Not by the place where I am, be intended, / But by that place which is my due: and when / With reverence thou farre off wouldst fall, / I will consent that thou me handle shall."[69] A theme is hinted at here that can be found in patristic and medieval

true knowledge and sense of sinne, is the onely way to comfort, *John* 16. 7, 8. Christ saith, the Spirit the Comforter which he would send, should reprove and convince the world. The Spirit of God never comforted any till he had first reproved and convinced them." *CVIII lectures upon the fourth of John* (London, 1632), 64–5.

[65] *Collected Works of Erasmus* (Toronto: University of Toronto Press, 1974),vol. 66, 72–3, cited in Kearney, *The Incarnate Text*, 62–3.

[66] Kearney, *The Incarnate Text*, 62.

[67] Erasmus points out in his commentary on John 20 that "fellowship" with Christ must await the arrival of the Comforter as Spirit: "But truely thine affeccion is yet somedeale carnall, because I have not yet ascended up to my father, whiche thyng once doen, I shall sende unto you the spirite that is the comforter, and he shall make you perfite and wurthy to have the spirituall felowship of me." *The first tome or volume of the Paraphrase of Erasmus upon the Newe Testamente* (London, 1548), 562.

[68] Miles Coverdale aptly uses Magdalene's inability to touch Christ to bolster his argument against the real presence: "Thus learne wee also, to knowe and honour Christ nowe no more after the flesh, and to shew no corporall outward service unto his person.... Thus may faith & love well use some outwarde things, not to doo service therewith unto God, but unto our selves, or to our neighbour As when we take and minister bread and wine about in the supper, distributing and eating it, the same is not done principally, to the intent to declare a service unto God: but somewhat to provoke our outward senses and flesh by the exteriour signes, that wee may the better consider and ponder the grace of God declared unto us in the death of Jesus Christ." *Fruitfull lessons, upon the passion, buriall, resurrection, ascension* (London, 1593), 91.

[69] Markham, *Seventh Lamentation*, 25.

commentaries on John 20: Mary must come to the knowledge of Christ's divine nature in order even to contemplate touching him (and even then touching might be reserved for the glorified afterlife, analogous to the elusive *visio dei*). Aquinas supports the interpretation of *noli me tangere* offered in Augustine's treatise on the Trinity: "It is that touch is the last stage of knowledge: when we see something, we know it to a certain extent, but when we touch it our knowledge is complete. Now this particular woman had some faith in Christ. . . . But she had not yet reached the point of believing that he was equal to the Father and one with God."[70] John's Gospel and the literary treatments of *noli me tangere* are promissory and eschatological. Through an appreciation of Christ's words, Mary undergoes a process of learning the nature of formed or true faith, which itself will enable her to acknowledge Christ's divinity. Only then will she be able to touch the object of her faith. The precise time at which that touching might ensue—during Mary's creaturely or ascended state—is left provocatively open.[71]

MAGDALENE'S DISCIPLESHIP FAILURE

I have been arguing that in their appropriations of material from John 20, the literary treatments of Magdalene at the tomb elevate faith through verbal testimony over signs. But the literary treatments are equally Johannine in their form—that is, in the manner in which the narrators and Christ instruct Mary. As I remarked in the Introduction, John's Gospel, more than any of the Synoptic Gospels or Paul's Epistles, relies on a rhetoric of irony and misunderstanding, among both Jesus' disciples and the disbelievers, as a mode of Christological pedagogy. Sent by the Father to enlighten a world mired in sin and darkness, Christ will often speak ironically and in a riddling or symbolic manner.[72] Only through a pedagogical sorting of ideas do his hearers alight upon the accurate meaning of Christ's words. When Christ remarks to the otherwise well-intentioned Pharisee Nicodemus that the kingdom can only be embraced by those who have been reborn, Nicodemus dimly takes Christ to mean a literal rebirth rather than being born "from above," after which Christ chastises him and provides clarification (3:4, 9). Other examples include the belief by the Samaritan woman that Christ's reference to "living water"

---

[70] Saint Thomas Aquinas, *Commentary on the Gospel of John, Chapters 13–21*, trans. Fabian R. Larcher and James A. Weisheipl (Washington, D.C.: Catholic University Press, 2010), 265.

[71] Thus a sermon on John 20:17 by John Seller explains that Mary cannot touch Christ because she is too "earthly-minded." For Seller, the entire pericope agrees with John's admonition against worldliness expressed throughout the Fourth Gospel: "First then when we see, after so many heavenly instructions, the earthly-mindednesse of *Mary,* that so are her thoughts fixt upon things below, and for this cause so is shee overjoy'd with the presence of her Master, as that hee is forc'd with a gentle checke to reprove her indiscretion, *Touch mee not.* This may teach us as St. JOHN hath already made the application to our hand, *that we love not,* love not too well, *the world, nor the things of the world." Five sermons preached upon severall occasions* (London, 1637), 236–7.

[72] A comprehensive discussion of Jesus' use of irony and of "catch riddles" in particular can be found in Tom Thatcher, *The Riddles of Jesus in John* (Atlanta: Society of Biblical Literature, 2000), chapter 5, *passim.*

describes a well or natural spring (4:10–15) rather than Christ's gift of salvation; the skepticism registered by Jesus' hearers that he would be able literally to construct a "temple" in three days (2:20) (Jesus clearly refers to a spiritual temple); and the disciples' assumption that the "asleep" Lazarus is resting rather than dead (11:13). The resolutions of these misconstruals typically signify that the brethren have properly understood (believed) Christ's saving words and so are well on their way toward achieving the promised eternal life.

Christ's hearers in the Johannine Gospel reveal again and again that they initially misunderstand his message. Because they typically take his words too literally, they fail to appreciate the symbolic context in which his words are spoken. Both Southwell and Markham are keenly attuned to this Johannine pedagogical strategy and recapitulate it in their reconstructions of John 20 that include but also extend beyond the hearing–seeing distinction. Consider Southwell's gloss on an important Johannine intertext, Christ's explanation, in response to Thomas's query— "Lord, we know not whither thou goest: and how can we know the way?"—that Christ is "the Way, the Trueth, and the Life" (14:5–6). Southwell complains on Mary's behalf: "Of thy selfe thou hast sayd, that thou art *The way, the truth and the life,* If then thou art a way easie to find & never erring, how doth shée misse thée? If a life giving life and never ending, why is shée ready to die for thée? If a true promising truth & never failing, howe is shée bereaved of thée? For if what thy tongue did speake, thy truth will averre, shée will never aske more to make her most happy."[73] It is important that these questions appear early in Southwell's treatise, for the remaining portions of his text indeed go on to explicate properly what these significant Johannine words mean. Southwell deliberately provides glib and overly literal explanations of the respective meanings of Christ as the way, the truth, and the life, as if he is playing the ignorant disciple (doubling with Mary herself), the naiveté of which his very text will relinquish for an appreciation of a richer and more symbolic explanation. Instead of assuming that Christ is the "way" because he is "easy" to find and unerring, the proper meaning is that Christ is the only way to God the Father—which in John is subsequently explained: "no man commeth unto the Father but by mee" (14:6). This is a lesson that Mary will eventually learn upon acknowledging the divinity of Christ subsequent to the *noli me tangere* admonition.

Regarding Christ as the "truth," Southwell's ambiguous gloss signifies an appreciation of Christ's dependability or authenticity. Southwell's text goes on to show, in keeping with the influential glosses on John 14, that Christ as the truth signifies the infallibility of his words. Thus Chrysostom paraphrases Christ's comments: "If I am also the 'Truth,' My words are no falsehoods," an association between truth and words that one finds in Aquinas's comment on John 14:5–6, where Aquinas

---

[73] Southwell, *Funerall Teares*, 11. Southwell's translation of verses such as John 14:6 probably stem from his familiarity, as McDonald and Brown note, with the Vulgate rather than the Douay Bible. His translation of 14:6 in particular actually conforms more to the 1537 Matthew Bible (itself based on Tyndale's Bible) than it does Cranmer's Bible, the Douay Bible, or the Geneva Bible. On Southwell's use of the Bible, see the short note in *The Poems of Robert Southwell, S.J.* eds. James H. McDonald and Nancy Pollar Brown (Oxford: Clarendon Press, 1967), xiv.

remarks that "truth belongs essentially to him because he is the Word."[74] Finally, Southwell's assumption that "life" doesn't reconcile with Mary's willingness to die for him is analogous to Nicodemus's misunderstandings. Life in this context refers to the recurring Johannine promise of everlasting life which refers to spiritual renewal, not to the avoidance of literal death. Southwell's strategy is akin to the Johannine one of airing naïve misunderstanding of tightly compressed symbolic words of Jesus in order to provide the occasion to clarify the true meaning of those otherwise gnomic statements.

Southwell extends this strategy of productive misunderstanding in his commentary on the *hortulanus* sequence and the events leading up to it. In response to Christ's question posed to Mary—"Woman, why weepest thou? whom seekest thou?" (20:15)—Southwell initially ventriloquizes Mary's confusions by marking her suffering and love and then plying Christ with questions to Christ's own question: "Full well thou knowest, that thée onely shee desireth, thée onely she loveth, all things besides thée she contemneth, and canst thou find in thy heart to ask hir whom she séeketh?"[75] But as expected, Southwell then answers his and Mary's question, again providing the underlying reason for Christ's query as to why Mary weeps, and again pointing out that Mary has been too literal, that she has missed the fundamental *irony* of Christ's death: "But *O Mary,* not without cause doth he aske thée this question. Thou wouldest have him alive, and yet thou wéepest because thou doest not finde him dead. Thou art sorie that hee is not here, and for this verie cause thou shouldst rather be glad. For if he were dead, it is moste likely hee should bee héere, but not being héere, it is a signe that hée is alive."[76] Mary needs to realize that the mortification of Christ's body is the proper entry into eternal life. Calvin conflates Christ's question with the angels' same preceding question regarding the cause of Mary's weeping, concluding that John designedly omits conversation and exfoliation at this point, determined as he is to spotlight Christ's resurrection: "From the other Evangelists it may be easily inferred that the angel said many things. But John gives a brief summary, sufficient to prove the Resurrection of Christ. He speaks reproof mingled with comfort."[77] Aquinas draws a distinction between the angels' and Christ's similar questions, observing John's pedagogical strategy: "Mary was advancing step by step: for the angels asked her why she was weeping, but Christ asked her whom she was looking for, for her weeping was caused by the desire which led her to look. Christ asked her whom she was looking for in order to increase this desire."[78] Sibbes further explains that Christ reveals himself only by "degrees," "darkly at first," not simply to "try and exercise" Mary's faith but because deferral enhances desire: "God to set a greater price on his presence, and that he would be held more strongly, when he doth reveal himself, he defers a long time."[79] The same stepwise process is outlined by Miles Coverdale, who says about Mary and the disciples that "godly wisedome lead

[74] Aquinas, *Commentary on the Gospel of John,* chapters 13–21, 55.
[75] Southwell, *Funerall Teares,* 44.   [76] Ibid., 45.
[77] *Calvin's New Testament Commentaries,* vol. 5, 197.
[78] Saint Thomas Aquinas, *Commentary on the Gospel of John,* 263.
[79] Sibbes, *A heavenly conference between Christ and Mary after His resurrection,* 23.

them still by little and little, to make them stronger, declaring unto them certaine assured evidences," as Christ eventually becomes a "schoole-master within" Mary's heart.[80] Southwell shares with Calvin, Aquinas, Coverdale, and Sibbes an appreciation of the staged and rhetorical structure of the scene: "That is one reason why he did defer revealing himself to *Mary,* that she might have the more sweet contentment in him, when he did reveal himself, as indeed she had."[81] By means of a Socratic method of sorts, Mary's misunderstanding regarding the location of Christ's body is gradually replaced not simply with her knowledge of the Resurrection but with an even more earnest affection for her Master.

Southwell draws attention to these strategies in his subsequent gloss on the *hortulanus* scene. His obligatory questioning as to why Mary would mistake Jesus for a gardener provides an occasion to explain that, although Mary's sight was deceived, her intellect was astute, for her "mistaking hath in it a farther mistery"— namely, the typological symbolism of Christ as gardener.[82] Here Southwell capitalizes on a long exegetical tradition that associates Christ as a gardener with a second Adam. If Adam was deceived in a garden, Christ was betrayed in a garden. If Adam sinned in the garden and was "apparelled in dead beastes skinnes," Christ, in defraying that debt, "in this garden…lay clad in the dead mans shrowd."[83] A brief gloss on Canticles follows in which Southwell remarks that Christ's body, sown in a garden, will reap everlasting life. Southwell's concluding comment again recalls Johannine tutelage: "For this also was *Mary* permitted to mistake, that we might be informed of the mystery, and see how aptly the course of our redemption did answere the process of our condemnation."[84] Mary's erroneous assumptions are not simply explained away but allowed to develop precisely so that the proper symbolic and/or typological explanation of events can unfold in their stead.

It has recently been said that Southwell's distinctiveness as a Jesuit missioner in England rests more in his pastoral concerns for Catholic compatriots than in his innovatory poetics: "Not a poet but a priest who—brilliantly, sensitively—includes poetry in his pastoral activity," remarks Anne Sweeney about Southwell's missionary devotion.[85] Because of his pastoral zeal, Southwell embraces a Jesuit-inspired conception of Magdalene that, against more traditional counter-Reformation portraits, depicts her less as a weeping, regretful, spiritually inadequate penitent, and more as an ardent, if puzzled, devotee of Christ, a saintly exemplar who could be used for spiritual consolation rather than chastisement. This is the Magdalene Southwell finds in his return to the Johannine sources—not just in John 20 but also in her appearance in the Lazarus pericopes where, as opposed to what we find in Matthew's account, Magdalene is more emotionally, pro-actively involved in tending to Jesus in Bethany after the death of her brother Lazarus.[86] If, in their emphasis on private emotionalism, the Jesuit exercises, so important to Southwell's pastoral sensibility, could appeal to a "Protestant and Catholic alike," so too might

---

[80] Coverdale, *Fruitfull lessons*, 89–90.   [81] Southwell, *Funerall Teares*, 25.
[82] Ibid., 46.   [83] Ibid., 46.   [84] Ibid., 47.
[85] Sweeney, *Robert Southwell: Snow in Arcadia*, 233.
[86] On the Johannine versus Matthean depictions of Magdalene in Bethany, see Sweeney, *Robert Southwell: Snow in Arcadia*, 148.

Southwell's Johannine Magdalene, a figure whose relationship to her Master is described less in doctrinal terms (despite passing references to her co-operative grace) than in terms of the high Christology inimitably located in the Fourth Gospel.[87]

What we find in *Marie Magdalene's Funerall Teares* is not a metanarrative of loss that assumes that Mary must accept the harsh reality of the inaccessibility of her master's body. We find, rather, a mostly unreconstructed Johannine narrative in which Mary is encouraged to appreciate that Christ's death has indeed been expedient. The angels at the tomb plead with her to "exchange [her] sorrow for our joy," reminding her that Christ's "business" has been "finished," that there is no "place more convenient for the Sonne, then to be with his Father."[88] Repeatedly, Mary is prompted to envisage the glory that Christ has achieved in death as she is asked, "Alas why bewaylest thou his glorie, as an injurie," and exhorted to visualize Christ "invested in the robes of glorie."[89] A belief in the testimony of Christ's continuing ministry will come from her recollection of Christ's own promises that his saving presence does not depend on corporeal accessibility: "Doest thou not beléeve my former promises? hast thou not a constant proofe by my present wordes? are not thy eies and eares sufficient testimonies, but that thou must also have thy handes & face witnesses of my presence?"[90] And here again, Mary's example will provide consolation to those readers who will recall her realization that sacred access inheres above all in Christ's words and promises: "If with *Marie* thou cravest no other solace of Jesus but Jesus himselfe, he will answere thy teares with his presence, and assure thée of his presence with his owne words, that having séene him thy selfe, thou maiest make him knowne to others: saying with *Marie. I have seene our Lord, and these thinges he sayd unto me.*"[91] Pastoral comfort is sourced not in Southwell's doctrinal dogmatism but in the manner in which Mary, like any believer across denominational divides, will come to find comfort in her savior's continuing, immaterial presence.

JOHANNINE INTERTEXTUALITY: *NOLI ME TANGERE*

In addition to recapitulating discipleship misunderstanding, most of the literary treatments of Mary at the tomb are also distinctly Johannine in their tendency to provide intertextual comparisons between John 20 and other Johannine sequences, symbols, and messages. Johannine intertextuality appears most significantly in Nicholas Breton's *Mary Magdalens Love* (1595). An establishing instance occurs when Breton comments on Mary's running to Simon Peter upon apprehending the empty tomb: "*Then shee ranne, and came to* Simon Peter, *and the other Disciple*

---

[87] Ibid., 144.

[88] Southwell, *Funerall Teares*, 26, 35. To argue that the theology of *Funerall Teares* is fundamentally Johannine is not to say that Southwell relied solely on John's brief account of Mary at the tomb. Southwell's narrative also is mediated by the Pseudo-Origenist's late medieval homily *A Homilie of Marye Magdalene* (London, 1565). For a brief discussion of Southwell's use of the homily, see Brownlow, *Robert Southwell*, 34–8.

[89] Southwell, *Funerall Teares*, 45, 57.   [90] Ibid., 62.   [91] Ibid., 76.

whom Jesus loved, and saide unto them."[92] Breton makes much of that fact that John's Mary was to have said anything to the disciples, given her shock and grief: "Now it is not said, shee cryed, or sighed, or sobbed, and coulde not speake a worde, or as a body halfe destraught, laide holde on the Disciples, to hale them to the place where shee had beene, but when shee came to them shee saide; which worde *saide*, encludeth a kinde of discreete delivery of speech."[93] For Breton, Mary's composure does not simply recall a speech "well delivered"; it echoes Christ's uniquely Johannine manner of address to the disciples: "Yea, Christ him-selfe, in heaven and earth, the glory of all wisedome, useth that worde in many places, as *Verelie, verelie, I say unto you, &c.* Many places coulde I sette downe where this worde is used to beautefie the speeche, with the Modestie in the delivery."[94] While Christ typically uses "verily" (truly) throughout the four Gospels, the "verily, verily" address prior to the "said" locution is unique to John's Gospel. Breton observes that Christ and Mary rely on this mode of address in order to provide subtlety, beauty, and modesty in their speeches. The point may seem to be a minor one but it illustrates that, for Breton, Mary's Christ is a uniquely Johannine one. This helps to contextualize some of the more important intertextual glossing that will ensue in the treatise.

One example of intertextuality occurs when Breton expatiates on the role of Peter at the tomb of Christ. The verse reads: "Peter therefore went forth, and that other disciple, and came to the Sepulchre. So they ranne both together, and the other disciple did outrun Peter, and came first to the Sepulchre" (20:3–4). In a veritable Petrine *excursus*, Breton remarks that Peter is significantly singled out as the dis-ciple whom Mary first addresses at the tomb. Peter's confession receives extended treatment:

> To which of them did he say as hee saide to *Peter* three times; Dost thou love mee *Peter?* Feede my flocke. Dost thou love me *Peter?* Feede my Lambes, &c. Who though hee answered him to both his questions, with Lorde thou knowest I love thee; yet hee treabled his question againe, asking him, Dost thou love mee *Peter?* And when hee had received his answere, that Lorde thou knowest all thinges, and thou knowest I love thee: Hee gave him this commandement, Feed my Lambs nowe, if wee bee Lambes of Christes flocke, where shall wee looke for the milke of his mercie, but out of the booke of his most holy and sacred Scriptures, & who can interpret them unto us? But his learned and holy Ministers, and such as will shewe Christe their love in instructing his flocke. Such a Disciple was Peter, and such a Lambe was Mary: God sende us many such Lambs as Mary, to run to such Disciples as Peter, to talke of nothing but Christ.[95]

While all four Gospels describe Peter's three-fold denial of Christ (although the details vary across the four depictions), only John records the restoration or rehabilitation of Peter, which Breton is concerned with here. After the disciples' miraculous catch of 153 fish, Jesus approaches Peter, asking for an affirmation of his love. Following Peter's pledge of love (which parallels his earlier denial), Jesus reinstates Peter's apostleship, appointing him shepherd (and symbolically leader of

[92] Nicholas Breton, *Marie Magdalens Love* (London, 1595), Uppon the seconde verse, 12.
[93] Ibid., 12.   [94] Ibid., 13.   [95] Ibid., 15.

the Church): "And he said unto him, Lord, thou knowest all things, thou knowest that I love thee. Jesus sayth unto him, Feed my sheepe" (21:17). Breton embellishes Peter's restoration as described in John 21 (which itself recalls the good shepherd discourse) in order to provide a further comment on Mary's encounter with Peter in John 20. His elaboration establishes the importance for Mary of following the lead of Christ's chosen ministers, although such instruction is initially lost on Mary, for she will fail to internalize the guidance of the angels who will later attempt to allay her grief.

But Breton has more to say about Peter's example for Mary. Several paragraphs later he returns to a seemingly minor detail of John's original text: "So they ranne both, but the other Disciple did outrunne Peter, and came first to the Sepulcher."[96] The fact that Peter stays back, allowing the other "beloved disciple" (identified as John in Breton's text) to run incautiously ahead, reveals the maturity and wisdom of Peter: "A light beleefe will make many men and women to runne them selves out of breath to see a May game...but heere was no such report, and therefore coulde bee no such beleefe: and therefore woulde to God the idle heades of the world would turne their mindes to better matters & leave such toyes...and rather bee delighted to talke with the Ministers of Gods holye worde, of the passion of Christ, & to seeke him in his worde; than to runne with wicked people to see a foole in a play."[97] Although John reaches the sepulchre first, he stops upon seeing the linen clothes, and so Peter enters instead. Peter's example represents for Breton mature or formed faith, naturally expected in one older than John or Mary. But Breton's larger project is to underline, as we have seen in Southwell's commentary, the importance of seeking Christ in his "holy word" rather than running headlong into matters the meaning of which one is unprepared to understand. The lesson that Breton would bequeath to his readers is just such a privileging of the Word of God over any other mode of witnessing: "As I said before, Marie did, and such as Marie will: shee ran to them to tell of Christ, & shee came with them to heare of Christ, would to God we could & would so run."[98]

The other important Johannine intertextual narrative that helps Breton illuminate Mary's plight is the death and raising of Lazarus. John 11 provides the only Gospel story of Jesus' raising of Lazarus of Bethany, the brother of Martha and Mary. Perhaps the most influential statement in John's description of Lazarus's resurrection is the well-known phrase "Jesus wept" (John 11:35). Breton refers to Jesus' weeping for Lazarus in order to distinguish the true nature of Mary's tears. After quickly dismissing the sentimentalist notion that Mary's tears represent excessive or false crying, Breton distinguishes tears of sorrow—as in Peter's denial of Christ and Christ's own weeping for Jerusalem—from tears of love: "Nowe there are teares of Love, and those proceed of the kinde nature of the hart, as Christ wept when hee sawe Lazarus dead, whom he loved, and now Mary wept when she saw her Lord dead, or at least, could not see him dead, or alive when shee lived."[99]

---

[96] Breton, *Marie Magdalens Love*, Upon the foure, five, sixe, seaven and eighth verses, 22.
[97] Ibid., 21.   [98] Ibid., 22.   [99] Ibid., 36.

To associate Christ's weeping with Mary's extends Breton's strategy of excusing Mary by identifying her with Christ, as Breton had established when comparing Mary's manner of linguistic address to Christ's address to his followers. This strategy marks a departure from the gentle rebukes and apologies for excessive weeping that we see in the other Magdalene portraits, especially Southwell's.

By identifying Mary's weeping with Christ's, Breton implicitly dignifies her weeping, casting her in a position of greater control than his contemporaries typically would allow. Jesus' weeping at Lazarus's tomb was understood by exegetes from the patristic through the early modern period as exemplary crying in that it is willed, intentionally directed, and moderate rather than excessive in nature: "Christ willed to be troubled and to feel sadness," Aquinas remarks, "so that by controlling his own sadness, he might teach us to moderate our own sadness.... Our Lord willed to be sad in order to teach us that there are times when we should be sad, which is contrary to the opinion of the Stoics; and he preserved a certain moderation in his sadness, which is contrary to the excessively sad type."[100] Calvin comes to much the same conclusion: "Our feelings are sinful because they rush on unrestrainedly and immoderately; but in Christ they were composed and regulated in obedience to God and were completely free from sin."[101] Breton trades on this understanding of Christ's tears in his understanding of Mary's weeping not as cautionary (in that it depicts excessive sorrow) but as instructive and worthy of emulation: "I beseech God to graunt us all Grace, so to sorrow for our sinnes, and to long for his comming, that seeking him as Mary did with teares, wee may see him with joy, and say with Mary, Master: which Master, Lord, King and God, be loved served, honoured praised and glorified."[102]

We have seen the extent to which the late-seventeenth-century treatments of Mary's contrition rely heavily on both the content and the rhetorical approach of the Fourth Gospel. Concerned as they are not only to emblematize her contrition but also to reconstruct the Johannine process by which she comes to appreciate that Christ's words are integral to her conversion, such treatments present a portrait of a Magdalene who is humble and loving but still fallibly human. After a brief, framing discussion of Hans Holbein's relevant depiction of Magdalene in his *Noli Me Tangere* painting, we will see that seventeenth-century poets tend to pick up the accounts of Mary's conversion where the earlier treatises and poems leave off. The Magdalene of Richard Crashaw's and Henry Vaughan's lyrics is a glorified figure who has achieved communion with Christ and God in heaven.[103]

---

[100] Aquinas, *Commentary on the Gospel of John*, chapters 6–12, trans. Fabian R. Larcher and James A. Weisheipl (Washington, D.C.: Catholic University Press, 2010), 241.

[101] *Calvin's New Testament Commentaries*, vol. 5, 12.   [102] Ibid., 39.

[103] Although I have not been concerned to draw out the eroticism of Magdalene's encounter with Christ in the Magdalene narratives, I agree with Debora Kuller Shuger that there is an anti-dualism or lack of transcendence in the recounting of John 20 that figures in the writings of Southwell, Markham, Walkington, and Breton. See Shuger, *The Renaissance Bible*, 175.

MAGDALENE'S DEVOTION: HANS HOLBEIN'S
NOLI ME TANGERE

Perhaps the best-known sixteenth-century artistic rendition of Mary's encounter with Christ in John 20 is Holbein's *Noli Me Tangere* painting dating from 1524–6. Holbein's work seems to have been commissioned by Thomas More, one of Holbein's principal patrons during Holbein's early stay in London (Fig. 2.3).[104]

Included in the royal collection of Henry VIII as early as 1540, the painting is remarkable historically for its departure from more typical late medieval and Italian Renaissance iconographic fifteenth- and sixteenth-century depictions of John 20, including versions of *noli me tangere* by Titian (1512–15) and Correggio (1525). The latter paintings position Mary beneath Christ, typically genuflecting in submission, Titian's depiction in particular situating Mary barely off the ground while she pleads to touch Christ (Fig. 2.4).

Fig. 2.3 Hans Holbein the Younger, *Noli Me Tangere* (1524–6), Royal Collection Trust/ © Her Majesty Queen Elizabeth II 2016.

---

[104] On the provenance of Holbein's painting, see Derek Wilson, *Hans Holbein: Portrait of an Unknown Man* (London: Weidenfeld & Nicolson, 1996), 135. See also the brief description of the commissioning of Holbein's painting in Susan Foister, *Holbein in England* (London: Tate Publishing, 2006), 127.

Fig. 2.4 Titian, *Noli me Tangere* © The National Gallery, London. Bequeathed by Samuel Rogers, 1856.

Holbein's version is unique in having Mary stand directly across from Christ, a posture that agrees with the choreography of John 20:16. Mary had been "standing" (20:14), although she stoops briefly to look into the tomb. Once Christ calls her name, she turns and addresses him as Rabboni, after which Christ warns her against touching him: "Jesus saith unto her, Mary. She turneth herself, and saith unto him in Hebrew, Rabboni; which is to say, Teacher" (20:16).

Not only does Holbein elevate Mary in compositionally placing the figures on equal planes, but he faithfully includes narrative details of the scene, including a view of the two well-lit angels in the tomb and the backset images of Peter and John. These are details that the more dramatic medieval-Renaissance depictions typically eschew in favor of a more eroticized tableau. While Titian and Correggio, both influenced by the sensual turn in humanist art, eroticize the encounter by depicting Mary pining for a semi-clad Christ, Holbein's Christ and Mary are fully clothed. The image, given the steady exchange of glances between Mary and her Master, conveys Mary's spiritual epiphany and understanding of the *noli me tangere* admonition rather than the erotics of an abortive touch.

Holbein's image is also remarkably faithful to the scriptural text in that it underscores, through Christ's posture and hand gestures, the absolute prohibition against a material encounter. In Titian's image, Christ avoids Mary's outstretched hand but Christ still leans toward her, his lower hand hardly pulling away and still within grasp. The palpable closeness of Mary and Christ in Titian's image is of a piece with the traditional Italian-Renaissance and medieval sense that, despite the warning, Mary might have indeed touched Christ. As Jeanne Nuechterlein has remarked, not only did devotional manuals such as *Meditations on the Life of Christ* doubt whether Christ would really have prohibited Mary's touch; several medieval devotional images depict Mary touching Christ's feet. Indeed, a mythographic tradition arose that imagined Christ had touched Mary on the forehead before he departed, a scene that Albrecht Dürer reimagines in his Small Woodcuts of 1511.[105] Against these embellishments, Holbein's "truth-seeking" sensibility, in Derek Wilson's words, positions Christ as lifting his hands away from Magdalene as he backs away from her, emphasizing the seriousness of the warning against contact before Christ's Ascension.[106]

Holbein's image legitimates what I have been describing as the fundamental, if paradoxical, Johannine focus on enchantment and sacred presence. Precisely because of the manifest distance that renders Christ's body unavailable to Mary, a distance clearly marked in Holbein's portrait as well as in the homiletic and poetic accounts of John 20 that we have been discussing, Mary can achieve intimate fellowship with Christ. Her spiritual uplift and personal ascension to the Father depend on her acknowledgement that Christ's presence is not materially required. And in its unstylized depiction of Mary's encounter with Christ, Holbein's vision agrees with what we find in both Crashaw's and Vaughan's later Magdalene poems, particularly the sense in which, once Mary comes to an understanding of the significance of the prohibition against touching, she can at least approach the spirituality of her Master.

THE GLORIFICATION OF MARY: CRASHAW, VAUGHAN, AND TRAPNEL

Richard Crashaw's "The Weeper," included in his *Steps to the Temple: Sacred Poems, With other Delights of the Muses* (1646), provides us with an example of the ways in which Johannine material merges with that of the Synoptics, in this case Luke 7, in order to present a portrait of Magdalene that also isolates her glorification and incorporation into Christ rather than her earthbound conversion. That the poem clearly is Lukan in some sense is evidenced by the last line. Mary's tears, now become two "bright brothers" (XXVIII, 1), will not fall on the merely earthly—the "rose's modest Cheek" (XXX, 3) or "violet's humble head" (XXX, 4)—but will "goe to meet / A worthy object, our lord's FEET" (XXXI, 6).[107] Luke's version of the

---

[105] Jeanne Nuechterlein, *Translating Nature into Art: Holbein, The Reformation, and Renaissance Rhetoric* (University Park: Penn State University Press, 2011), 196–7.

[106] Wilson, *Hans Holbein*, 136.

[107] All quotations from "The Weeper" are taken from *The Complete Poetry of Richard Crashaw*, ed. George Walton Williams (New York: NYU Press, 1972), 120–37.

anointing of Christ in Bethany by Mary is distinctive in recording Mary's weeping: "And behold, a woman in the citie which was a sinner, when shee knew that Jesus sate at meat in the Pharisees house, brought an Alabaster boxe of ointment" (Luke 7:37). John, who presumably locates the scene at Lazarus's house, also remarks that Mary anoints Christ's feet rather than head, although he makes no mention of Mary's weeping: "Then tooke Mary a pound of ointment, of Spikenard, very costly, and anointed the feet of Jesus, & wiped his feet with her haire: and the house was filled with the odour of the ointment" (John 12:3). Matthew and Mark (but not Luke) depict Mary as simply pouring the anointment on Jesus' head (Matthew 26:7, Mark 14:3).

In the context of Crashaw's poem, in which Mary's tears paradoxically flow heavenward rather than earthward, the closing Lukan sentiment seems to realize the main conceit of the poem. Crashaw's critics have pointed out that, since Christ's feet symbolize heaven, "Mary's tears in falling on them actually are rising," although George Walton Williams is correct in remarking that the idea is not typically "repeated in connection with the Magdalene."[108] In fact, there is nothing intrinsic to the Lukan account to signify that, through Mary's anointing of Christ's feet, she and Christ are at once transported to heaven. Luke represents the manner in which Mary, despite entering the scene as a sinner, displays more hospitality and reverence toward Christ than his Pharisaical host when she washes Christ's feet (itself a traditional ritual of respect). In anointing Christ, she reflects her faith and so deserves to be forgiven for her sins. According to Calvin, the fact that Mary anoints Christ's head is not even a significant symbolic difference across the four versions of the story: "Nor indeed is there any contradiction in Matthew and Mark relating that Christ's head was anointed, while our author [John] says it was His feet. Anointing was usually of the head, and for this reason Pliny regards it as extravagant when some anointed the ankles."[109]

The spiritual elevation of Mary in Crashaw's poem depends in part on the Johannine material that precedes it. By the last stanza, Crashaw has already drawn on two important narratives from the Fourth Gospel—the discourse of the vine and the miracle at Cana—in order to celebrate the achieved glorification of Mary. Stanza XI reads: "Such the maiden gemme / By the purpling vine put on, / Peeps from her parent stemme / And blushes at the bridegroome sun. / This watry Blossom of thy eyn, / Ripe, will make the richer wine" (XI, 1–6). John's vine discourse highlights the mutual fellowship of the believer in Christ: "I am the true vine, and my Father is the husbandman. Every branch in me that beareth not fruit, hee taketh away: and every branch that beareth fruit, he purgeth it, that it may bring foorth more fruit....Abide in me, and in you" (15:1–4). In Crashaw's poem, Christ has already brought Mary into this state of mutuality or participation: "Twas his well-pointed dart / That digg'd these wells, and drest this Vine" (XVIII, 1–2).

[108] George Walton Williams, *Image and Symbol in the Sacred Poetry of Richard Crashaw* (Columbia: University of South Carolina Press, 1963), 100, 102.
[109] *Calvin's New Testament Commentaries*, vol. 5, 25.

Incorporated into Christ, Mary's eyes will produce richer tears/wine than the natural vine.

This metaphor of engrafted union with Christ is developed further in the subsequent stanza in which Crashaw makes reference to the miracle at Cana: "When some new bright Guest / Takes up among the starres a room, / And Heavn will make a feast, / Angels with crystall violls come / And draw from these full eyes of thine / Their master's Water: their own Wine" (XII, 1–6). In the Johannine source narrative, Christ approaches a Samaritan woman at a dry well and assures her that he can provide the "living water" to quench the Samaritans' thirst:

> Jesus answered, and said unto her, If thou knewest the gift of God, and who it is that sayth to thee, Give me to drinke; thou wouldest have asked of him, and hee would have given thee living water. The woman saith unto him, Sir, thou hast nothing to drawe with, and the Well is deepe: from whence then hast thou that living water? Art thou greater then our father Jacob, which gave us the Well, and dranke thereof himselfe, and his children, and his cattell? Jesus answered, and said unto her, Whosoever drinketh of this water, shall thirst againe: But whosoever drinketh of the water that I shal give him, shall never thirst: but the water that I shall give him, shalbe in him a well of water springing up into everlasting life.   (4:10–14)

This "living water," typically understood to refer to the spirit of Christ (and the means by which the brethren's faith inheres in Christ), is reflected in Crashaw's phrase "master's Water," which itself serves to conflate Magdalene's sanctified tears and the spirit of God such that she has become incorporated into God. The frequent suggestion in the poem that the location of the site of incorporation is in heaven reflects a mutual ascension that Mary shares with Christ, an ethereal union that in itself agrees with the Johannine tendency to elevate the divine rather than the human aspects of the Son.[110]

Crashaw's critics have tended to pass lightly over the fact that much of the material that the longer version of "The Weeper" adds to the earlier version is distinctly Johannine material.[111] This material includes not only stanzas XI and XII but also stanza XVIII, which reiterates the vine metaphor, adding to it the lamb reference: "The lamb hath dipp't his white foot here" (XVIII, 6). We do not know exactly why Crashaw expanded the poem in this manner. He seemed to have found in the Johannine verses scriptural warrant for the otherwise inflated sense that Magdalene's tears (and Magdalene herself) join Christ in heaven. By the time the reader gets to the Lukan anointing at the end of the poem, an anointing that would not in itself evoke the ascended provenance of Mary and Christ, Crashaw

---

[110] In his excellent reading of the "The Weeper," which focuses very differently on the sacramental and Eucharistic mysteries of the real presence (79), Gary Kuchar also points out that, compared to Southwell's depiction of Magdalene's penance (at least in *St. Peter's Complaint*), Crashaw's Magdalene "is more idealized and thus more other-worldly." *The Poetry of Religious Sorrow in Early Modern England*, 78.

[111] Crashaw adds eight stanzas to the poem in the second edition of *Steps to the Temple* in 1648. Austin Warren correctly remarks that Crashaw's extensions display his desire to "dilate, to display further ingenuity," conducing to a "less staccato" and "more sequential" effect, but Warren makes no mention of the scriptural sources for the added material. See Warren, *Richard Crashaw: A Study in Baroque Sensibility* (Baton Rouge, LSU Press, 1939), 128–9.

has confidently placed Mary at God's right hand along with Christ. The paradoxicality of the movement downward as really being a movement upward is spiritually assonant despite its cognitive dissonance.

A similar use of the Johannine material as a means of lifting Mary's spiritual status is at work in Henry Vaughan's "St. Mary Magdalen," a poem included in Vaughan's *Silex Scintillans* (1650). At the outset of the poem, Mary is described as brighter, "more white then day" (1), a saint whose turn toward Christ has freed her from her own vanities—"not tutor'd by thy glass" (7)—but who nevertheless weeps: "But since thy beauty doth still keep / Bloomy and fresh, why dost thou weep?" (9–10).[112] There is more than a faint echo here of John's description of Mary at Christ's tomb. Magdalene's whiteness analogizes the whiteness of the angels who ask her, as does the speaker of Crashaw's poem, "Woman, why weepest thou?" (20:13). And as in John's account, so too in Vaughan's poem the interrogatives continue, though in varying form. As Christ asks again, "Woman, why weepest thou? whom seekest thou?" (John 20:15), so Vaughan's speaker likewise plies Mary with analogous questions, for example, "Why art thou humbled thus, and low / As earth, thy lovely head dost bow?" (24–5). Patricia Badir observes that "this is the Mary of John 20," although Badir goes on to argue that the "introverted clairvoyance characteristic of Southwell's solitary weeper is replaced here with unapologetic display."[113] Badir is certainly correct to point out the "disheveled contrition" of Mary here. Yet I would add that the Johannine signature resurfaces in Vaughan's reinscription of the mutual glorification of Christ and Mary.

Perhaps the most overt but typically passed over Johannine reference appears in the first of four short stanzas beginning at line 51: "Her Art! whose memory must last / Till truth through all the world be past, / Till his abus'd, despised flame / Return to Heaven, from whence it came" (51–4). As we have begun to see, John's is the only Gospel that, in celebrating the pre-existent, divine nature of Christ, foregrounds a descent and return motif. In his conversation with Nicodemus, Christ points out that "no man hath ascended up to heaven, but hee that came downe from heaven, even the Sonne of man which is in heaven" (3:13). Later, in his response to the Pharisees who remark that his record "is not true," Christ remarks: "Though I beare record of my selfe, yet my record is true: for I know whence I came, and whither I goe: but ye cannot tell whence I come, and whither I goe" (8:14). Vaughan's description of Christ as a flame that will "return to heaven, from whence it came" helps us to see that the Christ of his poem, quite like the Christ of Crashaw's Magdalene poem, is the divinely privileged Christ of the Fourth Gospel.

If the stanza invokes the Johannine Christ, it also places Mary, along with Christ, in a post-resurrection context quite like Crashaw's "The Weeper" but with a crucial addition. Through her "art," Vaughan's Mary will serve Christ's followers in the manner of the Comforter or Spirit-Paraclete once Christ has departed. Mary's eyes,

---

[112] All quotations from Vaughan's "St. Mary Magdalen" are taken from *The Works of Henry Vaughan*, ed. L. C. Martin (Oxford: Clarendon Press, 1957), 507–8.
[113] Badir, *The Maudlin Impression*, 163.

described as a "light" which will help "dark straglers to their sight" (59–60), will serve as a means of remembrance of the truths that Christ embodies: "Her Art! whose memory must last / Till truth through all the world be past" (51–2). Here we have an example of Vaughan's syncretistic use of biblical material. The lines recall Matthew's belief that Mary's anointing of Christ's head with the precious ointment will foster remembrance of her devotion: "Verely I say unto you, Wheresoever this Gospel shall be preached in the whole world, there shall also this, that this woman hath done, be told for a memoriall of her" (Matthew 26:13). Yet the Matthean sense is incorporated into the Johannine commissioning theme at lines 53–4 and into the apocalypticism of the final lines of the stanza: "And send a fire down, that shall bring / Destruction on his ruddy wing" (55–6). The Matthean focus on the remembrance of Mary slides into the Johannine-informed sense of the judgment that Christ will dispense once he returns to heaven "from whence" he comes, as in John 8:16: "And yet if I judge, my judgement is true: for I am not alone, but I and the Father that sent me." If the Matthean lines remind us of the glory that should redound to Mary particularly in a pre-resurrection context—that is, until Christ's "despised flame" (53) returns to heaven (54)—the superimposed Johannine lines signify that Mary will provide the light to darksome stragglers until Christ returns with fanfare. Consider Mary's role here alongside Christ's promise of the Paraclete to his disciples in John 16: "It is expedient for you that I goe away: for if I goe not away, the Comforter will not come unto you: but if I depart, I will send him unto you. And when he is come, he will reprove the world of sin, and of righteousness, and of judgment.... Howbeit, when hee the spirit of trueth is come, he wil guide you into all trueth" (John 16:7–13). As does the Paraclete, Mary functions as Christ's *anamnesis* as well as pedagogue to the faithful who are left behind. She will testify to Christ's example and his truths, and she will continue his missionary work through which those who are in darkness will be brought into her (and his) light.

In both Crashaw's and Vaughan's treatment of the Magdalene narratives, Mary has achieved more than the initial conversion testified in Luke's account of her weeping and anointing of Christ's feet. Mary enjoys in both poems more of a state of glorification than initiation into the arduous process of conversion. Both devotional poets extend the accounts of the *noli me tangere* narrative that we find in Southwell, Markham, Walkington, and Breton. While those four writers were concerned to reconstruct the ways in which Mary must first come to an understanding of the importance of hearing Christ's words (as opposed to touching or seeing her Master) before she can find conversion, Crashaw and Vaughan re-imagine a Magdalene who has acquired formed or proper faith. This is a Magdalene who enjoys not only a mystical union with Christ in the afterlife; she will also extend Christ's message to those whom he has left behind.

I turn lastly to the treatment of Mary at the tomb in the writings of the seventeenth-century enthusiast Anna Trapnel. Trapnel's brief but provocative references to *noli me tangere* extend further the treatments we have found in the emblematic and devotional assessments discussed so far. In *A Voice for the King of Saints and Nations* (1657), Trapnel remarks that Christ momentarily postpones the Ascension in order to mind Mary's tears and pity her weeping eyes: "When a weeping *Mary* comes, Hee'l not leave her alone / Without some words of comfort, O / He must to *Mary* talk, / And also send to Bretheren. / Who likewise love his walk / She cries *Rabbony,* and would touch, / But prethee *Mary* stay, / For I am not ascended yet / Saith he, but go that way."[114] At the outset Trapnel attends, as do the sixteenth-century accounts, to the exchange of words between Christ and Mary, stressing that Christ "must" talk to the weeping Magdalene, a focus that is intensified as Trapnel's narrative picks up: "He did not stay, I cant now talk; / But wipes away her teares, / And speaks most kindly unto her, / That so she might not fear; / O what a glorious Christ is this, / That doth say I am he, /And what'a bright and flaming love, / May poor hearts in him see. / While she was weeping he doth speak, / And unto her doth come, / While you have eares on cheeks for him."[115] Trapnel's recounting shuttles between her assertion that Christ could not "stay" with Mary and "talk" and her acknowledgement that he does indeed stay in order to speak kindly to her. What Christ offers is the simple and glorious proclamation of who he is—"That doth say I am he." The importance of Mary's hearing his words is brought out in Trapnel's remarkable, almost Crashavian conceit signifying that Mary will hear through her tears, now become "ears on cheeks" for Christ.

So much is what we might expect, given the importance of aurality throughout the "touch me not" sequence. But Trapnel, to a greater extent than we find in the earlier treatments, celebrates the spiritual "comfort" that Mary's dialogue with Christ confers on her: "He will bring comfort home / Unto your soul, and you shall drink, / And have your fill of love; / And it shall rise up to a flame, / And carry you above."[116] Mary's passing reference to spiritual comfort opens out to the larger context of Trapnel's exaltation of John as her most cherished spiritual guide, to whom a gendered paean appears elsewhere in *A Voice for the King of Saints and Nations.*[117] Trapnel cannot contain her enthusiasm for "My *John* to whom I am so dear, / He that shew'd love so high"; John is the apostle who will "shew this very Christ / To whom the Father spake," the apostle who tells of Mary, Christ's "hand-maid," the apostle who understands Christ's appreciation of all women comparable to the Magdalene: "John doth not disdain to take in, / The hand-maids which were there, / Who did so much love Jesus Christ, / And resurrection rare. / O *John* he did speak of hand-maids, / Whom Christ did love so dear, / And tells that Jesus Christ he did, / To hand-maids first draw near. / O *John* his record of the son, / Is very sweet indeed."[118] It is a short step from the spiritual benefits that Trapnel

---

[114] Anna Trapnel, *A Voice for the King of Saints and Nations* (London, 1657), 51.

[115] Ibid., 51.   [116] Ibid., 51.

[117] Trapnel's treatment of Magdalene's weeping as exemplary for other women is anticipated in *Elogium heroinum, or, The praise of worthy women written* (London, 1651), a pro-feminist treatise written by C. G. (Charles Gerber?):"But with what a blisse was this conversation crowned, when as Christ Jesus himself in person, would approve himself to be the chief in that heavenly conference and enquiry, by his saying, *Why weepest thou? whom seekest thou?* and so might he wel say indeed, since hee himself was there to bid them weep no more. Most blessed Sexe! though they were forbidden to weep, yet may all men continue the same for the backwardness of such as follow not the example of these pious and religious women" (149–50).

[118] Ibid., 35. Richard Sibbes likewise lingers over the fact that Christ reveals himself to a woman, although Sibbes more pointedly claims that, as a woman, Mary's affective bond with Christ is

imagines Mary had received from Christ to the comparable comfort that Trapnel herself finds in Johannine theology. Such comfort is outlined several times in her conversion narrative, *A Legacy for Saints* (1654). Here the comforts of Mary are personalized for Trapnel, as she joins ranks with her dissenting and antinomian compatriots in exalting the "free grace" and liberation from legalism so touted among the dissenters and in parading the pneumatological assurance and perseverance provided to her by the Paraclete:

> Free grace hath opened a fountain for to wash in, not onely your feet, but head and hands, yea your whole man; in this fountain I was cleansed, by this wine my drooping spirits were revived, Christ was that good *Samaritan,* that found me wounded, whom the Law nor Priest did not pitty; legall threatnings, and legall promises looked upon me.... Oh how comfortable was his oyl and wine to my wounds.... The Saints told me when I mourned for the loss of my tender mother, that Christ would be more tender, and would be all to me in the loss of earthly comforts; and he was more to me then they told me, he was double comfort, and a Comforter that hath tarried and abided with me, and will abide with me for ever, a Comforter that was still revealing love, and bringing love tokens to my soul.[119]

These are the words and experience of Anna Trapnel, but they are also the words and experience that Trapnel has projected onto Mary Magdalene and all such "hand-maids," an experience of mutual abiding in love through the agency of the Spirit that provides an unwavering assurance of salvation.[120] If the sixteenth-century emblematic and homiletic treatments of John 20 reconstruct the peda-gogical process by which Mary needs to re-learn the proper signification of Christ's words, and if the devotional poetry of the later seventeenth century further elevates Mary by imagining her in a post-resurrectional state with Christ, Trapnel provides the most personal testimony of an even more mystical encounter with the spiritual nourishment and love of Christ provided to herself, Mary, and all enthusiastic converts. But there is more to be said on the subject of the Paraclete and Johannine pneumatology, the subject to which we now turn.

---

exceptional: "Who is sent. A *woman,* a *woman* to be the Apostle of the Apostles.... *Mary Magdalen* was sent to instruct the Apostles in the great Articles of Christs Resurrection and Ascension to Heaven. By a Woman death came into the world, and by a woman life was preached to the Apostles; because indeed she was more affectionate, and affection taketh all. And that makes that sex more addicted to Religion, by the advantage of their affection; for Religion is meerly a matter of affection." *A heavenly conference between Christ and Mary after His resurrection* (London, 1654), 44–5.

[119] Anna Trapnel, *A legacy for saints; being several experiences of the dealings of God with Anna Trapnel* (London, 1654), 13.

[120] Sibbes's treatise on Mary at the tomb, *A heavenly conference between Christ and Mary after His resurrection* (London, 1654), published the same year as Trapnel's *A Legacy for the Saints*, also celebrates the sending of the Comforter following the Ascension: "And likewise he ascended to leave us his spirit, that he might send the Comforter. He taketh away himself that was the great Comforter, while he was below. He was the Bridegroom, and while the Bride-groom was present, they had not such a measure of the spirit, Christs presence supplyed all; but Christ ascended to Heaven, that his departure from them, might not be prejudiciall to them; but that they might have comfort through the God of com-fort, the spirit of comfort, the Holy Ghost" (93–4).

3

Spiritual Comfort and Assurance
The Role of the Paraclete in
Seventeenth-Century Poetry and Polemic

From the controversial Johannine Comma in the First Epistle to the fateful announcement at the outset of his Gospel—"And the Word was made flesh" (1:14)—John's writings exerted an unrivalled influence on patristic, medieval, and Reformed notions of the Trinity. Paul C. H. Lim has recently described the formative influence of several key Johannine passages on the Trinitarian-Socinian debates of the latter part of the seventeenth century, pointing out the malleable use of the Johannine discourses to prove and disprove the Trinitarian unity of God. While seventeenth-century English poets and theologians generally were, of course, engaged by much of the pre- and early modern polemicizing regarding the Trinity (the Racovian Catechism of the Socinians orients its anti-Trinitarianism around controversial interpretations of key Johannine texts), many such writers seem particularly engaged by Johannine pneumatology and the unique role of the Holy Ghost in providing spiritual comfort against backsliding and tribulations. In addition, Christ's promise of the arrival of the Paraclete, the favored Johannine term for the Spirit who will provide testimony of Christ's teachings and help establish and guide the future Church, becomes a polemical debating point in some of the period's most contentious conflicts between, on the one hand, Catholic pretensions regarding the infallibility of the Church and, on the other hand, the post-Reformed belief that the Church can and has often been seduced by false spirits.

This chapter therefore focuses on the uniqueness of the Johannine Paraclete (relative to the Synoptic presentation of the Holy Spirit) and the range of uses to which the Paraclete was put in post-Reformed, mostly seventeenth-century English discourse. What follows is a brief assessment of John's presentation of the third person, or "Comforter," and a set of close readings of the writings of John Donne and John Milton. Despite their widely differing literary sensibilities, Donne and Milton are included in this chapter because, among seventeenth-century poets and writers, both writers show an especially keen, if divergent interest in Johannine pneumatology. Donne believes that the Paraclete provides traditional assurance and perseverance against the well-known registration of filial and servile fear that so often turns up in his prose and poetry. Writing during the turbulent Interregnum and early Restoration periods, Milton's skepticism regarding the Church's claim to unerring spiritual truth leads him to question the role of the Paraclete in salvation.

THE JOHANNINE SPIRIT-PARACLETE

In the first half of John's Gospel, we find references to the Holy Spirit that can be found in comparable form in the Synoptic writings, although the Johannine content and message depart significantly from the Synoptics' presentation of the descent of the Spirit. The earliest reference in 1:32–3 of John the Baptist's witnessing of the Spirit's descent on Jesus in the form of a dove can be found in Matthew, Mark, and Luke. Other Spirit references in the early sections of the Fourth Gospel include Jesus' advice to Nicodemus that he needs to be born again of "water and of the Spirit" (3:5), Jesus' claim that his words are life-affirming in that they provide the Spirit (6:63), and Jesus' announcement of the future arrival of the Spirit (7:38–9).

The Holy Spirit becomes an especially prominent feature of the Johannine Farewell Discourse at 14:15–24. Here we find John's unique description of the Spirit as "Paraclete," a transliteration of the Greek word *Parakletos*, often translated as "Advocate" but more generally understood to mean one who will not only testify and inspire remembrance of Jesus' ministry but also provide spiritual ease and comfort: "And I will pray the Father, and hee shall give you another Comforter, that he may abide with you for ever. . . . The Comforter, which is the holy Ghost, whom the Father wil send in my name, he shal teach you al things, & bring al things to your remembrance, whatsoever I have said unto you" (14:16, 26). Akin to the designation as Comforter is the description of the third person as the Spirit of truth, as in 15:26–7: "But when the Comforter is come, whom I wil send unto you from the Father, even the Spirit of trueth, which proceedeth from the Father, hee shall testifie of me. And ye also shall beare witnesse, because ye have bene with me from the beginning." The Spirit is pivotal in the Farewell Discourse (as well as in the final commissioning scene at 20:22, in which Jesus breathes the Spirit onto the disciples) in that it will maintain continuity between Jesus' pre- and post-glorification teaching and enable communication between the adopted brethren and Christ after his departure.[1]

In addition to John's unique description of the Spirit as Comforter or Paraclete, John's discussion of the initial descent of the Spirit departs significantly from the Synoptics' account of the baptism of Jesus. According to Matthew, for example, after the Spirit descends like a dove, a heavenly voice proclaims that Jesus is the "beloved Sonne" (Matt. 3:16–17). As I remarked earlier, in John's version, instead of the announcement by a heavenly voice, the Spirit reveals to John the Baptist that Jesus is the Son of God. In the Fourth Gospel, the Baptist is the one to whom Christ is revealed (1:34), which in turn prompts the Baptist to realize that Jesus will be the one privileged to baptize and sanctify with the Holy Spirit (1:32–3). And the Johannine account, unlike the Synoptic narrative, maintains that the Spirit will *remain* on Jesus.

The Johannine departure from the Synoptics is subtle but has profound implications for our understanding of the unique role of the Spirit in Johannine theology.

---

[1] See Andreas J. Köstenberger, *A Theology of John's Gospel and Letters: The Word, The Christ, The Son of God* (Zondervan, 2009), 96–8.

In helping to reveal to John the Baptist Christ's role as redeemer, the lamb who takes away sin, the Spirit provides the testimony and knowledge of Christ as the Son of God.[2] The Johannine version departs from Synoptic pneumatology in emphasizing the power-affirming rather than the power-giving aspect of the Spirit once it descends on the newly arrived Christ. Throughout the Synoptics, the descent of the Spirit endows or "fills" Christ with divine power, as if the Spirit at some level alters Jesus' nature.[3] Markan Christology in particular holds that Jesus is impelled by the power of the Spirit, as in Mark's sense that the Spirit prompts Christ to wander in the wilderness: "And immediately the Spirit driveth him into the wildernesse" (Mark 1:12).[4] For John, however, the descent and divine anointing simply herald the arrival of the Son of God, recalling, as does the entire Fourth Gospel, the Son's prior relationship with the Father. "The Spirit descends," one commentator notes, "in order that Jesus 'might be revealed' as the Son of God to Israel. The emphasis falls on making Jesus known to others, and not on making of him something that he was not before."[5] That the Spirit remains on Jesus highlights the extent to which, although Jesus will confer the Spirit upon the faithful, the Spirit's permanence in him continually bears witness to his divinity.[6]

THE PARACLETE IN REFORMED ENGLISH THEOLOGY AND CULTURE

Early modern English commentators on the Fourth Gospel and First Epistle typically distinguish the three significations of the Paraclete as comforter, teacher or exhorter, and advocate. Thus Henry Hammond's paraphrase of John 16:15:

> And I will ask my Father, and when I am gone he shall send you the holy Ghost, who for the several parts of his office 1. to intercede as an advocate, 2. to exhort, 3. to comfort, is best exprest by the word [Paraclete] which in Greek signifies all these three, and he, when he cometh, shall abide with you forever, not departing, as I now doe, but continuing with you as long as you adhere and continue obedient to my precepts.[7]

Although Hammond will go on to describe the Paraclete's role as advocate or "interlocutor" of the "Christian's cause with God," most commentators shared

---

[2] See Marianne Meye Thompson, *The God of the Gospel of John* (Grand Rapids: Eerdmans Publishing Company, 2001), 161.

[3] Ibid., 164.

[4] As Gary Burge remarks of the Johannine Spirit, "The Spirit is not an alien force empowering the Messiah as, say, Markan Christology would have it. Jesus does not seem to 'have' the Spirit; instead the Spirit is an attribute of his very life." Burge, *The Anointed Community: The Holy Spirit in the Johannine Tradition* (Grand Rapids: Eerdmans Publishing Company, 1987), 72.

[5] Thompson, *The God of the Gospel of John*, 164. See also Albert Schweitzer, *The Mysticism of Saint Paul the Apostle*, trans. William Montgomery (New York: Henry Holt & Company, 1931), where Schweitzer remarks, "According to the view taken in the Gospel of John, the baptism of Jesus did not constitute a significant experience for Himself, nor an outstanding event of His Coming into the world, but only as a means of making known to the Baptist that he can thenceforth preach Jesus as Him who is to baptize with the Holy Spirit" (358–9).

[6] Thompson, *The God of the Gospel of John*, 164.

[7] Henry Hammond, *A paraphrase and annotations upon all the books of the New Testament* (London, 1659), 311.

John Owen's preoccupation, articulated later in the seventeenth century, with the Paraclete's comforting office.[8] In his lengthy treatise on the Spirit, Owen remarks: "The Work of a Comforter is principally ascribed unto him.... That he is principally under this Name intended as a *Comforter,* is evident from the whole Context and the occasion of the Promise. It was with respect unto the Troubles and Sorrows of his Disciples, with their Relief therein, that he is promised under this Name by our Saviour."[9] The office of assuagement suits the "principal work" of the Spirit, given the identification of the Spirit elsewhere in the Gospel as the Spirit of peace, love, and joy, whose role, Owen maintains, is "to communicate a Sense of Divine Love with Delight and Joy unto the Souls of Believers."[10] We will see momentarily that this affective and *agapic* service of the Paraclete is voiced by Calvin and Luther and informs Donne's conception of the Spirit in his sermons and *Holy Sonnets.*

An important question in the context of this and subsequent chapters is the Reformed and early modern perception of the relationship between the Johannine Spirit and personal assurance. Early modern and modern commentators often point out that the First Epistle provides the most detailed discussion of personal assurance across New Testament accounts.[11] For example, in his commentary on assurance and John's First Epistle—*Believers evidences for eternall life collected out of the first epistle of John* (1655)—Presbyterian clergyman Francis Roberts remarks, "The holy Ghost by the Apostle hath replenished this *precious Epistle* with more variety and plenty of pregnant *Marks, Signes, Characters or Evidences* of Believers spiritual estate, then any other Scripture of like quantity in the whole Book of God. So that it is a *Rich Treasury for Christian-Assurance.*"[12] Calvin assumes that assurance followed naturally from saving faith. His position is developed not only in the *Institutes* but also primarily in his commentary on John's First Epistle. An exemplary remark on assurance appears in the First Epistle at verses 3:18–19: "My little children, let us not love in word, neither in tongue, but indeede and in trueth. And hereby wee know that wee are of the trueth, and shall assure our hearts before him." This is a seminal passage which for Calvin implies that the ground of assurance lies not in sanctified works, love, or even within the conscience of the penitent but in God's free adoption by means of the Spirit: "In these words he tells us that faith does not exist apart from a good conscience. Not that assurance comes from it or depends on it; but because we are truly, and not falsely, assured of our union with God only when He manifests Himself in our love by the efficacy of His Holy Spirit."[13] While a good conscience cannot be separated from faith, Calvin

---

    [8] Ibid., 312.
    [9] John Owen, *Two discourses concerning the Holy Spirit, and His work the one, Of the Spirit as a comforter, the other* (London, 1693), 11–12.
    [10] Ibid., 13.
    [11] On the importance of John's First Epistle to personal assurance, see D. A. Carson, "Johannine Perspectives on the Doctrine of Assurance," *Explorations* 10 (1996), 59–97.
    [12] Francis Roberts, *Believers evidences for eternall life collected out of the first epistle of John* (London, 1655), 3.
    [13] John Calvin, *The First Epistle of John,* in *Calvin's New Testament Commentaries,* vol. 5, eds. David W. Torrance and Thomas F. Torrance, trans. T. H. L. Parker (Grand Rapids: Eerdmans Publishing Company, 1994), 278.

continues, assurance is not contingent on works or any further activity on the recipient's part.

The intimate relationship between assurance and saving faith is featured in Calvin's more wide-ranging use of Johannine material in the *Institutes*. Calvin points out that assurance cannot be found within us and that our election is grounded in Christ, the "mirror in which we ought, and in which, without deception, we may contemplate our election."[14] While Calvin refers here to the communion with God as depicted in Romans 8, several key Johannine pericopes from the Fourth Gospel help to underline his point. Our assurance is found in the promise of "everlasting life" (3:16), itself effected through the "bread of life." Our confidence in our election is tied to our callings as described in those Johannine passages (6:37–9 and 17:6–12) that relate the manner in which the faithful are admitted under God's guardianship and protection, about which Calvin concludes: "If we would know whether God cares for our salvation, let us ask whether he has committed us to Christ, whom he has appointed to be the only Saviour of all his people."[15] To look for assurance elsewhere, Calvin cautions, "we must ascend above Christ."[16]

Calvin makes clear in his Johannine commentaries and the *Institutes* that the Spirit's role in assurance is to provide the seal or witness of our adoption: "Every man's faith is an abundant witness to the eternal predestination of God, so that it is sacrilege to inquire further; and whoever refuses to assent to the simple testimony of the Holy Spirit does Him a horrible injury."[17] Assurance depends on the witness of the Spirit, but one should not assume that such a testimony is an additional conferral or action. The Spirit-Paraclete does not bequeath election so much as it provides the pledge of our election, especially the comforting knowledge that assurance has already been given.[18] Calvin will emphasize that the Spirit is not a "constructor of new revelations," that its peculiar office is to teach (remind) the apostles of Christ's mission, not to reveal "something higher" than "what they had already learned."[19] To the extent that the Paraclete adds anything new or additional to saving faith, it adds an *affective* component as a salve against despair and fear: "The Spirit is said to testify of Christ because He retains and settles our faith in Him alone, that we may not seek any part of our salvation elsewhere. Again he calls Him the Paraclete, that, relying on His protection, we may never be alarmed.... [W]herever He speaks, He frees men's minds from all doubt and fear of deception."[20] In an influential study, R. T. Kendall maintains that faith, for Calvin, is primarily cognitive or intellective rather than volitional or affective in nature.[21] As Richard

---

[14] John Calvin, *Institutes of the Christian Religion*, trans. Henry Beveridge (Grand Rapids: Eerdmans Publishing Company, 1995), Book III, chapter 24, 244.

[15] Ibid., 245.   [16] Ibid., 245.

[17] John Calvin, *The Gospel According to St. John*, in *Calvin's New Testament Commentaries*, vol. 4, eds. David W. Torrance and Thomas F. Torrance, trans. T. H. L. Parker (Grand Rapids: Eerdmans Publishing Company, 1994), 162.

[18] The role of the Spirit in providing a seal of assurance is described at length in A. N. S. Lane, "Calvin's Doctrine of Assurance," *Vox Evangelica* 11 (1979), 35.

[19] Calvin, *The Gospel According to St. John*, vol. 5, 11–21, 88.   [20] Ibid., 110.

[21] Kendall remarks that faith is above all equated with "knowledge" for Calvin, along with synonymous terms such as "recognition" or "illumination." *Calvin and English Calvinism to 1649*

A. Muller remarks, however, Calvin's mature conception of faith, especially as found in the 1539 edition of the *Institutes* (to which Calvin added verses both from Paul's epistles and John's Fourth Gospel), emphasizes the extent to which knowledge (*cognitionem*) is balanced with the sealing of faith on the heart (*cor*).[22] Susan Schreiner more specifically describes Calvin's notion of faith as the work of the Spirit in "both mind and heart."[23] Calvin shares this belief in the affective work of the Comforter with Luther. Also refusing to separate saving faith from assurance, Luther celebrates the intimacy and personhood of the Comforter in his description of the Paraclete as one who "will fill a saddened heart with laughter and joy toward God, bids you be of good cheer because of the forgiveness of your sins, slays death, opens heaven, and makes God smile upon you."[24] English divines such as the Puritan clergyman Stephen Jerome even more effusively evoke the affective work of the Paraclete: the heart of God's servant is the "hive into which the Spirit that *Paraclete,* the Comforter brings the sweet hony of Spirituall Comforts; it's the banqueting-house of the bridegroome, yea his nuptiall bed of heavenly desires, and delights."[25]

It is perhaps well known that those English Calvinists typically described as experimental Puritans or Pietists departed from Calvinist orthodoxy in sundering assurance from faith and in arguing that, through introspection or a reflex act as well as through the commission of moral works, one might strive toward personal knowledge of assurance. According to Kendall, for example, experimentalists such as William Perkins and Arthur Hildersam followed Beza rather than Calvin in their enthusiasm for 2 Peter 1:10—"Give diligence to make your calling and election sure: for if ye doe these things, ye shall never fall"—a remark that assumes that certainty of faith might be deduced from the effects of sanctification.[26] Omitted from such scholarly appraisals as Kendall's is the disposition of the experimentalists toward the Johannine conception of the Paraclete. As we might expect, Perkins's treatment of the Paraclete marks a departure from Calvin's and Luther's. Having associated in his 1595 commentary on the Apostle's Creed the Paraclete with the "Sanctifier," Perkins remarks in an anti-Catholic 1606 treatise on Revelation that only the apostles proper enjoy the salvific certainty promised by the Comforter: "Which promise some apply all Gods ministers; but if we marke the circumstances therof, we shall see that properly it agreeth to the Apostles: for though in others the

(Eugene: Wipf & Stock, 1997), 19. A critique of Kendall's presuppositions here can be found in Richard A. Muller, *The Unaccommodated Calvin: Studies in the Foundation of a Theological Tradition* (Oxford: Oxford University Press, 2000), 159–61.

[22] Muller, *The Unaccommodated Calvin*, 160.

[23] Susan E. Schreiner, "The Spiritual Man Judges All Things: Calvin and the Exegetical Debates about Certainty in the Reformation," in *Biblical Interpretation in the Era of the Reformation*, eds. Richard A. Muller and John L. Thompson (Grand Rapids: Eerdmans Publishing Company, 1996), 207–8, cited in Muller, *The Unaccommodated Calvin*, 161.

[24] Martin Luther, *Sermons on the Gospel of St. John*, in *Luther's Works*, vol. 24, ed. Jaroslav Pelikan (Saint Louis: Concordia Publishing, 1961), 115.

[25] Stephen Jerome, *The arraignement of the whole creature, at the barre of religion, reason, and experience* (London, 1632), 88.

[26] Kendall, *Calvin and English Calvinism to 1649*, 33.

certaintie hereof cannot be affirmed."[27] And elsewhere Perkins will remark that one must prepare oneself for the reception and inhabitation of the Paraclete: "If Christ have sent unto his church the holy Spirite to be our comforter, our duty is, to prepare our bodies and soules to be fitte temples and houses for so worthy a guest."[28] Implicit in this preparationism is Perkins's contention that the Comforter also aids us in "laboring" to find redemption: "Christ at his ascension sent his holy Spirite to be the comforter of his Church: & therefore when we are troubled in conscience for our sins, we should not seek ease by such slender means, but rather seeke for the helpe & comfort of the holy ghost, and labour to have our sinnes washed away."[29] The premise behind these comments is that the Comforter does not recall us to the assurance of saving faith that has already been granted; the Comforter rather reminds us of the manner in which we can strive to prepare, maintain, and evince salvation.

Doubts concerning assurance and hence a recontextualization of the Johannine passages among the experimentalists can be seen more clearly in the work of a follower of Perkins, the nonconformist clergyman Arthur Hildersam. For Hildersam, the comforts of the Paraclete need to be understood in the context of the countervailing possibility of false assurance: "The Spirit of God is called *the Comforter, John* 14 26. There is also an assurance and peace of the divells working, he can cause peace too.... But that peace cannot be found and true peace; that Spirit cannot be a true comforter.... Try thy assurance therefore whether it be of God yea or no."[30] Because of the chance of being seduced into assurance by the devil, individuals are exhorted to look for the signs of true assurance, to "examine diligently whether by them whether his assurance be sound or no."[31] One way of determining whether assurance is saving or not is to extrapolate from "the effects and fruits that this assurance produceth in him that hath it."[32] Such deductions are outlined in a lengthy explanatory section in which Hildersam preaches on the importance of loving conduct, an active and "operative" instead of idle "reformation" of one's own "heart and life," and an ongoing fear of offending God through sin; such self-scrutiny should lead to the "practice" of what is taught by the word in keeping with the recommendation in Psalm 26:3 to walk in the truth.[33] If Calvin respects the letter and Spirit of the Johannine passages on the Paraclete in his contention that personal assurance is conferred along with saving faith, Hildersam and Perkins typically invoke yet then veer from the Johannine conception of the Paraclete. They typically qualify John's theology of assurance and

---

[27] On Perkins's association of the Paraclete with sanctification, see *An exposition of the Symbole or Creed of the Apostles* (London, 1595), 30, 398. For Perkins's remarks on assurance and the apostles, see *A godly and learned exposition or commentarie upon the three first chapters of the Revelation* (London, 1606), 69.

[28] Perkins, *An exposition of the Symbole or Creed*, 350.   [29] Ibid., 349.

[30] Arthur Hildersam, *CLII lectures upon Psalme LI* (London, 1635), 621.

[31] Ibid., 620.   [32] Ibid., 621.

[33] Ibid., 626–8. On the importance in Hildersam's sermons of fear to the preparatory process, see Norman Pettit, *The Heart Prepared: Grace and Conversion in Puritan Spiritual Life* (New Haven: Yale University Press, 1966), 57–61.

comfort by referencing passages from Petrine theology and key Wisdom texts that exhort the elect to look for assurance, always precarious, in the fruits of faith and sanctified conduct.

We can begin to see a pattern here that will re-emerge throughout the following chapters, particularly in our discussion of the Johannine influence on early modern conceptions of free grace. To the extent that a theologian or poet remains close to the letter of John's references to the Spirit-Paraclete, personal assurance is indeed linked, as it is for Calvin and Luther, to justification by faith. Only when John is decontextualized and used polemically against Roman Catholicism, on the one hand, or antinomianism, on the other hand, are the Johannine passages marshaled against claims to certainty of election. We will see in Chapter 5 that, during the Antinomian Controversy in Boston, John Cotton, perhaps the period's most learned expositor of Johannine theology, will return again and again to both the First Epistle and Fourth Gospel (as well as Calvin's treatments of those texts) in his defense of free grace against the presuppositions of experimental Puritanism that are codified in the 1648 version of the Westminster Confession of Faith.

Yet there are early modern treatises and literary texts that embrace the psychological comforts promised by the Johannine Paraclete without also fussing over neo-scholastic distinctions among faith, assurance, and perseverance. Perhaps the most widely circulated early modern English presentation of the role of the Johannine Paraclete can be found in Francis Quarles's emblematic writings. In *Judgement and Mercie* (1646), Quarles brings together 1 John 2:27 (on the anointing of believers by the Spirit), John 14:26 (on the service of the Spirit to foster remembrance), and John 15:26 (on the testifying role of the Spirit) in order to assuage his readers' tribulations: "When sharp *Afflictions* shall plough up the sallows of thy heart, this Pearl shall then appear and comfort thee."[34] The related prayer attached to Meditation 5 of the treatise is a cobbling together of related verses on assurance and perseverance: "Remember thy word to thy servant, upon which thou hast caused me to hope. Behold I am weak, be thou my *helper*, Behold I am comfortlesse, be thy *Comforter*."[35] All such commentaries celebrate the role of the Paraclete in permanently providing comfort even to those recalcitrant saints who are prone to backsliding and who need to be reminded of the permanence of grace on their behalf. Quarles was a well-known Royalist who enjoyed court patronage. But we do not find in Quarles's writings, particularly in the *Emblemes* (1635) and *Judgement and Mercie* (both of which enjoyed popularity across denominational divides) the sort of polemical quibbling that sets Puritan Pietists against antinomians. Indeed, we would be wrong to argue that Johannine conceptions of assurance divide along ideological lines. As we will see later, John's comforting verses are embraced as readily by the high churchman Henry Vaughan as they are by a Ranter such as Lawrence Claxton or by the radical antinomian Anne Hutchinson. What we can say is that the closer one hewed to an experimentalist or federalist position that would separate faith from assurance (and justification from

---

[34] Francis Quarles, *Judgement and Mercie for Afflicted Souls* (London, 1646), 20–1.
[35] Ibid., 24.

sanctification), the more likely Johannine theology would be diluted with scriptural counter-texts.

It should also be noted that the Johannine Spirit-Paraclete takes on a slightly different political connotation throughout the English Interregnum. In this context, the Comforter is portrayed more as a protector of the church militant, one who serves to defend believers from corporeal encroachments, rather than simply as a provider of spiritual comfort. Typical of such rhetoric is a long treatise by the Independent minister Nicholas Lockyer, whose *Christ's Communion with his Church Militant* (1640) provides a hundred-page gloss on John 14:8 ("I will not leave you comfortless"). Lockyer assures readers that, because the "Spirit of delusion" is upon these "latter days," "Christ will come to his Church Militant as a Comforter.... He may stop the mouthes of all ungodly wretches, who say of the godly when in great distresses, *Persecute and take them.*"[36] Lockyer, who will eventually embrace the Solemn League and Covenant and defend the regicide as a vocal Engager, has in mind the role of the Comforter to provide a defense against "ungodly" Royalists and to discern such "false Christs" and "false comforters."[37] A similar bolstering rhetoric shows up in William Dell's troop-rousing sermon preached to Fairfax and the New Model Army generals in 1646 and in Lazarus Haward's inspirational address to war-torn Irish soldiers in 1647: "Every man whose eternall election and present justification is such, that he can call God father, his Saviour brother, and the Holy Ghost his Comforter, the terrors of death amaze him no."[38] Although not specifically grounding their usage in Johannine sources, Royalists, in turn, enlist the same rhetoric of the Comforter as protector. In *Eikon Basilke* (1648), for example, Charles I identifies his conscience as comforter upon retreating to the Scots—"My Conscience both My Counsellour and My Comforter"—after which royalist propagandists begin using the term to eulogize Charles, as in Robert Browne's *The Subject's Sorrow* (1649): "*I weep, mine eye, mine eye runneth down with water, because the Comforter* (King *CHARLES*) *that should relieve my soul is far from me.*"[39] In his versified history of the church militant, William Vaughan more exclamatorily projects the Paraclete onto Charles: "*Royall Charles, whose sweet and moderate / Condition yeeld us Hopes, that, like his Sire, / He will retaine unquencht the Sacred Fire, / Which in his Soule burnes calmely by the Heat / Of Heavens Flame, the Holy Paraclete.*"[40] That the Comforter is appropriated throughout the seventeenth century by writers of varying political and denominational allegiances is evidenced by its later appearance with fanfare in John Dryden's *Britania Rediviva* (1688), where Dryden, apologist for the tolerationism of James II, describes the birth of the new prince as effected by none other

---

[36] Nicholas Lockyer, *Christ's Communion with his Church Militant* (London, 1640), 69, 55.

[37] Ibid., 73.

[38] William Dell, *The building and glory of the truely Christian and Spiritual church* (London, 1646), 8. Lazarus Haward, *A few collections for Irelands souldiers* (London, 1647), 16.

[39] Charles I, *Eikon Basilke* (London, 1648), 198. Robert Browne, *The Subject's Sorrow* (London, 1649), 89, portions of which are reprinted as Richard Heyrick's *The paper called the Agreement of the people taken into consideration* (London, 1649).

[40] William Vaughan, *The Church militant historically continued from the yeare of our Saviours Incarnation* (London, 1640), 298–9.

than the Spirit-Paraclete: "Last solemn Sabbath saw the Church attend; / The Paraclete in fiery Pomp descend; / But when his Wondrous Octave rowl'd again, / He brought a Royal Infant in his Train. / So great a Blessing to so good a King / None but th' Eternal Comforter cou'd bring."[41]

In its multivocal role as guarantor of faith, anamnesis of Christ's mission, inspirational defender of the church militant, and legitimator of sovereignty, the Paraclete is put to a wide range of theological and political uses in seventeenth-century England. We turn now to the fuller engagements with Johannine pneumatology in the writings of both John Donne and John Milton. Although Donne, like Quarles, provides in his sermons an appreciative and largely traditional (not experimental) Calvinist understanding of the role of the Johannine Spirit in providing assurance and testimony, Donne wrestles with the more complex relationship among pneumatology, adoption, and *agape* in selections of the *Holy Sonnets*. Milton, too, offers a traditional understanding of Johannine pneumatology in *De Doctrina Christiana*, although Milton tends to degrade the role of the Spirit in his treatise and *Paradise Lost* due to his sense that the Paraclete has too often been suborned by false and seducing spirits, a fear sanctioned by several of his contemporaries in mid-seventeenth-century England.

JOHN DONNE: THE SPIRIT-PARACLETE AND ASSURANCE

Donne dedicates considerable space in his sermons to explicating key Johannine texts on the Trinity. Three sermons are devoted entirely to sections of Jesus' Farewell Speech at 14:20 and 14:26. Donne's further meditations on the Trinity are influenced by his reading of several other influential Johannine writings on the topic. Donne's various commentaries tend to fall under two conceptual categories: those sermonic glosses that focus on the role of the Holy Ghost in testifying to Jesus' ministry and those that focus on the Paraclete in his role as comforter. We will see that, in the *Holy Sonnets*, Donne follows Augustine in developing a psychological model of the Trinity, one that identifies the Holy Spirit with charity. Donne's Johannine Trinitarianism provides him (and his auditors) with the divine assurance that critics have typically argued is offset in Donne's work by his meditations on constitutional backsliding, fear, and death.

Donne's most extensive discussions of the Spirit appear in his two Pentecostal sermons delivered on Whitsunday within two years of one another in 1627–8, both of which gloss John 14:26. As we have seen, Jesus promises that the Holy Ghost will provide psychological ease to the brethren: "But the Comforter, which is the holy Ghost, whom the Father wil send in my name, he shal teach you al things, & bring al things to your remembrance, whatsoever I have said unto you" (14:26). Donne makes much of the fact that this statement is part of Jesus' last great sermon, which, Donne will add, uniquely elevates the divinity of Christ even

---

[41] John Dryden, *Britanica Rediviva* (London, 1688), 2.

as John's writings foster the spread of the Church: "This is a Sermon recorded only by that last Evangelist, who, as he considered the Divine Nature of Christ, more then the rest did, and so took it higher, so did he also consider the future state, and succession of the Church, more then the rest did, and so carried it lower."[42] Donne sees John as both evangelist and "prophet." In assigning to the Holy Ghost the role of missionary work, the Farewell Speech promises the seal and consummation of our redemption through the earthly ministry of the Church once Jesus is gone.

In his subsequent sermon on the theme of the Spirit's missionary role, Donne more generally focuses on the Spirit's role as teacher. Christ promises a teacher to the brethren who will instruct men how to preach to others about his ordinances: "This is the teaching of the Holy Ghost, promised and intended in this Text, and performed upon this Day, that he by his power enables and authorises other men to teach thee; That he establishes a Church, and Ordinances, and a Ministery, by which thou maist be taught how to apply Christs Merits to thy soul."[43] But Donne further describes the manner in which the Holy Ghost teaches by imparting to the disciples the proper memory of Christ: "The office of the Holy Ghost himself, the Spirit of all comfort, is but to bring those things to remembrance, which Christ taught, and no more."[44] And as a prompt to the remembrance of Jesus, the Holy Ghost above all serves as testifier of earthly ministry: "*He shall testifie of me*, saith Christ concerning the Holy Ghost; Now the office of him that testifies, of a witnesse, is to say all the truth, but nothing but the truth."[45]

Donne's systematic gloss on John's presentation of the Spirit closes with his less systematic and more creative and syncretistic identification of the Spirit with God's light. Donne incorporates into his interpretation of 14:26 one of his favorite Augustinian maxims—*Facies Dei est, qua nobis innotescit* ("That is alwaies the face of God to us, by which God vouchsafes to manifest himselfe to us")—to describe the ways in which our union with the Spirit helps to "see" God, at least God's face as manifested in "his Ordinance in the Church."[46] That metaphorical face is likened to the *Lux Dei*, the light of God that is contained in God's Word.[47] The Holy Spirit provides testimony that this illuminating (and illuminated) face of God is provided for the disciples' peace of mind: "The Evidence, the Seale, the Witnesse of all, that this face which I see by this light, is directed upon me for my comfort, is, The Testimony of the Holy Ghost, when that Spirit beares witnesse with our Spirit, that he is in us."[48]

Donne's understanding of the Spirit's role as testifier in particular also registers the Holy Ghost's equally important role as Comforter. Donne follows Athanasius in remarking that the designation "Comforter" is unique to the Gospel. In the Old Testament, including Genesis and the Psalms, the Holy Ghost is called variously the Spirit of God, the Holy Spirit, and the Principal Spirit, but never the

---

[42] *The Sermons of John Donne*, eds. Evelyn M. Simpson and George R. Potter (Berkeley: University of California Press, 1954), vol. vii, 439. Donne's translation of 14:26 conforms to the 1611 Authorized Version (the translation of which does not depart from the earlier Bishops' Bible of 1568).

[43] *Sermons of John Donne*, vol. viii, 260.

[44] Ibid., 263.   [45] Ibid., 262.   [46] Ibid., 266.

[47] Ibid., 266.   [48] Ibid., 266.

Comforter.[49] Unlike the Law, which "itself afforded not comfort," the Fourth Gospel, in conferring remission of sin (and not just conviction of sin) provides the "sustenation" and the "assurance of a Comforter."[50] Intent on further distinguishing the Paraclete's unique role in providing satisfaction, Donne contrasts an earlier reference to the Paraclete in John's First Epistle with the reference in 14:36 of John's Gospel. The former reference, in describing the Paraclete as "Advocate"—"If any man sinne, we have an Advocate with the Father" (1 John 2:1)—misses the "intire," "internall," and "viscerall" sense of the latter Gospel reference.[51] The important difference, for Donne, rests on the latter's sense that, once Jesus commissions the Comforter to provide testimony to the disciples, that spiritual presence will abide eternally. Also concerned with the means by which we can perceive the working of the Holy Ghost in us, Donne argues counterfactually that we can measure the depths of our apostasy according to the level of comfort that we find in and through the third person: "If I have no comfort from the Holy Ghost, I am worse, then if all mankinde had been left in the Putrifaction of *Adams* loynes, and in the condemnation of *Adams* sin.... Having had that extraordinary favour, of an offer of the Holy Ghost, if I feele no comfort in that, I must have an extraordinary condemnation."[52] Here again Donne will imagine a sanctified relationship with the Holy Ghost, a relationship so immediate that one should palpably feel the Spirit's presence when one is unburdened of sin: "The Holy Ghost is alwaies neare me, alwaies with me.... With me in my sleep, to keep out the Tempter from the fancy, and imagination."[53] So intimate is the relationship between the believer and Holy Ghost that the Sprit becomes more familiar with the believer than does Christ himself: "The Father is a Propitious Person; The Son is a Meritorious Person; The Holy Ghost is a Familiar Person."[54] To the extent that any person will see the face of God in a creaturely, temporal sense, that person will see God through the Spirit, since the vision of Christ is reserved for heaven: "The Heavens must open, to shew me the Son of Man at the right hand of the Father, as they did to *Steven*; But if I doe but open my heart to my self, I may see the Holy Ghost there, and in him, all that the Father hath Thought and Decreed, all that the Son hath Said and Done."[55]

Midway between his delivery of two Pentecostal Johannine sermons in 1627–8, Donne delivers a notable sermon early in 1628 on Saint Paul's conversion. The scriptural passage for the Pauline sermon is Paul's well-known farewell speech to the Ephesians as recorded in Luke-Acts: "And now, behold, I know, that all yee among whom I have gone preaching the Kingdome of God, shall see my face no more."[56] The instructions that Paul dispenses to the Ephesians regarding their conduct following his departure recall the instructions that Christ will provide to the disciples once he has been crucified. Donne's paraphrase of Paul's words, "Observe, recollect, remember, practice that which I have delivered unto you,"

---

[49] *Sermons of John Donne*, vol. vii, 449.   [50] Ibid., 449.
[51] Ibid., 450.   [52] Ibid., 439.   [53] Ibid., 439–40.
[54] Ibid., 440.   [55] Ibid., 440.
[56] *Sermons of John Donne*, vol. viii, 157.

indeed recalls the practices of the Johannine Paraclete to kindle remembrance of Jesus' ministry.[57] Gregory Kneidel has described Donne's rhetoric here as a "paraphrase of Paul's *parakleo*"; Paul would often use the term *parakleo* to exhort his listeners to continue to practice godly conduct, reminding them of the larger Christian mission to maintain faith during the period between the crucifixion and *Parousia*.[58] Despite Donne's seeming appreciation of the kinship between Pauline and Johannine *paraklesis*, I would point out that the special focus on spiritual comfort and assurance is a feature of the Johannine sermons, in particular. The sermons on Paul's conversion are focused more narrowly on the disciplined pastoral and moral life of the community once Paul has departed. Kneidel rightly suggests that the sermons on Paul are designed to offer the "mutual encouragement and consolation of Christian believers," but the consolatory rhetoric of the sermons is more typically Johannine than Pauline in emphasis.[59] Of course, Donne will make recourse in his sermons and *Holy Sonnets* to Paul's seminal verse on spiritual assurance in Romans 8:15—"For ye have not received the spirit of bondage againe to feare: but ye have received the spirit of adoption, whereby we cry, Abba, father"— but Donne is also acutely aware of those otherwise offsetting verses in Philippians and elsewhere that remind the penitent to carry out his salvation with fear and trembling. The appeal of the Johannine Paraclete to Donne is that there are no such soteriological qualifications in the Fourth Gospel. The Paraclete is uniquely sent to offset spiritual doubt.

The Paraclete as testifier of Christ's ways, witness of the sanctification of the faithful, and pathway of comfort and assurance—these Donnean presuppositions carry over into several of the *Holy Sonnets*, to which we now turn. What Donne adds to the poetry that is not prioritized in the sermons is the extent to which God's *agape*, itself associated with the Spirit and the glorification of the individual inhering in Christ, helps to provide the perseverance that serves as a spiritual balm to typical Donnean expressions of soteriological insecurity.

THE SPIRIT-RAVISHMENT OF "BATTER MY HEART"

Donne's critics have traditionally parsed the Trinitarian references in "Batter my heart" in discrete terms: "knocking" and "breaking" are ascribed to God, mending and burning are attributed to Christ, and "breathing" and "blowing" are attached to the operations of the Holy Spirit.[60] Yet the operations of the Spirit are arguably more fundamental in the poem than has traditionally been assumed. The opening quatrain reads: "Batter my heart, three-person'd God, for you / As yet but knock,

---

[57] Ibid., 160.

[58] Gregory Kneidel, *Rethinking the Turn to Religion in Early Modern English Literature: The Poetics of All Believers* (Basingstoke and New York: Palgrave Macmillan, 2008), 80.

[59] Ibid., 80.

[60] See, for example, Arthur L. Clements, "Donne's 'Batter my heart'," *Modern Language Notes* 76:6 (June, 1961), 484–9; and George Herman, "Donne's Holy Sonnets, XIV," *Explicator* 12 (December, 1953), Item 18.

breathe, shine, and seek to mend; / That I may rise, and stand, o'erthrow me; and bend / Your force to break, blow, burn, and make me new" (1–4).[61] The most important scriptural reference to the way in which the Spirit "blows" appears in Jesus' discussion with Nicodemus regarding spiritual rebirth: "The winde bloweth where it listeth, and thou hearest the sound thereof, but canst not tel whence it commeth, and whither it goeth: So is every one that is borne of the Spirit" (John 3:8). The conversation is designed to convey two essential truths to Nicodemus: that only the Spirit renews men and that the Spirit's operations are often miraculous and difficult to discern (in Henry Vaughan's "Regeneration," the Johannine "wind" or Spirit whispers that it blows "*Where I please*").[62] If renewal is the province of the Spirit, in the context of Donne's poem, which links such renewal ("make me new") to all of the several processes and operations adduced (knocking, breathing, shining, breaking, and blowing), we should consider the ways in which the Spirit carries out each process in addition simply to "blowing." That the Spirit "breathes" on the believer is itself declared toward the end of the Fourth Gospel when Jesus appears to the disciples: "Then said Jesus to them againe, Peace be unto you: As my Father hath sent me, even so send I you. And when he had said this, hee breathed on them, and saith unto them, Receive ye the holy Ghost" (20:21–2). The breathing of the Spirit onto the disciples provides comfort and enables them to carry out Jesus' teachings after his departure, particularly to protect the ministry of the Church. The Spirit provides the ability to testify on Christ's behalf, a theme sounded in Donne's sermons, as we have seen.

The important point about such breathing of the Spirit is that it does not yet represent a full renewal. Calvin describes it as a "sprinkling" that will reach fuller realization afterward, as depicted in Acts 2:3, when the Spirit will appear in "tongues of fire," which (along with the idea of rebirth through burning that echoes Isaiah 4:4) agrees with the "burning" and "shining" motions of the Spirit alluded to in Donne's first quatrain.[63] Even the act of "knocking" referenced in line 2 recalls the Spirit's activity, as in the Synoptic entreaty—"Aske, and it shalbe given you: seeke, and ye shal find: knocke, and it shalbe opened unto you" (Luke 11:9)—a passage that goes on to suggest that one needs to ask specifically for the Spirit to provide renewal: "For every one that asketh, receiveth: and he that seeketh, findeth: and to him that knocketh, it shalbe opened.... If ye then, being evill, know how to give good gifts unto your children: how much more shall your heavenly Father give the holy Spirit to them that aske him?" (Luke 11:10–13).

---

[61] All citations from Donne's *Holy Sonnets* will be taken from *John Donne's Poetry*, ed. Donald R. Dickson (New York: W. W. Norton, 2007). Dickson relies on the twelve-poem sequence of the 1633 manuscript of the poems, the version, as Dickson notes, that the Variorum editors believe to be Donne's final grouping. See n. 1, 136.

[62] About the "rushing wind," Vaughan's speaker remarks: "But while I listning sought / My mind to ease / By knowing, where 'twas, or where not, / It whisper'd; *Where I please*" (77–80). Henry Vaughan, "Regeneration," in *The Works of Henry Vaughan*, ed. L. C. Martin (Oxford: Clarendon Press, 1957), 397–9.

[63] Calvin, *The Gospel According to St. John*, vol. 5, 205.

If we return to Donne's sonnet, we can see that all of the various operations of the Spirit summoned by the speaker have been administered, yet the crucial "as yet" reminds us that these operations have failed to provide assurance and spiritual union due to backsliding and thralldom to God's "enemy" (10). I agree with Barbara Lewalski's notion that the poem "is explicitly about regeneration" rather than justification.[64] The speaker's imputed righteousness is not in question. He has been called by his triune God and he expresses genuine, if faltering, love for God, love presumably made possible by the Spirit's agency in loving God. This is not a depraved or hopelessly unregenerate creature but an embattled penitent, as the military metaphor makes clear: "I like an usurp'd town" (5). Such embattlements are conveyed in the very repetition at key syntactic moments of transitional phrases and prepositions: "As yet but knock" (2); "but oh, to no end" (6); "But is captiv'd" (8); "Yet dearly I love you" (9); "But am betroth'd" (10). The speaker seems to realize that, in order to maintain God's love, he requires an even stronger administration of the Spirit's power to renew, which is metaphorized in the well-known conceit of divine ravishment: "Take me to you, imprison me, for I, / Except you enthrall me, never shall be free, / Nor ever chaste except you ravish me" (12–14). We should not assume, as Lewalski does, that Christ does the ravishing: "Christ can become liberator of the soul only by becoming its jailer, and be its Bridegroom only by becoming its ravisher."[65] Nor should we accept too quickly the more typical assumption that God as such does the ravishing.[66] I suggest that the Spirit in particular is the agent of ravishment. This might seem to be a superfluous particularization of the agency of one person of the Trinity until we consider how important such a designation is for understanding the soteriological themes of the sonnet.[67]

One source text for "ravishment," the text that frames much of the final third of Donne's sonnet, is of course the Song of Solomon, particularly 4:9: "Thou hast ravished my heart, my sister, my spouse; thou hast ravished my heart, with one of thine eyes, with one chaine of thy necke." Early modern commentators extrapolate from this line (especially when read in conjunction with the subsequent line's reference to the spouse's "smell of ointments") that the Spirit is the agent of ravishment.

---

[64] Barbara Lewalski, *Protestant Poetics and the Seventeenth-Century Religious Lyric* (Princeton: Princeton University Press, 1979), 271.

[65] Ibid., 272.

[66] See, for example, Regina Mara Schwartz, *Sacramental Poetics at the Dawn of Secularism: When God Left the World* (Stanford: Stanford University Press, 2008): "The speaker says to God that he can never be 'chaste unless you ravish me'" (131). That God does the ravishing is argued in more detail by Lucio Ruotolo, who, acknowledging the irreducible Trinitarianism of the sonnet, finds it suitable that, as begetter and generator, God the Father ravishes the speaker. Ruotolo, "The Trinitarian Framework of Donne's Holy Sonnet XIV," *Journal of the History of Ideas*, 27:3 (1966), 445–6.

[67] Although I would not argue for a neat division of the quatrains according to the three persons of the Trinity, I agree with George Knox's belief that the Spirit does the "interpenetration" of the final quatrain of the sonnet: "The third exemplifies the reborn understanding (en*light*ened through the Son) conceiving the consubstantiality of man and God through imagery of interpenetration [the Holy Ghost]." "Donne's 'Holy Sonnets,' XIV," *Explicator* 15, Item 2, cited in John E. Parish, "No. 14 of Donne's Holy Sonnets," *College English* 24:4 (January, 1963), 299.

Hence the poet Phineas Fletcher's concluding prayer to the Spirit in *Joy in Tribulation* (a text published the year in which the first edition of Donne's *Holy Sonnets* appeared):

> Oh ravish my heart with thy beauty, and teach me to abhorre the painted harlotry of this sinfull world; unite my heart unto thee by faith, and knit it fast in love....Oh thou holy and blessed Spirit, who sealest unto mee those precious promises, apply powerfully this signet to my heart, and seale it up in thy Covenant. Open mine eyes, and fasten them on Christ, and those things where Christ sitteth at the right hand of God: Make mee to know, and remember that I can lose no good thing, so long as I enjoy thee.[68]

The ravishment of Fletcher's heart is achieved through the powerful operations of the Spirit, which in turn provide a seal through which he will steadfastly love God and enjoy the firm assurance of his ability to see God and Christ at God's right hand. Indeed, the phrase "Spirit-ravished" seems to have circulated in the early decades of the seventeenth century. Playwright and sometime poet Robert Davenport, in his versified reference to Revelation 20, allies himself with John of Patmos when describing the beatific vision: "As If I (with Spirit-ravish'd *John*) take view, Of thee in thy celestiall seat."[69] Thomas Middleton designates those who are confirmed in grace as "Spirit ravish'd."[70] And the religious controversialist Humphrey Sydenham remarks that he relies on his "Spirit" to "Ravish Scriptures" for meaning.[71]

One finds in early- to mid-seventeenth-century sermons and homilies the recurring idea that Spirit-ravishment provides comfort and fellowship with God. Thus remarks the Puritan divine Edmund Calamy, extrapolating from his commentary on John 14:16 ("And I will pray the Father, and hee shall give you another Comforter, that he may abide with you for ever"):

> Labour to get more communion from the Spirit of God. This will raise and sublimate your natural comforts, and turn them into Spiritual comforts. A man can never relish these outward comforts, till he come to taste the *ravishment* and sweetness of the holy Ghost, till he taste the love of God [italics mine].[72]

Implicit in Calamy's exhortation is the processual rather than once-and-for-all nature of union with the Spirit. Communion or indwelling with Christ and God follows from spiritual ravishment, which is itself a testament to God's answering love for the communicant. Bishop Joseph Hall reiterates this idea of fellowship through ravishment by the Spirit in his meditations on John's Farewell Discourse: "Oh the inexplicable joy of the ful & everlasting accomplishment of the happy union of Christ & the beleeving soule, more fit for thankfull wonder and *ravishment of Spirit* then for any finite apprehension!"[73] (italics mine).

---

[68] Phineas Fletcher, *Joy in Tribulation* (London, 1632), 321.

[69] Robert Davenport, *A crowne for a conquerour; and Too late to call backe yesterday* (London, 1639), 1.

[70] Thomas Middleton, *Two new playes* (London, 1657), 2.

[71] Humphrey Sydenham, *Sermons upon solemne occasions preached in severall auditories* (London, 1637), 258.

[72] Edmund Calamy, *A Compleat collection of farewel sermons* (London, 1663), 197.

[73] Joseph Hall, *Christ mysticall, or, The blessed union of Christ and his members* (London, 1647), 103.

The tenor and content of these references approximate the sense of Donne's final conceit. The speaker's chaste relationship with God can be achieved through the enthralling and ravishing of the Spirit, the very Spirit that has been working on his renewal all along. The theology of the poem is relatively straightforward once it is acknowledged that regeneration or an impartation of holiness works by means of such pneumatological motions. Richard Strier compellingly remarks that the speaker's problem is that he is "unable to accept the paradoxes of *simul justus et peccator*," but it is not as clear that the speaker's *agon* stems from any mixed doctrinal allegiances allegorized in the poem, which is what Strier goes on to observe: "Donne does not seem to know where he stands—with Luther and Calvin or (as Sherwood argues) with Saint Bernard."[74] The speaker's problem is that he wants an impartation of grace, full and assured righteousness, to follow from a once-and-for-all act, even though the fullness and freedom that he seeks is incremental or gradual. The imperative verbs and commands—"divorce me" (11), "untie" (11), "break" (11), "Take me to you" (12)—reflect a speaker who is not so much obtuse as he is impatient. The plea to have the Spirit "ravish" him, a theological commonplace, becomes a daring metaphor because of its terminal implications. In his belief that "chastity" can be achieved through this one decisive act, after which he will finally be "free" (13), the speaker imagines regeneration to be a complete (if paradoxical) *act* or *moment* of rebirth rather than an arduous, ongoing process of renewal riddled with backsliding and captivation by the enemy. Ramie Targoff aptly remarks: "Donne wants his imperfect flesh to be perfected. And he wants God to intervene not at the last day, but now."[75] I would refine this claim slightly by saying that Donne's speaker seems not to realize, or refuses to accept, that God does and will intervene before the last day, although not at the speaker's peremptory bidding.

The much less perverse and paradoxical choice of conceit (which would have obviously yielded a lesser poem) would have been a comparison of the divine rape to the once-and-for-all act of justification. The doubled conditionals in the final quatrain—"For I, / Except you enthrall me, never shall be free, / Nor ever chaste except you ravish me"—convey a forensic, declarative tone that would indeed be more fitting to describe the speaker's desire to be justified, not sanctified. More paradoxical than the sexual metaphor as such is the yoking of the sexual metaphor, the violence of this discrete act, to an ongoing process in the order of salvation. To put it crudely, regeneration is more akin to foreplay, a sexual relationship, than it is to consummation, a sexual act or event.

One way of thinking about the speaker's union with God is that the speaker is indeed "free" in some sense, his freedom inhering in the proclamation that he already loves God: "Yet dearly I love you, and would be loved fain" (10). The scriptural commonplace that seems lost on the speaker (but which will provide the pedagogical matter for the succeeding sonnet, "Wilt thou love God," as we will see)

---

[74] See Richard Strier, "John Donne Awry and Squint: The 'Holy Sonnets,' 1608–1610," *Modern Philology* 86:4 (May, 1989), 376. Strier's reference is to Terry G. Sherwood, *Fulfilling the Circle: A Study of John Donne's Thought* (Toronto: University of Toronto Press, 1984).

[75] Ramie Targoff, *John Donne, Body and Soul* (Chicago: University of Chicago Press, 2008), 122.

is that the speaker's self-proclaimed dear love to God itself testifies to God's love for him. 1 John 4:19, "We love him: because hee first loved us," reveals that, in the fuller context of the Johannine love commandments, Christ's satisfaction already evinces God's love: "Herein is love, not that wee loved God, but that he loved us, and sent his Sonne to be propitiation for our sins" (1 John 4:10). That the speaker misunderstands or ignores the proper circuit of *agape* is embedded in the diction and structure of line 10. When the speaker asks for God to love him "fain," which the OED defines adverbially as "gladly," he might as well be arguing that he wants God to love him "dearly." The parallelism implies a desired symmetry between the speaker's and God's love. Yet the fact that God's love is gratuitous and not reducible to merely dear or glad creaturely love suggests an asymmetry between human and divine love that seems lost on or willfully disregarded by the speaker, who can only project an accommodated and anthropomorphic love onto God with the ascription of the colloquial "fain." The speaker's minimal anthropomorphism at line 10 then gives way to the maximal anthropomorphism of the violent rape, as the speaker entreats for union by violent means what he has already begun to enjoy through God's loving grace.

When read in conjunction with Donne's keen appreciation in the sermons of the role of the Spirit-Paraclete, the richness of the poem can be seen to reside in the speaker's inability to pause and meditate on the ways in which regeneration is achieved gradually through the comforting and assuring operations of the Holy Spirit. That the speaker is able to love God despite his persistent tribulations might have provided a degree of spiritual comfort that would have mitigated the over-compensations of the sexual rape, or what Brian Cummings incisively describes as the over-determined "shouts in the dark" of the final quatrain.[76] Compare finally the last quatrain of "Batter my heart" to Bishop Hall's similar, if less eroticized, account of being ravished by God's infinite love:

> I am swallowed up, O God, I am willingly swallowed up in this bottomelesse abysse of thine infinite love; and there let me dwell in a perpetuall ravishment of spirit, till being freed from this clog of earth, and filled with the fulness of Christ, I shall be admitted to enjoy that, which I cannot now reach to wonder at, thine incomprehensible blisse, and glory which thou laid up in the highest heavens for them that love thee.[77]

Hall describes a state of being swallowed and ravished by God's love until he will be "freed" from earthly attachments, after which he will achieve glorification and the very beatific vision that now only exists in his imagination. An appreciation of God's love, described here as ravishment in spirit, is a step toward freedom, full union, and glorification, not the end itself. The speaker of "Batter my heart" wants his freedom now, and he asserts, desperately, dogmatically, that freedom rests in divine ravishment.

We turn now to two succeeding sonnets, "Wilt thou love God" and "Father, part of his double interest." Both sonnets depict speakers preoccupied with the Trinitarian

---

[76] Brian Cummings, *The Literary Culture of the Reformation: Grammar and Grace* (Oxford: Oxford University Press, 2002), 397.

[77] Hall, *Christ mysticall*, 212–13.

mystery and the role of the Spirit in salvation, but both depict speakers who reveal a more measured understanding of the Spirit's capacity as spiritual comforter.

DONNE BETWEEN JOHN AND PAUL: "WILT THOU LOVE GOD, AS HE THEE?"

Donne's critics have been right to point out the fundamentally Pauline disposition of the references to the Spirit and adoption in "Wilt thou love God" (Sonnet 11 in the 1633 manuscript). The first item to consider, according to Donne's "wholesome meditation" (2), is the manner in which "God the Spirit, by angels waited on / In heaven, doth make his temple in thy breast" (3–4), a line that clearly draws on Paul's testament in Corinthians: "Knowe yee not that yee are the Temple of God, and that the Spirit of God dwelleth in you?" (1 Cor. 3:16). The next lines transition into an explicit statement of the speaker's adoption—"The father having begot a son most blest, / And still begetting (for he ne'er begun) / Hath deign'd to choose thee by adoption, / Co-heir to his glory" (5–8)—itself a reference to Romans 8:15–17: "Ye have received the spirit of adoption, whereby we cry, Abba, father. The spirit it selfe beareth witnes with our spirit, that we are the children of God. And if children, then heires, heires of God, and joynt heires with Christ."[78]

Embedded within the Pauline lines of the poem, however, are also some key Johannine lines, also related to adoption, that have typically been passed over by Donne's editors. The language of "begetting" at line 5—"the father having begot a son most blest / and still begetting"—brings us directly to John, the only New Testament writer to use, in several instances, "beget" and its cognates to describe the eternal pre-existence of the Son and the filial union among God, the Son, and the brethren.[79] The *locus classicus* regarding pre-existence is the announcement in the Prologue of the Fourth Gospel of the Incarnation as *Logos*: "And the Word was made flesh, and dwelt among us (& we beheld his glory, the glory as of the onely begotten of the Father) full of grace and trueth" (1:14). In the context of Donne's poem, more relevant adoptive or relational descriptions of begetting appear in John's First Epistle and outline the process by which one becomes a member of God's holy family: "Whosoever beleeveth that Jesus is the Christ, is borne of God: and every one that loveth him that begate, loveth him also that is begotten of him. By this wee know that wee love the children of God, when we love God and keepe his commandements" (1 John 5:1–2). To be "born" of God is to love God, the begetter, and to love God is to love Christ, the begotten. To appreciate or "believe on" the fact that God's love for the world manifests in his sending of the begotten son is to achieve eternal life: "For God so loved the world, that he gave his only begotten Sonne: that whosoever beleeveth in him, should not perish,

---

[78] For a comprehensive annotation of the Pauline references, see *The Variorum Edition of the Poetry of John Donne*, vol. 7, Part I, ed. Paul A. Parrish (Bloomington: Indiana University Press, 2005), 553.

[79] Donne describes the "eternall generation of the Son" in his 1625 sermon on John 5:28–9 (*Sermons of John Donne*, vol. vi, 264).

but have everlasting life" (3:16). Sonship or adoption depends for John on our apprehension of God's love for us: "Beholde, what manner of love the Father hath bestowed upon us, that wee should be called the sonnes of God" (1 John 3:1).

What, then, is the relationship between the Pauline and Johannine references in the first two quatrains of "Wilt thou love God"? Why does Donne incorporate the Johannine notion of the begottenness of Christ into the Pauline lines of adoption? We should observe first the larger context of Paul's promise of adoption in Romans 8. After assuring his auditors that the Spirit can testify that they are the children of God, Paul shifts from the present to future tense, advising that adoption through the means of the Spirit and the concomitant glorification of the members of God's family have not yet been realized. "And if children, then heires, heires of God, and joynt heires with Christ: if so be that we suffer with him, that wee may be also glorified together. For I reckon, that the sufferings of this present time, are not worthy to be compared with the glory which shall be revealed in us" (Romans 8:17–18). Paul, like John, mingles a realized and futurist eschatology, Paul's realized eschatology being more prominent in later writings, such as Ephesians and Colossians, that focus on the death and resurrection of Christ as eschatological moments. Yet in this verse from Romans, the *eschaton* has not arrived. Paul focuses as much on empathetic suffering with Christ as he does on the future, post-resurrected glory that Christ and his co-heirs will achieve. In Donne's sonnet, though, the Johannine description of the eternal pre-existence of the Son, along with an equally important Johannine echo at line 11—"The son of glory came down and was slain"—gestures at a realized eschatology that is not as prominent in the Pauline source text on adoption.[80] The announcement that Christ has already arrived as "glorified," itself evidence of his eternal pre-existence, proclaims his divinity, elevating him in keeping with what I have been describing as John's high Christology. To the extent that the speaker and/or readers of the poem realize that they have already been chosen for adoption (12), and that they will partake of the "endless" Sabbath, God's Spirit already in their breasts (4), they have already at least begun to enjoy the mutual indwelling and everlasting life promised throughout the Johannine corpus.[81] That Donne believes strongly in the role of the Spirit

---

[80] As I remarked in the Introduction, the difference between John and Paul regarding realized and futurist eschatology is a matter of degree rather than kind. Most commentators acknowledge that, although both authors figure a realized eschatology, John's is more pronounced and radical than Paul's. For foundational studies on Johannine realized eschatology, see C. H. Dodd, *The Parables of the Kingdom* (New York: Charles Scribner's Sons, 1961), as well as Dodd's *The Apostolic Preaching and its Developments* (New York and London: Harper & Brothers, 1951). Rudolf Bultmann had earlier discussed the historicization of eschatology in *Theology of the New Testament*, 2 vols., trans. Kendrick Grobel (New York: Charles Scribner's Sons, 1951–5), in which he points out that John radicalizes Pauline eschatology. For the importance of Johannine realized eschatology to early modern secularization theses, see Hans Blumenberg's discussion of Bultmann's "demythologizing" project in *The Legitimacy of the Modern Age*, trans. Robert M. Wallace (Cambridge: M.I.T. Press, 1983), 39–44.

[81] Few themes are more pronounced in John's Gospel than the divinity of the Son, expressed most clearly in the ascription of the Son's glory despite the humbling of the Passion. At the outset of the Gospel, John celebrates the eternal begetting of the Son by drawing attention to the gloriousness of the Word made flesh: "And the Word was made flesh, and dwelt among us (& we beheld his glory, the glory as of the onely begotten of the Father) full of grace and trueth" (1:14). Elsewhere in the Gospel, John will even more directly link the Son to glory. Jesus predicts his own death with the words, "The

to grant eternal life to the penitent is brought out in Donne's own sermonic elevation of John 17:3: "How often doth the Sonne say, that the Father sent him? And
how often that the Father will, and that he will send the Holy Ghost? *This is life
eternall*, says he, *to know thee, the onely true God, and Jesus Christ, whom thou hast
sent.* . . . No man can call Jesus the Lord, but by the holy Ghost."[82]

If the Pauline lines alone do not help to explain the realized eschatology of the
sonnet, neither do they link to the opening query of the sonnet in which Donne
raises the question of divine *agape* relative to creaturely love: "Wilt thou love God,
as he, thee?" (1). None of the five Pauline references to adoption directly connects
filial union to *agape*; and, aside from remarking, as we will see in Chapter 4, that
divine *agape* is expressed in a theology of the cross (and that neighbor-love fulfills
the law), Paul has little to say about the reciprocal love among God, Christ, and the
penitent. While it would be misleading to say that the opening of Donne's sonnet
relies on Johannine verses on *agape* as source texts, the framing query is closer in
grammar and spirit to comparable Johannine texts than it is to any other scriptural
reference to *agape*. Consider the sense of the query "Wilt thou love God, as he,
thee?" in relation to 1 John 4:19: "We love him: because hee first loved us."
Consider further the syntax of the "as" comparatives in the two commandments
that Christ issues in the Fourth Gospel: "As the Father hath loved me, so have
I loved you" (15:9); "Love one another, as I have loved you" (15:12). Distinctive
about the Johannine love expressions is their focus on reciprocity. Christ loves
the brethren as God loves Christ, and the brethren love one another as Christ has
loved them. Donne's query might be understood as a play on this approach to
understanding God's love relative to creaturely love. The point of the sonnet is
to reveal the difficulty of returning love to God, given the asymmetry between God's
love for us and our responsive love for him. Indeed, the endpoint of the sonnet is
to have the speaker and reader realize exactly what 1 John 4:19 expresses—that we
can only love God *because* he has first loved us, that we would be presumptuous to
assume that we can simply love God "as" he loved us.[83] It is as if Donne is issuing
a lesson in the poem on the proper understanding of the Johannine love commandments (a lesson that, in its interrogative form, recalls the very Johannine
pedagogy of discipleship misunderstanding). Do not erroneously import the "as"
construction onto responsive love for God, Donne seems to be saying; although we

---

houre is come, that the Sonne of man should be glorified" (12:23), a focus on glorification through
death that is absent in the Synoptics, where Mark, for example, will note only that "the Son of man is
betrayed into the hands of sinners" (14:41). At various points in the Fourth Gospel, emphasis is placed
on the extent to which Jesus' disciples will have clearer knowledge of his divinity once he is glorified:
"These things understood not his disciples at the first: but when Jesus was glorified, then remembred
they that these things were written of him, and that they had done these things unto him" (12:16);
"If God be glorified in him, God shall also glorifie him in himselfe, and shall straightway glorifie
him" (13:32); and "Father, the houre is come, glorifie thy Sonne, that thy Sonne also may glorifie
thee" (17:1).

[82] *The Sermons of John Donne*, vol. ix, 55.

[83] Analogously, John Tobin correctly reads John 4:19 into the final, rhyming line of George
Herbert's "A True Hymn": *O, could I love*! And stops: God writeth, *Loved*." *George Herbert: The
Complete English Poems*, ed. John Tobin (London and New York: Penguin Books, 2005), 403, n. 20.

might model love of brethren on Christ's love for us, we cannot so simply model our love for God on his love for us unless we remind ourselves that, through the cross, God has loved us first (as stated in 1 John 4:10: "Herein is love, not that wee loved God, but that he loved us, and sent his Sonne to be the propitiation for our sins"). The main conceit of the poem, in which Christ as Lord of glory must buy back what Satan has stolen, reinforces this asymmetry between divine and creaturely love. An inestimable magnitude of difference stretches between the love of a God who must turn himself into a man to buy back his very creation, on the one hand, and the mere expression of loving thankfulness for having pulled this off at our behest, on the other hand. The message of the poem is clear. We can love God, through the adoptive effects of the Spirit, only because God has sent the eternally begotten son. This is consistent with Pauline theology, but the Johannine writings provide a clearer connection among filial union, Christ's eternality, and divine *agape*.

But this still leaves unaddressed the fundamental role of the Spirit in mediating adoption. As we have seen in our discussion of Donne's sermons, Donne is keenly interested in the role of the Spirit in providing assurance to the believer through the granting of eternal or everlasting life. That Sonnet 11 is working with a Johannine conception of the Spirit is reflected in what might otherwise seem an insignificant departure from the Corinthians reference to the "Spirit of God"; namely, that the sonnet invokes instead "God the Spirit" at line 3. The only biblical identification of God with the Spirit appears in John 4:24, when Jesus advises the Samaritan woman that the Messiah has already arrived: "God is a Spirit, and they that worship him, must worship him in spirit, and in trueth." The passage was frequently used by patristic writers against the Arians to legitimate the divinity of the Holy Spirit. Thus Ambrose: "The Lord Himself said in the Gospel: 'The Spirit is God.' Which passage you, Arians, so expressly testify to be said concerning the Spirit, that you remove it from your copies, and would that it were from yours and not also from those of the Church!"[84] Donne's identification of God with the Spirit, alongside both the poem's elevation of the divinity of the Son and its emphasis on divine *agape*, reflects the poem's implicit Trinitarianism. A brief detour into Augustine's interpretation of key Johannine texts will help clarify this claim.

Early in his treatise on the Trinity, Augustine makes clear that a proper under-standing of the nature of love is the starting point for any further theorizing about the Triune God: "In this enquiry concerning the Trinity and our knowledge of God, the first thing for us to learn is the nature of true love—or rather the nature of love."[85] What follows is a detailed explication of Johannine references to charity (especially the "God is love" verse at 1 John 4:7), from which Augustine concludes that love of neighbor and love of God are equivalent, since to love one's neighbor

---

[84] Saint Ambrose, *Of the Holy Spirit*, in *A Select Library of Nicene and Post-Nicene Fathers of the Christian Church*, eds. Philip Schaff and Henry Wace, vol. x (New York: The Christian Literature Company, 1896), 143.

[85] Saint Augustine, *The Trinity*, in *Augustine: Later Works*, ed. John Burnaby (Philadelphia: Westminster Press, 1955), 50.

is to love *love* and hence to love God.[86] When Augustine begins to extrapolate his conception of the psychological Trinity from the Johannine sources, he reasons that our love of neighbor and God is itself patterned on the shared love between the Father and Son. It is the Holy Spirit that provides the essential element, since he is the "Spirit neither of the Father alone nor of the Son alone, but of both; and so his being suggests to us that mutual charity whereby the Father and the Son love one another."[87] Yet Augustine is quick to add that, although the "proper nature" or "special fitness" of the Spirit is charity (the Father's is memory, and the Son's is understanding), all three persons of the Trinity may likewise be said to be identified with charity: "All and each possess all three characters in their proper nature; and…in them the three are not separate, as in ourselves memory is one thing, understanding another, and love or charity another: but that there is one single potency for them all."[88]

Augustine justifies the Spirit's "special fitness" as/for charity by turning to "a careful examination of the apostle John's way of speaking."[89] What follows is a series of deductions based on John's related descriptions of God as love, on the one hand, and of the love that is from God, on the other hand: "This makes it plain that the love which he calls God is the same love which he has said to be 'of God.' Love, then, is God of (or from) God."[90] The remaining question is: given that the Son is born and the Spirit proceeds from God, which person is referred to in John's commentary? Because John writes "he loved us, and sent his Son as expiator for our sins," Augustine continues that God exhorts us to love one another so as to achieve a mutual indwelling of charity, which is reflected in John's First Epistle: "Hereby know wee that we dwell in him and he in us, because hee hath given us of his Spirite" (1 John 4:13).[91] The conclusion is that in this special sense it is the Spirit that is referenced in the earlier statement that God is love: "Thus the Holy Spirit, of whom he has given us, makes us dwell in God, and God in us. But that is the effect of love. The Holy Spirit himself therefore is the God who is love.…It is the Spirit therefore who is signified in the text 'God is love.'"[92] The Spirit is not simply the means by which we love our neighbors but is himself the God of love that is both the cause and goal of charity.[93]

Returning to "Wilt thou love God," we can see that one of the pedagogical points of "this wholesome meditation" (2) is its Trinitarianism. To love God "as" he loves us is first to realize that the means of receiving and then returning such love is through the Spirit. Yet the Spirit is not described as an intermediate person or instrument so much as a manifestation of God himself. It follows (and this is Augustine's key observation) that, insofar as the channel of love requires the Holy

---

[86] Ibid., 53.   [87] Ibid., 157.   [88] Ibid., 158.   [89] Ibid., 160.
[90] Ibid., 160.   [91] Ibid., 160.   [92] Ibid., 160.
[93] In his *Sermons on the Gospel of St. John*, Luther goes so far as to identify the Comforter with God himself, although Luther reads Romans 15:5 into John 14:16: "There is surely no God besides Him who is a Comforter. And henceforth he who wants to know God aright and name Him appropriately must call Him 'Comforter' or, as St. Paul terms Him in Rom. 15:5, 'the God of Comfort,' namely, for those who are frightened and have no other comfort." *Sermons on the Gospel of St. John*, in *Luther's Works*, vol. 24, ed. Jaroslav Pelikan (Saint Louis: Concordia Publishing House, 1961), 113.

Spirit, no distinction should be drawn among God, the Spirit, and Love. To be chosen by adoption in the poem is to enjoy the indwelling of all such aspects of God within the temple in the speaker's "breast" (4). And the additional, crucial Trinitarian element in this substantial conflation is Christ, eternally begotten, whose pre-existent "glory" renders him divine. Donne's Augustinian position is summed up later in the century in John Owen's meditation on Johannine love and the role of the Spirit: "Unspeakable love accompanieth the Susception and Discharge of this Office; and that working by Tenderness and Compassion. The Holy Spirit is said to be the Divine, Eternal, mutual Love of the Father and Son."[94] We have already seen Donne's own statement about the Trinitarian unity expressed in a sermon on Genesis and justified by John 17:3: "life eternall" cannot be achieved "but by the holy Ghost."[95]

To what extent might we conclude that the Spirit referenced in Sonnet 11 also recalls Donne's sermonic preoccupation with the Spirit's dispensation as Comforter? Augustine remarks in a tractate on John that adoption turns on the role of Spirit as Comforter:

> So that no one may think that only the Father and the Son, without the Holy Spirit, make a dwelling place among those who love them, let him recollect what was said a little earlier about the Holy Spirit: 'Whom the world cannot receive because it does not see him or know him; but you will know him because he will abide with you and will be in you.' Look, in the saints, together with the Father and the Son, the Holy Spirit too makes a dwelling place, within, of course, as God in his *temple* [italics mine].[96]

That the Johannine and Pauline discourses on adoption could so easily dovetail is evidenced by Augustine's importing of the Pauline "temple" reference into his depictions of the Spirit-Paraclete as promised in John 14:19–24 (Donne himself superimposes John's version of the cleansing of the Temple, in which Christ describes himself as a Temple at 2:21, onto 1 Corinthians 3:16 in a 1623 sermon on the Feast of Dedication).[97] Additionally, Donne would certainly have known that the Geneva version of John 14:18 highlights the Paraclete's role in adoption by using the term "fatherless" rather than the King James Bible's term "Comfortless": "I will not leave you fatherles: but I will come to you" (Geneva Bible of 1587).[98] Aquinas's *Catena Aurea* quotes Augustine's view of the adoptive sense of the line

---

[94] Owen, *Two Discourses*, 27.   [95] *Sermons of John Donne*, vol. ix, 55.

[96] Saint Augustine, *Tractates on the Gospel of John*, 55–111, ed. John W. Rettig (Washington, D.C.: Catholic University Press, 2010), 99.

[97] Donne remarks: "Let this be the Feast of the Dedication of our selves to *God. Christ* calls him-selfe a *Temple, Solvite templum hoc*: Destroy this *Temple*. And *Saint Paul* call us so twice, *Know ye not that ye are the Temple of the Holy Ghost?*" (*Sermons of John Donne*, vol. iv, 378).

[98] In his discussion of John 17 (in the larger context of his treatise on *noli me tangere*), Richard Sibbes brings a distinctly Johannine conception of comfort and assurance together with spiritual adoption: "That whatsoever comfort we look for from God, and in God, we must see it in Christ first, before we see it in our selves; because we be but Sons by adoption, and we have all we have from God through Christ. Whatsoever we see in Christ, think this will belong to us. And whatsoever we look should belong to us, see it first in him." *A heavenly conference between Christ and Mary after His resurrection* (London, 1654), 151.

that is based on the Greek association of Paraclete with "wardship": "I will not leave you comfortless. The Greek word signifies 'wards.' Although then the Son of God has made us the adopted sons of the Father, yet here He Himself shows the affection of a Father towards us."[99] Of course, Donne does not explicitly effect such an integration in the poem. The Spirit reference at line 3 is not expressly connected to the comforts of the Paraclete.[100] Yet if the opening and closing lines of the poem remind the speaker of his humility in the face of God's ineffable love and the miracle of the Incarnation, that humility is infused with the speaker's sense that, according to the testimony of the Spirit within, he has already found entrance into God's holy family. I agree with Stephenie Yearwood, who finds in the omniscient voice of the sonnet tones of forgiveness and assurance: "By reminding the seeker that Christ is within him, the voice cultivates assurance and combats despair."[101] By the end of "Wilt thou love God," the speaker is reminded that he shares the glory enjoyed by the Son, and he expresses confidence in the presence of the loving Spirit of God in his breast.

We can see that if the immediate proof-texts for the sonnet's sense of adoption are Paul's epistles, the sonnet's disposition toward adoption and the speaker's psychology and overall mood are informed severally by the Johannine discourses on *agape*, the pre-existence of the Son, and the Trinitarian unity. For another instance of Donne's reliance on Johannine material to elevate the third person of the Trinity, we turn to Sonnet 12 in the 1633 manuscript, "Father, part of his double interest."

DONNE'S SERMONS AND "FATHER, PART OF HIS DOUBLE INTEREST"

Donne's elevation of the Spirit as the Trinitarian person responsible for providing comfort through the gift of love is reflected in Donne's most expressly Johannine sonnet, "Father, part of his double interest." Donne describes "two wills," one that corresponds to legalistic death, and one that corresponds to renovation through love: "Revive and quicken what law and letter kill. / Thy law's abridgement, and thy last command / Is all but love. Oh let that last will stand" (12–14). Helen Gardner has noted the formative influence of the several Johannine sources for the

---

[99] *Catena Aurea, Commentary on the Four Gospels Collected Out of the Works of the Fathers by Thomas Aquinas: Volume 4, St. John*, trans. John Henry Newman (London: John Henry Parker, J.G.F. and J. Rivington, 1841), reprinted by Veritatis Splendor Publications, 2012, 273.

[100] Consider that, as Robin Robbins has recently suggested, the reference to "digest" at the outset of the sonnet—"then digest, / My soul, this wholesome meditation" (1–2)—brings us to the Second Sunday Collect for the Common Book of Prayer: "Grant that we may in such wise hear them [the scriptures], read, mark, learn, and inwardly digest them, that by patience and comfort of thy holy Word, we may embrace, and ever hold fast, the blessed hope of everlasting life." To a certain extent, the language of the Collect recalls the Johannine rhetoric of comfort and everlasting life. See *The Complete Poems of John Donne*, ed. Robin Robbins (Abingdon and New York: Routledge, 2010), n. 1, 542.

[101] Stephenie Yearwood, "Donne's Holy Sonnets: The Theology of Conversion," *Texas Studies in Literature and Language* 24:2 (Summer, 1982), 218.

sonnet.[102] Christ's last command articulated to his disciples just before he promises the Comforter is the mandate to love one another as he has loved them: "A new commandment I give unto you, That yee love one another, as I have loved you, that yee also love one another. By this shall all men know that ye are my disciples, if yee have love one to another" (13:34–5). Gardner also finds a mingling of John 1:17 ("For the Law was given by Moses, but grace and trueth came by Jesus Christ") and 2 Corinthians 3:6 ("the letter killeth, but the spirit giveth life") as the basis for lines 11–12: "None doth, but thy all-hearing grace and Spirit / Revive again what law and letter kill."[103] And Gardner rightly points out that the overall rhetoric and content, the "theme" of Sonnet 12, can be found in Donne's 1630 sermon on another passage of the Fourth Gospel's Farewell Discourse in which Christ promises that, when he returns to his disciples, they will enjoy participation in one another and God: "At that day ye shall know, that I am in my Father, and you in me, and I in you" (14:20). The opening of the sermon, parts of which are cited by Gardner, is as follows:

> The two Volumes of the Scriptures are justly, and properly called two Testaments, for they are *Testatio Mentis*, The attestation, the declaration of the will and pleasure of God, how it pleased him to be served under the Law, and how in the state of the Gospell. But to speake according to the ordinary acceptation of the word, the Testament, that is, The last Will of Christ Jesus, is this speech. . . . By this Wil then, as a rich, and abundant, and liberall Testator, having given them so great a Legacy, as *a place in the kingdome of heaven*, yet he adds a codicill, he gives more, he gives them the evidence by which they should maintain their right to that kingdome, that is, the testimony of the Spirit, *The Comforter, the Holy Ghost*, whom he promises to send to them.[104]

"Donne expounds the theme of this sonnet at length" in this sermon, Gardner remarks, but the relationship among the sonnet, the sermon, and the Johannine material is left unaccounted for in her brief gloss.[105] The first point to make about the Johannine love commandment is that its goal is the awareness of the Father's love for the penitent who, through emulating Christ's love, will love the brethren. The causal nexus is laid out in 13:35: "By this shall all men know that ye are my disciples, if yee have love one to another." To emulate Christ's love through love of one another is to derive knowledge of Christ's love for the faithful who carry out the "new" commandment. But the loving circuit extends even further, since to derive Christ's love is thereby to acquire knowledge of God's love, which is the concluding sentiment of the verse that immediately succeeds 14:20 (the verse on which Donne's sermon is based): "He that hath my commandements, and keepeth them, hee it is that loveth me: and he that loveth me shall be loved of my Father, and I will love him, and will manifest my selfe to him" (14:21). The Johannine new

---

[102] Gardner, *John Donne: The Divine Poems*, 72–4. For a fuller range of editorial references to the Johannine sources for the sonnet, see *The Variorum Edition of the Poetry of John Donne*, 384–7.

[103] Gardner, *John Donne: The Divine Poems*, 74.

[104] *Sermons of John Donne*, vol. ix, 232–3, cited in a shorter version in Gardner, *John Donne: Divine Poems*, 72–3.

[105] Ibid., 72.

commandment is not simply a command to neighbor-love (it is not even that, since it narrows the recipients of love to "one another," assuming a close-knit community of disciples). The new commandment is the means by which the disciples can apprehend Christ's and God's love, and it is designed to provide comfort and advocacy once Christ has departed.

The difficulty in applying this interpretation to "Father, part of his double interest" is that Donne's sermon on John 14:20, which uses language so similar to that of the sonnet, is designed to highlight the role of spiritual assurance through the "last Will of Christ Jesus," while the sonnet seems more modestly to establish only the importance of the love commandment relative to the death of the law. The difficulty is only apparent, though, because the ending of the sonnet clarifies the nature of the gift that has been established at the outset of the poem. Despite the speaker's inability to understand the "knotty" Trinity (3), he realizes that he has received part of God's "double interest" (1) in the gift of the Son—"thy son gives to me" (2)—and that the Lamb has already "blest" the "world" with his life: "This lamb, whose death with life the world hath blest" (5). Renovation is effected not simply by "all-healing grace" (11) but by the all-important agency of the "Spirit" (11), the means by which the speaker can maintain the love commandment and find the confidence that he is part of the "world" that has been sanctified ("world" understood in the Johannine sense as the world of enlightened believers). And what implies that the speaker has derived for himself a degree of spiritual optimism (and what brings the poem into thematic connection with the sermon) is the enthusiastic proclamation expressed in the couplet, "Thy last command / Is all but love. Oh let that last will stand" (13–14). The rest on "stand" suggests, as do the Farewell Discourse and Donne's sermon, that the perseverance provided by the Spirit and love will indeed remain with the disciples. As Donne remarks: "Assurance of their right shall not be taken from them, till he himself return again to give them an everlasting possession."[106]

Read in the context of the Johannine source texts and Donne's sermons on the Paraclete, "Father, part of his double interest" relies on the gift of the Spirit to provide the speaker with a measure of spiritual confidence. The poem's conception of the Spirit is perhaps expected, given Donne's worry, expressed in his sermon on Genesis 1:26, that among the three persons of the Trinity, the Holy Ghost's singular role in sanctified perseverance has too often been overlooked. Cautioning his auditors that they do not often consider the Trinity to the extent that they should, Donne singles out the neglect of the Holy Ghost in particular: "But for the holy Ghost, who feels him, when he feels him? Who takes knowledge of his working, when he works? Indeed our Fathers provided not well enough for the worship of

---

[106] *Sermons of John Donne*, vol. ix, 232. Donne will go on to elaborate the theme of assurance with a gloss on John 16:7, emphasizing the equality among God, Christ, and the Spirit: *"If I goe not away,* says Christ, *the Comforter will not come to you.* How great a comfort must this necessarily be, which must so abundantly recompense the losse of such a comfort, as the presence of Christ was? This is that Spirit, who though hee were to be sent by the Father, and sent by the Son, yet he comes not as a Messenger from a Superiour, for hee was alwaies equall to Father and Son" (240).

the whole Trinity, nor of the holy Ghost in particular."[107] Especially neglected, Donne continues, is the role of the Holy Ghost in easing our consciences:

> Which of us doth truly, and considerately ascribe the comforts, that he receives in dangers, or in distresses, to that God of all comfort, the Comforter, the holy Ghost? We know who procured us our Presentation, and our dispensation: you know who procured you your offices, and your honours. Shall I ever forget who gave me my comfort in sicknesse? Who gave me my comfort, in the troubles, perplexities, and diffidencies of my conscience? The holy Ghost brought you hither. The holy Ghost opens your eares, and your hearts here.[108]

To contemplate the day of judgment is a "fearfull thing" but to consider that day without the Holy Ghost is a "thousand times" more fearful.[109]

Both "Father, part of his double interest" and "Wilt thou love God" reflect Donne's sermonic conception of the soteriological role of the Spirit. If the Spirit initially provides regeneration and renewal, its fuller and final operations foster the indwelling that will come to those who are (or will become) spiritually advanced. Despite the speakers' acknowledgment of their own passivity in the redemptive process, both sonnets suggest that the Spirit can allay the more typically Donnean concerns over servile fear and the uncertainties of assurance once the speakers have been imputed saving faith.[110] Both sonnets depict speakers who, like the speaker of "Batter my heart," understand the service of the Spirit to provide comfort but who, unlike the exigent speaker of "Batter my heart," also show a more considered understanding of the manner in which the Spirit, through a circuit of love, imparts comfort by degrees in the economy of salvation. The Johannine inflections of the latter two sonnets are distinct from the complaint of hardened sin and backsliding sounded mournfully elsewhere in Donne's verse: for example, in the couplet of "O might those sighs and tears"—"To poor me is allow'd / No ease; for long yet vehement grief hath been / The effect and cause, the punishment and sin" (12–14). This is one verse among many others that represents what Helen Gardner has described as, drawing on Paul's well-known verse in Philippians, the speaker's soul in anguish: "The image of a soul in meditation which the 'Holy Sonnets' present is an image of a soul working out its salvation with fear and trembling."[111] Suffice it to say that this portrait of the "persecutory imagination" depicts a speaker much

---

[107] *Sermons of John Donne*, vol. ix, 53.   [108] Ibid., 54.   [109] Ibid., 54.

[110] This is not to say that the *Holy Sonnets* as a group (at least the 1633 edition) depict a speaker entirely assured in his conversion. Perhaps the best recent account of the soteriological open-endedness of the *Holy Sonnets* can be found in Cummings's *The Literary Culture of the Reformation*, where Cummings, elaborating the manner in which the sonnets raise more questions than they answer, remarks: "screaming for conversion, the sonnets point to their sullen unconvertedness" (398). I have been suggesting only that, on the scale of conversion, the sonnets discussed above do indeed provide a greater measure of assurance, itself legitimated by the Johannine texts, than what is more typical of other sonnets in the sequence. A similar argument for an appreciation of the spiritual assurance imparted in sonnets 11 and 12 can be found in Yearwood, "Donne's Holy Sonnets: The Theology of Conversion," 208–21.

[111] Gardner, *John Donne: The Divine Poems*, xxxi, cited in F. W. Brownlow, "The Holy Sonnets," in *Donne and the Resources of Kind*, eds. A. D. Cousins and Damian Grace (Madison, N.J.: Fairleigh Dickinson University Press; London: Associated University Presses, 2002), 103, n. 16.

less confirmed in his belief that the unassailable Spirit will confer on him the rarity of eternal life.[112]

We turn now to a more skeptical outlook on the assuring promises of the Paraclete in the prose and poetry of John Milton. Approaching the Johannine Paraclete from the perspective of the post-Interregnum years and ongoing political turmoil in mid-seventeenth-century England, Milton, too, appreciates the unique role of the Spirit as Comforter, but he cautions against the appropriation of the Paraclete by false and seducing "Montanist" spirits who have corrupted the Spirit of truth and the Church itself.

JOHN MILTON, THE COMFORTER, AND FALSE SPIRITS

In *De Doctrina Christiana* Milton outlines a comprehensive and provocative account of the Holy Spirit. Although drawing on a full range of Old and New Testament references, Milton relies on Johannine pneumatology as the anchoring point for his multifaceted argument that the Spirit, although a person and not a simple power, is not divine and is thus subordinate to both God and the Son. At the beginning of his treatise, Milton establishes that those passages in the New Testament that seem to endow the Spirit with autonomous redemptive power—passages in Acts 10:38, 13:32, Luke 4:1, Matthew 12:28, and Luke 11:20—refer to the "power of the Father" rather than to the Holy Spirit himself.[113] Milton's justification for this questioning of the unassisted power of the Spirit is taken from

---

[112] On the use of this term to describe the English Puritan preoccupation with habitual sin and the fears of backsliding, see John Stachniewski, *The Persecutory Imagination: English Literature and the Literature of Religious Despair* (Oxford: Oxford University Press, 1991). For a discussion of the importance of comfort and assurance in Donne's theology (rightly attributed to Donne's partial embrace of Calvinism), see Richard Strier, "John Donne Awry and Squint: The 'Holy Sonnets,' 1608–1610," *Modern Philology* 86 (1989), 357–84. According to Catherine Gimelli Martin, the *Holy Sonnets* follow the theology of experimental predestinarianism in occupying a middle ground between excessive voluntarism and assurance, on the one hand, and abject despair, on the other hand. Martin appreciates R. T. Kendall's distinction between Calvin's doctrine of assurance (for whom assurance is granted with faith at the outset) and that of the Bezan reformers (including William Perkins), for whom assurance follows faith and needs to be worked out by the individual communicant. See Martin, "Experimental Predestination in Donne's Holy Sonnets: Self-Ministry and the Early Seventeenth-Century 'Via media,'" *Studies in Philology*, 110:2 (2013), 350–81. Yet when discussing the *Holy Sonnets*, particularly "Batter my heart," Martin tends to elide the Calvinist and Bezan distinctions, suggesting, for example, that "Batter my heart" is part of a standard "Calvinist or Bezan script" (369). I would argue that Donne's Johannine approach to assurance and pneumatology in "Wilt thou love God" and "Batter my heart" is Johannine–Calvinist (and not preparationist/experimentalist), for Calvin's doctrine of assurance as developed in the *Institutes* as well as in his commentary on the First Epistle of John fundamentally draws on Johannine proof-texts. For more on the "orthodox" nature of Donne's theology in relationship to Calvinism, see Jeffrey Johnson, *The Theology of John Donne* (Cambridge: D. S. Brewer, 1992). For a recent discussion of the role of fear in Donne's devotional verse, see Ryan Netzley, *Reading, Desire, and the Eucharist in Early Modern Religious Poetry* (Toronto: University of Toronto Press, 2011), chapter 3, *passim*.

[113] John Milton, *De Doctrina Christiana*, in *The Works of John Milton*, eds. Frank Allen Patterson et al. (New York: Columbia University Press, 1933), vol. 14, 367. Subsequent quotations from *De Doctrina Christiana* will be taken from this edition.

apposite passages in John, especially John 16:15 ("He shall take of mine"), that draw a fine but essential distinction between Christ's acquiring power because he is filled with the Spirit and Christ's use of the Spirit as a symbol of the Father's (and hence Christ's) intrinsic power:

> For how could it be necessary that Christ should be filled with the Holy Spirit, of whom he had himself said, John xvi. 15. 'he shall take of mine?' For the same reason I am inclined to believe that the Spirit descended upon Christ at his baptism, not so much in his own name, as in virtue of a mission from the Father, and as a symbol and minister of the divine power. For what could the Spirit confer on Christ, from whom he was himself to be sent, and to receive all things? Was his purpose to bear witness to Christ? But as yet he was himself not so much as known.[114]

As we have seen, in the Fourth Gospel, unlike in the Synoptic accounts, the descent of the Spirit on Christ in the likeness of a dove does not confer any particular power of the Spirit on Christ. The descent represents the affection of the Father for the Son. Milton has set up a tension between the intrinsic power of Christ, on the one hand, and that of the Spirit, on the other hand, a tension that the remaining sections of the treatise will help to slacken. Since the elevation of the Spirit as autonomous agent of salvation would diminish the power of Christ, the Spirit must be seen as subordinate to Christ, a holy "person" that Christ uses instrumentally in his missionary work. After multiplying additional scriptural examples according to which the Holy Ghost is seemingly granted autonomous power (as in 2 Peter 1:21, "to move" holy men, or described, as in Luke 2:25–6, as "upon him"), Milton asserts the priority and superiority of the agency of Christ: "It appears to me, that these and similar passages cannot be considered as referring to the express person of the Spirit…because Christ alone…is, properly speaking, and in a primary sense, the Word of God, and the Prophet of the Church."[115] The middle sections of the treatise are devoted to Milton's more explicit use of Johannine material in distinguishing the Spirit from God and in subordinating the Spirit to the Son. To those who would project divine attributes onto the Spirit, Milton first mentions Mark 13:32 (which points out that no person, angel, or even the Son has knowledge of the day that heaven and earth will pass) and then adduces John 16:14 to crown his argument: "If not even the Son himself, who is also in heaven, then certainly not the Spirit of the Son, who receiveth all things from the Son himself."[116] To those who would attribute the power of effecting divine works to the Spirit—which is suggested in additional passages from Acts and 2 Peter—Milton rests his rebuttal on the Johannine conception of the Paraclete:

> A single remark will suffice for the solution of all these passages, if it be only remembered what was the language of Christ respecting the Holy Spirit, the Comforter; namely, that he was sent by the Son from the Father, that he spake not of himself, nor in his own name, and consequently that he did not act in his own name; therefore that he did not even move others to speak of his own power, but that what he gave he had himself received.[117]

---

[114] Ibid., 367.   [115] Ibid., 369.   [116] Ibid., 387.   [117] Ibid., 389.

Throughout the treatise, Milton restates the strictly hierarchical relationship rather than Triune essentialism among the Father, Son, and Spirit: if the Son does "every thing in the name of the Father," the Spirit does "every thing in the name of the Father and the Son."[118]

Milton realizes, however, that if the Johannine material can easily be used to support his argument for the purely Christological and instrumental service of the Spirit, that same material might be used to argue for the Spirit's essential person-hood. The passage in question is the controversial Johannine Comma at 1 John 5:7: "For there are three that beare record in heaven, the Father, the Word, and the holy Ghost: and these three are one."[119] Milton chooses not to dismiss the passage out of hand, despite its questionable lineage. The lines do not appear in the earliest Greek editions of the Bible and may have been added by a Latin redactor in what some had argued was a gesture of counter-Arianism, although Erasmus controver-sially included the lines in his version of the New Testament.[120] Instead, Milton draws on Beza's translation to point out that "unum sunt," typically taken to refer to unity in essence, should be understood to mean "agree in one," signifying that the three witnesses all bear record.[121] The nature of that witnessing is described in the preceding verses at 1 John 5:5–6 that maintain that whoever believes that Jesus is the "anointed" Son of God will overcome the world. Milton deduces that the Son cannot be essentially one with God, since we see and hear the anointed "word" of God but cannot so access God himself. The same argument would seem to relate to the Holy Ghost: "The same has already been proved, by other arguments, with regard to the Spirit; it follows, therefore, that these three are not one in essence."[122] Milton has not spelled out in detail his argument by analogy but the implication is that, because the Spirit operates on behalf of God and Christ and is sent by God to disseminate Christ's message, the Spirit is not identical to either God or Christ.

If Milton appropriates key pneumatological passages from John to argue for the purely instrumental rather than autonomous and essential nature of the Spirit, his reference to the Comforter in *Paradise Lost* helps us to unravel why he holds so tightly to a relative derogation of the third person.[123] Toward the end of Book XII, after Michael has provided Adam with his cautionary tour of biblical history cul-minating in a promise of the protevangelium, Adam wonders who will guide God's faithful once Christ has departed. Michael's response makes pointed reference to the Paraclete: "From Heav'n / Hee to his own a Comforter will send, / The promise

---

[118] Ibid., 393.   [119] Ibid., 399.

[120] Donne, too, believed in the authenticity of the Johannine Comma, and he devotes a lengthy sermon on 1 John 5 in which he uses the lines to elaborate the two natures of Christ. See *The Sermons of John Donne*, vol. v, 13–50.

[121] Milton, *De Doctrina Christiana*, 401.   [122] Ibid., 401.

[123] Recent work on Milton's conception of the Holy Spirit tends to focus less on the role of the Paraclete and ecclesiology and more on the role of the Spirit in prophetic/poetic inspiration. See, for example, Barbara K. Lewalski, "Milton: The Muses, the Prophets, the Spirit, and Prophetic Poetry," *Milton Studies* 54 (2013), 59–78; and David Ainsworth, "Milton's Holy Spirit in *De Doctrina Christiana*," *Religion and Literature* 45:2 (Summer, 2015), 1–25. For an earlier account of the relationship between Milton's muse and the Holy Spirit, see Stevie Davies and William B. Hunter, "Milton's Urania: 'The Meaning, Not the Name I Call,'" *Studies in English Literature* 28:1 (Winter, 1988), 95–111.

of the Father, who shall dwell / His Spirit within them, and the Law of Faith / Working through love, upon thir hearts shall write, / To guide them in all truth, and also arm / With spiritual Armor, able to resist / Satan's assaults" (XII, 487–92).[124] Michael has compressed here several functions of the Paraclete: to provide comfort and assurance to the disciples so that they will continue to enjoy kinship with Christ; to provide them with the continuing means and lessons to deliver the "truth" of Christ's message; and to arm them against the mounting spiritual assaults of the reprobate world.

Yet as Michael embellishes his vision of the Comforter, we notice a refocusing on the Paraclete's role in protecting the faithful against the disbelief and spiritual encroachments of the world. Inspired and rewarded with "inward consolations" (495), Christ's faithful, with the help of the Paraclete, will fearlessly "quench" Satan's "fiery darts" (XII, 492). If for a time the warfaring Christians will success-fully evangelize, distributing Christ's gifts and miracles, they will eventually die off, as "grievous Wolves" will "succeed for teachers" (XII, 508). Beginning with the reference to the wolves, Milton's account of the Paraclete takes a topical and polit-ically allegorical turn. As is well known, Milton uses the reference to wolves else-where, as in "Lycidas" and his "Sonnet to Cromwell," to describe the corrupt clergy, but the political message acquires more specificity as Michael's prediction continues. The truthfulness of the Spirit—embodied not least in written testimony or scripture, the "written Records pure" (XII, 513)—will be held hostage to super-stition and tradition, by which Milton means any overly structured, top-down, institutionalized system of worship and Church governance that defies the rule of faith, most probably a reference to early seventeenth-century episcopacy and the yoking of secular power to matters of faith (XII, 517). The result is the constrain-ing of individual conscience and the persecution of those who worship in "Spirit and Truth" (XII, 533), a reference to John 4:23, until Christ's day of judgment and the eventual dissolution of the "perverted World" (XII, 547).

In his cynical portrayal of the overthrow of the Spirit by the world, Milton departs from the more canonical emphasis on the ways in which, despite worldly tribulations and unregeneracy, the Paraclete continues to provide unassailable comfort, truth, and testimony to Christ's circle of believers. Milton's Paraclete is vanquished by the world; the world impersonates or "appropriates" the "Spirit of God" (XII, 518–19). To the extent that truth and liberty of conscience re-emerge, that defeat of the world is reserved for Christ at the end-time; the Spirit does not re-emerge in a sustained manner in Michael's telescoped version of biblical history.[125]

---

[124] All quotations from Milton's poetry are taken from *John Milton: Complete Poems and Major Prose*, ed. Merritt Y. Hughes (New York: Macmillan Publishing Company, 1957).

[125] Phillip J. Donnelly argues convincingly that Milton's reference to the Comforter in *Paradise Lost* suggests an endorsement of the co-operation of the Father Son, and Holy Ghost and hence a Biblicist (I would say Johannine) defense of the economic, if not the immanent, trinity: "While Milton does not subscribe to extra-biblical formulations regarding relations internal to the being (or essence) of the Godhead—the 'immanent Trinity'—he clearly endorses biblical depictions of the Father, Son, and Holy Spirit working in co-ordination to bring about salvation history—the 'economic trinity.'" *Milton's Scriptural Reasons: Narrative and Protestant Toleration* (Cambridge: Cambridge University Press, 2009), 177. I would point out that the cynicism contained in the biblical paraphrase

In typical reconstructions of Milton's idealization of the Spirit and inward illumination, Milton's critics have tended to neglect this fact that, once Michael registers the overtaking of the Spirit of grace and truth by the "greater part" (XII, 533), the Spirit drops out entirely from Michael's end-time exposition. For an unspecified period between the Pentecostal bestowal of the Spirit and the Second Coming of Christ, the world will "Under her own weight" groan (XII, 539). Timothy Miller is correct to remark that, for Milton, the Spirit rather than clergy or institutional church will direct the faithful: "God's Spirit leads believers in 'all truth,' into direct knowledge of God and heavenly things. God's Spirit will also strengthen believers to strive against and break through the institutional repression of the Spirit in their lives."[126] Yet during the interim between the Apostolic age and the *Parousia*—in Milton's political allegory, beginning at least with the Restoration— those who remain guided by the Spirit are so eclipsed by the "far greater part" (XII, 533) that "works of Faith" (XII, 536) will "[r]arely be found" (XII, 537) until the heralded arrival of the Savior. For Adam, the approaching comforts of the "Comforter" must inevitably give way to the more distant comforts of the protevangelium.[127]

One explanation for the qualification of the Spirit is that the elevation of Christ is foremost here, as it is elsewhere in *Paradise Lost*, particularly in Milton's earlier depictions of the creation of the world, the resolution of the war in heaven, and the heavenly council in Book III at which God trots out the merits of his vicegerent Son. The ranked relationship between the Spirit-Paraclete and Christ is featured in another reference to the Johannine Paraclete in *Paradise Lost* at the beginning of Book XI, when Christ intercedes to present Adam and Eve's prayers to the Father and offers himself as "advocate": "Hear his sighs though mute; / Unskilful with what words to pray, let mee / Interpret for him, mee his Advocate / And propitiation" (XI, 31–4). The lines are taken from John's First Epistle—"And if any man sinne, we have an Advocate with the Father, Jesus Christ the righteous" (I John 2:1)—the only appearance of the Greek term *parakletos* in the First Epistle, which is typically translated as "advocate." We have seen in Donne's treatment of the passage that this forensic usage, which presents Christ as mediator, differs in connotation from the Fourth Gospel's accent on Christ's role as teacher and comforter. This difference helps explain the fact that, in the Fourth Gospel, the Spirit is "another" Paraclete who will substitute for Christ after the Ascension: "It is expedient for you that I goe away: for if I goe not away, the Comforter will not

---

that Michael continues to present to Adam after the reference to the Comforter reflects that, for Milton, a co-ordinated economic trinity was a foregone ideal rather than a post-Apostolic reality.

[126] Timothy C. Miller, "Milton's Religion of the Spirit and 'the state of the Church' in Book XII of *Paradise Lost*," *Restoration: Studies in English Literary Culture*, 13:1 (Spring, 1989), 12.

[127] I agree with Georgia B. Christopher's appraisal of Michael's notably cynical or "jaded" presentation of redemptive history: Milton puts "the question of faith in its harshest possible light. Not only does he pile up concrete woes as counter-evidence, but the angelic messenger himself becomes dejected over how the endgame of history is to be played out. Michael is a rather jaded minister who announces the gifts of the Comforter…but says less and less about 'inward consolations'…as he goes on." *Milton and the Science of the Saints* (Princeton: Princeton University Press, 1982), 189.

come unto you" (16:7).[128] If Christ serves as Paraclete in mediating creaturely sin to the Father, the later Spirit-Paraclete is designated to remind the disciples of this advocacy.

That Milton wants to emphasize the prototypical role of Christ as Paraclete is evidenced several lines later in Christ's address to the Father. Paraphrasing the Johannine language of abiding at verse 17:22 of the Fourth Gospel, the Son proclaims: "All my redeem'd may dwell in joy and bliss, / Made one with me as I with thee am one" (XI, 43–4). Merritt Hughes and Milton's editors have generally remarked on the paraphrase here of the influential Johannine prayer for believers.[129] Yet they have not noticed Milton's important departure from the original sense of the Johannine prayer. The relevant portion of the prayer to the Father begins in the Fourth Gospel as follows: "I pray for them, I pray not for the world: but for them which thou hast given me, for they are thine. And all mine are thine, and thine are mine: and I am glorified in them. And now I am no more in the world, but these are in the world, and I come to thee. Holy Father, keep through thine owne. Name, those whom thou hast given mee, that they may bee one, as we are" (17:9–11). Christ's believers, those in faith who have been sequestered from the world of unbelief, have already been glorified in Christ. In petitioning the Father to main-tain the status of the brethren after the Ascension, the prayer typifies the realized rather than futurist or apocalyptic eschatology of the Fourth Gospel. Additionally, the prayer needs to be seen intertextually as a continuation of the promissory emphasis on the Comforter already laid out in 16:7–16:15. The narrow focus on the disciples then opens out to the prayer for believers: "Neither pray I for these alone; but for them also which shall beleeve on me through their word: That they all may be one, as thou Father art in mee, and I in thee, that they also may bee one in us: that the world may beleeve that thou hast sent mee" (17:20–1). Although the tense has shifted to the future adoption of those who "shall" or will come to embrace the Word, such co-presence will be achieved while Christ is in heaven, presumably at some point after Pentecost but before the *Parousia*: "Father, I will that they also whom thou hast given me, be with me where I am" (17:24).

If we look back to the Son's paraphrase of the Johannine prayer to Christ in Book XI of *Paradise Lost*, we find that the realized eschatology of the prayer has been displaced by futurist or apocalyptic promise: mankind will receive the gift of adopted union with the Father and Son after his "number'd" (XI, 40) days lead to the "doom" (XI, 40) of death, yielding a "better life" (XI, 42). Omitted here is any sense of a realized glorification during the interim between Pentecost and final judgment. But this remarkable compression of redemptive history is understand-able in the context of the cynicism of that post-Apostolic era that Michael will later convey to Adam regarding the usurpation of the Comforter by seducing spirits in Book XII. It is as if the later cynicism of Book XII needs to be retroactively read

[128] I owe this understanding of the forensic versus counseling role of the Paraclete to Gary M. Burge's discussion of the several connotations and translations of the term in *The Anointed Community*, 6–7.

[129] Milton might have in mind either John 17:11 or 17:22–3. Hughes cites the former in *John Milton: Complete Poems and Major Prose*, 434, n. 43, while John Leonard cites the latter in *John Milton: The Complete Poems* (London and New York: Penguin Books, 1998), 854, n. 44.

into the exclusion of realized eschatology in Christ's self-designation as advocate in his speech to the Father at the opening of Book XI. In the relevant Johannine verses, Christ serves as advocate during his earthly ministry, after which he will send the Comforter (a second advocate) and eventually return in judgment. Milton's Son, by contrast, more unilaterally projects a dual role in which his advocacy is effectively followed by his judgment. The service of the Comforter is diminished in relation to the Son's other offices. Here again, the elevation of the Son relative to the Spirit agrees with what we have seen in *De Doctrina*. The Spirit remains instrumental and subordinate to the Son's intercessory role as advocate. Milton's cynicism regarding the continuing power of the Paraclete seems also to be of a piece with the mid-seventeenth-century English worldview concerning the fear of false spirits and false prophets, which a brief detour into the early modern appreciation of another key Johannine text on pneumatology can properly contextualize.

FALSE SPIRITS IN SEVENTEENTH-CENTURY ENGLISH POLEMIC AND *PARADISE LOST*

In the First Epistle, John remarks: "Beloved, beleeve not every spirit, but trie the spirits, whether they are of God: because many false prophets are gone out into the world. Hereby know ye the spirit of God.... And every Spirit that confesseth not that Jesus Christ is come in the flesh, is not of God: and this is that spirit of Antichrist, whereof you have heard, that it should come, and even now already is it in the world" (1 John 4:1–3). This fear of false or "private" Spirits proliferates throughout the middle decades of the seventeenth century. One notable example can be found in Thomas Bayly's controversial *Certamen Religiosum* (1651). The Royalist Bayly sets out to vindicate earlier charges made by the Marquesse of Worcester against King Charles I regarding the proper interpretation of scripture. The Marquesse had apparently argued that Charles referred to the apostles as "pen-men of the Holy Ghost" who were capable of error, to which Bayly responds:

> His Majesty was farre from thinking, that the Apostles, as Pen-men of the Holy Ghost, could Erre. For then there were no room for that inference, *That Truth is no where to be found but in Holy Scripture.* His Majesty spake not of any private Spirit, but of the Spirit of God leading us into all Truth.... It's true, if any under pretence of the Spirit goe contrary to the Word, (as too many doe) whether they be particular Persons, or generall Councells that doe so, it is a private Spirit, *viz.* their owne Spirit that they are guided by. Therefore Saint *John* bids, *Believe not every Spirit, but trie the Spirits, whether they be of God, because many false Prophets,* (many that falsly pretend the Spirit) *are gone out into the world,* 1 *John* 4. 1. But whoever they be that goe according to the Word, though they be particular and private persons, yet it is not their own particular and private Spirit, but the Spirit of God that doth guide them.[130]

---

[130] Thomas Bayly, *Certamen religiosum, or, A conference between the late King of England and the late Lord Marquesse of Worcester* (London, 1651), 120.

We cannot determine decisively whether Charles made such comments. Yet the polemic reveals the extent to which, in the tempestuous political climate of mid-century England and the Interregnum, a tension was registered between the proper, conscientious interpretation of scripture according to the Word (which would involve a reliance on an exercise of right reason for Independents like Milton) and a bastardized interpretation of scripture proffered by any number of individuals, sects, or conventicles that might harness the power of the incarnated Paraclete in their scriptural dictates.

A recurring trope in the pamphlet literature during the period is the ascription of Montanism to those who were accused of false spiritism and the appropriation of the Johannine Spirit. Montanus was a second-century self-styled prophet and enthusiast who contended that he was the inspired Paraclete. Early Christians argued that Montanus attempted to elevate the power of the Spirit over any apostolic witnessing and even over Christ himself.[131] The charge of Montanism surfaces frequently in a wide swath of polemical literature in the seventeenth century ranging from anti-Catholic polemic to diatribes against dissent and Protestant enthusiasm. In *Paradise Lost*, Michael's admonition to Adam about the Satanic appropriation of the Spirit echoes John Owen's concern as expressed in a 1657 treatise that "seducing Spirits" like Mahomet and other Montanists have steadily gone abroad in the world, "which have been exercising themselves at severall seasons, ever since the *Ascention* of Christ. The *iniquity* of the generation that is past, & passing away, lay in open cursed opposition to the *holy Ghost*. God hath been above them wherein they behaved themselves presumptiously. Satan, whose designe, as he is God of this world, is to be uppermost...hath now transformed himselfe into an *Angell* of light, and he will pretend the Spirit also."[132] The same year in which Owen's treatise was published saw the publication of Edmund Porter's *Trin-unus-deus, or, The trinity and unity of God* (1657), a defense of the Trinity against Millenarianism and Quaker enthusiasm in which Porter worries that "the new risen *Quakers* do harp upon the same string, shrew'd signs, that they are directed, and inspired by some *Montanistical, and earthly paraclete*."[133]

Perhaps the most detailed debates regarding the Paraclete surface in Catholic–anti-Catholic polemic during the earlier decades of the seventeenth century. In his 1620 treatise against the Catholic traditionalism of the Council of Trent, François de Cro remarks: "*Montanus* joyned with the old and new Testament certaine other observations of his pretended paraclete: is not this the very same that was said of

---

[131] Eusebius, drawing on fragments from Apollonaris of Hierapolis, provides a brief history of Montanism in *The history of the church from our Lords incarnation, to the twelfth year of the Emperour Maricius Tiberius*, trans. Valesius (Cambridge, 1683), chapter xvi, 80–2. For a late-seventeenth-century overview of Eusebius on Montanism, see Louis Ellies Du Pin, *A new history of ecclesiastical writers containing an account of the authors of the several books of the Old and New Testament* (London, 1693), 67–8.

[132] John Owen, *Of communion with God the Father, Sonne, and Holy Ghost* (Oxford, 1657), 297. Owen provides an extended commentary on the Paraclete in his *Two Discourses Concerning the Holy Spirit and His Work*. See 35–8 for his belief that the promise of the Spirit presupposes tribulations and false Spirits.

[133] Edmund Porter, *Trin-unus-deus, or, The trinity and unity of God* (London, 1657), 159–60.

that holy Ghost, that was carried by post from Rome to Trent in a cloake-bagge?"[134] Several years later William Laud assures his Jesuit controversialists that, although "infallibility" is accorded to the founding apostles, it is not granted to the Church: "If the *Holy Ghost* doth not *alwayes* abide in the *Preachers,* then most certainly he doth not abide in them to a *Divine Infallibility* alwayes. The *Third Place* is in *S. John* 14. where Christ sayes *The Comforter the Holy Ghost shall abide with you for ever,* Most true againe. For the *Holy Ghost* did abide with the *Apostles* according to *Christs* Promise there made, and shall abide with their *Successors* for ever....But here's no Promise of *Divine Infallibility* made unto them."[135] The same argument emerges in the backbiting polemic between the crypto-Arminian Richard Montagu and the Catholic apologist John Heigham. Arguing for the unerring nature of the Church, Heigham had maintained that the claim in John 14:6 that the Comforter will "abide forever" refers not simply to the apostles but also to their successors: "But the Apostles themselves aboad not for ever, therfore this is to be understood of the perpetuall aboad of the Spirit of Tru[t]h, with their Successors."[136] In his widely read *A Gagg for the New Gospel?* (1642), Montagu objects that the Paraclete passage promises only that the "Spirit of truth" cannot err, not the Church as such; furthermore, Montagu contends, the promise of the Spirit is for "comfort," not "instruction," a gift to the apostles in particular: "It was a temporary promise, a personall priviledge to the Apostles."[137]

About ten years later, Edward Knott, another Jesuit controversialist, summons the Paraclete in a related defense of the infallibility of the Catholic Church: "Because both Catholiques and Protestants, receive holy Scripture, we may thence also prove the infallibility of the Church in all matters which concerne Faith and Religion. Our Saviour speaketh cleerely: *The gates of Hell shall not prevaile against her.* And, *I will ask my Father, and he will give you another Paraclete, that he may abide with you for ever, the Spirit of truth.* And, *But when he, the Spirit of truth cometh, he shall teach you all truth.*"[138] Knott's treatise provoked the ire of the well-respected Laudian controversialist and rationalist William Chillingworth, whose influential *The Religion of Protestants* (1638) takes Knott to task for offering a truncated account of the Spirit. For Chillingworth, Knott removes the Johannine passage from its surrounding context, a context in which Christ expresses the contingent, non-absolute promise of the Paraclete:

> These words, *I will ask my Father, and he shall give you another Paraclete, that he may abide with you for ever, even the Spirit of Truth,* conceale in the mean time, the words before, and the words after; that so, the promise of Gods Spirit, may seem to be absolute, whereas it is indeed most cleerely and expresly conditionall: being both in

---

[134] François de Cro, *The three conformities. Or The harmony and agreement of the Romish Church with gentilisme, Iudaisme and auncient heresies* (London, 1620), 209.

[135] William Laud, *A relation of the conference betweene William Laud, then, Lrd. Bishop of St. Davids; now, Lord Arch-Bishop of Canterbury: and Mr. Fisher the Jesuite by the command of King James of ever blessed memorie* (London, 1639), 96.

[136] John Heigham, *The touch-stone of the reformed Ghospell* (St. Omer, 1634), 40.

[137] Richard Montagu, *A gagg for the new Gospell? No: a new gagg for an old goose* (London, 1624), 43.

[138] Edward Knott, *Mercy & truth. Or Charity maintayned by Catholiques* (St. Omer, 1634), 112.

the words before, restrained to those only, that *love God and keep his Commandements:* and in the words after, flatly denied to all, whom the Scriptures stile by the name of *the World....* Behold the place entire, as it is set down in your own Bible. *If ye love mee keep my Commandements, and I will aske my Father, and he shall give you another Paraclete, that he may abide with you for ever, even the Spirit of the Truth, whom the world cannot receive.* Now from the place there restored and vindicated from your mutilation, thus I argue against your pretence. We can have no certainty of the infallibility of your Church, but upon this supposition, that your Popes are infallible in confirming with the Decrees of Generall Councells.[139]

Given that no certainty of the Pope's heart can be discerned and that so many of the Roman See are "worldly, wicked, carnall, diabolicall men," the Spirit of truth identified with the Comforter cannot be associated with the so-described infallibility of the Church.[140] Indeed, the Spirit of truth is denied, not promised, to such worldlings, according to Chillingworth's invective.

Seventeenth-century polemic regarding the misuse of the Spirit by the infallible Church is echoed in Michael's tutelage to Adam in *Paradise Lost*. Milton, too, implies that the Spirit should not be used to claim the infallibility of the Church, since no institution can provide such certitude: "Who against Faith and Conscience can be heard / Infallible?" (XII, 529–30). And in his polemical treatises Milton will expand on the ways in which Church doctrine and hirelings have "undervalued" "Christ beneath Mahomet" and should therefore be reviled and ashamed for crying out with a distinct voice that "If ye settle not our maintenance by Law, farewell the Gospel; then which nothing can be uttered more false, more ignominious, and I may say, more blasphemous against our Saviour; who hath promised without this condition, both his holy Spirit, and his own presence with his Church to the worlds end."[141] Given the prevailing fear that false and seducing Paracletes have overtaken the Church of England, we can understand the qualification of the power of the Paraclete in Michael's speech to Adam in Book XII of *Paradise Lost.* This is not to say that the Paraclete is an ineffective advocate, teacher, or protector for Milton. Milton will argue in *The Treatise of Civil Power* (1659) that the Holy Spirit itself provides the freedom and liberty of conscience for individuals to interpret scripture according to their own lights: "Our beleef and practise, as far as we are able to apprehend and probably make appeer, is according to the will of God & his Holy Spirit within us, which we ought to follow much rather then any law of man."[142] And in the context of classical pagan–Christian tensions rehearsed in *Paradise Regained*, the Johannine "Spirit of truth" dwells instructively "[i]n pious Hearts, an inward Oracle / To all truth requisite for me to know" (I, 463–5). However, Milton worried, much in the manner of Chillingworth, that John's

---

[139] William Chillingworth, *The religion of protestants a safe way to salvation* (Oxford, 1638), 175–6.
[140] Ibid., 176.   [141] John Milton, *A supplement to Dr. Du Moulin* (London, 1680), 25.
[142] John Milton, *A treatise of civil power in ecclesiastical causes* (London, 1659), 4. Milton further argues that we have "no other divine rule or autoritie from without us warrantable to one another as a common ground but the holy scripture, and no other within us but the illumination of the Holy Spirit so interpreting that scripture as warrantable only to our selves and to such whose consciences we can so perswade" (4).

promise of the Paraclete was too often used to justify ecclesiastical Church government rather than liberty of conscience.[143]

Much of what I have argued regarding Milton's pneumatology has implications
more generally for our understanding of the role of the Spirit in *Paradise Lost*.
Extrapolating from seeming references to the Holy Spirit in relation to Milton's
invocation of the Muse in Books I and VII as well as references to the Spirit of
truth or Comforter in Book XII, Miltonists have typically assumed that Milton
held the Spirit in high regard as a source of inspiration and strength: "The Spirit
functions most pervasively and, in the human context, most significantly in the
inner workings of the godly," Thomas Corns maintains, adding that Milton typically opposes the "spirit within" to "carnal laws."[144] Yet we have seen that, given the
encroachments of false spirits and the very difficulty of discerning differences
between upright and misleading spirits, a reliance on the "spirit within" as a check
on carnal laws might mislead more often than properly guide any but the most
rarefied among the elect.

It is uncertain in *Paradise Lost* whether Milton believes that the true offices
of the Spirit-Paraclete, the offices of assuagement and comfort, can achieve their
affective work among the singularly faithful amid so much spiritual unregeneracy.[145]
Much of the consolation that Adam will take from Michael is cognitive rather than
affective in nature. Adam has learned that "to obey is best" (XII, 561) and that
"suffering for Truth's sake / Is fortitude to highest victory" (XII, 569–70). Michael
responds that, without questing after illicit knowledge, Adam has "attain'd the
sum / Of wisdom" (XII, 575–6) and that he will now need to "add / Deeds" to
such "knowledge answerable" (XII, 581–2). Any measure of affective consolation
added to this knowledgeable renewal is, as expected, forward-looking, as when Eve
remarks that the "consolation yet secure / I carry hence" (XII, 620–1) is tied
directly to the restoration of the protevangelium. The protevangelium, scripturally
sourced in Genesis, is typically associated not only with the vanquishing of Satan
during the end-time but also with the Crucifixion. Yet Michael's presentation of
the protevangelium, presumably the version here internalized by Eve, is trained
almost exclusively on final judgment. His earlier description of the day of "respir-
ation to the just / And vengeance to the wicked" (XII, 540–1), which has its scriptural
source in Acts 3:19, is quickly yoked to a description of Christ's return amid the
"Clouds from Heav'n" (XII, 545), a paraphrase of the apocalyptic verses of

---

[143] E. M. W. Tillyard, too, recognized Milton's ambivalence regarding the testimony of the Spirit,
but Tillyard believed that Milton's skepticism derived from his alliance of the Spirit with right reason:
"His words on scriptural corruption betray a doubt concerning a doctrine of Scripture whose very
strength was a rigidity and a confinement not really congenial to the free working of the Spirit.... If
man's reason, aided by the Holy Spirit, can interpret the canonical scriptures, why can it not interpret
other religious works?" *Studies in Milton* (London: Chatto & Windus, 1955), 152.

[144] Thomas N. Corns, *Regaining Paradise Lost* (London: Longman, 1994), 24–5.

[145] Louis L. Martz memorably describes the inescapable cynicism here as an irremediable fissure:
"The contradictions, the fissure in the poem's last two books cannot be healed; the weight of the woe
has gradually weakened the epilogue's connection with the poem's center, and here the epilogue at last
drops off." *The Paradise Within: Studies in Vaughan, Traherne, and Milton* (New Haven: Yale University
Press, 1964), 165.

Revelation 1:7 that herald the last judgment. If there is true spiritual comfort here, it is once again projected into the distant future. Michael so compresses salvific history as nearly to erase the spiritually infused period between Christ's Ascension and the *Parousia*.

The effacement of post-Apostolic earthly comfort by end-time hopefulness helps to explain, against the most optimistic readings of the final lines of Milton's epic, the uncertainty that even the recently tutored and presumably Spirit-guided Adam and Eve will face once they find themselves on the other side of the gates of Eden. We should recall the portentous and martial sense of the final expulsion. Michael hastens to grab the lingering Adam and Eve as the descending Cherubim, brandishing the "Sword of God" (XII, 633), ablaze like a fierce comet (the language of which recalls the dreadful encounter between Death and Satan in Book II), throng the Edenic gates (XII, 628–43). Michael had earlier been instructed by God to remove Adam and Eve "not disconsolate" (XI, 113). Yet what Michael has provided in consolation is displaced by the martial tableau imagined by Milton's qualifying narrator. The way ahead is slow and "solitary" (XII, 649).[146] It is diffi-cult for even the most optimistic of Milton's devout readers to believe that, although the paradise within awaits Adam and Eve should they remain faithful, they leave Eden with the emotional uplift and spiritual optimism that the Johannine Comforter is commissioned to bestow on the brethren.

The Spiritual comforts and advocacy that Donne finds in the Paraclete are qualified for Milton, given the seeming ease with which the soteriological and ecclesiological powers of the Spirit can be suborned by those outside the faithful community of independent thinkers. Johannine history repeats itself, not incidentally, for this is the sort of misappropriation that gives rise to the very conception of the First Epistle of John, which was written toward the end of the first century to expose false appropriations of the Spirit by those sects who were continuing to radicalize Johannine pneumatology. Milton's pneumatology affords us a glimpse of the seventeenth-century politico-theological implications of the Johannine discourses that, given their emphasis on the ongoing salvation of a sect of Christ's followers guided by the Paraclete after Jesus' departure, will often be appropriated as divisive, even dualistic scriptural sources. As we will see in Chapter 5, it is precisely an enthusiastic spiritism born of Johannine pneumatology that inspires seventeenth-century antinomian arguments for free grace and perfectionism. One standard antinomian claim is that the Spirit is sufficiently sanctifying and obviates the need for practical piety and moral habituation. But we turn now to the traces of such separatism and dualism that are often linked to another uniquely Johannine pre-supposition, the identification with God as *agape*, which for some interpreters entails a neglect of horizontal love expressed from the Johannine community toward perceived out-groups.

---

[146] In *Milton and Religious Controversy: Satire and Polemic in Paradise Lost* (Cambridge: Cambridge University Press, 2000), John N. King ends his critical assessment of Book XII by remarking: "Michael's consolation extends the promise that good works predicated upon faith will enable Adam and Eve" to possess a paradise within (188). Yet I would argue that the final narration of the expulsion qualifies the consolatory aspects of Michael's tutelage.

4

God is Love
Johannine *Agape* and Early Modern Devotional Poetry

John's uniqueness in comparison with the Synoptics' presentation of Jesus' ministry emerges most clearly in his multivocal presentation of love. The Synoptics and especially Paul focus on the ways in which God's spontaneous and unmotivated love, to which the Son's sacrifice for humankind testifies so clearly, is acknowledged primarily through the ethical action of neighbor-love. John, by contrast, more ontologically identifies God with love: "Hee that loveth not, knoweth not God: for God is love" (1 John 4:8). Additionally, John focuses more directly on the ways in which Jesus' brethren can enjoy the eternal love that God has expressed prior to the Incarnation toward the Son. In the Fourth Gospel, love of God is reached through the disciples' belief in Christ's words and hence their coming to a knowledge of God (at times described as fellowship with God or as an achievement of the beatific vision). Shared creaturely love within an immediate circle of believers is also essential, but John makes no mention of love for one's enemies, which has suggested from at least Augustine onward a particularistic, sectarian vision of love that is achievable only for the insular and enlightened Johannine community.[1]

In this chapter, I argue that early modern exegetes and devotional poets acknowledge the uniqueness of John's conception of love, celebrating its ontological focus and its troubling of neat distinctions between God's eternal love for Christ and his love for the community of believers. After a brief overview of the early modern acceptance of John's metaphysical and ontological conception of *agape*,

---

[1] For an influential discussion of the practical-ethical implications of Johannine sectarianism, see Wayne A. Meeks, "The Ethics of the Fourth Evangelist," in *Exploring the Gospel of John: In Honor of D. Moody Smith*, eds. R. Alan Culpepper and C. Clifton Black (Louisville: Westminster John Knox Press, 1996), 317–26. On the express "new" love commandment in the Fourth Gospel to "love one another," Meeks remarks: "It is this mutual love within the community that is set over against the world's hatred. The model is Jesus' love for those whom he names his friends and for whom he lays down his life (John 15:12–15). There is nothing in John, unlike the Synoptics, about loving one's enemies" (324). A critique of Meeks's position and a survey of the Johannine love ethic can be found in Andreas J. Köstenberger, *A Theology of John's Gospel and Letters: The Word, the Christ, the Son of God* (Grand Rapids: Zondervan, 2009), chapter 13, *passim*. The extent to which post-Reformed English writers might appropriate such exclusionism depends on context: although seventeenth-century dissenting writers will use Johannine insularism to justify the beliefs of their particular conventicles (as described in Chapter 5), other writers might use the more open-ended love verses from the First Epistle in order to exhort love of neighbors. See, for example, Naomi Tadmor's important discussion in *The Social Universe of the English Bible* (Cambridge: Cambridge University Press, 2010), 41–9, of the use of various English Bible translations to justify a morality of neighborliness, particularly regarding the use of John's First Epistle in a treatise entitled *A briefe discouse of two most cruell and bloudie murthers* (London, 1583).

I turn to three seventeenth-century poets, each of whom borrows a distinctive feature of Johannine *agape* in his own poetic vision of love. For George Herbert, love of God is the surest means of knowing (seeing) God, which is ideally attainable through the route of Christ. Henry Vaughan also makes much use of John's identification of God with love, although Vaughan's optimism is offset partly by skepticism concerning his (or his speakers') redemptive fitness. Vaughan's ontology of love is tempered by a poetics of servile and filial fear. Thomas Traherne shares with Herbert a Johannine appreciation of the indwelling of the convert with God, but to the extent that Traherne integrates a naturalistic theology (God's love is suffused throughout the created orders) with a high Christology, he syncretistically combines an *analogia entis* (analogy of being) with an *analogia fides* (analogy of faith).

GOD IS LOVE

Among New Testament accounts of *agape*, John's First Epistle uniquely identifies God with love as such: "And we have knowen and beleeved the love that God hath to us. God is love, and hee that dwelleth in love, dwelleth in God, and God in him" (1 John 4:16). The importance of this single passage is proclaimed by Augustine, who remarks in a tract on the First Epistle: "If nothing else were said in praise of love, in all the pages of this Epistle, nothing else whatever in any other page of Scripture, and this were the one and only thing we heard from the voice of God's Spirit—'For God is love'—we should ask for nothing more."[2] Early modern commentators agree with Augustine's esteem of the verse. For example, William Jones, an English clergyman leaning toward nonconformity, expressly privileges 1 John 4:15 over Pauline conceptions of agape: "*God is love*, saith Saint *John*; a golden sentence. Saint *Paul* in his whole Chapter of love, 1 *Cor.* 13. Spake not so much in the commendation of *love*, as Saint *John* doth in this one short and pithy sentence."[3]

What sets the Johannine verse apart from comparable New Testament passages is not simply its ontological-metaphysical association of God with love but the implications that such an approach has for our understanding of creaturely love toward God. To declare God's equivalence with *agape* raises the question, as do the immediately preceding verses of the First Epistle, of the nature of the relationship with God once creaturely love has been achieved. The First Epistle and John's dovetailing Gospel comments on love center on the manner in which, through an understanding of God's eternal love for Christ and of Christ's analogous love for the brethren, creatures can attain to something approaching knowledge of God or a witnessing of the beatific vision. The Fourth Gospel and First Epistle set up Christ as the one who has had privileged access to God and who is uniquely able to make God known to his believers. Accessible knowledge of the divine is achievable

    [2] Saint Augustine, *The Homilies of the First Epistle General of St. John*, in *Augustine: Later Works*, ed. John Burnaby (Philadelphia: Westminster Press, 1955), 314.
    [3] William Jones, *A commentary upon the Epistles of Saint Paul to Philemon, and to the Hebrewes* (London, 1635), 671.

through the vehicle of creaturely love: "No man hath seene God at any time. If wee love one another, God dwelleth in us, and his love is perfected in us. Hereby know wee that we dwell in him and he in us, because hee hath given us of his Spirit" (1 John 4:12–13). The Johannine approach to divine love raises the question, which exercises early modern and modern commentators, of how God's essence as love can be approached by humans whose fallible love will always fall short of the essential love that is God. Augustine establishes the implications for the ontological understanding of God's *agape* that will influence the early modern conception:

> 'God is love.' What outward appearance, what form, what stature, hands or feet, has love? None can say; and yet love has feet, which take us to the Church, love has hands which give to the poor, love has eyes which give intelligence of him who is in need....Love has ears....All these are not members set each in their own place; he that has charity sees the whole at once with the understanding's grasp. Dwell there, and you shall be dwelt in: abide, and there shall be abiding in you. My brothers, one does not love what one cannot see.[4]

For Augustine, the ideal result of *agape* is knowledge of God's essence. Although that essence cannot be directly known or experienced, we can, through church membership, responsive love for the Son, and love of one another in some sense "see" God's love dwelling within us. Augustine's commentary brings to the fore two Johannine questions on love: the ontological question of the nature of God's love relative to creaturely love; and the soteriological (and ethical) question of the manner in which creatures relate to God by means of horizontal fellowship.

Regarding the ontological question, most early modern commentators draw on neo-scholastic distinctions among substance, essence, and accidents in order to detail the asymmetries between divine *agape* and creaturely love. In a *Stock of Divine Knowledge* (1641), the moderately conforming Puritan Richard Stock cautions against conflating the essence of divine love with human love: "Let no man think when I speak of Gods love, that I mean qualities in God; for when I say God is love, I mean no new thing, but that same which the Apostle saith, 1. *Joh.* 4.16. *God is love:* now then there is a double love; there is love giving love, there is love the substance, & love the quality: If it be the name of the substance, it is given to God; if the name of the quality, it is given to man: and whatsoever is said of love, may be said of any other Attribute, as mercy, justice, &c."[5] Given the metaphysical divide between God's essence and contingent creaturely attributes, creaturely love will always remain imperfect in some sense, although we are encouraged to attempt to approach the elusive nature of love that is identical with God's irreducible essence. In his 1591 sermons on the sacraments, the Scottish Presbyterian minister Robert Bruce remarks: "Now says JOH. in his 1. epist. 4. 8. God is love; therefore,

---

[4] Saint Augustine, *The Homilies of the First Epistle General of St. John*, 317.
[5] Richard Stock, *A Stock of Divine Knowledge* (London, 1641), 88. On Stock's moderate Puritanism, see Jeffrey Alan Miller, "Milton and the Conformable Puritanism of Richard Stock and Thomas Young," in *Young Milton: The Emerging Author, 1620–1642*, ed. Edward Jones (Oxford: Oxford University Press, 2000), 72–106.

the more we draw neere to love, the more near are we to that happy life: for we are in God, & partaker of the life of God. When I speak this, ye mann not thinke, that love in God, & love in us, is an thing; for love is but a quality in us, & it is not a quality in God. ... [A]s love in God, is his own essence: Therefore, the more yee grow in love, the neerer ye draw to God, and to that happy and blessed life."[6] In his 1645 treatise *The Anchor of Hope* John Wells adds that, in consisting only of an action, creaturely love is fundamentally distinct from divine *agape*: "Because God is Love, and this is much more then to say God loves, it notes thus much that it is the very Essence and nature of God: Man may properly be said to love, but cannot be said to be love."[7] John Cotton's extensive commentary on the First Epistle perhaps sums up best the Johannine isomorphism between God and love. For Cotton, 1 John 4:16, which implies the simplicity of God's nature, suggests an analogy between "God is love" and "God is a Spirit" (4:24): "As our savior saith God is a Spirit, that is, its not a quality in him, that may be or may not be, but love is essential and nature to him, Gods love is in himself, and so his power and wisdom."[8] All such treatises highlight the asymmetry between creaturely love, which is at best a "quality," and divine *agape*, which, as unapproachable substance or essence, is irreducible to neoscholastic principles of accidents and qualities.

Early modern exegetes quibbled over these academic distinctions, but a more pressing issue, touched on in the treatises above, is the extent to which, through expressions of creaturely love to Christ and one's neighbor, one might approach union with God. Framing John's declaration that "God is love" in the First Epistle are his exhortations to the brethren to love one another, for only then will they come to know God: "Beloved, let us love one another; for love is of God: and every one that loveth, is borne of God and knoweth God" (1:4:7). A commandment along these lines is also issued in the Fourth Gospel: "A new commandement I give unto you, That yee love one another, as I have loved you, that yee also love one another. By this shall all men know that ye are my disciples, if yee have love one to another" (13:34–5). Drawing on Johannine commentaries by Augustine, Aquinas, and Peter Lombard, John Mayer, early seventeenth-century clergyman and prolific biblical commentator, remarks in *Ecclesiastica interpretatio* (1627): "God is said to be love in the abstract, as he is said to be goodnesse, justice, and wisdome, because he is infinitely loving, an example whereof is immediatly subjoyned, and such a fountaine of love, that they which are in him cannot but love one another."[9] Notable here is the ability with which converts, through love of the brethren, might achieve not simply knowledge of God but also participation and fellowship with God (and the Trinitarian unity). We have seen in earlier chapters that the rhetoric of abiding is used throughout the Johannine discourses, as in "If wee love

---

[6] Robert Bruce, *Sermons Upon the Sacrament of the Lord's Supper* (Edinburgh, 1591), 150. I have modernized slightly the language of this excerpt.

[7] John Wells, *The anchor of hope, for Gods tossed ones* (London, 1645), 89.

[8] John Cotton, *A practicall commentary, or An exposition with observations, reasons, and uses upon the first Epistle generall of John* (London, 1658), 317.

[9] John Mayer, *Ecclesiastica interpretatio: or The expositions upon the difficult and doubtful passages of the seven Epistles called catholike* (London, 1627), 208.

one another, God dwelleth in us, and his love is perfected in us" (1 John 4:12); "If ye keepe my Commandements, ye shal abide in my love" (15:11); and "These things have I spoken unto you, that my joy might remaine in you, and that your joy might be full" (15:10). To love God is to acknowledge Christ's love for his followers, itself patterned after God's love for Christ. Although "no man hath seene God at any time" (1:4:12), the result of belief in Christ's love for the brethren and love for one another is adoption into God's family through means of the Spirit.

The language of unitive abiding with God through expressions of horizontal love is unique to John. Paul tends to link neighbor-love explicitly to the fulfillment of the law (as in Romans 8), and the Synoptics tend to emphasize love of enemies (and to model horizontal love on self-love). There is indeed a mystical accent to the Johannine rhetoric of indwelling, but a distinction should be drawn between Hellenistic "unio mystica" and this particular manifestation of Johannine "communio mystica."[10] According to the former, the convert becomes so ecstatically absorbed into or possessed by Godhead as to leave off creaturely life entirely, ultimately deified in the process of self-emptying.[11] The latter, Johannine view is not contemplative but ethical-practical (the brethren dwell in God through Christ and one another) as well as communal or relational.[12] To dwell in Christ is to dwell also in God, such fellowship signifying union through shared *agape* but without relinquishing selfhood in the process.[13] And such interpersonal fellowship is always historically grounded, mediated through the revelation of the Son.[14] John has therefore been called at most a "semi-mystic"; C. K. Barrett, one of the leading modern commentators on the Fourth Gospel, points out that, in his immortality, essential oneness with God, and equality with God, the "one true mystic" in John's writings is Christ himself.[15] An especially clear early modern statement of this

[10] The use of the terms "unio mystica" and "communio mystica" frames Jey Kanagaraj's discussion of the critical appraisal of Johannine mysticism in *"Mysticism" in the Gospel of John: An Inquiry into its Background* (Sheffield: Sheffield Academic Press, 1998), 22–30.

[11] See James McPolin, "Johannine Mysticism," *Way* 1 (1978), 26, for a brief discussion of ecstasy and metaphysical pantheism in Hellenistic mysticism.

[12] This "relational" understanding of the reciprocal forms of love in the Fourth Gospel is discussed in Marianne Meye Thompson, *The God of the Gospel of John* (Grand Rapids: Eerdmans Publishing Company, 2001), who remarks, "The relationship between Father and Son is the reality in which those who have faith participate and dwell. This is the relationship or reality in which one finds 'life,' and whose fundamental commitment can be summarized in terms of 'love'" (100).

[13] In his commentary on John 6:56, Luther points out that medieval mysticism erroneously assumes that Johannine abiding signifies meditation or contemplation: "Contemplation and shadowy and erratic thoughts, which are but an imaginary indwelling and nothing but thoughts, will not do here." *Sermons on the Gospel of St. John, Chapters 6–8*, in *Luther's Works*, vol. 23, ed. Jaroslav Pelikan (Saint Louis: Concordia Publishing, 1959), 144–5. For Luther, "to abide" meant "to remain" or "to dwell" in a person.

[14] I owe these distinctions regarding Johannine mysticism to C. K. Barrett, *The Gospel According to John* (London: S.P.C.K., 1965), 71–4; C. H. Dodd, *The Interpretation of the Fourth Gospel* (Cambridge: Cambridge University Press, 1965), 197–200; and Kanagaraj, *"Mysticism" in the Gospel of John*, particularly his summary on pp. 32–3 of D. L. Mealand's "The Language of Mystical Union in Johannine Writings," *The Downside Review* 95 (1977), 19–34.

[15] See Barrett, *The Gospel According to John*, who concludes: "If John has borrowed from contemporary mystical thought he has done so not in his descriptions of Christians but in his portrait of Christ. The 'mystical' life of Christians (the word is misleading) is derivative and rests upon the essential relation of Jesus with the Father" (73–4).

distinctive form of Johannine mediated or semi-mysticism can be found in a treatise on *noli me tangere* and John 20 by the Puritian divine Richard Sibbes, who
remarks in *A heavenly conference between Christ and Mary after His resurrection*
(London, 1654):

> God in Christ is so near our nature, that there is an hypostatical union, they make one
> person, our nature being taken into the second person. By reason of this near union
> of the God-head to our nature cometh that comfort and near union between God and
> our nature, whereby *God* hath sweet communion with us in Christ. *God* by his spirit,
> though not hypostatically, yet gratiously is one with us, and hath communion with us
> now as his Children.[16]

Johannine mysticism offers not a deification or union between the individual
and God, which would assume that our nature might become one with God's
holy family, but rather a "nearness" to God achieved through a shared personhood with Christ, "in whom it is nearest of all, in whom it is advanced above the
angelical nature."[17] A similar conception of Johannine participation can be
found in the work of the early English Protestant John Merbecke, who remarks
in his commonplace book regarding the conception of dwelling in John 6 and
the vine metaphor:

> Which dwelling is neither corporall nor locall, but an heavenlie, spirituall and super-
> naturall dwelling whereby so long as we dwell in him, & he in us, we have by him
> everlasting life. And therfore Christ saith in the same place, that Christ is the Vine and
> we are the braunches, because that by him we have life. For as the braunches receive
> life and nourishment of the bodie of the vine, so receive we by him, the naturall prop-
> ertie of his bodie, which is life and immortalitie, and by these meanes, we being his
> members doe live and are nourished.[18]

Through this supernatural rather than corporeal mode of participation, Christ
dwells in us, according to Merbecke's paraphrase of Peter Martyr, only by faith
and spirit. Hence it does not follow that "either his body or his soule dwelleth in
our harts really as I may cal it & substancially. It is enough that Christ be said to
be in us by his divine presence, & that he is by his spirit grace & gifts, present
with us."[19]

Without expressly describing John's conception of *agape* in mystical terms,
early modern commentators with broad and varying denominational affiliations

---

[16] Richard Sibbes, *A heavenly conference between Christ and Mary after His resurrection* (London, 1654), 175–6.

[17] Ibid., 176.   [18] John Merbecke, *A booke of notes and common places* (London, 1581), 188.

[19] Ibid., 187. Quick to reject any notion that verses on corporate unity in Corinthians, Ephesians, and Galatians (especially 3:28) describe substantial, ontological, or mystical alteration, William Perkins uses John's conception of dwelling to argue that scriptural "unity" with Christ is mediated and pneumatological: "The substance of the godhead of Christ is incommunicable....Beleevers are not one with Christ by transfusion of the properties and qualities of the godhead, or manhood unto us. It may be said how then are they one with him? I answer by one and the same spirit dwelling in Christ and in all the members of Christ. 1. Cor. 6. 17. *he that cleaveth to the Lord, is one spirit.* Paul saith in this sense, Eph. 2. 14. that Christ maketh the two [20] distinct nations of Iewes and Gentiles *one new man.* S. John saith, that *Christ dwells in us and we in him by the spirit.* 1. John 3. 23." *A commentarie or exposition, upon the five first chapters of the Epistle to the Galatians* (London, 1604), 265.

elaborated the language of participation used in John's key passages on *agape*, particularly the First Epistle's advisement that to know or dwell in the God who is love is to abide in him.[20] In his paraphrase on John's First Epistle, Erasmus describes participation through *agape* in terms of a metaphor of bodily incorporation: "If we love our neighbour...than the love of God is perfite in us, declaryng also that God hymselfe is in us. Lyke as all one spirite knytteth the membres of the body together, and maketh them one body: even so the spirite of god doeth in a maner glue together and knytte bothe us with hym, and every one to other."[21] If Erasmus's rhetoric has a practical-ecclesiastical end in its suggestion of corporate church membership, Thomas Collier, mid-seventeenth-century Baptist minister, approaches a mystical understanding when noting the ways in which, through faith, love brings the soul up to God: "*We have known & beleeved the love that God hath to us: and God is love, and he that dwelleth in love, dwelleth in God, and God in him:* It acts the soule above it selfe, and causeth it to dwell in God, and so to dwell in his love, and this is an exceeding glorious effect."[22] Collier's strong inflection toward mysticism is a radicalizing gesture that, as we will see at length in Chapter 5, appears frequently in antinomian and dissenting treatises on free grace.[23]

William Tyndale's exposition on 1 John 4 also celebrates the fellowship that results from an emulation of Christ's love. Yet Tyndale's text, like so many comparable glosses, focuses epistemologically on the knowledge of God to be gained in the

[20] Medieval mystics such as Nicholas of Cusa were fond of the quasi-mystical passages of John's Farewell Discourse. Yet they too drew a distinction between an ontological and a participative relationship with the deity. Jaroslav Pelikan remarks: "Contrary to a mysticism that was in danger of heresy, the 'mystical theology' that was at the same time churchly and orthodox took the favorite proof text for deification, the words of the psalm, 'You are gods' [Pelikan also cites John 10:34], to mean a change that was not ontological but 'participative and assimilative.'" Pelikan, *The Christian Tradition: A History of the Development of Doctrine, Volume 4: Reformation of Church and Dogma (1300–1700)* (Chicago: University of Chicago Press, 1984), 66. Thus Cusa, who in *On Learned Ignorance* relies on key verses in Corinthians and John's Farewell Discourse, among other seeming mystical texts: "Each of the blessed, while the truth of each's being is preserved, exists in Christ Jesus as Christ and through him in God as God." *Nicholas of Cusa: Selected Spiritual Writings*, trans. H. Lawrence Bond (New York: Paulist Press, 1997), 2004.

[21] Desiderius Erasmus, *The seconde tome or volume of the Paraphrase of Erasmus upon the Newe Testament* (London, 1549), 338. When Erasmus uses terms such as "dwelling" to describe Johannine participation with Christ, as in his gloss on John 6, his primary concern is typically with corporate fellowship and the body of the Church. For example: "Ye shal through my spirite, live everlastingly: like as the membres of one bodye lyveth by one common spirite, so long as they do adhere and cleave fast together. And I shall leave unto you my fleshe and blood as a hid secret mystery, and mistical token of this copulacion and felowship: which selfe thing although ye do receive it, yet will it not profit you unles ye receyve it spiritually." *The first tome or volume of the Paraphrase of Erasmus upon the Newe Testamente* (London, 1548), 490. On Erasmus and Eucharistic incorporation, see Thomas J. Davis, who remarks, "Yes, there is union with Christ, but Erasmus emphasized the union of one Christian with another; the Sacrament is individual, but it is also social." *This Is My Body: The Presence of Christ in Reformation Thought* (Grand Rapids: Baker Academic, 2008), 151–2.

[22] Thomas Collier, *The marrow of Christianity: or, A spirituall discoverie of some principles of truth* (London, 1647), 34.

[23] Albert Schweitzer describes this form of Johannine love mysticism as follows: "To be 'in-love' signifies, according to the preaching of the Logos-Christ, not only to exercise love in the ethical sense, but above all to continue steadfast in the true fellowship of the Elect, and through it to remain united to Christ and God." *The Mysticism of Saint Paul the Apostle*, trans. William Montgomery (New York: Henry Holt & Company, 1931), 352.

process: "For the love of a mans neighbour unfaynedly spryngeth out of the unfayned knowledge of God in Christes bloud. By which knowledge we be borne of God & love God and our neighbours for his sake. And so he that loveth hys neighbour unfaynedly, is sure of him selfe, that he knoweth God, and is of God unfaynedly."[24] For Tyndale, one extrapolates knowledge of God from the evidence of neighbor-love. In an earlier treatise pitched against Stephen Gardiner's defense of the Mass, Edward Gilby makes the same point, although counterfactually, and he more directly integrates the epistemological and ontological registers: "Let us love together, for love is of God, and euerie one that loveth is borne of God. He that loveth not knoweth not God, for God is love. If we love together God dwelleth in us, and his love is perfec[t] in us."[25]

That John's comments on the language of fellowship through love could be interpreted for varying ends is evidenced in Miles Coverdale's use of 1 John 4 to justify his Johannine–Augustinian notion that belief is equivalent to eating the host and participating with God: "He gave himselfe whole unto us: so ought we to give our selves whole unto him, and to our neighbour. To him through beleefe, to our neighbour through charitable love. Through faith we abide in him: by working love hee abideth in us. The more wee love, the more enjoy we of this meate: the more wee beleeve, the more we love."[26] To love Christ and God is not simply to understand and believe in the love extended from the Father to the Son and from the Son to the disciples (and hence to enjoy union with the holy family). It is also to partake of the sacramental "eating" (in terms of the spiritual not local presence) of Christ's body, a position described at length in Chapter 1.

The language of adoption, fellowship, and dwelling in the several Johannine love discourses raises the question of John's conception of the relationship among personal assurance, love, and faith, particularly as expressed in the First Epistle. As with so many Johannine themes, the relevant verses caused a significant amount of debate among Reformed and post-Reformed commentators. 1 John 4:15 reads: "Whosoever shall confesse that Jesus is the Sonne of God, God dwelleth in him, and he in God," a testament that suggests that the surety of abiding depends on a confession of faith in Jesus. Yet consider the sense of the succeeding verse: "And we have knowen and beleeved the love that God hath to us. God is love, and hee that dwelleth in love, dwelleth in God, and God in him" (1 John 4:16). This verse describes a narrow circuit of assurance that depends primarily on loving and receiving love from God. "Boldness" before God at judgment day follows from the perfections afforded by *agape*: "Herein is our love made perfect, that wee may have boldnesse in the day of Iudgement, because as hee is, so are we in this world" (1 John 4:17). Luther had trouble harmonizing these passages with one another and with his cherished Pauline belief (itself directed against the medieval Catholic notion that faith is "formed" in love) that love is a fruit of faith or that, according

[24] William Tyndale, *The whole workes of W. Tyndall, John Frith, and Doct. Barnes* (London, 1573), 416.

[25] Edward Gilby, *An answer to the devillish detection of Stephane Gardiner* (London?,1528), xiv.

[26] Miles Coverdale, *Fruitfull lessons, upon the passion, buriall, resurrection, ascension* (London, 1593), 10.

to Galatians 8, faith manifests or is active in love.[27] One way around the seeming tension was to posit two separate courts of appeal for the communicant. Faith renders the individual assured in front of God, while love and works present the individual as assured in front of the community: "Through faith I glory in the fact that I belong to God; through my works and love I glory in the fact that no one has anything against me."[28] Yet as Paul Althaus rightly observes, John does not draw rigid distinctions between assurance in front of God and assurance in front of the congregation. Nor can we deny that 1 John 4:15 elevates the role of love relative to faith in the economy of salvation. For Luther, another way around the conundrum was to read the sense of John's earlier verses on assurance into the meaning of 1 John 4:15.[29] A seemingly clearer statement of the subordination of love to faith that was more congenial to Luther's Pauline conception of justifying grace is found in 1 John 3:18–19: "My little children, let us not love in word, neither in tongue, but indeede and in trueth. And hereby wee know that wee are of the trueth, and shall assure our hearts before him." Certainty of election depends on horizontal love toward the community. Given the absence of any mention of prior faith, even these lines, if taken out of context, might suggest an elevation of love regarding personal assurance. As Nigel Smith has pointed out, Robert Gell's *An Essay Toward the Amendment of the Last English-Translation of the Bible* (1659) maintains that the Authorized Version should be retranslated to include "in the truth of love" as an addendum to verse 20 in order to highlight the importance of love in allaying fear.[30] Still, the larger context brings faith into view. We know from 1 John 3:23 and comparable verses that horizontal love itself issues from a faithful acknowledgement of Christ's precipitating love: "And this is his commandement, that we should beleeve on the Name of his Sonne Jesus Christ, and love one another, as hee gave us commandement."

The Johannine verses are open-ended and malleable enough to warrant, if not a prioritization of love over faith, at least an ambiguation of the precise relationship between the two and hence a placement of one on equal footing with the other. 1 John 3:19 was indeed used by English and Continental exegetes to underscore the singular role of love in assurance. Lancelot Andrewes conjoins the Johannine verse with Luke 7:27 in his focus on the role of love in remitting sins and providing spiritual conviction: "When we love the brethren, not in word, and tongue onely, but in deed and truth, that is a meanes for us, to perswade our hearts before him.... So our Saviour affirmeth of the woman, because *she loved much, she had many sinnes forgiven her, Luke 7.27.*"[31] For the Puritan divine John Dod, loving mercifully is a sure path to certainty of election: "Hereby shall we assure our harts

---

[27] For an extended discussion of Luther's changing disposition toward the Johannine verses on assurance and love, see Paul Althaus, *The Theology of Martin Luther*, trans. Robert C. Schultz (Philadelphia: Fortress Press, 1966), Appendix Two, 446–58.

[28] Cited in Althaus, *The Theology of Martin Luther*, 455.   [29] Ibid., 455–6.

[30] See Robert Gell, *An essay toward the amendment of the last English-translation of the Bible* (London, 1659), (b) 2. Nigel Smith discusses the translation in "Retranslating the Bible in the English Revolution," in Kevin Killeen, Helen Smith, and Rachel Willie, eds. *The Oxford Handbook of the Bible in Early Modern England, c.1530–1700* (Oxford: Oxford University Press, 2015), 101.

[31] Lancelot Andrewes, *The morall law expounded* (London, 1642), 106.

before God, that we are of the truth... & this every Christian that hath any acquaintance with his own heart, will confesse, that when hee is most mercifull and most ready to put up injuries & indignities, then he hath most comfortable assurance of his own salvation."[32] In a treatise on the conversion of Zacchaeus, John Wilson puts the point concisely when remarking that loving the brethren in deed and truth "furthers our assurance of eternall life."[33] While we would be wrong to argue that these passages decisively downgrade faith in relation to love (context in each passage dictates a focus on love rather than faith), other commentators will bring the discourse of horizontal love in 1 John 3 into dialogue with the more ontological and vertical discourses of 1 John 4 to make the still more radical suggestion that love plays a formative role in assurance. Thus the Puritan divine Paul Baynes in an extended commentary on 1 John 3:16, *The mirrour or miracle of Gods love unto the world of his elect* (1619):

> This point touching Gods love toward us, doth shew whence it is, that our love to God & our neighbour is engendred; even hence doth it proceed from Gods loving of us. Saint *John*...doth prove and conclude that wee are in God, and have the knowledge and faith of Gods love to us, even from our love to God, and our Brethren. For God is love: yea, that maine and vast sea of love, from whom all those streames and rivelets of love that are in men do issue and flowe.[34]

Against what we have seen in Luther's handling of comparable passages, Baynes draws no fundamental distinction between love of God and neighbor. Baynes also suggests, given the force of "even," that knowledge and faith of God's love (and the assurance that this knowledge affords) itself flows from love to God and the brethren. Although Baynes's is a more radical post-Reformed position on love and faith than one typically finds during the period, the assumption that love bequeaths assurance of faith is frequently voiced, as in Johann Gerhard's remark that "By faith we are made partakers of the divine nature: But *God is love*. Therefore where charitie sheweth not itself without, let no man beleeve that there is faith within."[35] Compare these comments to Calvin's countervailing position that clearly subordinates love to faith: "*God is love*. This is to say, the minor proposition in the syllogism. For he reasons from faith to love like this: By faith God dwells within us. But God is love. Therefore, wherever God abides, love must also flourish."[36] Faith necessarily assures, for Calvin. It makes sense that Calvin would assert, more in keeping with the Pauline disposition on faith and love, that mutual indwelling is faith-based. Yet in so many Reformed and post-Reformed Johannine commentaries, love not only confirms faith or contributes to personal assurance but can also provide certainty of election. I will return to these competing conceptions of

---

[32] John Dod, *A remedy against privat contentions* (London, 1614), 12.

[33] John Wilson, *Zacheus converted: or The rich publicans repentance* (London, 1631), 328.

[34] Paul Baynes, *The mirrour or miracle of Gods love unto the world of his elect Preached on the third of John, verse the sixteenth* (London, 1619), 9.

[35] Johann Gerhard, *Gerards meditations* (Cambridge, 1638), 216.

[36] John Calvin, *The First Epistle of John*, in *Calvin's New Testament Commentaries*, vol. 5, eds. David W. Torrance and Thomas F. Torrance, trans. T. H. L. Parker (Grand Rapids: Eerdmans Publishing Company, 1959), 294.

the triangulated relationship among faith, love, and assurance when discussing George Herbert's poetic meditations on *agape* and personal assurance.

We have seen that the Johannine conception of *agape* has primarily an ontological and relational focus. The additional feature of Johannine *agape* not yet discussed is John's presentation of the love of God for Christ relative to his love for the world. John follows Paul, both of whom depart from the Synoptics, in stating forthrightly that God's love for the world manifests in a theology of the cross.[37] Insofar as God acts lovingly, that action is revealed in the sacrifice of the Son: "Herein is love, not that wee loved God, but that he loved us, and sent his Sonne to be the propitiation for our sins" (1:4:10). What John adds to Paul, however, is the equally important proclamation that God's love also manifests itself primordially in his eternal love for the Son: "Father, I will that they also whom thou hast given me, be with me where I am, that they may behold my glory which thou hast given mee: for thou lovedst mee before the foundation of the world" (17:24). In none of the Synoptics or in Paul do we get this clear an expression of God's foundational love for the Son and, by implication, humankind. Calvin recognized that this passage from the prayer for believers is difficult to square with earlier passages in John's Gospel itself—"For God so loved the world, that he gave his only begotten Sonne" (3:16), for example—in which God's love for the world emerges most prominently at the Incarnation:

> An apparent contradiction arises here, however. For, as we have seen elsewhere, Christ declares the infinite love of God towards the world was the reason why He gave His only-begotten Son. If the cause must precede the effect, we infer that God the Father loved men outside of Christ; that is, before He was appointed the Redeemer. I reply: In that and similar passages love means the mercy with which God was moved toward the unworthy, and even towards His enemies, before He reconciled them to Himself. It is a wonderful goodness of God and incomprehensible to the human mind, that He was benevolent towards men whom He could not but hate and removed the cause of the hatred that there might be no obstruction to His love.[38]

In using this passage to point out the expansiveness of God's love for humankind, love that pre-exists the redemptive Incarnation, Calvin to a certain extent follows Augustine, who likewise exalts God's love for humankind that is expressed prior to the creation of the world: "Therefore, the love by which God loves is incomprehensible and unchangeable. For he did not begin to love us from the time when we were reconciled to him through the blood of his son; but before the foundation of the world he loved us, that we, too, might be his sons together with

---

[37] For Anders Nygren, Paul's distinctive contribution to the development of the *agape* motif is an integration of a theology of the cross with divine love: "Agape and the theology of the Cross are for him [Paul] quite simply one and the same thing. . . . Without the Cross of Christ we should never have known God's love and learnt its deepest meaning; and, conversely, without God's Agape Christ's way would not have led to the Cross." *Agape and Eros*, trans. Philip S. Watson (London: S.P.C.K., 1953), 117.

[38] John Calvin, *The Gospel According to St. John*, in *Calvin's New Testament Commentaries*, vol. 5, eds. David W. Torrance and Thomas F. Torrance, trans. T. H. L. Parker (Grand Rapids: Eerdmans Publishing Company, 1959), 150.

the Only-Begotten, before we were anything at all."[39] Calvin and Augustine each go on to provide clever elaborations of the manner in which God simultaneously (and eternally) loves what he hates (Calvin attempts to harmonize the Johannine passages with Pauline theology by using Ephesians 1:4 and Romans 5:10 to help clarify a seeming incongruity). But we can see that John's privileging of God's love for the pre-incarnated Son raises important questions regarding the precise nature of *agape* and just how creaturely love for one another might be analogized to that mystical love between God and the Son.

This is a question that led Anders Nygren to conclude that Johannine theology idiosyncratically reworks the early Christian *agape* motif, revealing a dualism of *agape* and *eros* that is itself a residue of John's Hellenistic orientation. For Nygren, one of the reasons that *agape* occupies in John a "somewhat uncertain position between unmotivated and motivated love" is that John's metaphysical premise that God "before the foundation of the world" expresses eternal love for the Son has something rationalizing and motivated about it: "Is it not...the case that the inherent worth of the Son is what makes Him the object of the Father's love? If so, will not this have its effect, at least in some measure, on God's love towards men, so that not even it is conceived as altogether spontaneous and unmotivated?"[40] The prototypical relationship of love between Father and Son, not entirely unmotivated, becomes the example on which more creaturely analogues of love in the Johannine corpus are based. As the Father loves the Son, so the Son loves the disciples who in turn love their brethren, conveying a circuit of love that is not so much value-creating as value-inhering. For Nygren, the ensuing love of the world directs *agape* too much toward objects, and so creaturely love threatens to turn love for God into the very forms of acquisitive love that it, by definition, countermands.

At stake here is a proper understanding of John's unique Christology, particularly his tendency to focus on the glorification rather than sacrificial and debasing nature of Jesus' death on the cross. As we have seen, in John's hands the Passion does not simply mark Christ's sacrificial death for us (and serve therefore as an example of God's spontaneous and unmotivated love for humankind). The Passion also serves to glorify the Son and redound to God's joy. To locate the source or genesis of *agape* in the eternal Triune relationship is to elevate what Augustine describes as the nature of God's love for himself/the Son as not only immutable but incomprehensible to God's creatures. And for Christ to claim that he will love his disciples after God's love for him and that the disciples should love their brethren after Christ's love for them is to claim the same ineffability for lesser forms of love, all based on God's metaphysical love for the Son.

In sum, the Johannine conception of *agape* is distinctive in providing an ontological conception of God as love, the essence or substance of which is distinct from the accidental or qualitative nature of creaturely love. The promised consequence of love of Christ and his followers (John is not as concerned as are the

[39] Saint Augustine, *Tractates on the Gospel of John*, 11–55, trans. John W. Rettig (Washington, D.C.: Catholic University Press, 1994), 296.
[40] Nygren, *Agape and Eros*, 152.

Synoptics with loving out-groups or enemies) is both the knowledge of God and interpersonal fellowship with the Father and Son. All such loving relationships are reciprocal, based on the eternal love of Father and Son. Although internally consistent, even programmatic, the Johannine conception of *agape* is provocative for several reasons. Experientially, what would be entailed by such a state of mutual indwelling, mystical or otherwise? In what measure can any loving creature appreciate the beatific vision of God as love? These and related questions on the relationship between faith and love orient the poetic treatments of the love theme in the works of George Herbert, Henry Vaughan, and Thomas Traherne. We begin to address some of these questions in our turn to the *agape* motif in George Herbert's *The Temple*.

GEORGE HERBERT'S KNOWLEDGE OF *AGAPE*

In keeping with the Johannine love discourses, Herbert's most *agapic* poems position a speaker who determines that knowledge of God will issue from an understanding of God's inimitable love. The speaker of "Mattens" who asks at the outset "what is a heart" (9) quests to know why God would single out any heart on which to pour all his art (10–11).[41] The speaker realizes that the answer as to why God loves him rests not in a direct apprehension of God but through the created orders: "He did not heav'n and earth create, / Yet studies them, not him by whom they be" (15–16). Yet a poem that might turn neo-Platonic in focusing on a re-ascent by the means of God's creation, especially given the intimation of *eros* at the close—"Then by a sunne-beam I will climbe to thee" (20)—changes course in the final stanza. In place of a diligent studying of "heaven and earth" on his own terms, the speaker requests to be taught to know God's love: "Teach me thy love to know" (17). That divine pedagogy is embodied in the emerging morning light that the speaker celebrates in the opening lines: "I Cannot ope mine eyes, / But thou art ready there to catch / My morning-soul and sacrifice" (1–3).

"Daylight" is reprised as the "new light" in the last stanza: "That this new light, which now I see, / May both the work and workman show: / Then by a sunne-beam I will climbe to thee" (18–20). The association of Christ with the epiphanic light is a recurring theme in John's First Epistle and Gospel. The First Epistle announces early on that Christ, as true light, implicitly described as love, has opened the eyes of the brethren: "Againe, a new commandement I write unto you, which thing is true in him and in you: because the darkenesse is past, and the true light now shineth. He that saith he is in the light, and hateth his brother, is in darkenesse even untill now" (1 John 2:8–9). John's Gospel, too, proclaims at the outset that, if John the Baptist will bring light to the darkened world, he will do so through his teaching about Christ, who is the true light: "That was the true light, which lighteth every man that commeth into the world" (1: 9). Further associations

---

[41] *The Works of George Herbert*, ed. F. E. Hutchinson (Oxford: Clarendon Press, 1941), 62. All quotations of Herbert's verse will be taken from this edition.

of Christ's ministry of love with light appear throughout the remainder of the Fourth Gospel: "In him was life; and the life was the light of men" (1:4); "Light is come into the world, and men loved darknesse rather then light, because their deedes were evill" (3:19); "I am the light of the world: he that followeth mee, shall not walke in darkenesse, but shall have the light of life" (8:12); "As long as I am in the world, I am the light of the world" (9:5); and "I am come a light into the world, that whosoever beleeveth on me, should not abide in darkenesse" (12:46).

In the context of Herbert's poem, Christ as the new light becomes the means through which the speaker might understand "both the work and workman," which entails knowledge of and love toward both the creaturely world and God himself. The only slightly ambiguous aspect of the final stanza is the causal nature of the pedagogy. The speaker first asks God to teach him to know God's own love and then implies, given the transitional "That" at line 18, that God's teaching will help him to understand the "new light" that will reveal God's love. God will provide the gracious means to the speaker for a proper understanding of Christ as new light, who will then teach the speaker about the work and workman. That sense is justified by the final line: to know God's love is to know that love through Christ's love for God's creatures. Only through Christ's light/love will the speaker be able to "climbe" toward God. There is little concern here to explicate the forensic or sacrificial nature of Christ's saving work. Nor is there any bother to prioritize neighbor love or love for the "work" as a means of loving God. The speaker has access to the loving God directly through the illuminating example of the Son.[42]

Herbert's more directly ontological treatment of God as love appears in the related poem "Even-song." After much perturbation and hand-wringing, the speaker exclaims, "My God, thou art all love" (29). En route to this ontological epiphany, the speaker will muse on the same themes of "Mattens," including the relationship of day and night to *agape*, although Christ's sacrifice becomes more prominent in "Even-song." "Even-song" opens with what Helen Vendler has described as a "toneless, unfelt, and unpromising" beginning: "Blest be the God of love, / Who gave me eyes, and light, and / power this day, / Both to be busie, and to play" (1–4).[43] One way of reading the opening is to associate this God of love with a lesser god such as Cupid, as in John Tobin's notion that Herbert refers to "a kind of Christian Cupid who blinds himself."[44] On this reading, the paganized "God of love" in the opening is contrasted with the God who is love itself at line 28, the implication being that the power granted to the speaker at the outset "to be busy" and "to play" describes impious creaturely pastimes that need to be displaced by sanctified pursuits. On Vendler's reading, however, God intends for the speaker

[42] In "George Herbert and *Caritas*," in *Essays by Rosemond Tuve: Spenser, Herbert, Milton*, ed. Thomas P. Roche, Jr (Princeton: Princeton University Press, 1970), 167–206, Rosemond Tuve does acknowledge that "the conception of *Agape* is in general markedly Johannine" (182), yet Tuve focuses less on the ontological implications of Johannine love and more on the asymmetries between God's love for creatures and creaturely love for God.

[43] Helen Vendler, *The Poetry of George Herbert* (Cambridge, MA: Harvard University Press, 1975), 158.

[44] John Tobin, *George Herbert: The Complete English Poems* (Penguin, 2005), n. 1 to "Evensong," 356.

to carry on during the day in this manner, but the speaker falls into sin instead: "But to be busy, to play—God's intent for man—has been vitiated by the sins committed this day."[45]

One way of extending Vendler's analysis is to see the poem as privileging a Johannine, ontological conception of God as love as such over the Synoptic and apostolic reference to the God of love, as in the farewell testimony of Paul's second letter to the Corinthians: "Finally, brethren, farewell: Bee perfect, bee of good comfort, bee of one minde, live in peace, and the God of love and peace shalbe with you. Greet one another with an holy kisse" (2 Corinthians 13:11–12). The last stanza of "Even-song" makes clear that to understand love as part of God's essence (rather than as a particular action of God) is properly to see love as transcending earthly oppositions between day or night, light or darkness: "I muse, which shows more love, / The day or night" (25–6).[46] The speaker will come to rest not because of the night-time, when God's love allows him to escape from his impious days, but because God's love lifts him out of daily, cyclical change: "Not one poore minute scapes thy breast, / But brings a favour from above; / And in this love, more than in bed, I rest" (30–2). Love is not connected to any action of God that would control the speaker's days and nights, bringing order "to our disorder'd clocks" (24). Love issues from the speaker's brightening awareness that he resides in God when he dwells in "all love" (29).[47]

However, the speaker's achievement of this union with God's *agape* depends on a series of subtle transitions regarding the speaker's understanding of the virtues of seeing properly. The particular emphasis on Christ's day-work that terminates at night and the general theme of spiritual blindness (despite the speaker's gift of the power of sight, he only plays idly during the day) bring us to Jesus' healing of the blind man in John 9. That Herbert is in some capacity thinking of John 9 in the poem is suggested by the resemblance between the speaker's sense that Christ rests his work at night-time—"And now with darknesse closest wearie eyes" (18)—and Christ's declaration that his work (as light of the world) is carried out during the day: "I must worke the workes of him that sent me, while it is day: the night commeth when no man can worke" (9:4). Once he has healed the blind man, Jesus explains the lesson of day-work to the uncomprehending Pharisees: "I am come into this world, that they which see not, might see, and that they which see, might be made blind" (9:39). Herbert's speaker comes to realize that seeing in the light has brought him precious little more than "fome" (12). The speaker then muses that, if the day has its virtues (only if one sees properly), so too does the night,

---

[45] Vendler, *The Poetry of George Herbert*, 158.

[46] The poem is as much theological as it is Christological, a duality missed in Barbara Lewalski's assumption that the poem focalizes a "savior-redeemed relation" in which the speaker's opening apostrophe, "'Blest be the God of Love,' grounds that title upon God's gift of his Son and his constant favors." *Protestant Poetics and the Seventeenth-Century Religious Lyric* (Princeton: Princeton University Press, 1979), 294.

[47] Here I agree with Stanley Fish, for whom the last lines suggest the absorption or consumption of the self in God. Fish, *Self-Consuming Artifacts: The Experience of Seventeenth-Century Literature* (Berkeley: University of California Press, 1972), 162–4, referenced in Wilcox, *The English Poems of George Herbert*, 231.

perhaps because, as John 9 suggests, to "not see" is itself an almost *apophatic* route to Christ. But the speaker's more profound *volta* occurs in the final stanza when his preoccupation with the limits of subjective seeing is displaced by an emphasis on being seen by God: "Not one poore minute scapes thy breast, / But brings a favour from above" (30–1). Wilcox rightly points out that John 3:16 frames the poem— "For God so loved the world, that he gave his only begotten Sonne: that whosoever beleeveth in him, should not perish, but have everlasting life."[48] But lines 30–1 specifically bring us to the revelation in 3:21–2 that to come into the light signifies a revealing of oneself to God: "For every one that doeth evill, hateth the light, neither commeth to the light, lest his deeds should be reproved. But hee that doeth trueth, commeth to the light, that his deeds may be made manifest, that they are wrought in God." As in lines 30–1 of "Even-song," the point made here is that coming out of the darkness and into the light signifies not necessarily a proper see-ing of Christ or God but an opening up of oneself and one's works in such a way that one is exposed under God's purview. And it is at this moment that one finds participation with God. The phrase "wrought in" God is comparable to Herbert's sense that enlightened exposure allows one to "rest" in God's love (32). We have seen such an intricate use of Johannine material in other poems of Herbert, particularly in "Peace." "Even-song" is not simply influenced or inspired by key Johannine verses. It rather derives through its own tropes responses to the questions that John's verses themselves raise and answer. In this case, if foundational verses such as "God is love" direct both the Johannine and Herbertian conceptions of *agape*, John explains further through intertextual amplifications, as Herbert does throughout his poem, the means by which the penitent might find participation in divine *agape*.

The subtle shift in Herbert's lyrics from depicting *agape* as an act or quality to *agape* as God's ontology or essence is a feature of several of Herbert's best lyrics. One of Herbert's most thoroughgoing Johannine poems is "The Call," which in its brief span of twelve lines brings together John 2:10, 14:6, 15:11, and 16:22:

> Come, my Way, my Truth, my Life:
> Such a Way, as gives us breath:
> Such a Truth, as ends all strife:
> Such a Life, as killeth death.
>
> Come, my Light, my Feast, my Strength:
> Such a Light, as shows a feast:
> Such a Feast, as mends in length:
> Such a Strength, as makes his guest.
>
> Come, my Joy, my Love, my Heart:
> Such a Joy, as none can move:
> Such a Love, as none can part:
> Such a Heart, as joyes in love.

The immediate context for the poem is Jesus' address to Thomas, who, upon hear-ing that Jesus will be departing, puzzles over Jesus' advice to the apostles that they

---

[48] See Wilcox, *The English Poems of George Herbert*, 232.

can follow him. Thomas asks, "Lord, we know not whither thou goest: and how can we know the way?" to which Jesus responds, "I am the Way, the Trueth, and the Life: no man commeth unto the Father but by mee" (14:5–6). Calvin and Luther provide overlapping commentaries on the verse, both aligning the way, the truth, and the life with Christ's role as the "beginning, the middle and the end."[49] For Calvin, Christ is the way to attain eternal life, truth implying a "perfection of faith."[50] Luther, more extensively than Calvin, relates the manner in which, only through Christ, one might come to the Father and acquire eternal joy: "What does coming to the Father mean? Nothing else that has often been stated: to pass from death into life, from sin and damnation into innocence and piety . . . into eternal joy and bliss."[51]

If the lesson of 14:6 is that the joy of abiding eternally with God is achieved solely through the means of Christ, succeeding verses and chapters of the Farewell Discourse explain more fully the means by which the brethren can unite with Christ and thence God. To keep Christ's commandments and attest belief is to love Christ, the result of which is the love of the Father and Son: "He that hath my commandements, and keepeth them, hee it is that loveth me: and he that loveth me shall be loved of my Father, and I will love him, and will manifest my selfe to him" (14:21). The vine discourse develops further the reciprocity among Father, Son, and believer, emphasizing fellowship between the believer in Christ and God, which is itself a material cause of the everlasting joy that is promised in the earlier description of Christ as the way, the truth, and the life: "If ye keepe my Commandements, ye shal abide in my love, even as I have kept my Fathers Commandements, and abide in his love. These things have I spoken unto you, that my joy might remaine in you, and that your joy might be full" (15:10–11). The promise that joy will persevere, especially through the gracious service of the Comforter, is reprised when Christ reminds the disciples that he will return to them: "I will see you againe, and your heart shall rejoyce, and your joy no man taketh from you" (16:22). This verse as well as the "fullness" reference at 15:11 signified to early modern exegetes the semi-mystical union that I have described in the first section of this chapter. So Thomas Gataker, an Episcopalian clergyman, remarks in his 1623 treatise on joy: "Untill wee come all to meet and partake together in that *fulnesse of Joy,* which shall never againe be interrupted or eclipsed in us, shall never in whole or in part be taken againe away from us."[52] Importantly, especially in the context of Herbert's "The Call," love is treated as both a means and an end throughout these verses. Creaturely love, manifested as belief and obedience, will secure Christ's and God's love (14:21), which itself leads to participation *in* or with Christ and God (15:10–11). Love is simultaneously an answering action of Christ and God and an ontological quality of the Father and the resurrected Son.[53]

[49] Calvin, *The Gospel According to St. John*, vol. 5, 76.   [50] Ibid., 77.
[51] Martin Luther, *Sermons on the Gospel of St. John*, chapters 14–16, in *Luther's Works*, vol. 24, ed. Jaroslav Pelikan (Saint Louis: Concordia Publishing, 1961), 52.
[52] Thomas Gataker, *The joy of the just with the signes of such* (London, 1623), 163.
[53] Meister Eckhart goes so far as to connect the "fullness of joy" metaphor in John 16 to the "full of grace and truth" reference in "The Word was made flesh" verse at John 1:14: "Informed by that

Herbert's poem cleverly manipulates the Johannine sources at the outset by having the speaker summon Christ through the iterated "come." An understanding of Christ as the way and means through which one comes to God in the Johannine verses is transposed in the poem into the speaker's desire to have Christ heed his call. The speaker can licitly and amiably effect this transposition because he draws no distinction between Christ and God. The poem reads as a prayer-like testament of his assured belief that he so understands what it means to view Christ as the only way, truth, and life—the one who can provide him "strength" (8) to persevere and grant eternal life in killing death (4)—that the call to Christ is at the same time a call to God. This is a mature speaker who has already learned the lesson needed to be explained to Thomas and Philip. Although they don't realize it, those disciples do indeed "know" and have seen Christ and are ready to witness the Father: "Have I bin so long time with you, and yet hast thou not knowen me, Philip? he that hath seene me, hath seene the father, and how sayest thou then, Shew us the father?" (14:9). If Philip and Thomas scratch their heads at Christ's meaning, Herbert's speaker approaches Christ with arms open, eager to embrace the fullness of joy that is his assured gift.[54]

The manifestation of that gift is, as we have seen in Herbert's other poetic treatments of *agape*, a loving participation of speaker with Father and Son: "Such a Love, as none can part: / Such a Heart, as joyes in love" (11–12). Vendler rightly points out the shift in the poem from a verbalized to nominalized status of love in the closing phrase, "joyes in love," which posits a metaphysical absorption of the speaker into Christ and God: "This is a figure for total self-completion, when the subject and his actions are perfectly congruent, and when the actions and their object are also perfectly congruent."[55] But Vendler goes on to conclude, much less convincingly, that in its development away from the so-called "stern implication of the original Gospel source" (by which she means "the way, the truth, and the life" verse) to an "identity of self and Jesus," the "ending is far less 'Biblical' and far more 'Herbertian' than the beginning."[56] In her zeal to unfold for the reader a uniquely Herbertian developmental logic—the forlorn speaker, alienated from Christ at the outset, eventually comes to a realization of his intimacy with Christ—Vendler erroneously projects "strife" onto the opening stanza and Herbert's use of John

---

Word, like its only-begotten he sees its glory, since he is full of grace and truth.... The Savior speaks of this fullness in chapter sixteen when he says, 'Ask and receive, that your joy may be full.'" *Meister Eckhart: The Essential Sermons, Commentaries, Treatises, and Defense*, trans. Edmund Colledge and Bernard McGinn (Mahwah: Paulist Press, 1981), 172.

[54] Chrysostom's paraphrase of 14:6–8 points out that the brethren only partly knew Christ: "They did know Him, but not as they ought to do. Nor was it till afterwards, when the Spirit came, that they were fully enlightened." See *Catena Aurea, Commentary on the Four Gospels Collected Out of the Works of the Fathers by Thomas Aquinas: Volume 4, St. John*, trans. John Henry Newman (London: John Henry Parker, J. G. F. and J. Rivington, 1841), reprinted by Veritatis Splendor Publications, 2012, 266.

[55] Vendler, *The Poetry of George Herbert*, 208. In *Love Known: Theology and Experience in George Herbert's Poetry* (Chicago: University of Chicago Press, 1983), 227, Richard Strier provides a brief and approving comment on Vendler's interpretation of the last line of the poem. For another interpretation of the poem's shifting between abstract nouns and verbs, see Arnold Stein, *George Herbert's Lyrics* (Baltimore: Johns Hopkins University Press, 1968), 146.

[56] Vendler, *The Poetry of George Herbert*, 209.

14:6. And she neglects to read the closing stanza in the context of the unmistakable Johannine references to 15:11 and 16:22, references that Hutchinson had already clarified in the standard edition of its time. It is not that the poem becomes less scriptural and more Herbertian as it unfolds. The ending of the poem uses John's comments on the fullness of joy (15:11, 16:22) to help explain Christ's earlier designation of himself as the way, the truth, and the life.[57]

This is not to say that, in its rigorous use of the Johannine material, the poem does realize the fear that motivates Vendler's elaboration—namely, that without Herbert's "redefinition" of Jesus and himself, the poem "would remain piety and no more, the sort of versification of the Gospels found often in hymns."[58] Structurally, as John Drury has recently said so elegantly, the poem's resituating of its three guiding nouns in respective lines with motion verbs, and then the transformation at the end of the nominalized "Joy" into its verb form, reflects "economy pitched to ecstasy, craft expressing emotion."[59] And the originality of the poem, what saves it from formulaic hymnic piety, lies in its direct call for Christ to come to him and in its compact shift in emphasis, in keeping with the very arc of the Johannine discourses, from love as issuing in an action and quality—"Such a Love, as none can part" (11)—to love as a substance metaphysically linked to the fullness of joy. Even more ingeniously, the speaker's address to Christ through the anaphoric use of "come" in each stanza, culminating in the joy found in God's *agape*, recalls Christ's own intercessory prayer to the Father in verse 17 of the Fourth Gospel: "And now come I to thee, and these things I speak in the world, that they might have my joy fulfilled in themselves" (17:13). As Christ comes to the Father, enabling the brethren to joy in the Father's love, so Herbert's speaker imagines that Christ comes to him, enabling his participation in divine *agape*. The analogy is not at all audacious on Herbert's part. The speaker seems to realize that the reason that he can ask Christ to come to him is that Christ has already come to the Father on his behalf. Here, relevant Johannine verses such as 14:6 do not merely inspire the content of the poem. Additional verses such as 17:13 provide the occasion for Herbert's speaker to emulate Christ's manner of address—in this case, Christ's prayer to the Father.

In the very unfolding of the poem, the speaker does not develop soteriologically and psychologically so much as he clarifies the meaning that is implicit in the opening use of "the way, the truth, and the life" verse. The message of that verse is that Jesus' otherwise parabolic words already carry with them the promise of intimate fellowship. Thus Calvin supposes that the eternal life promised in

---

[57] Much of my interpretation of "The Call" parallels Chana Bloch's incisive critique of Vendler's reading. For Bloch, too, Vendler too quickly opposes the "biblical" and the "Herbertian," and so Vendler's reading "rests on an inadequate accounting of just how much Herbert owes to the Bible." *Spelling the Word: George Herbert and the Bible* (Berkeley: University of California Press, 1985), 84.

[58] Vendler, *The Poetry of George Herbert*, 205.

[59] John Drury, *Music at Midnight: The Life and Poetry of George Herbert* (Chicago: University of Chicago Press, 2014), 348. Drury, too, recognizes the transition to a metaphysic of indwelling in the last lines: "In the last verse, this inherent dialogue between poet and Jesus melts into identity as the happiest feelings of the human heart are also the qualities of its indwelling, divinity, Jesus" (348).

John 14:6 is "to be found in" Christ.[60] The Scottish divine William Cowper concludes similarly: "Since he is life, we must walke to him, since hee is the way, and the verity, wee must walke in him, and be in him, & then do we walke in him, when we beleeve in him."[61] In Herbert's poem, later Johannine verses are used to help decipher just this meaning of John 14:6. "The Call" does not so much appropriate Johannine sources as it poetically explains them. Like Herbert's "Peace" (discussed in Chapter 1), it is a poem that is at once lyrically bracing, original, *and* exegetical.[62]

Several other lyrics of Herbert have as their endpoint an ontology of love in keeping with the joyful Johannine message of "The Call." The speaker of "Dulnesse" petitions God to provide him with the "quicknesse" (3) to praise God without having to resort to the mundane expressions of a "wanton lover" (5). He realizes that an expression of his love for God cannot rival his intuition that Christ embodies that inexpressible, perfect love: "Thou art my lovelinesse, my life, my light, / Beautie alone to me" (9–10). It is through his understanding of Christ's love that he will at least be able to look toward God: "Lord, cleare thy gift, that with a con-stant wit / I may but look towards thee: / *Look* onely; for to *love* thee, who can be, / What angel fit?" (25–8). This appears to be a straightforward description of unmerited, top-down *agape* in that the speaker recognizes that he cannot directly return God's love as it is perfected in Christ. But the verb form of "who can be" reveals the speaker's intuition that, in order to love God, one must be God, thus implicitly identifying God with love. The speaker's pause results from his realization not that he cannot *love* properly, but that he cannot *be* properly, since to love God is to have Christ and God dwelling within him. Only with assurance and adoption by God would the speaker be included in God's irreducible quality as love. The speaker of "Dulnesse" will look forward to the ontological surety enjoyed by the speaker of "Assurance," who realizes that, despite tribulations, "What for it self love once began, / Now love and truth will end in man" (41–2). Here again we have an elevation of a metaphysical conception of God as love. For love to begin for "itself" might involve the speaker's *amor sui*, but it more compellingly tells of God's prior love for Himself expressed through Christ, which now will redound to the benefits of man.

The experience of abiding through both horizontal and vertical love brings us finally to the role of *agape* in Herbert's more fully articulated conception of per-sonal assurance. Herbert's celebrated poem "Assurance," arguably an improvement on "Perseverance" from the Williams manuscript, poeticizes the speaker's agonistic struggle with a "Spitefull bitter thought" (1). Along the way, the speaker convinces himself that God, without force of contract, gratuitously provides the spiritual bulwark to protect him against his "foes" (which seem to include his recalcitrant thoughts). The speaker realizes by the final couplet that his personal assurance is

    [60] Calvin, *The Gospel According to St. John*, vol. 5, 76.
    [61] William Cowper, *A defiance to death Wherein, besides sundry heavenly instructions for a godly life* (London, 1610), 279.
    [62] I agree with Chana Bloch's interpretation of the final stanza of "The Call," about which she concludes, "Indeed the intimacy and certainty of the final stanza are firmly rooted in Scripture." *Spelling the Word*, 84.

sourced unmistakably in God's *agape*: "What for it self love once began, / Now love and truth will end in man" (41–2). Despite the surprisingly straightforward title of the poem and the importance of "truth" and "love" in conducing to assurance (which I have described at length in the first section of this chapter), Herbert's editors and critics typically pass over the relevance to the poem of 1 John 3:18–20, perhaps the most important New Testament verses on assurance: "My little children, let us not love in word, neither in tongue, but indeede and in trueth. And hereby wee know that wee are of the trueth, and shall assure our hearts before him. For if our heart condemne us, God is greater then our heart, and knoweth all things."[63] As discussed earlier, the verses prompted post-Reformed exegetes to argue that assurance is contingent on the reciprocal love between God and the penitent as well as between the penitent and the Christian community. Being assured of one's salvation through love is intimately connected to dwelling in the "truth," precisely the sense of the last two stanzas of Herbert's "Assurance": "Wherefore if thou canst fail, / Then can thy truth and I" (31–2). By the end of the poem truth expands to include love, and both truth and love have found their habitation in "man." Chana Bloch has argued that the turning point in the poem occurs at the fourth stanza, in which the speaker finds an escape from the "enemy within" through his brightening faith: "Then suddenly the speaker brightens ('But I will to my Father,' 19), turning to God with the confidence of a child who knows that his father is powerful and that he himself is loved. In the act of turning the eyes of the mind, he is lifted up by faith."[64] No doubt the speaker evinces faith in the final three stanzas of the poem. But there is no clear crisis of faith or moment of the speaker's awareness of justifying grace that would constitute a conversion *volta* as suggested by Bloch. Given that the speaker's uplift comes from a more fundamental awareness of divine *agape*, there is much to credit in Richard Strier's remark that this is one of Herbert's most antinomian moments. Assurance comes not from any forensic or contractual act or even from self-examination. Rather, the speaker "takes the 'antinomian' position; he turns wholly outside himself—to God."[65] In his denial of any two-way contract, the speaker does indeed seem antinomian. Yet his turn is not purely outward since, as in 1 John 3, assurance comes particularly from the "heart," itself expressed in the poem's transition from the forensic cavils of the speaker in the early stanzas to his awareness that assurance depends on a simple transition from self-love to a truthful love that, in ending in man, provides a guarantee of his election.[66]

---

[63] Although he does not draw out its Johannine implications, Gene Edward Veith, Jr. prefaces his interpretation of "Assurance" with a quote from Richard Hooker's *Of the Lawes of Ecclesiastical Politie* that directly basis its claims about assurance on 1 John 3. See Veith, *Reformation Spirituality: The Religion of George Herbert* (Eugene: Wipf & Stock, 1985), 97.

[64] Bloch, *Spelling the Word*, 274.

[65] Strier, *Love Known*, 109. Veith sees the speaker's complete turn toward God as expressing less of an antinomian posture than it does an anti-Arminian, Calvinist belief that "God provides everything necessary to salvation—not only good works, but even faith itself." *Reformation Spirituality: The Religion of George Herbert*, 99.

[66] In agreement with Strier, Daniel W. Doerksen remarks on Herbert's Calvinist turn against self-examination: "In line with Calvin's warning against the 'sure damnation' of contemplating the self

Yet if this were all "Assurance" offered, we would have little more than an unin-spired paraphrase of relevant verses of 1 John 3. "Assurance" is one of Herbert's most puzzling, hieroglyphic poems. Its unfolding but always abstract narrative in which the speaker contends with the poisonous, bitter thought raises more ques-tions than most readings of the poem have compellingly addressed. Why the speaker's preoccupation with the singular "thought?" The chiasmic repetition in the first two lines and doubled exclamation marks—"O Spitefull bitter thought! / Bitterly spitefull thought!" (1–2)—almost dare the reader to guess at what that thought might be. Why a "spiteful" thought in particular? If we assume that we are getting merely the subvocal dialogue of the speaker's tortured soul, the personified "enemy within" suborning the speaker's league with God, we are led into at best a mazed reading. How to reconcile the singular "thought" with the speaker's later references to his plural "foes" (24, 26)? Bloch's refusal to acknowledge the lack of grammatical agreement seems forced: "The speaker's 'foes' are given their proper name here: 'spitefull bitter thought,' 'bitterly spitefull thought.'"[67] Why not "thoughts" and "foes," or "thought" and "foe?"[68] And the shifting time frame of the poem itself raises questions that a reading of the poem as a simple interior mono-logue does not satisfactorily explain; "even now" (7) the spiteful thought reminds the speaker that "all was not so fair" (8) with his God, as if the speaker has in mind not simply an earlier apostate life that subverts his devotion but a haunting event that he fears might raise its devilish designs again. The speaker's statement, "I see, I know, / I writ thy purpose long ago" (18), reiterates the sense that he at some past time has given voice to this particularized thought, again encouraging the reader to coax this thought out of the narrative. And how to understand the "bone" refer-ence in the final stanza: "For thou hast cast a bone / Which bounds on thee, and will not down thy throat" (39–40)? Should we just uncritically accept Hutchinson's reliance on Heywood's *Proverbs* (1526) in concluding that this "bone" refers to a proverbial "bone of contention?"[69]

Assuming that Herbert must have had a deep familiarity with the Johannine verses on *agape* and assurance, we should revisit some of those verses in the fuller context of 1 John 3:

> For this is the message that yee heard from the beginning, that wee should love one another. Not as Cain, who was of that wicked one, and slewe his brother: and where-fore slewe hee him? because his owne workes were evill, and his brothers righteous. Marveile not, my brethren, if the world hate you. Wee know that wee have passed

---

apart from Christ…Herbert always proceeds beyond self-examination…to seek help in God." *Picturing Religious Experience: George Herbert, Calvin, and the Scriptures* (Newark: University of Delaware Press, 2011), 190.

[67] Bloch, *Spelling the Word*, 274.

[68] To read the poem, as Jane Wolfe does, as a morality play in which Herbert's goal is the "shaming of Satan," the principal enemy or foe conjured in the poem, is too allegorically tidy. See Jane E. Wolfe, "George Herbert's 'Assurance,'" *College Language Association Journal* 5 (1962), 221.

[69] On the "bone of contention," see Hutchinson, *The Works of George Herbert*, 531–2; Wilcox, *The English Poems of George Herbert*, 536, n. 39; Tobin, *George Herbert: The Complete English Poems*, 398, n. 39; and Strier, *Love Known*, 113.

from death unto life, because wee love the brethren: he that loveth not his brother, abideth in death. Whosoever hateth his brother, is a murtherer, and yee knowe that no murtherer hath eternall life abiding in him. Hereby perceive wee the love of God, because he layd downe his life for us, and wee ought to lay downe our lives for the brethren. But who so hath this worlds good, and seeth his brother hath need, and shutteth up his bowels of compassion from him; how dwelleth the love of God in him? My little children, let us not love in word, neither in tongue, but indeede and in trueth. And hereby wee know that wee are of the trueth, and shall assure our hearts before him. (1 John 3:11–19)

Readers might ask what Cain is doing in this well-known New Testament passage on personal assurance. Although Hebrews 11:4 and 12:24, Matthew 23:35, and Luke 11:51, make passing reference to Abel, 1 John 3:12 is the only New Testament reference to Cain. The point of the reference is obvious in the context of the abiding Johannine dualism that we will track in Chapter 5. Cain's example is antithetical to the commandment to love the brethren and Jesus, and his example is certainly antithetical to the granting of personal assurance of salvation. In this passage and so many comparable ones in the First Epistle and Fourth Gospel, the world, itself of the tribe of Cain, is sunk in sin. The Johannine believer is able, through *agape*, to lift himself out of the world of disbelief and into the rarefied world of Christian fellowship.

If we understand the speaker's narrative in "Assurance" as less of an interior monologue about his sinful thoughts and more as veiled typology and allegory, we might begin to see faint echoes of the Cain reference in Herbert's poem. Consider that the speaker is not merely engaging with a personified thought. He is typologically situating himself as a descendant of Cain whose "spiteful" thought recalls Cain's plotting and the perceived unfairness of God as well as the speaker's fear that his evil thought will breach his covenant with his Father: "Thou said'st but even now, / That all was not so fair, as I conceiv'd, / Betwixt my God and me" (7–9). To act on the spiteful thought would indeed raise or re-raise the very "devils" with which the speaker's impersonation has long been familiar: "Wouldst thou raise devils? I see, I know, / I writ thy purpose long ago" (17–18). One of the difficulties in understanding the speaker's thoughts as foes is the sense in which, at line 24, the speaker does not need God to oppose his foes. He rather needs God to protect him from the *objection* of his foes. Despite the invading threats of his foes, his "gracious Lord" (20) has opposed his enemies on his behalf: "I had not half a word, / Not half a letter to oppose / What is objected by my foes" (23–4). Recall the immediate aftermath of Cain's murder of Abel. Cain faces persecution from his newfound foes who object to his conduct, but God gratuitously promises to save him from his enemies:

And Cain said unto the LORD, My punishment is greater, then I can beare. Behold, thou hast driven me out this day from the face of the earth, and from thy face shall I be hid, and I shall be a fugitive, and a vagabond in the earth: and it shall come to passe, that every one that findeth me, shall slay me. And the LORD said unto him, Therefore whosoever slayeth Cain, vengeance shalbe taken on him seven fold. And the LORD set a marke upon Cain, lest any finding him, should kill him. (Gen. 4:13–15)

If in stanza four of "Assurance" the speaker recalls to himself such a one-sided and gratuitous covenant that God has made with him despite his actions, in stanza five he shifts to the present tense, questioning for a moment whether this covenant still holds. He realizes that, although he has yet another spiteful thought, God will not simply reassert the covenant but will provide him with the very power to resist his enemies (whether "enemies" refers to interior motions or external foes): "Thou art not onely to perform thy part, / But also mine" (27–8). This is arguably the typological crystallization in the poem, the moment when the speaker accepts that, to the extent that he can choke down the spiteful thought, he has been afforded this ability gratuitously rather than covenantally.

Reading the poem's allegory of assurance in the context of the reference to Cain in 1 John 3 has the virtue of explaining not only the bone reference in the final stanza but also the ambiguous reference to self-love in the penultimate line. Medieval and early modern iconography routinely assumed that Cain murdered Abel with a jaw-bone, as when Shakespeare's Hamlet exclaims during the graveyard scene: "That skull had a tongue in it, and could sing once. How the knave jowls it to the ground, as if 'twere Cain's jaw-bone, that did the first murder!"[70] Even the proverbial understanding of casting a bone of contention could be paired with Cain's murder of Abel. Thus John Trapp remarks: "The Divel doth what he can to cast a bone betwixt brethren, to make those that should love most dearly, to hate one another most deadly. See this exemplified in *Cain* and *Abel, Esau* and *Jacob, Joseph* and his Brethren."[71] The speaker has been able to quell the spiteful thought and to refrain allegorically from duplicating Cain's evil. He instead follows the strictures of 1 John 3 that dictate that he assure his heart to God by means of *agape*. The bone will rebound not merely on the bitter thought. It will rebound on the "self-love" that is (or was) instanced most primordially by Cain's evil but that now will be reversed by the speaker's shared love with God.

None of this is to say that "Assurance" univocally recapitulates the Cain and Abel narrative in its appreciation of 1 John 3. I suggest only that the narrative is faintly suggested in the very plotline of the poem (for the poem does chronicle a plot), even as the poem might be read as a more abstract self-soul dialogue that is self-referential regarding Herbert's perturbations on how properly to write assuredly of God. The important theological point is that "Assurance" is another of Herbert's thoroughly Johannine meditations on the priority of *agape* in the scheme of salvation, in this case certainty of election. And here again we can see that Herbert's Johannine sources are never used merely as occasional prompts to devotional verse; nor do the poems themselves serve simply as proof-texts of the Johannine sources. If "Assurance" is indeed "living" and "active," as Frances Cruickshank remarks

---

[70] William Shakespeare, Hamlet, ed. Susanne L. Wofford (New York: Bedford Books, 1994), Act 5, Scene 1, 72–4. For a study of the use of the jaw-bone image in medieval and early modern art and literature, see Meyer Schapiro, "'Cain's Jaw-Bone that Did the First Murder,'" *The Art Bulletin* 24:3 (1942), 205–12.

[71] John Trapp, *Commentary or exposition upon the books of Ezra, Nehemiah, Esther, Job and Psalms* (London, 1647), 4.

about devotional lyrics generally, it is a poem that serves simultaneously as a palimpsest of the Johannine verses that originally animate it.[72]

If the preceding poems are written in the spirit of Johannine conceptions of *agape*, "Love-Joy" follows John's conception of love to the letter. The short poem provides a veritable paraphrase of John's allegory of the vine, the latter of which reads:

> I am the true vine, and my Father is the husbandman. Every branch in me that beareth not fruit, hee taketh away: and every branch that beareth fruit.... I am the vine, ye are the branches: He that abideth in me, and I in him, the same bringeth forth much fruit.... Herein is my Father glorified, that ye beare much fruit, so shall ye bee my Disciples. As the Father hath loved me, so have I loved you: continue ye in my love. If ye keepe my Commandements, ye shal abide in my love, even as I have kept my Fathers Commandements, and abide in his love. These things have I spoken unto you, that my joy might remaine in you, and that your joy might be full. (15:1–11)

The vine discourse provides one of the clearest statements of the uniquely Johannine conception of love. The Fourth Gospel sets out to provide knowledge of God to the disciples, but such knowledge can only be gleaned through a proper understanding of Christ's words and actions. As we have seen in relation to the "The Call," to understand God's love is to understand the way in which God eternally loves the Son, and God's love for the Son is reiterated in Christ's love for his followers. One loves God when one recognizes that Christ is the embodiment of that love, after which one experiences the fullness of joy that signals a sharing of love among God, Christ, and the brethren.

Herbert's "Love-Joy" extends the metaphor of the Johannine vine narrative. Christ as vine bears fruit in the form of grapes "with *J* and *C* / Anneal'd on every bunch" (2). Asked by "one standing by" (3) what the letters mean, the speaker responds: "It seem'd to me / To be the bodie and the letters both / Of *Joy* and *Charitie*. Sir, you have not miss'd, / The man reply'd; It figures *JESUS CHRIST*" (5–8). While Galatians 5:22 provides an important source for the poem, so too does the Johannine vine discourse. Herbert's critics, who typically pass over the relevance of the vine discourse, have described the poem as one in which the speaker's and/or the reader's misjudgment is corrected, given that the speaker might have associated the letters with Jesus Christ from the opening of the poem.[73] Yet Herbert's devout seventeenth-century readers, who would have been quite familiar with the metaphor of the vine, would not find the unfolding of the poem surprising. Given that the brethren are the fruit and Christ is the vine, the J and C annealed on the grapes evoke the interpersonal relations that Jesus describes in the vine narrative. The fact that such abiding has been achieved at the outset signifies

---

[72] Frances Cruickshank, *Verse and Poetics in George Herbert and John Donne* (Aldershot and Burlington: Ashgate Publishing, 2010), 1.

[73] Stanley Fish, *The Living Temple: George Herbert and Catechizing* (Berkeley: University of California Press, 1978), 27–9. Helen Wilcox acknowledges the vine discourse more to contrast its meaning with the sense of the poem than to locate the discourse as one of the poem's sources: "In contrast to the 'withered branches' condemned in *John* xv 2 and 6, this is a vine which bears fruit." *The English Poems of George Herbert*, 414, n. 2.

that the promised fullness of joy for Christ's believers has already been achieved. This explains why the letters are attached to joy and charity before they are to Jesus Christ. To denote the letters as joy and charity signals that the speaker has indeed understood the meaning of the vine metaphor. Those who recognize Christ as the true vine will already have achieved such unabating joyfulness. Even in this compact lyric we can see the larger Johannine love theme at work. To love God is to understand the significance of Christ's saving work as well as the elevation of Christ in John's treatment of the theme. While the grapes might recall the sacrament, they are linked directly to joy rather than to any forensic ransoming or sacrifice.

Herbert's Johannine optimism regarding the ease with which the communicant unites with the loving essence of God/Christ is not shared by all seventeenth-century devotional appropriations of Johannine notions of *agape*, even among those poets such as Henry Vaughan who were directly influenced by Herbert's example. In the writings of Vaughan, to which we now turn, we find that Vaughan's speakers, despite their understanding of a Johannine poetics of love, cannot escape from a servile and filial fear of backsliding and hence a depletion of their fund of God's love.

HENRY VAUGHAN: BETWEEN LOVE AND FEAR

Henry Vaughan's approach to John departs from Herbert's in that Vaughan's speakers recapitulate the ignorance, questioning, and fear that Christ's auditors and disciples themselves express in John's Gospel despite Christ's otherwise comforting words. Another way of saying this is that, due to his failure of confidence in his own and his speakers' piety, Vaughan will typically communicate a Johannine theme even as he signals his inability to understand and/or follow the message of that theme. A good example of this scriptural departure occurs in "The Law, and the Gospel," which takes as its source text John's description of Christ's promise of the Holy Spirit to those who maintain his commandments. The passage opens with Christ's proclamation, directly referenced in Vaughan's poem, "If ye love me, keepe my commandements" (John 14:15). Those commandments include, as Christ has earlier established in John 13, horizontal love of one another: "A new commandement I give unto you, That yee love one another, as I have loved you, that yee also love one another" (John 13:34). To keep the commandment to love one's brethren, which avows the penitent's love for Christ, has as its result the pledge that God and Christ love the believer: "He that hath my commandements, and keepeth them, hee it is that loveth me: and he that loveth me shall be loved of my Father, and I will love him, and will manifest my selfe to him.... If a man love mee, he will keepe my wordes: and my Father will love him, and wee will come unto him, and make our abode with him. He that loveth mee not, keepeth not my sayings" (14:21–4). There is no fundamental distinction between law and gospel here. Christ's "law" is to love one another, from which follows love of Christ and God.

The speaker in Vaughan's "The Law, and the Gospel" initially represents himself as well on his way to witnessing the manifestation of God that should issue from the proper love and understanding of Christ's words. Unlike those individuals under the yoke of the fearsome Mosaic Law who, due to terror and fear, "whisper'd obedience, and their heads Inclin'd" (10), Vaughan's speaker acknowledges that, because of Christ's "bloud" (12), he is in a privileged position to see and touch God: "And through thy bloud thy glory see, / With filial Confidence we touch ev'n thee; / And where the other mount all clad in flame, / And threatening Clouds would not so much / As 'bide the touch, / We climb up this, and have too all the way / Thy hand out stay" (12–18).[74] Embarrassed to the point of guilt for his gifts and acknowledged presumptuousness, reminding himself and his readers that he is a "brute" like any other creature, the speaker apologizes in advance for asking one additional favor of God—that God provide him with both the Gospel and law: "O plant in me thy *Gospel*, and thy *Law*, / Both *Faith*, and *Awe*; / So twist them in my heart, that ever there / I may as well as *Love*, find too thy *fear*!" (27–30). The speaker, who has been enjoying the fruits and "ful Comfort" (19) of God's love, is worried that, without the requisite reverential fear of the law (the very fear that the Gospel helps to displace), he will backslide. Backsliding is described in the poem as his inability to honor the Eucharistic meal. His shame would be evidenced by his spilling rather than drinking the blood and by a scattering of his food (31–4). Without the proper legalistic fear, he cannot even be sure that he loves God: "For while I fear, / I know, thou'lt bear, / But should thy mild Injunction nothing move me, / I would both think, and Judge I did not love thee" (37–40). Here and throughout the poem, Vaughan cleverly plays on distinctions between servile and filial fear. While the former is typically associated with fear of God's punishment (and is highlighted in the Old Testament terror and fear described in the first stanza), filial fear is routinely associated with the fear of losing God's favor. Vaughan's speaker realizes that, although he is well beyond servile fear, he is bereft of the appropriate filial fear that would keep him from sliding into sin. The result is his plea to have God provide that fear (in the form of the law) as yet another gift of grace, a bittersweet bestowal that would follow upon God's gift of love (shown most clearly in Christ's sacrifice). The scriptural source text from John 14:15—"If ye love me, keepe my commandements"—has been modified into "If ye love me, fear me." The speaker's final statement is the contrapositive of that very restatement of the source: "If you do not fear me, you have not loved me," which is versified as "But should thy mild Injunction nothing move me, / I would both think, and Judge I did not love thee" (39–40).

Vaughan deviates creatively from his Johannine source. As I have already remarked, the principal Johannine commandment is to love one another. This would include all of Jesus' teachings, of course, and his overall example, but it would not specifically be tied to fearing God. Indeed, John is notable for suggesting that love expels fear: "There is no feare in love, but perfect love casteth out feare: because feare hath torment: hee that feareth, is not made perfect in love" (1 John 4:18). The passage troubled Augustine, who understood the value of fear

---

[74] All quotations are taken from L. C. Martin, *The Works of Henry Vaughan* (Oxford: Clarendon Press, 1957).

as promoted elsewhere in scripture.[75] Augustine pointed out, for example, that John's emphasis on casting out fear implies that fear, as Psalm 11:10 proclaims, is the "beginning of wisdom," an important "starting point" that "prepares the place for charity."[76] Proper charity, however, should displace or "cast" fear out entirely. And when faced with reconciling the Johannine dismissal of fear with those scriptural passages that claim the importance of enduring fear—for example, Psalm 19:9, which reads "The feare of the Lord is cleane, enduring for ever"—Augustine will resort to the familiar distinction between pure or filial fear and impure or servile fear.[77]

We should note, however, that neither way of integrating love and fear applies whole cloth to Vaughan's "The Law, and the Gospel." The speaker is certainly more advanced in the order of salvation than one who is just "starting" out (in Augustine's terms). And the filial fear of losing God's favor fails to agree with the speaker's final sentiment that, without the sanctioned fear, he cannot be sure that he loves God (the loss of filial fear should bring with it the loss of God's love for the speaker, not the speaker's answering love for God). By claiming that an inability to keep God's commandment broadcasts the speaker's lack of love for God, Vaughan is able to stick close to the letter of the Johannine source text, even though his insertion of fearing God as an example of such a commandment departs significantly from that source. Recall that John 14 makes clear that those who do not follow Jesus' words do not love him and will not be able to access the Father: "He that loveth mee not, keepeth not my sayings" (14:24). Those words or "sayings" have everything to do with the testaments of love sounded elsewhere in the Fourth Gospel, fear having no pride of place. It is as if Vaughan clearly understands the uniqueness of John's account of *agape*—when we love our brethren, we love Christ, and when we love Christ, we can approach God—but Vaughan finds John's account too idealistic, too easily issuing in the complacency of the speaker as shown in the second stanza of the poem. Fear is poetically imported into the Johannine context as a way of reminding the speaker of his apostasy. The subtle but diffuse quality of this fear is incorporated into the syntax and punctuation of the poem. Vaughan's habit of separating coordinated doublets with a comma preceding the "and" conjunction becomes insistent here. The pauses at the commas in lines such as "O plant in me thy *Gospel*, and thy *Law*, / Both *Faith*, and *Awe*" (27–8) mark several long pauses that prompt the reader to imagine that the speaker needs to remind himself that he needs the requisite fear, legalistic and otherwise, as a supplement to the comforts

---

[75] The interplay between love and fear is a frequent concern of John Donne, who tends to collapse distinctions between proper or filial fear and love of God. Donne concludes his sermon on Psalm 34:11 by assuring his auditors that, whether they come away from this text fearing or loving God, he has done his duty as preacher: "If I send you away in either disposition, *Timorous*, or *amorous*; possessed with either, the fear, or the love of God; for, this fear is inchoative love, and this love is consummative fear; The love of God begins in fear, and the fear of God ends in love; and that love can never end, for God is love." *Sermons of John Donne*, vol. VI, eds. Evelyn M. Simpson and George Potter (Berkeley: University of California Press, 1953), 113.

[76] Augustine, *The Homilies of the First Epistle General of St. John*, in *Augustine: Later Works*, 332.

[77] Ibid., 333–5.

of the Gospel. The only exclamatory line in the poem itself hints that the speaker has to bind himself to fear as much as to love: "find too thy *fear*!" (30).

"Love-sick" provides another example of Vaughan's inability to find unwavering consolation in God's *agape*. "Jesus, my life! how shall I truly love thee?" (1), the speaker initially asks. He recognizes, as we find in John, that Christ's love enters into the convert by means of the Holy Spirit—"O that thy Spirit would so strongly move me.... As to make man all pure love, flesh a star!" (2–4). Yet the speaker is so barred in by his "narrow skies" (7) that he is at war with himself (9). The antidote is the purification of his heart by Christ's "refining fire" (13), a use of Isaiah that one finds elsewhere in Vaughan's poetry (and a source text for Herbert's "Love unknown"). The refined product would allow for the speaker's renovated heart to be sealed with Christ's blood. The sacramental union is made explicit at the close: "Thy blood which makes thee mine, / Mine ever, ever; And me ever thine" (20–1). The poem reads as the speaker's recognition that, although Christ loves him, he cannot accept that love until he asks for and receives the grace that would prepare his "love-sick" heart for a proper bestowal. Vaughan seems to separate faith and grace, on the one hand, and love, on the other hand. Love is the consequence of his petitioning for grace, a belief that brings out Vaughan's abiding sense of the asymmetry between Christ's love for us and our love for him and God. Implicit in the poem is the Johannine ontology of love. The love that the speaker recognizes in Christ and that remains out of reach (indeed, even after his engrafting in Christ, the speaker might not have overcome his lovesickness) is a "pure love" (4) that is not simply expressed in loving deeds but is transformative of man himself: "As to make man all pure love, flesh a star!" (4).

Vaughan's cynicism regarding his own salvation, as well as his appreciation of the elusive nature of *agape*, is reflected in his meditation on John's telling of the death of Lazarus. "Jesus weeping" (the version that includes the relevant Johannine verses as an epigraph) is one of the few extended seventeenth-century devotional meditations on John 11:35. John remarks that Jesus weeps upon learning of the death of his friend Lazarus and the sadness of Mary Magdalene, Lazarus's sister. In Vaughan's handling of the theme, Jesus' love is so bound up with grief that Vaughan's speaker has trouble distinguishing the two or understanding their proper relationship: "Dear Lord! Thou art all grief and love, / But which thou art most, none can prove. / Thou griev'st, man should himself undo, / And lov'st him, though he works thy wo" (22–5). The speaker reasons that Jesus' grief is motivated by his love for Lazarus—"'Twas thy love that (without leave,) / Made thine eyes melt, and thy heart heave" (32–3)—itself remarkable given that Christ can and will restore us: "Yet, thou so full of pity art / (Pity which overflows thy heart!) / That, though the Cure of all mans harm / Is nothing to thy glorious arm, / Yet canst not thou that free Cure do, / But thou must sorrow for him too" (38–43). Despite the speaker's earlier avowal that no one can prove whether love or grief predominates in Jesus' response, he complains that grief is the more remarkable, given that it persists despite Jesus' power to provide a "free Cure" of death (42). The point of the speaker's seeming sleight toward the close of the poem is not that he believes that Jesus' grief is more notable than his love, but rather that he believes that Jesus' grief is the surest means of representing the elusive quality of Jesus' love. It is as if the speaker realizes that, while he cannot directly emulate Christ's love, he can at least trace the contours of that love as Christ's grief, which he will take on henceforth: "My business here shall be to grieve: / A grief that shall outshine all joys / For mirth and life, yet without noise....A grief so bright / 'Twill make the Land of darkness light" (45–52). Through grief, the speaker believes that he will bring the light to a darkened world, light that is typically associated with Christ's light. Unable to access Christ's love directly, the speaker takes a synecdochal approach. Through that part of love that is expressed in grief, he can manifest the very love that serves as grief's irreducible and inaccessible source. The Johannine Lazarus narrative, one of the few instances in John's Gospel when Jesus' humanity is unexceptionally brought out, provides the speaker with a palpable manifestation of Christ that allows him to approach the otherwise inaccessible nature of *agape*.[78]

What we find in Vaughan's tentative approach to the Johannine love discourses is similar to what we found in our assessment in Chapter 1 of Vaughan's approach to the sacramentalism of John 6. In respect of both the Eucharist and divine *agape*, Vaughan, alienated from the comforting rituals of the Prayer Book, constructs an intensely personal Christology that forces him to reflect upon and ultimately question at every move his spiritual standing. In Chapter 5, we will see the same self-scrutiny bred of skepticism emerging in Vaughan's most politically allegorical and dualistic verses from *Silex Scintillans*, Part II.

If Vaughan approaches the Johannine love discourses cautiously, even skeptically, Thomas Traherne, to whose work we now turn, rejoins Herbertian optimism. However, we will see that, unlike both Herbert and Vaughan, Traherne's lens for the Johannine conception of God is a neoscholastic, analogical understanding of the way in which creatures continue to participate in God's love even in a post-lapsarian context. Such a participatory and naturalistic theology renders God's *agape* accessible to creatures among the created orders. What especially sets Traherne's conception of love apart from Herbert's and Vaughan's is that Traherne uses the Johannine material syncretistically in his integration of Christology and the *analogia entis* (analogy of being).

THOMAS TRAHERNE AND *ANALOGIA*

In the opening sections on divine love in *Christian Ethicks* (1675), Traherne draws explicitly on John's First Epistle in order to establish a conception of *agape* that will recur throughout the treatise:

> The Apostle saith, *GOD is Love*: By Loving he begot his Love. And if his Love be his Godhead, his Essence is an infinite and Eternal Act of Love, by extending which through all infinity, and by Loving Eternally, he begot his infinite and Eternal Essence:

---

[78] For more on Jesus' love for Lazarus, see Philip F. Esler and Ronald A. Piper, *Lazarus, Mary and Martha: Social-Scientific Approaches to the Gospel of John* (London: S.C.M. Press, 2006), 76–86.

which is the Love that filleth all Worlds with Beauty and Glory. When you consider it well, An Act of Love is begotten by *Loving*.[79]

Traherne develops the Johannine ontology into a précis on the self-begetting nature of Love. God "begets" his own infinite essence by his eternal love, which includes the Son: "For GOD enjoyeth all Things by his Love, which is his Eternal Son," from whom he begets creaturely life.[80] All created orders flow naturally from God's eternal love, through which he communicates his goodness: "Had not GOD from all Eternity Loved, had he never desired, nor delighted in any thing; he had never exerted his Almighty Power, never communicated his Goodness."[81] Traherne then imagines, using as his inspiration the exaltation of the lamb from Revelation 5:13, that, since all things are created from God's diffusive love and goodness, all creatures retain that loving aspect and so can re-attain God's love: "There is some Hope, that the same Felicity is prepared for the soul which is made in his Image, and that every thing, being fit for GOD, is full of infinite Depth and Beauty."[82] But to what extent, and through what means, can creatures participate in God's love?

Prior to his invocation of John in *Christian Ethicks*, Traherne points out that, although in terms of the "love of Reason," human affection and divine love are "near allyed," human love ultimately differs from divine love "in a lower Acceptation," given that human love is founded upon "Temporal Causes, Vivacity, Wit, Learning, Beauty" (although such creaturely affections, once sanctified, might be exalted and rendered "Divine by the superadded concurrence of Coelestial Causes").[83] Traherne elaborates the discussion later in the treatise, where he notes that, although God loves by his "essence," angels and men love primarily by inclination. He reinstates the neo-scholastic distinction between accident and essence in remarking that, because human affections are accidental, they tend to alter and cease over time and are subject to the vagaries of chance, obligation, and reward.[84] But he unmistakably sees the relationship as one of analogy and proportion: "In many things there is a great Agreement and proportion between them [human and divine love]. For GOD has made the love of Angels and men so like his own, by extending their Knowledge to all objects, that infinite Perfections are contained in their love. It is as GODLIKE as any Thing created is capable of being."[85] This extension of knowledge reflects Traherne's sense of the infinite capacity of creaturely love (as against the love of beasts) to extend infinitely the power of love by way of the imagination: "man can see, and know, and love any object, in any Age or Kingdom in the World."[86] The *telos* of any loving creature is the Soul's overflow of love such that, because it is made in the image of God, it strives to imitate the power and inclination of God and to "love after his similitude."[87]

Divine love turns out to be the linchpin in Traherne's metaphysical account of creaturely participation in Godhead. In the *Select Meditations*, he elaborates a

---

[79] Thomas Traherne, *Christian Ethicks*, eds. Carol L. Marks and George Robert Guffey (Ithaca: Cornell University Press, 1968), 50.
[80] Ibid., 50.   [81] Ibid., 51.   [82] Ibid., 54.   [83] Ibid., 46.
[84] Ibid., 47.   [85] Ibid., 47.   [86] Ibid., 48.   [87] Ibid., 48.

complex process by which, through the vehicle of love itself, creatures are able to receive and understand at least the similitudes of God's otherwise incommunicable attributes. These attributes or divine names, including God's infinity, eternity, sovereignty, and power, are presented in two ways, either by expressing them to sight and making them objects of creaturely enjoyment (by which Traherne means modes of revelation) or "by obliging us more to Lov Him then our very Selves. [T]he natural consequent of which is, to Delight in them more for being his, then For being ours. It being Impossible that they Should be made ours, but they must be made more. More then ours by obliging us more to Lov their Possessor."[88] Love is a vehicle not to a direct participation in or a sharing of God's attributes but to an appreciation of the infinite and ultimately inaccessible nature of those attributes. Love can exalt itself, as it exalts God, but the essence of God's noumenal attributes will always remain out of reach: "For while God satisfieth infinit Love, He Satisfieth Lov in Him and us. O my God, Thou hast given us the Similitude of Thine Incommunicable Attributes."[89]

We can begin to see that, through an initial appreciation of the Johannine ontological identification of God as love, Traherne develops a view of the creature–creator relationship that is describable as an *analogia entis* (analogy of being), itself consistent with neo-scholastic naturalistic theology. As I have argued elsewhere, the timeworn critical assumption that Traherne's poetry is mystical or neo-Platonic in orientation has overlooked the neo-scholastic terminology and conceptual bases of so much of his poetry and prose.[90] A brief review of the analogy of being will help resituate the theological orientation of Traherne's writings.

In his commentary on Boethius's *De Trinitate*, Aquinas explains the metaphysical foundation for what will become his distinctly analogical mode of talking about God. Following Dionysius, Thomas notes that we know God via three paths, the way of transcendence, of causality, and of negation: "The human mind advances in three ways in knowing God . . . first by knowing more perfectly His power in producing things, second, by knowing Him as the cause of the more lofty effects which, because they bear some resemblance to Him, give more praise to His greatness, and third, by an ever-growing knowledge of Him as distant from everything

---

[88] Thomas Traherne, *Select Meditations*, in *The Works of Thomas Traherne*, vol. 5, ed. Jan Ross (Cambridge: D. S. Brewer, 2005), 359.

[89] Ibid., 360.

[90] Several critics have argued for the influence of neo-Platonism and mysticism on Traherne's poetry and prose. This includes A. L. Clements, *The Mystical Poetry of Thomas Traherne* (Cambridge, MA: Harvard University Press, 1969); Stanley Stewart, *The Expanded Voice: The Art of Thomas Traherne* (San Marino: Huntington Library Press, 1970), 125–9; and more recently, Sarah Hutton, "Platonism in some Metaphysical Poets: Marvell, Vaughan and Traherne," in *Platonism and the English Imagination*, eds. Anna Baldwin and Sarah Hutton (Cambridge: Cambridge University Press, 1994). Pushing slightly against this critical presupposition, K. W. Salter acknowledges the neo-Scholastic and Thomistic influence on Traherne's works in *Thomas Traherne: Mystic and Poet* (London: Edward Arnold, 1964), 33–7. I have argued at length for the influence of Thomism on Traherne in "Thomistic Metaphysics and Ethics in the Poetry and Prose of Thomas Traherne," *Literature and Theology* 16:3 (2002), 248–69; and Benjamin J. Barber has recently questioned the attribution of neo-Platonism to Traherne in "Syncretism and Idiosyncrasy: The Notion of Act in Thomas Traherne's Contemplative Practice," *Literature and Theology* 28:1 (2014), 16–28.

that appears in His effects."[91] Aquinas will derive a linguistic epistemology from his metaphysics of expressive causality. Since we know that effects resemble and participate in their causes, we can work back from the nature of creaturely attributes—goodness or love, for example—and derive some sense of God's analogous attributes, even though God's pre-existent perfections will be supereminent versions of the creaturely attributes.

Aquinas's is an *a posteriori* rather than an *a priori* argument for discerning God's perfections. Although ontologically speaking God is prior to his creatures, linguistically speaking we derive a sense of God's priority from participating effects. Expressive causality and linguistic priority are the cornerstones of the analogy of proportion:

> Whenever a word is used analogically of many things, it is used because of some order or relation to some central thing.... When we say that He is good or wise we do not simply mean that he causes wisdom or goodness, but that he possesses these perfections transcendently. We conclude, therefore, that from the point of view of what the word means, it is used primarily of God and derivatively of creatures.[92]

When we speak of the love or goodness of God in relation to his creatures, we necessarily predicate those qualities to God perfectly and infinitely, bearing in mind that these attributes are not to be confused with accidents or qualities that might be added to his substance in the manner in which they are predicated of creaturely life. More counterintuitively, while we can make approximations of the nature of infinite attributes through analogy, we can never discover their true, univocal essence, hence Aquinas's notion that expressive causality and the analogy of proportion lead to negative rather than positive theology.

Before returning to Traherne's appropriation of the analogy of being, it is worth pointing out that one of the overarching premises of the negative and analogical way is a Johannine one. As the Pseudo-Dionysius remarks, despite the unique revelation of God to the Son, God's essence remains unknowable and hidden to every creature: "Someone might claim that God has appeared to himself and without intermediaries to some of the saints. But in fact it should be realized that scripture has clearly shown that 'no one has ever seen' or ever will see the being of God in all its hiddenness."[93] If 1 John 4:12 and John 1:18 explain God's hiddenness for Dionysius, the Johannine contention that God's knowledge is infallible (21:17) prompts Dionysius to explain how God can have this knowledge without "intellectual activity" and with a transcendence of the "domain of sense": "As I have often said previously, we must interpret the things of God in a way that befits God, and when we talk of God as being without mind and without perception, this is to be taken in the sense of what he has in superabundance and not as a defect."[94]

---

[91] Cited in Roger M. White, *Talking about God: The Concept of Analogy and the Problem of Religious Language* (Aldershot and Burlington: Ashgate Publishing, 2010), 84.

[92] Ibid., 89.

[93] *Pseudo-Dionysius: The Complete Works*, ed. Paul Rorem, trans. Colm Luibheid (New York: Paulist Press, 1987), 157.

[94] Ibid., 107.

If we return to Traherne in the context of the *analogia entis*, we can begin to understand the process by which he believes creatures can attain to the knowledge of God. Traherne is as concerned to provide instruction on how to attain to the perfections of God as he is to explain the genesis of God's creation. Throughout the *Kingdom of God*, typically relying on pivotal Johannine passages, especially 1 John 1:5, Traherne points out that the way back to God is through an appreciation of the manner in which God instantiates not only love but also light, glory, wisdom, and goodness, which all are rendered synonymously: "The Wisdom of God is GOD, the Goodness of God is GOD, the Glory of God is GOD, the Love of God is GOD, for God is Lov, Saith the Divine, and Beloved Apostle. The Light of God is GOD. for God is Light, and in him is no Darkness at all."[95] In terms of achieving the knowledge of God, "we must set his Perfections before our Eys, and in their Nature discover his Essence.... It is a Wise, and Holy thing to meditate on these Divine and Single perfections, becaus it is the Way to the Knowledge of GOD, which is Life Eternal. For in the Intuition of them (when we are informed with the Knowledg of their Greatness and Perfection) we are made partakers of the Beatifick Vision."[96] Traherne does not explain in this passage exactly how any creature is able to contemplate God's perfections. Yet his use of the term "intuition" reflects again his reliance on an analogy of proportion. To acquire an intuition of God's attributes is to acquire a sense of the multifarious ways in which we are both like and unlike God.

Analogical thinking is a notable feature of the *Commentaries of Heaven*, Traherne's recently discovered collection of topics in which alphabetical entries that describe human and divine qualities or attributes typically follow a commonplace book pattern. Traherne's specific procedure in the *Commentaries* is to provide a comparative account of a range of qualities, typically weighing the human versions against the foundational divine versions and then describing the means and ends of such qualities. His definition of "Accesse" is exemplary in this regard. Defined at the outset as "an Approaching to remote and Desirable Things," Access is described in terms of kinds and instances—bodily and spiritual, for example—and then, most importantly, in terms of God and human beings. Among human beings, our nature desires a "corporeal access" in order to satisfy creaturely appetite and senses."[97] Yet spiritual access is Traherne's larger concern. While a servant's access to his lord is mean and contemptible, a bride's access to her bridegroom or a Queen's to a King is the proper spiritual exemplar: "She can enter into his Soul and see his Lov.... Her Soul entereth into his, her Affection Dwelleth in the chambers of his Mind, her Desire is Satisfied in the Interior Court, She reigneth in his Understanding."[98] When Traherne shifts to God's access, he reasons that, although God's omnipresence would seem to allow for infinite access to the divine, God is often excluded by the memory and understanding. God limits and confines

---

[95] Thomas Traherne, *The Kingdom of God*, in *The Works of Thomas Traherne*, vol. I, 317.
[96] Ibid., 317.
[97] Thomas Traherne, *Commentaries of Heaven*, in *The Works of Thomas Traherne*, vol. II, Part I, 97–101.
[98] Ibid.,102.

himself, accommodating himself to our circumstances, in order to allow us to approach him: God "stoopeth down to the Estate of his Creatures…that He might Convers with us: and that we might be Exalted to the Highest Degree of Glory and Honor.…For this End He made us Capable of all His Glory, His Infinity, Eternity…and gav us the Power of Seeing, Admiring, Loving, Esteeming, Enjoying, etc."[99] Divine access is an accommodated adjunct to God's omnipresence—"Divine Access is the Approach of His Glory whose Omnipresence was there before"—and of course transcends human access as well as angelical access, the latter of which, despite being spiritual in nature, fundamentally differs from divine access. Angelical access "differeth from Divine, becaus tho it be purely Spiritual, as GODs is, yet it is not attended with that Power which accompanieth His, either to prevail, or Delight.…The Power they hav is Borrowed and Derived."[100] The important point is that access is not described as wholly other or irrelevant when we speak of our approach to God; it is defined as different in degree relative to the modes of access that are predicated of angels and creatures. God, angels, and man share a plane of resemblance or analogy in possessing similar but ultimately disproportionate abilities when it comes to granting and achieving modes of accessibility.

To take another example of analogical thinking from the *Commentaries*: the entry "Affections" compares in abundant detail the nature of the affections of inanimate objects, brutes, humans, and angels and then compares all to the nature of divine affections. Stones show affects (a stone's propensity to descend is described as an affection); bees, ants, and doves exercise passions that are circumscribed within narrow limits, the ends of such passions "feeble"; men's passions are superior in that they can "pitch upon Invisible and Intelligible things as well as Material"; and angelical passions are unique in being purely intellectual and without sense. When it comes to love, in particular, men tend toward the self-serving and acquisitive. Their love unavoidably is inflected by their "Will which produceth Love."[101] Graduating to a discussion of divine affections, Traherne remarks that, while all other affections are predicated as accidents of creatures and objects, God's seeming "affections" are identical with his substance: "Tho therfore there be no Affections in God there must be some thing in their Steed that is infinitly higher. for he does infinitly love infinitly desire infinitly rejoyce infinitly hate.…All these in him are but one by a happy and transcendent Union simplicity and Perfection.…And all that Sence we have is but a little Spark of his Life, and all our Affections but dimm and feeble shadows of his Strong and Infinit Resentments."[102] If human love attaches to discrete objects, God's love is not so divided: "He Loves and desires and Enjoys Eternally, and all at once, even as he sees an Object in all its Appearances."[103] Here again, although Traherne only reluctantly uses the term "affections" to describe these unchangeable essences of God, he notes a proportionality between human and Godly affects, the former being pale approximations of the latter. He concludes with a contrast between the contingent, changeable, and accidental

---

[99] Ibid., 98.   [100] Ibid., 99.
[101] Ibid., 286–7.   [102] Ibid., 289.   [103] Ibid., 289.

nature of human affections and the essential and eternal nature of God's: "As Powers exercised immutably and for ever these are in him, and so far are Affections. but they are not divers from him, or Accidental, or Changeable, as they are in men, from whose Essence they are distinct."[104]

That Traherne understands the path to beatitude as proceeding through analogy and similitude is shown in his passages on the achievement of the *visio dei*. John 1:16 and 2 Corinthians 3:18 allow him to project a state of glorification in which penitents ideally share not only the fullness of God but also the discrete attributes of God in equal terms: "*For of his fullness we hav all received, even Grace for Grace.* and in the Transformation affected by the Beatifick Vision, *we Shall be changed into the same Image from Glory to Glory.*"[105] That Traherne believes that such a perfect likeness to God has not yet been achieved, that the authentic vision of God is still awaiting us, is illustrated in his commentary on 1 John 3:12:

> We are so Mysterious that S. John saith, Behold what Manner of Lov the father hath bestowed upon us, that we should be called the Sons of God: Therfor the World Knoweth us not, because it knew him not. Beloved now are we the sons of God, and it doth not yet appear what we Shall be, but we know, that when he Shall appear, we shall be like him.[106]

If now we can understand our resemblance to God through analogy (our loving affections are types, shadows, and accidents of the perfect love that he embodies), we will eventually come to realize our perfect likeness to God such that, according to Traherne's neo-scholastic terminology, our essence will become equivalent to our existence.

But readers at this point might ask where the presence of Christ is in Traherne's *analogia entis*. We notice that in none of the Johannine glosses above does Traherne remark that the Incarnation and Christ's redemptive gifts provide the means by which we can return love to God. Despite the centrality of Christology to all the Johannine material, Christ seems to fade behind Traherne's metaphysical conception of the creature–God relationship—as if the simple meditative turn toward God, through an appreciation of the fundamental continuities that creatures share with God, can impel a re-approach to the loving deity. One might make at this point the sort of criticism against Traherne that Karl Barth famously made about the *analogia entis*.[107] In imagining a metaphysical link between the creatures and God even in a postlapsarian context, Traherne seems to have neglected a theology

---

[104] Ibid., 289.   [105] Traherne, *The Kingdom of God*, 448.   [106] Ibid., 479.

[107] Barth's notorious comment was that the analogy of being was the invention of Antichrist, by which he meant that Erich Pryzwara's understanding of the analogy of being neglected the Reformed notion of the analogy of faith and a theology of the cross. Pryzwara's original conception of the analogy of being can be found in Erich Pryzwara, *Analogia Entis: Metaphysics—Original Structure and Universal Rhythm*, trans. John R. Betz and David Bentley Hart (Grand Rapids: Eerdmans Publishing Company, 2014). Barth's development of an alternative analogy of faith appears throughout his lectures and writings, but it is formulated clearly in the Preface to the first volume of his *Church Dogmatics*. See Barth, *Church Dogmatics*, trans. G. T. Thompson (T&T Clark, 1956–75), vol. I, Part I. The most influential critique of Barth's analogy of faith can be found in Hans Urs von Balthasar, *The Theology of Karl Barth*, trans. John Drury (New York: Holt, Rinehart & Winston), 1971, especially Part Two, 43–147.

of the cross altogether. At times, for example, in the poem "Felicity," Traherne's poetic speakers simply prompt themselves to appreciate that "Sphere of Lov" (10), equivalent to the "Mind of God" (10), through an embrace of "Dame Nature" (4), nature referring variously to the cosmos, blissful happiness or felicity, or the speaker's nature itself.[108]

But while it is true that in the passages so far culled from *Christian Ethicks, The Kingdom of God*, and the *Commentaries of Heaven* Christology seems to be displaced by natural theology, Christ does become a focal point in several key writings of Traherne, especially *The Centuries of Meditation* and the poetry. The question is, then, to what extent is Traherne's neo-scholastic metaphysics reconcilable with his Christology? I would suggest that Traherne is able to incorporate his Christology into his metaphysics and naturalism because, again following the Johannine tradition, he emphasizes the pre-existence of Christ as Word over an incarnational poetics that might focus on sin, justifying faith, and atonement. Traherne's most sustained discussion of Christ's relationship to God appears in his entry "Assumption" in the *Commentaries*, a discussion that is extended to the *Centuries of Meditation*, especially the *First Century*. That Traherne is drawing on a Johannine conception of deity is evident in his belief in the pre-existence of the Son: "In the Beginning was the Word, and the Word was with GOD, and the Word was GOD: etc. And the Word was made flesh. Jo. 1.1.14."[109] What follows from Christ as pre-existent *Logos* is Traherne's positing of the divinity of the Son, the Son as the manifestation of God's fullness, as against the Socinian and Arian heresies that Traherne strives to undermine in "Assumption." The fullness metaphor, drawn from both John 1:16 and Paul's Ephesians 3:14, is one of Traherne's recurring tropes—for example, the "fullness of the GODHEAD dwelled in Bodily."[110] Traherne then paraphrases Athanasius's Trinitarian creed for the unity of God's personhood: "GOD of the Substance of the Father, begotten before the Worlds, and MAN of the substance of his Mother born in the World: Perfect GOD and Perfect Man... Equal to the Father as touching his GODHEAD, and inferior to the Father as touching his Manhood."[111] But it is the Son's equality with the Father that Traherne will track throughout his prose writings. The *First Century* explains the paradox that God reveals himself as most divine when he is humbled as the Son: "In this Death is His Lov painted in most lively colours. GOD never shewd Himself more a GOD, then when He appeared man. Never gained more Glory then when He lost all Glory."[112] In an embedded prayer for an infusion of Christ's righteousness, the speaker continues: "Let thy Merits justify me, O Thou who art Equal unto GOD, and didst suffer for me."[113] Given the divinity of the Son as well as Traherne's analogical conception of the human–God relationship, we would expect that Traherne would extend the analogical process to his account of the Son.

---

[108] All quotations from Traherne's poetry will be taken from *The Poetical Works of Thomas Traherne*, ed. Gladys I. Wade (London: P. J. & A. E. Dobell, 1932).

[109] Traherne, *Commentaries of Heaven*, in *The Works of Thomas Traherne*, vol. III, Part 2, 280.

[110] Ibid., 284.   [111] Ibid., 279.

[112] Thomas Traherne, *Centuries of Meditations*, in *The Works of Thomas Traherne*, vol. V, 44.

[113] Ibid., 45.

The first thing to note is that the Incarnation is analogically related to creation itself: "The Condescension of the Eternal GOD to the low Estate of an Instant, was like that of his Stooping down to Nothing for the Creation of the World; and must have an End proportionable to it."[114] If the end of the creation is to diffuse God's love and goodness and to glorify God in the process, the Incarnation achieves much the same effect: "That his Love might be satisfied, and his Mercy Glorified in the Welfare of his Great and Principal Work, in the Honor due unto his Name....Many more Ends might be premised, as the Manifestation of Gods Goodness to Sinners, of Mans Excellency, of the Seriousness of Gods Love, of the Dignity of Nature, the Glory of the Universe."[115] For Traherne, the Incarnation is more of an extension of God's creationist impulse to disseminate his love (Himself) than it is a punitive corrective to fallen creaturely life. The Incarnation by necessity serves to manifest God's goodness to sinners. The forensic aspects of the Incarnation that preoccupy, for example, Pauline theology—sacrifice, ransoming, justification, conversion—are displaced by the more fundamental end of communicating God's love and glory.

This plane of resemblance between creation and the Incarnation itself funds one of Traherne's otherwise startling analogies:

> The Deitie suffered in the Humanitie, and lived in the Humanitie; and if it lived in the Humanitie, in the Human Nature it died. Hence it followeth that the Sufferings of the Humanitie are of infinit Valu, bec. they are indeed the very Passion of the Deitie. The Deitie of the Son felt all the Resentments of our Saviors Soul, as much as other Mens Souls feel the Affections and Passions of their Body. Whence it further followeth that his Dolors were infinitly Mysterious as well as Sacred, being as Incomprehensible to us, as Ineffable.[116]

God is to the Son as creaturely souls are to their bodies. The analogy of resemblance permits just such a proportionality between God and his creatures' "souls." Not only does God suffer through the Son's body but we can at least approach understanding this "resentment" if we consider the ways in which we contend with our corporeal passions. This plane of resemblance helps to explain Traherne's account of the role of creaturely will in re-ascending to the divine. After asserting that Christ's (and therefore God's) will and his spirit are one—"Thy Will O Christ and thy Spirit in Essence are one"—Traherne will draw another analogy of resemblance between the divine and creaturely will: "As therefore thy Human Will is conformable to thy Divine; let my Will be conformable to thine."[117] By simple transposition, if Traherne can emulate Christ's will, he would by extension be approximating God's will. How exactly might such a conformability be achieved? Traherne realizes that Christ's merits must become his own, but his theology is certainly not one of alien righteousness or total depravity of the will: "Let they Righteousness clothe me. Let thy Will imprint the Form of it self upon mine; and let my Will becom Conformable to thine: that thy Will and mine, may be united,

[114] Thomas Traherne, *Commentaries of Heaven*, in *The Works of Thomas Traherne*, vol. III, Part 2, 284.
[115] Ibid., 285.   [116] Ibid., 284.   [117] Thomas Traherne, *Centuries of Meditations*, 46.

and made one for evermore."[118] The rhetoric of imprinting or copying suggests that, through his conformity to Christ, Traherne can emulate God's will. Christ's example and Traherne's faith provide the means by which Traherne's own will can be renovated. Traherne has not lost entirely the created grace and *imago dei* that he has already received from God. The very acknowledgment that God is the "Sphere of Lov" is itself a means to participate in that plenary loving union among God, Christ, the world, and the Church. As Traherne remarks in "Felicity": "There in the Mind of God, that Sphere of Lov…A Man may see Himself, the World, The Bride" (10–13).

One of the recurring ideas paraphrased in the *Centuries* is John's notion that only those reborn in faith can see God:

> Wisely doth S. John Say, We are the Sons of God; but the World knoweth us not becaus it knew Him not. He that Knoweth not the Spirit of God, can never Know a Son of GOD, nor what it is to be His Child. He made us the Sons of God in Capacity by giving us a Power, to see Eternity, to Survey His Treasures, to love his children, to know and to lov as He doth, to becom Righteous and Holy as He is.[119]

Such loving capacities are actualized by the Holy Ghost (who makes us the "Sons of God in Act"), after which we are called "out of Darkness, into His Marvellous Light."[120] But we should additionally note that, despite Traherne's confidence that he can be reunited with God through the means of the Holy Ghost, itself the vehicle of Christ's grace and subsequent renovation of his natural (rather than alien) righteousness, Traherne does not assume that this process will make God more epistemologically available. As we have seen in the above passages, the Incarnation makes Christ/God more "divine" by reinstating his ineffability: "Whence it further followeth that his Dolors were infinitly Mysterious as well as Sacred, being as Incomprehensible to us, as Ineffable."[121]

Perhaps the clearest example of Traherne's refusal to displace a naturalistic theology by a theology of the cross occurs in his poem "Meditations on the Six Days of the Creation." Having followed the Genesis creation narrative, Traherne describes the fifth day of creation: "The Waters now are truly living made, / But how is this? / Th' Almighty Word has said; / He said, *Now let the Waters living be*. / Th' admiring Angels then did Wonders see" (1–5). Genesis narrates the manner in which the waters bring forth creaturely life: "And God said, Let the waters bring foorth aboundantly the moving creature that hath life, and foule that may flie above the earth in the open firmament of heaven. And God created great whales, and every living creature that moveth, which the waters brought forth aboundantly after their kinde, and every winged foule after his kinde: and God saw that it was good" (Genesis 1:20–1). Note that Traherne twice ascribes "life" to the waters themselves. The waters are made "truly living"; the "Waters living be." "Living waters," a phrase that appears in Leviticus, Zechariah, and Canticles, typologically forecasts the association of the Johannine Christ with the living water during the Samaritan

---

[118] Ibid., 45.   [119] Ibid., 48–9.   [120] Ibid., 49.
[121] Thomas Traherne, *Commentaries of Heaven*, vol. III, Part 2, 284.

episode: "Jesus answered, and said unto her, If thou knewest the gift of God, and who it is that sayth to thee, Give me to drinke; thou wouldest have asked of him, and hee would have given thee living water. The woman saith unto him, Sir, thou hast nothing to drawe with, and the Well is deepe: from whence then hast thou that living water?" (4:10–11). That Traherne associates the Genesis waters with the Christological living water might be seen as a minor use of poetic typology. Yet it reflects his habit of collapsing distinctions between the role of Christ as the Word in creation and the redemptive role of the incarnated Christ in the Passion. Christ as redeemer is read back into the *Logos* account of Christ as pre-existent Word expressed in the Prologue to John's Gospel. There is no firm break in Traherne's writings such that the fallen world has been fundamentally severed from God and can only work back to deity through a theology of the cross. Redemption is built into the role of the pre-existent *Logos* and manifests itself in the created orders and through the service of the redeeming Son. This is an analogy of faith folded into the analogy of being.

If we turn to some of Traherne's poetic figurations of *agape*, we find that he incorporates an appreciation of the love of God found among the created orders into the love of God granted to the speakers through the vehicle of Christ.[122] In "Goodnesse," the elusive "Face of GOD" (I, 5), twinned with "His Burning love" (IV, 6), shines upon the "Soft and Swelling Grapes" (V, 1) and even infinitely beyond the "Ends / Of Heaven and Earth" (IV, 7–8); yet it also shines more strongly "above," where the natural orders are relocated to heaven: "Far Better Wines do flow / Above, and while / The Sun doth Smile / Upon the Lillies" (V, 9–11). The speaker does not mark any essential distinction between the natural vine and the Christological "true vine." God's love is located in and through both nature and Christ. Although at times, as in "Goodnesse," the Christological way is privileged over the naturalistic, at other times, as in "Nature," Traherne can apprehend God's love in his own and in external nature: "For Nature teacheth Nothing but the Truth.... The very Day my Spirit did inspire, / The Worlds fair Beauty set my Soul on fire.... His Greatness Wisdom Goodness I did see, His Glorious Lov, and his Eternitie" (3–10).

To the extent that Traherne's understanding of divine love is represented as more firmly Christological he shifts focus away from John's ontological conception of love and more toward the ethical conception registered in John 15:12–13. Thus Traherne remarks in the *Centuries*, "Thou commandest us Saying, *As I hav loved you, so do ye also love one another.* Wherin Thou hast Commanded all Men, so to lov me, as to lay down their Lives for my Peace and Welfare. Since Lov is the End for which Heaven and Earth was made, enable me to see and discern the Sweetness

---

[122] In *The Paradise Within: Studies in Vaughan, Traherne, and Milton* (New Haven: Yale University Press, 1964), Louis L. Martz also remarks on the importance of Traherne's naturalistic theology to an understanding of *agape*: "All creation becomes a channel of Love's 'streaming,' a means, a nexus between the Love of God and the love of man. ... Man's present power of realizing the Love of God through the creation serves as a constant reminder of the Love of God shown in the redemption" (75). However, Martz tends to underemphasize the extent to which this naturalistic theology is integrated with Traherne's Christology.

of so great a Treasure."[123] Given the attention here to horizontal love among neighbors (as opposed to the ontological conception of God as love), we can understand why Traherne will recast the Johannine passages with a Pauline emphasis: "Give me the Grace which S. Paul prayed for, that I may be Acceptable to the Saints."[124] But even in the ethical register we can see the ontological and naturalistic seeping through. Love is not simply the message that Christ himself embodies. It is also the end for which "heaven and Earth was made." To understand Christ's love is to understand not simply the proleptic Passion but also the retroactive creation of the world by the Word of God that instantiates eternal love.[125]

Traherne's refusal to collapse distinctions between an ontological and ethical conception of love and between an analogical/naturalistic and Christological/incarnational poetics returns us, finally, to the question that has exercised Nygren and other Johannine commentators. What is the relationship between God's eternal love for the pre-existent Son, on the one hand, and God's love for creaturely life, on the other hand? Traherne follows a Johannine–Augustinian–Calvinist line in positing both that God is love and that God expresses love eternally toward the Son. The question of how and why we receive love is not a pressing issue because Traherne does not assume any fundamental break in the circuit of eternal love that flows through God and Christ to nature and creaturely life. All creatures participate in God's love in virtue of having been created. Although our loving capabilities pale in comparison to the perfections of God/Christ, our return of God's love is effected through a belief both in the goodness we share with God, itself manifested in the created orders, and in the clearest example of that goodness embodied in the teachings of the Son.

Traherne's critics have traditionally described his body of work as neo-Platonic and mystical in orientation. In a recent collection of essays, Jacob Blevins, drawing on earlier studies by Carol Marks and Gladys Wade, remarks that the references in Traherne's notebooks to Theophilus Gale, Marsilio Ficino, Henry More, and Hermes Trismegistus "suggest a strong interest in Christian mysticism and Platonism."[126] There is no doubt that one finds neo-Platonic resonances in the *Centuries*. Louis Martz rightly notes that the repetitive, even dizzying form of those prose pieces shows the influence of Augustinian reminiscence in which the cogitating mind "draws together, re-collects, the fragmentary hints of truth scattered about in the things that are made."[127] When we push the neo-Platonic influence too far, however, we neglect to appreciate, as I have argued elsewhere, Traherne's neo-scholastic account of the perfective nature of the theological virtues, the Aristotelian conception of ethical habituation that runs throughout *Christian*

[123] Thomas Traherne, *Centuries of Meditation*, 47.

[124] Ibid., 47.   [125] Ibid., 47.

[126] Jacob Blevins, *Re-reading Thomas Traherne: A Collection of New Critical Essays* (Tempe: Arizona Center for Medieval and Renaissance Studies, 2007), xi. Blevins cites Carol Marks, "Thomas Traherne's Commonplace Book," *Papers of the Bibliographical Society of America* 58 (1964), 458–65, as well as Gladys Wade, *Thomas Traherne* (Princeton: Princeton University Press, 1944), 250–7.

[127] Martz, *The Paradise Within*, 47.

Ethicks, and the persistent use of the neo-scholastic notions of God as "pure act" that one finds in Traherne's poetry and prose.[128]

The virtue of returning to the scriptural, Johannine sources for Traherne's ontology and soteriology, especially regarding the nature of perfective love, is that such an approach helps us to avoid, on the one hand, reductively pinning a particular denominational ideology to Traherne (Pelagian, Arminian, or Cambridge-Platonist, for example), or, on the other hand, throwing up our hands and declaring that his work is irreducibly syncretistic or eclectic in theological orientation. To describe Traherne's theology of love as Johannine is to appreciate its theological fundamentals. God's eternal love is readily available to creatures, not through a purely meditative or ecstatic return to the unitive One or emanationist deity, but instead through the vehicles of both the creation of the world and the Incarnation (with less of an emphasis on the Atonement or expiatory sacrifices of Christ).[129] The beatific vision, even for those glorified saints who participate or dwell with Christ and God, will always recede from view. The creaturely *imago* at best approximates the attributes of a supereminent God. In Traherne's and John's theology, the direct *visio dei* is reserved for the Son.

* * *

We have seen that, in their varying treatments of *agape*, Herbert, Vaughan, and Traherne all reveal an ontological conception of Johannine love in their conception of love as a divine essence. Of course, each poet's distinctive sensibility inflects the Johannine material. Herbert concludes that the surest route to the loving essence of God is through a belief in the pedagogical lessons and missionary work of Christ (which displaces in many of his poems a thorough meditation on the expiatory sacrifices of the Son). Less confident and optimistic than Herbert is Vaughan, whose optimism is tempered by both filial and servile fear, skeptical postures fostered by what we might describe as productive misunderstandings of Christ's work (as if Vaughan's speakers allegorize those original Johannine auditors and disciples who were arduously taught how to leave off skepticism and heed Christ's words). Traherne resumes Herbert's optimism, although his integration of the *analogia entis* with high Christology assumes a neo-scholastic appropriation of the Johannine material. What the three poets share, ultimately, is a prioritization of a metaphysics of love over the more practical-ethical horizontal conception of love that one finds more typically in both Synoptic and Pauline theology. And in such a prioritization we can begin to discern the politico-theological cast to the Johannine worldview.

---

[128] Cefalu, "Thomistic Metaphysics and Ethics in the Poetry and Prose of Thomas Traherne," 248–9. For other assessments of Traherne's neo-scholasticism, see n. 90 above.

[129] Perhaps the most subtle discussion of Traherne's principle of plenitude, an argument that I find congenial even though it is focused less on biblical poetics and more on Traherne's anti-dualism and elevation of the object world, is Robert N. Watson's chapter on Traherne in *Back to Nature: The Green and the Real in the Late Renaissance* (Philadelphia: University of Pennsylvania Press, 2009), chapter 9, *passim*. Watson denies that Traherne's theology is *apophatic*, pointing out that sacred presence, even divine intention, inheres in the created orders (300).

Harmony among a mutually loving in-group that abides in Christ is prioritized over ecumenical relations with perceived worldlings who have not expressed proper belief in Christ.[130] Another way of saying this is that the Johannine love discourses are often indicative of a more overarching Johannine dualism that, as we will see in Chapter 5, is enthusiastically sanctioned by a broad group of sixteenth-and seventeenth-century English dissenters and antinomians.

---

[130] As Wayne A. Meeks remarks regarding the countercultural stance of the Johannine community: "Loyalty to the Son of God … binds together all those whom he 'chose' and 'sent into the world' as he was 'sent from the Father.' To abide in Jesus' logos entails abiding in the community, and 'to abide' carries the strong connotation of resistance to the dark and hostile world." "The Ethics of the Fourth Evangelist," 323.

5

Johannine Dualism, Antinomianism, and Early Modern English Radical Dissent

During the past few decades, several important studies have focused intensively on the otherwise neglected body of politically dissenting literature that emerges in seventeenth-century England.[1] The writings of the Familists, Ranters, Seekers, Diggers, Grindletonians, and antinomians in general have been given due attention. Religious historians now view antinomianism (which typically downgrades legalism and elevates free grace) as an influential and formidable opponent to Puritan Pietism, which more typically attempts to integrate justification with practical divinity, especially sanctified moral renovation and the commission of good works. However, very little of this scholarship has drawn attention to the foundational influence on such dissenting literature of the Johannine tradition, particularly the dualistic orientation of John's Gospel and First Epistle.[2]

Johannine thought is unique among New Testament writings in promoting a cosmic dualism rather than the temporal eschatology that one more typically finds in the Synoptic tradition. Since the Johannine corpus assumes a partly realized rather than a futurist/apocalyptic eschatology, modes of historical dualism that weigh the sinful present against a redeemed future are transposed into a vertical dualism that typically contrasts two realms of being: the sphere of immemorial light, divinity, and Sonship is counterpoised to the contingent, worldly Pharisaical sphere of darkness. As the one privileged being who has seen God, having descended from above, the Son's mission is to enlighten those who live under the created order of falsehood and then to re-ascend to the Father. Typical concerns of Synoptic eschatology—the overcoming of Satan during the end-time, for example—are of secondary concern in the Johannine literature.[3]

---

[1] See, for example, Theodore Dwight Bozeman, *The Precisianist Strain: Disciplinary Religion and Antinomian Backlash in Puritanism to 1638* (Chapel Hill: University of North Carolina Press, 2003); and David Como, *Blown by the Spirit: Puritanism and the Emergence of an Antinomian Underground in Pre-Civil-War England* (Stanford: Stanford University Press, 2004).

[2] The most extensive study to date of the influence of the Bible on the literature of dissent is Christopher Hill's *The English Bible and the Seventeenth-Century Revolution* (London: Penguin Books, 1993). In his discussion of radical millenarian politics, Hill is not as concerned with Christology and New Testament influence as he is with Old Testament myths and Wisdom literature as they are radicalized in millenarian writings. See chapter 8, *passim*, for Hill's discussion of the influence of the myths of Cain, Abel, Esau, and Jacob on seventeenth-century radicalism.

[3] Robert Kysar, *John, The Maverick Gospel* (Louisville: Westminster John Knox Press, 2007), 77–9.

An anthropological approach to Johannine thought takes such cosmic dualism a step further in drawing attention to its radically sectarian implications. John's "maverick Gospel," as it has come to be known among some commentators, depicts Jesus' ministry of believers, possibly newly expelled from the synagogues, as an anti-community contending with the hostilities of the world of unbelievers.[4] Jesus' circle of believers is an idiosyncratic linguistic community forced to develop a veritable anti-language, or at least linguistic innovations, that can only be understood by a discipleship of insiders.[5] Prominent linguistic features of Johannine anti-language include relexicalization, in which new phrases stand in for familiar ones, and overlexicalization, in which multiple terms signify one particular belief or concept. An example of the former would be John's uses of the phrases "believing on" or "believing into" Jesus as a substitute for the more straightforward Pauline notion of "faith in Christ"; an example of the latter would be the multiplication of terms for John's conception of light, including the designations "above," "spirit," "life," "freedom," "truth," and "love."[6] The upshot of these idiosyncratic linguistic features is that John's Gospel is often less concerned with the ideational (what the Evangelist and Jesus say in terms of content) than it is concerned with the interpersonal (who is speaking to whom and why?) and the textual/formal (in which manner does one speak?).[7]

Johannine dualism provides antinomians with a uniquely insular, dualistic, and semi-mystical conceptual apparatus that is seen as akin to their vision of themselves as marginalized, warranting their separation from both conformist church dogma and nonconformist Pietism during the early to middle decades of the seventeenth century. While Johannine dualism underwrites much of the antinomian dispensation, a wealth of Johannine material influences the full range of early Stuart and mid-seventeenth-century antinomian positions on justification, perfectionism, and eschatology. For example, those antinomian treatises that advance a doctrine of free grace refer with astonishing frequency to the trope of "walking in the light" and a "cleansing" from all sins that has its origin in John's First Epistle: "But if wee walke in the light, as he is in the light, wee have fellowship one with another, and the blood of Jesus Christ his Sonne clenseth us from all

---

[4] Ibid., chapter 2, *passim*.

[5] See Norman R. Petersen, *The Gospel of John and the Sociology of Light: Language and Characterization in the Fourth Gospel* (Eugene: Wipf & Stock, 2008), chapter 4, *passim*. Richard Bauckham argues differently that the Fourth Gospel is addressed not to a specific enclave or sequestered Johannine community but rather to a "broad, general Christian audience." "The Audience of the Fourth Gospel," in *Jesus in Johannine Tradition*, eds. Robert T. Fortna and Tom Thatcher (Louisville: Westminster John Knox Press, 2001), 102. Rather than take sides in the ongoing debate about the composition of the ancient Johannine community, I more modestly suggest that early modern Johannine enthusiasts did find in the Fourth Gospel a sectarian language and *ethos* that they considered appropriate for their own conventicles.

[6] Bruce J. Malina and Richard L. Rohrbaugh, *Social-Science Commentary on the Gospel of John* (Philadelphia: Fortress Press, 1998), 5. A more recent assessment of the Johannine community hypothesis as it relates to sectarian anti-language can be found in the work of David A. Lamb, whose *Text, Context and the Johannine Community: A Sociolinguistic Analysis of the Johannine Writings* (London: Bloomsbury T&T Clark, 2014) employs sociolinguistic theories of register to supplement reductive historical-critical assumptions about Johannine sectarianism.

[7] Malina and Rohrbaugh, *Social-Science Commentary on the Gospel of John*, 5.

sinne" (1 John 1:7). Related antinomian views on perfectionism and union with God and Christ rely heavily on a suite of Johannine citations, especially the narrative of the vine (John 15), the bread of life discourse (John 6), and the Farewell Discourse (John 13–17). More radical pneumatological or "spiritist" conceptions of grace, which are especially prominent in the writings of Hendrik Niclaes, John Everard, and Gerrard Winstanley, all recur to several Johannine passages, especially 4:9, 15:5–10, and 17:21. Antinomian realized eschatology appropriates key passages at 8:51 and 17:4 (Christ's proclamation that his work is "finished"), and, as I remarked above, the basic light/dark dualism of two worlds that runs throughout all of the dissenting literature is shaped by key passages from John 1:9, 3:21, 8:12, 15:18 and 1 John 2:8–15. Finally and perhaps more familiarly, the early Quaker belief in universal enlightenment rests squarely on the recurrent use of John 1:9 in the writings of George Fox, Robert Barclay, and others. It is not an exaggeration to say that the early Stuart and mid-seventeenth-century antinomian sensibility could not have been formulated in the manner it was without such a heavy reliance on the Johannine discourses. And this Johannine material shapes both the radical perfectionist strains of antinomianism (according to which believers achieve an inherent perfection in this life) as well as less radical, "imputative" incarnations of antinomianism (which claim that believers are not inherently pure but are cleansed only in front of God).[8]

The detailed exegeses that I provide in this chapter might seem tedious to some readers. But I believe that dedicated attention to the multivariate antinomian uses of scripture is warranted if we are to take seriously Nicholas McDowell's revisionist argument that such enthusiastic writers were not rude or uneducated "mechanic" preachers.[9] The image of the illiterate or artisanal enthusiast, perpetrated by contemporary heresiographers, modern scholarship, and, oftentimes in ironic reversals, mid-century enthusiasts themselves, does not square with the subtle attention among the antinomian writers to both the thematic content and the form of the Johannine discourses.[10] I agree with McDowell and others that such enthusiasts should be seen as *bricoleurs* who often fuse rude and elite discourses or combine proclamations of ignorance with the "display of learning" in order to disrupt cultural authority during the period.[11] One seeming incongruity that I address below is the integration in so many antinomian discourses of a purely

[8] On the differences between perfectionist or inherentist and imputative antinomianism, see Como, *Blown by the Spirit*, 39–40.

[9] In *The English Radical Imagination: Culture, Religion, and Revolution, 1630–60* (Oxford: Clarendon Press, 2003), McDowell remarks that "university-educated radicals draw on their knowledge of learned culture and their experience of institutional education to expose those systems and structures of knowledge as a means of preserving hierarchical and antichristian relations of power" (9).

[10] For a discussion of the perceived allegorical use of scripture by such "mechanic laymen" as the Diggers and Levellers, see Christopher Hill, *The World Turned Upside Down: Radical Ideas During the English Revolution* (London: Penguin Books, 1975), 143. For a discussion of Hill's perception of the unbookish quality of radical ideas during the Interregnum, see McDowell, *The English Radical Imagination*, 2–5.

[11] McDowell borrows the term "radical bricoleurs" from John Mee's *Dangerous Enthusiasm: William Blake and the Culture of Radicalism in the 1790s* (Oxford: Oxford University Press, 1992), 8–10. McDowell, *The English Radical Imagination*, 19.

affective, pneumatological, and anti-scriptural posture with the very nuanced and lettered use of scripture that this radical pneumatology supposedly eschews. This often involves attention to the historicity of the prototypical Johannine community. Gerrard Winstanley, John Everard, and George Fox, for example, will rely heavily on the Johannine discourses not merely to argue for scriptural allegoresis but to make a case that the mid-century radicals and sectarianism more generally analogize the sectarianism outlined in both the Fourth Gospel and the First Epistle of John.

Given that antinomian claims regarding free grace, spiritism, and the more mystical assumption that particular brethren mutually dwell with Christ are premised on a more basic Johannine account of the ways in which believers are separated from the world of the unregenerate, I begin this chapter with a brief contextualization of the use of the *kosmos* motif in John's writings and in early modern theological discourse. I then reconstruct the ways in which Johannine world-withdrawal is mingled in the separatist writings with the more nuanced accounts of perfectionism that are typically pitched against Puritan Pietism and mainstream Protestant practical divinity. While the detailed analyses that follow are designed to clarify the Johannine influence on mid-century enthusiasm as such, I also believe that these assessments can provide a fresh historical context in which to rethink some of the most Johannine tropes, images, and poetic sensibilities of two contemporary but very different devotional poets: Richard Crashaw and Henry Vaughan. The last three sections of the chapter evaluate some antinomian leanings in Crashaw's otherwise Laudian-inspired verse—a revisionist understanding of Crashavian Christology already begun by Thomas F. Healy and Nicholas McDowell—followed by a discussion of the anti-enthusiasm of some of Vaughan's topical and most politically charged poems of *Silex Scintillans*.[12]

THE JOHANNINE WORLD

The term "world" (*kosmos*) appears no fewer than fifteen times in the Fourth Gospel. While the term is sometimes used in a neutral sense to describe the created world (1:9, 3:16, and 16:21), it is more typically used to designate the realm of darkness or unbelief in which reside those who disregard Jesus' teachings. In this context, Jesus addresses the world of outsiders who have come to hate his ministry (and who will continue to threaten his disciples after his departure):

> If the world hate you, yee know that it hated me before it hated you. If ye were of the world, the world would love his owne: But because yee are not of the world, but I have chosen you out of the world, therfore the world hateth you. Remember the word that I said unto you, The servant is not greater then the Lord: if they have persecuted me, they will also persecute you: if they have kept my saying, they will keepe yours also.
>
> (15:18–19)

---

[12] See McDowell, *The English Radical Imagination*, and Thomas F. Healy, *Richard Crashaw* (Leiden: Brill, 1986).

The stark dualism of this passage is seized on by Augustine, who remarks: "But this world, which God reconciles to himself in Christ, and which is saved through Christ, and for which all sin forgiven through Christ, has been chosen apart from the hostile, damned, contaminated world. For indeed out of that lump, which totally perished with Adam, were formed vessels of mercy in which is found the world that belongs to reconciliation; and this the world hates."[13] Martin Luther goes so far as to recommend that the faithful should find in 15:18 a justification actively to disdain the world: "Christ says all this for the comfort of His own, that they, in turn, may learn to disdain the world with its envy and hatred and whatever harm it may do them."[14] Yet Luther's vehement dualism should not distract us from the fact that, in the Johannine context, the world has not been designated by God as unredeemably fallen. The world is sunk in sin because it has consciously rejected the Son who has been sent to save it: "For God sent not his Sonne into the world to condemne the world: but that the world through him might be saved. He that beleeveth on him, is not condemned: but hee that beleeveth not, is condemned already, because hee hath not beleeved in the Name of the onely begotten Sonne of God" (3:17–18). The dualistic implications of the Gospel's depiction of the world occur most clearly when Jesus addresses unbelievers: "And hee said unto them, Yee are from beneath, I am from above: Yee are of this world, I am not of this world" (8:23). In other instances, the world is associated more directly with Satan and judgment: "Now is the judgement of this world: now shall the prince of this world be cast out" (12:31). These passages might seem to convey a dualism between heaven and earth. Yet in the Johannine context, Jesus' believers have already removed themselves from the temporal world and dwell in the Son who is of another realm entirely. While the term "world" might refer to the created or temporal world, that demarcation narrowly separates the faithful from the enemies of the Johannine community rather than from the world of human beings as such.[15] We will see later that this sectarian, realized eschatology and mystical language/conceptual apparatus encourages the use of Johannine tropes in the writings of Hendrik Niclaes, who persists in claiming that members of the Family are uniquely chosen and adopted ("Godded") into the family of Christ and God.

A brief look at sixteenth- and seventeenth-century English commentaries on two representative Johannine references to the world—15:18 and 17:14—can help clarify the extent to which John's references to the world were so wide-ranging that they could be used in several separatist registers. In his treatise *A Second Champion* (1653), the Baptist Richard Stooks bases his lengthy justification for separation on John 15:18–19. Remarking that those who follow Jesus' ministry will naturally be expelled from the world of unbelievers—"Those that imbrace the Gospel, loose the

---

[13] Saint Augustine, *Tractates on the Gospel of John, 55–11*, ed. John W. Rettig (Washington, D.C.: Catholic University Press, 2010), 148–9.

[14] Martin Luther, *Sermons on the Gospel of St. John*, in *Luther's Works*, vol. 24, ed. Jaroslav Pelikan (Saint Louis: Concordia Publishing House, 1961), 272.

[15] Ibid., 245–6. Cited in Jerome H. Neyrey, *The Gospel of John* (Cambridge: Cambridge University Press, 2007), 262.

savour and esteeme of the World, and are hated of all men"[16]—Stooks enlists John
15:18–19 to justify separatism:

> Because the Gospel holds forth separation, that Gods people ought to be a separated
> people, in respect of worship from all the people in the Earth, which is a way that most
> men abhorre; and therefore it is that so few obey the Truth; because separation is a
> hainous thing in the Worlds Eye.... *John 15. 18. 19. and therefore doth the World hate*
> *you.* And thus you see, there is a Gospel command for separation; as also there is example;
> for what did Christ and his Apostles preach, but away of separation from the World,
> both in their doctrine and practise?[17]

For Stooks, not to be separated from the "unequal yoke of unbelievers" is to force
concord between the "Gospel of light with the way of darkness," itself an implicit
appropriation of Johannine dualism.[18] Samuel Rutherford, a Presbyterian minister
and another nonconformist, albeit less radical than Stooks, devotes several pages of
his sermons on John 12 to describing the many denotations and connotations of
the term "world" in Johannine discourse: "The World," for Rutherford, is "the black
company that lyes in sinne, 1 John 5.9," and "haters of Christ, and all his, John
15.18"; such individuals are "a number uncapable of grace, or reconciliation."[19]
Rutherford ascribes pro-activity to the members of the world who would persecute
those who have removed themselves from the realm of unbelief. Thus the world is
"one of the professed enemies on Christs contrary side that he overcommeth, and
wee in him."[20]

 From overzealous Puritans to extremist dissenters, enthusiasts of otherwise antithetical denominational allegiances would similarly appropriate Johannine dualism.[21] The fanatical Puritan William Prynne recalls the marginalized community
of John 15:18–20 in order to convey to readers that John, too, would be ostracized
as a hater of the world for embracing piety after the fashion of Prynne's militant
Puritanism: "Yea, were our Saviour Christ, St. Paul, St. John…now living here
among us, I doubt not but they would all be pointed at, hissed, reviled, hated,
scorned, if not persecuted, as the very Archest Puritans, for their transcendent
holinesse, and rebukes of sin & sinners: since those poore Saints of God, who have
not attained to the moity of their transcendent grace and purity."[22] Later in the
century, the Leveller John Lilburne will similarly use John polemically to point out
the ways in which upright ministers of Christ will be persecuted by the rest of the

---

[16] Richard Stooks, *A second champion, or, Companion to truth* (London, 1653), 19.
[17] Ibid., 32–3.   [18] Ibid., 33.
[19] Samuel Rutherford, *Christ dying and drawing sinners to himself, or, A survey of our Saviour in his*
soule-suffering (London, 1647), 194.
[20] Ibid., 194–5.
[21] In *Moderate Puritans and the Elizabethan Church* (Cambridge: Cambridge University Press,
1982), Peter Lake describes a much earlier appropriation of Johannine dualism in Laurence Chaderton's
moderate Puritan attack on the established Church in the later decades of the sixteenth century. In his
lectures on the Pharisees' refusal to acknowledge Christ's healing of the blind man, Chaderton draws
an analogy between the obtuse worldliness of the Papists (and implicitly the Church of England) and
the Johannine Pharisees, all of whom refuse to communicate with the godly who possess, as Lake
describes, the "gifts of God's Spirit" (49–53).
[22] William Prynne, *Histrio-mastix: The players scourge* (London, 1633), 801.

world: "The naked purity and Truth of the Gospell of Christ, is too homely a thing, for the great learned Doctors of the world, to imbrace, stoope and submitt unto; for Christ hath said, that the professors of it shall be hated of all men, yea of their parents, kindred, and Friends…and are accounted as Sheepe to the slaughter… whose condition is to be afflicted and persecuted here by the men of the world, John 15.18.19, and 16.2."[23] For Lilburne, the world designates not a particular place so much as the inhabitants of sin.

An especially lucid use of Johannine dualism to justify radical dissent appears in Laurence Claxton's *A Paradisical Dialogue Betwixt Faith and Reason* (1660). The Ranter Claxton, after elaborating his conception of hell, has his polemical inter-locutor remark that not "one in 20 thousand will believe anything" contained in his discourse, to which Claxton's mouthpiece responds that his opponents' "seed" was not meant to understand "this Doctrine, no more then the Jews were to under-stand Christ": "It was not given to they seed to understand the Mysteries of the Kingdom of Glory; therefore I say, as *John* said, *We are of God, and the whole world lyeth in wickedness*, so I infallibly know, that almost the whole world will perish, save those few that believed in the last spiritual Commission."[24] Claxton's is a more fevered version of the dualism that one typically finds in other Ranter writings. Richard Coppin's *Divine Teachings* (1649), for example, builds its dualistic case on John 2:6 and 1 John 1:3–5. If the former verse justifies Coppin's conception of Antichrist—"What is born of the flesh is flesh, but that which is born of the spirit is spirit…& now this Flesh, together with Antichrist and fleshly things, shall be destroyed by the coming of Jesus Christ into the soul"—the latter verse justifies "the main drift" of Coppin's discourse, the distinction between the light of God and the darkness of the world without God: "In this God all things appear to be lovely, full of flight and joy: but out of this God, that is, in anything below himself, and anything in but himself, there all things appear hatefull, and full of darknesse and trouble."[25]

Realizing the radical use to which Johannine dualism could be put, more con-forming seventeenth-century theologians would typically provide lengthy exegeses in order to temper these fractious uses of the Fourth Gospel. George Downame, chaplain to King James and staunch defender of episcopacy, explicitly acknow-ledges the separatism implied in John 15:17–18 and 17:14, but he remarks in his lectures on the Psalms: "The world doth love her owne, but hateth those which are Christs," quickly providing caveats against judging the world too harshly, given that we cannot discern properly who is included or excluded from the gathered Church. Since "many are in the Church, which be not of it," the only "judgement of certaintie" belongs to God, the only "searcher of the heart."[26] While Downame

[23] John Lilburne, *[Come out of her my people] or an answer to the questions of a gentlewoman* (Amsterdam, 1639), 18.

[24] Laurence Claxton, *A paradisical dialogue betwixt faith and reason disputing the high mysterious secrets of eternity* (London, 1660), 22.

[25] Richard Coppin, *Divine Teachings in Three Parts* (London, 1649), 60–1.

[26] George Downame, *Lectures on the XV. Psalme read in the cathedrall church of S. Paule, in London* (London, 1604), 19–20.

accepts the Johannine separation of the elect and unbelieving but warns that we cannot be certain of anyone's reprobation, Arthur Hildersam, moderately noncon-formist clergyman, questions whether those who remove themselves from the world can be certain of their own election: "Nay if thou be but a meere naturall man unregenerated, unconverted, there is no love of God in thee, but thou hatest him in thy heart. For so saith our Saviour, John 15.18. of the whole world, of all men in their naturall estate, Yee know that the world hated me, before it hated you. And verse 23. He that hateth me, hateth my father also. Neither is this the state of the reprobate in the world onely, but even of Gods elect also."[27] We can see in Hildersam's cautionary interpretation of John 15:18 that the Evangelist's dualism could be used *against* sectarianism when one considers those earlier passages in the Fourth Gospel that set Christ against the world prior to the assembling of his dis-cipleship on Earth. According to John 3:17, for example, the Son is sent to judge (although not sentence) the entire world: "For God sent not his Sonne into the world to condemne the world: but that the world through him might be saved." In the first half of the Fourth Gospel, Jesus stands against the world and yet reaches out to it; in the second half of the Gospel, the part of the world that has honored his Word sections itself off. While all such passages connote dualism, only the latter half of John's Gospel is typically appropriated by mid-century radical sectar-ians. We turn now to the more sustained and innovative use of Johannine dualism that one finds in the dissenting tradition beginning with the Familist works of Hendrik Niclaes in the middle decades of the sixteenth century and extending to the latter part of the seventeenth century in the mystical and millenarian writings of John Everard and Gerrard Winstanley.

HENDRIK NICLAES: GODDED WITH JOHN

Hendrik Niclaes, who established the Family of Love in the 1550s and 1560s in northern Europe, achieved lasting influence in England when his works were republished in the early decades of the seventeenth century. Despite the Laudian attempt to curtail the seditious dissemination of Niclaes's writings and despite the spate of pamphlets denouncing the seeming libertinism of the Familists (which we realize now is something of a pejorative caricature of the sect), the writings of Niclaes, or "H.N.," exerted a powerful influence over the most perfectionist and mystical English antinomian writings, particularly the work of John Eaton and John Everard. Scholars typically posit a syncretistic influence on Niclaes and the radical antinomians, often mentioning the *Theologia Germanica* as well as the writ-ings of Hermes Trismegistus, Nicholas of Cusa, and the Pseudo-Dionysius as important sources for the evident mysticism, illuminism, and prophetism that one finds in the writings of the Familists and antinomian underground.[28] Although

---

[27] Arthur Hildersam, *CLII lectures upon Psalme LI preached at Ashby-Delazouch in Leicester-shire* (London, 1635), 391.

[28] On the genesis and influence of Niclaes's writings, see Como, *Blown by the Spirit*, 169–73; Nigel Smith, *Perfection Proclaimed: Language and Literature in English Radical Religion, 1640–1660* (Oxford:

Nigel Smith has noted in passing the importance of John to the Familist heritage, scholars of early modern culture have not generally discussed the profoundly shaping influence of the Johannine discourses on the radical strains of antinomianism.[29] I begin this section, therefore, with an assessment of the influence of both John's Gospel and the First Epistle on Niclaes's dualistic worldview as well as on his influential perfectionist soteriology and realized eschatology.

In *The Prophecy of the Spirit of Love* (1649) Niclaes draws directly on 1 John 2:15–17 (Jesus' "Do Not Love the World" pericope) to justify the Family's separation from worldly reprobates: "All such unbelievers, and resisters of the Love and her Service, may be right-easily known by their wicked deeds and inclination; for such false hearts...do all make themselves manifest, that they all (against the Truth, and against the Spirit or Mind of the supream God) are or stand with the perverse World."[30] Niclaes does not imagine merely a sequestration of believers from unbelievers. All who resist the evangelizing efforts of the Family are "worthy of the fire" and "everlasting condemnation."[31] In this passage and elsewhere in his writings, Niclaes capitalizes on the realized eschatology conveyed in John's most dualistic passages, especially 1 John 2:15–17 (which segues from a commentary on the perverse world to Jesus' warning that the last times have arrived) and John 12:31: "Now is the judgement of this world: now shall the prince of this world be cast out." The latter verse serves as the epigraph to the allegorical image of the Lamb of God destroying sin that is used as either a frontispiece or an inserted illustration in at least six of Niclaes's extant treatises (Fig. 5.1).[32]

The illustration compresses John 12 not only with Revelation 12:10 but also, given the radiant image of Christ atop the beast, Niclaes's reliance in his writings on the Johannine trope of Christ as "true light" as well as, given the inset inscription on the flanking scroll, Christ as the "Way, the Trueth, and the Life" from John 14:6. In addition to these foundational verses from the Fourth Gospel and a stream of verses on judgment from Revelation, a related important Johannine theme on judgment for Niclaes is Jesus' conversation with Nicodemus in John 3, particularly Jesus' assertion that God condemns those worldlings who reject the light and continue to embrace darkness. This is a passage that, for Niclaes, again looks toward the apocalyptic election of the Familists: "O ye beloved and good-willing hearts, what an heart, lust, and love God hath turned or born towards us all, for to rid and lead us all, now in these last perillous times through his Service of Love, out of the abominations of the perverse world."[33]

Clarendon Press, 1989), chapter 4, *passim*; and Christopher Marsh, *The Family of Love in English Society, 1550–1630* (Cambridge: Cambridge University Press, 1994). In *The World Turned Upside Down*, 185, Christopher Hill also argues for the influence of Hermeticism on the Familists as well as on the work of John Everard.

[29] See Smith, *Perfection Proclaimed*, 151.

[30] Hendrik Niclaes, *The prophecy of the spirit of love* (London, 1649), 7.   [31] Ibid., 7.

[32] Versions of the image are included in *Fidelitas* (Cologne, 1574), *Cantica Certen* (Cologne, 1574), *Epistolae HN* (Cologne, 1575), *The prophetie of the spirit of love* (Cologne, 1574), *A publishing of the peace upon earth* (Cologne, 1575), and *Revelatio Dei* (Cologne, 1575).

[33] Niclaes, *The prophetie of the spirit of love*, 49.

Now goeth the Judgment ouer the World :
Now becometh the Prince of this
World cast-out. Iohn. 12.

Now is the Saluation/ the Power/ and the
Kingdom, becom our Gods : and
the Might his Christes.
Apoca. 12.

Fig. 5.1 Christ as Lamb of God, in Hendrik Niclaes, *Cantica Certen of the songes of HN*
(Cologne, 1575), RB 31644, The Huntington Library, San Marino, CA.

In order to justify the separation of the Family from outsiders, Niclaes does not merely reference those Johannine passages that overtly address the world. In *Terra pacis* (1643), he appropriates the good shepherd allegory to exhort those who would leave the world to enter the right door of the Family: "Let him study or endeavor himself to enter into the upright Christian life, and to the true understanding of God, through the right door of the Humility and Obedience of *Jesus Christ*, and to become assembled in the family of love."[34] Niclaes returns to John 10 in his *Dicta* (1574) where he more explicitly uses the passage to separate insiders from outsiders: "And if they will not by any-meanes enter with you; at the right Doore of the Sheepe-folde of Iesu Christ: but chuse them an other Way / to breakein unto you / or that they likewise turne them away from us Elders and from our Ministration of the Woord and Requiring of the Seruice of Love / so turne you then also away from them / and let them then hardelie / depart from you."[35] At other times Niclaes will thread several key Johannine passages and motifs together, including light/dark dualism (John 3), the motif of blindness/darkness (John 9), and the sense in which the enlightened man does not stumble (John 11):

> For whosoever doth not forsake the same Land and his darkneses, as also the blinde guides in the same, and suffereth not himself to be led into the true light, by the seeing guides of the Family of Love; he must oftentimes stumble or become offended, and also many times stagger and fall, and that altogether; because he is not taught, nor led to the cleerness of the true Light, nor to the truth of the upright Life, whereby to behold the same true Light, in his upright Righteousness, and to inherit the upright Life, in his peaceable Being.[36]

This passage is instructive not merely because it represents the centrality of Johannine sources to Niclaes's prophetism, but also because it hints at Niclaes's assumption that he and the Familists have been incorporated into Christ and God or veritably united with God. The phrase "seeing guides of the Family" posits that Niclaes is able to see clearly the "true light," which pairs Niclaes's power of vision with Christ's as a vehicle for communicating God's message. On Niclaes's tendency to associate himself with the true light, the clergyman John Knewstubs, who worked for the crown in investigating Familist practices in the 1580s, assures his readers that the Family and Niclaes should not arrogate to themselves the light that is reserved in John for Christ and God:

> [Niclaes] challengeth againe, that which is proper and peculiar onely unto Christ in that he is God, that is, to be the true light of the perfect being.... What will this man bee ashamed of, who dare to say of himselfe, that he is that true light, which lighteneth everie man that commeth into the worlde, for so be the very wordes of that place, whereunto he sendeth us? What can bee more blasphemous, then to lay claime to that, which belongeth not unto Christ himselfe but onely in respect of his Godhead. This blasphemie is yet more evident in that which foloweth. For there it is thus written:

---

[34] Hendrik Niclaes, *Terra pacis a true testification of the spiritual land of peace* (London, 1643), 27.

[35] Hendrik Niclaes, *Dicta HN. Documentall sentences eauen-as those-same were spoken-fourth by HN* (Cologne, 1574), 39.

[36] Hendrik Niclaes, *Terra pacis*, 24–5.

God is light, and in him is no darkenesse at all, thereupon H. N. concludeth himselfe to be the true light.[37]

This sort of presumptuous claim to unity with God is made clearer in Niclaes's use of the Johannine language of abiding that he borrows from the vine discourse. Niclaes writes in his *Prophecy of the Spirit of Love* (1649) that those who give themselves over to the whole obedience of the "requiring of the Word" will show themselves "uprighter & lovelier, then that which ye have had out of the will or self-mindedness of the flesh: For, doing even so, ye shall, through the obedience of the requiring of the gracious Word and of his Service of *Love,* become incorporated to the lovely Nature of God, and to the everlasting peaceable Being of the holy Spirit of *Love.*"[38] One of Niclaes's favorite terms, "incorporation," has been fashioned out of his use of the related language of dwelling and communion that he finds in John 15 and 17. In his *Dicta*, Niclaes more explicitly derives union with God from a sense of having been "planted" with God: "Thanke God / for that Hee through the serviceable Woord of his Love; riddeth or leadeth us Unworthyons therout / and planteth us againe in his godlie Beeing / for to bring-fourth the Fruites of Righteousnes."[39] To have been "planted" in God's "Being" implies an engrafting that would erase substantial distinctions between the brethren and the deity.

Not surprisingly, 1 John 4:8—"God is love"—becomes a pivotal passage for the Familists' contention that they have been united with God. Here again Knewstubs calls Niclaes to task for self-deification:

They terme them selves the family of love, but their meaning is that they bee more then the Familie even the love it self: for though they agre not alwayes & in al places with themselves, & sometyme they take this word love, as is standeth, for love in deed, yet in other places they take it after the woordes of John, where he saith: *God is love,* so making themselves, not the householde of God, but god himselfe. This they vouch in many places of their writings, in saying that they are deified, that is made and become gods, & God is hominified.[40]

The particular heresy here, Knewstubs maintains, is that Niclaes has overpassed the Incarnation entirely and instead has drawn on the erroneous Mosaic assumption that "Adam was al that God was, & God al that Adam was."[41] Yet Niclaes's radical understanding of 1 John 4:8 survives well into the Interregnum years, typified in

---

[37] John Knewstubs, *A confutation of monstrous and horrible heresies* (London, 1579), 6.
[38] Hendrik Niclaes, *The Prophecy and Spirit of Love* (London, 1649), 95.
[39] Niclaes, *Dicta*, 11.   [40] Knewstubs, *A confutation*, 93.
[41] Ibid., 93. In *A confutation*, Knewstubs had earlier exclaimed against Niclaes's assumption that 1 John 4:8 refers to a singular essence of God: "*That God is love,* but no woorde heard that his being shoulde be no other thing beside love it selfe, which is the matter that he woulde willingly establish. Now this is his accustomed craftie and subtile dealing.... [W]hen hee setteth downe most absurde thinges, albeit there be no parte of his opinion established thereby, It sufficeth him if there be founde in the Scripture one of those woordes that hee useth, howe farre soever hee swarve in sense and meaning from the purpose of that place from whence hee taketh it. For what reason is there in this, to say, because GOD is love, therefore his essence and beeing is love" (23). Knewstubs goes on to argue that, in addition to instantiating love, God also embodies mercy, wisdom, strength, holiness, etc. and hence should not be reduced to a particular ontological quality.

the Leveller William Walwyn's exclamation that "God is love, and love makes man God-like."[42]

This persistent use of John to justify the Familist claim of radical union with God relies on an exegetical sleight of hand on Niclaes's part that prompted the polemic of several other vehement opponents of the Familists. In the metaphorical vine discourse, Jesus draws a fundamental distinction between himself as the vine and the disciples as branches—"I am the vine, ye are the branches"—pointing out that they can do nothing without him (15:5). Contrary to Niclaes's assertion, this does not mean that the disciples are one with or "planted" in God. On Niclaes's further contention that the vine metaphor signifies that the branch of the vine is somehow "vined" to the vine, another Familist prosecutor, William Wilkinson, remarks:

> The vine braunche is vined into the vine. I finde no such wordes in the place by you quoted out of S. John, neither doth the Gréeke or Latin translation afford any such termes of vinyng into a vine as ye seme to import. There is to abyde or remaine in the vine.…Christ is not sayd to bee a naturall vine, but is by some qualitie of the vine resembled unto us: So are not we *naturally Godded* with God in his substaunce, but *in qualitie with the image.*[43]

The distinction, admittedly a nuanced one, is that the vine does restore the branch and a resemblance to God (a restoration of the *imago dei*) but does not also unite us with God in substance, as Niclaes implies in his well-known creative metaphors of transmutation: vined in the vine, or Godded with God.

Niclaes further manipulates the language of fellowship in 1 John 1:3 to justify the unique fellowship in love that the Family has with God's holy family. John's sentiments on adoption warrant Niclaes's comment that "The faithfull have fellowship with the Apostles and God the Father, in or with Christ Jesus: Therfore this fellowship is in the familie of your love onely, and there is no societie in truth but yours."[44] This sentiment is reframed by Wilkinson, who first defines "community" and fellowship in the proper Johannine context—"This worde *fellowship* geveth us to understand, that among the godly there ought to be a mutuall féelyng of infirmities, with a supplying of all comfort both in thynges spirituall and temporall"—and then advises Niclaes that the Family is not the first to find fellowship with Christ and God.[45] In any case, Wilkinson continues, Niclaes's notion of fellowship is far removed from the Evangelist's purported meaning: "For many a day before HN. was heard of was there a Communialitie of Saintes, neither was it a Communialitie of goodes, of which the Anabaptistes did dreame, neither that filthy and graceles Communialitie of the Femal kinde of wives, virgins &c. whiche the Nicholaitanes did dote of."[46] Whether or not Wilkinson has caricatured the libertinism of the Familists, his point is clear. The Familist community of love is neither prototypical nor sanctified.

---

[42] William Walwyn, *The Power of Love* (London, 1643), 36.
[43] William Wilkinson, *A confutation of certaine articles delivered unto the Familye of Love with the exposition of Theophilus* (London, 1579), 5, 16.
[44] Ibid., 7.   [45] Ibid., 7.   [46] Ibid., 7.

We can begin to see from such polemic that a play on Johannine language is endemic in Niclaes's writings, particularly in his most prophetic work, *Revelatio Dei* (1649). A good example of this inventive approach to John's writings is Niclaes's recurring appropriation of the language of the Samaritan episode in which Christ provides his own "living water" to the Samaritans. In the Fourth Gospel, the Samaritan women asks Jesus, "How is it that thou, being a Jewe, askest drinke of me, which am a woman of Samaria?" (4:9). Jesus responds: "If thou knewest the gift of God, and who it is that sayth to thee, Gave me to drinke; thou wouldest have asked of him, and hee would have gaven thee living water" (4:10). In Niclaes's recasting of the key Johannine notion of living water, we find "through the outflowing Waterstreames of thy gratious Woorde and Testimonies of thy holie Spirit and Service of Love."[47] Niclaes has taken a phrase that is unique in the New Testament to John's Gospel and refashioned it into his own neologism, "outflowing waterstream," a term and symbol that he repeats in slightly varied form several times in *Revelatio Dei*. In Niclaes's allegorical reconstruction of the Samaritan episode, the woman "opens her mouth, and there...outflowed, the Word of God, and the true bread and life"; she promises to provide the "water of refreshing for to feed all thirsty souls"; and she later remarks that, from her body, her hearers will receive a "floud of living waters" to refresh their souls.[48] From a single episode and key Johannine phrase, Niclaes will develop his own related but idiosyncratic vocabulary that gains momentum through its varied repetitions.

Consider another of Niclaes's basic and recurring metaphors, that of "walking in the light": "Therfore respect-well now this same New Daye, that thou mayst walke in his Light."[49] Niclaes's immediate source is John 8:12: "Then spake Jesus againe unto them, saying, I am the light of the world: he that followeth mee, shall not walke in darkenesse, but shall have the light of life." Niclaes's mutual identification of Christ and Family members with the "light" or the "true light" also finds its intertexts in John's many references to light, particularly 1:9, 3:21, and 1 John 2:8. For a stretch of about ten pages of *Revelatio Dei*, Niclaes will play creatively with the identification of Christ as true light:

> I Heare heere before the Iudgment, a Complaint against Mee: To-wit, that I; with the Light of my Woorde; should have made an entrie, into anothers Light, Wisdom, & Peace. and so have brought-in Distourbaunce and Dissention by the Man, in hys Understandinge: Wherto I rightlie make-answer, that I knowe not of anye other Light, but my Life: and the Life, which proceedeth or floweth from Mee, that same is the true Light of the Man: and is to an Illuminating of him in his Understanding, and ther is none other Light more....Also I knowe not of any other Wisdome, but the holie Understandinge, which also is a Life of my Life, and for that cause likewise, a Light of my Light.[50]

Niclaes manipulates John 8 in order to elevate himself to the status of "Man" or the true light that Christ proclaims for himself. And he does so not simply through repetition but also through chiasmus and inversion (typical rhetorical strategies

---

[47] Hendrik Niclaes, *Revelatio Dei* (London, 1649), 30.
[48] Ibid, 40–1, 44.   [49] Ibid., 61.   [50] Ibid., 87.

that one finds in John's writings): "true light" transmutes into "light of my word," "life of my life," "light of my light," and then, on the subsequent page, "light, which is that true life it selfe."[51] In later formulations, Niclaes will have God himself speak in the language that Niclaes has just co-opted for himself: "This same Life of myne, is the true Light. This same Light of myne, is my true Woorde; my only begotten Sonne, which floweth-fourth from Mee, to the Peace and Salvation of Men."[52] Throughout his polemical writings, Niclaes will reshape Johannine language and concepts to justify the unique ontological/metaphysical relationship that Family members purportedly enjoy with Christ and God. Knewstubs was particularly vexed by Niclaes's tendency to assume for himself the privileged position of providing comfort and testimony of Christ's ways, thereby competing with the office of the Holy Ghost: "He chalengeth that promise, which our saviour Christ made unto his Apostles in John (for the sending of a comforter unto them, and not leaving of them comfortlesse) to be now verified, at the breaking out of this doctrine, which hee hath broched nowe of late."[53] Notable again is the extent to which Niclaes does not merely affiliate himself with Johannine concepts and its sectarian implications; he actually imitates the use of language that one finds in John, as if to forge an insider's perspective on an insider's Gospel. Wilkinson puzzles over Niclaes's creative use of language:

> Let the diligent Reader pare and set aside his wrested and violent Allegories, his unusuall and insignificant phrases, of beyng united into the perfect beyng of the love in the spirite, his scripture scripture quoting, incorporatyng into God, consubstantiatyng with Christ, &c, and such lyke wordes of course, he shall finde small substaunce and litle stuffe in matter that may be gathered by the order of readyng by pen or memory, and sometyme he shal be so plunged in the wordes, and wander for matter, that hee shall very hardly or not at all make sence of that hee readeth.[54]

John's Gospel itself is noteworthy for generating several synonymous terms for a single established idea and term that might otherwise be found in the Synoptic writings and Pauline theology. As I remarked earlier, for the simple term "light," John substitutes a string of different terms that can all connote "light," including "above," "spirit," "life," "freedom," "truth," and "love." In his creative phrases and neologisms—"Godded with God," "vined in the vine"—and in his idiosyncratic application of more familiar terms such as "communalitie," "outflowing," and "fellowship," Niclaes appropriates the Johannine style of address rather than simply the content of the Fourth Gospel. Especially notable in several of the passages quoted is Niclaes's reliance on rhetorical staples of the Fourth Gospel, themselves derived from Greek rhetorical theory. These include amplification (*amplificatio*), in which, through repetition, synonymy, and refining (*expolitio*), Niclaes

---

[51] Ibid., 88.   [52] Ibid., 92.   [53] Knewstubs, *A confutation*, 9.

[54] Wilkinson, *A confutation*, 32. Wilkinson's complaints about Niclaes's preoccupation with words rather than matter and about the redundancy of Niclaes's coinages are echoed by at least one modern commentator, J. D. Moss, who charges Niclaes, as Nigel Smith records, with redundantly using a wealth of related phrases to describe a straightforward experience. See J. D. Moss, "'Godded with God': Hendrik Niclaes and His Family of Love," *Transactions of the American Philosophical Society*, 71:8 (Philadelphia, 1981); cited in Smith, *Perfection Proclaimed*, 175.

(like the Evangelist) dwells on selected choice terms—light and life, for example—and reconfigures them syntactically as if to suggest some new thought or idea.[55] Nigel Smith rightly notes that Niclaes's tendency to invent terms and then employ them redundantly is "part of a generally consistent and well-planned whole where associated meanings of a central tenet (begoddedness) are developed successively and concentrically outwards from the central truth";[56] in so noting, Smith is unintentionally describing the rhetorical process on which John's Gospel relies as well. And when Wilkinson complains that, in Niclaes's writings, there is little "matter" or substance but only unusual phrases into which the reader is "plunged," he too might as well have been describing the Johannine approach, which is to de-emphasize the ideational and focus instead on the interpersonal and the linguistic/textual manner of address to one's communicants.[57] In his relative eschewal of scriptural matter and his emulation of the Johannine mode of address, Niclaes fascinatingly bears out Rudolf Bultmann's famous comment about the Fourth Gospel—namely, that Jesus provides little content in his teachings beyond the fact that his mission is to make God's ways known: "Jesus as the Revealer of God, *reveals nothing but that he is the Revealer.*"[58]

FREE GRACE: JOHN TRASKE
AND RETURNE HEBDON

Religious historians have at times argued that early Stuart antinomianism—especially its emphasis on believers indwelling with the Spirit of God and its belief in repentance preceding faith—was influenced by English and continental Familism. David Como has recently remarked that Niclaes's writings inspire the perfectionism of the writings of both the early Stuart antinomian John Traske and his disciple, Returne Hebdon, both of whose writings influence the later development of antinomian dogma in the less radical works of John Eaton and the so-called Eatonites.[59] Traske, an itinerant and unlicensed preacher who is pilloried at the hands of the Star Chamber in 1618, is more technically and complexly antinomian than Niclaes, since he rabidly supports what seemed like a reversion to Old Testament

---

[55] On the use of classical rhetorical figures in the Fourth Gospel, particularly *amplificatio*, see the important essay by C. Clifton Black, "'The Words That You Gave to Me I have Given to Them': The Grandeur of Johannine Rhetoric," in *Exploring the Gospel of John: In Honor of D. Moody Smith*, eds. R. Alan Culpepper and C. Clifton Black (Louisville: Westminster John Knox Press, 1996), especially 224–9.

[56] Smith, *Perfection Proclaimed*, 175.

[57] Malina and Rohrbaugh, *Social-Science Commentary on the Gospel of John*, 5.

[58] Rudolf Bultmann, *Theology of the New Testament,* vol. II, trans. Kendrick Grobel (New York: Charles Scribner's Sons, 1955), 66. For recent assessments of the influence of Bultmann's account of the revelatory quality of the Fourth Gospel, see D. Moody Smith, "Johannine Studies since Bultmann," *Word and World* (2001), 21:4, 343–51; and John Ashton, *Understanding the Fourth Gospel* (Oxford: Clarendon Press, 1991), 545–3. In an influential revision of Bultmann's theory, Wayne A. Meeks suggests that Jesus reveals not only that he is the revealer but also that he is an "enigma." "The Man from Heaven in Johannine Sectarianism," *Journal of Biblical Literature* 91:1 (1972), 57.

[59] See Como, *Blown by the Spirit*, 167–73.

legalism.[60] In fact, his legalism stemmed from his belief that true believers inhered in Christ and God so unassailably that the law, inscribed in their hearts, could and should be obeyed effortlessly. In their perfectionism both Traske and Hebdon do seem to follow Niclaes, although I would argue that, in terms of direct influence, they principally follow John, whose writings, as we have seen, were fundamental to Niclaes's enthusiasm.

Like Niclaes's writings, John Traske's *Heaven's Joy, or Heaven Begun Upon Earth* (1616) is shaped by the Fourth Gospel and First Epistle. Traske's goal, however, is to outline the various forms of theological assurance that Johannine theology offers to the believer. Like Niclaes, Traske separates those who enjoy eternal life from those who remain in thrall to worldly sin: "He that heareth my word (saith Christ) and beleeveth on him that sent me, hath everlasting life; and shall not come into condemnation.... He that beleeveth not on the Sonne, shall not see Life, but the wrath of God abideth on him."[61] Beyond the evident dualism, what gives this line (and Traske's entire treatise) a Johannine pedigree is its emphasis on revealed rather than end-time eschatology. Traske does not merely project an apocalyptic separation of believers from unbelievers. Believers have received a foretaste of things to come, enjoying "even here" the benefits of service to Christ. The faithful "shall be clearely seene of such as are spirituall, at the last Day: yet because the beginnings of it are here, even upon Earth, and they that will ever see, and enjoy the fulnesse of it hereafter, must bee acquainted with the Beginnings here."[62] Fulfillment theology is underlined in the very title of Traske's treatise. Heavenly joy begins for the faithful during their temporal sojourn and discipleship on earth.[63]

Traske then outlines the distinctive benefits that fulfilled believers will confidently enjoy, including peace, joy, and truth, all of which are promised for Traske in key Johannine texts. After a gloss on Isaiah's comparison of peace for the Church to a river, Traske uses John 14:27 to assure his auditors of the fearless peace that will be entrusted to believers: "And this is that Peace which our blessed Redeemer speaketh of, where he saith: Peace I leave with you, my Peace I gave unto you, not as the world gaveth, gave I unto you, let not your hearts be troubled, neither let it be afraid."[64] The assured peace derives from the love of God that provides the fount of unwavering joy to the believer, a process related for Traske in John 15:9–11 and 16:22: "Joy shall be upon their Heads: they shall obtaine joy, and gladnesse, and sorrow, and sighing shall flye away. It shall never be taken from them....As my Father hath loved mee, so have I loved you, continue yee in my Love."[65] Uppermost in Traske's mind is not only personal assurance and perfectionism but a clear distinction between insiders and outsiders. He goes on to distinguish the manner in which his or "our" joy inevitably increases while the joy of hypocrites is fleeting: "This is the first difference, betweene the Joy of Hypocrites, and our Joy. Theirs is

---

[60] Ibid., 138–40.
[61] John Traske, *Heaven's Joy, or Heaven Begun Upon Earth* (London, 1616), 5.
[62] Ibid., 6.
[63] For more on antinomian conceptions of spiritual assurance, see Mark Jones, *Antinomianism: Reformed Theology's Unwelcome Guest?* (Phillipsburg: P&R Publishing, 2013), 98–110.
[64] Traske, *Heaven's Joy*, 13.   [65] Ibid., 17.

short or momentany, ours everlasting; Single illegible letterheirs is taken from them, ours never; theirs vanisheth, ours increaseth."[66] Far from admitting the backsliding of the elect, as most mainstream or experimental Puritans would, Traske presupposes the assurance of Christ's brethren, noting above all the "inseparability" of the faithful "from righteousness, peace, and the Holy Ghost."[67] It is a short leap from such an unswayable experience of personal assurance to the enjoyment of inseparable union with God and Christ. At his most Familistic moments, Traske will rely heavily on Isaian, Pauline, and Johannine proof-texts in his contention that the faithful are no "lesse then heires with *God*";[68] that they have the "mind of Christ";[69] and that, because they cannot fail in completing their work, their estates are built upon the "Rocke Christ."[70]

While Traske complements the familiar horizontal dualism that we find in the Familists with a vertical dualism that distinguishes the elevated spirit of the elect from the fleshly world (those converts who are truly "free" are not born of men, blood, or the will of the flesh, but of the spirit and God), his most ardent follower, Returne Hebdon, gives fuller expression to a Johannine dualism of flesh and spirit.[71] At the outset of his *Guide to the Godly* (1648), Hebdon relies on the bread of life narrative in his argument that true believers commingle with the spirit of God:

> And thus he is the food of immortality which nourisheth the Devine nature in man, to every one to whom he is communicable both in flesh, and spirit; for the word is now both flesh, spirit and life.... He which eateth naturall bread is quickned mortally for the time of a day &c. much more shall he live to immortallity, and to God that applyeth to himself the body and spirit of Jesus Christ: the manifestation of which life of Christ is effectuall to every true member of his body, in that such are made of God to some end in the flesh.[72]

The presence of the phrase "divine nature of man" is itself ambiguous enough to avoid heterodoxy. But the idea that the flesh of man is in some sense transformed or "made of God" conveys the perfectionism that recalls Niclaes's writings. Hebdon legitimates his claims with several more passages from John, including 1 John 3:37 and John 20, which convince him that God's chosen and holy vessels enjoy the spirit of Christ while on Earth: "the same spirit of Jesus Christ which is in heaven liveth in them."[73]

Framing Hebdon's perfectionism and featured throughout his entire treatise is, as we might expect, a clear polarity according to which believers are the children of light, while unbelievers are the children of darkness.[74] Several Johannine passages compress in Hebdon's dualistic vision:

> All the world is darke, and is laid in wickednesse, and for this their sins are condemned and dead in the Law before Christ Jesus came, when he came in the flesh, he was the light of the world, and all that by the discovery of that light, hated their evil workes,

[66] Ibid., 17–18. [67] Ibid., 18. [68] Ibid., 80.
[69] Ibid., 69. [70] Ibid., 114.
[71] John Traske, *A Treatise of Libertie from Judaisme* (London, 1620), 12.
[72] Returne Hebdon, *A Guide to the Godly* (London, 1648), 6.
[73] Ibid., 7. [74] Ibid., 14.

did come unto the light, and love to walke in it, doing the truth, that their workes may be manifested to be done in God; but on the other side, there were and are another seed that have enmity against the light, and the Children of light, and these will not come unto the light, but hate the light, because they love their own evill workes of darknesse: this light then is the confirmation of their former condemnation without any remedy.[75]

From Jesus' conversation with Nicodemus (which, as we will see, is one of John Eaton's favorite pericopes), Hebdon imagines two countervailing winds corresponding to light and dark or to spirit and flesh: "I understand from John 3.8. That there is a twofold wind or spirit. The one is called the common wind, spirit, or ayre; whereby all flesh do breath, and live the naturall and mortall life.... The other is called the holy wind of spirit whereby such as are begotten from above by the spirit do breath and live the spirituall and immortall life."[76] Johannine dualism is used by Hebdon to help explain to his readers the conundrum of how the newly regenerated man is able to vanquish the stubborn old man. The polemic here is against a much earlier treatise by the sixteenth-century Reformed martyr John Bradford, *A frutefull treatise and ful of heavenly consolation against the feare of death* (1564). Bradford had taken an extreme Lutheran position on the co-existence of the old and new man in the regenerated creature. If Luther had argued that sin and election uneasily co-exist, rendered in his influential phrase *simul justus et peccatorum*, Bradford, drawing on an analogy between David and Goliath, pursued a more cynical line. Since the old man is likened to a giant and the new man to a little child, "the olde man therefore is more stronger, lusty, and stirring, then is the new man, because the birth of the newe man is but begonne now, and the olde man is perfectly borne."[77] Against Bradford's claim for the resilience of the old man and his notion that the old and new man are in "continuall conflict and warre most deadly," Hebdon asserts that the newly regenerated believer will easily be able to overcome the recalcitrances of the old man: "But seeing that which is borne from above after the spirit of Christ, is of the spirit, and that which is after the flesh is flesh, distinctly as are flesh and spirit; mortall and immortall distinct, the least part of that immortall spirit must needs be stronger then the strongest flesh of the body, for it is stronger then all the fleshly power of the world."[78] The conclusion, drawn with further evidence from 1 John 5, is that Satan can never assail the "divine nature" that inhabits a "renewed minde."[79]

Crystallized in Hebdon's polemic is a strategy that one finds in so many antinomian treatises. Two starkly opposed worlds are established—the world of light, spirit, eternal life, and perfect union with God (through Christ) against the world of darkness, flesh, and alienation from Christ and God—after which the writer will turn to crucial Johannine passages in order to develop a soteriology of assurance and perseverance. Because those who abide in Christ have already achieved

---

[75] Ibid., 11.   [76] Ibid., 11.

[77] John Bradford, *A frutefull treatise and ful of heavenly consolation against the feare of death* (London, 1564), 44. Hebdon bases his account of Bradford's position on the 1655 edition of Fox's *Book of Martyrs*.

[78] Ibid., 28–9.   [79] Ibid., 31.

perfection through free grace, the chosen should not fret over backsliding or the need for sanctified renovation, although as we will see in the next section, Hebdon does not resort to forensic jargon in the manner of John Eaton or John Cotton.

JOHN EATON AND THE CLEANSING OF SIN

If the works of the Familists and the early antinomian Traskites advance an inherentist notion of free grace, union with God, and realized eschatology, a second group of still influential antinomians, those who adhere more closely to mainstream Puritan Pietism, develop an imputative form of antinomianism according to which even the elect were still tainted by sin.[80] In the early decades of the seventeenth century, John Eaton, the Oxford trained Protestant, began preaching a doctrine of free justification that would find him disciplined by the High Commission in 1619.[81] Eventually, having communed for a time with the Traskites, Eaton published two influential treatises, *The Honey-combe of Free Justification* (1642) and the *Discovery of the Most Dangerous Dead Faith* (1641), each of which presents a distinctive position on justification that veers slightly but consequentially from the dogma of Puritan practical divinity. English Calvinists such as William Perkins and William Ames had argued that justification describes an imputation of grace that bestows on the passive believer the extrinsic righteousness of Christ. Often described by Luther, for example, as alien righteousness, justification so understood did not entirely cleanse the communicant from heritable sin (the arduous process of sanctification at least contributed to the subsequent renovation of the believer's moral character). As we will see, Eaton contributes to an antinomian counter-Puritanism in arguing that an imputation of grace purified the sinner in God's eyes, even though, from a creaturely vantage point, the penitent would still harbor sin. In this nuanced departure from English Calvinism, the Eatonists were less radical than the Familists and Traskites, although they share the same dualism and anti-legalism that finds its legitimation in the Johannine discourses.

Eaton will use Johannine texts more pointedly than his antinomian forebears in support of the controversial claim that free justification abrogates the law entirely. Key passages cited throughout his work are taken from John's First Epistle. After establishing the basic light/dark dualism that suffuses the Epistle, John advises that Christ has removed sin entirely from his believers: "But if wee walke in the light, as he is in the light, wee have fellowship one with another, and the blood of Jesus Christ his Sonne clenseth us from all sinne. If we say that we have no sinne, we deceive our selves, and the trueth is not in us. If we confesse our sinnes, hee is faithfull, & just to forgave us our sinnes, and to cleanse us from all unrighteousnesse"

---

[80] See Como, *Blown by the Spirit*, 40–1, and chapter 6, *passim*. See also T. D. Bozeman, "The Glory of the 'Third Time': John Eaton as Contra-Puritan," *Journal of Ecclesiastical History*, 47 (1996), 638–54; and W. Stoever, *"A Faire and Easie Way to Heaven": Covenant Theology and Antinomianism in Early Massachusetts* (Middletown: Wesleyan University Press, 1978), 138–47.

[81] For biographical information on Eaton, see Como, *Blown by the Spirit*, 176–80.

(1 John 1:7–9). Related passages frequently cited by Eaton and the antinomians appear in chapter 8 of the Fourth Gospel, where Jesus warns the Pharisees that they will die in sin: "Ye are from beneath; I am from above: ye are of this world; I am not of this world" (8:23); "I said therefore unto you, that ye shall die in your sinnes. For if yee beleeve not that I am hee, yee shall die in your sinnes" (8:24). Christ's warning here is counterpoised to the subsequent passage in which he again promises freedom from sin to the faithful: "And the servant abideth not in the house for ever: but the Sonne abideth ever. If the Sonne therfore shall make you free, ye shall be free indeed" (8:35–6). For Eaton, this light/dark dualism, which itself corresponds to the vertical dualism of heaven and the world, is modified into a free/unfree dualism that hinges on the niceties of justification. Early in *The Honey-combe*, Eaton explains his position on free justification: "For the blood of Jesus Christ the Sonne of God doth make us cleane from all sinne. . . . This does our good physician Jesus Christ most effectually cleanse the spirituall leprosie of our sins, because by his own blood he has made us cleane from all sin."[82] Further support for Eaton's position is found in Christ's proclamation in John 19:30—"It is finished or perfect"—which signifies to him Christ's "fulfillment" of free grace.[83]

It is worth pausing, given Eaton's recurrence to the Johannine reference to sinful cleansing, to put 1 John 1:7 in a larger exegetical context. Augustine's gloss on the passage is exemplarily balanced when weighed against the often biased and decon-textualized interpretations that one finds in early modern dissenting writings. On the particular sentiment that "the blood of Jesus Christ his Son cleanseth us from all sin," Augustine remarks: "Great is the confidence that God has given us. Well may we celebrate our Paschal sacrifice, in which the Lord's blood is shed to cleanse us from all transgression. Let us rest confident: the devil held against us a bond of slavery, but Christ's blood has wiped it out."[84] But regarding this justifying removal of sin, Augustine reminds his auditors that the very next line in the First Epistle seems to give back the sins that we have been assured Christ has expiated: "If we say that we have no sinne, we deceive our selves, and the trueth is not in us" (1 John 8): "If then you confess yourself a sinner," Augustine concludes, "the truth is in you, for the truth itself is light. Your life is not yet perfect in brightness, for there are sins in it: yet your enlightenment has begun with your confession of sin."[85] Augustine's point is that the cleansing of sin, which restores the individual, still assumes the possibility of sinful degeneracy: "After the forgiving and wiping away of all sin, our life amidst the temptations of this world may not avoid all stain."[86] The forensic terminology is absent here, but Augustine does provide the ingredients for a more formal distinction between justified and sanctified right-eousness. Sanctified righteousness, at least according to the experimental Puritan tradition, involves not only obsessive self-monitoring (applying the practical

[82] John Eaton, *The Honey-combe of Free Justification by Christ Alone* (London, 1642), 26–7.
[83] Ibid., 26.
[84] Saint Augustine, *Ten Homilies on the First Epistle General of St. John*, in *Augustine: Later Works*, trans. John Burnaby (Philadelphia: Westminster Press, 1955), 263.
[85] Ibid., 263.   [86] Ibid., 263.

syllogism to one's conscience, for example) but also the commission of works and moral rigorism.[87]

Radical dissenters tended to seize on the cleansing aspect of 1 John 1:7 while neglecting the overt language of backsliding and the implicit language of sanctification in 1 John 1:8. A typical antinomian complaint was that too much self-scrutiny and fretting over sinful behavior would meddle with the pledge of 1 John 1:7. Excessive hand-wringing over "relapsing & fallings again into the same sins," the antinomian Seeker John Saltmarsh cautions, will "bring such anguish and terrour upon such *souls*, even almost to *confusion of face*.... [A]s if it were in vain for them to perswade themselves of *Christ* or the *love* of God, but rather to sin it out in this life, not considering *that the Blood of Christ cleanseth us from all sin*."[88] It is a short step from Saltmarsh's caution against self-scrutiny to, for example, the Familist presumption that sacramental "cleansing" is tied to spiritual perfection. According to Henry Ainsworth, a much less radical separatist, this claim was yet another specious antinomian posture. To be cleansed and baptized into Christ does not lead, Ainsworth remarks in a 1608 epistle, to "*the forgiving and releasing of their synns, as H. N. Pharisaically inferreth; but to shew forth the fruit and force of faith wherby the just doe live*."[89] Again the passage in question is 1 John 1:7, manipulated by Niclaes, Ainsworth avers, to justify freedom from moral obligation: "A vain perswasion of our own obedience righteousnes and sanctification to wash our selves in; and hath roiled with his feet the pure fountain of Christs blood which clenseth all beleevers from all sin."[90]

Later in the century, Anthony Burgess, Presbyterian nonconformist, makes a similar argument against the antinomians. Burgess reminds his readers that John's conception of Christ as continuing advocate qualifies any measure of sinlessness following justification: "Christ is said still to be *an Advocate,* and *to make Intercession* for *believers* after they are *justified,* which would be altogether needless, if God did not take notice of their sins....*John* having said, *That Christs bloud cleanseth us from all sin*...a place the antinomian much urgeth, not considering that at the same time the Apostle *ver.* 9. requireth *confession* and *shame* in our selves."[91] Burgess has in mind not simply the antinomian heresies but also the Quaker portrayal of Christ as advocate to argue the countervailing position that advocateship proves rather than disproves that the elect are cleansed once and for all. Thus the Quaker George Whitehead contends that the apostles Paul, James, and John evinced purity because of Christ's advocacy following cleansing: "What one sin or sins can they lay to their charge, or to any of them which they were not freed from before their

---

[87] For an example of the experimental Puritan position on John's discussion of sin in the First Epistle, see William Perkins, *A golden chaine: or The description of theologie* (London, 1600), 685–9.

[88] John Saltmarsh, *Free grace, or, The flowings of Christs blood free to sinners* (London, 1646), 55.

[89] Henry Ainsworth, *An epistle sent unto two daughters of Warwick from H.N., the oldest father of the Familie of Love* (London, 1608), 43.

[90] Ibid., 43.

[91] Anthony Burgess, *The true doctrine of justification asserted and vindicated, from the errours of Papists, Arminians, Socinians, and more especially antinomians* (London, 1651), 66. The most extensive late-seventeenth-century commentary on 1 John 2 and Christ's advocacy is John Bunyan's *The advocateship of Jesus Christ clearly explained* (London, 1688).

decease? Let them prove some sin which was not destroyed in any of these before their decease, (and who can lay any thing to the charge of Gods elect?)."[92] Whitehead's tendency to cherry-pick the sweetest verses from John brings us back to Augustine by means of Whitehead's opponent, the mid-century nonconformist John Horn. Horn reminds the Quakers of the fuller context of the Johannine verses that charge the individual with self-deceit when imagining purity from sin. For Horn, the Johannine verses serve summarily as a warning against further sin: "He [John] writ those things as a warning of men to take heed of sinning, for it tends to make men the more watchful, to know that there is such an Enemy in their bosom, that is so dangerous to them."[93] We can see the circularity of such polemic. Horn articulates the very mode of affective individualism and self-scrutiny that is rejected by the antinomian sensibility.

If we return to Eaton and his imputative understanding of justification, we can begin to appreciate the ways in which his use of 1 John 7–8 departs from more radical antinomian and Quaker appropriations of that controverted verse. In anticipating objections to his arguments for free grace, Eaton further uses John to distinguish a "mystical" from a "gross and palpable" cleansing of sin. If 1 John 1:7 and John 1:29 ("Behold the Lambe of God, which taketh away the sinne of the world") reflect a mystical or secret abolishing of sins because cleansing is "wrought, seen, and apprehended above reason, sense, and feeling; that is, by faith," other passages, especially 1 John 3:3 ("And every man that hath this hope in him, puri-fieth himselfe, even as he is pure"), comport more with sanctification that "will never feele to be perfected in us" until the life to come.[94] Eaton needs to retain the distinction, for he distinguishes between what God sees in us regarding sin and what we see in ourselves and one another, the former linked to justification, the latter linked to sanctification: "Is God not able to abolish those sins that we feele daily dwelling in us, out of his own sight, although he doth not abolish them out of our sight, that we may here live by the faith of his power?"[95] And Eaton further uses John, particularly 8:24 ("I said therefore unto you, that ye shall die in your sinnes. For if yee beleeve not that I am hee, yee shall die in your sinnes"), to justify his related contention that the wicked do know/see their sins, albeit God knows their sins "more perfectly" than they themselves do.[96] Eaton's nuanced gloss on the Johannine material is put more concisely by another imputative mid-century English antinomian, Robert Towne, who mingles Johannine assurance with relevant verses from Pauline theology:

> It is true God accounts not us non-sinners in our selves, and free from all indwelling sinne; for that were an untruth; but he both justifieth us by faith in Christ, and makes us pure and free from all spot of sinne, before his Judgement seat... *The blood of Jesus cleanseth us from all sinne.* Now you are pleased... to wrest our words; as if we did not

---

[92] George Whitehead, *A brief discovery of the dangerous principles of John Horne* (London, 1659), 3.

[93] John Horn, *The Quakers proved deceivers and such as people ought not to listen to, or follow, but to account accursed, in the management of a charge formerly given out against them to that effect* (London, 1660), 3. For more on the controversy over the Quaker understanding of sinful cleansing, see William Penn, *The Christian-Quaker and his divine testimony vindicated by Scripture* (London, 1674).

[94] Eaton, *The Honey-combe*, 51.   [95] Ibid., 48.   [96] Ibid., 71.

hold the good works of the regenerate to be faulty in themselves. As if we meant by the removal (as you call it) or abolition of sinne, such an annihilation of sinne in its essence root and branch, that it should not dwell in us here; whereas you know and read the contrary.[97]

Here again a line is drawn between the vantage point of God—from which God sees only purity in the communicant—and the judgment seat of everyone else, for whom the sanctified moral character of the sinner will always remain in question.[98]

Eaton legitimates his creative interpretation of familiar doctrine by comparing his opponents' outworn belief system to Johannine discipleship failure. When summarizing the overarching "Protestant" resistance to his newfangled interpretation of free justification, Eaton describes the opposition as mired in "Nicodemicall" misunderstanding, unable to appreciate the nuances of his linguistic reconstructions. These "Protestants" are those who "especially being tried, as Nicodemus was, with a new phrase which they have not heard of expressing but the old matter, which like blind Mille-horses they daily run around in; and have daily heard, then with Nicodemus, they count it absurd, and doe judge it very foolishnesse it selfe...and do not keep neither in word nor deed that which they hold."[99] Here and elsewhere Eaton, like Niclaes, will rely on both the letter and the spirit of the Johannine worldview to support his idiosyncratic positions on grace, sin, and law, separating those in the minority who understand the subtleties of Jesus' words from those who cling to an unenlightened approach to those words and meanings.[100]

---

[97] Robert Towne, *The re-assertion of grace, or, Vindiciae evangelii a vindication of the Gospell-truths* (London, 1654), 24.

[98] Eaton's related use of the recurring trope of the "wedding garment" is itself influenced by the larger sectarian argument that he appropriates from Johannine sources. His antinomian brethren are distinguished from all of those Protestants of the "dead faith," those of the "world" who cannot see the extent to which the faithful are clothed with the garment of Christ's righteousness: "The fourth enimy...is the great multitude, commonly called the world; of whom S. John speaketh" (*The Honey-combe*, 198). Eaton will then bring John 3:32 into his argument as a means of arming the antinomian listeners against this "great multitude" who do not believe the "mysteries of Christ": "Against this scandal we are...fore-armed with that one watch-word of the Holy Ghost saying, That Christ brings the most certain testimony of himself and of his benefits, from his Father, *but no man receiveth his testimony, John 3.32* which...must not be understood, as if no man at all doth receive Christ's testimony, but...because very few in comparison do receive it, who if they be compared with the huge multitude, that make a shew of receiving it, by the dead faith, but in truth doe not" (*The Honey-combe*, 199). Eaton compares his rarefied knowledge of free justification to the sort of privileged knowledge entrusted to the apostles who receive from the Paraclete the secret mysteries of faith.

[99] Eaton, *The Honey-combe*, 46.

[100] Eaton's use of "Nicodemicall" is not equivalent to the charge of Nicodemism that, beginning during the Marian persecution, was leveled against those dissimulators who secretly held Protestant beliefs even though they publically confessed Catholic doctrine. The most influential early-sixteenth-century anti-Nicodemite work is Calvin's 1544 treatise *Excuse à messieurs les Nicodemites*. Representative descriptions of English Nicodemism can be found in George Gillespie's *A dispute against the English-popish ceremonies* (London, 1637): "The...Nicodemite, holdes it enough to yeeld some secret assent to the trueth, though neither his profession nor his practise testify so much. He, whose minde is possessed with praejudicate opinions against the truth, when convincing light is holden forth to him, looketh asquint, and therefore goeth away" (3). See also Anthony Burgess's *The Scripture directory for church-officers and people* (London, 1659): "There were some who have held, That they might do any external acts of Idololatrical worship, be at Masse (say they) believe any thing, so that they keep their

But this still leaves unaddressed Eaton's understanding of the imputed sinner's body once justified and his considered view of sanctification as a stage in the order of salvation. If the experimental Puritans typically argued that sanctification, which issues from justification, involves the gradual but not step-wise renovation of sinful flesh, Eaton claims that converts are sanctified the moment that they are justified. They have taken on the body of Christ, their own bodies not subject to mortification or renewal so much as covered over, hidden from creaturely view by the "wedding garment" (although utterly abolished from God's sight).[101] This position finds its warrant, Eaton believes, in another of his favorite passages from the Fourth Gospel: "Behold the Lambe of God, which taketh away the sinne of the world" (1:29).[102] As if realizing that the claim that we are spotless in front of God but not in front of ourselves or one another might defy logic, Eaton will spend much of the last two-thirds of *The Honey-combe* in an attempt at elucidation. One of his explanations is that, according to 1 John 3:5, Christ has no sin; it follows that, since we take on Christ entirely, our bodies, too, as well as the Church entire, must also be washed of sin in God's eyes.[103] In terms of the tension that inevitably exists between the lived experience of one's own sinfulness and the belief that one is completely sinless in front of God, Eaton will recommend not a mortification of the flesh so much as a perspectival shift away from the flesh and toward the Word: "But if thou ask me, how, and by what meanes may I mortifie my reason, sense, and feeling, and come to believe the contrary unto them? I answer, by removeing what they pretend, out of thy sight and minde; as Abraham did the deadnesse of his body, and the deadness of Sarah wombe, but not considering the same."[104] Even Peter, Paul, and John lived with sin, Eaton maintains, but they were able to set the Word and wedding garment against their "lives," trusting only to grace that they were "perfectly good."[105]

Noteworthy is Eaton's strategy of preempting objections by simply declaring the "mystical" and mysterious nature of the process by which Christ's wedding garment abolishes sin from God's vantage point. Such passages as these are typical in *The Honey-combe*: "the second part of Free Justification, is a wonderfull, mysticall work and benefit of the Gospel"; and we are "mystically formed with Christ's own

---

consciences and minds pure" (167). The history of continental and English Nicodemism is rich and well attended to in the critical heritage. See, for example, Carlos M. N. Eire, *War Against the Idols: The Reformation of Worship from Erasmus to Calvin* (Cambridge: Cambridge University Press, 1989), chapter 7, *passim*. Karl Gunther has recently argued that, for many ecclesiastical and social Protestant activists, anti-Nicodemism extends well into the seventeenth century in England. Gunther, *Reformation Unbound: Protestant Visions of Reform in England, 1525–90* (Cambridge: Cambridge University Press, 2014), especially chapter 3, *passim*.

[101] Typical Puritan accounts of the manner in which sanctified righteousness follows from justification can be found in John Preston, *The Saint's Qualification* (London, 1637); Thomas Taylor, *The Progress of Saints to Full Holinesse* (London, 1630); and Jeremiah Lewis, *The Right Use of Promises, or A Treatise of Sanctification* (London, 1632).

[102] Eaton, *The Honey-combe*, 37.

[103] Ibid., 41. For a brief discussion of free justification and sanctification in the works of Eaton, Traske, and Tobias Crisp, see William B. K. Stoever, *"A Faire and Easie Way to Heaven": Covenant Theology and Antinomianism in Early Massachusetts* (Middletown: Wesleyan University Press, 1978), 138–47.

[104] Eaton, *The Honey-combe*, 181.   [105] Ibid., 184.

righteousness."[106] That Eaton attaches a mystical process of sanctification to the Fourth Gospel becomes especially evident toward the end of *The Honey-combe* when he overtly resorts to the language of indwelling from Jesus' prayer for believers. Having described free justification as a wonderful "union into Christ" whereby we are, through the holy ghost, "mystically and spiritually, yet, truly, really and substantially so ingraffed and united into Christ, that wee are made one with him, and he one with us," Eaton reasons that such a union does not consist merely in charity, love, or affection; this is a real and "substantial union," made evident by "that excellent prayer that Christ made for all the faithful, John 17, 20, 21, 22, 23."[107] We have seen the enthusiastic embrace of this Johannine rhetoric of indwelling in Niclaes's writings and the work of the Traskites. Yet Eaton, more than other nonconformists, will marvel at the mystical, ineffable quality of such a process, using it as a source text for his idiosyncratic conception of God's-eye sanctification.

Eaton's *The Honey-combe of Free Justification* brings us again to the question of the distinctiveness of Johannine mysticism and the manner in which such Christ-mysticism appealed to the antinomian tradition.[108] As I remarked in the preceding chapter on Johannine *agape*, we do not find in the Johannine writings the ecstatic or vision-mysticism typical of the medieval tradition or the writings of Teresa d'Avila. The direct apprehension of God is emphatically not part of the Johannine worldview. The Father is apprehended through the Son, and the Son is the only one who has seen the Father.[109] Although the language of self-emptying and ecstatic absorption is suggested in the most radical antinomian appropriations of John's writings (hinted at in Niclaes's works and here in Eaton's *The Honey-combe*), most antinomians found in John's Fourth Gospel the semi-mystical language of mutuality and immanence that allowed for an analogical, fundamentally Christological approach to union with God. The oneness that Christ enjoys with the Father can itself be duplicated in the oneness that the believer can achieve with Christ.[110] This sort of Johannine mediated mysticism has been connected to various sources, including the Hermetic writings, the neo-Platonism of Philo, Mandean dualism,

---

[106] Ibid., 51, 257.   [107] Ibid., 429.

[108] Although she does not focus specifically on the Johannine influence on mid-century mysticism, Sarah Apetrei makes a convincing argument that "mysticism should be rehabilitated as an important theme in the scholarship of early modern English religion," remarking that "the turn to mysticism was part of the same movement that led to a radical critique of Christian orthodoxy." " 'Between the Rational and the Mystical': The Inner Life and the Early English Enlightenment," in *Mysticism and Reform, 1400–1750*, eds. Sara S. Poor and Nigel Smith (Notre Dame: University of Notre Dame Press, 2015), 202–3.

[109] C. H. Dodd distinguishes ecstatic versions of mysticism from the Johannine union with God in *The Interpretation of the Fourth Gospel* (Cambridge: Cambridge University Press, 1965), 197–200. More recent studies of the distinctiveness of Johannine mysticism include Jey J. Kanagaraj, *"Mysticism" in the Gospel of John: An Inquiry into its Background* (London: Bloomsbury T&T Clark, 1998), which traces Johannine mysticism to first-century Palestinian-Jewish mysticism, and April D. DeConick, *Voices of the Mystics: Early Christian Discourse in the Gospels of John and Thomas and Other Ancient Christian Literature* (London: Bloomsbury T&T Clark, 2004), which discusses John's distance from vision mysticism, chapter 3, *passim*.

[110] On mutual indwelling, see Dodd, *The Interpretation of the Fourth Gospel*, 195.

and more generally Hellenistic mysticism.[111] Yet the antinomians, even those who directly revive some of these traditions (such as John Everard, to whose work we turn momentarily) find their Christ-mysticism directly in the Johannine writings, which provide sufficient sources from which to fashion a perfectionistic theology.[112]

Just what, finally, does Eaton's imputative disposition on justification achieve beyond a polemical defense of moderate antinomianism against charges of radicalism by the Pietists? Given that Eaton and Towne do not deny the importance of sanctified works, the imputative line is not, behaviorally speaking, notably different from the inherentist position. Certainly the assumption that the sinner is seen as pure by God, if not by the Christian community, helps the Eatonists to imagine a reliably comforting rather than an unpredictably punitive *deus absconditus*. But more than this, such a position allows the Eatonists, garbed in their sanctified wedding clothing, to imagine themselves as the privileged few who, from their own divinely sanctioned perspective, can distinguish those who are alive from those who are dead in faith. The Eatonists find in the Johannine material as rigid a dualistic worldview as do their seemingly more radical Familist progenitors.

JOHN EVERARD: JOHANNINE PEDAGOGY

Among mid-seventeenth-century dissenters, perhaps the most subtle but also the most sustained attention to Johannine theology is found in the sermons of John Everard. Everard, who did not forthrightly advance a separatist ideology, was an enthusiastic preacher and prolific writer whose presence was felt most strongly in the 1620s in England, during which time he was under the watchful eye of King James's Laudian conformists for his seditious writings.[113] Religious historians have had some trouble situating Everard's theology in relation to prevailing dissenting and more conforming early modern religious worldviews. Given Everard's evident

---

[111] A foundational study of the influence of Hellenistic mysticism on Johannine theology is Dodd's *The Interpretation of the Fourth Gospel*, especially 10–73.

[112] The most radical appropriations of Johannine notions of union and dwelling occasion the invective of anti-separatists such as Anthony Burgess, who devotes an entire treatise to the perceived misappropriations of the language of dwelling and participation in John 17. Burgess believes, for example, that verse 17:23—"I in them, and thou in mee, that they may bee made perfect in one, and that the world may know that thou hast sent me, and hast loved them, as thou hast loved me"—gives rise to "*erroneous and dangerous conceits about Christs being in his people*," pointing out that "When Christ is said to be in his people, *That is not to be understood, as if there were a confusion of their beings, or as if they were made one reall and physical person with him*; for thus some have dangerously affirmed, That we are *Christed* with *Christ*, and made one reall person with Christ. It is true, Christ and his people make up one spiritual and mystical Person; They are not to be considered as two, no more then the Head and the body, yet it's an hainous errour, as also high non-sense, to affirm such a being of Christ in us, as that we are turned into Christ" (621–2). Against such "nonsensical" notions of being "transessentiated" into God, Burgess argues that the Evangelist often speaks metaphorically and that union typically signifies to be "with" rather than "in," the former suggesting that Christ "operates" through individuals rather than dwelling within them (623). *CXLV expository sermons upon the whole 17th chapter of the Gospel according to St. John, or, Christs prayer before his passion explicated* (London, 1656).

[113] On Everard's biography, see Smith, *Perfection Proclaimed*, 110–14, as well as Como, *Blown by the Spirit*, 219–28.

interest as translator in the neo-Platonic works of the Pseudo-Dionysius as well as his engagement with the alchemical writings of Hermes Trismegistus, David Como and others have declared Everard's indebtedness to a broad sectarian tradition of mysticism that includes the influential *Theologia Germanica* and source texts by Nicholas of Cusa and Maimonides.[114]

Yet Everard's perfectionism—his diminution of legalism and moralism in favor of free justification—also places him in a line of continuity with the Familists and Eatonists. Everard, too, advances a view of the perfect life of the believer in Christ, but he enhances his perfectionism with a realized eschatology that has already separated those who are in Christ from those who are not. That Everard's theology is built upon a Johannine edifice is suggested in the following exaltation of John's theology over any other, a passage that I quote at length because Everard's heavy reliance on John has gone mostly unnoticed among religious historians:

> Yet I must tell you more, That this word and Christ and the Spirit All dwell Among us, dwell In us, and we know them not: as John 1. 10. He was in the world, and the world was made by him; He dwels among us, and yet the world knows him not; nay, He came among his Own, and his Own received him not: These are strange expressions; what may be the meaning of this Divine high-flowen Eagle? (for that is his Embleme:) I conceive it was, to shew that he soared and flew higher in Divine contemplations of truth, and in the knowledge of the Mystery, then all the rest of the Evangelists; This was he of whom it is said, The Disciple whom Jesus loved, and this is he that leaned on his breast at supper: This was he that had all those divine visions and Secret mysteries revealed to him in the Isle of Pathmos, who writ the Revelation, and was therefore called JOHN the Divine. I conceive his meaning is (when he saith, He came and dwelt among us, and yet the world knew him not, although it was made by him) was this, that God in Jesus Christ dwells in every creature, but the creature comprehends it not, Because the light shineth in darkness, and the Darkness cannot comprehend the light.[115]

It makes sense that Everard would hold up John as the most visionary and illuminating apostle. John speaks not literally of God's and Christ's ways but indirectly through mysteries and riddles; this is an approach to divulging and sorting out knowledge that Everard favors throughout his sermons. One of those mysteries has to do not simply with the indwelling nature of God in believers but with our inability fully to discern God's presence, given that we do not fully understand the light that is the Son.

Earlier in his sermons, Everard provides glosses on Johannine scenes such as Christ's encounter with the woman at Samaria in order to explain the importance of pedagogical lessons culled from discipleship misunderstanding, particularly the sense that one must experience Christ rather than merely read or hear about him: "If thou knowest the Letter of the Scriptures never so exactly...thou never yet understoodst what the Word of God was: but finding these things in thee, thou wilt say as those Samaritans said to the woman of Samaria, who told them she had

---

[114] See Como, *Blown by the Spirit*, chapter 7, *passim*.
[115] John Everard, *The Gospel treasury opened* (London, 1657), 349–50.

met with Christ the Messiah: but when they themselves had conferred with him, say they, now we believe him to be so, not because thou saidst so, but because we have seen him and found him so to our selves: so mayest thou say, now I believe, not only because it is written in Gen, but because I have felt it, and seen it written & fulfilled in mine own soul."[116] The sentiment here is consistent with Everard's abiding belief that traditional scripturalism takes the words of the Bible too literally. Traditional or overly literal exegesis neglects to acknowledge that Christ's experiences (which believers should be able to recreate within themselves) are the route to Godhead:

> Yet much ado there hath been among many men about this Letter of the word, who pretend to know much in Gods word, as if they knew whatever were to be known.... And in our dayes, and in our Nation, what talk is there everywhere of Gods word, when indeed and in truth most men are ignorant of Gods word? [A]nd all is, because they take these Literal, black letters to be The word of God.... These Letters cannot be The word of God.... The letter doth but bear Witness to the truth; Christ is the Truth, and the letter gives Testimony to him: See what the Evangelist sayes The Word is, Joh. 1. In the beginning was the word (Bibles were not then) and the word was God.[117]

Informing Everard's critique of scriptural literalism is an accommodationist approach to interpretation. The words in the Bible do not contain unassailably literal truths. Scripture offers at best concessions to the limits of creaturely sensibility in appreciating the extent to which Christ as the Word can be found within the believer.[118]

But if John's Gospel underlies Everard's anti-literal understanding of the mysterious nature of Christ's teachings, that same Gospel provides perseverance to the faithful who worry that the path to righteousness is too arduous. After outlining the path toward the mystical emptying of the sinner in the face of God—which includes "self-annihilation" (accounting of our souls as "nothing"), abdication of the world, indifference to all things, and conformity with Christ—Everard provides a crucial "qualification" to provide "comfort and encouragement": "God is in you, although you know it not; as you know there are in us all those parts, those organs and instruments of life by which we breath and live.... As John said concerning Christ, There is one in the midst of you whom you know not... I say so of you, there is one among you, and yet alas, you see him not, you know him not."[119] Anticipating that these stark words might seem elusive or too lofty, Everard makes recourse again to Nicodemus in order to describe the ways in which John and he, Everard himself, rely on a principle of accommodation to make Christ's ways palatable to those novices in faith: "But these things are somewhat too high, and you cannot conceive (it may be) what I mean by these expressions. But I shall come

---

[116] Ibid., 288.   [117] Ibid., 347–8.

[118] Ibid., 288, where Everard remarks: "Thus God is pleased, for our capacities and comprehensions, to convey to us the knowledge of this inward work within us, by *external representations* to our understanding; that so we may comprehend *Those things,* that are so far above us."

[119] Ibid., 134.

lower to your capacities, and shall make you acquainted with these hidden things, and make them familiar to you."[120] In addition to his repeated references to the Samaritan episode—a staple of discipleship misunderstanding—Everard recounts the ways in which Christ renders the nature of conversion understandable to Nicodemus:

> Saith our Saviour to Nicodemus....Except a man be born again, he cannot see the Kingdom of God; Christ was now too high for him: See (for all he was such a great and learned man among the Jews) what an ignorant and a fleshly answer he makes Christ, Can a man enter into his mothers womb and be born again? Christ falls lower to his understanding; (saith he) That which is born of flesh is Single illegible letterlesh, and that which is born of the Spirit is Spirit: He falls lower still, to familiar comparisons to make him understand; Marvel not that I said unto thee, ye must be born again. The wind (now I am in thy element wherein thou understandest, even among the creatures) It bloweth whither it listeth, and thou hearest the sound, but knowest not whence it cometh or whither it goeth; so is every one that is born of the Spirit.[121]

Everard here and elsewhere will not borrow the marrow of a key Johannine text so much as he will refashion the structure, style, and form of Johannine address, in this case positioning himself as Christ and drawing a comparison between the way in which Christ instructs Nicodemus and the way in which he, Everard, will instruct his auditors: "So, would you know of me how far these *high* truths may be dispensed with, and what is the *lowest* degree in grace you must come to, if ye would be saved? Thus; though God call you not to that degree of suffering, as he doth some others; yet there ought to be a propension and an Affection to it, to aim at it, though you reach it not."[122] Everard relies here on the pedagogical rhetoric of Johannine theology. He has translated high matters to a bottom-line conception of grace in order to make a relatively simple accommodative point. Like "babes" we must stake an ardent disposition toward Christ, since "Christ will *perfect that disposition* in his due time."[123]

The final thoroughly Johannine aspect of Everard's sermons is their realized eschatology, which provides additional comfort to those who would doubt their salvation. Everard relies on John 8:51 and 18:36 in order to advise his devoted readers that they need not fret about apocalyptic events, since they have already been saved:

> Whatever is externally done in the world, and expressed in the Scriptures, is but Typical and Representative and points out, A more spiritual and saving salvation, and a more Divine fulfilling of them....Christ takes them off from all those things; and saith, My Kingdom is not of this world, for them would my servants fight to obtain this their Kingdome; but the Kingdome of heaven is within you; for men may have their part in these external Powers, Scepters, Crowns and Kingdoms, and have no part in Christs Kingdom; Therefore all those thoughts are but Literal and low, and poor, and childish: but let us mind such a Kingdom, wherein if we have but the least part,

---

[120] Ibid., 135.   [121] Ibid., 135–6.   [122] Ibid., 136.   [123] Ibid., 136.

the least share, that if we be but Door-keepers, then we are Happy for ever, and shall never perish, neither in this world, nor in that to come.[124]

Here we have an additional reason to maintain assurance, Everard concludes. Scripture is "already fulfilled" for the faithful (Everard earlier echoes the perfectionist contention that, as Eaton maintains, Christ has purged all sin from believers). Informing this eschatology is the dualism that we have seen in so much of the dissenting literature. Yet Everard will spend more time outlining the nature and reach of Antichrist, reminding his brethren of the contemporary relevance of 1 John 2:18. Although there may be many Antichrists among them (and not only far removed in Rome), they will remain safe from worldliness if they remember that Christ is within them.[125]

Everard does not develop a systematic doctrine of assurance or perseverance, but his theological sureties depart from the covenant theology that is enshrined in the Westminster Confession of Faith of 1648. That formulary, heavily influenced theologically by the federalism of William Perkins, is established by Presbyterians and Nonconformists in Scotland who rejected the Act of Uniformity. The Confession distinguishes in Chapter XVIII assurance from faith, pointing out the difficulty of perseverance even among the saints: "Infallible assurance does not so belong to the essence of faith, but that a true believer may wait long, and conflict with many difficulties, before he be partaker of it."[126] What Everard and radical dissenters took from John was the dogma, if not doctrine, that with faith, described as belief in Christ's mission and his Word, assurance would inevitably follow.

Perhaps because of the syncretistic nature of Everard's theology—at once mystical, Hermetic, antinomian, and perfectionistic—religious historians have overlooked the important influence of John on Everard's theology. When Everard's apostolic sources are adduced, Saint Paul emerges as the most influential on Everard's thinking, particularly because Everard reverts to some key Pauline passages on the law–gospel relationship that help to justify his anti-legalism. David Como remarks that one of Everard's references to Galatians 5:18, which Como describes as the "most unequivocally 'antinomian' passage of the Pauline epistles"— "But if yee be lead of the spirit, yee are not under the Law"—is a "basic indicator of English antinomianism" that one finds in Everard's sermons.[127] In terms of the question of how the simple "power of love" might guide believers without clear legal precepts for action, Como continues, "How, without a law (and hence an external compulsion) of some sort, were believers to know what to do? Everard, like other antinomians—and indeed like Saint Paul himself—provided no concrete answer to this question. Those who were inhabited and ruled by Christ would simply know."[128] Yet I would suggest that, if Paul's letters and the Synoptic Gospels provide source texts for Everard for an understanding of the way in which faith

---

[124] Ibid., 94–5.   [125] Ibid., 179.

[126] On the covenantalism of the Westminster Confession, see Graham Redding, *Prayer and the Priesthood of Christ in the Reformed Tradition* (London: Bloomsbury T&T Clark, 2003), 166–78. See also R. T. Kendall, *Calvin and English Calvinism to 1649* (Eugene: Wipf & Stock, 1997), chapter 13, *passim*.

[127] Como, *Blown by the Spirit*, 260.   [128] Ibid., 261.

displaces law, John's theology more readily provides confidence to converts that they can indeed act properly once they acknowledge the benefits of loving and believing in Christ. These benefits would include a sense of rarefied, even exclusive communality with other believers and confidence that the *eschaton* has already arrived. Everard's relationship to his apostolic sources realizes the ways in which John's theology relates to Paul—namely, that as is often noted in Johannine studies, John in a sense completes Paul. Everard fashions from Johannine material a distinctive approach to understanding scripture that is not a primary concern of Paul. This includes an awareness of the purely symbolic and figural understanding of Christ's messages and the need, given the ease with which believers misunderstand or take too literally Christ's words, for an enlightened interpreter like Everard himself. It is not simply that John provides Everard and his readers with decisive answers to the questions that, for Como, remain unanswered in Everard's sermons. John endows Everard and his readers with the confidence to believe that, through a methodical process of self-questioning, they can *experience* and at least approach an understanding of God's will for them.[129]

THE DIVINE ANOINTING: GERRARD WINSTANLEY'S JOHANNINE *ESCHATON*

From Everard's illuminism we move fittingly to the related millenarian and visionary writings of the True Leveller or Digger, Gerrard Winstanley. Winstanley's writings throughout the English Interregnum are well known for their political activism, even proto-communism. Not surprisingly, given Winstanley's outspoken sectarianism, we find a number of Johannine themes converging in some of his most theologically focused treatises, including *The Breaking of the Day of God* (1649) and *The New Law of Righteousness* (1649). Unlike most other mid-century sectarians, Winstanley uniquely incorporates John's Gospel and First Epistle into the Book of Revelation. The millenarianism of the latter is often read into and hence radicalizes the more qualified eschatology of the Fourth Gospel and the First Epistle. Winstanley, like Everard but in contrast to the mainstream of English writings on John, ambiguates any distinction between John the Evangelist and John of Patmos, even though he at times will refer to the former as the "Evangelist" and the latter as "St. John."[130]

At the outset of *The Breaking of the Day*, Winstanley offers the usual antinomian fare on world-withdrawal and union with God, drawing especially on 1 John 5:5: "The Saints break the Serpents head by Christs strength in them, even the same Anointing: and hence it is that Christ the head, That his Disciples, or body mystical, might be one with him, as he and his Father were one....And so again, who is he that overcometh the world, but he that believeth that Jesus the Anointed is

---

[129] Ibid., 260–1.
[130] Gerrard Winstanley, *The Breaking of the Day of God* (London, 1649), 19.

the Son of God."[131] So much is what we would expect from Winstanley's familiarity with 1 John 2:27, 1 John 5:5, and John 17:21. But in Winstanley's topical use of the Johannine material, one additionally finds (reminiscent of Everard's approach) a direct analogy between the ways in which Jesus and his ministry are hated by the Pharisees, according to John's historical presentation, and the manner in which Winstanley's sectarian auditors are vilified by seventeenth-century Presbyterians and Conformists:

> But what's the reason, the world doth so storm against you; but because you are not of the world, nor cannot walk in the dark wayes of the world; they hated your Lord and Master, Jesus Christ, and they hate you; they knew not him, and they know not you; for if they had known him, they would not have crucified him; and if they did truly know the power of that God, that dwels in you, they would not so despise you. But well: these things must be; it is your Fathers will it shall be so, the world must lie under darkness for a time, that is Gods dispensation to them; and you that are Children of light, must lie under reproach and oppressions of the world; that is Gods dispensation to you. But it shall be but for a little time. What I have here to say, is to bring you glad tydings, that your redemption drawes neer.[132]

Here in Winstanley's proclamation in the epistle to the reader, addressed to the "despised sons and daughters of Zion, scattered up and down the kingdome of England," we have an explicitly stated correlation between the hostility toward and lack of knowledge of Christ's ways among the Pharisees (John 15:19 and 1 John 3:1) and the marginalization of Winstanley's own emergent dissenting community.[133] This framing analogy, which is implicit throughout the entire treatise, allows Winstanley not only to dismantle chronological, then/now distinctions between the secessionism of the first-century Johannine conventicle and his own dissenting community but also to proclaim the *Parousia* for his own time. And like Everard and Niclaes, Winstanley will co-opt the power of light, the province of the Johannine Christ, for Winstanley will "only hold forth to my fellow creature, man; not customarily to make a trade of it, for fleshly ends, but occasionally as the Light is pleased to manifest himself in me; that others from me, and I from them may be witnesses each to other."[134]

Winstanley's apocalyptic strategy is not simply to gloss key texts from Revelation but to integrate Revelation with John's Gospel and First Epistle. The putative subject of *The Breaking of the Day* is an explication of the two witnesses referred to in Revelation 11:3 ("And I will give power unto my two witnesses, and they shall prophesie a thousand two hundred and threescore dayes clothed in sackcloth").

---

[131] Ibid., 11–12.   [132] Ibid., second page.

[133] I agree with John Richard Gurney's belief that, although Winstanley's early works tend toward mysticism, such works are also politically engaged. See Gurney, *Brave Community: The Digger Movement in the English Revolution* (Manchester: Manchester University Press, 2007), 97. In *Uncloistered Virtue: English Political Literature, 1640–1660* (Oxford: Clarendon Press, 1992), Thomas N. Corns tends to undervalue the theological integrity and political import of the early pre-Digger tracts, remarking that "the early pamphlets manifest difficulties in structure, in clarity of exposition, and in the image of the author produced within them, and Winstanley seems to have a poor notion of whom he is addressing and what effect he wishes to have upon them" (151–2).

[134] Gerrard Winstanley, *The New Law of Righteousness* (London, 1649).

Revelation records that the witnesses will prophesy on behalf of the world for 1260 days, after which they will be killed by the beast but rise quickly in three and a half days. Winstanley argues that the role of the witnesses is to bear testimony to the eternal will of God, especially the protevangelium or promise that the seed of the woman shall bruise the serpent's head (Gen. 3:15). Yet he emphasizes, drawing on Corinthians and Ephesians, that the serpent will be defeated by the entire city of Zion, one corporate spiritual body, the "Spirit of the Father."[135] The identities of the two witnesses (typically associated with the prophets, Moses and Elijah) are, according to Winstanley's typological vision, Christ and the faithful saints who have been anointed with Christ's spirit.[136] These two witnesses provided visible testimony of both Christ's glory and the "mysteries of the Kingdom of God" for the designated 1260 days, but they were eventually slain by the "beast."[137] However, according to Winstanley's topical shift of the narrative in real time, they are about to rise as predicted: "I believe they have lien dead, well nigh their full time, if not compleat; for I believe they are upon their rising."[138] England is currently living under the "day of the Beast," in which "under the name of Round-heads," the Saints of God have been condemned to death. Yet Babylon is falling, "for the spirit of life appears in some already, and will appear in more ere long, (when the showre of hayl falls,) And God takes up his Saints to himself."[139]

If Revelation provides Winstanley with the overall framework for his apocalyptic narrative, including the appropriate symbols, chronology of the rising of the witnesses, and the eventual overcoming of the beast, John's Gospel and First Epistle provide him with the content and personnel, the veritable flesh of that narrative. Revelation dictates *why* and *when* the witnesses will return, but the Fourth Gospel and First Epistle delineate *who* will return. The discourse of the vine helps to legitimate Winstanley's claim that the second witness consists of Christ's original faithful ministry/Winstanley's devout readers and followers: "Those whom the Father hath chosen and given to *Jesus* the anointed, and writ their names in him, the Lambs Book, makes up but one Son of God, being all partakers of one Spirit."[140] Similarly, the Longinus piercing of Christ, which allows for the flowing of water and blood from Christ's side, reflects the extent to which the two witnesses are really one in Christ: "This is he that came by water and bloud, and not by water only, but by water and bloud; and this Christ came not only in himself, but in his Saints, whom he sanctifies and washeth in his bloud; and it is the spirit that beares witness, because though the bodies be weak."[141] Indeed, John's Gospel at times serves as the interpretive key and proof-text for Revelation, as when Winstanley will explain functional symbols from Revelation 11—the two olive trees and candlesticks, for example—in terms of John 1:16 ("And of his fulnesse have all wee received, and grace for grace"): "Now brethren you know, that the Church and Saints doe not receive light, life & grace, from any other but from Christ; *Of his fulnesse we receive grace for grace:* Therefore these two *Olive-trees,* these two *Candlestickes* which *John* speaks of, and these two *Witnesses* which God glories in,

[135] Winstanley, *Breaking of the Day of God*, 9.   [136] Ibid., 32.   [137] Ibid., 44.
[138] Ibid., 86.   [139] Ibid., 97.   [140] Ibid., 9–10.   [141] Ibid., 22.

and calleth *His Witnesses,* must needs be meant Christ and his Spirit."[142] At other times, Winstanley advances a nuanced typological understanding of the eschatological relationship between John's Gospel and First Epistle, on the one hand, and more overtly apocalyptic narratives of Revelation, Ezekiel, and Zechariah, on the other hand.

It is not the case that Revelation simply continues or realizes what is expressed in the Fourth Gospel and First Epistle. Revelation rather makes available to believers and nonbelievers what John's Gospel and First Epistle entrust to a select ministry of Christ's devoted followers. John 14 and 16 warrant Winstanley's proclamation that, after the death of Christ, the faithful will be entrusted to the Paraclete who will maintain the covenant of grace for believers: "God sent his Spirit the comforter, to testifie his unchangeable love to the Church, and to lead her into all truth; because he is the Spirit of truth: And so in the bodily absence of Christ, the Spirit, which is the *Lord our Righteousnesse,* ruling as a King in love in them, doth counsell, comfort, sanctifie, and remaines with the Church for ever."[143] Christ's work has already been realized and will be maintained by the ongoing mission of the Spirit in Christ's stead. According to the promissory terms of 1 John 5:10, those who believe have already achieved a state of perfect witnessing. These same believers now function as witnesses of the world-changing events recorded in Revelation 11:6:

> God proves Christ in his two-fold appearance, that is, in his own person, and in flesh, or persons of his Saints, to be his two witnesses; for saith he in the 6. verse of the eleventh chapter of the *Revelations. These have power to shut Heaven, that it raine not in the dayes of their Prophesie; and have power over waters to turn them into bloud; and to smite the Earth with all plagues as oft as they will.*[144]

The metaphor of shutting heaven from rain is further interpreted by Winstanley to signify the means by which the "beast is destroyed" by the witnesses: "The Witnesses have a power to shut the Church, or Heaven, from raining in this kind, till their Prophesie be ended, as God appointed: And then (I believe) there shall appear plentifull manifestations of Gods love in the Church."[145] The net result is both the destruction of the beast and an increase of the number of Saints in the latter days.[146]

We can see that John's Gospel and First Epistle have been transformed into prophetic texts or at least enlisted in the service of explaining the prophecies of Revelation that will come to pass. But more than this, the Gospel and Epistle establish the community of disciples who will then expand in strength and number as the testifiers of Revelation. This entails their own acquisition of clearer knowledge of what is originally provided to them in the earlier texts: "To hear that Christ was raised from death, and from the grave, is joy. But to see and feel Christ the Anointing, raised upon me; and to feel him who is the spring of life, to be opened in me, and to send forth sweet manifestations of God to my soul, this is much more joyous."[147] Winstanley compares here the knowledge of the anointing

---

[142] Ibid., 27.   [143] Ibid., 26.   [144] Ibid., 36.   [145] Ibid., 40.
[146] Ibid., 36.   [147] Ibid., 65.

and union with God that he has acquired from John's First Epistle with the experience and spoken expression of the knowledge of the overcoming of the serpent that is predicted in Revelation 2:17. Revelation serves not merely as a fulfillment text relative to the earlier Johannine material; it allows for the Johannine ministry (maintained since Christ's Ascension by the anointing of the continual presence of the Paraclete) to acquire more refined knowledge of what constitutes fit membership in that community.

What finally brings Winstanley together with Everard, beyond their shared eschatology, is Winstanley's anti-literal understanding of scripture, itself informed by his distinctive concept of spirit-anointing.[148] In the *Mysterie of God* (1649), Winstanley cites the Johannine belief that God's anointing provides a sufficient pedagogy for the saints: "But the anointing which ye have received of him abideth in you, and ye need not that any man teach you: but as the same anointing teacheth you of all things, and is truth, and is no lie, and even as it hath taught you, ye shall abide in him" (1 John 26).[149] From this text Winstanley concludes that only hirelings preach from the "book" rather than from the "anointing":

> Now the Church is at a stand, and the worship is partly light, and partly dark; some resting upon the bare letter, according to the example of Christ, and the Apostles only, which is a worship after the flesh, and was true, and was of *God* in the time of its dispensation. And others do acknowledge *God,* not exemplarily, but by the faith, the name, and anointing of Jesus Christ, ruling, teaching, acting, and dwelling in them.[150]

Legitimating Winstanley's anti-scripturalism is again a direct analogy between the original Johannine context and the mid-seventeenth-century turmoil in England. The same true testimony is "suppressed," then and now, "for the same spirit of the world, the serpent, does still persecute the same anointing of *God* in this, as in the former dispensation."[151]

In *The New Law of Righteousness*, Winstanley boldly proclaims the power of each individual to provide his or her own spiritual tutelage, to script his or her own sermons, as against the "publique preachers" who profess Christ without the proper knowledge gained from spiritual anointing:

> A Sermon is a speech made from the man-seer, which is Christ within; for this anointing sees the Father in every thing.... Now that man or woman that sees the Spirit, within themselves, how he enlightens, how he kils the motions of the flesh, and makes the flesh subject to Righteousnesse, and so can see *light in his light;* this man or woman is able to make a Sermon, because they can speak by experience of the light and power of Christ within them.[152]

Several Johannine proof-texts converge to justify this conclusion. From John 10:13 Winstanley takes the metaphor of the hireling as poor shepherd and applies it to England's "blind guides"; from John 1:9 he borrows the language of Christ as "true

---

[148] For more on Winstanley's anti-formalism and quest for experimental knowledge, see Gurney, *Brave Community*, 91.

[149] Gerrard Winstanley, *The Mysterie of God* (London, 1649).   [150] Ibid., 34.

[151] Ibid., 34–5.   [152] Winstanley, *The New Law of Righteousness*, 69, 74.

light" to justify the personal light of each believer; and from John 3:11 he takes the notion of inward testimony to provide the credibility for each saint to construct his or her own sermon or homily.[153] And what knits together the entire narrative of scriptural autodidactism is the theme of anointing with the spirit that threads through all of Winstanley's millenarian writings. Winstanley's vision is the pedagogical apotheosis of the antinomians' typical projection of the Christological light onto themselves. The faithful have so internalized that light of truth that they are rendered suitable to preach their own Gospel.

THE LIGHT WITHIN: GEORGE FOX AND QUAKER SECTARIANISM

Winstanley's appropriation of the true light metaphor from the Johannine Prologue brings us finally to early modern English Quaker apologetics. Religious historians have spent more time outlining the Johannine influence on the early Quaker movement than on any other seventeenth-century separatist group.[154] Surveying the recurring use of the Fourth Gospel in the Quaker writings of George Fox, Robert Barclay, and others, Howard Brinton remarks: "It is fair to comment that the theology of the Society of Friends is essentially Johannine theology."[155] Brinton has in mind not only the seminal verse at 1:9—"That was the true light, which lighteth every man that commeth into the world"—but also the entire Prologue of the Fourth Gospel as well as Johannine dualism and pneumatology more generally. Many of the cherished beliefs of Quaker theology—universal enlightenment, the active presence of Christ, the elevation of the experimental rather than the scriptural-historical witness of the Spirit—have been traced back in one form or another to Johannine theology. This seems to be particularly true of the epistles and notable *Journal* of George Fox, about which Douglas Gwyn remarks, "Fox follows the radical Christology of John in believing Christ to be the Word of God who, in his incarnation, life, death, and resurrection, has fulfilled the history and scriptures of Israel. Then, in his revelation within the individual, this same Word recapitulates history in personal experience."[156] This cornerstone of Fox's theology—his refusal to separate the historical Christ and the spirit of truth within the believer—bears some additional scrutiny, as does the often-noted Quaker identification of the Friends as indwelt lights. We will see that the Quaker reception of the controverted text, John 1:9, itself opens out to larger separatist concerns regarding the authority of scripture relative to experimental piety.

---

[153] Ibid., 74.

[154] See, for example, Howard H. Brinton, *The Religious Philosophy of Quakerism: The Beliefs of Fox, Barclay, and Penn as Based on the Gospel of John* (Wallingford, PA: Pendle Hill Publications, 1973).

[155] Howard H. Brinton, *Friends for 300 Years: The History and Beliefs of the Society of Friends since George Fox Started the Quaker Movement* (New York: Harper & Brothers, 1952), 38.

[156] Douglas Gwyn, *Apocalypse of the Word: The Life and Message of George Fox (1624–1691)* (Richmond, Indiana: Friends United Press, 1986), 95.

That John 1:9 was the pivotal Quaker text is acknowledged by the most analytically erudite spokesperson for the early Quaker movement, Robert Barclay. Barclay's *An apology for the true Christian divinity* (1678) approaches more closely a formulaic Quaker statement of faith than does any other influential Quaker writing, including Fox's more popularly accessible *Journal*. In the *Apology* Barclay states forthwith that John 1:9 has rightfully been deemed the Quakers' text: "This place doth so clearly favour us, that, by some, it is called *the Quaker[s'] Text*, for it doth evidently demonstrate our Assertion, so that it scarce needs either consequence or deduction."[157] The verse needs no special elaboration, Barclay believes, because it serves as an "inference" of the two preceding verses at 1:4–5: "In him was life, and the life was the light of men. And the light shineth in darknesse, and the darknesse comprehended it not."[158] All men who walk in the light, which is "communicated" to them by Christ, enjoy "fellowship and communion" with Christ. Only spiritual obstinacy would prevent one from walking in the saving light: "So that it is plain, there comes no Man into the World, whom Christ hath not enlightened, in some measure, and in whose dark Heart this *Light* doth not shine, though the Darkness comprehend it not, yet it shineth there."[159]

Yet John 1:9 was not so axiomatically clear to Barclay's Puritan and Conformist interlocutors, many of whom followed Calvin in distinguishing the divine light of Christ from the natural light of human reason.[160] Addressing those "fanatics" who "seize" on the verse and "twist it" into signifying that the grace of illumination is offered to all without distinction, Calvin points out that "it is only referring to the common light of nature, a far lowlier thing than faith."[161] And this lowlier light of reason, Calvin reminds his readers, has of course been so dimmed by sin that only a "few meager sparks" remain amid such an abyss of errors.[162]

William Allen, a nonconforming Parliamentarian at the outbreak of the civil war, occupies the Calvinist position in *The danger of enthusiasm discovered in an epistle to the Quakers* (1678): "Christ indeed…doth enlighten every man that comes into the world, with the faculty of Reason and Understanding, by which he may know that there is a God, and that he is to be worshipped, and that he is placable; and the difference between moral good and evil in many things.…Yet this

---

[157] Robert Barclay, *An apology for the true Christian divinity* (London?, 1678), Fifth Proposition, 103. Barclay's estimation of John 1:9 is cited in D. Elton Trueblood, *Robert Barclay* (New York: Harper & Row, 1968), 155.

[158] Barclay, *An apology for the true Christian divinity*, 103.   [159] Ibid., 103.

[160] In response to Richard Baxter's distinction between the light of nature and the supernatural light of revelation, George Fox replies that Baxter is a "man not fit to teach," for he is "ignorant of *Johns* doctrine, and the Scriptures." *The great mistery of the great whore unfolded* (London, 1659), 28. A detailed discussion of this debate between Fox and Baxter can be found in Geoffrey Nuttall, *The Holy Spirit in Puritan Faith and Experience* (Oxford: Basil Blackwell, 1947), 47–8.

[161] *The Gospel According to St. John*, in *Calvin's New Testament Commentaries*, vol. 4, eds. David W. Torrance and Thomas F. Torrance, trans. T. H. L. Parker (Grand Rapids: Eerdmans Publishing Company, 1959), 15.

[162] Ibid., 15.

Natural Light is *not sufficient* to direct those that live under the Gospel, to believe and do what they are bound to believe and do."[163] The natural light needs supplementing with supernatural revelation, by which Allen means external and mediate scriptural revelation tied to obedience and faith, precisely the mode of biblical testimony that is rejected by Quaker experimentalism.[164] Dozens of extant, late-seventeenth-century tracts against enthusiasm reiterate the point. To take just two examples: against his adversaries who would conclude that this "Light is Christ himself, the true Light," Edward Beckham, in *The principles of the Quakers further shewn to be blasphemous and seditious* (1700), concludes that such a light is "but a Ray from that Sun, an Illumination from the Father of Lights," and hence men come into the world with only the "Light of Reason, human Understanding, and natural Conscience."[165] William Mather, a disillusioned Quaker himself, ranges Proverbs against the Quaker conception of John 1:9: "It appears they own but *one Light* that we were born with. This *Light*, or Understanding, tho it be called, *The Candle of the Lord, Prov.* 20.27. which reproves for some sins, yet is but a dim Light to see spiritual things by."[166] The only means by which God's candle is "lightened" further is through divine grace and the Holy Scripture.[167]

Quakers certainly did attribute the light within to Christological illumination and universal enlightenment rather than right reason, a heritable divine spark or, in neo-scholastic jargon, the *synderesis*. And Quaker rhetoric on the subject of enlightenment at times approaches the Familist understanding of divine immanence and a mystical incorporation into Christ's true light. Drawing on some well-known comments in Fox's *Journal* in which Fox remarks, "The Father and Son are one, and we are of his flesh and of his bone," one scholar of early modern Quakerism describes Fox's Christology as "integrated immanence," in which Christ is "substantially as well as spiritually present to the believer."[168]

And yet Fox typically offers a less ontological, and more epistemological and relational (and hence less tendentious) understanding of John 1:9 than either his contemporary adversaries or religious historians have acknowledged.[169] Oftentimes the enlightenment promised in John 1:9 is pedagogically linked in Fox's *Journal* to belief, self-knowledge, and knowledge of Christ and God: "God who lightneth every man [that] cometh into the world [that] all men through him might

---

[163] William Allen, *The danger of enthusiasm discovered in an epistle to the Quakers* (Amsterdam, 1674), 42.

[164] Ibid., 44.

[165] Edward Beckham, *The principles of the Quakers further shewn to be blasphemous and seditious* (London, 1700), 4.

[166] W. Mather, *An answer to the switch for the snake* (London, 1700), 14.

[167] Ibid., 144.

[168] Hilary Hinds, *George Fox and Early Quaker Culture* (Manchester: Manchester University Press, 2011), 17.

[169] The relational and adoptionist rhetoric of Quaker participation should be weighed against the critical contention that Quaker theology offered a radical "Christopresent" conception of, as Richard Bailey has argued, "celestial inhabitation" or "cohabitation" of the body of Christ and the believer. *New Light on George Fox and Early Quakerism: The Making and Unmaking of a God* (San Francisco: Mellen Research University Press, 1992), 78–9.

beeleeve."[170] With belief come self-scrutiny and an awareness of sin: "with which light they might see there sinns & with the same light they might see there savior {Christ Jesus} to save [them] from there sinns."[171] Once so illuminated, Fox's audi-tors are encouraged to missionize and to disseminate the light and spirit of truth abroad: "In the *Light, Life* and *Power* of *God* you may *spread* his *Truth* abroad, and be valiant for it upon the Earth."[172] When Fox employs the term "union," he typ-ically means incorporation into the gathering Society of Friends: "Walking in this light it enlightens your consciences & understandings, walking in it you have union one with another for the light is but one which will discover all imagned light false worships"; and "every one" who is "in the Light he is in the wisdome of God, & these are they [that] doe well & are in unity one with another."[173]

When Fox does project mutuality among the Friends and Christ/God, the rhet-oric of union shades into the rhetoric of fellowship: "Walk in the light that you may have fellowshipp with the son & with the father and come all to wittnes his image his power and his law which is his light."[174] Detectable here is a distinction between the light within the believer and the light proper to Christ/God, the for-mer allowing for the testimony of the latter. Fellowship with the Son and the Father describes more of an adoption of the enlightened believer into the holy family than it does a substantial or corporeal union: "And therefore every one must believe in the *Light*, if they do receive *Christ Jesus*; and as many as receives him, he gives them *Power to become the Sons of God*."[175] Precisely because it is not typically a theology of divine immanence or purely mystical absorption, Fox's participatory theology is consistent with Johannine theology as I have been reconstructing it throughout the preceding chapters. Christ, the only one who has seen the Father, fosters belief in his way, truth, and life, illuminating those mired in darkness, encouraging the brethren or Friends to love one another as he has loved them, through which they can enjoy the same fellowship with the Son that the Son is privileged to enjoy with the Father.

Yet Fox's interest in John 1:9 stretches well beyond his Christology and his views on saving grace. The verse at 1:9 and related verses are mentioned with astonishing frequency to exact judgment on those reprobates who, due to obstinacy or ignor-ance, refuse to accept Christ's enlightenment. To this end, John 1:5—"And the light shineth in darknesse, and the darknesse comprehended it not"—is often mentioned in tandem with 1:9 as well as with the dualistic sentiments of 3:20: "For every one that doeth evill, hateth the light, neither commeth to the light, lest his deeds should be reproued." The vitriol expressed for those who reject the light is evident in Fox's *Truth's defence against the refined subtilty of the serpent* (1653). Those who hate the light will not merely "stumble"; they will perish in accordance

---

[170] George Fox, *The Journal of George Fox*, vol. 1, ed. Norman Penney (New York: Octagon Books, 1973), 206. When citing Penney's edition, I have slightly modernized the spelling here and throughout.
[171] Ibid., 50.
[172] George Fox, *A journal or historical account of the life, travels, sufferings, Christian experiences and labour of love in the work of the ministry, of ... George Fox* (London, 1694), 415.
[173] *The Journal of George Fox*, vol. 1, ed. Penney, 97, 218.   [174] Ibid., 145.
[175] Fox, *A journal or historical account*, 629.

with John 11, and the "Eternal pure Light shall be... [their] condemnacion."[176] On the one hand, Fox's dualism is a reiteration of the broad antinomian dualism of two worlds that we have been tracking throughout this chapter. On the other hand, Fox, more specifically and overtly than even Everard and Winstanley, will analogize the sectarianism of the early Johannine community to his own mid-century radical break with Puritan nonconformity. Consider passages such as the following: "All stumbling is by being disobedient to the Light, as the *Jews* who stumbled at *Christ* who sayd, he was *the Light that enlightneth every one that cometh into world,* so thou dost now at the same Light, which shall be thy condemnacion, eternally thou shalt witness me; it is the same Light as ever was: to that which should exercise your consciences do I speak, which will witness me, and condemn you."[177] John 1:9 is not used here in a purely Christological register. Fox turns to Johannine history in order to parallel the way in which "the Jews" stumbled at the light and the way in which Fox's adversaries stumble at Fox himself, who comes to represent for the gathering Friends that unchanging light.

This politicizing of John 1:9 and the unashamed anti-Semitism informing such an appropriation run throughout several of Fox's writings. Fox refers frequently to what is known among modern Johannine commentators as the "expulsion" topos in the Fourth Gospel. On three occasions the Fourth Gospel makes mention of the Christ-confessors' excommunication from the synagogues. The *locus classicus* is John 9:22, which describes the refusal of the parents of the former blind man to explain the miracle performed by Jesus on their son's behalf, lest they might suffer removal from the synagogal culture: "These words spake his parents, because they feared the Jewes: for the Jewes had agreed already, that if any man did confess that he was Christ, he should be put out of the Synagogue." Regarding the tentative belief in Christ's miracles, the narrator of the Fourth Gospel remarks, "Neverthelesse, among the chiefe rulers also, many beleeved on him; but because of the Pharisees they did not confesse him, lest they should be put out of the Synagogue" (12.42). Later, in the Farewell Discourse at 16:2, Jesus himself warns the disciples: "They shall put you out of the Synagogues: yea, the time commeth, that whosoever kil-leth you, will thinke that hee doeth God service."

Fox seizes on the expulsion motif, demonizing the Pharisees and the synagogal culture as a means further to vilify his contemporary adversaries who, although they might know the letter of scripture, fail to understand its spiritual message. That Fox is acutely aware of the Gospel verses warning of excommunication is clear from his discussion of the "outward Professors" of Christ in *Concerning such as have forbidden preaching or teaching in the name of Jesus* (1684):

> And the *Jews,* which were the greatest outward Professors, agreed, *That if any Man did Confess that he was the Christ, they should be put out of their Synagogue,* John 9.22. *And many of the Chief Rulers Believed on him, but because of the Pharisees, they did not Confess him,* namely Christ, *lest they should be put out of their Synagogue,* John 12.42. So here were them that did Believe, both Rulers and others in Christ, but they were

---

[176] George Fox, *Truth's defence against the refined subtilty of the serpent* (London, 1653), 86.
[177] Ibid., 86.

afraid to Confess Christ, lest they should be Excommunicated, or put out of their Synagogues.[178]

Fox will resort repeatedly to the expulsion narrative in order to legitimate the basic Quaker distinction between letter and spirit, between scripture and the personal experience of the light. Toward the end of his *Journal* he compares the Jewish and Pharisaical "professors" of the Word to his hostile opponents: the "people do not become the Sons of God" and heed the true light because they "do not receive Christ. The *Jews*, the great *Professors*, which had the *Promises, Propheicies, Figures* and *Shadows* of him, they would not *receive* him, when he came. And now the *Priests*, and high *Professors* of Christ, they are so far from receiving the *Light* of *Christ* and Believing in it that they have *hated* the *light*."[179] Fox does not merely draw parallels between the dualism of his and the historic Johannine community. Acutely aware of the pejorative connotations of "sect," he actually manipulates the Johannine narrative in such a way as to level the charge of sectarianism not against the Christian Jews of the Fourth Gospel but against the dominant culture of the first-century Pharisees. His epistle on John 4 is analogously devoted to projecting the concept of sectarianism ironically away from the marginalized Friends and toward all those who seemingly reject the true light: "And there are all the *Sects,* and such as grieves and quenches the Spirit, and comes not to the Truth in their Inward Parts, and such as stop their Ears, and close their Eyes to that of God in them, like the *Jews* and *Pharisees,* and kicks against that which pricks them, like *Saul,* and such as hates the true Light that enlightens every one that comes into the World."[180] Using as a refrain the truth set up by Christ "1600 years ago" (by which Fox means, in this particular narrative context, the founding Johannine community of dissenters), Fox concludes that it is not Christ who "makes Sects"; rather, sect-makers and schismatics are those who depart from the measure of truth and ability that "Christ has given unto them."[181]

Yet despite this persistent disparaging of the perceived exclusionary Judean culture of the Fourth Gospel, we also find the otherwise well-documented philo-Semitism not only in George Fox's treatises on the conversion of mid-seventeenth-century Jews but also in Margaret Fell Fox's hortative writings on re-admitting contemporary Jews into post-Cromwellian society. George Fox's epistles typically distinguish the "Jew inward" from the "Jew outward":

> And so *Christ's* Worship in the Spirit and Truth is set above the Jews outward Worship at *Jerusalem,* and the Mountain Worship near *Samaria;* and the Jew inward is set above the Jew outward; and above the Jews outward Offering in his outward Temple, and the Priest having Chambers in the Temple, that was the Place of their Offering; the Jew inward, he offers in his Temple the Spiritual Sacrifices; and no where else doth he offer but in his Temple; for by the Spirit, doth he offer to God who is a *Spirit.*[182]

---

[178] George Fox, *Concerning such as have forbidden preaching or teaching in the name of Jesus* (1684), 1.

[179] Fox, *A journal or historical account*, 575.

[180] George Fox, *An epistle to all professors in New-England, Germany, and other parts of the called Christian world also to the Jews and Turks throughout the world* (London?, 1673), 7.

[181] Ibid., 11.

[182] George Fox, *A collection of many select and Christian epistles, letters and testimonies written on sundry occasions* (London, 1698), 244.

The text that warrants Fox's distinction between Pharisaical worship in the outward Temple and the Christian belief in the internal spirit is John 4. After turning water into wine for the Samaritans, Jesus outlines a distinction between outward worship at Jerusalem and inward worship of the Father "in spirit, and in trueth" (4:23). As Fox glosses the passage: "*Spiritual Man*, set up above *Sixteen hundred* Years since… when he denied the *Mountain Worship*, where *Jacob's* Well was, and the Temple Worship of the outward *Jews* at *Jerusalem*, where they went to the outward *Temple* Yearly to Worship. And so every one are to *Worship* in the *Spirit*, and come to the Spirit and Truth in their own Hearts."[183] We find the same anti-Temple Christology in Margaret Fell Fox's exhortation to Menasseh Ben Israel, who is told that the Lord should be worshipped not in outward Temples or "outward Synagogues made with hands," for the time has arrived that the Lord should be worshipped in Spirit, "in the inward man."[184] Based on these writings and several others, Elizabeth Sauer has recently argued that, given their marginalized status in mid-century England, the early Quakers "saw some affiliations between themselves and the Jews attributable to their related millenarian interests, as well as their mysticism, skepticism, and shared sense of persecution."[185] Fox and other Quakers do take an interest in the Hebrew language, and Margaret Fell Fox, in the treatise quoted above, *For Manasseth Ben Israel. The call of the Jewes out of Babylon* (1656), does attempt to open dialogue with the Portugese kabbalist Menasseh Ben Israel.

Yet how to reconcile such shared millenarianism with the evident hostility expressed toward the historic Judean culture of the Fourth Gospel? We should not overestimate the extent of Quaker philo-Semitism. While Margaret Fell Fox's tone in her writings is perhaps, as one historian has remarked, "unusually conciliatory," readers of George Fox's writings will not be able to ignore Fox's tendency to cast the Johannine Judeans as themselves unenlightened sectarians who bear the responsibility for the crucifixion.[186] The widely held "two-level" account of Johannine sectarianism provides a means of understanding how Fox depicts both Johannine and seventeenth-century Jewish culture. On the one hand, the Fourth Gospel should be (and was) read as purely Christological in nature. The Prologue's descent and return motif, the emphatic designation of Christ as true light, and the healing examples of Christ at verses 9 and elsewhere, extend the Synoptics' often symbolic presentation of Christ as Messiah, a narratively rich depiction of Christ's mission that is not reducible to historical contingency. On the other hand, the Gospel records the sociopolitical experience of the late first-century Johannine community, members of which, according to

---

[183] Ibid., 265.

[184] Margaret Askew Fell Fox, *For Manasseth Ben Israel. The call of the Jewes out of Babylon* (London, 1656), 14.

[185] Elizabeth M. Sauer, "Milton's Peculiar Nation," in *Milton and the Jews*, ed. Douglas A. Brooks (Cambridge: Cambridge University Press, 2008), 44. For more information on Menasseh ben Israel, see Achsah Guibbory, *Christian Identity, Jews, and Israel in Seventeenth-Century England* (Oxford: Oxford University Press, 2010), 224–31.

[186] Judith Kegan Gardiner, "Margaret Fell Fox and Feminist Literary History: A 'Mother in Israel' Calls to the Jews," in *The Emergence of Quaker Writing: Dissenting Literature in Seventeenth-Century England*, eds. Thomas M. Corns and David Loewenstein (London: Frank Cass & Co., 1995), 47.

some biblical scholars, were threatened with excommunication from the communal life of the synagogues for their increasingly sectarian and radical confessing of Christ. At this level the Gospel should be understood as a rallying cry to bolster the confidence and solidarity of the encroached-upon Johannine community: "The Gospel was written in order to strengthen the faith of the Johannine Christians in this dire situation (20:30–1) and to provide them with arguments against their Jewish opponents."[187] The two-level approach to interpreting the Fourth Gospel (literary historians would more typically use the phrase "political allegory") assumes that the rupture between Christians and Jews provides an additional occasion to write the Gospel in a way that extends beyond the fundamental narration of Christ's mission, and that the most politically charged testaments in the Gospel were probably redactions interpolated into the narrative at a later date.[188]

In his selective focus on the expulsion motif and anti-Temple rhetoric of the Fourth Gospel, Fox reads the Fourth Gospel as a political and racialized sectarian document. Yet in his focus elsewhere on universal grace provided by Christ as true light, Fox presents the Fourth Gospel as the open-ended, catholic "spiritual Gospel" it was deemed to be by patristic and Reformed commentators. This is not to say that the two levels do not interpenetrate. When Fox distinguishes internal and external Jewishness in his treatises on conversion, the missiological, soteriological, and political registers clearly converge; and although the two-levels approach helps us to understand Fox's anti-Judean sentiment, it does not mitigate that sentiment. What we can say is that Fox found in the historical circumstances that shaped the emergence of the Johannine community a specific enactment of dualism that he believed was being re-enacted in the mid-seventeenth century tensions between Quaker prophesying and more traditional forms of piety.

An especially notable treatment of Johannine particularism, and perhaps the most subtle found in any early modern turn to the Fourth Gospel, is Fox's ironic projection of sectarianism away from the Quaker minority and toward the Pietist majority. This mode of ironic reversal has been described as one of the most significant elements of Johannine sectarianism:

> Granted that John is, in sociological terms, a sectarian document, of what significance is this theologically? In essence, it means that John portrays a conflict over sectarian heresy from the *heretics'* point of view. When John railed against those who reject its theological claims, it does not do so in defense of established orthodox dogma against

---

[187] Adele Reinhartz, "The Johannine Community and its Jewish Neighbors: A Reappraisal," in *"What is John?" Volume II. Literary and Social Readings of the Fourth Gospel*, ed. Fernando F. Segovia (Atlanta: Scholars Press, 1999), 119.

[188] On the reconstruction and redaction of the politically charged material in John 9 and elsewhere, see J. L. Martyn, *History and Theology in the Fourth Gospel* (Louisville: Westminster John Knox Press, 2003). Raymond E. Brown provides a thorough discussion of the increasing sectarianism of the Fourth Gospel in *The Community of the Beloved Disciple* (New York: Paulist Press, 1979). For a discussion of the integration of the two-levels of interpretation, the spiritual and the sociological, see David Rensberger, *Johannine Faith and Liberating Community* (Philadelphia: Westminster Press, 1988). A detailed commentary on the synagogue expulsion theme can be found in D. Moody Smith, *John* (Nashville: Abingdon Press, 1999), 194–8.

heretical innovation. Rather, the Fourth Gospel represents a heretical offensive against orthodoxy, i.e., the orthodoxy of the synagogue authorities.[189]

When Fox argues in *An Epistle to all Professors* (1673) that "there would be no *Sect* in *Christendom,* nor in the World, nor among the *Jews,* if they all would come to the Truth in their Inward Parts," he indeed launches, as does the prototypical Johannine community, a heretical offensive against orthodox "sectarianism."[190] In self-consciously transmuting sectarianism into universalism, Fox's strategy is a departure from the more typical antinomian tendency simply to co-opt language from the Fourth Gospel and then coalesce around an in-group sensibility (which is what we find in Familism). Religious historians have often raised the question of why, among so many emergent radical prophesiers in the later seventeenth century, the Quakers flourished and continued to find adherents in the New World. While several explanations for the later Quaker efflorescence have been offered—the lasting influence of Robert Barclay's *Apology* and the eventual leadership of well-connected luminaries such as William Penn, among other reasons—at least one contributing factor to Fox's lasting legacy is his subtle understanding and recapitulation of the history of Johannine sectarianism.[191]

JOHANNINE DUALISM: BEYOND ENGLISH DISSENT

We have seen that the antinomian and separatist worldview was fundamentally shaped by Johannine material—perfectionism, a mystical or semi-mystical union with God through the historical Christ, realized eschatology, horizontal and vertical dualism, even the rhetorical approach of particular treatises are all indebted to the particularities of the Fourth Gospel and First Epistle. And John's writings are malleable enough that dissenters could occupy nonconformist although not always radical or separating positions. John does become further radicalized in some of the Familist and Ranter writings, but John becomes perhaps most radicalized in the Antinomian Controversy in Boston during the years 1636–8. A detailed assessment of the Antinomian Controversy is beyond the scope of this chapter, but a brief outline of the debates between John Cotton, a Puritan clergyman who emigrates to the Massachusetts Bay Colony in 1613, and the more mainstream Boston Congregationalists highlights just how important the Johannine

---

[189] David Rensberger, "Sectarianism and Theological Interpretation in John," in Segovia, ed., *"What is John?"* 143.

[190] Fox, *An Epistle to all professors,* 11.

[191] The Quaker legacy is addressed briefly in Trueblood, *Robert Barclay,* 2–3, where Trueblood cites Lord Macauley's estimation of the ability of Quakerism to thrive relative to comparable fanatical groups: "Fox made some converts to whom he was immeasurably inferior in everything except the energy of his conviction. By these converts his rude doctrines were polished into a form somewhat less shocking to good sense and taste." On Quaker resilience and influence, see also Rosemary Moore, "The Inevitability of Quaker Success?" in *The Creation of Quaker Theory: Insider Perspectives,* ed. Pink Dandelion (Aldershot and Burlington: Ashgate Publishing, 2004), 48–60. On the cultural reach of seventeenth-century English Quakers, see B. Reay, "Quakerism and Society," in *Radical Religion in the English Revolution,* eds. J. F. McGregor and B. Reay (Oxford: Oxford University Press, 1984), 141–64.

material, particularly its pneumatology, could be to the community of dissenters in England and abroad, especially regarding the status of regeneration in the economy of salvation.

At issue during the Antinomian Controversy is the role of sanctification in the *ordo salutis*. The Congregationalists held to the Pietist belief that practical, sanctified conduct can serve as a sign and assurance of justification. Embracing what was deemed a radical conception of sanctification, John Cotton repeatedly makes recourse to John 3:8, 8:36, 14:16, 16:22, and 1 John 5:13 in his claim that sanctification occurs when the Holy Ghost, administered to the elect through Christ, provides an "internal concourse" that steadies the belief and salvation of the recipient.[192] For Cotton, although the Spirit is only one of three Trinitarian witnesses, it serves as the agent of free grace and "truth": "And all these works of the Father and of the Son, of the Spirit the Spirit witnesseth in promises of free grace without respect to work."[193] The upshot of Cotton's pneumatology is that the Spirit, not the believer, effects sanctified holiness, a subtle point that depends on his particular reading of John's First Epistle. While his Congregationalist objectors would argue that the Epistle (especially passages such as 1 John 5:13) holds that believers know that they have eternal life through a belief in the name of the Son of God, Cotton advises caution: "It will not thence follow that beleevers do come on first to believe ... by their witness of their works of Sanctification: But that coming to believe, and to know thay they do beleeve by the unctions of the Spirit revealed in the word of grace that abideth in them, they may be further confirmed in faith by the same Spirit."[194] Comments such as these reveal that the Antinomian Controversy gives more overt expression to the salient question that underlies all of the English dissenting treatises: to what extent does the believer have agency to effect, maintain, and display salvation, and to what extent does salvation require the practical divinity and disciplinary reformation so beloved of the experimentalists and Pietist Puritans?

As I have argued, John's theology provides the dissenting tradition with the nuanced, sometimes riddling evidence to proclaim that unqualified agency at any point during the *ordo salutis* is illusory. So while Cotton's opponents might point to John 14:21, which warns that no man can keep the commandments of Christ except one who loves Christ, Cotton will rejoin with 1 John 4:16–19, the gist of which is that our knowledge of Christ's and God's love toward us precedes our answering love. And while Cotton's opponents will reference 1 John 2:3, which holds that we know Christ if we keep his commandments, or recall 1 John 3:14, which maintains that we are translated from death to life because we love the brethren, Cotton will respond, leaning heavily on Calvin, that these signs of one's good estate are not given to all Christians as a means of acquiring assurance but are given only to those who are already assured by the indwelling of the Spirit and

---

[192] See *Mr. Cotton's Rejoynder* in *The Antinomian Controversy, 1636–38: A Documentary History*, ed. David D. Hall (Middletown: Wesleyan University Press, 1968), 103. For an excellent discussion of the originality of Cotton's antinomian spiritism, see Bozeman, *The Precisianist Strain*, chapters 11–14, *passim*.

[193] Hall, *The Antinomian Controversy*, 115.   [194] Ibid., 107.

hence "would declare their election to the world."[195] Suffice it to say that Cotton's radicalism stems from a subtle understanding of John, the sort of fine-grained understanding that is jettisoned when Johannine theology is used by the even more zealous radicalism of his disciple, Anne Hutchinson, who tends to erase distinctions entirely among the mystical believer, Christ, and the Holy Spirit.[196]

In Cotton's apology for free justification during the Antinomian Controversy, we have the most erudite and sophisticated antinomian interpreter of the Johannine writings (he had already written a several-hundred-page commentary on John's First Epistle).[197] Especially noteworthy is his tendency throughout the controversy to align Calvin's doctrine of assurance with the Johannine corpus, an affiliation that had not been made to any detailed degree in the more enthusiastic English antinomian writings. Cotton rightly focuses on the First Epistle, since passages such as 1 John 3:19 ("And hereby wee know that wee are of the trueth, and shall assure our hearts before him") do indeed suggest for Calvin that assurance does not proceed from works or conscientiousness.[198] And although Cotton does not refer as frequently to the *Institutes*, Calvin relies in that text heavily on John (as we have seen in Chapter 3) to argue that we cannot find the certainty of election in ourselves but only in Christ who mirrors our election, who has promised everlasting life, and who, as the bread of life, provides witness that we are included as heavenly sons by the Father. To ask for more, Calvin warns, is to "ascend above Christ."[199] Cotton was wise to bring the authority of Calvin to bear on the Johannine proof-texts for personal assurance, thereby achieving more than any other seventeenth-century antinomian a near-legitimation of the unorthodoxies of free grace.[200]

Throughout this chapter I have made scant reference to the use in antinomian, nonconformist, and dissenting literature of key scriptural texts other than John's theology. To be sure, as I noted above, Pauline theology is mined for much of the

---

[195] Ibid., 106.

[196] See chapters 9–10 in Hall, *The Antinomian Controversy*. What separates Cotton from his more radical followers is his belief that the rigor of legalism precedes effectual conversion, even though assured sanctification inevitably follows from the external call. On Cotton's distinctive legalist position on free grace, one that ironically would inspire enthusiastic antinomianism, see Norman Pettit, *The Heart Prepared: Grace and Conversion in Puritan Spiritual Life* (New Haven: Yale University Press, 1966), 130–41.

[197] John Cotton, *A practical commentary, or, An exposition with observations, reasons, and uses upon the First Epistle generall of John* (London, 1656).

[198] As Calvin remarks on 1 John 3:19: "Although a good conscience cannot be separated from faith, none should conclude from this that we must look to our works for our assurance to be firm." *Commentary on the First Epistle of John*, in *Calvin's Commentaries: The Gospel According to St. John 11–21 and the First Epistle of John*, vol. 5, eds. David W. Torrance and Thomas F. Torrance, trans. T. H. L. Parker (Grand Rapids: Eerdmans Publishing Company, 1959), 278.

[199] John Calvin, *Institutes of the Christian Religion*, trans. Henry Beveridge (Grand Rapids: Eerdmans Publishing Company, 1995), Book III, 244–5. Calvin will also note that a confirmation tending toward confidence in election derives from one's calling, referencing as proof-texts John 6, 7, and 10. *Institutes*, Book III, 245.

[200] Kendall provides an account of Calvin's doctrine of faith and assurance in *Calvin and English Calvinism to 1649*, chapter 1, *passim*. On Calvin's use of John in his doctrine of personal assurance, see D. A. Carson, "Johannine Perspectives on the Doctrine of Assurance," *Explorations* 10 (1996), 59–97; and A. N. S. Lane, "Calvin's Doctrine of Assurance," *Vox Evangelica* 11 (1979), 32–4.

content for the antinomian positions regarding the law–gospel relationship. David Como rightly concludes that Galatians 5:18 is the Pauline source used by Everard and others to warrant the displacement of legalism entirely. But while such verses in Paul, the Synoptics, Isaiah, and other New and Old Testament passages appear with frequency in the nonconforming and dissenting literature of the seventeenth century, Johannine theology provides the antinomians with a distinctive set of passages that are used to justify their belief in free grace. Even more importantly, the Johannine tradition inimitably provides, through the very example of the marginalization of the historical Johannine community, a spiritual legitimation of the dissenters' conviction that they share an intimate (and insular) union with Christ and God.

Patrick Collinson and Peter Lake have recently employed the term "conventicle" to describe the unique social formation of mid-century sectarian or "heretical" congregations.[201] An ambiguous designation for godly membership, the conventicle might be deemed the sacred locus of truth and redemption when viewed from the inside. From the outside, however, the conventicle might be seen as a deeply subversive and punishable threat to piety and ecclesiastical uniformity.[202] Lake is particularly interested in the ways in which, despite their evident differences on fine points of theology, Puritans and Familists—each group gathering in their respective conventicles, each group part of an amorphous "Puritan Underground"—share a common distance from the national Church and so emerge during the period as veritable "mirror images" of one another.[203] We have seen that the Fourth Gospel and First Epistle comprise at least one set of important scriptural texts for the very conception of such conventicalism. The Johannine emphasis on a horizontal rather than vertical dualism enables the Puritan underground to justify an "us versus them" political theology. And the same dualism could also be used to legitimate membership distinctions based on nuanced points of theology. John Coffey has rightly remarked that, "although historians have concentrated on their debates over church government, the divines actually spent more time arguing over points of theology."[204] Depending on the theological point in question—the nature of free grace, the Trinity, sacramentalism, legalism, justification versus sanctification, realized versus futurist eschatology, *sola scriptura*, discernment of the spirit, etc.—conventicles might just as easily distinguish themselves from one another as find common cause with one another against the codified statements of orthodox faith, such as the Canons of Dort (1619), the Westminster Confession

---

[201] See Patrick Collinson, "The English Conventicle," in *Voluntary Religion*, eds. W. J. Sheils and Diana Wood, *Studies in Church History* 23 (Oxford: B. Blackwell for the Ecclesiastical History Society, 1986), 223–59, on which Peter Lake draws in "Puritanism, Familism, and Heresy in Early Stuart England: The Case of John Etherington Revisited," in *Heresy, Literature, and Politics in Early Modern English Culture*, eds. David Loewenstein and Johan Marshall (Cambridge: Cambridge University Press, 2006), 91–2.

[202] See Lake, "Puritanism, Familism, and Heresy in Early Stuart England," 91–2.

[203] Ibid., 92.

[204] John Coffey, "A Ticklish Business: Defining Heresy and Orthodoxy in the Puritan Revolution," in *Heresy, Literature, and Politics*, eds. Loewenstein and Marshall, 114.

(1647), and the Larger Catechism (1648).[205] We have become accustomed by now to appreciating the difficulty of defining heresy or even Puritanism during the period, given the frequency with which individuals, sects, and conventicles might shift political or theological alliances.[206] It is evident that the ancient Johannine verses on dualism and conventicalism provided important scriptural material for such theological maneuvering not least in the ways in which Hendrik Niclaes arrogates for himself and the Familists the rhetoric of Christological illumination, Gerrard Winstanley and John Everard liken their insular communities to the gatherings of the ancient Johannine brethren, and George Fox charges Presbyterian orthodoxy itself with sectarianism or heresy. As I noted in the Introduction, these politico-theological appropriations of the very historicity of Johannine sectarianism suggest a political theology based on historical analogy, even though dissenters might further radicalize and distort the Johannine material on which their views are based.

We turn now to two near-contemporary devotional poets writing in the early through the middle decades of the seventeenth century: Richard Crashaw and Henry Vaughan. Both poets, although for much different reasons, show an interest in several of the antinomian topics described above. If Crashaw's verse shows unexpected overlap with the works of the antinomian John Saltmarsh, particularly on the topic of free grace, Vaughan's writings reveal the extent to which Johannine dualism was malleable enough to be used against the antinomian dualists themselves.

RICHARD CRASHAW, JOHN SALTMARSH, AND ANTINOMIAN FREE GRACE

In a recent essay, Nicholas McDowell provocatively describes some "unexpected conjunctions" found between the antinomian writings of mid-century New Model Army chaplain John Saltmarsh and the Laudian, "finally Catholic" poetry of Richard Crashaw.[207] After observing that a volume of George Thomason's collected tracts pairs the second edition of Crashaw's *Steps to the Temple* (1648) with Saltmarsh's 1645 edition of *The fountaine of free grace*, McDowell goes on to describe some of the liberal and antinomian leanings of both writers' works: an emphasis on Christ crucified and the assurance of salvation as well as a "resolution of contraries in divine love."[208] Although he cautiously advises that Crashaw's sacramentalism and Arminian emphasis on works are difficult to reconcile with the

---

[205] On the declarations of orthodoxy in these formularies and others, see Coffey, "A Ticklish Business," 113–14.

[206] For a comprehensive account of the protean uses of terms such as "heretic" and "blasphemer," see David Loewenstein, *Treacherous Faith: The Specter of Heresy in Early Modern English Literature and Culture* (Oxford: Oxford University Press, 2013), especially the Introduction, *passim*.

[207] Nicholas McDowell, "The Beauty of Holiness and the Poetics of Antinomianism: Richard Crashaw, John Saltmarsh, and the Language of Religious Radicalism in the 1640's," in *Varieties of Seventeenth- and Early Eighteenth-Century English Radicalism in Context*, eds. Ariel Hessayon and David Finnegan (Abingdon and New York: Routledge, 2011), 31–50.

[208] Ibid., 38.

free grace theology of Saltmarsh, McDowell invites us to appreciate the ways in which Crashaw's poetic expressions of ecstatic union with Christ found example and warrant not only in the writings of Saltmarsh but also in a stream of mid-century antinomian controversialist literature.[209]

What brings Crashaw's work into harmony with antinomian writings on free grace is their shared interest in the basic Johannine verses, images, and tropes that I have been discussing throughout this book, especially a recurring interest in the Christological doublet "water and wine" and its bearing on the etiology of personal assurance. In order to put a finer point on some of these shared theological concerns, I will focus much of the initial discussion on Crashaw's and Saltmarsh's use of the Johannine writings on the question of the role of mortification and regeneration in the economy of salvation. After a discussion of both writers' understanding of the Johannine conception of the piercing of Christ (and the attendant water and blood imagery), we can assess the relationship between justification and sanctification in this seemingly shared antinomianism. Mindful of the difficulty of squaring Crashaw's engagement of Laudian fundamentals with mid-century conceptions of free grace, I proceed cautiously in tagging Crashaw as an antinomian poet. My argument is that, on narrow theological questions of the relationship between grace and regeneration, especially the question of the penitent's active or passive role in sanctified holiness, Crashaw's poems do tend toward antinomianism or mid-seventeenth-century enthusiasm more generally. But given how far removed Crashaw's devotional poetry is from mid-century sectarian rhetoric bred of the sort of horizontal dualism reconstructed in this chapter, we would be wrong to describe Crashaw as antinomian in a more thoroughgoing sense.

One of Crashaw's many sacred poems on the symbolic wounding of Christ, "Song upon the Bleeding Crucifix" (1648/52), finds its source material in several important Johannine verses, including the wounding of Christ at 19:34 and the Samaritan reference to the well of living waters at 4:14 (as well as the rivers of water at John 7:38). Stanza five, serving as a midpoint in the revised version, directly references the piercing: "But o / thy side, thy deep-digg'd side! / That hath a double Nilus going" (V, 1–2).[210] Depictions of the interfusion of the blood imagery and otherwise traditional water imagery continue—the "double Nilus" becoming the "red sea of thy blood" (VI. 2) and then "thy blood's deluge" (IX. 1)—leading to the culminating image of the well of living waters taken from the Samaritan reference (itself prefigured in Isaiah) in the couplet following stanza xi: "N'ere wast thou in a sense so sadly true, / The WELL of living WATERS, Lord, till now" (IX, 5–6). I have already remarked in Chapter 1 on Crashaw's post-Reformed, Augustinian conception of the piercing of Christ. Typologically, the wound or opening is prefigured by the opening provided by Noah (which also anticipates the gathering Church). Symbolically, the double wound, which emits blood and water, represents

---

[209] In *Richard Crashaw*, 61–2, Thomas F. Healy also finds similarities between the work of Crashaw and Saltmarsh, particularly regarding the imagery in both writers' works of mixed blood and water.

[210] All references to Crashaw's poetry are taken from *The Complete Poetry of Richard Crashaw*, ed. George Walton Williams (New York: N.Y.U. Press, 1972).

the sacraments of the Eucharist and Baptism; yet it more generally recalls justifying grace and sanctified holiness. In Crashaw's hands, the typological and symbolic understandings inform the poem's controlling conceit of abundance. The depiction of Noah as a typological figure for Christ is suggested in "A deluge of Deliverance; / A deluge least we should be drown'd" (IX, 3–4); and Crashaw's reference to the "double Nilus" (V, 2) flowing from Christ's "deep-digg'd side" (V, 1) reflects Crashaw's appreciation of a long tradition according to which both the blood and the water are emitted from the heart-wound. On the one hand, then, the elongated epigram is fairly predictable in some of its imagery once the reader appreciates the yoking of Crashavian excess to John 19:34. The phrase "hands to give" (IV, 1), as Rosemond Tuve and others have remarked, is commonly used to describe the Eucharistic offering, and the justifying signification of the "red sea" of blood is suggested by the "deluge of deliverance."[211]

On the other hand, we should not too quickly assume a neat progression of such imagery in the poem, as Williams does when observing "the cumulative profession in water imagery in the latter part of the poem: Nile, red sea, one [river] all ore, overflowed rivers, deluge, Well of living Waters."[212] We find instead an accumulation of sacramental and Eucharistic imagery. The various bodies of water referenced in the poem flow with Christ's justifying blood. Yet the final couplet marks a shift from the focus on Christ's body-as-blood to the different Samaritan reference to Christ as the fountain of living waters. The water imagery does not exactly accumulate in the poem; the poem moves from a persistent focus on the alteration of water into blood to an image that leaves off the blood imagery and culminates in Christ as living water.

The image of Christ as living water is typically associated neither with Christ's justifying grace nor even narrowly with baptismal renewal. It more frequently voices the Johannine proclamation of eternal life—"The water that I shall give him shall be in him a well of water springing up into everlasting life" (4:14). As Calvin remarks: "These next words express more clearly what has been said already. They indicate a continual watering which sustains in believers a heavenly eternity during this mortal and perishing life. Christ's grace therefore does not flow to us only for a little while but pours on into a blessed immortality."[213] Another way of saying this is that, as we have seen in so many of the antinomian references to the Samaritan episode, the living waters symbolize the realized as opposed to end-time or futurist eschatology of the Johannine confessions. The poem does not end with the Samaritan reference or any relevant symbolic glosses. After five preceding stanzas with no offsetting punctuation in the respective final lines, the couplet halts with the interposed "Lord"—"The WELL of living WATERS, Lord, till now" (X, 6). The "now" marks the present as the eschatological moment in which Christ as continually flowing fountain, to use Calvin's terms, provides everlasting life.

---

[211] See Williams, *The Complete Poetry of Richard Crashaw*, note to stanza IV, 111.

[212] Ibid., 111.

[213] *Calvin's Commentaries: The Gospel According to St. John 1–10*, vol. 4, eds. David W. Torrance and Thomas F. Torrance, trans. T. H. L. Parker (Grand Rapids: Eerdmans Publishing Company, 1961), 93.

We might ask whether there is a poeticized moment of regeneration in the poem that accompanies the images of justifying grace. One candidate would be stanza VIII: "Rain-swoln rivers may rise proud, / Bent all to drown and overflow. / But when indeed all's overflow'd / They themselves are drowned too" (VIII, 1–4). We might see this as a symbol of spiritual renewal. The swollen rivers are akin to the puffed-up old man in need of renovation, in this case through the fate of drowning— hence the emphasis on "deliverance" in the penultimate stanza. But Crashaw draws no distinction between justifying grace and sanctified or baptismal renewal. The overflowing river is nothing other than the "blood's deluge" that achieves renewal through drowning. That the two salvific motions are interfused has already been hinted at earlier in the poem. When Crashaw remarks that there is "but one" river (VII, 3), he means most immediately that all worldly tributaries meet in the one that is "all ore" (VII, 4). Yet he also means that the earlier referenced "double" Nilus is, itself, one. The deliverance by the river is a complete and unified motion. Blood and water have become one, an interfusion that sets up the final reference to the eternally flowing life sourced in the well of living waters.

One finds this collapsing of both the blood and water images elsewhere in Crashaw's poetry, in "Vexilla Regis," for example, where Crashaw again focuses on the twin effusion following the Passion: "Lo, how the streames of life, from that full nest / Of loves, thy lord's too liberall brest, / Flow in an amorous floud / Of WATER wedding BLOOD" (II, 1–4). The conceit of an amorous wedded union between the water and the blood (and not simply the more traditional image of Christ as bridegroom and Church as bride) symbolically brings together justification and regeneration. What follows is Crashaw's largely unpoeticized description of the way in which the wounds, recast as "wounds of love" (III, 6), allow for participation via engrafting in Christ: "The while our hearts and we / Thus graft our selves on thee" (VII, 3–4). McDowell finds an Arminian "emphasis on works" in the phrasing of the first stanza of "one long Debt" (I, 4), yet the reference to expiation or atonement does not necessarily suggest works-righteousness.[214] The "debt" owed to Christ is simply "love to Him" (I, 5), which in the context of the subsequent reference to engrafting and then inheritance of the kingdom of Christ (VIII, 5) conveys, if not a realized eschatology proper, at least a belief in the self-sufficiency of Christ's saving work for the lovingly faithful. In both "Vexilla Regis" and "Upon the Bleeding Crucifix" there is much to warrant Thomas Healy's observation that, in Crashaw's poetry, especially the sacred epigrams, one finds a "confidence in salvation unusual in Protestant writing."[215]

The forensic terminology of works-righteousness and more technical distinctions between justification and sanctification or imputed and imparted righteousness are beyond anything that one expects to find in Crashaw's lyric repertoire. I use the terms here because it is in the poems' imagistic refusal to separate grace and holiness that Crashaw's work recalls the more legalistic debates between antinomians and experimental Puritans on the disputed relationship between justification and sanctification. Recall that for so many of the antinomian writers described

---

[214] Ibid., 38.   [215] Healy, *Richard Crashaw*, 26.

above, sanctification or perfect regeneration occurs at the moment of justification. Sanctification as a discrete stage in the order of salvation is associated with works-righteousness, moral progress, and spiritual presumptuousness. Saltmarsh's position is summed up in two concluding points in *Free grace*: "The Scriptures lay down these following things. 1. *Christ's sanctification* to ours, or his true holinesse. 2. *Faith* about our own *sanctification*."[216] To tie sanctification to personal effort or self-renewal or to even question one's sanctified status is to elevate the penitent's active righteousness over Christ's: "These *Teachers* bid you see *something* in your self; so as the leaving out Christ in *sanctification*, is the foundation of all *doubts, fears*, and *distractions*."[217] Such comments fueled the notion, articulated most clearly by Samuel Rutherford, that Saltmarsh's conceptions of free grace led inexorably to moral perfectionism: "So *Saltmarsh* willeth us not to repent, nor beleeve, nor mortifie sinne in our owne person, but to beleeve Christ hath done these for us perfectly, and then we beleeve, repent, and mortifie sin perfectly."[218]

Saltmarsh will at times rely on imagery similar to Crashaw's in order to depict figuratively some of his otherwise technical conceptions of free grace. One of Saltmarsh's clearest statements against a step-wise or staged conception of spiritual progress can be found in the preface to *Free grace*:

> If any man *sin* more freely because of *forgivenesse of sins*, that man may suspect himself to be *forgiven*; for in all *Scriptures* and *Scripture-examples*, the more *forgivenesse*, the more *holinesse; Mary* loved much, because much was forgiven to her; and *righteous* and *holinesse, blood* and *water, Jesus* and *Lord* and *Christ, called* and *justified*, are still to be found together in the *Word*.[219]

Rather than draw distinctions between discrete moments of renewal such as forgiveness and holiness—which tend to align sacramentally with blood and water—Saltmarsh locates the moment of full conversion in the Word as such.[220] This is the sort of intermixing of figures and steps in the economy of salvation that provokes the ire of heresy-seekers such as Thomas Gataker, who attempts to bend Saltmarsh's logic here to mean exactly what Saltmarsh polemicizes against—namely, that sanctified holiness can evince justification: "*Righteousnesse and Holines, blood and water, Jesus and Lord Christ, called and justified, are stil to be found together in the word. And if they go thus together*, then the one may with good ground evidence the other."[221] For Saltmarsh, however, a desire to draw distinctions between blood and water and related distinctions between justification and sanctification reveals

---

[216] John Saltmarsh, *Free grace, or, The flowings of Christs blood free to sinners being an experiment of Jesus Christ upon one who hath been in the bondage of a troubled conscience* (London, 1646), 83.

[217] Ibid., 85.

[218] Samuel Rutherford, *A survey of the spirituall antichrist opening the secrets of familisme and antinomianisme in the antichristian doctrine of John Saltmarsh and Will. Del* (London, 1648), 195.

[219] Saltmarsh, *Free grace*, A5.

[220] For more on Saltmarsh's conception of grace and assurance, see C. Fitzsimmons Allison, *The Rise of Moralism: The Proclamation of the Gospel from Hooker to Baxter* (Wilton: Morehouse Barlow, 1966), 170–2.

[221] Thomas Gataker, *Antinomianism discovered and confuted: and free-grace as it is held forth in Gods word* (London, 1652), 28.

instead our own sense of righteousness and threatens our Christ-given personal assurance: "I dare not deal in any such way of our own *righteousnesse*, because I finde no *infallible mark* in any thing of our own *sanctification*."[222]

Saltmarsh's polemical positions are at times expressed poetically in some of his Johannine-inspired water images that indeed anticipate Crashaw's devotional range. Saltmarsh's *A Divine Rapture Upon the Covenant* (1644) encourages the children of Sion to "Bathe in pure waters every day, / Waters of Life, and happinesse, which have / A Chrystall Grate in every wave."[223] Once upon the city of God, the faithful will "See here a chain of Pearl, and watry dew / Wept from the side of God for you; / See here a chain of Rubies from each wound, Let down in Purple to the ground."[224] McDowell is correct to note that, in terms of imagery at least, *A Divine Rapture* bears a startling resemblance to some phrasings in Crashaw's "On the wounds of our crucified Lord" (Epigram 45), which closes with "The debt is paid in *Ruby*-Teares, / Which thou in Pearles did'st lend" (19–20). But in terms of its orientation toward salvation, *A Divine Rapture* resembles as well both Crashaw's "Vexilla Regis" and his "Upon the Crucifixion." Drawing together the image of the river of the water of life from Revelation 22:1 as well as several related references to the Samaritan episode of the Fourth Gospel, Saltmarsh, like Crashaw, shows confidence in the sufficiently regenerating actions of Christ symbolized in the interfusing of water and blood: the chains of watery dew and rubies eventually thread on one "golden string." Correlating with Crashaw's notion of engrafting through love is Saltmarsh's metaphor for union: "Come tye your hearts with ours, to make one Ring, / And thred them on our golden string: / Great God, let down some glorious beam of thine, / To winde about his soul and mine."[225] If Crashaw believes, along with Saltmarsh, in the sufficiently regenerating actions of the Passion, Saltmarsh more directly asserts that personal assurance issues as a consequence: "And every ones; then we shall joyfull be, / Made sure to heaven and Thee."[226]

McDowell argues convincingly that Crashaw shares with the antinomian sensibility a high Christology and confidence in free grace and personal assurance. What gets left out of McDowell's discussion is the pathway by which one earns or arrives at sufficiently renovating grace. Crashaw voices along with Saltmarsh and other enthusiasts not merely the Johannine notion that assurance naturally follows from faith but also a conception of faith as simple *belief* in Christ's message. We recall Augustine's influential mantra culled from his understanding of John 6: "eating is believing." For Crashaw and the antinomians, the stumbling blocks to personal assurance include a failure to stake belief in Christ's message and a tendency to search for evidentiary signs of grace (as if the analogous antinomian mantra would be "to believe is to be assured"). Consider Saltmarsh's remarks in *Free grace* on the short work of finding personal assurance:

---

[222] Ibid., 31.
[223] John Saltmarsh, *A solemn discourse upon the sacred league and covenant of both kingdoms* (London, 1644), 8.
[224] Ibid., 8.   [225] Ibid., 8.   [226] Ibid., 8.

Salvation is not made any puzzeling work in the *Gospel*; it is *plainly, easily*, and *simply* revealed; *Jesus Christ was crucified* for *sinners*; this is *salvation*, we need go no further; the *work* of *salvation* is past, and finished; *sins* are *blotted out*....And now if you ask me what you must *do to be saved*, I answer, *Beleeve in the Lord Jesus Christ, and thou shalt be saved*. All that is to be done in the *work of salvation*, is to *beleeve* there is such a *work*, and that *Christ died* for *thee*, amongst all those other *sinners* he *died* for. To *beleeve* now, is the onely *work* of the *Gospel*; *This is the work that ye beleeve on him whom he hath sent*. Joh. 6.29. *This is the Commandment, that ye beleeve on his Son Jesus Christ.* 1 Joh. 3.23.[227]

Much of the edifice of Saltmarsh's conception of free grace is founded on this basic assumption that Christ's work is to get the faithful to believe in or "on" Christ's sufficiently saving work. Saltmarsh elaborates on this Johannine notion of efficacious belief: "The *Word* says, To *beleeve*, is to *receive*, or put *confidence* in, or *trust*, as in *John* 1.12."[228] Personal assurance naturally follows from ardent belief without the need for self-scrutiny, external witnessing, or signs of justification: "What way of assurance would you commend to a soul thus troubled? I answer, Christ in the Word and Promise to beleeve in for assurance. This was that way the *Lord* himself commended to his *Disciples*."[229] The antinomian conception of Johannine dualism is typically used to legitimate this conception of spiritual perseverance. To believe in Christ's righteousness, which is itself "complete" and "perfect," is to find eternal life. To refuse to believe, or to remain mired in darkness, is to find damnation: "To *beleeve* is life *eternal*, and not to *beleeve* is *condemnation*; He that *beleeveth hath everlasting life*, and *he that beleeveth not is condemned*; and this being a Scripture way, I would leave the soul upon these *principles*, and under this *Commandment, Beleeve on the Lord Jesus Christ*; for *this is the Comandment that ye beleeve on his Son, &c.*"[230]

We have already seen in Chapter 1 that Crashaw's divine epigrams on the bread of life emphasize the importance of proper belief for the faithful. But Crashaw's interest in the Johannine conception of assurance following belief is most often suggested in those verses that acknowledge the centrality of belief to salvation, even as they recognize the difficulty in achieving the transition from ignorance to belief. This is a transition most typically troped as the challenge of moving from darkness to illumination. If Crashaw shares with seventeenth-century enthusiasts the idea that assurance is subsequent to proper belief in Christ's righteousness, Crashaw is not always as confident that the transition out of darkness is readily achievable. Crashaw devotes four Latin epigrams to John 3–4, most verses of which are directly concerned with the difficulty of lifting the recalcitrant world out of Pharisaical ignorance and into the true light. Thus Sacred Epigram 132 on John 3:4, "How can a man be born who is old," which parodies Nicodemus's ignorant questioning to Christ, raises a series of riddles on the topic of rebirth—for example, "Why with its dying beak does the savage bird preying on its own old age gather more time with its impetuous mouth?" (5–6)—and concludes: "Do you not know, Pharisee? that is enough. You will learn to believe: *he who is properly ignorant has half of his faith*" (9–10). Half-belief or persistent ignorance is rejoined in Sacred Epigram

---

[227] Saltmarsh, *Free grace*, 191–2.   [228] Ibid., 156.   [229] Ibid., 32.   [230] Ibid., 31.

134 on John 3:19: "Behold God comes with his light and shines in the world: / yet still the world continues to love its darkness. / But for this reason the world will be condemned to the Stygian shades: does the world still continue to love its darkness?" (1–4). In Sacred Epigram 135, Crashaw is similarly interested in John 4:47, which describes the plea of a Capernaite nobleman for Jesus to heal his son. Jesus questions the courtier's belief, upbraiding him for wanting to witness a miracle, but he then heals the son from a physical distance, at which point the courtier achieves proper belief in Jesus' far-reaching power. Crashaw's epigram on John 4:47 plays on the theme of Christ's refusal to travel with the man to perform the miracle. Crashaw's speaker advises the man: "Here is Christ to whom you make your petitions / but—believe me—the same Christ who will grant these petitions is there" (9–10). The speaker plays here the role of the gently rebuking Christ who must enforce the man's belief that the savior's healing power extends beyond the physical realm. All such epigrams meditate on the profound importance of simple belief in Christ's righteousness to effect salvation. Yet these epigrams remind readers of the stubborn refusal, typically of the Capernaites and Pharisees, to see and believe properly. In these early writings, Crashaw does seem interested in the very Johannine material so dear to the enthusiasts. But the epigrams do not so much assert the bestowal of free grace through belief as they question the world's ability to make the gestalt shift necessary to seeing that Christ's righteousness unilaterally imparts grace and sanctification.

In Crashaw's longer, more meditative and hymnal works, the theme of proper belief versus ignorance rejoins much of the Johannine material, especially the dualism of worlds and the conception of Christ as true light. The *Hymn in the Glorious Epiphanie* has divided critics at least since Ruth Wallerstein complained that the poem's reference to Pseudo-Dionysius is incongruous with its eschewal of negative theology.[231] Recent criticism has claimed either that the poem appropriates Dionysian conceptions in the service of positive or cataphatic theology or that it gives voice to a thoroughgoing Dionysian revival popular among Caroline Laudians.[232] I would argue that a description of the poem as fundamentally Johannine reveals the extent to which the poem's distinctive form of Christ-mysticism, which does borrow from the Dionysian tradition, comports with some of the antinomian tenets that I have been describing in this chapter.

One of Crashaw's most insistently dualistic poems, the Epiphany hymn develops strong, sometimes paradoxical antitheses between the natural/pagan sun and the supernatural light of the Son. That Crashaw is working with a Johannine conception of Christ as the one who brings light to a darkened world is signified in the direct reference to the new "sun" as "true light": "As by a fair-ey'd fallacy of day / Mis-ledde before they lost their way, / So shall they, by the seasonable fright / Of

[231] Ruth C. Wallerstein, *Richard Crashaw: A Study in Style and Poetic Development* (Madison: University of Wisconsin Press, 1959), 143.

[232] On competing interpretations of the use of Dionysius in the Epiphany hymn, as well as the Dionysian revival in Caroline England, see Gary Kuchar, "A Greek in the Temple: Pseudo-Dionysius and Negative Theology in Richard Crashaw's 'Hymn in the Glorious Epiphany,'" *Studies in Philology* 108:2 (Spring 2011), 261–98.

an unseasonable night, / Loosing it once again, stumble'on true LIGHT" (163–7). The trajectory of the poem—that Christ as true light provides the proper way, but the world resists and continues to languish in darkness—is based on a compendium of key Johannine verses. This includes the verse so popular among enthusiasts such as the Quakers—"That was the true light, which lighteth every man that commeth into the world" (1:9)—but also key verses that compare the light of Christ to the darkened ignorance of the world, most obviously the Nicodemus encounter in John 3 as well as verses from John 8: "I am the light of the world: he that followeth mee, shall not walke in darkenesse, but shall have the light of life" (8:12). In heralding Christ at the outset of the poem as the world's sure way— "Welcome, the world's sure Way! / HEAVN'S wholsom ray" (60–1)—Crashaw also recalls the well-known Johannine conception of Christ as the way, the truth, and the life: "I am the Way, the Trueth, and the Life: no man commeth unto the Father but by mee. If ye had knowen me, ye should have knowen my Father also: and from henceforth ye know him, and have seene him" (14:6–7).

Despite these obvious Johannine sources (as well as the Apocalyptic imagery found elsewhere in the poem), what gives the hymn its distinctive quality— rendering it much more than a mechanical paraphrase of source texts—is the equally obvious reliance on paradox. The sun and daylight keep the otherwise faithful in the dark, for the ignorance and presumption of the sun need to be eclipsed by the "supernaturall DAWN of Thy pure day" (174). Yet we need not resort to the paradoxes and negative processes of Dionysian mysticism to appreciate the fundamental Johannine orientation of the paradox. Consider Crashaw's description of the blindness of the sun and its Gentile followers: "And as before his too-bright eye / Was Their more blind idolatry, / So his officious blindnes now shall be / Their black, but faithfull perspective of thee" (168–71). The theme of acquiring a faithful perspective on Christ only when one can no longer see is the theme of spiritual blindness at the conclusion of John 9: "For judgment I am come into this world, that they which see not, might see, and that they which see, might be made blind" (9:39). Worldly wisdom, in both Crashaw's Epiphany hymn and John 9, is associated with spiritual blindness. Only when the sun goes dark and they can no longer see will the worldly-wise begin to see Christ.

Throughout the Epiphany hymn's various restatements of illumination through darkness, Christ provides the spiritual way because he retains his glorified and visible status as the fount of illumination, whether cast as "true LIGHT" (167), "originall Ray" (211), or "day's light" (246). This consistent high Christological emphasis on Christ as true light keeps the poem from realizing its seeming Dionysian and apophatic tendencies toward the later parts of the poem. At line 191 we are introduced to the Pseudo-Dionysius, the "right-ey'd Areopagite" (191) who, through witnessing the eclipse, is able to "descant THEE" (195) beyond the "obsequious cloud" (200) that was once called the sun. Yet, if the Dionysian reference were to open out to an endorsement of the Dionysian tradition of negative theology, this would entail not merely an appreciation of the paradox of spiritual illumination amid darkness but also a step-wise ascent through which basic distinctions between light and dark are transcended. The processual endpoint or "supreme cause" for

Dionysius is the unsayable or unnamable, beyond creaturely antinomies, beyond any dialectics of negation. As Dionysius remarks, this incomprehensible endpoint is neither "spirit" nor even "sonship or fatherhood": "Darkness and light, error and truth. It is none of these. It is beyond assertion and denial."[233] It is difficult to reconcile this conception of the apophatic way with the more cataphatic sense of Christological transference or substitution that closes Crashaw's hymn. As the sun is shorn of its "pretence" (245), it defers to a subordinate position of, at best, a "brighter SHADOW (sweet) of thee" (249). Christ is now fully illuminated as the new "day's light" (246) and "our own sun" (252). Such metaphors are recast only slightly in the accompanying dedicatory poem to Queen Henrietta Maria, "To the Queen's Majesty," in which Christ is the "day-break of the nations" (3). What emerges at the end of the hymn is a straightforward Johannine vindication of Christ as true light who, unlike in Crashaw's more skeptical and ironic sacred epigrams, is able successfully to convert those stragglers such as Nicodemus and the Samaritans who would otherwise remain under the cover of darkness. Given this high Christological conclusion to the poem, Dionysius seems retroactively as an ideal follower, another "eagle" (232) that has shut its eyes so that it can see. Dionysius is cast as a glorified disciple who is invoked more for the example of his faith than for the prescriptive mystical process about which he writes.

What, if anything, about the Epiphany hymn is reminiscent of the work of antinomian enthusiasts on the question of the relationship between grace and mortification? Consider the final emergence and then supercession of the otherwise illuminated wise men in the poem: "Thus we, who when with all the noble powres / That (at thy cost) are call'd, not vainly, ours / We vow to make brave way / Upwards, and presse on for the pure intelligentiall Prey" (219–22). These are the regenerate faithful who erroneously assume that the "powers" they have received from the true light will now allow them actively to "peep and proffer at thy sparkling Throne" (225). In place of any notion that Christ's actions enable us actively and independently to see God, we find here the subtly different notion, in keeping with antinomian substitutionism, that Christ's powers work through us or supersede our own. The transference of powers is troped as an admission of our inability to see the proper sun through our own devices: "In stead of bringing in the blissfull PRIZE / And fastening on Thine eyes" (226–7). This acknowledgment that regenerative powers are nothing more than Christ's active righteousness working through the faithful accords with Saltmarsh's conception of self-negation: "The *Scriptures* bid you see *nothing* in your self, or *all* as *nothing*. These *Teachers* bid you see *something* in your self; so as the leaving out Christ in *sanctification*, is the foundation of all *doubts, fears,* and *distractions*."[234] In keeping more closely with the language and imagery of the poem, the antinomian belief in passive but complete and Christ-centered righteousness is described more aptly in John Winthrop's notion that a belief in one's imparted righteousness leads to darkness rather than illumination:

---

[233] *Pseudo-Dionysius: The Complete Works*, trans. Colm Luibheid and Paul Rorem (New York: Paulist Press, 1987), 141.

[234] Saltmarsh, *Free grace*, 85.

"Sanctification is so farre from evidencing a good estate that it darkens it rather, and a man may more clearly see Christ, when he seeth no sanctification then when he doth, the darker my sanctification is, the brighter is my justification."[235] And this idea that the proper way to see Christ's righteousness is to eschew rather than to seek for evidence from our own sense of righteousness is again put in terms close to Crashaw's Epiphany hymn by the enthusiast Peter Sterry. Describing the ways in which one attempts to see Christ through a natural and a divine eye, Sterry remarks:

> The *Naturall Eye* is that of Reason, which is alwayes open in all Men, so farre as they are Men. The *Divine Eye* is for many yeares, many ages, quite shut up in the Soul ever since the Creation, untill the Regeneration. This Eye is a *Divine Principle or Faculty* of seeing Things; the *Supreame Power* of Knowing, as God Knows and is Known. Saint *John* speaks of this Eye, *John*, 3.2. *When He appeares, we shall be like Him, For we shall see Him as He is.* The Proper Light and Object of This Eye is Jesus Christ in the Spirit, as He is the Brightnesse and Image of the God-head. As a Sun-beame beating with a strong Light upon the Naturall Eye; So shall the Lord Jesus awaken this Eye in Man, by setting Himselfe in it.[236]

Here we have, as in Crashaw's poem, an account of the overcoming of the "natural eye," figured in the Epiphany hymn as the "fair-eyed fallacy of day" (163), by the stronger light of Christ as sun-beam from which can emerge the divine eye, itself exemplified by the "right-ey'd" (191) Areopagite. These substitutions allow the light of the proper Sun/Son to set himself in the illuminated light of man.

Crashaw's seeming antinomian leanings stem more specifically from the enthusiasm for key Johannine tropes that he shares with antinomian Christology than from any wholesale embrace of the many anti-legalist and politically inflected aspects of antinomian theology. Crashaw shares with Saltmarsh and others a distinctive form of Christ-mysticism that maintains a high Christological conception of Christ as true light whose perfect obedience remits sins and mortifies the flesh. Those moments when Crashaw's verse most leans toward antinomianism are ones in which Christ provides full satisfaction to the faithful. At these moments distinctions between imputed or imparted righteousness, justification and mortification, vivification, or application break down. Another way of saying this is that Crashaw is most antinomian when he seems most mystical, when the faithful are united with Christ such that distinctions between self and Christ are diluted, and Christ's righteousness substitutes for the active righteousness of Crashaw's penitential speakers. Yet this substitutionism or Christ-mysticism typically sustains a high Christological focus on the limitations of creaturely ecstatic vision and self-purgation relative to the exaltation of Christ as the only figure who can properly find glorification and witness the beatific vision.

One reason we would be wrong to describe Crashaw's poetry as antinomian in a more exacting sense is that the evident dualism of worlds that runs throughout

---

[235] John Winthrop, *Antinomians and familists condemned by the synod of elders in New-England* (London, 1644), 15.

[236] Peter Sterry, *The clouds in which Christ comes opened in a sermon before the Honourable House of Commons* (London, 1648), 25–6.

his sacred poetry typically represents a vertical distinction between a glorified heaven and a corrupt world. This is not equivalent to the horizontal and politically/topically oriented dualism that informs antinomian conventicalism during the Interregnum years. It makes sense that when Crashaw turns to those passages in the Johannine writings that justify dualism, he typically seizes on verses such as John 3:19—"Light is come into the world, and men loved darknesse rather then light, because their deedes were evill"—rather than on more "separatist" verses such as 15:19: "If ye were of the world, the world would love his owne: But because yee are not of the world, but I have chosen you out of the world, therfore the world hateth you."

If such horizontal dualism does not exercise the imagination of Crashaw, it does inform the more politically engaged devotional poetry of his near contemporary, Henry Vaughan. Vaughan's most topically oriented poems often respond directly to those Johannine passages that seem to legitimate mid-century separatism and enthusiasm. If on fine points of Christology Crashaw will show his antinomian leanings, on even finer points of political eschatology Vaughan will show his leanings against enthusiasm and separatism generally. We turn now to the most politically and eschatologically resonant poems of Vaughan's *Silex Scintillans*.

HENRY VAUGHAN AND THE JOHANNINE WORLD

If Johannine dualism structures much of the approach and content of the antinomian disposition, it need not be the sole province of nonconformist separatism or dissent. The dualism we have been discussing throughout this chapter can be appropriated analogously by very different denominational affiliations (assuming that these positions tend toward extremism in either the radical or the conformist direction). Having fought for the Royalists during the English Civil War, Henry Vaughan wrote from the political margins, typically mourning in his most overtly political poems the death of political allies and supporters of the crown. In his prayer manual *The Mount of Olives* (1652) and elsewhere in his writings, Vaughan attempts to find alternative forms of Anglican worship once the Book of Common Prayer and several Anglican rites had been forbidden during the Interregnum. Because Vaughan was a disenfranchised Royalist, much of his work, however theological in focus, is thus keenly political in both its grief over the loss of the kingship and its hope for restoration. "So much in [Vaughan's work] is hidden," Alan Rudrum remarks, "quietly biding its time, waiting for a new life, that the alert and sympathetic contemporary reader may have seen in such images hidden and buried royalism and Anglicanism waiting for their potentialities to be actualized, for their new day to dawn."[237] We will see that when Vaughan advances his interpolated apologies and complaints for a lost political regime, he frequently turns to the themes and language of Johannine dualism.

---

[237] Alan Rudrum, *Henry Vaughan*, in *Oxford Dictionary of National Biography* (Oxford: Oxford University Press, 2014).

The opening of Vaughan's *The Mount of Olives* so parallels the beginning of the Fourth Gospel that one wonders whether Vaughan is approximating a translation of his source: "O God the Sonne! light of light," Vaughan exclaims, "thou, that art the light shining in darknesse, Inlightning every one that cometh into this world, expell from me all Clouds of Ignorance, and give me true understanding."[238] Vaughan hails both the spirit and the letter of the dualism of John 1:4–5, a theme that he develops further: "O God the Holy Ghost…shed into me thy most sacred light, that I may know the true Joyes of Heaven, and see to escape the illusions of this world. Ray thy selfe into my soul that I may see what an Exceeding weight of glory my Enemy would bereave me of for the meer shadowes and painting of this world."[239] A few pages later, after reiterating the importance of retreating not merely from the allurements of the world but also from any converse with the enemies of the world—"Remember that thou art to come forth into the *World*, and to Converse with an Enemy; And what else is the World but a Wildernesse"— Vaughan turns to the Johannine understanding of God as "the Way, the Trueth, and the Life" (14:6) as a means of protecting him spiritually from his worldly enemies: "Almighty and everlasting God, who art the *Way*, the *Life* and the *Truth*; look down from heaven, and behold me now betwixt the Assaults of the Devil, the allurements of the World, and my own inclinations."[240] Later in the text, cautioning his readers to avoid "dangerous medling with the world," Vaughan cites the important passage at 1 John 2:15—"Love not the world, neither the things that are in the world. If any man love the world, the love of the Father is not in him"— about which he concludes: "We should therefore be very cautious how we deal with it, or with the followers and favourites of it."[241] We can see from this remark that the world for Vaughan signifies not simply vain allurements (as in a *contemptus mundi* conception) but also base and untoward people, those "followers" and "favourites" he would consider his adversaries. If the world is Vaughan's enemy, it is so in a topical and sociopolitical, rather than in a materialist, register.

Vaughan's dualism surfaces elsewhere in *The Mount of Olives*—for example, in his "Prayer Before Going to Church": "O thou most mild and merciful *Lamb of God*…grant, I beseech thee, that the seed which falls this day upon my heart, may never be choak'd with the Cares of this world, nor be devoured by the fowles of the aire, nor wither away in these times of persecution and triall."[242] These persecutory worldlings are more directly addressed at the close of the treatise, following the "Prayer in Adversity, and Trouble Occasioned by Our Enemies": "Thou seest, O God, how furious and Implacable mine Enemies are, they have not only rob'd me of that portion and provision which thou hadst graciously given me, but they have also washed their hands in the blood of my friends, my dearest and nearest relatives."[243] Given the importance of John's writings to much of what has preceded this complaint in *The Mount of Olives*, it is understandable that Vaughan will

---

[238] Henry Vaughan, *The Mount of Olives, or Solitary Devotions*, in *The Works of Henry Vaughan*, ed. L. C. Martin (Oxford: Clarendon Press, 1957), 143–4.
[239] Ibid., 144.   [240] Ibid., 146.   [241] Ibid., 185.   [242] Ibid., 149.
[243] Ibid., 167.

find solace in the "beloved disciple," a veiled reference to John (cryptically referred to in the Fourth Gospel at 13:23): "I know, O my God, and I am daily taught by that disciple who thou did'st love, that no murderer hath eternal life abiding in him."[244] On the one hand, John provides Vaughan with the language to justify his world-withdrawal and even his hostility toward his implied political enemies. On the other hand, John provides Vaughan with the Christological material not only to refrain from any further violence or untoward action toward his perceived foes but also to petition God to forgive them and show charity: "Give me thy grace, and such a measure of charity as may fully forgive them."[245] This petition might seem perfunctory or even in bad faith, but Vaughan has found John's writings sufficiently capacious to warrant the language of both separation and conciliation, an approach that we can further track in his poetry.

SILEX SCINTILLANS: JOHANNINE DUALISM AND ESCHATOLOGY

Although Vaughan's "The Stone" takes its guiding metaphor of the testimony of a stone from Joshua 24—"Behold, this stone shalbe a witnesse unto us; for it hath heard all the words of the Lord which hee spake unto us; it shall be there for a witnesse unto you, lest ye deny your God"—the dualistic judgment placed upon unbelievers is derived from two of John's most politically charged pericopes: Jesus' defense to the Jews after the miracle at Bethesda (5:30–45) and Jesus' remarks on judgment that are prompted by his hearers' refusal to believe his prediction of his own death: "And if any man heare my words, and beleeve not, I judge him not; For I came not to judge the world, but to save the world. He that rejecteth me, and receiveth not my words, hath one that judgeth him: ye word that I have spoken, the same shall judge him in the last day" (12:47–8). In the Bethesda pericope, Jesus defends himself against the accusation that he has transgressed the Sabbath, to which he responds that his will is not his own. In the latter narrative, Jesus addresses those auditors who persist in their apostasy even after hearing his words. To claim that he has not come to judge the world implies both that God will do the judging and that he will judge harshly only stubborn unbelievers.

"The Stone" is pointedly about judging those "wilde men" (42) who fail to realize that their sins are recorded by Christ, he who "knows / All that man doth" (30–1) and who judges by a fair and deliberate process. The witnesses of this judgment might include not only "sand and dust" but seemingly dead stones as well (37–9).[246] When Vaughan invokes John 5—"But he that judgeth as he hears, / He that accuseth none, so steers his righteous course" (28–9)—the implication, given the larger Johannine context, is that those who would judge Jesus are themselves being judged by Jesus and by the very stones that have become registering "Scribes":

---

[244] Ibid., 167.   [245] Ibid., 167.
[246] All quotations from Vaughan's poetry are taken from *The Works of Henry Vaughan*, ed. L. C. Martin (Oxford: Clarendon Press, 1957).

"Each thing turns Scribe and Register, / And in obedience to his Lord, / Doth your most private sins record" (43–5). In the Johannine narrative, the Scribes are those who would too quickly question, accuse, and incriminate Jesus. Vaughan's ironic approach to the source material is to imagine that Christ (who has been accused by the Pharisaical scribes) will become not the accuser (since "accusation" implies an impetuous or unfair judgment) but the deliberate judge of those actions of the referenced "wilde men" (42).

Although Vaughan's references to John 5 and 12 frame rather than directly appear in the fourth stanza, the sense of that particular stanza is thoroughly influenced by the source passages: "The Law delivered to the Jews, / Who promis'd much, but did refuse Performance / will for that same deed / Against them by a stone proceed; / Whose substance, though 'tis hard enough, / Will prove their hearts more stiff and tuff" (46–51). The reference to the failure to obey the law and the trope of the hardened heart are grounded in both John 5 and John 12. In the former verse, Jesus remarks that he need not accuse the Pharisees, since, ironically, they have already been accused by Moses, the one whom they would otherwise follow: "There is one that accuseth you, even Moses, in whom ye trust? For had ye beleeved Moses, ye would have beleeved me: for he wrote of me. But if ye beleeve not his writings, how shall ye beleeve my words?" (5:45–6). The resultant hardened hearts of the Jews, a clear reference to Isaiah, is at the same time a reference to John 12, which directly recalls the Isaian context:

> But though he had done so many miracles before them, yet they beleeved not on him: That the saying of Esaias the Prophet might be fulfilled, which hee spake, Lord, who hath beleeved our report? and to whom hath the arme of the Lord beene revealed? Therefore they could not beleeve, because that Esaias said againe, He hath blinded their eyes, and hardned their heart, that they should not see with their eyes, nor understand with their heart, and be converted, and I should heale them.   (12:37–40)

Vaughan borrows the stone motif from Joshua. Yet the development of the poem, which is trained on the judgment of God through the testimony of Jesus and his naturalistic scribes (the very stones that will not simply judge but actually pulverize the stony hearts into dust), is a development sourced in John 5 and 12, both of which are only briefly referenced in the poem. When Vaughan remarks that the Gospel will judge and soften the hardened hearts of the "wilde men," he is not programmatically playing the Old against the New Testament. He is measuring the unbelief of the Mosaic dispensation as well as of the contemporary "wilde men" against the Gospel of John, particularly the notion that the legacy of Christ's Word, the Word that will be diffused through the testimony of his disciples and the Paraclete, will survive his death: "The *Gospel* then (for 'tis his word / And not himself shall judge the world) Will by loose *Dust* that man arraign, / As one then dust more vile and vain" (56–9).

"The Stone" uses Johannine material to describe the severity but also the fairness of God's judgment. It also draws a sharp distinction between those who will be judged harshly and those who will not. Vaughan's use of Johannine dualism can help us re-evaluate a recently emerging conundrum in Vaughan studies. While

Claude Summers rightly points out Vaughan's heavy reliance on the Apocalyptic writings and "Anglican survivalism," Vaughan's use of Apocalyptic material has become the subject of some debate.[247] Nigel Smith remarks that "the apocalypse is the Day of Judgement, not the Second Coming of Christ. The millennium is subjugated to the always present, gradual slowing down of the world."[248] Agreeing with Smith's appreciation of Vaughan's anti-millenarian rhetoric, Philip West responds that, if Vaughan's writings are pointed against millenarian enthusiasm, they nevertheless link that anti-millenarianism to the Second Coming of Christ: "Both parts of *Silex Scintillans* yearn passionately for the Second Coming, so that to correct Smith, one must say that Vaughan's Apocalypse is *both* the Second Coming of Christ *and* the day of Judgement."[249] The issue pivots on a precise understanding of the mid-seventeenth-century notion of the *Parousia*. According to Revelation 20 and related verses, the Second Coming refers to the thousand-year rule on Earth by Christ and the Saints, after which Satan is released for a time (along with the resurrection of all souls), the eventual outcome of which is Judgment Day and a second resurrection. While Smith is correct to note that Vaughan's writings do not foresee the Second Coming in the temporal and earthly sense of the vanquishing of the beast and Christ's reign on Earth (as predicted in Matthew 25, for example), West is also correct to note that Vaughan does yearn for the re-emergence of Christ and worldly judgment. How to reconcile the difference of opinion? I would suggest that Vaughan's eschatology, despite his generous use of verses from Revelation, is more accurately described as futurist than apocalyptic proper (if we include under the purview of apocalyptic the *Parousia* and millenarian reign of Christ and the Saints on Earth). Vaughan does envision a return of Christ and the resurrection of devout souls. But the Second Coming is more often understood as an ongoing vertical experience that the faithful enjoy with Christ and God in heaven than as a chronologically specific event that takes place on Earth.[250] Such a futurist eschatology is particularly (even peculiarly) located in the Fourth Gospel, as opposed to what one finds in Revelation (indeed the eschatology of the former was included by John to soften the martial and sublunary implications

---

[247] Claude J. Summers, "Herrick, Vaughan, and the Poetry of Anglican Survivalism," in *New Perspectives on the Seventeenth-Century English Religious Lyric*, ed. John R. Roberts (Columbia: University of Missouri Press, 1994), 51, 67. "Anglican survivalism" is John Morrill's term to describe the manner in which, despite the forbidding of Anglican rites, festivals, and the comforts of the official Prayer Book, high Anglican and Royalist adherents covertly continued to worship as if the national Church were still viable during the early Interregnum period. See Morrill, "The Church in England, 1642–1649," in John Morrill, ed., *Reactions to the English Civil War, 1642–9* (Basingstoke and New York: Palgrave Macmillan, 1982), 89–114. Philip West discusses Vaughan's survivalism in *Henry Vaughan's Silex Scintllans: Scripture Uses* (Oxford: Oxford University Press, 2001), 148–50. On the emergence of radical "new lights" in the 1650s, see West, *Henry Vaughan's Silex Scintllans*, chapter 5, *passim*.

[248] Nigel Smith, *Literature and Revolution in England, 1640–1660* (New Haven: Yale University Press, 1991), 269, cited in West, *Henry Vaughan's Silex Scintillans*, 194.

[249] West, *Henry Vaughan's Silex Scintillans*, 194.

[250] In claiming that Vaughan's vision mingles presentism and futurism but remains largely non-apocalyptic, I agree with Jonathan F. S. Post's attentive discussion in *Henry Vaughan: The Unfolding Vision* (Princeton: Princeton University Press, 1982), 128, of the "unprophetic" nature of Vaughan's Christ.

of the latter). A brief review of Johannine eschatology can help better contextualize Vaughan's anti-millenarianism.

As I mentioned in the Introduction, the Fourth Gospel ambiguates neat distinctions between realized and futurist eschatology. On the one hand, several passages maintain that everlasting life has already been bestowed on Jesus' believers (3:36, 10:27, 5:25). On the other hand, several other passages project future judgment on the "last day" (5:28–9, 6:39–40, and 12:48). Verses on realized salvation are sometimes placed in such close proximity to those on future judgment as to suggest a downright contradiction. Defending himself against the charge that he has broken the Sabbath by conducting healing miracles, Jesus warns the Pharisees: "Verily, verily I say unto you, The houre is comming, & now is, when the dead shall heare the voice of the Sonne of God: and they that heare, shall live" (5:25). But consider Jesus' proclamation that the hour of judgment "now is" alongside the statement expressed just three verses earlier: "Marveile not at this: for the houre is comming, in the which all that are in the graves shall heare his voice" (5:28). Here both the resurrection of life and the resurrection of the dead are predicted to "come foorth" (5:29) at some unspecified future date.

Johannine scholars have advanced any number of theories to explain the seemingly self-contradictory nature of John's eschatology. Rudolf Bultmann argues that Christ's descent and the phraseology of 5:25 signifies the arrival of the eschatological hour; hence the futurist verses were added by a later redactor in order to integrate the more "dangerous" aspects of realized eschatology with traditional Jewish eschatology and Synoptic apocalyptic.[251] Other, less radical views, such as C. H. Dodd's, contend that the contradiction between realized and end-time eschatology is only apparent. The gift of eternal life in the present anticipates and is continuous with the resurrection at Judgment Day: "The evangelist agrees with popular Christianity that the believer will enter into eternal life at the general resurrection, but for him this is a truth of less importance than the fact that the believer already enjoys eternal life, and the former is a consequence of the latter."[252] For Dodd, the Christ-event itself inaugurates the offer and presence of eternal life. The apocalyptic language of the Fourth Gospel is used only symbolically to describe a transcendent Kingdom of God.[253] The authentic "coming" of Christ has already transpired in the Fourth Gospel and will be apotheosized with the subsequent arrival of the Spirit-Paraclete in Christ's stead. To the extent that one finds more overtly apocalyptic language in the Fourth Gospel, that language is included to

---

[251] Bultmann, *The Gospel of John*, 261. Refuting Bultmann, C. K. Barrett sees the co-presence of realized eschatology and Synoptic apocalyptic: "John has not so radically transformed the synoptic eschatology that he ceases to regard the final judgement as the supreme act of Jesus the Son of man. There is no reason whatever for regarding vv. 28f. [5:28] as a supplement to the original Johannine discourse unless it is held incredible that John should have thought of resurrection and judgement under both present and future aspects." *The Gospel According to St. John* (London: S.P.C.K., 1965), 219.

[252] Dodd, *The Interpretation of the Fourth Gospel*, 148.

[253] For this summary of Dodd's position, see George Eldon Ladd, *A Theology of the New Testament*, revised edition (Grand Rapids: Eerdmans Publishing, 1993), 335.

satisfy habituated expectations of a "second, more glorious coming in the future—at first, in the near future; then, in the distant future."[254]

Critical to all such discussions of John's twofold eschatology is a distinction between futurist and apocalyptic theology. Most modern scholars accept that the Fourth Gospel brings together present and futurist elements. Because physical death will obviously befall the disciples who enjoy "eternal" life here and now, the "full gift" of life will not come until the resurrection.[255] And perhaps the most important futurist aspect of John's eschatology is the promise that, once Jesus has re-ascended to the Father, he will prepare a dwelling place in heaven to which he will bring his believers (14:2–3 and 17:24).[256] If the futurist elements seem to sit uneasily with realized eschatology, there is still less of a consensus that the Fourth Gospel offers a final eschatology or apocalyptic narrative. To the extent that verses such as 5:28, 6:44, and similar references to the last day do exist in the Fourth Gospel, those passages (either included originally to appease those followers who expected a more traditional apocalypse, or added later by an ecclesiastical redactor) are shorn of the martial drama, cataclysm, and millennial zeal that one finds in Daniel, Ezekiel, Revelation, and Synoptic apocalyptic. Not only are there far fewer references to the coming Kingdom of God in the Fourth Gospel relative to the Synoptics, but such a Kingdom describes not a post-resurrectional reign on Earth just before the end-time but an otherworldly celestial Kingdom that is promised to the brethren. When Raymond Brown remarks that "in Johannine thought the ultimate goal of the disciples is to be withdrawn from the world," he is recalling the basic premise of John's distinctive dualism, which distinguishes not a diachronic present from a future age but the world of believers from the world of unbelief.[257]

Returning to Vaughan's poetry, we can see that his distinctive *non-apocalyptic eschatology* in selected poems is thoroughly Johannine in orientation. Consider the compact set of references in stanza 4 of "The Agreement": "Thine are the present healing leaves, / Blown from the tree of life to us / By his breath whom my dead heart heaves" (20–2). The healing leaves and tree of life certainly recall the apocalyptic language of Revelation 22:2 (as well as comparable verses in Ezekiel). And while the references to Christ's breath and the blown leaves might bring to mind Genesis 2:7, they typologically look forward to John 20 and Jesus' appearance to the apostles in which he breathes onto them the Holy Ghost: "And when he had said this, hee breathed on them, and saith unto them, Receive ye the holy Ghost" (20:22). The Johannine inflection is further realized in the speaker's acknowledgement of the "comfort" provided by Christ described later in the poem—"For until thou didst comfort me, / I had not one poor word to say" (37–8)—and it is realized in the references to John 6 that close the poem: "So thou, who didst the work

---

[254] Raymond E. Brown, *The Gospel According to John*, vol. 1 (i–xii) (Garden City, N.Y.: Doubleday & Company, 1966), cxviii.

[255] Ibid., cxviii.   [256] Ibid., cxviii.

[257] Raymond E. Brown, *The Gospel According to John*, vol. 2 (xiii–xxi) (Garden City, N.Y.: Doubleday & Company, 1966), 852, cited in Armando J. Rodriguez, Jr., *Life from on High: The Eschatology of the Gospel of John in Light of its Vertical Dimension* (Ann Arbor: ProQuest L.L.C., 2008), 92–3.

begin / (*For I till drawn came not to thee*) / Wilt finish it, and by no sin / Will thy free mercies hindred be" (67–70). As the Revelation references shade into the Fourth Gospel verses, the poem displaces apocalyptic scenery with a typical Johannine concatenation of realized and futurist elements. The preliminary comforts provided or "begun" by Jesus ratify the speaker's conviction that his faithful "silence" will prevail over his foes and prepare him for his own death. Eventually, according to the promise of John 6:44 (footnoted by Vaughan himself), he will come to the Father through Christ: "No man can come to me, except the Father which hath sent me, draw him: and I will raise him up at the last day" (6:44). If Vaughan seems more interested in this first clause of 6:44 than the second clause—"and I will raise him up at the last day" (6:44)—this is because "last day" in the context of the poem signifies little more than the speaker's personal resurrection and joining of God in heaven. Vaughan's non-apocalyptic use of John 6:44 is echoed in an important mid-century Johannine commentary by George Hutcheson, Scottish resolutioner and fellow anti-enthusiast, for whom the last day addition to the granting of everlasting life as promised in John 6 offers personal assurance of salvation rather than apocalyptic judgment:

> For the further assuring of beleevers of their eternal happinesse, it is also covenanted, that they shall have this life in present possession, in the earnest and first fruits thereof; for, they *have everlasting life,* even here, and before their raising up. Christ, having given an earnest-penny of salvation, will not suffer it to be lost by any difficulty or impediment in the way; but will carry beleevers through all difficulties, till he destroy death and the grave, and raise up their very dust, that in body and soul they may partake of that blisse.... Therefore it is added, *and I will raise him up at the last day.*[258]

That the typical fearsomeness and judgment associated with the "last day" might be bleached of cataclysmic overtones is similarly voiced in Edward Hyde's *A Christian Legacy* (1657). In the section subtitled "The Comforts of the Soul against Judgement," Hyde remarks on John 12:48 (another "last day" reference in the Gospel): "The sentence at the last day shall be but a declaration and confirmation of the sentence that is already spoken in the Word: And haply in this respect it is said, That the Apostles shall Judge the world, Wherefore if we can have comfort from the sentence that is already passed upon us by the Apostles, we may have also comfort from the sentence that will be passed upon us by their Master."[259] For Hutcheson and Hyde as well as for Vaughan, the last day reference is added by the Evangelist simply to bolster confidence in the faithful that, through the comforts of the Spirit, they will retain after death the eternal life that has already been covenanted to them in their present life.

---

[258] George Hutcheson, *An exposition of the Gospel of Jesus Christ, according to John* (London, 1657), 109.

[259] Edward Hyde, *A Christian legacy consisting of two parts* (London, 1657), 234. In other treatises, the "last day" reference in John 12:48 should principally prompt self-judgment, as in Ralph Robinson's *Panoplia. Universa arma. Hieron. Or, The Christian compleatly armed* (London, 1656): "This is that which our Saviour saith, *John* 12. 48. Now every man must come to judgement for himself, *Ergo,* its necessary, that he should know that word, by which God will judge him" (140).

This is not to say that all of Vaughan's eschatological verse is non-apocalyptic. Alan Rudrum, Philip West and others have described the overt apocalypticism of poems such as "Ascension-day," "Ascension Hymn" and "White Sunday." West provides attentive interpretations of the ways in which these otherwise apocalyptic poems promote anti-millenarianism by defusing verses in Revelation often cited by radical prophesiers.[260] I would only add that these poems typically carry out a tempering of millenarian fire through their embedded references to the Fourth Gospel. And such poems gesture at modes of realized eschatology that are unaccounted for in West's contention that the "anti-millenarian force of *Silex Scintillans* resides largely in its scriptural metaphors, which establish that Christ's Second Coming will mark the start of eternal life and not the beginning of an earthly millennium."[261]

We have seen that in poems such as "The Agreement," eternal life does not await the Second Coming. It is a here-and-now possibility for those saints who look forward to a continuation of life in heaven in a post-resurrectional future. At the outset of "Ascension-day" the speaker imagines that, although the glorious Ascension is "remo'ved / So many Ages" from him, it is "so prov'd / And by thy Spirit seal'd to me, that I / Feel me a sharer in thy victory" (5–8). This is not a passive speaker who awaits the heralded eternal life at judgment day; it is a pro-active speaker whose "sharing" of Christ's glory has already been "sealed" by the Spirit, one who appreciates the "perfect gifts" (4) offered to him by Christ. He can "walk the fields of Bethani" (37) following Christ as "true light" (13) because he has projected himself into an achronological future. In his ardent, even ecstatic testimony of Christ as "true light," the speaker himself provides an additional "witness" to the two Johannine witnesses referenced in the penultimate lines of the poem: "*What two attest, is true*, / Was thine own answer to the stubborn Jew" (59–60). In John 8, after Jesus has pardoned the adulterous woman and proclaimed himself the "light of the world" (8:12), the Pharisees accuse him of falsely bearing record of himself, to which Jesus responds: "I am one that beare witnesse of my selfe, and the Father that sent mee, beareth witnesse of me" (8:18). When the Pharisees ask, "Where is thy Father," Jesus responds: "Ye neither know me, nor my Father: if ye had knowen mee, yee should have knowen my Father also" (8:19). Vaughan's speaker, unlike the Pharisees, is wholly prepared to meet the Father. His sharp vision of the Ascension itself bears record to his assured belief in Christ as true light.

Even in a poem such as "The Men of War," which is thematically forward-looking in the speaker's repeated request for the "patience" (37) to see his "Crown / as near / And Almost reach'd" (38–9) and in his diligent awaiting of judgment during which he will see the setting of Christ's "Throne" (47), we detect the speaker's already-achieved enlightenment. The poem draws its language of enlightenment from the Fourth Gospel: "Were not thy word (dear Lord!) my light, / How would I run to endless night, / And persecuting thee and thine, / Enact for *Saints* my self and mine. / But now enlighten'd thus by thee, / I dare not think such villany" (9–14). More assured of his divine illumination than is the speaker of "The World,"

---

[260] West, *Henry Vaughan's Silex Scintillans*, 194–229.   [261] Ibid., 195.

the speaker here, without recapitulating Quaker perfectionism, expresses the rhetoric of the indwelt light from John 1:9. West is correct to observe Vaughan's "special use of John's gospel" (as well as the First Epistle) in the poem, particularly in respect of the speaker's realization that overcoming the world requires patience and firm belief rather than martial affronts—as in "But patient, meek, and overcome / Like thee" (19–20), and "Who by no blood (here) overcame / But the blood of the *blessed Lamb*" (51–2).[262] Here again we should consider the larger context of the Johannine verses on which the poem's Christology is based. Jesus' farewell comment to the brethren (16:33) follows from an immediately preceding exchange in which the brethren avow that they do believe in him and hence can understand the Father "plainly" and without recourse to Proverbs: "Now are we sure that thou knowest al things, and needest not that any man should ask thee: By this we beleeve that thou camest foorth from God. Jesus answered them, Doe yee now beleeve? Behold, the houre commeth, yea is now come, that ye shall be scattered, every man to his owne, and shall leave me alone: and yet I am not alone, because the Father is with me. These things I have spoken unto you, that in me ye might have peace" (16:30–3). Vaughan's speaker here is much like the brethren. Having received illumination through belief, he is far along in the order of salvation, and he is prepared to survive the tribulations that await him. The sense of "overcame" in the last lines—"I may be found (preserv'd by thee) / Amongst that chosen company, / Who by no blood (here) overcame" (48–50)—predict not that he will eventually overcome his opponents after judgment day but that he *will have* overcome them by that projected last day of judgment. The poem provides solace to the speaker. He will be able to maintain the saving faith (and, implicitly, eternal life) that he and Christ's original disciples have begun to experience.

We return, finally, to Vaughan's use of Johannine dualism in relation to the antinomian separatist usage of the equivalent material. Vaughan finds in the Johannine writings the same spiritual comfort and perseverance as his opponents, even as he uses verses in the Fourth Gospel to ameliorate the apocalypticism of the dissenters. In this approach he reverses Winstanley, who enlists the Fourth Gospel in the service of millenarian projections. This is not to say that Vaughan arrogates to himself the perfectionism of Niclaes, Fox, Everard, and others. In his most politically allegorical poems in *Silex Scintillans*, Vaughan will rest his hopes on the comforts of realized eschatology. At times, however, the Fourth Gospel also prompts Vaughan to self-reflection, even fostering a questioning of his own spiritual standing in relation to the "worldlings" for whom his speakers express pity at best, disdain at worst. The speaker of "The World," perhaps Vaughan's most insistently dualistic poem, expresses a wondrous and vivid image of eternity—"A great *Ring* of pure and endless light" (2)—but that speaker needs to be reminded by a final interlocutor just why some "prefer dark night / Before true light" (49–50): "One whisper'd thus, / *The Ring the Bride-groome did for none provide / But for his bride*" (59–61). We cannot be sure, given the speaker's obtuseness (recalling the spiritual lassitude

---

[262] Ibid., 227. In *Henry Vaughan's Silex Scintillans*, West describes at some length the ways in which "The Men of War" follows Johannine theology in the latter's "comfortable doctrine" (228).

of, say, the speaker in Herbert's "Love unknown"), whether he understands what it takes to become united with Christ. The speaker intuits, in keeping with the eschatology of several of Vaughan's other poems, that the coming of Christ has already arrived. Eternal life is figured forth in the Ring of endless light and refigured in the marriage union of Canticles. Yet he is not entirely sure whether he has found his way out of the darksome realm of worldlings and into the illuminated ring of eternity.[263] We will continue to interpret in Chapter 6 this same self-reflexive turn in which Vaughan's speakers find themselves recapitulating some of the Johannine misunderstandings that are articulated by both the faithful disciples and the uncomprehending Pharisees such as Nicodemus.

---

[263] This helps to explain the seeming disunity, so often discussed by Vaughan's critics, between the inspired vision of eternity in the first seven lines and the less vaulted imagery and language of the remaining lines of the poem: the speaker's divided vision itself reflects his own spiritual tentativeness. On the perceived disunity of "The World," see James D. Simmonds, "Vaughan's Masterpiece and Its Critics: 'The World' Revaluated," *SEL* 2 (1968), 77–93; Leland B. Chambers, "Vaughan's 'The World': The Limits of Extrinsic Criticism," *SEL* 8 (1968), 137–50; and Post, *Henry Vaughan: The Unfolding Vision*, 129–30.

6

Discipleship Misunderstanding and Johannine Irony in the Poetry of George Herbert and Henry Vaughan

I have discussed in the preceding chapters the ways in which Johannine depictions of Mary Magdalene's grief, the bread of life narrative, the *agape* motif, the role of the Paraclete, and radical dualism coalesce around John's high Christology. We have also seen the importance of Johannine style and rhetoric—particularly the use of discipleship misunderstanding and dramatic irony—to the early modern treatments of Magdalene and to the recasting of Johannine Christology in seventeenth-century dissenting literature. Yet Johannine irony is especially evident in some well-known poems of both George Herbert and Henry Vaughan. I offer below close readings of three poems of Herbert—"The Bag," "The Bunch of Grapes," and "Love unknown"—as well as a reading of Vaughan's "The Night" in terms of our continuing focus on Johannine devotional poetics and high Christology but with particular attention to parallels between discipleship misunderstanding and the use of dramatic irony in these poems.

In *Overheard by God*, an underappreciated study of the voicing of God/Christ in Herbert's *The Temple*, among other texts, A. D. Nuttall complains that, because he deigns to put words in God's mouth, Herbert shows bad faith and a "sense of impropriety" in poems such as "Dialogue," "The Collar," and "Love unknown."[1] Despite the humble redemptive strategies behind the tactic (the divine interlocutor typically corrects or gently rebukes the speaker), divine voicing seems problematic to Nuttall because in a poem such as "Dialogue," Herbert "does not simply submit himself to the will of God; he personally supplies the divine correction."[2] I hope to show that the voicing of Christ and God in Herbert's best poems should be seen not as spiritual presumptuousness or what Nuttall describes as "false intimacy" on Herbert's part but as an emulation of the tonality and structure of Johannine dialogism and accompanying dramatic irony.[3]

---

[1] A. D. Nuttall, *Overheard by God: Fiction and Prayer in Herbert, Milton, Dante and Saint John* (London: Methuen, 1980), 9.

[2] Ibid., 3. Nuttall observes that a similar use of divine voicing occurs in the Fourth Gospel, where Christ, often the purveyor of discontinuous dialogue, logical ellipses, and dramatic irony, relies on a technique of "deliberate transcendence" that seems to justify his non-answers to his interlocutor's questions (131). Yet Nuttall neglects to consider the ways in which Christ typically goes on to resolve or clarify some of the mysteries and ironies that the Fourth Gospel raises.

[3] Ibid., 59.

We will see that critical debates regarding Herbert's vacillating or alternating style—described by Helen Vendler as Herbert's tendency to "reinvent" his speakers/ poems and by Stanley Fish as catechizing—miss the Johannine orientation of Herbert's rhetoric of productive misunderstanding.[4] And we will see that such irony is redoubled in Vaughan's treatment of the role of Nicodemus in "The Night." I have paired Herbert and Vaughan not merely because of the unmistakable stamp of the former on the latter, but also because both poets show a deep appreciation of both the spirit and the letter of the Johannine tradition.[5]

CHRIST'S DIVINITY IN HERBERT'S "THE BAG"

The clearest reference in Herbert's "The Bag" to John's Gospel appears midway in the speaker's very compressed Passion narrative: "But as he was returning, there came one / That ran upon him with a spear" (25–7).[6] The so-called Longinus piercing, which appears in New Testament theology only in John (and is prefigured slightly in the prophetic book of Zechariah), receives copious glossing beginning with the patristics and extending throughout the seventeenth century. The significance of the reference, typically overlooked by Herbert's modern commentators, will be accounted for momentarily, as will the other unmistakable reference to John in the poem: Christ's fashioning of himself as an open door through which the faithful can gain entry to glorification. But since the use of one or two scriptural references to John does not necessarily make a poem Johannine in orientation, we should track back from the piercing reference in order to clarify the Johannine implications of the poem's earlier recounting of the Incarnation.

After reminding himself and his readers not to despair, given God's concern for us despite tribulations, the speaker divulges a "strange storie" (8) in response to his own question, "Hast thou not heard, that my Lord JESUS di'd?" (7): "The God of power, as he did ride / In his majestick robes of glorie, / Resolv'd to light; and so one day / He did descend, undressing all the way" (9–12). Herbert's initial focus on God's light brings us immediately to John. As we have seen in the preceding chapters of this book, no other Synoptic or apostolic explication of the divinity of Christ is as concerned as John with the manner in which Christ, identified at the outset with God, brings light to a darkened world: "In him was life, and the life was the light of men. And the light shineth in darknesse, and the darknesse comprehended it not" (1:4–5). John the Baptist is then referred to as the witness of Christ as the true light: "That was the true light, which lighteth every man that

---

[4] See Helen Vendler, *The Poetry of George Herbert* (Cambridge, MA: Harvard University Press, 1975); and Stanley Fish, *The Living Temple: George Herbert and Catechizing* (Berkeley: University of California Press, 1978).

[5] On the influence of *The Temple* on *Silex Scintillans*, see Kenneth Friedenreich, *Henry Vaughan* (Boston, MA: G. K. Hall, 1978), 122–6, as well as Joan Bennett, *Four Metaphysical Poets* (New York: Vintage Books, 1960), 83–103.

[6] All quotations are taken from *The Works of George Herbert*, ed. F. E. Hutchinson (Oxford: Clarendon Press, 1941).

commeth into the world" (1:9). In addition to these opening references to light, there are several more invocations of light in John 3 and 12, all of which suppose that Christ's arrival brings illumination in the form of revelation-as-knowledge, yet the recalcitrant auditors such as Nicodemus remain in ignorance: "Light is come into the world, and men loved darknesse rather then light, because their deedes were evill" (3:19).[7] Herbert's "The Bag" plays on the theme in several ways. The phrase "resolv'd to light" (11) identifies God with light even as it affirms that he will bring light to the world upon which he descends. To be resolved to light presumes that God and light are one, soluble in one another; it also bespeaks God's very decision—his resolution—to bring light downward. That God descends at night-time is evidenced by the relinquishing of his crown, once amidst the clouds, to the stars: "The starres his tire of light and rings obtain'd" (13).

God's transformation into Christ is so telescoped in the poem as to happen in an instant or not happen at all, the implication being that the two are one. Happy and smiling, God genially disrobes, assuring us that he has new clothes on earth—referencing the scriptural (and Donnean) trope of God wearing our flesh in order to become human—and then lights upon "an inne" (20) only very quickly to be crucified and then resurrected: "Both then, and after, many a brunt / He did endure to cancell sinne: / And having giv'n the rest before, / Here he gave up his life to pay our score. / But as he was returning, there came one / That ran upon him with a spear" (21–6). Consider the "strangeness" of this astonishing compression of the Incarnation, Passion, and Resurrection. In the span of seven lines, God bears brunts, cancels sin, and then, upon re-ascending, is (potentially) interrupted by the piercing of his side. The Passion, along with any elaboration of the creaturely tribulations that Christ suffers, is not the concern of this section. The concern is rather with the Resurrection and its implications, conveyed by the pause introduced with the "but" at line 25—"But as he was returning…" (25). Herbert's speaker tells us that all was going unproblematically as planned (the "all" referring to the crucifixion itself, glancingly referenced here) until, on the cusp of re-ascension, Jesus' side is pierced by one who would determine thus whether he had yet died. The consequence of that piercing provides the matter for the remaining two stanzas of the poem. By means of the ensuing wound, Christ will provide a pouch or bag in which to deliver messages from creatures to God. The message that Christ would convey to his listeners (the message of the poem itself) is that Christ will continue to provide such a door to God even for those who abuse him in the manner of an unregenerate Longinus.

The rapidity with which God descends and then re-ascends, the privileging of the Resurrection over the cross, and the revelation of the significance of the piercing all suggest the poem's fundamental Johannine orientation. As I have discussed in earlier chapters, the basic presupposition of John's Christology is that Christ, because he has descended from God, is singularly prepared to impart knowledge to

---

[7] John Donne devotes an entire 1621 sermon to John 1:8 and the nature of Christ as "true light" (*Sermons of John Donne*, eds. George R. Potter and Evelyn M. Simpson (Berkeley: University of California Press, 1957), vol. iii, especially 353–4).

a darkened world and then re-ascend. That Herbert emphasizes this descent and return theme is further conveyed by Christ's repairing "unto an inne" (20), which meaningfully swerves from Matthew's and Luke's account of the birth of Jesus. In Luke 2:7, for example, Mary brings her newborn child to the manger because there was no room at the inn: "And she brought foorth her first borne sonne, and wrapped him in swadling clothes, and laid him in a manger, because there was no roome for them in the Inne" (2:7). The site of the manger is where the neighboring, humble shepherds witness the newborn Christ, after which they spread the good news abroad. The protracted and detailed homely birth narrative in Luke intimates the kenotic emptying of God into the vulnerable humanity of the newborn Jesus. In John's version the nativity scene is expectedly passed over. John has already established the pre-existence of the incarnate Christ, his analogous "birth" scene described in the Prologue to the Fourth Gospel: "In the beginning was the Word, & the Word was with God, and the Word was God" (1:1). The fact that Herbert, too, leaves out the nativity scene does not render the poem Johannine (or Markan by default). But that Christ rests directly in an inn is another way in which the speaker elevates Christ in the sense that, unlike the "homeless" wanderers, Joseph, and the newborn Jesus who were turned away from the inn, Herbert's divine Christ will directly repair to the inn and therefrom begin his sojourn.

In its compression of the Incarnation and Resurrection and its relative neglect of the cross, "The Bag" is richly Johannine in its preoccupation with the divinity of Christ and salvation as revelation rather than expiation and atonement. Yet it is true that Herbert references the Atonement in several lines in stanza four: "He did endure to cancell sinne: / And having giv'n the rest before, / Here he gave up his life to pay our score" (22–4). Ransoming does transpire, but it is stated in such a matter-of-fact manner as to dilute its importance relative to both the majestic disrobing of God that precedes the Atonement and the complexly symbolic piercing that occurs just after the Crucifixion. The *fact* of the Atonement is integral to the poem but it is treated here, as it is in John, as less of an abasing act through which Christ, in his humanity, suffers, and more as an exalted event that issues in God's revelation of love and glory for his believers. To so "happily" descend comports with the fundamental Johannine notion, as represented throughout the good shepherd narrative, that Christ willingly "chooses death": "No man taketh it from me, but I lay it downe of my selfe: I have power to lay it downe, and I have power to take it againe. This commandement have I received of my father" (10:18). The hurriedness of the lines in Herbert's poem and their generic formulations—"cancell sinne" (22) and paid "our score"(24)—render Jesus much less human than one would expect from an otherwise moving account of the Passion.

In regard to the Passion reference and the wound created by the piercing (the latter not described viscerally), Herbert's critics at times project anthropomorphic suffering onto Herbert's Jesus that the poem does not warrant. In keeping with Robert Graves's belief that the wound of Jesus has "distinct feminine characteristics," Michael Schoenfeldt remarks that "The Bag" illustrates Herbert's tendency to "comprehend the mystery of Christ's descent into vulnerable flesh": "The poem's details—the action of 'undressing,' the placement in an 'inne,' the emphasis upon pregnability, the seductive promise that 'the doore / Shall still be open'—all connote a sexual scenario which never fully surfaces, but which suffuses the process by which the almighty God of power becomes a vulnerable and compassionate deity."[8] Whether or not Herbert is conjuring a feminized Christ here, it does not follow that the deity is represented as "vulnerable." As we have seen, the undressing is done "happily," the locus of the inn, in its play on Luke's homespun account, elevates rather than debases Christ, and neither the Passion nor the sword-wound is rendered viscerally or even corporeally. The poem is not especially concerned to represent the "blatant violence" attributed to it by Schoenfeldt.[9] Despite her acknowledgement that, in "The Bag," Herbert's Christ "assumes heroic proportions" rather than victimhood, Jeannie Sargent Judge also assumes that a suffering Christ is at the heart of the poem: " 'The Bag' shows us a speaker whose emotional recovery of a suffering, accessible Jesus effects his spiritual recovery."[10] Yet such suffering is more attributed by Herbert's critics than illustrated in the poem itself. "The Bag" presents not a suffering Christ but a glorified one, again in keeping with Johannine theology. Chana Bloch is correct to note the "upbeat" tone of "The Bag," but she too neglects to consider that the confident "certainties" of such a poem do not stem from, as she suggests, the comparable certainty of the Psalms but rather from the joyful descent and return of the Johannine God as Christ.[11]

Is it not the case that the major conceit, the open wound of Christ serving as a bag in which to carry messages to God, is itself graphic and brutal (or violent)? Perhaps graphic, but Herbert is more interested in the Johannine symbolism of the wound than its corporeality and brutality. Herbert and his contemporaries closely follow Augustine's influential interpretation of the Johannine account of Christ's wound. The depiction in the Fourth Gospel is as follows:

> But one of the soldiers with a speare pierced his side, and forthwith came there out blood and water. And he that saw it, bare record, and his record is true, and he knoweth that hee saith true, that yee might beleeve. For these things were done, that the Scripture should be fulfilled, A bone of him shall not be broken. And againe another Scripture saith, They shall looke on him whom they pierced. (19:34–7)

The soldiers had planned to break Jesus' legs (which would typically expedite the death of the crucified), but they abstain because Jesus seems to have already died. One of the soldiers pierces Jesus' side in order to determine whether Jesus has actually expired. Commentators such as Augustine were preoccupied not only

---

[8] Michael C. Schoenfeldt, *Prayer and Power: George Herbert and Renaissance Courtship* (Chicago: University of Chicago Press, 1991), 249.

[9] Ibid., 249.

[10] Jeannie Sargent Judge, *Two Natures Met: George Herbert and the Incarnation* (New York: Peter Lang, 2004), 59–60.

[11] Chana Bloch, *Spelling the Word: George Herbert and the Bible* (Berkeley: University of California Press, 1985), 240, 278–9.

with the symbolism of the outpouring blood and water but also with the signification of the open wound itself. Augustine writes in a tractate on the Passion:

> The Evangelist used a wide awake word so that he did not say, 'pierced his side' or
> 'wounded' or anything else, but 'opened,' so that there, in a manner of speaking, the
> door of life was thrown open from which the mystical rites of the Church flowed,
> without which one does not enter into the life which is true life. That blood was shed
> for the remission of sins; that water provides the proper mix for the health-giving cup;
> it offers both bath and drink. There was a foretelling of this in that Noe was ordered
> to make a door in the side of the ark where the animals that were not going to perish
> in the flood might enter, and in these [animals] the Church was prefigured. For this
> reason the first woman was made from the side of a sleeping man....For indeed it
> signified a great good, before the great evil of collusive transgression. Here the second
> Adam, his head bowed, slept on the cross in order that from there might be found for
> him a wife—that one who flowed from the side of the One sleeping. O death from
> which the dead live again! What is cleaner than this blood? What is more healthful
> than this wound?   (50–1)[12]

As I discussed in Chapter 1, Augustine's emphasis on the result of the wounding
rather than on the piercing itself allows for his typological and intertextual glossing
of the passage. From the opening flow the sacraments, vehicles of the blood (justification) and water (baptismal sanctification). The opening recalls the door provided by Noah, itself a prefiguration of the visible and invisible Church. Celebrated
as the harbinger of life through death—Eve from the opening of Adam, Christ's
espousal of the Church—the wound "lifts up" in Johannine spirit; its link to the
mortification of the flesh is judged as secondary to its resurrectional vitality.

Early modern commentators embellished on Augustine's symbolic and typological interpretation. Lancelot Andrewes, Bishop of Winchester, remarks: "Saith
Saint Augustine...the Apostle was well advised, when he used the word opening;
for, there issued out water and blood....Marke it running out, and suffer it not
to runne waste, but receive it....Of the fulnesse whereof we all have received, in
the Sacrament of our Baptisme. Of the later (the blood)...we may receive this
day."[13] Early-seventeenth-century English writers and theologians with varying
denominational allegiances converged on the opinion that the piercing represents
the glory rather than the debasement of Christ. In his popular and widely
reprinted *Practice of Piety* (1613), Anglican Bishop Lewis Bayly imagines a dialogue in which Christ informs an interlocutor that the piercing is significant
because "by my Blood shedding, Justification and Sanctification were effected to
save thee: secondly, that my Spirit by the consciable use of the Water in
Baptisme, and bloud of the Eucharist will effect in thee righteousnesse and holinesse by which thou shalt glorifie mee."[14] John Clarke, English schoolmaster,
remarks similarly: "Out of whose pierced side, issued forth water and bloud, for

---

[12] Saint Augustine, *Tractates on the Gospel of John, 111–24*, ed. John W. Rettig (Washington, D.C.:
Catholic University Press, 1995), 50–1.

[13] Lancelot Andrewes, *XCVI Sermons* (London, 1629), 345.

[14] Lewis Bayly, *The practise of pietie directing a Christian how to walke that he may please God*
(London, 1613), 1014.

the sanctifying, and justifying, of thine Elect. To *whom,* with *thee,* and the Holy *Spirit,* be all glory, service, thanksgiving, and dominion."[15] In his treatise on the Virgin Mary, Anthony Stafford urges Mary to "Fixe thine eyes upon / This glorious Throne, / And on the right hand, there behold thy Sonne. / Behold his hands, his feet, his pierced side, / That for us dide, / Whose very wounds in heaven are Deifide."[16] And in his lengthy commentary on John 19 and the Longinus piercing, Robert Rollock, Ramist Minister of Scotland, concludes: "If thou feelest that Justice of God, and the terrours of Hell before thee, the sight of the death of Jesus would be the most joyfull and comfortable sight that ever thou sawest, and all thy joy & glorie would be in that death of Christ."[17] Because of the glorified result of the death and superfluous wounding (commentators were quick to point out that the wound actually helped to keep Christ's body intact, as his legs were not broken), Christ experiences the wound with joy rather than shame and abasement. Thus a 1603 sermon by a Protestant polemicist and rector in Lincolnshire Francis Trigge on the relationship between the piercing and justification: "*He beholds the holy bloud to boile out of his side, not onely valiantly, but joyfully.*"[18]

Herbert follows Augustine and early modern exegetes in focusing more on the final rather than on the efficient and material cause of the wound. The resultant opening allows Christ immediately to turn the wound to profit for his brethren— "And straight he turn'd" (30)—as if the wound had been expected and embraced once sustained. The wound-as-bag will provide a safe conduit for both the penitent and unregenerate: "Or if hereafter any of my friends / Will use me in this kinde, the doore / Shall still be open" (37–9). In keeping with the Augustinian interpretation of the passage (although Augustine focuses typologically on Noah's open door), Herbert has superimposed a later Johannine episode and motif, that of the good shepherd, onto the prototypical Longinus piercing: "Then said Jesus unto them againe, Verily, verily I say unto you, I am the doore of the sheepe. All that ever came before me, are theeves and robbers: but the sheepe did not heare them. I am the doore by me if any man enter in, he shall be saved, and shall goe in and out, and find pasture" (10:7–9). The point of the Johannine verses is the same as Herbert's notion. To enter the proper way is to enter through the door. Unrepentant thieves and robbers "climeth up some other way" (10:1), but anyone who enters properly through the door will receive benefits.

Throughout Herbert's poeticization of the image of the wound/bag, Christ's divinity is lodged in the vehicle of his body. The contents of the bag will be "safely" (34) delivered to God precisely because the bag is intimately connected to Christ's "heart" (36). This reflects not a transmission of the communicant's message through the pouch (as in Rosemond Tuve's notion that the bag represents a mail or "carrying pouch" for requests to the Father) but a suturing of the message in the

---

[15] John Clarke, *Holy incense for the censers of the saints* (London, 1634), 170.

[16] Anthony Stafford, *The femall glory* (London, 1635), 40.

[17] Robert Rollock, *Lectures upon the history of the Passion, Resurrection, and Ascension* (Amsterdam, 1616), 230.

[18] Francis Trigge, *The true Catholique formed according to the truth of the Scriptures, and the shape of the ancient fathers* (London, 1602), 63.

very flesh, specifically the heart that God has temporarily assumed.[19] The divinity
here is in the details. Early modern commentators typically located the site of the
wound in the "pericardion" or "pericardium," variously described as a "cawl," "pannicle," or "casket" that surrounded and protected the heart. In describing the site
of the wound as a bag, Herbert is not being especially inventive, since all of these
terms evoke the protective, sack-like aspect of the pericardium. In his annotations
on John, Edward Leigh approximates Herbert's designation as "bag" in his own use
of the term "purse" to describe the piercing of Jesus' pericardium: "It is very likely
that the very *Pericardium* was pierced, a filme or skin like unto a *purse*, wherein is
contained cleare water to coole the heate of the heart" (italics mine).[20] The important point is that, in Herbert's poem, the messages that are placed in Christ's wound
are not carried to his heart (literally and figuratively) and thence to God, as if the
route to God is through the separate medium of the flesh; such messages are placed
directly there and hence within the flesh that God has taken on. In locating the
divinity of Christ in and through the wound, Herbert follows those commentators
such as Aquinas, whose commentary on John points out that the prophetic
books—Zechariah 12:2, for example—describe a metaphorical piercing of God's
side, itself a prefiguration of the piercing of Christ and testament to Christ's
Sonship: "If we join the statement of the Prophet to what the Evangelist says, it is
clear that the crucified Christ is God, for what the Prophet says he says as God, and
the Evangelist applies this to Christ."[21]

The identification of the pre-incarnated and post-resurrected Christ with God
signals the "The Bag's" partially realized eschatology. As I noted earlier, the reference
in the poem to Christ's door—"the doore / Shall still be open" (38–9)—recalls
John's good shepherd narrative: "I am the doore of the sheepe" (10:7). As good
shepherd, Jesus announces that those who enter through the door properly (because
they have been raised up) receive eternal life: "My sheepe heare my voyce, and
I know them, and they follow me. And I give unto them eternall life, and they shall
never perish, neither shall any man plucke them out of my hand. My father which
gave them me, is greater then all: and no man is able to plucke them out of my
fathers hand" (10:27–9). Although John will elsewhere remark that eternal life
awaits the faithful who have died, the good shepherd discourse reveals eternal life to

---

[19] See John Tobin's note in *The Complete Poems of George Herbert*, ed. John Tobin (London and
New York: Penguin Books, 2005), 396.

[20] Edward Leigh, *Annotations Upon All the New Testament* (London, 1650), 168. On the association between the pericardium or pericardion and the site of the piercing, see William Perkins, *The
Golden Chaine* (London, 1600), where Perkins describes the pericardion as a casket or "coate": "For
seeing that water and blood gushed forth together, it is very like, the casket or coate which investeth
the heart called *Pericardion*, was pierced" (31). Comparable descriptions of the pericardion appear in
manuals on health and the humours—for example, in Levinus Lemnius's *Touchstone of Complexions*
(London, 1576), where the pericardion is described as a "pannicle or coffyn," (113), and William Vaughan's
The Soul's Exercise (London, 1641), where the pericardion is described as a "skinne about his heart"
(214). The use of "cawl" to describe the pericardion itself derives from Hos. xiii:8, as noted in the
OED: "I...will rent the kall of their hearts."

[21] Saint Thomas Aquinas, *Commentary on the Gospel of John* (Washington, D.C.: Catholic University
Press, 2010), 249.

be a present reality that will be fulfilled in the future.[22] In Herbert's poem, the secure conveyance of the messages of the devotees to the "Fathers hands and sight" (33) recalls the Johannine notion that the sheep who have entered through the door will find a place alongside God and the Son, secure in the Father's hands. The temporal change marked by "hereafter any of my friends" (37) reveals that the secure salvation and life for those faithful converts is a present rather than future state. Those who abuse Christ will still find the door open and will be able to enter when they disabuse themselves of their recalcitrant sighs. The poem integrates realized and future eschatology in keeping with the eschatological message of the shepherd source text.

In the context of the Johannine content of the poem, the very structure and narrative of "The Bag" is consistently Johannine. As we have seen in several earlier chapters, a hallmark of the Johannine approach is the use of multiple forms of irony that typically issue from discipleship misunderstanding. Nicodemus, who mistakenly associates rebirth with a literal process of being born again, is just one example of someone whose inability to understand Christ's message impedes his ability to acknowledge Christ as the true light. Nicodemus's ignorance provides Christ with the occasion to further reveal, although indirectly and symbolically, efficacious knowledge of Christ's role in relation to the Father. When we encounter such examples of narrative irony and misunderstanding, we are made aware that Christ relies on a well-structured literary approach. Through Christ's use of dramatic irony, symbolism, double-entendre, repetition, and metaphor, his hearers are Socratically coaxed into understanding and assimilating his words and lessons.

The speaker of Herbert's "The Bag" sets out not merely to assure himself and his readers that tribulations are ultimately the "triumph" of God's art (5) but to demonstrate that such an overcoming is the case. To the basic question, "Hast thou not heard, that my Lord JESUS di'd?" (7), the speaker realizes that he will need to provide a narratively rich answer. Yet to arrive properly at illumination requires the telling of a mysterious and "strange storie," the true significance of which will be clarified by the poem's close. The pivotal image and sign is the piercing of Christ's side. Rather than intuitively suggesting the abasement of Christ's body, it signifies the lifting up of Christ; and it does so through the provision of an opening by which penitents might communicate with God and through which Christ provides justifying and sanctifying grace. Gene Veith remarks that the strange story makes scant "reference to the stated problem of the poem, which is despair."[23] Yet once explicated properly, the wound helps to explain why the speaker and the poem's readers should leave off the despair that otherwise seems too quickly explained

---

[22] John makes a distinction between present eternal life and the *eschaton* that follows the resurrection of the dead. As R. Alan Culpepper remarks, "Believers who 'see the Son' and participate in the community's sacred meal have eternal life (now), and Jesus will raise them up on the last day." "Realized Eschatology in the Experience of the Johannine Community," in *Resurrection of Jesus in the Gospel of John*, eds. Craig R. Koester and Reimund Bieringer (Tübingen: Mohr Siebeck, 2008), 255. On John's realized eschatology, see also C. H. Dodd, "The Kingdom of God has Come," *Expository Times* 48 (1936), 138–42.

[23] Gene Edward Veith, Jr., *Reformation Spirituality: The Religion of George Herbert* (Eugene: Wipf & Stock, 1985), 224.

away early in the poem. Christ, through the vehicle of the wound and its significance, provides the efficacious knowledge of why his communicants should neither despair over his death nor for their own tribulations. And I emphasize the
phrase *efficacious knowledge*, because the idea is that the simple understanding of
and belief in the imparted knowledge of Christ's intimate relationship both with
God and with sinners is sufficient assurance that they either have been saved (the
faithful) or will be saved (those whose sighs represent spiritual lassitude).

"The Bag" tells a strange story, the proper explication of which is required in
order to arrive at the rather counterintuitive Johannine association of the wound
with Christ's divinity rather than his corporeality. This strangeness is what no
doubt gives "The Bag" the provisional, open-ended quality that one finds in so
many of Herbert's lyrics. Initially, we think we are reading, as Helen Vendler
remarks, a "denatured fairy tale," only to be then confronted with the unspeakable piercing of Christ's side which turns out to be the very means by which our
fears are allayed and Christ's divinity is assured.[24] But if the poem unsettles us,
changes course, or, in Vendler's terms, "re-invents" itself afresh, this revisionism
and irony do conduce to stable meaning. Such a process of clarification through
irony is precisely what Herbert would have inherited from the Johannine imagery
and atmosphere on which the poem is based.[25] This does not mean that Herbert
self-consciously imitates the style of Johannine accommodation and pedagogical
misdirection. It suggests only that, because Herbert's Christology is Johannine in
orientation, the irony that accompanies his use of Johannine motifs is more plaus-
ibly connected to the irony intrinsic to his scriptural sources than it is attributable
to an idiosyncratic tendency of his poems to "re-invent" themselves or, in Stanley
Fish's terms, to present themselves as deconstructive, "self-consuming artifacts."[26]
Nor does the Johannine temper detract from the shining originality of Herbert's
poem. On the one hand, the strange story at the outset is founded on the mysteriousness of the Johannine source narrative: the *Logos* theme, the descent and return
motif, the high divinity of the Son, all contribute to the widespread early modern
view of the Fourth Gospel as the most lofty and spiritual of the Gospel narratives.
On the other hand, Herbert further estranges the story with the inventive conceit
of the vehicular pericardium/bag, as if the mysteriousness of John's story gives
Herbert license to further occult the source narrative. Yet Herbert's Christ, like
the Johannine Christ, goes on to reveal and resolve the mysteries that the high
Christological narrative raises.

The overlap between Johannine and Herbertian irony can be made clearer if we
distinguish between stable and unstable irony. Stable irony, intended in nature, is
finite in the sense that it does not frustrate our desire to find meaning: "Once a

---

[24] Vendler, *The Poetry of George Herbert*, 175.
[25] For a concise definition of Vendler's conception of Herbert's "re-invented" poems, see her essay,
"The Re-Invented Poem: George Herbert's Alternatives," in *Essential Articles for the Study of George
Herbert's Poetry*, ed. John R. Roberts (Hamden: Archon Books, 1979), 181–98.
[26] On the tendency of Herbert's poems to deconstruct or "consume" themselves, see Stanley Fish,
Self-Consuming Artifacts: The Experience of Seventeenth-Century Literature (Berkeley: University of
California Press, 1973), chapter 3, *passim*.

reconstruction of meaning has been made, the reader is not then invited to under-mine it with further demolitions and reconstructions."[27] Unstable irony, on the other hand, will continually elude fixed meaning or propositional knowledge: "The truth asserted or implied is that no stable reconstruction can be made out of the ruins revealed through the irony."[28] The stabilities of Johannine irony, as R. Alan Culpepper remarks, derive from a basic presupposition of Johannine theology, especially as related in the Prologue to the Fourth Gospel. As the Word made flesh, and the only one who has ever seen God, Christ occupies an Olympian position (John's Prologue is itself influenced by Greek and Hellenistic sources). His mission is to address those "who dwell in error," to correct the misjudgments of his brethren, themselves victims of irony, and to teach them to "[j]udge not according to the appearance, but judge righteous judgement" (7:24).[29] The process relies on stable irony because, by the end of discrete pericopes throughout the Fourth Gospel, discipleship misunderstanding is clarified or corrected rather than suspended in paradox or instability. It is precisely this culmination of meaning through the route of misunderstanding that one finds in "The Bag": the meaning of the piercing becomes more, not less stable as the speaker and reader come to greater knowledge of its significance as the poem unfolds.

CHRIST AS TRUE VINE: "THE BUNCH OF GRAPES" AND "THE AGONIE"

In "The Bag," Herbert is interested more in the mysterious, even anti-passible, div-inity of Christ, in keeping with Johannine theology, than he is in the humanity of the savior. Yet biblical scholars have at times maintained that what makes John distinctive and irreducible is that his Gospel is as interested in elevating Christ as God-man as it is in depicting Jesus' low-born humanity (Jesus' weeping is typically mentioned as evidence of Jesus' humanity, a topic on which John Donne spends an entire Lenten sermon in 1622).[30] Such ambiguity renders Johannine Christology central to the Trinitarian–Socinian debates during the latter part of the seventeenth century. As Paul C. H. Lim remarks, "One of the reasons the Gospel of John became a veritable minefield for both anti-Trinitarian and Trinitarian exegesis was that this Gospel, more than any other New Testament book, affirmed—often within the same pericope, if not the same verse(s), the Son's subordinate and eco-nomic status and his equal status vis-à-vis the Father."[31] Here I continue to follow

---

[27] Wayne C. Booth, *A Rhetoric of Irony* (Chicago: University of Chicago Press, 1974), 6, cited in R. Alan Culpepper, "Reading Johannine Irony," in *Exploring the Gospel of John: In Honor of D. Moody Smith*, eds. R. Alan Culpepper and C. Clifton Black (Louisville: Westminster John Knox Press, 1996), 193.

[28] Booth, *A Rhetoric of Irony*, 240, cited in Culpepper, "Reading Johannine Irony," 193–4.

[29] Culpepper, "Reading Johannine Irony," 194.

[30] Donne's Lazarus sermon was preached at Whitehall in 1622/3. See John Donne's *Sermons on the Psalms and Gospels*, ed. Evelyn M. Simpson (Berkeley: University of California Press, 1963), 157–77.

[31] Paul C. H. Lim, *Mystery Unveiled: The Crisis of the Trinity in Early Modern England* (Oxford: Oxford University Press, 2012), 274.

those early modern and modern commentators who, acknowledging the presence of the human Christ in the Fourth Gospel, point out that even in his most crea-turely manifestation Jesus is not shamed or rendered vulnerable to the extent that he is in the Passion narratives of the Synoptics.[32] The distinction bears directly on our Johannine interpretation of Herbert. Herbert, too, is as preoccupied with the humanity of Jesus as much as he is with the Son's divinity. Yet even when put in the poetic contexts of abasement (rendered as the Man of Sorrows in the iconographic winepress, for example), Herbert's Christ remains principally a God of joy, love, and glory.

The typology of Herbert's "The Bunch of Grapes" has received much critical attention.[33] The standard reading is that Herbert's speaker, who has lost possession of joy, meditates on the Pauline notion that Israel's sojourn to the Promised Land presaged the New Testament wandering from sin to atonement. The Old Testament hieroglyph, the cluster of grapes, refers to the grapes that the elders of the tribes of Israel secured from Canaan as proof of the fertility and bounty of that land. Yet because the elders perceived that Canaan was populated with giants and estab-lished tribes, they deemed the land uninhabitable for themselves. Against God's instruction to Abraham to enter into the New Jerusalem, they retreat, after which God punishes them by forcing them to wander in the desert for forty years.

Herbert's speaker recognizes that his movement from joy to sin and backsliding recapitulates the godliness but ultimate disobedience of the Israelites: "For as the Jews of old by Gods command / Travell'd, and saw no town; / So now each Christian hath his journeys spann'd" (8–10). Yet he also realizes that, in acquiring the giant cluster of grapes at Eshcol, the elders experienced at least a foretaste of things to come should they remain constant in their devotion. If his life does recapitulate the Israelites', then should not he experience such momentary joy alongside his sorrows?—"But where's the cluster? where's the taste / Of mine inher-itance? Lord, if I must borrow, / Let me as well take up their joy, as sorrow" (19–20). However, the speaker quickly realizes that, as the fulfillment of the vine, Christ has already produced the saving wine that is sourced from the foundational vine and grape: "But can he want the grape, who hath the wine? / I have their fruit and more" (22–3). One reference here is to Christ's self-designation as the true vine in John 15: "I am the true vine, and my Father is the husbandman. Every branch in me that beareth not fruit, hee taketh away: and every branch that beareth fruit, he purgeth it, that it may bring foorth more fruit. Now ye are cleane through the word which I have spoken unto you" (15:1–3). As we have seen in earlier chapters, the image of Christ as true vine is exegeted frequently during the sixteenth and seventeenth centuries. The vine discourse is typically understood to be a reference to the formation of the true Church (the gathered fruit signifying the earnest

---

[32] On the divinity of Christ in John, see Ernst Käsemann, *Testament of Jesus: Study of the Gospel of John in Light of Chapter 17*, trans. G. Krodel (Minneapolis: Augsburg Fortress, 1978).

[33] See, for example, Joseph Summers, *George Herbert: His Religion and Art* (Cambridge, MA: Harvard University Press, 1968), 126–8. Rosemond Tuve provides a thorough account of the emblem-atic and iconographical tradition behind the grape image in *A Reading of George Herbert* (Chicago: University of Chicago Press, 1952), 112–37.

members thereof), but it was also frequently understood to reflect the regeneration of converts, fruit glossed as good works resulting from the gracious powers of Christ as vine.[34] The vine narrative is particularly relevant to Herbert's poem for what it concludes about joy. In the Fourth Gospel, after establishing that the bearing of fruit leads to the glorification of the Father, Jesus' focus shifts quietly to the love and joy that the vine image expresses:

> As the Father hath loved me, so have I loved you: continue ye in my love. If ye keepe my Commandements, ye shal abide in my love, even as I have kept my Fathers Commandements, and abide in his love. These things have I spoken unto you, that my joy might remaine in you, and that your joy might be full. This is my Commaundement, that ye love one another, as I have loved you. Greater love hath no man then this, that a man lay downe his life for his friends.   (15:9–13)

The vine discourse informs Christ's hearers that, should they obey his one command to abide in his love, they can be assured of the fullness of joy. It is the coming and going of joy about which the speaker of Herbert's poem complains and which motivates his analogy/disanalogy with the Israelites as a means to reinstate the joy that he has lost. In the further context of the poem, the vine metaphor helps the speaker to see that he must above all love Christ, love presented in the poem as adoration—"But much more him I must adore" (26)—if he is to recollect the joy that he once possessed. The Johannine vine narrative extends beyond the simple reference to typological fulfillment of the vine in Christ. It explains the poem's thrust to explain why the speaker's equanimity has been lost and the means by which that equanimity can be regained.

But "The Bunch of Grapes" does not rest on its own Johannine exegesis. The final image of the winepress is drawn from a range of Old Testament sources and ensuing iconographical tradition: "Who of the Laws sowre juice sweet wine did make, / Ev'n God himself being pressed for my sake" (27–8). Herbert's multivalent use of the grape and wine imagery allows him to superimpose the more widespread winepress image onto the Johannine one of Christ as the true vine. Serving as a typological palimpsest, the Johannine ambience seeps through the superimposed image of the winepress. The winepress image is typically employed to depict the sorrows of a suffering Christ, and it often puts into relief the blood and graphic wounds of Christ. But in keeping with the privileging of the divinity of Christ, Herbert bleaches the image of its graphic violence by first putting God instead of Jesus on the press and then simply conjuring the image rather than embellishing it. The force of "Ev'n" has a paradoxical value. On the one hand, it exclaims the astonishing and exceptional fact that "God himself" is "pressed" for the speaker's sins; on the other hand, it protects Christ (God himself) from the

---

[34] On the relationship between the "true vine" and regeneration, see, for example, Henry Burton, *The Christians bulwarke, against Satans battery* (London, 1632): "As the branch cannot beare fruit of it selfe, except it abide in the vine: no more can ye, except ye abide in mee: or without me yee can doe nothing. Therefore while a man is out of Christ, untill by faith he be ingrafted into Christ, the true Vine, from whom hee receiveth the lively sappe of a new life, hee can doe nothing; nothing that is good, nothing that is acceptable to God; no worke of new obedience or sanctification" (31).

illustrative debasement and suffering typically associated with the image and Christ's agony at Golgotha.

In terms of the structure and style of the poem, Stanley Fish is correct to note that the poem offers certain patterns and modes of understanding, only then to falsify or at least gently correct such misconstruals: "We too enjoy apparent (interpretive) successes and achieve supposedly full understandings, only to find again and again that the successes are temporary and the understandings partial."[35] Yet such construals and misconstruals, the poem's very "restlessness," to use a phrase introduced in a related context by Louis Martz, stem not from Herbert's poeticization of catechistical theory or meditative practice but more fundamentally from Herbert's desire to have a single Johannine theme—the divinity of Christ—emerge from a host of references and symbols that might otherwise cause the reader to question that very Christological exaltation.[36]

What of the other, more graphic recounting of the winepress motif in Herbert's "The Agonie?" Here, too, a Johannine interpretation puts the use of the image in its proper theological context. Opening as an Augustinian meditation on the virtues of self-scrutiny, "The Agonie" compresses the winepress and piercing image within two stanzas. If one needs to be reminded of sin, cautions Herbert, one should repair to Mount Olivet and apprehend "[a] man so wrung with pains, that all his hair, / His skinne, his garments bloudie be. / Sinne is that presse and vice, which forceth pain / To hunt his cruell food through ev'ry vein" (9–12). Here Herbert provides an unquestionably graphic and moving depiction of Christ's suffering on the cross, recalling a tradition of representing the humility of the cross that finds its *locus classicus* in Bernard of Clairvaux's *On the Song of Songs*.[37] But as soon as the image is presented, it is conflated with the love that Christ's blood and sacrifice signify. Rather than read a forensic meaning into the significance of the winepress image—as expiatory sacrifice and atonement—Herbert writes that, alongside the image of the piercing of Christ's side, the blood produced from both is nothing other than the love, that "liquour sweet and most divine," which "God feels as bloud; but I, as wine" (17–18). The intimate relationship between the Passion and love is a recurring Johannine theme, expressed clearly, for example, in chapter 3 of the Fourth Gospel: "For God so loved the world, that he gave his only begotten Sonne: that whosoever beleeveth in him, should not perish, but have everlasting life" (3:16); and, as might be expected, the same sense is conveyed in the continuation of the allegory of the true vine in which Christ remarks, "Greater love hath no man then this, that a man lay downe his life for his friends" (15:13).

---

[35] Fish, *The Living Temple*, 125.

[36] Louis Martz, "The Action of the Self: Devotional Poetry in the Seventeenth Century," in *Metaphysical Poetry, Stratford-Upon-Avon Studies* 11, eds. Malcolm Bradbury and David Palmer (London: Edward Arnold Publishers, 1970), 108. Cited in Fish, *The Living Temple*, 5.

[37] On the use of the winepress image in seventeenth-century theology, particularly in relation to Milton's *Paradise Regained*, see Russell M. Hillier, "The Wreath, The Rock, and the Winepress: Passion Iconography in Milton's *Paradise Regained*," *Literature and Theology* 22:4 (2008), 387–405. On the use of graphic representations of Christ in Bernard and then later in Lancelot Andrewes, Aemelia Lanyer, and others, see Femke Molekamp, "Reading Christ the Book in Aemelia Lanyer's *Salve Deus Rex Judaeorum*: Iconography and the Cultures of Reading," *Studies in Philology* 109:3 (2012), 321–4.

"The Agonie" begins with the graphic image of the winepress and agony of Christ's human body (as it appears in the Old Testament, Luke, and elsewhere), but it gradually shifts to both a Johannine image (the piercing) and a Johannine temper. Christ's mortifying sacrifice is an act (event) principally of divine love that exalts the body under stress, as if the poem provides its own Johannine antidote to the portrait of an overly suffering Jesus.

DISCIPLESHIP MISUNDERSTANDING AND "LOVE UNKNOWN"

"Love unknown" opens with the speaker's earnest plea for help. While sighing and fainting he proffers a gift to his lord—"a dish of fruit" (6)—only to find that God's servant rejects the fruit, seizing on his heart instead: "Seiz'd on my heart alone, / And threw it in a font, wherein did fall / A stream of bloud, which issu'd from the side / Of a great rock" (12–15). The image of the gashed rock is taken from Isaiah: "And they thirsted not when he led them through the deserts; he caused the waters to flow out of the rocke for them: he clave the rocke also, and the waters gushed out" (Isa. 48:21). Importantly, the Isaian eschatological rock is the Old Testament image that presages the uniquely Johannine image of the Longinus piercing of Christ's side that I have discussed in the first section of this chapter. Subsequent lines of "Love unknown" bring out the baptismal significance of the Johannine fulfillment of the Isaian image: "There it was dipt and dy'd, / And washt, and wrung: the very wringing yet / Enforceth tears. *Your heart was foul, I fear*" (16–18). If read solely in the context of the Isaiah reference, the lines raise something of a puzzle. While the blood is clearly the justificatory (if not sacramental) blood into which the heart is "dipt" and "dy'd," the "washing" and "wringing" that follow, in conjunction with the speaker's "tears," evoke an image of water alongside the blood. We recall that in John's fulfillment of the image of the piercing, blood *and* water pour forth from Jesus' side, a joint effusion that exercises the creative exegeses of John's early and later commentators, who assert that while the blood signifies justification, the water signifies baptism and sanctification: "*That the Sacraments of the new Law flowed out of Christ's side:* now none issued thence, but the Sacrament of water, which is Baptisme, and the Sacrament of bloud in the Supper."[38] Although Herbert appropriates the Isaian imagery to begin his narrative, the fulfilling significance of that imagery is taken from John's expression of the image in 19:34–5.[39]

The speaker quickly reveals that he has not entirely understood the significance of the cleansing of his heart. In particular, he acknowledges that he cannot be

---

[38] Simon Birckbek, *The Protestants evidence taken out of good records* (London, 1635), 119.

[39] On the extensive influence of Isaiah on John, see Daniel J. Brendsel, "Isaiah Saw His Glory": *The Use of Isaiah 52–53 in John 12* (Berlin: De Gruyter, 2014); Catrin H. Williams, "Isaiah in the Gospel of John," in *Isaiah in the New Testament*, eds. Steve Moyise and Maarten J. J. Menken (London: Bloomsbury T&T Clark, 2005), 101–16; and James Hamilton, "The Influence of Isaiah on the Gospel of John," *Perichoresis* 5/2 (2007), 139–58.

assured of his spiritual standing and that backsliding is a constitutional possibility. In response to his misunderstanding of the significance of the small miracle that he has just experienced and his overly assured belief that his "heart was well, / And clean and fair" (22–3), the speaker is presented with another cautionary image: "A boyling caldron, round about whose verge / Was in great letters set *AFFLICTION*. / The greatnesse shew'd the owner" (27–8). Still naive as to his spiritual progress, he presumptuously offers his newly cleansed heart as a sacrifice, only to have it thrown into the scalding pan because it remains too callous: "My heart, that brought it (do you understand?) / The offerers heart. *Your heart was hard I fear*" (36–7). Much of the remainder of the poem fixes steadily on the manner in which the speaker's heart remains, despite his seemingly best efforts at renewal, callous and dull, for he tends to pray lazily: "Though my lips went, my heart did stay behinde" (59).

The identification of the hardened heart with spiritual recalcitrance is an important Isaian theme, but here again it serves as a type for the theme's much fuller Johannine treatment that helps to shape the fulfillment theology of Herbert's poem. Describing Jesus' relationship to his disciples toward the end of his public ministry, John remarks that, even after having witnessed several miracles, his hearers still do not believe him (12:37). John believes that this tragedy of unbelief comes as no surprise because Isaiah has already recorded the comparable unbelief of the Israelites. At this point John directly quotes Isaiah on the hardened hearts of Moses's followers: "Therefore they could not beleeve, because that Esaias said againe, He hath blinded their eyes, and hardned their heart, that they should not see with their eyes, nor understand with their heart, and be converted, and I should heale them" (12:39–40). Importantly, given Herbert's figuration of the hardened heart throughout "Love unknown," John substitutes "hardened heart" for Isaiah's reference to making the Israelites' heart "fat": "Make the heart of this people fat, and make their eares heavy, and shut their eyes: lest they see with their eyes, and heare with their eares, and understand with their heart, and convert and be healed" (Isa. 6:10). John also grants more agency to God as the source of the hardening and blinding. In the Isaian prototype, the hardening and blinding are described passively through the use of indirect commands.

John's message in 12:39–41 is that Christian unbelief, foretold in Isaiah, is expected and natural. Christ's hearers cannot simply rely on their own senses and devotional aspirations to bind themselves to God, despite the signs and wonders that Christ has already displayed to them. "We must first understand," Calvin remarks, "that it was not Christ's fault that the Jews did not believe in Him. He abundantly testified who He was.... John goes further and says that faith is not begotten of an ordinary human faculty but is a unique and rare gift of God."[40] It is this uncommonness and difficulty of maintaining belief that is at question in Herbert's "Love unknown." Despite the miraculous workings of the Spirit and

---

[40] John Calvin, *The Gospel According to St. John*, in *Calvin's New Testament Commentaries*, vol. 5, eds. David W. Torrance and Thomas F. Torrance, trans. T. H. L. Parker (Grand Rapids: Eerdmans Publishing Company, 1959), 45.

sacrament on the speaker's behalf, he remains naive as to the significance of his witnessing; that ignorance is represented in the persistent failure of the various processes of suppling that are offered in the poem.

Like "The Bag," "Love unknown" also intimates, through its prophetic and Johannine imagery, a partially realized eschatology. The Isaian figure of the furnace of affliction, recalled in lines 26–9 of Herbert's poem, conveys the message of refining and purifying that is cross-referenced in several prophetic and apocalyptic books, most notably Jeremiah, Zechariah, and Daniel. In Daniel, for example, the theme of afflictive purifying and refining is sounded in Michael's deliverance during the end-time: "Many shalbe purified, and made white and tried: but the wicked shall doe wickedly: and none of the wicked shall understand, but the wise shall understand" (Dan 12:10). The narrative trajectory in Herbert's poem that moves from the image of the fountain to the furnace is paralleled in Zechariah 13. The chapter in Zechariah opens with a reference to the fountain offered to the Temple of David that is to provide spiritual washings of the faithful—"In that day there shalbe a fountaine opened to the house of David, and to the inhabitants of Jerusalem, for sinne, and for uncleannesse" (Zec 13:1)—and closes with a reference to refinement through burning that is applied to the remaining third of the faithful: "And I will bring the thirde part through the fire, and wil refine them as silver is refined, & will try them as gold is tried: they shall call on my Name, and I wil heare them" (Zec 13:9). The Zechariah passages on the scattered sheep are themselves the typological sources for the burning and refining of the third portion of the earth that is described throughout Revelation 8. If this seems to take us far from John's Gospel, recall that John provides the principal New Testament pericope that fulfills the Isaian notion of suppling and refining through affliction that is central to Herbert's "Love unknown." The poem's imagery harks back to the Prophets via John and then, in the scriptural connotations of the flaming furnace, gestures toward Revelation.

This is not to argue that "Love unknown" is an apocalyptic poem, but it does suggest that the poem has eschatological resonances, not all of which are future-oriented. The speaker of the poem needs to realize that the fulfillment of the symbolic function of the furnace of affliction, to refine and supple his heart, has already been undertaken on his behalf: "*Truly, Friend, / For ought I heare, your Master shows to you / More favour then you wot of*" (63–4). The speaker's plight is not that he is a hardened sinner, but that he is unaware of the fact that the renewing and quickening have already transpired, such actions placed in the past tense in the poem. Christ's redemptive death does not simply have forensic effects; it has sanctifying effects that have already taken place on the speaker's behalf, making his renewal a present rather than a future accomplishment. Certainly the speaker has not achieved anything like the everlasting life that Jesus promises to the faithful in the Fourth Gospel. But the process toward that attainment has already begun. A foretaste of eternal life has been made available to the speaker (given that the eschatological refining on his behalf has already been undertaken) in his creaturely present rather than his post-resurrectional future.

Finally, the very title, "Love unknown," captures the Johannine structure of misunderstanding that is recapitulated in the dialogical structure of the poem.

The obtuseness of the speaker as to the workings of Christ's love is reiterated again and again by the interlocutor, who never directly identifies himself as Christ. The speaker's "servant" or "friend" provides several explanations of the speaker's ignorance and presents the speaker with miraculous symbolic accounts of regeneration. Yet the speaker cannot extract the symbolic meaning from what he perceives as literally disturbing afflictions. Helen Vendler has recently observed that, in compensation for the inconstancy of God's presence, Herbert develops a model of divine intimacy based on friendship: "Herbert's most credible dramatic model is one of almost horizontal intimacy with the God who writes, or speaks, as a friend."[41] Yet Vendler draws no distinction between Christ and God as friend, and she overlooks the scriptural bases for the friendship theme. The idea of Christ as "friend" of the apostles is unique to Johannine theology, particularly John 15:14–15: "Ye are my friends, if ye do whatsoever I command you. Henceforth I call you not servants, for the servant knoweth not what his lord doth, but I have called you friends: for all things that I have heard of my Father, I have made knowen unto you." As friend, Christ in Herbert's poems clarifies seeming riddles for Herbert's speakers, as in Jordan (II): "But while I bustled, I might heare a friend / Whisper, *How wide is all this long pretence*!" (15–16).[42] The friend in "Love unknown" helps the speaker realize that the fountain, cauldron, and bed of thorns are connected in the speaker's mind with his inability to rest because he cannot put together their typological and symbolic significance. The poem reads as a veritable series of riddles posed to the speaker, the resolutions of which are explained only by the poem's direct address at the end: "*Mark the end. / The Font did onely, what was old, renew: / The Caldron suppled, what was grown too hard: / The Thorns did quicken; what was grown too dull*" (65–7). The title of Herbert's poem alerts us to the fact that that the approach and content of the poem will be, through the routes of irony and misunderstanding, the speaker's gradual illumination regarding the proper knowledge of the way of God through the divinely incarnated Word. What looks like Herbert's idiosyncratic tendency to reinvent his poem or to provide Socratic lessons for his speakers is explainable from his use of Johannine theology, this time superimposed on Isaian sources.[43]

The above readings of "The Bag," "The Bunch of Grapes," and "Love unknown" assume that Herbert's poetry is often *revelatory* rather than simply paradoxical in nature. The poems seek to illuminate knowledge of God's mysteries and Christ's redemptive actions, and they do so through the route of stable irony in which meaning/knowledge increases as a particular poem's theological crux or spiritual conflict works toward resolution.[44] This does not mean that all crises are neatly

---

[41] Helen Vendler, *Invisible Listeners: Lyric Intimacy in Herbert, Whitman, and Ashberry* (Princeton: Princeton University Press, 2005), 16.

[42] The Johannine theme of Christological friendship is explicitly stated in "The Church-Porch," where Herbert draws on the legacy of John as beloved disciple and friend of Christ: "But love is lost, the way of friendship's gone, / Though *David* had his *Jonathan, Christ* his *John*" (274–5).

[43] Vendler's brief discussion of "Love unknown" can be found in "The Re-invented Poem," 184.

[44] On the use of stable irony and revelation in Johannine theology, see Culpepper, "Reading Johannine Irony," 193–207.

resolved in a given poem; it does assume, though, that not all of the poems purposefully (catechistically, for example) frustrate meaning or move toward paradox and instability. It is precisely this revelatory aspect that, among other qualities, renders the poems discussed above more Johannine than Pauline in orientation. In both John and Herbert a revelatory poetics actually presupposes the use of the stable ironies that I have described above. Paul's fondness for paradox is well known, evidenced by the difficulty of finding congruity (as Luther struggled to do) between Romans 2:13 ("the doers of the Law shalbe iustified") and Romans 3:28 ("Therefore wee conclude, that a man is justified by faith, without the deeds of the Law"). Given such paradoxicality (and Paul's concern to exfoliate the intricacies of the faith, grace, and law relationship), a Pauline poetics would expectedly rely on unstable irony, as in so many of John Donne's *Holy Sonnets*, which meditate directly on Pauline paradoxes as well as on the fundamentally ironic nature of God becoming man: "'Twas much, that man was made like God before, / But, that God should be made like man, much more" ("Wilt thou love God," 13–14).[45] In Herbert's most revelatory poems, however, the primary objective is not to meditate on the irreducible nature of faith or even on the paradox of God made flesh. The concern is to depict poetically the fundamentally divine nature of Christ, someone who, because he alone descends from above and has experienced the beatific vision, is in a privileged position to remedy misjudgment and dispense an accommodated form of redemptive knowledge to the poems' speakers and readers. To Heather Asals's observation that "instructive, indeed, corrective, the voice of Christ frequently breaks through the poet's eudaemonistic, self-satisfied, and self-justifying voice," and to Vendler's remark that "Jesus' function in 'Love unknown' is that of a *viva voce* interpreter of the narrator's complaints, making love unknown into love known," I would suggest that at such moments Herbert's Christ sounds more like the Christ of the Fourth Gospel than any other scriptural voicing of the Son.[46] And such divine voicing typically relies on dramatic irony in order to provide corrections and illumination not to Herbert's implied readers (who would be expected to have sifted through the complexities of Johannine irony) but to the recalcitrant speakers of a given poem.

To explain further the importance of Johannine irony to such devotional verse, we turn now to Henry Vaughan, much of whose poetry is directly influenced by Herbert's style and thematic range. I have chosen for a close reading Vaughan's "The Night," a poem that, like so many of Herbert's poems, centers on unique Johannine images and pericopes but that also relies on forms of irony that are still more complex and open-ended than Herbert's use of stable irony.

---

[45] From the 1633 edition included in *John Donne's Poetry*, ed. Donald R. Dickson (New York: W. W. Norton, 2007).

[46] Heather A. R. Asals, *Equivocal Predication: George Herbert's Way to God* (Toronto: University of Toronto Press, 1981), 39. I would not conflate the "corrections" of the speaker or *persona* with the corrections of the poet/Herbert as Asals does. Vendler's remark can be found in *Invisible Listeners*, 20.

DARKNESS AND JOHANNINE IRONY
IN VAUGHAN'S "THE NIGHT"

Critical debates about the theological and philosophical background of Vaughan's "The Night" seem to have established that, if the poem is not firmly Hermetic in orientation, Vaughan at least borrowed fundamental motifs from the Hermetic and Cabbalistic traditions. What such debates have neglected to consider, however, is the Johannine foundation of much of the poem (which informs more than simply the opening reference to Nicodemus in John 3:2). This includes Vaughan's use in "The Night" of Johannine notions of darkness, light, *gnosis*, the divinity of Christ, and the hiddenness of God generally. The next section aims to resituate the focus on Vaughan's overt and veiled use of the Fourth Gospel as a means of explaining his complexly original account of the early modern Reformed notion of the *deus absconditus*.

One of the limitations of the Hermetic and Dionysian interpretation of "The Night" as against the Johannine is that the former, mystical interpretation understands the paradox of seeing God in or through darkness as a purgative process through which darkness becomes a means to witness God's light. Because Vaughan's poem serves as an apology for darkness throughout, and its final stanza celebrates a unitive process in which the speaker hides in God's "dazzling darkness," the poem at most borrows the trope of light-in-darkness from a broad neo-Platonic tradition. A better approach to interpreting Vaughan's vision is to see it as a digression from but then a return to its self-proclaimed Johannine sources. One way of reading "The Night" in relation to Johannine approach and form is to see it as resorting to forms of linguistic re-appropriation analogous to what one finds in the Fourth Gospel itself.

"The Night" opens with a direct reference to Nicodemus and an allusion to the scriptural notion of Christ-as-veil: "Through that pure *Virgin-shrine*, / That sacred vail drawn o'r thy glorious noon, / That men might look and live, as Glo-worms shine, / And face the Moon, / Wise *Nicodemus* saw such light / As made him know his God by night (1–6)."[47] Before attending to the veil reference, we should remind ourselves of the standard scriptural portrait of Nicodemus. Vaughan's projection of "wisdom" onto the Pharisee is an interpretive departure, an example of Vaughan's manipulation of the ordinary construal of Nicodemus as uncomprehending or ignorant. To Christ's advisement that "except a man be borne againe, he cannot see the kingdome of God" (3:3), Nicodemus pathetically responds, "How can a man be borne when he is old?" (3:4), representing a gross literalism, to which Christ responds, "Art thou a master of Israel, and knowest not these things?" (3:10). Christ then points out that if Nicodemus cannot understand the earthly accommodations to his sensibility, he will not be able to understand "heavenly things" (3:12).

Nicodemus's approach to Christ under cover of darkness exemplified for Reformed commentators cowardice and a fear of alienation from the Sanhedrin.

---

[47] All quotations from "The Night" are taken from *The Works of Henry Vaughan*, ed. L. C. Martin (Oxford: Clarendon Press, 1957), 522–3.

In his New Testament *Annotations* (1650), Edward Leigh, Puritan divine and Parliamentarian, remarks that Nicodemus was "ashamed openly to come to Jesus who was poor, and to be his disciple when he was a master in Israel."[48] George Hutcheson makes much the same point: "Nicodemus came to Jesus by night, as fearing to lose his name and reputation with the rest, or to sustain some damage, or being unwilling to be found ignorant, and one that needed come to be taught."[49] Both commentaries bring out one aspect of Nicodemus's motivation for visiting Christ at night that is featured in several of the more lengthy early modern commentaries on the Pharisee. Given that he is considered a learned pedagogue among the Sanhedrin, Nicodemus fears being deemed ignorant of Christ's coming. Thus Calvin:

> From his coming by night we infer that he was very faint-hearted; his eyes were daz-zled as it were by his own distinction. Perhaps, too, he was hindered by shame, for ambitious men think that their reputation is ruined if they once descend from the elevation of master to the rank of scholar. There was no doubt he was puffed up with a foolish opinion of his learning.[50]

Calvin shifts the vantage point slightly from Nicodemus's fear and shame to his arrogance bred of erudition. Nicodemus arrives under cover of darkness because he needs to protect his reputation for knowledge. His ignorance of Christ's ways would pose a threat to his standing in the community as a learned educator. To follow Nicodemus was, for most commentators, to remain in thrall not only to a covenant of works but also to a false conversion in which the very meeting with Christ at night might achieve satisfaction.[51] As the nonconformist John Udall remarks: "We seeke how to serve God and Mammon too: we labour to become religious in shewe, and covetous in deede: We desire to come to Christ by night with Nicodemus, for feare of worldly losses, we seeke to crie Lord, Lord, but we have no care to do the works of the Lord."[52]

Given this standard interpretation of Nicodemus's arrogance and ignorance, why does Vaughan praise Nicodemus's wisdom, holding him up as someone who, hidden in darkness, was not only able to "see" (9) God but was also, as a "blest believer" (7), able to "know" (6) God? The Johannine source text points out that Nicodemus has not at all "seen" (3:3) the kingdom of God because he has not been born again. Vaughan seems deliberately to conflate the fact of Nicodemus's literal speaking with Christ with Nicodemus's knowledge and understanding of God.

---

[48] Edward Leigh, *Annotations upon all the New Testament philologicall and theologicall* (London, 1650), 80.

[49] George Hutcheson, *An Exposition of the Gospel According to St. John* (London, 1657), 21.

[50] John Calvin, *The Gospel According to St. John*, in *Calvin's New Testament Commentaries*, vol. 4, eds. David W. Torrance and Thomas F. Torrance, trans. T. H. L. Parker (Grand Rapids: Eerdmans Publishing Company, 1959), 61.

[51] Luther's commentary on the Nicodemus pericope, concerned as it is to emphasize the failure of good works to achieve salvation outside of faith, tends to praise highly Nicodemus's character: "He lived a holy and honorable life in the world and gave due attention to good works." *Sermons on the Gospel of St. John*, in *Luther's Works*, vol. 22, ed. Jaroslav Pelikan (Saint Louis: Concordia Publishing House, 1957), 276.

[52] John Udall, *Peters fall. Two sermons upon the historie of Peters denying Christ* (London, 1584), A. iii.

Instead of providing some explanation for these departures, Vaughan's commentators have either marginalized the role of Nicodemus and the influence of Vaughan's source texts or offered creative resolutions. Puzzling over Vaughan's elevation of Nicodemus, Jonathan Post maintains that "the answer to this problem lies in Vaughan's view of history, one that affects the structure of the poem: there has been a general dimming of the lights, and if Vaughan were to pause over the Pharisee's own problems of understanding, he would fail to establish firmly at the outset a model of past piety away from which both the poem and the ages have moved."[53] For Post, Vaughan deliberately falsifies Nicodemus's piety in order to set up a stark contrast between past devotion and present backsliding. Yet if that were Vaughan's intention, one wonders why he would have chosen John 3 as a source text in the first place.

Vaughan's overriding concern in the poem to rehabilitate spiritual darkness underwrites his falsification of the Nicodemus story as well as his borrowing from the Hermetic tradition. Part of what happens in the opening two stanzas of the poem is that Vaughan's poetic treatment of the paradox of light-in-darkness ends up simplifying a more fundamental theological paradox, quite obviously misunderstood by Nicodemus, of the *theologia crucis* or the hiddenness of God in Christ. Consider Vaughan's facile use of the veil imagery in the opening stanza: the "*Virgin-shrine*" (1) that serves as a veil to allow creatures to look upon the otherwise too-bright resplendence of the deity (a common notion that one finds in Exodus, Colossians, and Hebrews) allows Nicodemus to "know his God by night" (6). But the veil image is typically tied to the clothing or flesh, as in Hebrews 10:19, that is worn by the incarnate God. The paradox of the metaphor is that the veil does not so much reveal God as reveal God's very hiddenness, consistent with the chiasmic Lutheran notion of the revelation of hiddenness and the hiddenness of the revelation. To see God by means of a veil is to see him darkly—that is, to be reminded that God is indeed much more than the debased form in which he has clothed himself. Thus John Cockburn notes, "For by becoming Man, his God-head was put under the Veil of Flesh, and the Majesty and Glory which belonged to him were for so long time eclipsed; which was certainly a stupendous Debasement."[54] Earlier in the century, Thomas Myriell exclaims: "O the power of the Majestie of Christ hidden in the vaile of our flesh."[55] An appreciation of Christ as veiled or clothed with virgin-born flesh ideally prompts faith in an unseen God, as in John Cotton's gloss on a later Johannine passage: "Though he be vailed with humane frailties... *Yet he is the way, the truth, and the life.*"[56] Because Vaughan's speaker desires to celebrate the epistemological gains that darkness provides, he manipulates the veil imagery to suggest the opposite of what it ordinarily signifies: not the fundamental distance and hiddenness of God but the accessibility of God once God's brightness has been dimmed.

[53] Jonathan Post, "Vaughan's 'The Night' and his 'late and dusky' Age," *SEL* 19 (1979), 135.
[54] John Cockburn, *Fifteen sermons preach'd upon several occasions* (London, 1697), 108.
[55] Thomas Myriell, *The devout soules search with the happie issue of comfort found* (London, 1610), 50.
[56] John Cotton, *A practicall commentary, or an exposition with observations, reasons, and uses upon the First Epistle generall of John* (London, 1658), 287.

Of course, we should not hold Vaughan to the letter of the Johannine and scriptural passages that he references at the outset. It is true that his poeticization of darkness and the knowledge of God partly derives partly from the mystical and Hermetic tradition. Yet Vaughan also swerves from this tradition in his zeal to rhapsodize about darkness. The clearest Hermetic reference to the paradox of God's illuminated darkness appears at the end of the poem: "There is in God (some say) / A deep, but dazling darkness; As men here / Say it is late and dusky, because they / See not all clear; / O for that night! where I in him / Might live invisible and dim." (49–54). The dazzling darkness reference is undoubtedly influenced by Dionysius's meditations on God's darkness in *Mystical Theology*, in which the Areopagite describes the unknown God as the "deep, but dazzling darkness" "which exceedeth light and more than exceedeth knowledge, where the simply, absolute, and unchangeable mysteries of heavenly Truth lie hidden in the dazzling obscurity of the secret Silence."[57] The Dionysian negative way describes a purgative experience, in keeping with its neo-Platonic (especially Porphyrian) pedigree, through which the initiate passes through the "dark night" of the soul in order at least to hope for a union with God. The important point is that any dialectic between light and dark needs to be surpassed in order to attain the "perfect day" with God: "There is no speaking of it, nor name nor knowledge of it. Darkness and light, error and truth—it is none of these. It is beyond assertion and denial."[58] The negative way might posit darkness as the negation of light and as an approach to Godhead, but oppositions between light and darkness, indeed all contraries, need to be negated as a final approach. The dazzling darkness of God is neither a *terminus* nor even a particular site of contemplation; it is more like an epistemological step to be surmounted. Close in spirit here to Dionysius is the anonymous author of the mystical *Cloud of Unknowing*, for whom the contemplation of darkness is a purgative or privative step in one's appreciation of the unknowability of God: "Now when I call this exercise a darkness or a cloud do not think that it is a cloud formed out of the vapours which float in the air, or a darkness such as you have in your house at night.... When I say 'darkness,' I mean a privation of knowing, just as whatever you do not know or have forgotten is dark to you, because you do not see it with your spiritual eyes."[59] Vaughan departs from the *apophatic* sense of God's "dazzling darkness" in his hypostasizing of what should be a step in an arduous epistemological process. Drawing on the foundational work of St. John of the Cross, R. A. Durr maintains that Vaughan elsewhere acknowledges such a process, although Durr fails to tie such an acknowledgement to "The Night": "Vaughan had known the first night of the soul, the sensual night, 'wherein the soul is purged according to sense'... but he hungered for the experience of the second night, which 'is the portion of the very few,' in order that he might pass through it into the Perfect Day."[60] But the sense of God's night as

---

[57] Cited in R. A. Durr, "Vaughan's 'The Night,'" *Journal of English and Germanic Philology* 39:1 (1960), 40.

[58] *Pseudo-Dionysius: The Complete Works*, trans. Colm Luibheid (New York: Paulist Press, 1987), 141.

[59] *The Cloud of Unknowing*, ed. James Walsh, S.J. (Mahwah, N.J.: Paulist Press, 1981), 128.

[60] Durr, "Vaughan's 'The Night,'" 40.

transitional or simply as a processual first night is not reflected in the speaker's desire to unite with God in order to "live invisible and dim" (54). How can we reconcile Vaughan's understanding of the dazzling darkness as an escape or retreat with both the Johannine and the Hermetic contexts of the poem? A return to the Johannine understanding of Nicodemus and conversion will help to clarify Vaughan's creative use of his sources.

NICODEMUS AND CONVERSION IN "THE NIGHT"

If we return to John's presentation of Nicodemus, we find that the narrative reveals not just Nicodemus's cowardice in seeking out Jesus under cover of darkness but his failure to understand even an accommodated notion of regeneration. Jesus relates that a man cannot enter the kingdom of God unless his birth of the flesh is displaced by a rebirth of "water and of the spirit" (3:5). Responding to Nicodemus's ignorance, Jesus questions whether, given that Nicodemus cannot process the "earthly" or accommodated notion of regeneration, Nicodemus would better understand if Jesus were to speak more directly of arcane or "heavenly things" (3:12). What is accommodated to Nicodemus is the notion of rebirth as cleansing or baptism, an "ordinary thing," Henry Hammond remarks in his annotations on John, rather than a "higher celestial doctrine" that would need to be revealed.[61] Nicodemus's extreme literalism regarding rebirth, despite Jesus' accommodations, warrants early modern comments such as John Trapp's that Nicodemus "understands no more of the doctrine of Regeneration then...a common cowherd doth the darkest precepts of Astronomy."[62]

Regeneration is integral to Vaughan's "The Night" not only because of the direct Johannine treatment of Nicodemus but also because of the other scriptural references to conversion. The night-time hour at which the speaker searches for Christ (which parallels Nicodemus's search) is described as Christ's "knocking time": "When my Lords head is fill'd with dew, and all / His locks are wet with the clear drops of night; / His still, soft call; / His knocking time; The souls dumb watch, / When Spirits their fair kinred catch" (32–6). The scriptural reference here is the Song of Solomon (5:2): "I sleepe, but my heart waketh: it is the voyce of my beloved that knocketh, saying, Open to me, my sister, my love, my dove, my undefiled: for my head is filled with dewe, and my lockes with the drops of the night." This verse is typically interpreted to signify a process of conversion, as in Henry Finch's 1615 commentary on Canticles: "The principal cause of this our conversion is the Spirit of Christ knocking at the doore of our heart."[63] But it is important not to take the passage out of context. The subsequent Canticles verses point up the lapsed or missed opportunity on the part of the beloved to respond to

---

[61] Henry Hammond, *The Gospel According to S. John*, in *A paraphrase and annotations upon all the books of the New Testament* (London, 1659), chapter 3, A.

[62] John Trapp, *A brief commentary or exposition upon the Gospel according to St John* (London, 1646), 14.

[63] Henry Finch, *An exposition of the Song of Solomon* (London, 1615), 101.

Christ's knocking: "I opened to my beloved, but my beloved had with drawn himselfe, and was gone: my soule failed when hee spake: I sought him, but I could not find him: I called him, but he gave me no answere" (5:6). The verse in context clarifies that the beloved delays too long due to lingering sin and will have to await another opportunity to respond to Christ's unsolicited call. The Puritan divine Thomas Taylor believes that hardness of heart might cause the delay: "Oh heare at length Christ knocking, & resolve presently to open: If thou hearest his voyce this day, harden thy heart no more. How long shall he be with thee? how long shall he suffer thee?"[64]

Elsewhere in scripture the motif of God's or Christ's knocking is more explicitly linked to the non-responsiveness of the beloved. Revelation 3.2 expands on the typical allegory of Christ as bride and Church as reluctant bridegroom: "Behold, I stand at the doore, and knocke: if any man heare my voyce, and open the doore, I will come in to him, and will sup with him, and he with me." William Perkins offers an extended commentary on this allegory of conversion: "Heere is a further signification of his desire of their conversion. Wherein we may behold his great & unspeakable mercie towards this Church, and in them towards all other his Children. This Church had bard out Christ by their sinnes: and yet he pursues them, he *knockes*."[65] Most commentators remind readers of the persistence of Christ's entreaties despite the addressee's failure to open the door and initiate conversion: "The doore here is our heart," remarks Hezekiah Holland, "which is naturally shut against Christ, yet Christ knocks more than once or twice, even till it be opened, it notes the assiduity and constant or continued care Christ hath of us."[66] The reference to Christ's knocking in Vaughan's poem represents a solicitation to initiate the difficult process of conversion. That the speaker is in need of Christ's saving knocking at his heart is revealed in the subsequent stanzas; the speaker confesses that he would like to remain under his Lord's "dark Tent" (38), but that during daylight he tends to consent "and run / to ev'ry myre" (45–6), the "ill-guiding light" (47) motoring his Donnean wandering almost against his will. The abrupt shift from the stillness of the night and the "soft" (34) sound of the "knocking time" (35) to the speaker's haunted, "loud, evil days" (37) implies that he finds himself unable to respond to Christ's knocking, that he remains unresponsive. By the end of the last two-thirds of the poem, the reader realizes that the speaker resembles more closely the scriptural Nicodemus than he does the elevated (and fictitious) Nicodemus that is constructed in the opening stanzas of the poem.

But the most profound shift in the poem is marked by the speaker's much different treatment of darkness in the last stanza relative to the earlier, paradoxical treatment of light-in-darkness in the preceding stanzas. In its proper Dionysian and mystical context, the "dazzling darkness" would not be understood as some

---

[64] Thomas Taylor, *The parable of the sower and of the seed Declaring in foure severall grounds* (London, 1621), 386.

[65] William Perkins, *A godly and learned exposition or commentarie upon the three first chapters of the Revelation* (London, 1606), 215.

[66] Hezekiah Holland, *An exposition, or, A short, but full, plaine, and perfect epitome of the most choice commentaries upon the Revelation of Saint John* (London, 1615), 30.

safe haven in which the believer might hide from the light of the world and his errant ways. The Dionysian darkness describes more of a privation of knowledge, a point in a step-wise process of abstractive contemplation that should precede at least a clearer illumination of God's remaining ineffability. The facile retreat into darkness is a desideratum more for the unregenerate sinner than for the mystical initiate. In terms of spiritual progress, Vaughan's speaker has done little more than acknowledge his recalcitrance. The last lines of the penultimate stanza—"And by this worlds ill-guiding light, / Erre more then I can do by night" (47–8)—should trouble those readers who would otherwise posit the speaker's progress or his keen appreciation of the paradoxical benevolence of night. The contrastive "more" signifies that to sin by night is the lesser evil compared to sinning by daylight. On one interpretation of the line, the speaker is closer to his otherwise veiled God during the evening hours; on another interpretation, however, his sins will go relatively unnoticed, rendered dim, even invisible to those who cannot see during this "dusky" (51) time.

The sense of night introduced in the last two stanzas recalls the period's common, not very paradoxical association of night with the hiddenness of one's apostasy. This is the more typical Johannine (rather than mystical or Hermetic) conception of night that is reflected in the Nicodemus passage that Vaughan borrows for the opening of his poem. Consider Jesus' concluding comments to Nicodemus in which he expands a bit on those heavenly things that seem beyond Nicodemus's ken: "And this is the condemnation, that light is come into the world, and men loved darknesse rather then light, because their deedes were evill. For every one that doeth evill, hateth the light, neither commeth to the light, lest his deeds should be reproved. But hee that doeth trueth, commeth to the light, that his deeds may be made manifest, that they are wrought in God" (3:19–21). The trope of darkness as a hiding place is abundantly found in early modern treatises and sermons. John Bunyan's *Resurrection of the Dead* (1665) provides one incisive gloss: "Here will be no hiding your selves behind Curtains, nor no covering your selves with the black and dark night. If I say, surely the darkness shall cover me even the night shall be light about me; yea, (O God) darkness hideth not from thee, but the night shineth as the day, the darkness and light are both alike unto thee."[67] Regarding Nicodemus and the Sanhedrin, Calvin remarks on the same sense of concealment under darkness: "Those men act wickedly who prefer darkness to light and flee from the light freely offered to them," a statement that is echoed in Thomas Granger's gloss on John 3:20 in *The Bread of Life* (1616): "If the world frowne on us, as it alwaies hath done on the children of God, wee are ready to give over, to dissemble, and conceale our selves with *Nicodemus*."[68] Of course, Vaughan's darkness is associated with God rather than with a place of sin and concealment. But the poem conflates the paradoxical sense of the benevolent darkness of God with the more straightforward sense of darkness as a hiding place.

---

[67] John Bunyan, *The resurrection of the dead and eternall judgement* (London, 1665), 124.
[68] *Calvin's New Testament Commentaries*, vol. 4, 77; Thomas Granger, *The bread of life, or Foode of the regenerate* (London, 1616), 18.

The middle sections of the poem, in which Vaughan naturalizes his theology, help set up the conflated ending by establishing a contrast between the relative accessibility of Christ, on the one hand, and the distance (and hence hiddenness) of God, on the other hand. The speaker questions whether he can find Christ amid the symbolism of nature: "What hallow'd solitary ground did bear / So rare a flower, / Within whose sacred leafs did lie / The fulness of the Deity…/ But his own living works did my Lord hold / And lodge alone; / Where *trees* and *herbs* did watch and peep / And wonder, while the *Jews* did sleep" (15–24). This section has at times been glossed as an example of the naturalism that one can find in several other poems of Vaughan. Theologically speaking, the section seems to offer a version of immanence that contrasts with the transcendence that emerges by the end of the poem. Ross Garner sees Vaughan's paradoxical treatment of night as the bridge between immanence and transcendence: "The juxtaposition of the last stanza of the first section (stanza 4), in which Christ is said to be found in the things of nature, with the opening of the second section…makes *night* the link between the immanent God of the first section…and the transcendent God of the second section and the epilogue.…Christ is both immanent and transcendent, both the earthly Jesus and the God the Father, and we arrive at the second by the first."[69] Such critical appraisals tend to conflate Vaughan's naturalism and his emphasis on the creaturely aspects of Christ with divine immanence. Immanence is a Johannine presupposition, represented most clearly in Vaughan's description of the "fulness of the Deity" (18) in Christ. But neither Dionysius nor the Johannine tradition is especially concerned with the corporeality or materiality of Christ. Dionysius, often described as a monopsychist, rejects Trinitarianism altogether. And we have seen that the distinguishing feature of the Fourth Gospel is that it is not especially concerned with the creaturely or historical Jesus. For both traditions, Christ is an accommodated deity whose nature can be glimpsed through his symbolic words and the brethren's pious belief. This is entirely consistent with Vaughan's opening description of Christ as a veil symbolically clothed with human flesh.

Most important is the fact that the paradoxical sense of God's presence in darkness depends on the notion of a divinely immanent God who is revealed even as he is concealed by and through Christ. To appreciate God's darkness in this paradoxical sense is to see that darkness as an immanently accessible rather than transcendent quality set apart from the natural and creaturely realms. Garner is correct to note that the immanence of the poem's middle stanzas is distinct from the transcendence of the final stanzas, the latter of which seem to leave off the naturalized Christ for a *deus absconditus* in whom the speaker might find refuge. But it is precisely because of such dualism that the paradoxical sense of night as God's dazzling darkness loses its force and gives way to a more straightforward sense of darkness as a place of hiding for the unregenerated speaker. The dazzling darkness of God *is* the divine *Logos*, Christ as the veiled fullness of God's being: such darkness exists through, not beyond Christ. When

---

[69] Ross Garner, *Henry Vaughan: Experience and the Tradition* (Chicago: University of Chicago Press, 1959), 140.

Vaughan escapes from the world of errant daylight to a transcendent night, he divides starkly the mundane from the supramundane. Darkness becomes a safe haven from the very creaturely realm that should be the site of the renovation that never adequately takes place in the poem.

We have traced the speaker's complex process in the poem. At the outset Vaughan's speaker reimagines Nicodemus as wise in order to mingle the Johannine source with the Dionysian approach to darkness. Given that Vaughan re-appropriates the Johannine understanding of Nicodemus in order to make such an integration cohere, this intermingling turns out to be more of a yoking. But as the poem unfolds, the paradoxicality of the Dionysian approach to light-in-darkness loses force and the more traditional Johannine conception of night as a place of unregeneracy emerges in its stead. It is as if Vaughan's speaker initially veers from the Johannine conception of Nicodemus only to derive that same conception by the poem's close. The supreme irony of the poem is that the speaker turns out be quite like John's Nicodemus, after all, not quite sure of his conversion status, a bit like the speaker of "The World" who, as we have seen in Chapter 5, by the end of that poem has qualified his own ability and spiritual license to disseminate Christ's message. The speaker of "The Night" reinstates typical Johannine dualisms—between the immanence of the world and the transcendence of Christ—only to question by the end his placement amid that dualistic division.

Despite the speaker's uncertainty over his conversion status, however, we would be wrong to argue that the message of "The Night" is itself rendered unstable or paradoxical. The Johannine rather than Dionysian conception of darkness is restored (or derived) by the poem's close, even if the speaker cannot be sure whether he deserves to be situated there or within the true light that shines on the unknowing Nicodemus. Ultimately, "The Night" shares with Herbert's "The Bag," "The Bunch of Grapes," and "Love unknown" a poetics that is revelatory rather than simply paradoxical in nature. All of these poems seek to illuminate knowledge of God's mysteries and Christ's redemptive actions, and they do so through the path of stable irony in which meaning/knowledge increases as a particular poem's theological crux or spiritual conflict works toward resolution. This does not mean that all such crises are neatly resolved in a given poem, but it does assume that selected poems do not purposefully frustrate meaning or move toward paradox and instability.

Afterword
The Johannine Enchantment of the World

In several recent articles and books, Alexandra Walsham, drawing on foundational work by Robert Scribner and others, has argued convincingly that the Protestant Reformation in England did not contribute to the so-called "disenchantment of the world." Instead of assuming, as the traditional disenchantment narrative has posited, that Protestant iconophobia, anti-ritualism, and virulent critiques of the real presence removed sacred presence from Reformed and post-Reformed culture, Walsham's revisionist narrative finds continuity rather than rupture between medieval and Reformed epistemes. The Reformed assault on the medieval economy of salvation paradoxically produced a "heightened sense that supernatural or preternatural forces were at work in the world."[1] Fueled by the growing fear of the immanence of Antichrist and accompanying eschatological anxieties, Reformed providentialism was keenly attuned to the fateful, manifestly ominous presence of God's agency. Far from removing divine presence, early modern Protestant culture paradoxically intensified that presence, helping to "expand the category of the preternatural and to collapse the miraculous into the natural."[2]

I hope to have shown throughout this book that the post-Reformed English enthusiasm for the Johannine confessions of Christ likewise contributes in profound ways to an enchantment narrative that typically exalts sacred presence. From Augustine through Ratramnus, Thomas Cranmer, and later English divines and literary authors, eating Christ's "flesh" means, according to John 6, little more than spiritual eating manifested as faith and belief. Yet in its very insistence that Christ's body is not corporeally available and that in a post-resurrection context Christ's body remains in heaven during the sacramental offering, John 6 enthusiastically, if paradoxically, testifies to divine presence. Participating or dwelling with God, the achievement of "eternal life" in Johannine parlance, is offered through the Incarnation itself rather than through the Communion or comparable ritualistic ordinances. One of the reasons that John 6 was often read in conjunction with the Farewell Discourse (John 13–17) and with the *noli me tangere* pericope of John 20 is that the latter verses legitimate and extend the incarnational sacramentalism of John 6. Not only does Magdalene dwell in Christ through faith rather than through

---

[1] Alexandra Walsham, "The Reformation and 'The Disenchantment of the World' Reassessed," *The Historical Journal* 51:2 (2008), 508.

[2] Ibid., 509.

contact with his material body, but as so many post-Reformed exegetes contend (seizing on the careful wording and logic of John 16:7) Christ's departure from the world is "expedient," for only then can the Spirit-Paraclete arrive in Christ's stead. This exchange of the Christological for the pneumatological presence is itself paradoxical, but such a transfiguration needs to be understood in the context of the Johannine insistence that even the most well-disposed brethren could never fully understand Christ's accommodated messages during his earthly ministry. The Paraclete will be even more present to the believers because the Spirit will further clarify Christ's messages and hence maintain the brethren's immaterial union or dwelling following the Ascension.

An understanding of the ways in which access to God through the Johannine Christ does not depend on a materialist ontology requires an appreciation of the Johannine conception of mutual indwelling with the Father and Son. As we have seen, Johannine participation or indwelling does carry a mystical orientation. Yet C. K. Barrett's advisement that Johannine participation is at best a "semi-mysticism" puts into proper context the uniqueness of the Christ-mysticism of the Fourth Gospel.[3] When Barrett remarks that, despite the mystical overtones of so much of the Johannine discourses, the only true mystic is Christ, he reminds us that Christ is the only one who can capably witness the beatific vision. To the extent that earthbound penitents dwell in God they do so adoptively and relationally rather than ontologically in the sense that they escape their bodies or negate creaturely life through ecstatic contemplation. In its pastoral and moralistic grounding, Johannine Christ-mysticism assumes that the route to Godhead is through the witness of the historical Christ (though as we have seen, none of the governing Johannine images, tropes, or parables presupposes a necessary communion with Christ's fleshly materiality). "Against a vision mysticism," Charles H. Talbert remarks, "the Fourth Gospel tells of a preexistent Logos who cohabited with God and was given the sole visionary experience of that God."[4] That such cohabitation is reserved for the Son is suggested throughout the Fourth Gospel, most particularly at verse 3:13: "And no man hath ascended up to heaven, but hee that came downe from heaven, even the Sonne of man which is in heaven."

Continental and English Reformed exegetes used varying metaphysical language to describe the distinctive quality of the penitent's union with divine presence. As we have seen, the early Reformer John Merbecke exemplarily defined such co-presence as shared "personhood" rather than "substantial" union, pointing out that Christ dwells in us by faith and spirit; hence it does not follow that "either his body or his soule dwelleth in our harts really as I may cal it & substancially. It is enough that Christ be said to be in us by his divine presence, & that he is by his spirit grace & gifts, present with us."[5] Later English Reformers with different denominational leanings, Richard Sibbes, for example, more specifically describe

---

[3] C. K. Barrett, *The Gospel According to John* (London: S.P.C.K., 1965), 73–4.

[4] Charles H. Talbert, *Reading John: A Literary and Theological Commentary on the Fourth Gospel and the Johannine Epistles* (Macon: Smyth & Helwys, 2005), 106.

[5] John Merbecke, *A booke of notes and common places* (London, 1581), 187.

Johannine indwelling as pneumatological: "*God* by his spirit, though not hypostatically, yet gratiously is one with us, and hath communion with us now as his Children."[6] Sibbes articulates the more commonly found English Reformed conception of Johannine Christ-mysticism that historically comports with versions of mediated mysticism that one finds in the work of Bernard of Clairvaux and in Johannes Tauler's sermons on the mystical itinerary: this is a *voluntas communis*, a coincidence of wills between the creaturely and the divine without assuming a mixing or confusing of substances.[7]

None of this is to say that the Johannine conception of indwelling is formulaically or straightforwardly presented in the Fourth Gospel. We have seen that Johannine metaphysics could easily be radicalized in dissenting writings prior to and during the English Interregnum, as when Hendrik Niclaes and like-minded zealots used the Johannine discourses to argue that they were "Godded with God" or "vined in the vine." The mid-century moderate nonconformist Anthony Burgess devotes an entire treatise to the ways in which the language of dwelling and participation of John 17 might be manipulated into justifying what he deemed to be "nonsensical" notions of converts being "transessentiated" into God. Against the more radical appropriations of Johannine union, Burgess follows earlier Reformers in arguing that John typically speaks metaphorically. The concept of union signifies that the communicant resides "with" rather than "in" Christ.[8]

That John's Christ-mysticism was the source of significant debate and that it might easily be misunderstood or caricatured by early modern and modern critics is especially evident in the difficulty that religious historians have had in agreeing on the metaphysical presuppositions of Thomas Cranmer's mature conception of the spiritual or true presence. Cyril Richardson's hand-wringing over Cranmer's elliptical metaphysics is a case in point. Richardson finds three clear and consistent presuppositions in Cranmer's mature theology: Christ is present during the Eucharist by his divinity rather than his humanity; the elements of institution are at most instruments for God's work rather than bare tokens; and eating Christ's body signifies only spiritual feeding. Beyond these premises Richardson finds Cranmer's central ontological presupposition of indwelling with Christ to be much

---

[6] Richard Sibbes, *A heavenly conference between Christ and Mary after His resurrection* (London, 1654), 175–6.

[7] On the distinction between volitional and substantive union, see, for example, Etienne Gilson, who writes about Bernard's mysticism: "The mystical union...is neither a confusion of the two substances in general, nor a confusion of the substances of the two wills in particular; but it is their perfect accord, the coincidence of two willings." *The Mystical Theology of Saint Bernard*, trans. A. H. C. Downes (Kalamazoo: Cistercian Publications, 1990), 123. On the *unio mystica* in Bernard and Tauler, see Steven E. Ozment, *Homo Spiritualis: A Comparative Study of the Anthropology of Johannes Tauler, Jean Gerson and Martin Luther (1509–16) in the Context of their Theological Thought* (Leiden: Brill, 1969), chapter 3, *passim*. Ozment argues that, for Tauler, the *unio mystica* is yet a preparatory stage to be superseded by a higher "unity in the divine being" (36). The question of the role of historical Christology in Tauler's mysticism is discussed at length in Bernard McGinn, *The Harvest of Mysticism in Medieval Germany (1300–1500)*, vol. iv of *The Presence of God: A History of Western Christian Mysticism* (New York: Crossroad Publishing, 1991), 271–96.

[8] Anthony Burgess, *CXLV expository sermons upon the whole 17th chapter of the Gospel according to St. John, or, Christs prayer before his passion explicated* (London, 1656), 623.

less clear and even internally contradictory.[9] How can Cranmer maintain, Richardson asks, both the belief that Christ's body, which remains in heaven during the Eucharist, is only spiritually eaten, and the belief that communicants are incorporated into Christ?: "The problem...arises from his [Cranmer's] constant emphasis upon the fact that such believing, such exercising of the mind on the Passion, has the consequence that Christ really, substantially and naturally, dwells in us and we in him. The theme of the double indwelling is as favourite a one in Cranmer as is that of the absence of Christ's body, and it is difficult to reconcile them."[10] Commenting on Cranmer's description in his *Answer* to Bishop Gardiner of the ways in which those who receive the Eucharist are "knitted and united spiritually to Christ's flesh and blood," Richardson adds that such language is irreconcilable with the notion that Christ's body remains at the right hand of God.[11] Yet if Richardson had acknowledged the Johannine influence on Cranmer's nominalism, he would perhaps have realized that because Cranmer often collapses distinctions between the Incarnation and more particularized sacraments, Cranmer understands participation, incorporation, and indwelling in the context of what I have been describing as the distinctiveness of Johannine Christ-mysticism.[12]

Again, this is not to argue that one finds in the Johannine literature an unambiguous signification of indwelling or incorporation. The open-endedness of such language is what makes the Johannine literature attractive to so many competing confessional and denominational biases during the early modern period. What we can say is that the Johannine writings were indeed enchanting in offering the possibility during creaturely life of incorporation with God through the Son. The perception that this sort of indwelling was actually experienced by the ancient Johannine community inspires so many Reformed and post-Reformed writers, especially within sectarian circles, to revive and emulate the prototypical Johannine approach to adoption into God's holy family. Not so much the sacralization of the world ("world" typically carrying the neo-Platonic connotation of fallenness in Johannine theology) but the sacralization of many disparate and competing conventicles, each with its own idealized conception of eschatological hope, is what the Evangelist offered to post-Reformed English culture.

Devotional poets of the period in particular found in the Johannine discourses an idiom of divine fellowship and participation that eschews the extremes of Christological materialism (eating or touching Christ's flesh), on the one hand, and vision mysticism (negating creaturely life in order to find absorption directly into God), on the other hand. In terms of what we might describe as Christological anti-materialism, devotional verses of writers such as Herbert, Crashaw, Taylor, and, to a more qualified extent, Vaughan, are intensely sacramental but not because they justify any particularized Church ordinance such as the Eucharist.

---

[9] Cyril C. Richardson, "Cranmer and the Analysis of Eucharistic Doctrine," *Journal of Theological Studies*, New Series, 16:2 (1965), 425–9.

[10] Ibid., 429.   [11] Ibid., 430.

[12] For Richardson's fuller discussion of Cranmer's nominalism in relation to his mature view of the Eucharist, see Cyril C. Richardson, *Zwingli and Cranmer on the Eucharist: Cranmer Dixit et Contradixit* (Evanston: Seabury-Western Theological Seminary, 1949), 36–49.

The sacramentalism of such work derives from an acknowledgment of the Incarnation and the accessibility to the Father that the Johannine Christ offers to those who cultivate the requisite belief in the mission of the divinely sent Son. We have seen that all of these poets rely on John 6, aptly described by Jaroslav Pelikan as the "iron wall" of the Reformed position on the Eucharist. John 6 allows these poets to develop a revelatory Christology that is deeply personal in the several manifestations of fellowship that the poetic personae enjoy with Christ despite the presence of the Son in heaven at the right hand of the Father.[13]

That Johannine divine fellowship is fundamentally Christological is important to bear in mind, for many of the devotional poets discussed in the preceding chapters have been described in one way or another as mystics in their theological orientation, especially Vaughan, Crashaw, and Traherne.[14] Yet each poet's rhapsodizing about the *visio dei* and divine participation is often Johannine (and hence only qualifiedly mystical) in acknowledging the mediatorial presence of the historical Jesus as a means to the beatific vision that typically remains on the horizon. In "The Night," Vaughan envisions a wondrous immersion in the "dazzling darkness" of God, yet that mystical union is achievable not through creaturely purgations or direct absorption with God but only through a realization that the incarnated Christ *is* the veiled fullness of God. And Crashaw's seemingly most mystical poem, "A Hymn to Sainte Teresa," closes not with a poeticization of Teresa's rapturous and unmediated union with the One or emanationist deity but with a paraphrase of 1 John 1:7 that describes her walking with Christ: "Thou with the LAMB, thy lord, shalt goe; / And whereso'ere he setts his white / Stepps, walk with HIM those ways of light" (178–80). We have seen the frequency with which the Johannine trope of walking in the light is mentioned during the period, a verse that above all highlights fellowship with one another and thence with Christ: "If wee walke in the light, as he is in the light, wee have fellowship one with another" (1 John 1:7). In Crashaw's poem, the route to heavenly access is not Teresa's flaming but "gentle HEART" (105) or any direct vision of God's illuminated face; it is rather her ascension with Christ through whose light she can begin to access God's light. Mario Praz once said about Crashaw's "Hymn": "There is still something detached and of a descriptive nature in this composition: the poet does not yet possess the adequate lyric heat for the mystical experience. Very likely Crashaw never reached that state of ardent rapture."[15] One wants

---

[13] Jaroslav Pelikan, *The Christian Tradition: A History of the Development of Doctrine, Volume 4: Reformation of Church and Dogma (1300–1700)* (Chicago: University of Chicago Press, 1984), 195.

[14] On the influence of mysticism and Hermeticism on Vaughan, see, for example, Elizabeth Holmes, *Henry Vaughan and the Hermetic Philosophy* (New York: Haskell House, 1966). Traherne's seeming mysticism is the topic of A. L. Clements, *The Mystical Poetry of Thomas Traherne* (Cambridge, MA: Harvard University Press, 1969). Crashaw's perceived mysticism is described in Frank J. Warnke, *European Metaphysical Poetry* (New Haven: Yale University Press, 1961), 892, cited in Lorrain M. Roberts, "Crashaw's Sacred Voice: 'A Commerce of Contrary Powers,'" in *New Perspectives on the Life and Art of Richard Crashaw*, ed. John R. Roberts (Columbia: University of Missouri Press, 1990), 68, where Roberts pushes against the contention that Crashaw's poetry is mystical in orientation.

[15] Mario Praz, *The Flaming Heart: Essays on Crashaw, Machiavelli, and other Studies in the Relations between Italian and English Literature from Chaucer to T. S. Eliot* (Garden City, N.Y.: Doubleday & Company, Inc., 1958), 261.

to respond that the reason neither Crashaw nor his rapturous Teresa attains to the heights of mystic contemplation is that, here again, that undiluted mystical vision is reserved for the only-begotten Son.

Traherne, perhaps even more so than Crashaw or Vaughan, has been placed in a mystical, sometimes more broadly neo-Platonic tradition. Yet we have seen that underlying his distinctive vision of felicity is a neo-scholastic *analogia entis* that is itself centered on the Johannine identity of God and *agape*. Although Traherne's body of work is not as elementally Christological as Herbert's, Vaughan's or Crashaw's, it is equally concerned with a poetics of indwelling or divine participation. The Johannine discourses, in this case relevant verses on God's love for Christ and humankind before the creation of the world, enable Traherne to imagine divine participation without assuming the ritualized negations of meditative, *apophatic*, or mystical theology through which his poetic speakers might find an ethereal oneness with God. Participation and fellowship are based rather on a series of analogies/disanalogies between creaturely and divine attributes. We participate with God in virtue of being created in God's loving image, although we can never be truly apotheosized given that creaturely attributes will at best approximate the divine names of a supereminent deity. And yet, despite this immeasurable distance from God, Traherne's work, like that of the earlier devotional poets discussed above, is enchanted and "felicitous" in that sacred presence never recedes from his fertile theological imagination.

We have seen that Johannine enchantment manifests in several particularized theological registers, including a high Christology, a revelatory soteriology rather than one shaped by forensic ransoming, a predominantly realized as opposed to futurist eschatology, a robust theology of assurance and comfort, and, stylistically, a rhetorical reliance on discipleship misunderstanding and stable irony. In terms of John's influence on early modern conceptions of political theology, there is clearly more to be said. As I remarked in the Introduction (and as our discussion of the dissenting writings referenced in Chapter 5 attests), Johannine sacrality or enchantment entails a conception of political theology that diverges from the work of Hans Blumenberg and from recent early modern studies on the question of theological legitimation and the transition to modernity. To a certain extent, in questioning Schmitt's secularization thesis, Blumenberg relies on a disenchantment narrative: in erecting an absolutist and hidden God, medieval nominalism inadvertently leads to the sundering of God from the creaturely realm, which in turn opens up a space for human invention and pragmatism. Yet despite its skepticism toward linearity and its designation as a "reoccupation" rather than secularizing theory, Blumenberg's narrative is consistent with the metanarrative of desacralization that the Johannine confessions call into question. Because God becomes intimately present through an indwelling with the divinely sent Son, Johannine theology erects a personal God for so many mid-century dissenters (heresy-seekers would say a too-personal God). In outlining a stark dualism that separates edified and spirit-filled believers from the hostile world of unbelievers, the Johannine confessions offer scriptural and historical legitimation for mid-seventeenth-century sectarianism.

I have spent more time outlining the Johannine influence on fine points of antinomian theology than on politics, but future work might productively weigh the extent to which the political beliefs of mid-century separatists, including the writings of New Model Army chaplains such as William Dell and John Saltmarsh, relied on the Johannine confessions to advance their views on the separation of spiritual and civil magistracy or on anti-Erastianism more generally. For example, when Dell advances his argument against the Westminster Assembly's notion of external uniformity, he invokes at the outset John 4:23—"But the hour cometh, and now is, when the true worshippers shall worship the Father in spirit and in truth"—a verse that shows up frequently in mid-century arguments in favor of freedom of conscience: "In which words it is most evident, that the worship of God in the time of the New Testament, is inward and spirituall, consisting in faith, hope, love, and prayer, the operation of the three former, &c. And so, is so far from *Uniformity* as hath been explicated, and as they understand it, that it is not at all capable of it."[16] The politico-theological writings of dissenters such as Dell and Saltmarsh, in which Johannine pneumatology and conceptions of fellowship are marshaled against decrees of civil and ecclesiastical uniformity, suggest that an early modern Johannine political theology might be seen as an important historical complement to the more frequently described political theologies found in the work of canonical political and philosophical thinkers such as Machiavelli, Hobbes, and Spinoza.[17]

Additional work might also be done on John's related influence on early modern Trinitarian–anti-Trinitarian debates. John's fateful words at the outset of his Gospel, the notorious crux of the Johannine Comma at 1 John 5:7–8, and several other relevant Johannine verses all ground the rhetoric of seventeenth-century dissenting Socinian treatises such as Johann Crell's *The Unity of God* (1691) as well as the mid-century anti-Socinian polemic of tracts such as Anthony Burgess's *CXLV expository sermons upon the whole 17th chapter of the Gospel according to St. John* (1656), just two polemical works among several that are focused on John and the Trinity.[18]

More attention might also be given to the importance of the Johannine material to conversion narratives and spiritual autobiographies of the period. As we have seen, the spiritual obtuseness of the well-meaning Pharisee Nicodemus, who fails to understand the conception of rebirth, is referenced again and again during the period. The Pharisee serves as a cautionary example for those who would otherwise find rebirth through Christ. In his *A Call to the Unconverted* (1658), Richard Baxter exhorts his unconverted readers to consult, among a "hundred" texts, John 3:3 in order to begin the arduous conversion process.[19] Like Baxter, the separatist

---

[16] William Dell, *Uniformity Examined* (London, 1651), 41–2.

[17] An excellent discussion of antinomianism in the writings of New Model Army chaplains such as Dell and Saltmarsh can be found in Leo F. Solt, *Saints in Arms: Puritans and Democracy in Cromwell's Army* (Stanford: Stanford University Press, 1959).

[18] For a comprehensive survey of the use of Johannine material in Trinitarian and anti-Trinitarian debates during the period, see Paul C. H. Lim, *Mystery Unveiled: The Crisis of the Trinity in Early Modern England* (Oxford: Oxford University Press, 2012), chapter 6, *passim*.

[19] Richard Baxter, *A call to the unconverted to turn and live and accept of mercy while mercy may be had* (London, 1658), 11.

Robert Purnell, in *The Way Step by Step to Sound and Saving Conversion* (1659), also centers his conversion treatise not merely on John 3 and comparable passages in Matthew and Luke but on the full range of relevant passages from the Fourth Gospel and First Epistle.[20] An especially noteworthy use of John in a spiritual autobiography occurs toward the end of John Bunyan's *Grace Abounding* (1666), where Bunyan holds out John 6:37—"All that the Father giveth mee, shall come to mee; and him that commeth to me, I will in no wise cast out"—as one pivotal text that provides him with confidence of Christ's promise of comfort: "O! many a pull hath my heart had with Satan, for that blessed sixth of *John*: I did not now, as at other times, look principally for comfort (though O how welcome would it have been unto me!) but now a Word, a Word to lean a weary Soul upon, that I might not sink for ever."[21]

In addition to the use of Johannine material in nonconformist confessionals such as Bunyan's, a particularly important appropriation of John's writings appears in the conversion narratives and treatises of seventeenth-century radicals such as Anna Trapnel and Anne Hutchinson. The roiling political climate of the seventeenth century gives voice to female authors who find in the author of the Fourth Gospel and First Epistle an apostle of gender egalitarianism. We have already seen that for Trapnel John reveals that Christ's treatment of Mary represents his favoring of all such "hand-maids": "O *John* he did speak of hand maids, / Whom Christ did love so dear, / And tells that Jesus Christ he did, / To hand-maids first draw near."[22] Thomas Walkington's *Rabboni* (1620), too, makes much of the fact that a woman appears first to Christ after his resurrection: "To *Mary* alone, not to the Disciples, but to *Mary* first. To a woman: as a woman was, *Nuncia mortis in Paradiso, The messenger of mortality, of death in Paradise.*"[23] We know that Anne Hutchinson, an ardent follower of John Cotton, used key passages of John's First Epistle to argue for free grace issuing from the Spirit. Hutchinson was brought to trial for relying on 1 John 3:14 ("Wee know that wee have passed from death unto life, because wee love the brethren") and related scriptural verses to advance anti-legalist and eschatological beliefs.[24] And Hutchinson's incendiary claim that "those which did not teach the new covenant had the spirit of antichrist" derived from her interpretation of 1 John 2:18.[25] While Hutchinson did not use any of these extant testimonies in an overtly gendered manner, she was found especially troublesome by the Boston elect because her fluid knowledge of these scriptural texts was deemed dangerous to other women: "She is of a most dayngerous Spirit and likely with her

---

[20] Robert Purnell, *The way step by step to sound and saving conversion, with a clear discovery of the two states* (London, 1659), 1.

[21] John Bunyan, *Grace abounding to the chief of sinners* (London, 1666), 70.

[22] Anna Trapnel, *A Voice for the King of Saints and Nations* (London, 1657), 33.

[23] Thomas Walkington, *Rabboni: Mary Magdalens teares, of sorrow, solace* (London, 1620), 7. See also Margaret Askew Fell Fox's discussion of Magdalene at the tomb in *Womens speaking justified, proved and allowed of by the Scriptures all such as speak by the spirit and power of the Lord Iesus* (London, 1667), 7.

[24] See *The Antinomian Controversy, 1636–1638: A Documentary History*, ed. David D. Hall (Middletown: Wesleyan University Press, 1968), 322.

[25] Ibid., 336.

fluent Tongue and forwardness in Expressions to seduce and draw many, Espetially simple Weomen of her owne sex."[26]

A more manifestly gendered use of the Johannine discourses can be found in an earlier treatise by Rachel Speght. Her *A Mouzell for Melastomus* (1616) was written in response to the vitriolic anti-feminist tract by Joseph Swetnam, *The Arraignment of Lewd, Idle, Froward, and Unconstant Women* (1615). In her quest to legitimate equal partnership in marriage, Speght relies heavily on John's presentation of Christ's turning water into wine at the wedding feast at Cana: "Marriage is a merriage, and this worlds Paradise, where there is mutuall love. Our blessed Saviour vouchsafed to honour a marriage with the first miracle that he wrought, unto which miracle matrimoniall estate may not unfitly bee resembled: For as Christ turned water into wine, a farre more excellent liquor; which, as the Psalmist saith, *Makes glad the heart of man;* So the single man is by marriage changed from a Batchelour to a Husband."[27] John counts this as Christ's first miracle by which he manifests his glory, a fitting example for Speght to reference in her desire to sanctify wedded union. The Cana reference then opens out in Speght's treatise to a discussion of the extent to which the Fourth Gospel evidences God's equal love toward men and women: "For whosoever, whether it be man or woman, that doth *beleeve in the Lord Jesus,* such *shall bee saved.* And if Gods love even from the beginning [John 3:18], had not beene as great toward woman as to man, then would hee not have preserved from the deluge of the old world as many women as men."[28] And against the sentiment expressed by Paul in 1 Corinthians that man is the woman's "head," Speght will marshal John 15:13: "*Greater love then this hath no man, when he bestoweth his life for his friend,* saith our Saviour: This president passeth all other patterns, it requireth great benignity, and enjoyneth an extraordinary affection, For *men must love their wives, even as Christ loved his Church.*"[29] Speght's tract deserves attention not least for such a use of Johannine material as a counter to the more frequently cited Pauline letters on the question of marital equality. In the section on the perils of married life, Swetnam's treatise enlists Paul to justify extreme caution when marrying: "*Saint Paul* saith those which marry doe well, but he also saith, those which marry not doe better; but yet also he sayeth, that it is better to marry then to burne in lust."[30] If in Swetnam's hands Paul legitimates a skeptical approach to marriage, in Speght's hands John elevates the sanctity of wedded union. It is worth investigating further not only the manner in which John tends to be ranged against Paul and other apostolic witnesses on the subject of gender relations, but also the ways in which early modernists interpreted John's evident elevation of the several referenced women in the Fourth Gospel, including the Samaritan woman, Martha and Mary of Bethany, and Mary, the mother of Jesus.[31]

[26] Ibid., 365. [27] Rachel Speght, *A Mouzell for Melastomus* (London, 1616), 14.
[28] Ibid., 16. [29] Ibid., 16–17.
[30] Joseph Swetnam, *The Arraignment of Lewd, Idle, Froward, and Unconstant Women* (London, 1615), 50.
[31] Paul's most controversial comments on marriage occur in 1 Corinthians 7, where he remarks that married life is best suited to those who cannot control their temperaments when unwed: "I say

In terms of literary genre, I have limited my study due to space constraints to some of the most influential devotional poetry and prose of the sixteenth and seventeenth centuries. But the influence of John's writings on the dramatic literature of the period is also worth serious attention. Johannine material emerges importantly in several of Shakespeare's plays, most notably *King Lear*, *Richard II*, *Richard III*, *2 Henry VI*, and *Measure for Measure*. And John's foundational verses on Antichrist in the First Epistle influence late medieval and early modern dramatizations of hell and the devil, most clearly in Christopher Marlowe's *Doctor Faustus*. Closer attention to such texts might reveal the extent to which the Fourth Gospel and First Epistle are as important to the dramatic literature of the period as they are to the devotional poetry.

We have for some time described a large body of canonical early modern devotional texts as Protestant or more specifically Protestant-Pauline in theological orientation. I hope to have shown throughout this book that an important portion of such early modern literature deserves to be called Johannine in nature. We have seen the ways in which John, the "beloved disciple" of Christ, the Eagle who sang of Christ's divinity, offered a revelatory theology and spiritual comfort to an early modern culture too often beset by ecclesiological turmoil and soteriological despair. William Alabaster, the sixteenth-century English sonneteer, expresses best the early modern enthusiasm for John in "St. John the Evangelist": "High towering eagle, rightly may thy feast, / Be held so near to Christ's solemnity, / That to his Godhead didst aspire so nigh, / That at his Passion by his side wast pressed, / That at his Supper didst lean on his breast" (1–5).[32] Alabaster and many other writers of the time found that they could abide in Christ through an emulation of John's very intimacy with the Savior. They leaned on John the way that John alone, the beloved disciple, could lean on Christ's breast.

therefore to the unmaried and widowes, It is good for them if they abide even as I. But if they cannot conteine, let them marry: for it is better to marrie then to burne" (1 Corinthians 7:8–9). For a good account of the Cana episode and John's conception of marriage (particularly according to Wolfgang Musculus), see Craig S. Farmer, *The Gospel of John in the Sixteenth Century: The Johannine Exegesis of Wolfgang Musculus* (Oxford: Oxford University Press, 1997), chapter 1, *passim*. For a comprehensive study of the positive light in which these Johannine women are cast in the Fourth Gospel, see Colleen M. Conway, *Men and Women in the Fourth Gospel: Gender and Johannine Characterization* (Atlanta: Society of Biblical Literature, 1999). A notable example of the use of Paul to justify wifely submission can be found in William Gouge's *Of domestical duties* (London, 1634), which draws on key verses from Ephesians and 1 Corinthians. Excerpts from Gouge's text, along with several other marital conduct books, can be found in *Renaissance Woman: A Sourcebook*, ed. Kate Aughterson (London: Routledge, 1999), chapter 3, *passim*.

[32] *The Sonnets of William Alabaster*, eds. Helen Gardner and G. M. Story (Oxford: Oxford University Press, 1959).

Selected Bibliography: Primary Works

Ainsworth, Henry. *An epistle sent unto two daughters of Warwick from H.N., the oldest father of the Familie of Love*. Amsterdam, 1608.

Ainsworth, Henry. *Annotations upon the five bookes of Moses*. London, 1627.

Allen, William. *The danger of enthusiasm discovered in an epistle to the Quakers*. London, 1674.

Andrewes, Lancelot. *XCVI Sermons*. London, 1629.

Aquinas, Saint Thomas. *Commentary on the Gospel of John, Chapter 13–21*, trans. Fabian R. Larcher and James A. Weisheipl. Washington, D.C.: Catholic University Press, 2010.

Arrowsmith, John. *Theanthropos, or, God-Man*. London, 1660.

Attersoll, William. *The badges of Christianity. Or, A treatise of the sacraments fully declared out of the word of God*. London, 1606.

Augustine. *Ten Homilies on the First Epistle General of St. John*, in *Augustine: Later Works*, ed. John Burnaby. Philadelphia: Westminster Press, 1955.

Augustine. *The Trinity*, in *Augustine: Later Works*, ed. John Burnaby. Philadelphia: Westminster Press, 1955.

Augustine. *Tractates on the Gospel of John, 1–10*, ed. John W. Rettig. Washington, D.C.: Catholic University Press, 1988.

Augustine. *Tractates on the Gospel of John, 11–27*, ed. John W. Rettig. Washington, D.C.: Catholic University Press, 1988.

Augustine. *Tractates on the Gospel of John, 55–11*, ed. John W. Rettig. Washington, D.C.: Catholic University Press, 1994.

Barclay, Robert. *An apology for the true Christian divinity*. London?, 1678.

Baxter, Richard. *The great mistery of the great whore unfolded*. London, 1655.

Baxter, Richard. *A call to the unconverted to turn and live and accept of mercy while mercy may be had*. London, 1658.

Baxter, Richard. *Making light of Christ and salvation*. London, 1691.

Bayly, Lewis. *The practise of pietie directing a Christian how to walke that he may please God*. London, 1613.

Bayly, Thomas. *Certamen religiosum, or, A conference between the late King of England and the late Lord Marquesse of Worcester*. London, 1651.

Beckham, Edward. *The principles of the Quakers further shewn to be blasphemous and seditious*. London, 1700.

Bilson, Thomas. *The True Difference Between Christian Subjection and Unchristian Rebellion*. Oxford, 1585.

Birckbek, Simon. *The Protestants evidence taken out of good records*. London, 1635.

Brathwaite, Richard. *A spiritual spicerie containing sundrie sweet tractates of devotion and piety*. London, 1638.

Brenz, Johannes. *A verye fruitful exposicion upon the syxte chapter of Saynte Iohn*. London?, 1550.

Brightman, Timothy. *Revelation of S. John*. London, 1619.

Browne, Robert. *The Subject's Sorrow*. London, 1649.

Bruce, Robert. *Sermons Upon the Sacrament of the Lord's Supper*. Edinburgh, 1591.

Bullinger, Heinrich. *Fiftie Godlie and Learned Sermons*. London, 1577.

Bullinger, Heinrich. *A most excellent sermon of the Lordes Supper*. London, 1577.

Bunyan, John. *The resurrection of the dead and eternall judgement*. London, 1665.

Bunyan, John. *Grace abounding to the chief of sinners*. London, 1666.

Bunyan, John. *The advocateship of Jesus Christ clearly explained*. London, 1688.

Burgess, Anthony. *The true doctrine of justification asserted and vindicated, from the errours of Papists, Arminians, Socinians, and more especially Antinomians*. London, 1651.

Burton, Henry. *Truth's Triumph Over Trent*. London, 1629.

Burton, Henry. *The Christians bulwarke, against Satans battery*. London, 1632.

Byfield, Nicholas. *An exposition upon the Epistle to the Colossians*. London, 1615.

Byfield, Nicholas. *A commentary upon the three first chapters of the first Epistle generall of St. Peter*. London, 1637.

Calamy, Edmund. *A Compleat collection of farewel sermons*. London, 1663.

Calvin, Jean. *The comentaries of M. John Calvin upon the First Epistle of Sainct Ihon*. London, 1580.

Calvin, Jean. *The Gospel According to St. John*, trans. T. H. L. Parker. *Calvin's New Testament Commentaries*, vols. 4–5, eds. David W. Torrance and Thomas F. Torrance. Grand Rapids: Eerdmans Publishing Company, 1959–61.

Calvin, John. *Institutes of the Christian Religion*, trans. Henry Beveridge. Grand Rapids: Eerdmans Publishing, 1995.

Chillingworth, William. *The religion of protestants a safe way to salvation*. Oxford, 1638.

Clarke, John. *Holy incense for the censers of the saints*. London, 1634.

Claxton, Laurence. *A paradisical dialogue betwixt faith and reason disputing the high mysterious secrets of eternity*. London, 1660.

Cockburn, John. *Fifteen sermons preach'd upon several occasions*. London, 1697.

Collier, Thomas. *The Marrow of Christianity*. London, 1647.

Coppin, Richard. *Divine Teachings in Three Parts*. London, 1649.

Cotton, John. *A practicall commentary, or an exposition with observations, reasons, and uses upon the First Epistle generall of John*. London, 1658.

Coverdale, Miles. *Fruitfull lessons, upon the passion, buriall, resurrection, ascension*. London, 1593.

Cranmer, Thomas. *An aunswere by the Reuerend Father in God Thomas Archbyshop of Canterbury, primate of all England and metropolitane, unto a craftie and sophisticall cavillation, devised by Stephen Gardiner Doctour of Law*. London, 1580.

Cranmer, Thomas. *The Work of Thomas Cranmer*, ed. G. E. Duffield. Philadelphia: Fortress Press, 1965.

Crashaw, Richard. *The Complete Poetry of Richard Crashaw*, ed. George Walton Williams. New York: New York University Press, 1972.

Cro, Francoise de. *The three conformities. Or The harmony and agreement of the Romish Church with gentilisme, Iudaisme and auncient heresies*. London, 1620.

Davenport, Robert. *A crowne for a conquerour; and Too late to call backe yesterday*. London, 1639.

Dell, William. *The building and glory of the truely Christian and spiritual church*. London, 1646.

Dell, William. *Uniformity Examined*. London, 1651.

Donne, John. *Sermons of John Donne*, eds. George R. Potter and Evelyn M. Simpson, 10 vols. Berkeley: University of California Press, 1953–62.

Downame, George. *Lectures on the XV. Psalme read in the cathedrall church of S. Paule, in London*. London, 1604.

Downame, John. *The Christian warfare wherein is first generally shewed the malice, power and politike stratagems of the spirituall ennemies of our salvation*. London, 1604.

Downame, John. *Annotations upon all the books of the Old and New Testament*. London, 1657.

Dryden, John. *Britanica Rediviva*. London, 1688.

Du Pin, Louis Ellies. *A new history of ecclesiastical writers containing an account of the authors of the several books of the Old and New Testament.* London, 1693.

Eaton, John. *The Honey-Combe of Free Justification by Christ Alone.* London, 1642.

Egerton, Stephen. *The boring of the eare contayning a plaine and profitable discourse by way of dialogue.* London, 1623.

Erasmus, Desiderius. *The first tome or volume of the Paraphrase of Erasmus upon the Newe Testamente.* London, 1548.

Etherington, John. *The defence of Iohn Etherington against Steven Denison.* London?, 1641.

Everard, John. *The Gospel Treasury Opened.* London, 1657.

Featley, Daniel. *Ancilla pietatis: or, The hand-maid to private devotion presenting a manuell to furnish her with necessary principles of faith.* London, 1626.

Featley, Daniel. *Transubstantiation exploded: or An encounter with Richard the titularie Bishop of Chalcedon concerning Christ his presence at his holy table.* London, 1638.

Finch, Henry. *An exposition of the Song of Solomon.* London, 1615.

Fletcher, Phineas. *Joy in Tribulation.* London, 1632.

Fox, George. *Truth's defence against the refined subtilty of the serpent.* London, 1653.

Fox, George. *An epistle to all professors in New-England, Germany, and other parts of the called Christian world also to the Jews and Turks throughout the world.* London?, 1673.

Fox, George. *Concerning such as have forbidden preaching or teaching in the name of Jesus.* London, 1684.

Fox, George. *A journal or historical account of the life, travels, sufferings, Christian experiences and labour of love in the work of the ministry, of … George Fox.* London, 1694.

Fox, George. *A collection of many select and Christian epistles, letters and testimonies written on sundry occasions.* London, 1698.

Fox, George. *The Journal of George Fox*, ed. Norman Penney. New York: Octagon Books, 1973.

Gardiner, Stephen. *An explication and assertion of the true Catholique fayth, touchyng the moost blessed sacrament of the aulter.* Rouen, 1551.

Gataker, Thomas. *Antinomianism discovered and confuted: and free-grace as it is held forth in Gods word.* London, 1652.

Gerhard, Johann. *Gerhards Meditations.* London, 1638.

Gilby, Edward. *An answer to the devillish detection of Stephane Gardiner.* London?, 1528.

Gouge, William. *The whole-armor of God: or A Christians spiritual furniture.* London, 1619.

Granger, Thomas. *The bread of life, or Foode of the regenerate.* London, 1616.

Hall, Joseph. *Christ mysticall, or, The blessed union of Christ and his members.* London, 1647.

Hammond, Henry. *The Gospel According to S. John*, in *A paraphrase and annotations upon all the books of the New Testament.* London, 1659.

Haward, Lazarus. *A few collections for Irelands souldiers.* London, 1647.

Hebdon, Returne. *A Guide to the Godly.* London, 1648.

Heigham, John. *The touch-stone of the reformed Ghospell.* St. Omer, 1634.

Herbert, George. *The Works of George Herbert*, ed. F.E. Hutchinson. Oxford: Clarendon Press, 1941.

Heyrick, Richard. *The paper called the Agreement of the people taken into consideration.* London, 1649.

Hildersam, Arthur. *CLII lectures upon Psalme LI preached at Ashby-Delazouch in Leicestershire.* London, 1635.

Holland, Hezekiah. *An exposition, or, A short, but full, plaine, and perfect epitome of the most choice commentaries upon the Revelation of Saint John.* London, 1615.

Horn, John. *The Quakers proved deceivers and such as people ought not to listen to, or follow, but to account accursed, in the management of a charge formerly given out against them to that effect.* London, 1660.

Howe, Obadiah. *The Universalist Examined and Convicted*. London, 1648.

Hutcheson, George. *An exposition of the Gospel of Jesus Christ According to John*. London, 1657.

Hyde, Edward. *A Christian legacy consisting of two parts*. London, 1657.

Jerome, Stephen. *The arraignement of the whole creature, at the barre of religion, reason, and experience*. London, 1632.

Jewel, John. *A Defence of the Apologie of the Churche of England*. London, 1567.

Knewstubs, John. *A confutation of monstrous and horrible heresies*. London, 1579.

Knight, Edward. *The triall of truth wherein are discovered three greate enemies unto mankind*. London, 1580.

Knott, Edward. *Mercy & truth. Or Charity maintayned by Catholiques*. St. Omer, 1634.

Leigh, Edward. *Annotations Upon All the New Testament*. London, 1650.

Lemnius, Levinus. *Touchstone of Complexions*. London, 1576.

Lewis, Jeremiah. The *Right Use of Promises, or A Treatise of Sanctification*. London, 1632.

Lilburne, John. *[Come out of her my people] or an answer to the questions of a gentlewoman*. Amsterdam, 1639.

Lockyer, Nicholas. *Christ's Communion with his Church Militant*. London, 1640.

Luther, Martin. *Sermons on the Gospel of St. John*, in *Luther's Works*, vol. 24, ed. Jaroslav Pelikan. Saint Louis: Concordia Publishing House, 1961.

Markham, Gervase. *Marie Magdalens lamentations for the losse of her master Iesus*. London, 1601.

Marlorat, Augustin. *A catholike and ecclesiasticall exposition of the holy Gospell after S. Iohn*. London, 1575.

Mason, Henry. *Hearing and doing the ready way to blessednesse*. London, 1635.

Merbecke, John. *A booke of notes and common places*. London, 1581.

Middleton, Thomas. *Two new playes*. London, 1657.

Milton, John. *A treatise of civil power in ecclesiastical causes*. London, 1659.

Milton, John. *A supplement to Dr. Du Moulin*. London, 1680.

Milton, John. *De Doctrina Christiana*, in *The Works of John Milton*, vol. XIV, eds. James Holly Hanford and Waldo Hilary Dunn. New York: Columbia University Press, 1933.

Milton, John. *John Milton: Complete Poems and Major Prose*, ed. Merritt Y. Hughes. New York: Macmillan Publishing Company, 1957.

Montagu, Richard. *A gagg for the new Gospell? No: a new gagg for an old goose*. London, 1624.

Myriell, Thomas. *The devout soules search with the happie issue of comfort found*. London, 1610.

Niclaes, Hendrik. *Dicta HN. Documentall sentences eauen-as those-same were spoken-fourth by HN*. Cologne, 1574.

Niclaes, Hendrik. *Terra pacis a true testification of the spiritual land of peace*. London, 1643.

Niclaes, Hendrik. *The prophecy of the spirit of love*. London, 1649.

Niclaes, Hendrik. *Revelatio Dei*. London, 1649.

Norris, John. *Reason and religion, or, The grounds and measures of devotion*. London, 1689.

Origen. *Origen against Celsus*, trans. James Bellamy. London, 1660.

Owen, John. *Of communion with God the Father, Sonne, and Holy Ghost*. Oxford, 1657.

Owen, John. *Two Discourses Concerning the Holy Spirit and His Work*. London, 1693.

Patrides, C. A., ed. *The English Poems of George Herbert*. London: J. M. Dent, 1974.

Penn, William. *The Christian-Quaker and his divine testimony vindicated by Scripture*. London, 1674.

Perkins, William. *A golden chaine: or The description of theologie containing the order of the causes of salvation and damnation, according to Gods word*. London, 1600.

Perkins, William. *A godly and learned exposition or commentarie upon the three first chapters of the Revelation*. London, 1606.

Perkins, William. *A cloud of faithfull witnesses*. London, 1607.

Porter, Edmund. *Trin-unus-deus, or, The trinity and unity of God*. London, 1657.

Powell, Vavasor. *God the Father Glorified*. London, 1649.

Preston, John. *The Saint's Qualification*. London, 1637.

Prynne, William. *Histrio-mastix The players scourge*. London, 1633.

Purnell, Robert. *The way step by step to sound and saving conversion, with a clear discovery of the two states*. London, 1659.

Quarles, Francis. *Judgement and Mercie for Afflicted Souls*. London, 1646.

Ratramnus. *A booke of Bertram the priest, concerning the body and blood of Christ written in Latin to Charles the Great*. London, 1623.

Ressold, William. *Four Sermons*. London, 1627.

Robinson, Ralph. *Panoplia. Universa arma. Hieron. Or, The Christian compleatly armed*. London, 1656.

Rollock, Robert. *Lectures upon the history of the Passion, Resurrection, and Ascension*. Edinburgh, 1616.

Ross, Jan, ed. *The Works of Thomas Traherne*, 5 vols. Cambridge: D. S. Brewer, 2005.

Rutherford, Samuel. *Christ dying and drawing sinners to himself, or, A survey of our Saviour in his soule-suffering*. London, 1647.

Rutherford, Samuel. *A survey of the spirituall antichrist opening the secrets of familisme and antinomianisme in the antichristian doctrine of John Saltmarsh and Will. Del*. London, 1648.

Saltmarsh, John. *A solemn discourse upon the sacred league and covenant of both kingdoms*. London, 1644.

Saltmarsh, John. *Free grace, or, The flowings of Christs blood free to sinners*. London, 1646.

Sclater, William. *The worthy communicant rewarded Laid forth in a sermon*. London, 1639.

Shakespeare, William. *King Lear*, ed. Alfred Harbage. London and New York: Penguin, 1970.

Sibbes, Richard. *A heavenly conference between Christ and Mary after His resurrection*. London, 1654.

Smith, Henry. *Treatise of the Lord's Supper*. London, 1591.

Smith, Henry. *The sermons of Maister Henrie Smith gathered into one volume*. London, 1593.

Smith, William. *The day-spring from on high visiting the world*. London, 1658.

Speght, Rachel. *A Mouzell for Melastomus*. London, 1616.

Stafford, Anthony. *The femall glory*. London, 1635.

Stanford, Donald E., ed. *The Poems of Edward Taylor*. New Haven: Yale University Press, 1960.

Sterry, Peter. *The clouds in which Christ comes opened in a sermon before the Honourable House of Commons*. London, 1648.

Stock, Richard. *A Stock of Divine Knowledge*. London, 1641.

Stooks, Richard. *A second champion, or, Companion to truth*. London, 1653.

Swetnam, Joseph. *The Arraignment of Lewd, Idle, Froward, and Unconstant Women*. London, 1615.

Sydenham, Humphrey. *Sermons upon solemne occasions preached in severall auditories*. London, 1637.

Taylor, Edward. *Treatise Concerning the Lord's Supper*, ed. Norman S. Grabo. East Lansing: Michigan State University Press, 1966.

Taylor, Thomas. *The parable of the sower and of the seed Declaring in foure severall grounds*. London, 1621.

Taylor, Thomas. *The Progress of Saints to Full Holinesse*. London, 1630.

Tobin, John, ed. *George Herbert: The Complete English Poems*. London and New York: Penguin, 2005.

Towne, Robert. *The re-assertion of grace, or, Vindiciae evangelii a vindication of the Gospell-truths*. London, 1654.

Traherne, Thomas. *The Poetical Works of Thomas Traherne*, ed. Gladys I. Wade. London: P. J. & A. E. Dobell, 1932.

Traherne, Thomas. *Christian Ethicks*, eds. Carol L. Marks and George Robert Guffey. Ithaca: Cornell University Press, 1968.

Trapnel, Anna. *A legacy for saints; being several experiences of the dealings of God with Anna Trapnel*. London, 1654.

Trapnel, Anna. *A Voice for the King of Saints and Nations*. London, 1657.

Trapp, John. *A brief commentary or exposition upon the Gospel according to St John*. London, 1646.

Traske, John. *Heaven's Joy, or Heaven Begun Upon Earth*. London, 1616.

Traske, John. *A Treatise of Libertie from Judaisme*. London, 1620.

Trigge, Francis. *The true Catholique formed according to the truth of the Scriptures, and the shape of the ancient fathers*. London, 1602.

Tuke, Thomas. *A fit guest for the Lords table. Or, a treatise declaring the true use of the Lords Supper Profitable for all communicants*. London, 1609.

Udall, John. *Peters fall. Two sermons upon the historie of Peters denying Christ*. London, 1584.

Vaughan, Henry. *The Works of Henry Vaughan*, ed. L.C. Martin. Oxford: Clarendon Press, 1957.

Vaughan, William. *The Church militant historically continued from the yeare of our Saviours Incarnation*. London, 1640.

Vaughan, William. *The Soul's Exercise*. London, 1641.

Vennar, Richard. *The right way to heaven and a good presedent for lawyers and all other good Christians*. London, 1602.

Vermigli, Pietro Martire. *The common places of the most famous and renowmed divine Doctor Peter Martyr*. London, 1583.

Walkington, Thomas. *Rabboni: Mary Magdalens teares, of sorrow, solace*. London, 1620.

Walwyn, William. *The Power of Love*. London, 1643.

Whitehead, George. *A brief discovery of the dangerous principles of John Horne*. London, 1659.

Wilcox, Helen, ed. *The English Poems of George Herbert*. Cambridge: Cambridge University Press, 2007.

Wilkinson, Robert. *A Jewell for the Eare*. London, 1602.

Wilkinson, William. *A confutation of certaine articles delivered unto the Familye of Love with the exposition of Theophilus*. London, 1579.

Winstanley, Gerrard. *The Breaking of the Day of God*. London, 1649.

Winstanley, Gerrard. *The Mysterie of God*. London, 1649.

Winstanley, Gerrard. *The New Law of Righteousness*. London, 1649.

Winthrop, John. *Antinomians and familists condemned by the synod of elders in New-England*. London, 1644.

Wotton, Anthony. *Sermons Upon a Part of the First Chapter of the Gospell of S. John*. London, 1609.

Zepper, Wilhelm. *The art or skil, well and fruitfullie to heare the holy sermons of the church*, trans. Thomas Wilcox. London, 1599.

Zwingli, Ulrich. *Commentary on True and False Religion*, eds. Samuel Macauley Jackson and Clarence Nevin Heller. Durham: Labyrinth Press, 1981.

Selected Bibliography: Secondary Works

Aers, David. *Sanctifying Signs: Making Christian Tradition in Late Medieval England.* Notre Dame: University of Notre Dame Press, 2004.

Agamben, Giorgio. *The Time That Remains: A Commentary on the Letter to the Romans*, trans. Patricia Dailey. Stanford: Stanford University Press, 2005.

Ainsworth, David. "Milton's Holy Spirit in *De Doctrina Christiana*," *Religion and Literature* 45:2 (Summer, 2015), 1–25.

Anderson, Paul N. *The Christology of the Fourth Gospel: Its Unity and Disunity in the Light of John 6.* Third printing. Eugene: Cascade Books, 2010.

Asals, Heather A. R. *Equivocal Predication: George Herbert's Way to God.* Toronto: University of Toronto Press, 1981.

Ashton, John. *Understanding the Fourth Gospel.* Oxford: Clarendon Press, 1991.

Badiou, Alain. *St. Paul: The Foundation of Universalism*, trans. Ray Brassier. Stanford: Stanford University Press, 2003.

Badir, Patricia. *The Maudlin Impression: English Literary Images of Mary Magdalene, 1550–1700.* Notre Dame: University of Notre Dame Press, 2009.

Bailey, Richard. *New Light on George Fox and Early Quakerism: The Making and Unmaking of a God.* San Francisco: Mellen Research University Press, 1992.

Barber, Benjamin J. "Syncretism and Idiosyncrasy: The Notion of Act in Thomas Traherne's Contemplative Practice," *Literature and Theology* 28:1 (2014), 16–28.

Barrett, C. K. *The Gospel According to St. John.* London: S.P.C.K., 1965.

Barrett, C. K. *Essays on John.* Philadelphia: Westminster Press, 1982.

Bennett, Joan. *Four Metaphysical Poets.* New York: Vintage Books, 1960.

Blevins, Jacob. *Re-reading Thomas Traherne: A Collection of New Critical Essays.* Tempe: Arizona Center for Medieval and Renaissance Studies, 2007.

Bloch, Chana. *Spelling the Word: George Herbert and the Bible.* Berkeley: University of California Press, 1985.

Blumenberg, Hans. *The Legitimacy of the Modern Age*, trans. Robert M. Wallace. Cambridge, MA: M.I.T. Press, 1983.

Bozeman, Theodore Dwight. *The Precisianist Strain: Disciplinary Religion and Antinomian Backlash in Puritanism to 1638.* Chapel Hill: University of North Carolina Press, 2003.

Bradstock, Andrew. *Faith in the Revolution: The Political Theology of Muntzer and Winstanley.* London: S.P.C.K., 1997.

Brinton, Howard H. *Friends for 300 Years: The History and Beliefs of the Society of Friends since George Fox Started the Quaker Movement.* New York: Harper & Brothers, 1952.

Brinton, Howard H. *The Religious Philosophy of Quakerism: The Beliefs of Fox, Barclay, and Penn as Based on the Gospel of John.* Wallingford, PA: Pendle Hill Publications, 1973.

Brown, Raymond E. *The Community of the Beloved Disciple: The Life, Loves, and Hates of an Individual Church in New Testament Times.* New York: Paulist Press, 1979.

Brown, Raymond E. *The Gospel and Epistles of John: A Concise Commentary.* Collegeville: Liturgical Press, 1988.

Brownlow, F. W. *Robert Southwell.* New York: Twayne Publishers, 1996.

Bultmann, Rudolf. *Theology of the New Testament*, 2 vols., trans. Kendrick Grobel. New York: Charles Scribner's Sons, 1951–5.

Bultmann, Rudolf. *The Gospel of John: A Commentary*. Philadelphia: Westminster Press, 1971.

Burge, Gary. *The Anointed Community: The Holy Spirit in the Johannine Tradition*. Grand Rapids: Eerdmans Publishing Company, 1987.

Clements, Arthur L. "Donne's 'Batter my heart'," *Modern Language Notes* 76:6 (June, 1961), 484–9.

Clements, Arthur L. *The Mystical Poetry of Thomas Traherne*. Cambridge, MA: Harvard University Press, 1969.

Colwell, Ernest Cadman and Eric Lane Titus. *The Gospel of the Spirit: A Study in the Fourth Gospel*. New York: Harper & Brothers, 1954.

Como, David. *Blown by the Spirit: Puritanism and the Emergence of an Antinomian Underground in Pre-Civil-War England*. Stanford: Stanford University Press, 2004.

Coolidge, John S. *The Pauline Renaissance in England: Puritanism and the Bible*. Oxford: Oxford University Press, 1970.

Corns, Thomas N. *Uncloistered Virtue: English Political Literature, 1640–1660*. Oxford: Clarendon Press, 1992.

Corns, Thomas N. *Regaining Paradise Lost*. London: Longman, 1994.

Cummings, Brian. *The Literary Culture of the Reformation: Grammar and Grace*. Oxford: Oxford University Press, 2002.

Culpepper, R. Alan. *Anatomy of the Fourth Gospel: A Study in Literary Design*. Philadelphia: Fortress Press, 1983.

Davies, Stevie and William B. Hunter. "Milton's Urania: 'The Meaning, Not the Name I Call,'" *Studies in English Literature* 28:1 (Winter, 1988), 95–111.

Davis, David J. *Seeing Faith, Printing Pictures: Religious Identity during the English Reformation*. Leiden: Brill, 2013.

Davis, Thomas J. *This Is My Body: The Presence of Christ in Reformation Thought*. Grand Rapids: Baker Academic, 2008.

DeConick, April D. *Voices of the Mystics: Early Christian Discourse in the Gospels of John and Thomas and Other Ancient Christian Literature*. London: Bloomsbury T&T Clark, 2004.

Dodd, C. H. *The Apostolic Preaching and its Developments: Three Lectures*. New York and London: Harper & Brothers, 1951.

Dodd, C. H. *The Interpretation of the Fourth Gospel*. Cambridge: Cambridge University Press, 1968.

Doerksen, Daniel W. *Picturing Religious Experience: George Herbert, Calvin, and the Scriptures*. Newark: University of Delaware Press, 2011.

Donnelly, Phillip J. *Milton's Scriptural Reasons: Narrative and Protestant Toleration*. Cambridge: Cambridge University Press, 2009.

Drury, John. *Music at Midnight: The Life and Poetry of George Herbert*. Chicago: University of Chicago Press, 2014.

Dubrow, Heather. *The Challenge of Orpheus: Lyric Poetry and Early Modern England*. Baltimore: Johns Hopkins University Press, 2008.

Duke, Paul D. *Irony in the Fourth Gospel*. Atlanta: John Knox Press, 1985.

Dugmore, C. W. *The Mass and the English Reformers*. London: Macmillan, 1958.

Eagleton, Terry. *The Event of Literature*. New Haven: Yale University Press, 2012.

Edwards, Richard M. *Scriptural Perspicuity in the Early English Reformation in Historical Theology*. New York: Peter Lang, 2009.

Eire, Carlos M. N. *War Against the Idols: The Reformation of Worship from Erasmus to Calvin*. Cambridge: Cambridge University Press, 1989.

Empson, William. *Seven Types of Ambiguity*. New York: New Directions, 1966.

Farmer, Craig S. *The Gospel of John in the Sixteenth Century: The Johannine Exegesis of Wolfgang Musculus*. Oxford: Oxford University Press, 1997.

Fish, Stanley. *Self-Consuming Artifacts: The Experience of Seventeenth-Century Literature*. Berkeley: University of California Press, 1972.

Fish, Stanley. *The Living Temple: George Herbert and Catechizing*. Berkeley: University of California Press, 1978.

Fortna, Robert T. and Tom Thatcher, eds. *Jesus in Johannine Tradition*. Louisville: Westminster John Knox Press, 2001.

Freinkel, Lisa. *Reading Shakespeare's Will: A Theology of the Figure from Augustine to the Sonnets*. New York: Columbia University Press, 2002.

Friedenreich, Kenneth. *Henry Vaughan*. Boston, MA: G. K. Hall, 1978.

Frye, Northrop. *The Anatomy of Criticism: Four Essays*. Princeton: Princeton University Press, 1957.

Gardner, Helen, ed. *John Donne: The Divine Poems*. Oxford: Clarendon Press, 1978.

Garner, Ross. *Henry Vaughan: Experience and the Tradition*. Chicago: University of Chicago Press, 1959.

Gerrish, B. A. *Grace and Gratitude: The Eucharistic Theology of John Calvin*. Eugene: Wipf & Stock, 1993.

Gilson, Etienne. *The Mystical Theology of Saint Bernard*, trans. A. H. C. Downes. Kalamazoo: Cistercian Publications, 1990.

Gregory, Brad S. *The Unintended Reformation: How a Religious Revolution Secularized Society*. Cambridge, MA: Harvard University Press, 2012.

Guibbory, Achsah. *Christian Identity, Jews, and Israel in Seventeenth-Century England*. Oxford: Oxford University Press, 2010.

Gunther, Karl. *Reformation Unbound: Protestant Visions of Reform in England, 1525–90*. Cambridge: Cambridge University Press, 2014.

Gurney, John. *Brave Community: The Digger Movement in the English Revolution*. Manchester: Manchester University Press, 2007.

Gwyn, Douglas. *Apocalypse of the Word: The Life and Message of George Fox (1624–1691)*. Richmond, Indiana: Friends United Press, 1986.

Hakola, Raimo. *Identity Matters: John, the Jews, and Jewishness*. Leiden: Brill, 2005.

Hall, David D., ed. *The Antinomian Controversy, 1636–38: A Documentary History*. Middletown: Wesleyan University Press, 1968.

Haller, William. *The Rise of Puritanism*. New York: Harper & Row, 1957.

Hamilton, James. "The Influence of Isaiah on the Gospel of John," *Perichoresis* 5/2 (2007), 139–58.

Healy, Thomas F. *Richard Crashaw: A Biography*. Leiden: Brill, 1986.

Hill, Christopher. *The World Turned Upside Down: Radical Ideas During the English Revolution*. London and New York: Penguin, 1972.

Hill, Christopher. *The English Bible and the Seventeenth-Century Revolution*. London and New York: Penguin, 1993.

Hillier, Russell. "The Wreath, The Rock, and the Winepress: Passion Iconography in Milton's *Paradise Regained*," *Literature and Theology* 22:4 (2008), 387–405.

Hillier, Russell. *Milton's Messiah: The Son of God in the Works of John Milton*. Oxford: Oxford University Press, 2011.

Hinds, Hilary. *George Fox and Early Quaker Culture*. Manchester: Manchester University Press, 2011.

Howard, W. F. *Christianity According to St. John*. London: Duckworth, 1943.

Hunt, Arnold. *The Art of Hearing: English Preachers and Their Audiences, 1590–1640*. Cambridge: Cambridge University Press, 2010.

Johnson, Jeffrey. *The Theology of John Donne*. Cambridge: D. S. Brewer, 1992.

Johnson, Kimberly. *Made Flesh: Sacrament and Poetics in Post-Reformation England*. Philadelphia: University of Pennsylvania Press, 2014.

Judge, Jeannie Sargent. *Two Natures Met: George Herbert and the Incarnation*. New York: Peter Lang, 2004.

Kahn, Victoria. *The Future of Illusion: Political Theology and Early Modern Texts*. Chicago: University of Chicago Press, 2014.

Kanagaraj, Jey J. *"Mysticism" in the Gospel of John: An Inquiry into its Background*. London: Bloomsbury T&T Clark, 1998.

Käsemann, Ernst. *Testament of Jesus: Study of the Gospel of John in Light of Chapter 17*, trans. G. Krodel. Minneapolis: Augsburg Fortress, 1978.

Kearney, James. *The Incarnate Text: Imagining the Book in Reformation England*. Philadelphia: University of Pennsylvania Press, 2009.

Kendall, R. T. *Calvin and English Calvinism to 1649*. Eugene: Wipf & Stock, 1997.

Killeen, Kevin, Helen Smith, and Rachel Willie, eds. *The Oxford Handbook of the Bible in England, c.1530–1700*. Oxford: Oxford University Press, 2015.

King, John N. *Milton and Religious Controversy: Satire and Polemic in Paradise Lost*. Cambridge: Cambridge University Press, 2000.

Kneidel, Gregory. *Rethinking the Turn to Religion in Early Modern English Literature: The Poetics of All Believers*. Basingstoke and New York: Palgrave Macmillan Press, 2008.

Koester, Craig R. *Symbolism in the Fourth Gospel: Meaning, Mystery, Community*. Minneapolis: Augsburg Fortress, 2003.

Koester, Craig R. *The Word of Life: A Theology of John's Gospel*. Grand Rapids: Eerdmans Publishing Company, 2008.

Köstenberger, Andreas J. *A Theology of John's Gospel and Letters: The Word, the Christ, the Son of God*. Grand Rapids: Zondervan, 2009.

Kruse, Colin G. "Paul and John: Two Witnesses, One Gospel," in *Paul and the Gospels: Christologies, Conflicts and Convergences*, eds. Michael F. Bird and Joel Willitts. London: T&T Clark, 2011, 197–219.

Kuchar, Gary. *The Poetry of Religious Sorrow in Early Modern England*. Cambridge: Cambridge University Press, 2008.

Kuchar, Gary. "A Greek in the Temple: Pseudo-Dionysius and Negative Theology in Richard Crashaw's 'Hymn in the Glorious Epiphany,'" *Studies in Philology* 108:2 (Spring, 2011), 261–98.

Kysar, Robert. *John, The Maverick Gospel*. Louisville: Westminster John Knox Press, 2007.

Lake, Peter. *Moderate Puritans and the Elizabethan Church*. Cambridge: Cambridge University Press, 1982.

Levy, Ian Christopher. *John Wyclif: Scriptural Logic, Real Presence, and the Parameters of Orthodoxy*. Milwaukee: Marquette University Press, 2003.

Lewalski, Barbara K. *Protestant Poetics and the Seventeenth Century Religious Lyric*. Princeton: Princeton University Press, 1979.

Lewalski, Barbara K. "Milton: The Muses, the Prophets, the Spirit, and Prophetic Poetry," *Milton Studies* 54 (2013), 59–78.

Lim, Paul C. H. *Mystery Unveiled: The Crisis of the Trinity in Early Modern England*. Oxford: Oxford University Press, 2012.

Loewenstein, David. *Treacherous Faith: The Specter of Heresy in Early Modern English Literature and Culture*. Oxford: Oxford University Press, 2013.

Loewenstein, David and Johan Marshall, eds. *Heresy, Literature, and Politics in Early Modern English Culture.* Cambridge: Cambridge University Press, 2006.

Low, Anthony. *Love's Architecture: Devotional Modes in Seventeenth-Century English Poetry.* New York: New York University Press, 1978.

Lupton, Julia Reinhard. *Citizen-Saints: Shakespeare and Political Theology.* Chicago: University of Chicago Press, 2005.

MacCulloch, Diarmaid. *Thomas Cranmer: A Life.* New Haven: Yale University Press, 1996.

Malina, Bruce J. and Richard L. Rohrbaugh. *Social-Science Commentary on the Gospel of John.* Philadelphia: Fortress Press, 1998.

Marsh, Christopher. *The Family of Love in English Society, 1550–1630.* Cambridge: Cambridge University Press, 1994.

Martin, Catherine Gimelli. "Experimental Predestination in Donne's Holy Sonnets: Self-Ministry and the Early Seventeenth-Century 'Via media,'" *Studies in Philology* 110:2 (2013), 350–81.

Martyn, J. Louis. *History and Theology in the Fourth Gospel.* Louisville: Westminster John Knox Press, 2003.

Martz, Louis L. *The Poetry of Meditation: A Study in English Religious Literature of the Seventeenth Century.* New Haven: Yale University Press, 1962.

Martz, Louis L. *The Paradise Within: Studies in Vaughan, Traherne, and Milton.* New Haven: Yale University Press, 1964.

McDowell, Nicholas. *The English Radical Imagination: Culture, Religion, and Revolution, 1630–60.* Oxford: Clarendon Press, 2003.

Meeks, Wayne A. "The Man from Heaven in Johannine Sectarianism," *Journal of Biblical Literature* 91:1 (1972), 44–72.

Molekamp, Femke. "Reading Christ the Book in Amelia Lanyer's *Salve Deus Rex Judaeorum*: Iconography and the Cultures of Reading," *Studies in Philology* 109:3 (2012), 311–32.

Moody Smith, D. *John.* Nashville: Abingdon Press, 1999.

Muller, Richard A. *The Unaccommodated Calvin: Studies in the Foundation of a Theological Tradition.* Oxford: Oxford University Press, 2000.

Netzley, Ryan. *Reading, Desire, and the Eucharist in Early Modern Religious Poetry.* Toronto: University of Toronto Press, 2011.

Neyrey, Jerome. *An Ideology of Revolt: John's Christology in Social-Science Perspective.* Philadelphia: Fortress Press, 1998.

Neyrey, Jerome. *The Gospel of John.* Cambridge: Cambridge University Press, 2007.

Nuechterlein, Jeanne. *Translating Nature into Art: Holbein, The Reformation, and Renaissance Rhetoric.* University Park: Penn State University Press, 2011.

Nuttall, A. D. *Overheard by God: Fiction and Prayer in Herbert, Milton, Dante, and St. John.* London: Methuen, 1980.

Nuttall, Geoffrey. *The Holy Spirit in Puritan Faith and Experience.* Oxford: Basil Blackwell, 1947.

Nygren, Anders. *Agape and Eros*, trans. Philip S. Watson. London: S.P.C.K., 1953.

Ozment, Steven E. *Homo Spiritualis: A Comparative Study of the Anthropology of Johannes Tauler, Jean Gerson and Martin Luther (1509–16) in the Context of their Theological Thought.* Leiden: Brill, 1969.

Parish, John E. "No. 14 of Donne's Holy Sonnets," *College English* 24:4 (January, 1963), 299–302.

Pelikan, Jaroslav. *The Christian Tradition: A History of the Development of Doctrine, Volume 4: Reformation of Church and Dogma (1300–1700).* Chicago: University of Chicago Press, 1984.

Perkins, Pheme. *Gnosticism and the New Testament*. Minneapolis: Augsburg Fortress, 1993.

Petersen, Norman R. *The Gospel of John and the Sociology of Light: Language and Characterization in the Fourth Gospel*. Valley Forge: Trinity Press International, 1993.

Pitkin, Barbara. "Calvin as Commentator on the Gospel of John," in *Calvin and the Bible*, ed. Donald K. McKim. Cambridge: Cambridge University Press, 2006.

Pryzwara, Erich. *Analogia Entis: Metaphysics—Original Structure and Universal Rhythm*, trans. John R. Betz and David Bentley Hart. Grand Rapids: Eerdmans Publishing Company, 2014.

Ramm, Bernard. *Protestant Biblical Interpretation: A Textbook of Hermeneutics*. Ada: Baker Academic, 1980.

Read, Sophie. *Eucharist and the Poetic Imagination in Early Modern England*. Cambridge: Cambridge University Press, 2013.

Reinhartz, Adele. "The Johannine Community and its Jewish Neighbors: A Reappraisal," in *"What is John?" Volume II: Literary and Social Readings of the Fourth Gospel*, ed. Fernando F. Segovia. Atlanta: Scholars Press, 1999, 111–38.

Reinhartz, Adele. *Befriending the Beloved Disciple: A Jewish Reading of the Gospel of John*. London: Bloomsbury Press, 2002.

Reinhartz, Adele. "Building Skyscrapers on Toothpicks: The Literary-Critical Challenge to Historical Criticism," in *Anatomies of Narrative Criticism*, eds. Tom Thatcher and Stephen D. Moore. Atlanta: Society of Biblical Literature, 2008, 55–76.

Ridderbos, Herman N. *Paul: An Outline of His Theology*, trans. John Richard De Witt. Grand Rapids: Eerdmans Publishing Company, 1975.

Ridderbos, Herman N. *The Gospel According to John: A Theological Commentary*, trans. John Vriend. Grand Rapids: Eerdmans Publishing Company, 1997.

Ross, Malcolm Mackenzie. *Poetry and Dogma: The Transformation of Eucharistic Symbols in Seventeenth-Century Poetry*. New Brunswick: Rutgers University Press, 1954.

Ryrie, Alec. *The Gospel and Henry VIII: Evangelicals in the Early English Reformation*. Cambridge: Cambridge University Press, 2003.

Ryrie, Alec. *Being Protestant in Reformation Britain*. Oxford: Oxford University Press, 2013.

Salter, K. W. *Thomas Traherne: Mystic and Poet*. London: Edward Arnold, 1964.

Sauer, Elizabeth M. "Milton's Peculiar Nation," in *Milton and the Jews*, ed. Douglas A. Brooks. Cambridge: Cambridge University Press, 2008, 35–56.

Schaff, Philip. *History of the Christian Church*, vol. VI. Grand Rapids: Eerdmans Publishing Company, 1963.

Schmitt, Carl. *Political Theology: Four Chapters on the Concept of Sovereignty*, trans. George Schwab. Chicago: University of Chicago Press, 1985.

Schmitt, Carl. *Political Theology II: The Myth of the Closure of any Political Theology*, trans. Michael Hoelzl and Graham Ward. Cambridge: Polity Press, 2016.

Schoenfeldt, Michael C. *Prayer and Power: George Herbert and Renaissance Courtship* Chicago: University of Chicago Press, 1991.

Schreiner, Susan. *Are You Alone Wise? The Search for Certainty in the Early Modern Era*. Oxford: Oxford University Press, 2011.

Schwartz, Regina Mara. *Sacramental Poetics at the Dawn of Secularism: When God Left the World*. Stanford: Stanford University Press, 2006.

Schweitzer, Albert. *The Mysticism of Saint Paul the Apostle*, trans. William Montgomery. New York: Henry Holt & Company, 1931.

Scribner, Robert W. "The Reformation, Popular Magic, and the 'Disenchantment of the World,'" *Journal of Interdisciplinary History* 23:3 (1993), 475–94.

Scroggs, Robin. *Christology in Paul and John: The Reality and Revelation of God*. Eugene: Wipf & Stock, 1988.

Segovia, Fernando F., ed. *"What is John?" Volume II: Literary and Social Readings of the Fourth Gospel*. Atlanta: Scholars Press, 1999.

Shell, Alison. *Catholicism, Controversy, and the English Literary Imagination, 1558–1660*. Cambridge: Cambridge University Press, 1999.

Sherwood, Terry G. *Herbert's Prayerful Art*. Toronto: University of Toronto Press, 1989.

Shuger, Debora Kuller. *The Renaissance Bible: Scholarship, Sacrifice, and Subjectivity*. Berkeley: University of California Press, 1994.

Simpson, James. *Burning to Read: English Fundamentalism and its Reformation Opponents*. Cambridge, MA: Harvard University Press, 2007.

Smith, Nigel. *Perfection Proclaimed: Language and Literature in English Radical Religion, 1640–1660*. Oxford: Clarendon Press, 1989.

Smith, Nigel. *Literature and Revolution in England, 1640–1660*. New Haven: Yale University Press, 1991.

Solt, Leo F. *Saints in Arms: Puritans and Democracy in Cromwell's Army*. Stanford: Stanford University Press, 1959.

Stachniewski, John. *The Persecutory Imagination: English Literature and the Literature of Religious Despair*. Oxford: Oxford University Press, 1991.

Stewart, Stanley. *The Expanded Voice: The Art of Thomas Traherne*. Los Angeles: Huntington Library Press, 1970.

Stoever, William S. *"A Faire and Easie Way to Heaven": Covenant Theology and Antinomianism in Early Massachusetts*. Middletown: Wesleyan University Press, 1978.

Strier, Richard. *Love Known: Theology and Experience in George Herbert's Poetry*. Chicago: University of Chicago Press, 1983.

Strier, Richard. "John Donne Awry and Squint: The 'Holy Sonnets,' 1608–1610," *Modern Philology* 86 (1989), 357–84.

Strier, Richard. *Resistant Structures: Particularity, Radicalism, and Renaissance Texts*. Berkeley: University of California Press, 1995.

Summers, Joseph H. *George Herbert: His Religion and Art*. London: Chatto & Windus, 1954.

Sweeney, Anne. *Robert Southwell: Snow in Arcadia—Redrawing the English Lyric Landscape, 1586–1595*. Manchester: Manchester University Press, 2006.

Tadmor, Naomi. *The Social Universe of the English Bible*. Cambridge: Cambridge University Press, 2010.

Talbert, Charles H. *Reading John: A Literary and Theological Commentary on the Fourth Gospel and the Johannine Epistles*. Macon: Smyth & Helwys, 2005.

Targoff, Ramie. *John Donne, Body and Soul*. Chicago: University of Chicago Press, 2008.

Thatcher, Tom. *The Riddles of Jesus in John*. Atlanta: Society of Biblical Literature, 2000.

Thatcher, Tom and Stephen D. Moore, eds. *Anatomies of Narrative Criticism: The Past, Present, and Futures of the Fourth Gospel as Literature*. Atlanta: Society of Biblical Literature, 2008.

Thompson, Marianne Meye. *The God of the Gospel of John*. Grand Rapids: Eerdmans Publishing Company, 2001.

Trueblood, D. Elton. *Robert Barclay*. New York: Harper & Row, 1968.

Veith, Gene Edward, Jr. *Reformation Spirituality: The Religion of George Herbert*. Eugene: Wipf & Stock, 1985.

Vendler, Helen. *The Poetry of George Herbert*. Cambridge, MA: Harvard University Press, 1975.

Vendler, Helen. "The Re-Invented Poem: George Herbert's Alternatives," in *Essential Articles for the Study of George Herbert's Poetry*, ed. John R. Roberts. Hamden: Archon Books, 1979, 181–98.

Vendler, Helen. *Invisible Listeners, Lyric Intimacy in Herbert, Whitman, and Ashberry*. Princeton: Princeton University Press, 2005.

Waetjen, Herman C. *The Gospel of the Beloved Disciple: A Work in Two Editions*. London: Bloomsbury T&T Clark, 2005.

Wahlde, Urban C. von. *Gnosticism, Docetism, and the Judaisms of the First Century*. London: Bloomsbury T&T Clark, 2015.

Waldron, Jennifer. *Reformations of the Body: Idolatry, Sacrifice, and Early Modern Theater*. Basingstoke and New York: Palgrave Macmillan Press, 2013.

Wallerstein, Ruth C. *Richard Crashaw: A Study in Style and Poetic Development*. Madison: University of Wisconsin Press, 1959.

Walsham, Alexandra. "The Reformation and the 'Disenchantment of the World' Reassessed," *Historical Journal* 51:2 (2008), 497–528.

Walsham, Alexandra. "Migrations of the Holy: Explaining Religious Change in Medieval and Early Modern Europe," *Journal of Medieval and Early Modern Studies* 44:2 (2014), 241–80.

Warnke, Frank J. *European Metaphysical Poetry*. New Haven: Yale University Press, 1961.

Warren, Austin. *Richard Crashaw: A Study in Baroque Sensibility*. Baton Rouge: LSU Press, 1939.

West, Philip. *Henry Vaughan's Silex Scintillans: Scripture Uses*. Oxford: Oxford University Press, 2001.

Whalen, Robert. *The Poetry of Immanence: Sacrament in Donne and Herbert*. Toronto: University of Toronto Press, 2002.

Wolfe, Jane E. "George Herbert's 'Assurance,'" *College Language Association Journal* 5 (1962), 213–22.

Young, R. V. *Richard Crashaw and the Spanish Golden Age*. New Haven: Yale University Press, 1982.

Young, R. V. *Doctrine and Devotion in Seventeenth-Century Poetry: Studies in Donne, Herbert, Crashaw, and Vaughan*. Cambridge: D. S. Brewer, 2000.

Index